Constitutional Law: Principles and Practice

DELMAR CENGAGE Learning

Options.

Over 300 products in every area of the law: textbooks, online courses, CD-ROMs, reference books, companion websites, and more – helping you succeed in the classroom and on the job.

Support.

We offer unparalleled, practical support: robust instructor and student supplements to ensure the best learning experience, custom publishing to meet your unique needs, and other benefits such as Delmar Cengage Learning's Student Achievement Award. And our sales representatives are always ready to provide you with dependable service.

Feedback.

As always, we want to hear from you! Your feedback is our best resource for improving the quality of our products. Contact your sales representative or write us at the address below if you have any comments about our materials or if you have a product proposal.

Accounting and Financials for the Law Office • Administrative Law • Alternative Dispute Resolution • Bankruptcy Business Organizations/Corporations • Careers and Employment • Civil Litigation and Procedure • CLA Exam Preparation • Computer Applications in the Law Office • Constitutional Law • Contract Law • Court Reporting Criminal Law and Procedure • Document Preparation • Elder Law • Employment Law • Environmental Law • Ethics Evidence Law • Family Law • Health Care Law • Immigration Law • Intellectual Property • Internships Interviewing and Investigation • Introduction to Law • Introduction to Paralegalism • Juvenile Law • Law Office Management • Law Office Procedures • Legal Nurse Consulting • Legal Research, Writing, and Analysis • Legal Terminology • Legal Transcription • Media and Entertainment Law • Medical Malpractice Law Product Liability • Real Estate Law • Reference Materials • Social Security • Sports Law • Torts and Personal Injury Law • Wills, Trusts, and Estate Administration • Workers' Compensation Law

DELMAR CENGAGE Learning
5 Maxwell Drive
Clifton Park, New York 12065-2919

For additional information, find us online at:
www.cengage.com/delmar

DELMAR
CENGAGE Learning·

Constitutional Law: Principles and Practice

Joanne Banker Hames

Yvonne Ekern

DELMAR
CENGAGE Learning

Australia • Brazil • Japan • Korea • Mexico • Singapore • Spain • United Kingdom • United States

Constitutional Law: Principles and Practice, Second Edition
Joanne Banker Hames and Yvonne Ekern

Vice President, Editorial: Dave Garza

Director of Learning Solutions:
Sandy Clark

Senior Acquisitions Editor:
Shelley Esposito

Managing Editor: Larry Main

Senior Product Manager: Anne Orgren

Editorial Assistant: Diane Chrysler

Vice President, Marketing:
Jennifer Baker

Marketing Director: Deborah S. Yarnell

Senior Marketing Manager: Mark Linton

Marketing Coordinator: Erin DeAngelo

Production Director: Wendy Troeger

Production Manager: Mark Bernard

Senior Content Project Manager:
Betty Dickson

Senior Art Director: Riezebos Holzbaur
Group

Senior Technology Project Manager:
Joe Pliss

For product information and technology assistance, contact us at
Cengage Learning Customer & Sales Support, 1-800-354-9706

For permission to use material from this text or product,
submit all requests online at **www.cengage.com/permissions**.
Further permissions questions can be e-mailed to
permissionrequest@cengage.com

Library of Congress Control Number: 2012932697

ISBN-13: 978-1-111-64854-1

ISBN-10: 1-111-64854-9

Delmar
Executive Woods
5 Maxwell Drive
Clifton Park, NY 12065
USA

Cengage Learning is a leading provider of customized learning solutions with office locations around the globe, including Singapore, the United Kingdom, Australia, Mexico, Brazil, and Japan. Locate your local office at: **www.cengage.com/global**

Cengage Learning products are represented in Canada by
Nelson Education, Ltd.

To learn more about Delmar, visit **www.cengage.com/delmar**

Purchase any of our products at your local college store or at our preferred online store **www.cengagebrain.com**

Notice to the Reader

Printed in the United States of America
2 3 4 5 6   23 22 21 20 19

Table of Contents

Chapter 3   Federal Judicial Power 56

Chapter 8 Equal Protection   196

Constitutional law is sometimes thought of as an area that focuses on important legal and moral principles with little application to the day-to-day practice of law. Certainly, constitutional law does involve such principles, but those principles do not exist in a vacuum. Constitutional principles affect numerous areas of law, including criminal law, family law, employment law, and personal injury litigation. Procedures in the courts as well as in administrative agencies must adhere to constitutional safeguards. Anyone who works in the legal field must be familiar with constitutional law. Yet the relevance of the Constitution in American life reaches far beyond those who work in the legal system. The individual whose property is taken by a redevelopment agency, the business that must accommodate disabled employees, even the children who recite the Pledge of Allegiance in a classroom are affected by constitutional law. Knowledge of constitutional law is important to everyone.

The Plan in Developing
Constitutional Law: Principles and Practice

Many excellent scholarly treatises on constitutional law are available for law students and legal scholars. Our objective in writing this text was not to create another such treatise. Instead, our goal was to write a text for students interested in various law-related careers. Our basic approach was to explain important constitutional principles and to put these principles into a practical, everyday context. The result, we believe, makes the text appropriate for a variety of students including legal studies, paralegal, pre-law, and administration of justice students.

Any text on constitutional law must, of course, refer not only to the Constitution but also to the Supreme Court cases that interpret the Constitution and form the basis for most of what we refer to as constitutional law. This text is no exception. We realize, however, that many students of constitutional law have little, if any, experience reading Supreme Court cases. Therefore, we do not attempt to include full Court opinions. Instead, for many Supreme Court cases we provide brief summaries or discussions. For some of the more major cases we also provide carefully edited opinions or excerpts. For some of the more recent cases we provide the Supreme Court's official syllabus. Several charts and boxes provide Supreme Court rulings in an easy-to-read format.

At the end of each chapter are several features such as review questions, analysis questions, and vocabulary terms to help students determine if they understand the concepts in the chapter. Assignments and projects at the end of each chapter help students see the practical applications of the chapter principles. A group activity is included to encourage class discussion and collaborative learning.

The Organization of
Constitutional Law: Principles and Practice

This book contains fourteen chapters, each dealing with a different area of constitutional law. All of the major areas of constitutional law are included. The first two chapters provide an introduction to the Constitution and to the federal government. Chapters Three through Six deal with the organization and powers of the judicial, legislative, and executive branches of the federal government, along with the constitutional limits on the power of state governments. Among some of the specific topics covered in these chapters are the power of judicial review, the commerce power, the tax power, and war powers. Chapters Seven through Fourteen deal with numerous constitutional rights and liberties, including equal protection, due process, economic protections, freedom of speech, privacy, and criminal procedure.

Additional material is found in the appendices to the text. Included here are the Constitution and selected historical documents including the Magna Carta, the Declaration of Independence, and the Articles of Confederation. Since one of our goals is to demonstrate the practical nature of constitutional law, also included in the appendix material are sample legal documents including an application and affidavit for a search warrant, an excerpt from a petition for writ of certiorari, an excerpt from a petition for commutation of sentence, a petition for writ of habeas corpus, a complaint form from the Department of Justice related to a discrimination claim, and a civil rights complaint. Other appendices include a noted petition for writ of habeas corpus, a partial transcript of testimony in the famous *Scopes* trial and excerpts from various attorney briefs to the Supreme Court. A complete glossary of terms is also included.

Chapter Organization

Each chapter begins with a chapter outline and a list of chapter objectives. In this way the student immediately identifies the chapter's learning goals. This is followed by a brief hypothetical situation illustrating the practical context of the chapter material. In most chapters this is followed by a short review of some of the principles and concepts covered in previous chapters that have relevance to the current chapter. Text material is presented with charts, tables, and other exhibits illustrating the text material. Interspersed are edited Supreme Court opinions Legal terms are bolded and defined. Special features in each chapter include an application of the text material to some area of legal ethics and a reference to a historical event or person connected to the text. Each chapter ends with a chapter summary, a list of key terms, questions for review, questions for analysis, practical assignments and projects, and a group activity.

Teaching and Learning Features

- **Chapter Outline** Each chapter points out the major topics to be covered in the chapter.
- **Chapter Objectives** Each chapter identifies the learning goals of the chapter.
- **Living with the Constitution** A hypothetical situation provides a practical introduction to each chapter, enabling students to identify the relevance of the material.

- **Looking Back** Most chapters contain a summary of previously covered terms and concepts that are relevant to new material in the chapter.
- **Something to Consider** Questions in the chapters follow selected cases and ask students to develop opinions about issues raised by the case.
- **A Point of Law** Most chapters contain brief summaries of the legal rulings found in cases discussed in the chapter.
- **Vocabulary** Legal terms in each chapter are bolded and defined and again listed at the end of each chapter.
- **Ethical Decisions—Everyday Choices** In each chapter students are presented with a problem based on a brief factual situation illustrating ethical concerns related to the chapter material.
- **Did You Know?** An interesting historical fact concerning constitutional law is found in each chapter.
- **Chapter Summary** Each chapter ends with a narrative summary of the chapter material.
- **Key Terms** Each chapter contains a list of legal terms found in the chapter, providing students with an opportunity to test their recollection of important legal vocabulary.
- **Questions for Review** Questions at the end of each chapter allow students to determine if they have successfully achieved the chapter objectives.
- **Questions for Analysis** These questions at the end of each chapter test the student's understanding of chapter material, especially Court decisions found in the chapter. These questions provide the student with the opportunity to apply the chapter material to the hypothetical situation found at the beginning of the chapter.
- **Assignments and Projects** Assignments and projects including briefing cases and Internet research provide students with the opportunity to expand their analytic, writing, and research skills.
- **Putting It into Practice** A practical assignment at the end of each chapter is designed to illustrate how the Constitution affects the day-to-day practice of law.
- **Group Activity** An activity or discussion at the end of each chapter appropriate for small–group classroom work or, in some cases, online discussion boards.
- **Glossary** A complete glossary of legal terms is included in the text.

New to This Edition

The second edition of *Constitutional Law: Principles and Practice* reflects the ever-evolving area of Constitutional law by adding discussions referring to over fifty Supreme Court cases decided since the publication of the first edition. For many of these cases, excerpts from the opinion or syllabus are included. These new cases include such noteworthy cases as *Boumediene v. Bush*, (2008), *District of Columbia v. Heller*,(2008), *McDonald v. City of Chicago*, (2010), *Skilling v. United States*, (2010), *Morse v. Frederick*, (2007), *Medellin v. Texas*, (2008), *Exxon Shipping v. Baker*, (2010), *Roper v. Simmons*, (2005), *Graham v. Florida*, (2010) *Brown v. Entertainment Merchant's Assoc.*, (2011), *Citizens United v. Federal Election Com'n*, (2010), *Kennedy v. Louisiana*, (2008), and *Graham v. Florida*, (2010). A complete list of all cases in this edition is found in the Table of Cases. The second edition continues to include excerpts or discussions of all the landmark and important decisions found in the first edition, although many of these have been carefully reedited to facilitate student understanding.

Pedagogical features at the end of each chapter are substantially revised. A new feature, Group Activity, is added to each chapter. Also added to each chapter are additional questions for review and analysis and additional or revised assignments and projects. Where needed, tables were updated or added. All forms in the appendix materials were updated and a new Appendix G contains selections from attorney briefs submitted to the Supreme Court. The briefs are incorporated in various end-of-chapter assignments. The second edition features the following chapter-by-chapter enhancements.

Chapter 1: Introduction to Constitutional Law—This chapter contains updated hypothetical situations reflecting contemporary constitutional issues and more focused editing of the federalist paper. Material on locating and reading cases was revised and expanded to include the nature and role of the Supreme Court Syllabus. A new case, *Ontario v. Quon*, 560 U.S. ___ (2010), is used to illustrate the features of a case.

Chapter 2: The Constitution and the Federal Government: An Overview—The organization of Chapters 2 and 5 was substantially revised so as to present a more complete topical *overview* of the office of the president in Chapter 2 and a more focused discussion of presidential powers in Chapter 5. Chapter 2 now addresses characteristics of the presidential office including executive privilege, immunity, impeachment, and presidential orders and proclamations. New cases include *Free Enterprise Fund* v. *Public Company Accounting Oversight Bd.*, (2010).

Chapter 3: Federal Judicial Power—Added to this chapter is a discussion of the current Supreme Court case detailing the rules for determining corporate diversity of citizenship. In addition, the chapter contains an expanded discussion of the Court's current view related to standing and jurisdiction. Excerpts and discussion of several new cases have been added. New cases include *Hertz v. Friend*, (2010), *Free Enterprise Fund v. Public Company Accounting Oversight Bd.*, (2010), *Elk Grove Unified School Dist. v. Newdow*, (2004), *Massachusetts v. E.P.A.*, (2007), and *Marshall v. Marshall*, (2006).

Chapter 4: Federal Legislative Powers—This chapter contains an expanded discussion of the Necessary and Proper Clause including recent case law, *United States v. Comstock*, (2010). Additional legislative topics are presented including universal health care and legislative involvement in the war on terror.

Chapter 5: Federal Executive Power—Along with Chapter 2, this chapter was reorganized. In addition, it contains a new section on executive power and the war on terror, covering such subjects as due process, the president's power to order military trials, and the Suspension Clause. Also new to the chapter is a discussion of the state's obligations to follow treaties negotiated by the president. New cases include *Hamdan v. Rumsfeld*, (2006), *Boumediene v. Bush*, (2008), and *Medellin v. Texas*, (2008).

Chapter 6: State Power and the Constitution—As with all of the chapters, the case law in this chapter was updated and includes new cases on federal preemption and state-enacted immigration laws. This chapter also now includes a discussion of the right of states to tax Internet sales. Related case law dealing with the right of states to tax mail order businesses is included. New cases include *Bruesewitz v. Wyeth LLC*, (2011), *Williamson v. Mazda Motor of America*, (2011), *C & A Carbone v. Town of Clarkstown*, (1994), *United Haulers Assoc. Inc. v. Oneida-Herkimer Solid Waste Mgmt. Auth.*, (2007), *Quill v. North Dakota*, (1992), *Chamber of Commerce of The United States of America v. Whiting*, (2011).

Chapter 7: Constitutional Protections of Civil Rights and Liberties—Added to this chapter are two Supreme Court cases explaining the Second Amendment right to bear arms. Excerpts from *District of Columbia v. Heller*, (2008), and *McDonald v. City of Chicago* (2010) discuss the Second Amendment as applied to both federal and state governments. Also added is a discussion of same-sex marriages and lower court decisions related to this, including *Perry v. Schwarzennegar,* a decision from the District Court of Northern California.

Chapter 8: Equal Protection—This chapter contains an expanded discussion of voting rights including the right of states to require photo IDs for voting. Also included is updated case law on the use of race as a factor by schools in admissions policies. New cases include *Crawford v. Marion County Election Bd.,* (2008), and *Parents Involved In Community Schools v. Seattle School,* (2007).

Chapter 9: Due Process—Added are cases and discussion of the following due process topics: punitive damages, vague statutes, juvenile death penalty and life imprisonment sentences, and the right to counsel in family law contempt proceeding. *Gonzales v. Oregon,* (2006), *State Farm Mut. Auto. Ins. Co. v. Campbell,* (2003), *Exxon Shipping v. Baker,* (2008), *Skilling v. United States,* (2010), *Roper v. Simmons,* (2005), *Graham v. Florida,* (2010) and *Turner v. Rogers,* (2011).

Chapter 10: Economic Freedom and Property Rights—A new section in this chapter contains a discussion of "takings" as a result of judicial action rather than legislative or executive. An excerpt from *Stop the Beach Renourishment, Inc. v. Florida Dept. of Environmental Protection,* (2010), helps to explain.

Chapter 11: Freedom of Expression—Since the publication of the first edition, the Supreme Court was very active in relationship to First Amendment cases. This chapter discusses several new cases and rulings, including the right of government to limit pure and expressive speech on public property, campaign finance, hate speech, harmful or violent conduct related to animal cruelty and violent video games, and commercial speech. The new cases include *Pleasant Grove City, Utah v. Summum,* (2009), *Christian Legal Soc. Chapter of Univ. of Cal. Hastings College of Law v. Martinez,* (2010), *Davenport v. Washington Educ. Ass'n,* (2007), *Ysursa v. Pocatello Educ. Ass'n,* (2009), *Citizens United v. Federal Election Com'n,* (2010), *United States v. Williams,* (2008), *Snyder v. Phelps,* (2011), *United States v. Stevens,* (2010), *Brown v. Entertainment Merchant's Assoc.,* (2011), *Morse v. Frederick,* (2007), and *Sorrell v. IMS Health Inc.,* (2011).

Chapter 12: Freedom of Religion—This chapter now contains a discussion of the relationship between the Establishment Clause and government display of the Ten Commandments. Current law on Religious Freedom Restoration Act was added as was a new section on the Religious Land Use and Institutionalized Persons Act. New cases include *McCreary v. ACLU,* (2005), *Van Orden v. Perry,* (2005), and *Gonzales v. O Centro Espirita Beneficiente Uniao Do Vegetal,* (2006).

Chapter 13: The Right to Privacy Under Due Process and Equal Protection Clauses—Added to the chapter are new Supreme Court cases ruling on the constitutionality of Partial-Birth Abortion Ban Act of 2003. Topics also now discussed include same-sex marriage as a privacy right, state laws recognizing the right to physician-assisted suicide, and the use of medicinal marijuana. New cases include *Gonzales v. Planned Parenthood,* (2007), *Gonzales v. Oregon,* (2006), and *Gonzales v. Raich,* (2005).

Chapter 14: Criminal Justice and the Constitution—This chapter has expanded discussion of several topics including good faith exceptions to the Exclusionary Rule, up-to-date search and seizure cases, the use of confession in violation of right to counsel for impeachment, effective counsel, pretrial publicity, the death penalty in child rape case, and the relationship of a juvenile's age to the *Miranda* requirements. New cases include *Herring v. U.S.* (2009), *Brendlin v. California,* (2007), *Arizona v. Gant,* (2009), *Safford Unified School District v. Redding,* (2009), *Kansas v. Ventris,* (2009), *Bobby v. Van Hook,* (2009), *Wong v. Belmontes,* (2009), *Skilling v. U.S.,* (2010), *Kennedy v. Louisiana,* (2008), *Graham v. Florida,* (2010), and *J.D.B. v. North Carolina,* (2011).

Supplements to the Textbook

- Instructors' resources for this text are available on a password-protected website. These resources include an instructor's guide with chapter-by-chapter analysis as well as lecture outlines, teaching tips, and suggested discussion questions. The instructors' website also includes PowerPoint® lecture slides and a test bank with answers. Go to login.cengage.com and sign in with your Single Sign-On (SSO) account to access these resources.
- A free companion website for students includes practice quizzes and chapter resources. To access these materials, visit www.cengagebrain.com and search for the title or ISBN (9781111648541) of this book.

Acknowledgments

No textbook can be produced through the sole effort of its authors. *Constitutional Law: Principles and Practice* is no exception. We would like to thank several individuals whose recommendations, assistance, and encouragement have made this work possible and enjoyable. Daily contributions came, first and foremost, from our husbands, Mark Hames and Bill Ekern: they have each contributed their special talents and knowledge to improve this text. More importantly, they have been a constant source of encouragement and support. Special thanks are also extended to Maria Soria.

The authors and Cengage Learning would also like to thank the following reviewers:

Sally Bisson
College of Saint Mary
Omaha, NE

Leslie "Les" Sturdivant Ennis
Samford University
Birmingham, AL

Kristine Mullendore
Grand Valley State University
Grand Rapids, MI

Barbara A. Ricker, J. D.
Kaplan University
Lewiston, Maine

William Weston
Kaplan University
Fort Lauderdale, FL

Anita Whitby
Kaplan University
Fort Lauderdale, FL

About the Authors

Joanne Banker Hames is an attorney who has been actively involved in paralegal education since 1977. Until 2004 she was a full-time instructor and the coordinator for the ABA-approved paralegal program at DeAnza Community College located in the heart of Silicon Valley. She continues to teach part time for the paralegal program and is also an adjunct instructor at Santa Clara University Law School. She earned her J.D. from Santa Clara University Law School and has been an active member of the California Bar since 1972. Prior to her involvement in paralegal and legal education, she practiced law in a firm specializing in litigation. She is also the coauthor of *Civil Litigation, Introduction to Law* and *Legal Research, Analysis, and Writing: An Integrated Approach*.

Yvonne Ekern is a full-time member of the law faculty of Santa Clara University Law School and adjunct faculty of DeAnza Community College Paralegal Program. For many years she was the chairperson of an ABA-approved Paralegal Program and division chair of the Applied Arts and Sciences Division of West Valley Community College. She graduated from the University of Idaho School of Law in 1985 and then worked in criminal and family offices. Prior to completing law school, she taught high school English and math in California and Missouri. She is the coauthor of *Introduction to Law* and *Legal Research, Analysis, and Writing: An Integrated Approach*. She has over thirty years of teaching experience.

Table of Cases

Bolded cases indicate that either an opinion excerpt or a court syllabus is found in the chapter.

1 Introduction to Constitutional Law

We must indeed all hang together, or, most assuredly, we shall all hang separately.

Benjamin Franklin, July 1776, at the signing of the Declaration of Independence

Exhibit 1-1

Courtesy of National Archives and Records Administration

Chapter Outline

Historical Background
Magna Carta
English Bill of Rights
Declaration of Independence
Articles of Confederation
The Constitutional Convention

The U.S. Constitution
Preamble
Articles
Amendments

The Constitution and Case Law
How Case Law Originates
The Court Syllabus
Locating Supreme Court Cases

How to Read a Supreme Court Case
Become Familiar with the Terminology
Used by the Court
Distinguish the Syllabus and Editorial
Enhancements from the Court's Opinion
Distinguish the Majority Opinion from
Concurring and Dissenting Opinions
Identify the Case Name and Citation
Identify the Various Parts of the Court's
Opinion

The Constitution and Other Sources of U.S. Law
Statutory Law
State Constitutions
Case Law

Chapter Summary

Chapter Objectives

When you complete this chapter, you should be able to

1. explain the purpose of the U.S. Constitution.
2. list the various historical documents and incidents that gave rise to the Constitution.
3. describe the general content and organization of the Constitution.
4. differentiate between the Constitution and constitutional law.
5. read a U.S. Supreme Court case.
6. describe the relationship of constitutional law to other U.S. law.

Living with the Constitution

Professor Bryce Springer was recently hired by a leading state university to teach English poetry. As part of the hiring process, he was required to go to the personnel office and complete a number of forms. In addition to the expected tax and insurance forms, he found that he was also expected to sign the following loyalty oath: "I do solemnly swear that I will support and defend the Constitution of the United States and the Constitution of this state against all enemies, foreign and domestic; that I will bear true faith and allegiance to the Constitution of the United States and the Constitution of this state; that I take this obligation freely, without any mental reservation or purpose of evasion; and that I will well and faithfully discharge the duties upon which I am about to enter." Springer was a little surprised. He thought that only the president and Supreme Court justices were required to take this oath.

BEFORE TAKING OFFICE, elected officials, judges, and public employees such as Springer are sometimes required to swear allegiance and to defend the U.S. Constitution. (See Exhibit 1-1.) Obviously, this document has extraordinary importance for those who hold public office. It is, in a sense, a symbol of the United States of America itself. Its importance, however, is not limited to politicians. The U.S. Constitution is important to every individual living in the United States for the simple reason that the Constitution, by its own terms, is the supreme law of the land. That does not mean that the Constitution contains all our laws. In fact, the Constitution is a relatively short document containing relatively few laws, most of which are related to the organization, operation, and powers of the federal government. Nonetheless, the Constitution affects people in a number of different ways. It controls the types of laws that both federal and state legislatures can enact. It applies to traffic stops for offenses as minor as failing to wear a seat belt as well as to major business transactions. In addition, even though the document is more than 200 years old, it also applies to current uses of new technology.

Consider the following situations that present some examples of cases involving the Constitution:

1. In view of recent shootings on school grounds, Congress wants to pass a federal law outlawing the possession of guns within 1000 feet of any school. Is this law enforceable?
2. A state legislature wants to make it a crime to burn or deface the American flag. Is this law enforceable?
3. A man is arrested for drug dealing. A cell phone in his pocket is seized and the contents searched without a warrant. An incriminating text message is found. Is the search of text messages legal?
4. An individual works for the government and is provided with a "tablet" type computer having email capabilities. The tablet is intended for work use but employees are allowed to take it home for work. Can the government employer search personal emails sent outside the scope of the normal workday?
5. Passengers boarding airplanes in a particular airport are required to submit either to body scans using small amounts of radiation or to physical pat-downs. Does this procedure violate a passenger's rights?
6. Smith is suspected of growing large amounts of marijuana in his home. Police use a high-tech thermal-imaging device to measure the heat radiating from the home so as to detect the presence of heat lamps known to be used in the cultivation of marijuana. The police have no warrant. The thermal imaging confirms the presence of high amounts of heat. Smith is arrested. Was the search legal?
7. Can a seventeen-year-old be imprisoned for life without the possibility of parole for committing a violent felony?

Each of these situations presents possible constitutional issues. One important purpose of the Constitution is that it establishes the power of the federal government to make laws. Thus, the right of Congress to make the laws described above are only valid if they are within that power. The Constitution also provides individuals with various rights and liberties. If the government violates these rights, it may be subject to civil liability. A violation of these rights can also negatively affect a criminal prosecution.

The Constitution also affects the rights of states to make laws. By its own terms, the U.S. Constitution is the supreme law of the land. Although states have the right to make laws, those laws cannot conflict with the U.S. Constitution. For example, one right guaranteed under the Constitution is the right to free speech. Thus, a state law prohibiting burning of the American flag would be unenforceable if burning the flag were an exercise of a person's right of free expression.

Constitutional questions often arise in criminal cases. Whenever police make an arrest, they normally have a right to conduct a limited search without a warrant. This search is usually limited to the area around the suspect. But does this allow an officer to take a cell phone from the suspect and search text messages? The development and use of technology have created many new constitutional questions. These examples are only a few of the situations that are controlled by the Constitution.

The Constitution has a tremendous influence not only on our legal system but also on our daily lives. It applies in civil cases and in criminal cases. It applies to actions by individuals, corporations, law enforcement officers, and politicians. Understanding the Constitution is fundamental to understanding the U.S. government and the U.S. legal system.

Historical Background

TO UNDERSTAND THE U.S. CONSTITUTION it is helpful to briefly review the historical environment surrounding its adoption as well as several documents that predated the Constitution. The Constitution, which provides the framework for the federal government, was drafted in 1787 and ratified by the states in 1789. Although the American colonies were well established by that time, the need for a federal or national government did not arise until the time of the Revolutionary War. Prior to this time, the American colonies operated as separate entities. Although the colonies were under English rule, each colony had its own local government and its own laws. For the most part, until the middle of the eighteenth century, the colonies were satisfied with this arrangement.

In the mid-1700s, territorial conflicts arose between the French and the English colonists. This conflict resulted in the French and Indian Wars, which precipitated events that contributed to the Revolutionary War. For the first time, the American colonies banded together to fight an enemy. Out of the conflict, a young general, George Washington, achieved prominence throughout the colonies. An additional result of the conflict with the French over American territories was that the English sent troops to help the colonists. After the war, England demanded a financial contribution from the colonies to defer the costs of the war by imposing various taxes on the colonists. The colonists resisted the imposition of these taxes, and hostilities between the colonies and England escalated. England passed laws restricting trade, prohibiting town meetings, and requiring that the colonists house or "quarter" British soldiers in their homes. Finally, the colonies rebelled and declared their independence from England.

The colonies were now ready to unite, and they needed a constitution to set out the framework of this union. From the very beginning, however, the founders recognized that this newly formed government had the potential for abusing the power given to it. Having suffered because of the many abuses imposed by the English government, they were determined not to create a powerful new government that could do the same. The first attempt at a national constitution resulted in the **Articles of Confederation** in 1781. The articles formed a national government but gave it very little power. The Articles of Confederation were soon discarded, and the Constitution as it exists today was written in 1787 and ratified by the states in 1789.

After more than 200 years, the Constitution remains as important to U.S. law in the twenty-first century as it was in the eighteenth century. The government, as structured in the Constitution, survives and flourishes today. The individual rights and freedoms found in the Constitution are still cherished, especially in an age when privacy is almost impossible.

The framers of the Constitution possessed a great deal of foresight for drafting such a document. The U.S. Constitution, however, was not the first document in history to show concern over such issues as personal liberties. In fact, the Constitution was influenced by many preceding documents, including the Magna Carta, the English Bill of Rights of 1689, the Declaration of Independence, and the Articles of Confederation.

🏛 **Articles of Confederation**
The document that held together the thirteen original American colonies before the adoption of the Constitution.

Magna Carta

Because the original colonies were English, it is not surprising that among the documents influencing the founders are two well-known English documents: the Magna Carta and the English Bill of Rights. Both of these documents were responses to abuses of royal power. The Magna Carta, which dates to 1215, was prepared by the nobles of England and presented to King John, whose abuses had greatly angered the English nobles. It contained provisions limiting the right of the king to tax and protecting the property rights of the barons. It also limited the right of the government to punish alleged criminals, providing that no freeman should be imprisoned "except by lawful judgment of his peers or by the law of the land."

[handwritten margin note: Basically them standing up against the monarchy]

English Bill of Rights

In 1689, England again found itself subject to abuses by the king. The country had recently undergone power struggles for the monarchy, and the result was the elimination of many rights. In particular, the English nobles complained that the king did the following without the proper authority from Parliament:

- suspended laws
- enacted taxes
- established and maintained a standing army
- quartered soldiers
- took arms away from Protestants but not Catholics
- violated the freedom of election of members of Parliament
- conducted arbitrary prosecutions
- allowed corrupt and unfair juries
- required excessive bail
- imposed excessive fines and cruel punishments

As a result of these complaints, the English lords demanded and were promised various rights by the new monarchy. See Exhibit 1-2 for a list of the rights found in the English Bill of Rights of 1689. The similarity between these rights and many of those found in the U.S. Constitution is apparent.

Exhibit 1-2   English Bill of Rights, 1689

- That the pretended power of suspending of laws, or the execution of laws, by regal authority, without consent of parliament, is illegal.
- That the pretended power of dispensing with laws, or the executions of laws, by regal authority, as it hath been assumed and exercised of late, is illegal.
- That the commission for erecting the late court of commissioners for ecclesiastical causes, and all other commissions and courts of like nature are illegal and pernicious.
- That levying money for or to the use of the crown, by pretence of prerogative, without grant of parliament, for longer time, or in other manner than the same is or shall be granted, is illegal.
- That it is the right of the subjects to petition the King, and all commitments and prosecutions for such petitioning are illegal.
- That the raising or keeping a standing army within the kingdom in time of peace, unless it be with consent of parliament, is against law.
- That the subjects which are protestants, may have arms for their defence suitable to their conditions, and as allowed by law.
- That election of members of parliament ought to be free.
- That the freedom of speech, and debates or proceedings in parliament, ought not to be impeached or questioned in any court or place out of parliament.

(continued)

(continued)

- That excessive bail ought not to be required, nor excessive fines imposed; nor cruel and unusual punishments inflicted.
- That jurors ought to be duly empanelled and returned, and jurors which pass upon men in trials of high treason ought to be freeholders. That all grants and promises of fines and forfeitures of particular persons before conviction, are illegal and void.
- And that for redress of all grievances, and for the amending, strengthening and preserving of the laws, parliaments ought to be held frequently.

© Cengage Learning 2013

Declaration of Independence

By the second half of the eighteenth century, the American colonists had many of the same complaints against England and the English king as did the English lords and nobles of the thirteenth and seventeenth centuries. In 1775, the Revolutionary War began. The next year, 1776, saw the leaders of the American colonies sign the **Declaration of Independence** setting forth the reasons for the Revolutionary War, including some of the fundamental principles that shaped the later-adopted Constitution. Some of those principles are as follows:

- Governments are formed to secure rights such as life, liberty, and the pursuit of happiness.
- Governments derive their power from the people who are governed.
- The abuse of power by a government justifies changing the government.

The Declaration of Independence also listed several of the abuses attributable to the king of England, including the following acts by the king:

- not ruling for the public good
- interfering with the people's right of a representative government
- refusing to establish a judiciary
- denying fair trials
- requiring a standing army in peacetime
- requiring quartering of soldiers
- cutting off trade
- taxing without consent of the people
- taking away colonial charters and interfering with local rule

All these abuses were considered when the Constitution was finally drafted and submitted for ratification by the states. See Exhibit 1-3 for the opening paragraphs of the Declaration of Independence in which the founding fathers state philosophical beliefs that form the basis of the Constitution. The entire text of the Declaration of Independence is found in Appendix B. See Exhibit 1-4 for a photograph of Independence Hall.

🏛 **Declaration of Independence**

The July 4, 1776, announcement by the Continental Congress (representatives of the thirteen colonies) that because of specified grievances the colonies were no longer subject to British rule but were free states. The Declaration of Independence is not a part of U.S. law, but its principles are reflected in the U.S. Constitution.

Exhibit 1-3   Declaration of Independence

IN CONGRESS, JULY 4, 1776

The unanimous Declaration of the thirteen united States of America,

When in the Course of human events, it becomes necessary for one people to dissolve the political bands which have connected them with another, and to assume among the powers of the earth, the separate and equal station to which the Laws of Nature and of Nature's God entitle them, a decent respect to the opinions of mankind requires that they should declare the causes which impel them to the separation.

We hold these truths to be self-evident, that all men are created equal, that they are endowed by their Creator with certain unalienable Rights, that among these are Life, Liberty and the pursuit of Happiness. That to secure these rights, Governments are instituted among Men, deriving their just powers from the consent of the governed, that whenever any Form of Government becomes destructive of these ends, it is the Right of the People to alter or to abolish it, and to institute new Government, laying its foundation on such principles and organizing its powers in such form, as to them shall seem most likely to effect their Safety and Happiness.

© Cengage Learning 2013

Exhibit 1-4   Independence Hall—Location of signing of both
Declaration of Independence and the Constitution

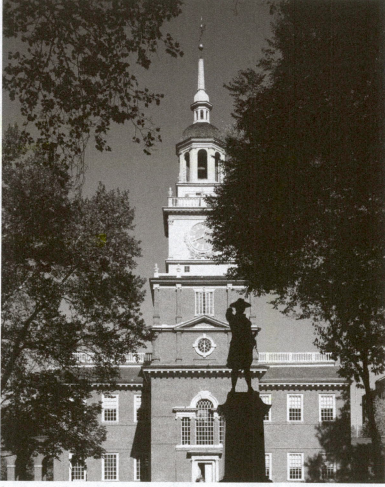

Courtesy of C. Borland/PhotoLink/Getty Images

Articles of Confederation

The European colonization of America resulted not in the creation of one new nation but in the creation of thirteen very separate colonies. Although each colony was subject to English rule, each had its own local government and laws. Each printed its own money and imposed taxes. Most had their own military. With the start of the Revolutionary War and the subsequent adoption of the Declaration of Independence, however, the colonies were forced to unite to gain their independence. This unification did not immediately result in a unified or national government. Although the need for a national government was obvious, the implementation of such a government posed a major problem for the colonists.

They were in the midst of fighting a war against a powerful government to remedy England's history of abuse. The last thing they wanted was to create a new government having the same potential.

The first attempt to unite the colonies and form a national government occurred in the Second Continental Congress with the drafting and ratification of the Articles of Confederation. The Articles of Confederation, which were ratified in 1781, formed a national government but did not give it much power. The new government was to act through a Congress, with each state having one vote. A president was to be selected by the Congress but could only serve one three-year term and, in actuality, did not have any power. When Congress was in recess, the government was to be ruled by a "Committee of the States." Most acts required a vote of nine of the states. The United States, as the new nation was referred to, was granted the exclusive power to declare war and enter into treaties. It did not, however, have the power to draft individuals to serve in the army or navy. These powers were to be provided by the states. In addition, even though the United States negotiated treaties, it could not interfere in the rights of the states to impose taxes or duties on imports. One major problem was that the new government had no power to impose direct taxes. It could assess a tax on the states, but it had no effective way of collecting. The Articles of Confederation created a national government but left most of the true governing power to the states. Another major problem with the Articles of Confederation was that it required a unanimous vote of the states to be amended. See Exhibit 1-5 for a summary of the provisions of the Articles of Confederation. A copy of the Articles of Confederation is found in Appendix B.

Exhibit 1-5   Articles of Confederation: Key Features

Adopted the name "The United States of America"

Features of new government:
- federal government to operate through a Congress
- each state to have one vote in Congress
- Congress to select a President to serve one three-year term
- a Committee of the States to govern when Congress is in session
- disputes between states to be resolved by Congress

Powers of new government:
- exclusive rights to declare war
- exclusive right to enter into treaties, subject to rights of states to impose duties and restrictions
- right to regulate value of coin and fix standards of weights and measures
- right to borrow money
- right to spend money
- right to raise an army and navy with forces to be supplied by states, but not to draft individuals
- right to request money from states, but not to tax individuals directly

Rights of states:
- states retain sovereignty, freedom and independence
- states retain right to regulate interstate and foreign commerce
- states retain all powers not expressly delegated to United States

Amendments to Articles:
- required unanimous consent of thirteen states

The Constitutional Convention

The founding fathers soon recognized that the Articles of Confederation would not be a workable constitution for the new nation. In May 1787, delegates from twelve states met in Philadelphia to revise the Articles of Confederation. Among the delegates were George Washington, Benjamin Franklin, Alexander Hamilton, and James Madison. The state of Rhode Island was not represented. The delegates decided very early that the Articles of Confederation should not be amended. Instead they decided to draft a new constitution.

Before this document was completed, the delegates debated several key issues. Probably the most important issue concerned the amount of power that should be given to the federal government. Many believed that the new federal government had to have power to tax, to regulate money, and to regulate commerce. Others still feared a central government with too much power. Another key point concerned the amount of representation each state should have in the new legislature. Smaller states favored equal representation among the states, whereas larger states called for representation based on population. A compromise was reached by creating a **bicameral** or two-house legislature, one house based on population and the other with equal state representation. A third issue during the constitutional convention surrounded the question of slavery. Many delegates and states opposed slavery. Other states depended on slavery for their economic survival. It was generally recognized that requiring all states to abolish the practice would prevent the formation of one national government. Yet the slave practice did affect the question of representation. How were slaves to be counted? States in which slavery existed would benefit in a representative legislature if slaves were counted. On the other hand, states in which slavery was prohibited did not view this method as fair. As a result, a compromise on this issue was also achieved. Each slave would count as three-fifths of a person. After months of debate and compromise, in September 1787 a new constitution was finally drafted and signed by representatives of the twelve states.

Before the new U.S. Constitution could take effect, it had to be ratified by nine of the states. This process was not easy because there was still a great deal of opposition to a strong central government. Extensive debate took place in all states, with strong arguments for each side being made. Those who supported the new U.S. Constitution were known as **federalists**. Arguments in favor of this new Constitution were published and became known as the Federalist Papers. James Madison, Alexander Hamilton, and John Jay were the authors. People who opposed the new Constitution were known as **antifederalists**. An excerpt from one of the Federalist Papers follows. In this paper, Hamilton supports the adoption of the new proposed constitution.

To secure the necessary vote of nine states, the federalists were forced to support amendments to the Constitution limiting the powers of the government and assuring certain basic rights and freedoms to the people. These ten amendments became the Bill of Rights. The new Constitution was finally **ratified** by the necessary majority in June 1788.

bicameral
Having two chambers. A two-part legislature, such as the U.S. Congress, is bicameral; it is composed of the Senate (the "upper house" or "upper chamber") and the House of Representatives (the "lower house" or "lower chamber").

federalists
Those persons supporting the ratification of the U.S. Constitution.

antifederalists
Those persons opposing the ratification of the U.S. Constitution.

ratified
(ratification) Confirmation and acceptance of a previous act.

Federalist Paper 1 (Hamilton)

To the People of the State of New York:

AFTER an unequivocal experience of the inefficiency of the subsisting federal government, you are called upon to deliberate on a new Constitution for the United States of America. The subject speaks its own importance; comprehending in its consequences nothing less than the existence of the UNION, the safety and welfare of the parts of which it is composed, the fate of an empire in many respects the most interesting in the world. It has been frequently remarked that it seems to have been reserved to the people of this country, by their conduct and example, to decide the important question,

(continued)

(continued)

whether societies of men are really capable or not of establishing good government from reflection and choice, or whether they are forever destined to depend for their political constitutions on accident and force. If there be any truth in the remark, the crisis at which we are arrived may with propriety be regarded as the era in which that decision is to be made; and a wrong election of the part we shall act may, in this view, deserve to be considered as the general misfortune of mankind....

Yes, my countrymen, I own to you that, after having given it an attentive consideration, I am clearly of opinion it is your interest to adopt it. I am convinced that this is the safest course for your liberty, your dignity, and your happiness. I frankly acknowledge to you my convictions, and I will freely lay before you the reasons on which they are founded. My arguments will be open to all and may be judged of by all. They shall at least be offered in a spirit which will not disgrace the cause of truth.

I propose, in a series of papers, to discuss the following interesting particulars:

THE UTILITY OF THE UNION TO YOUR POLITICAL PROSPERITY, THE INSUFFICIENCY OF THE PRESENT CONFEDERATION TO PRESERVE THAT UNION, THE NECESSITY OF A GOVERNMENT AT LEAST EQUALLY ENERGETIC WITH THE ONE PROPOSED, TO THE ATTAINMENT OF THIS OBJECT THE CONFORMITY OF THE PROPOSED CONSTITUTION TO THE TRUE PRINCIPLES OF REPUBLICAN GOVERNMENT, ITS ANALOGY TO YOUR OWN STATE CONSTITUTION and lastly, THE ADDITIONAL SECURITY WHICH ITS ADOPTION WILL AFFORD TO THE PRESERVATION OF THAT SPECIES OF GOVERNMENT, TO LIBERTY, AND TO PROPERTY.

In the progress of this discussion I shall endeavor to give a satisfactory answer to all the objections which shall have made their appearance, that may seem to have any claim to your attention.

It may perhaps be thought superfluous to offer arguments to prove the utility of the UNION, a point, no doubt, deeply engraved on the hearts of the great body of the people in every State, and one, which it may be imagined, has no adversaries. But the fact is, that we already hear it whispered in the private circles of those who oppose the new Constitution, that the thirteen States are of too great extent for any general system, and that we must of necessity resort to separate confederacies of distinct portions of the whole. It will therefore be of use to begin by examining the advantages of that Union, the certain evils, and the probable dangers, to which every State will be exposed from its dissolution. This shall accordingly constitute the subject of my next address.

PUBLIUS.

Something to Consider

Hamilton obviously believed that the adoption of the proposed Constitution would result in an effective government. If a country were developing a new constitution today, should it pattern it after the U.S. Constitution? What factors might influence the decision?

I believe that if a country were developing a new constitution they should consider SOME of the u.s. constitution but not all.

The U.S. Constitution

THE U.S. CONSTITUTION IS organized into three main parts: the preamble; the body of the document, divided into seven articles; and the twenty-seven amendments to the original document. The short preamble sets out the purpose and general intent of the Constitution. The articles are divided into sections and provide the guidelines for the structure and organization of the federal government. They also detail the authority and powers that the federal government has. The twenty-seven amendments to the Constitution contain various changes to the original Constitution. The first ten amendments are called the Bill of Rights.

Preamble

The preamble to the Constitution is a short statement explaining the general intent behind the Constitution. The document was drafted to form a workable federal government that would benefit Americans by assuring their safety, providing for their general welfare, and protecting their liberty. More specifically, the goals are stated as the following:

1. to form a more perfect union; that is, to form a workable federal government
2. to establish justice
3. to ensure domestic tranquility
4. to provide for the common defense
5. to promote the general welfare
6. to secure the blessings of liberty

See Exhibit 1-6 for the preamble to the Constitution.

Exhibit 1-6   Preamble to United States Constitution

We the People of the United States, in Order to form a more perfect Union, establish Justice, insure domestic Tranquility, provide for the common defence, promote the general Welfare, and secure the Blessings of Liberty to ourselves and our Posterity, do ordain and establish this Constitution for the United States of America.

© Cengage Learning 2013

Articles

Following the purpose stated in the preamble, the body of the Constitution is divided into seven articles; it sets forth the organizational structure for the federal government, establishes the powers of the federal government, defines the relationship between the federal and state government, and provides some rules for the relationship among the various states. The specific provisions of the seven articles are discussed in detail in subsequent chapters. Table 1-1 provides a general description of each article.

Table 1-1 Articles of the Constitution	
Article I	The organization and powers of the legislative branch
Article II	Selection and duties of the president
Article III	Functions of the Supreme Court
Article IV	Responsibilities of one state to another
Article V	Requirements for amending the Constitution
Article VI	Supremacy of the Constitution
Article VII	Procedure for ratification of the Constitution

© Cengage Learning 2013

Amendments

Since its ratification in 1788, twenty-seven amendments have been added to the U.S. Constitution. The first ten amendments, known as the Bill of Rights, were adopted soon after the Constitution itself, and, as the name suggests, they contain a list of rights that people have in relation to the federal government. These rights include the right to free speech, assembly, and religion; the right to bear arms; and numerous rights for those suspected or accused of committing crimes. The other amendments deal with a variety of topics, including the abolition of slavery, the right to impose income tax, various voting rights, and presidential term limits. The amendments to the Constitution are discussed in more detail in later chapters of this text. See Table 1–2 for a historical timeline.

Table 1-2 Historical Timeline	
1215	Magna Carta
1689	English Bill of Rights
1754–1760	French and Indian Wars
1775–1783	Revolutionary War
1776	Declaration of Independence
1781	Articles of Confederation
1787	U.S. Constitution drafted
1788	U.S. Constitution ratified
1791	Bill of Rights
1795–1992	Amendments XI through XXVII

© Cengage Learning 2013

The Constitution and Case Law

CONSTITUTIONAL LAW IS BASED ON the provisions set forth in the Constitution. Because many of the provisions in the Constitution are subject to various interpretations, constitutional law also includes numerous court decisions interpreting those provisions. Review the factual situations set forth earlier in the chapter. Consider the situation where a police officer searches text messages on a cell phone seized without a warrant from an individual who was arrested. The Fourth Amendment prohibits unreasonable searches but does not define the term unreasonable. Thus, whether this individual's Fourth Amendment rights were violated must ultimately be answered by the courts. In the U.S. legal system, courts have the power to interpret laws, including the Constitution. The U.S. Supreme Court has the final say regarding interpretation of the U.S. Constitution. A study of constitutional law therefore requires not only an examination of the Constitution but also a review of the many Supreme Court decisions that are based on various constitutional provisions. In fact, there is a great deal more constitutional law in **case law** than in the Constitution itself.

How Case Law Originates

Because the study of constitutional law requires one to read Supreme Court cases, a general understanding of case law is needed. Case law is found in written and published opinions deciding actual disputes that were heard in state and federal appellate and supreme courts. Although most cases start in a trial court, case law does not arise unless the decision of the trial court is appealed. When a case is appealed, it is heard before a panel of justices. At the first appellate level (normally in a court of appeals), a three-judge panel hears a case. In the U.S. Supreme Court, nine justices usually hear each case. After the parties submit written briefs and oral arguments regarding the issues, the justices vote to decide the case. The party receiving a majority of votes wins the case. At this point, one justice from the majority is assigned to write an **opinion** that contains the decision and the reason for the decision. The opinion from a court of appeals becomes case law if the court determines that the case should be **published** and if it is not appealed to a higher court. An opinion from the Supreme Court always becomes law. In addition to the opinion containing the decision of the court, any justice who hears the case is allowed to write a concurring or dissenting opinion. While concurring and dissenting opinions can be important, they are not cited as controlling case law.

🏛 **case law**
All reported judicial decisions; the law derived from judges' opinions in lawsuits (as opposed to, for example, the laws passed by a legislature).

🏛 **opinion**
A judge's statement of the decision he or she has reached in a case.

🏛 **published**
When an appellate court decides that a decision in a case should become case law, it orders the case "published." The case then appears in case reporters.

In an opinion, the appellate or Supreme Court usually describes the procedural and factual background of the case, the legal issue or question presented to the court, the holding or decision in the case, and the reason for the decision. Attorneys and judges look for these elements when they read court opinions. Sometimes they prepare written summaries of the cases, called **case briefs,** that contain a short description of these features.

The Court Syllabus

When the Supreme Court reaches a decision, it releases a written copy of its opinion, sometimes called a slip opinion. The Supreme Court's written decision is often preceded by a short summary of the case called a **syllabus.** The Court's Syllabus provides the reader with a summary of the important facts, the decision, and the reasons for the decision. It can be very helpful in understanding the entire opinion. However, the syllabus is not part of the opinion, and language from the syllabus is never cited by attorneys as law. Not all Supreme Court cases have an official syllabus.

Locating Supreme Court Cases

Supreme Court opinions are published in numerous sources. The U.S. government publishes an official print version of the cases in a case reporter known as the United States Reports. Private companies also publish print versions of Supreme Court cases. Two popular print sources are The Supreme Court Reporter and Supreme Court Reports, Lawyer's Edition. These publishers add unique editorial enhancements to aid the reader. References to these reporters are called **parallel citation.**

Today, Supreme Court cases are also found in numerous sites on the Internet. The official Web site for the U.S. Supreme Court contains recent and older cases. Search for "opinions." The publishers of the Supreme Court Reporter and the Lawyers' Edition (West and Lexis) maintain fee-based databases containing all Supreme Court cases. Numerous law school Web sites (such as Cornell Law School) provide free access to Supreme Court cases. A feature on the popular search engine Google, called "Scholar," also provides free access to Supreme Court cases. Cases can often be located online by using the citation to the print version of U.S. Reports. The citation includes the volume, the abbreviation for the U.S. Reports (U.S.) and the starting page number for the case (e.g., 347 U.S. 483). Cases can also be located online by searching for the name of the case or by the topic of the case. An excerpt from a Supreme Court case, *Ontario v. Quon*, 560 U.S. (2010), is found later in this chapter.

How to Read a Supreme Court Case

READING A SUPREME COURT CASE can be a challenge. The following are some guidelines to use when reading a case.

Become Familiar with the Terminology Used by the Court

Unless you have developed an extensive legal vocabulary, reading a Supreme Court decision is like reading a foreign language. If you do not understand the words, you will not understand the meaning of the case. You may need to have a legal dictionary available as you read cases. Exhibit 1-7 contains a list of terms often found in court decisions. Read the list and familiarize yourself with the terms.

🏛 case brief

A summary of a published opinion in a case. Preparing the summary helps in understanding the opinion and simplifies later review.

🏛 syllabus

A headnote, summary, or abstract of a case.

🏛 parallel citation

An alternate reference to a case (or other legal document) that is published in more than one place. There is usually one official publication of a court case or a statute. If so, that is the *official* or primary citation, and all others are *parallel citations.*

Exhibit 1-7 Case Vocabulary and Abbreviations

The following abbreviations commonly appear in citations within cases.

Id.	(Latin abbreviation) The same thing;the same citation as the one immediately before.
Infra	1. Below or under. 2. Within. 3. Later in this book. For example, "infra p.236" means "look at page 236, which is further on."
Cf.	(Latin abbreviation) Compare.
Ibid	(Latin) The same; in, from, or found in the same place (same book, page, case, etc.).
Supra	(Latin) Above; earlier (in the page, in the book, etc.).
Ante	(Latin) Before.
Post	After.
U.S.	United States Reports.

The following words and phrases appear commonly in judicial opinions:

Cert.	Abbreviation for certiorari.
Certiorari	(Latin) "To make sure." A request for *certiorari* (or "cert." for short) is like an appeal, but is one in which the higher court is not required to take for decision. It is literally a writ from the higher court asking the lower court for the record of the case. [pronounce: sir-sho-rare-ee]
Declaratory judgment	A judicial opinion that states the rights of the parties or answers a legal question without awarding any damages or ordering that anything be done. A person may ask the court for a declaratory judgment only if there is a real, not theoretical, problem that involves real legal consequences.
Holding (hold or held)	The core of a judge's decision in a case. It is that part of the judge's written opinion that applies the law to the facts of the case and about which can be said, "The case means no more and no less than this." When later cases rely on a case as precedent, it is only the holding that should be used to establish the precedent.
Injunction	A judge's order to a person to do or to refrain from doing a particular thing. For example, a court might issue an injunction to "enjoin" (prevent) a company from dumping wastes into a river. An injunction may be *preliminary* or *temporary* (until the issue can be fully tried in court) or it may be *final* or *permanent*.
Inter alia	(Latin) "Among other things."
Issue	Legal question that the appellate court (or Supreme Court) is asked to decide.
Motion	A request that a judge make a ruling or take some other action. For example, a *motion to dismiss* is a request that the court throw the case out.
Petitioner	One who has filed a petition such as a petition for a writ of certiorari. As used in Supreme Court opinions, the one asking the Court for a hearing.
Precedent	A court decision on a question of law (how the law affects the case) that is binding authority on lower courts in the same court system.
Question presented	The legal issue that the appellate court must decide.
Remand	Send back. For example, a higher court may remand (send back) a case to a lower court, directing the lower court to take some action.
Respondent	The person against whom an appeal is taken. (This person might have been either the plaintiff or the defendant in the lower court.)
Summary judgment	A final judgment (victory) for one side in a lawsuit (or in one part of a lawsuit), without trial, when the judge finds, based on pleadings, depositions, affidavits, and so forth that there is no genuine factual issue in the lawsuit (or in one part of the lawsuit.)

Distinguish the Syllabus and Editorial Enhancements from the Court's Opinion

Before reading a Supreme Court case, you must identify the Court's opinion and distinguish it from the Court's Syllabus and other editorial enhancements. Publishers of case law often add editorial enhancements to their publication of a case. Editorial enhancements may include a summary of the case, written by the publisher, and **headnotes**, or brief summaries of the law found in the case, also added by the publisher. Although reading the case summaries and headnotes help you understand the case, you must remember that the rules of law are found in what the Court writes, not what a publisher writes. Usually, the Supreme Court's decision will be labeled "opinion" and will contain the name of the justice writing the opinion for the court.

Distinguish the Majority Opinion from Concurring and Dissenting Opinions

When the Supreme Court decides a case, one justice is selected to write the Court's opinion. If all justices agree, this opinion becomes the opinion of the Court. Supreme Court cases are decided by a majority vote, and often the Court's decision is not unanimous. In such a case, the Court's opinion is called the **majority opinion** as long as a majority of the justices agree with the reasons expressed in the opinion as well as with the result. If a majority of the justices agree with the result but not the reasons for it, a **plurality opinion** or decision results. If justices agree with the result but not the reason for the decision as stated in the Court's opinion, they usually write a **concurring opinion**. A justice who does not agree with the result writes a dissenting opinion. Concurring and **dissenting opinions** are published with the Court's opinion. Case law is only found in the majority or plurality opinion, which is always published first.

Occasionally a Supreme Court case is a **per curiam** decision. This means that the opinion comes from the Court as a whole. Authorship of the opinion is not identified.

Identify the Case Name and Citation

Every U.S. Supreme Court case begins with a case title. The case title provides the information necessary to identify the name of the case and the citation. The case name and citation are important whenever you refer to the case. This information is used by lawyers and judges to locate a copy of the case. The citation provides the names of the case reporters or databases in which the case is published. If a reference is made to a case reporter, then the citation also includes the volume, an abbreviation for the case reporter, the series of the case reporter, and the page. The common Supreme Court case reporters are abbreviated as follows:

United States Reports	U.S.
Supreme Court Reporter	S. Ct.
Supreme Court Reports, Lawyer's Edition	L. Ed.

United States Reports, published by the U.S. government, is the official publication of Supreme Court cases. It should always be used when citing cases to a court. The other citations are called parallel citations. Prior to the 1880s, Supreme Court decisions were published privately. These books are referred to as nominative reporters because they are named after individuals who served as court reporters. These names include Dallas, Cranch, Wheaton, Peters, Howard, Black, and Wallace. When citing to early cases, the Supreme Court often refers to these publications. See Exhibit 1-8 for the proper format for citing Supreme Court cases.

Exhibit 1-8 Citing the Constitution and Cases

CITING THE CONSTITUTION
All legal authorities have accepted citations or shorthand references. When referring to specific parts of the United States Constitution, you should use the following format:

Preamble	U.S. Const. pmbl.
Articles	U.S. Const. art. III § 2
Amendments	U.S. Const. amend. XIV

CITING SUPREME COURT CASES
United States Supreme Court cases are referenced by standard citations. The citation for a Supreme Court case follows this format:

Name	Official Citation	Parallel Citations	Year
Kyllo v. U.S.,	533 U.S. 27,	121 S. Ct. 2038,150 L. Ed. 2d 94	(2001)

Official and parallel citations are in the following format:

Volume	Reporter	Series (if applicable)	Page
533	U.S.		27
121	S. Ct.		2038
150	L. Ed.	2d	94

The case of Kyllo versus the United States can be found in volume 533 of the United States Reports at page 27. It can also be found in volume 121 of the Supreme Court Reporter page 2038 and in volume 150 of the second series of the U.S. Supreme Court Reports, Lawyer's Edition at page 94. The case was decided in the year 2001.

Identify the Various Parts of the Court's Opinion

The most important part of the case is, of course, the opinion in which the Court tells how and why it decided the case. A Supreme Court opinion usually contains the following information.

THE JUDICIAL HISTORY OF THE CASE

In the opinion, the Court gives the legal history of the case. The Court explains which lower courts heard this case and what those lower courts did and said. It is important not to confuse this history with what the Supreme Court does and says.

THE FACTUAL DISPUTE

The Court describes the nature of the factual dispute that resulted in the appeal to the Supreme Court.

THE ISSUE OR QUESTION PRESENTED

The issue or question presented is the legal question the Court is being asked to decide. A case may have more than one issue or question. Most of the time, in the opinion, the Court will clearly identify the issue with language such as "The issue before us …" or "The question presented here is …."

THE HOLDING

The holding is the way in which the Court resolves the issue or question presented. It is the rule of law that results from the case.

THE RATIONALE

The rationale is the reason for the Court's decision. Usually, the Court describes the law or rules that it relied on in making its decision. The Court refers to constitutional provisions, statutes, and other cases that apply to the factual dispute before it. The Court might also refer to other sources that it considered. In discussing the law and other sources, the Court explains how and why the laws apply. (see Exhibit 1-9)

Exhibit 1-9   How to Read a Supreme Court Case: *Ontario v. Quon*

As you read the following case, *Ontario v. Quon*, note that the Court:

- identifies the issue or question for decision in the first sentence;
- in section I presents the factual background in detail before discussing the law;
- in section I also presents the judicial history of the case, telling the reader what happened at the trial and appellate levels;
- in section II discusses existing rules of law that it will apply to the case;
- later in section II applies the rules of law to the facts of this case;
- finally in section II reaches its conclusion.

As you read the opinion, make notes in the margin indicating specifically where the Court identifies the issue, presents the factual background, presents the judicial history, discusses the law, applies the law, and reaches its conclusion.

Note that following the conclusion, Justice Stevens wrote a concurring opinion. He agreed with the decision, but had other points he wanted to make.

In writing an opinion, a court frequently uses legal abbreviations and citations. In this case the following appear:

App. to Pet. for Cert. 152a—This is a reference to an appendix to the petition for the writ of certiorari and usually contains documents and transcripts from the lower courts.

Id.—*Id.* is a legal abbreviation and refers to the previously cited citation.

© Cengage Learning 2013

ONTARIO v. QUON
560 U.S. ___ (2010)

JUSTICE KENNEDY delivered the opinion of the Court.

This case involves the assertion by a government employer of the right, in circumstances to be described, to read text messages sent and received on a pager the employer owned and issued to an employee. The employee contends that the privacy of the messages is protected by the ban on "unreasonable searches and seizures" found in the Fourth Amendment to the United States Constitution, made applicable to the States by the Due Process Clause of the Fourteenth Amendment. *Mapp v. Ohio*, 367 U.S. 643 (1961). Although the case touches issues of far-reaching significance, the Court concludes it can be resolved by settled principles determining when a search is reasonable.

I

The case arose out of incidents in 2001 and 2002 when respondent Jeff Quon was employed by the Ontario Police Department (OPD). He was a police sergeant and a member of OPD's Special Weapons and Tactics (SWAT) Team. The City, OPD, and OPD's Chief, Lloyd Scharf, are petitioners here. In October 2001, the City acquired 20 alphanumeric pagers capable of sending and receiving text messages. Before acquiring the pagers, the City announced a Computer Policy that applied to all employees. Among other provisions, it specified that the City "reserves the right to monitor and log all network activity including e-mail and Internet use, with or without notice. Users should have no expectation of privacy or confidentiality when using these resources." App. to Pet. for Cert. 152a. Although the Computer Policy did not cover text messages by its explicit terms, at an April 18, 2002, staff meeting at which Quon was present, Lieutenant Steven Duke, the OPD officer responsible for the City's contract with Arch Wireless, told officers that messages sent on the pagers "are considered e-mail messages."

(continued)

(continued)

FACTUAL BACKGROUND *(handwritten margin note)*

Within the first or second billing cycle after the pagers were distributed, Quon exceeded his monthly text message character allotment. Duke told Quon about the overage and reminded him that messages sent on the pagers were "considered e-mail and could be audited." *Id.*, at 40. Duke suggested that Quon could reimburse the City for the overage fee rather than having Duke audit the messages. Quon wrote a check to the City for the overage. Duke offered the same arrangement to other employees who incurred overage fees.

Over the next few months, Quon exceeded his character limit three or four times. Each time he reimbursed the City. Quon and another officer again incurred overage fees for their pager usage in August 2002. At a meeting in October, Duke told Scharf that he had become "tired of being a bill collector." *Id.*, at 91. Scharf decided to determine whether the existing character limit was too low—that is, whether officers such as Quon were having to pay fees for sending work-related messages—or if the overages were for personal messages. Duke reviewed the transcripts and discovered that many of the messages sent and received on Quon's pager were not work related, and some were sexually explicit. Duke reported his findings to Scharf, who, along with Quon's immediate supervisor, reviewed the transcripts himself. After his review, Scharf referred the matter to OPD's internal affairs division for an investigation into whether Quon was violating OPD rules by pursuing personal matters while on duty. The report concluded that Quon had violated OPD rules. Quon was allegedly disciplined.

Quon filed suit against petitioners in the United States District Court for the Central District of California. Among the allegations in the complaint was that petitioners violated respondents' Fourth Amendment rights by obtaining and reviewing the transcript of Jeff Quon's pager messages. The District Court held that petitioners did not violate the Fourth Amendment. It entered judgment in their favor. The United States Court of Appeals for the Ninth Circuit reversed in part. 529 F.3d 892 (2008). The panel agreed with the District Court that Jeff Quon had a reasonable expectation of privacy in his text messages but disagreed with the District Court about whether the search was reasonable. Even though the search was conducted for "a legitimate work-related rationale," the Court of Appeals concluded, it "was not reasonable in scope." *Id.*, at 908. This Court granted the petition for certiorari challenging the Court of Appeals' holding.

II

The Fourth Amendment states: "The right of the people to be secure in their persons, houses, papers, and effects, against unreasonable searches and seizures, shall not be violated . . . ." It is well-settled that the Fourth Amendment's protection extends beyond the sphere of criminal investigations. *Camara v. Municipal Court of City and County of San Francisco*, 387 U.S. 523, 530. The Fourth Amendment applies as well when the Government acts in its capacity as an employer. *Treasury Employees v. Von Raab*, 489 U.S. 656, 665 (1989).

The Court discussed this principle in *O'Connor v. Ortega*, 480 U.S. 709 (1987). The *O'Connor* Court did disagree on the proper analytical framework for Fourth Amendment claims against government employers. A four-Justice plurality concluded that the correct analysis has two steps. First, a court must consider whether "an employee has a reasonable expectation of privacy." *Id.*, at 718. Next, where an employee has a legitimate privacy expectation, an employer's intrusion on that expectation "for noninvestigatory, work-related purposes, as well as for investigations of work-related misconduct, should be judged by the standard of reasonableness under all the circumstances." *Id.*, at 725–726.

III

Before turning to the reasonableness of the search, it is instructive to note the parties' disagreement over whether Quon had a reasonable expectation of privacy. The Court must proceed with care when considering the whole concept of privacy expectations in communications made on electronic equipment owned by a government employer. The judiciary risks error by elaborating too fully on the Fourth Amendment implications of emerging technology before its role in society has become clear. See, e.g., *Olmstead v. United States*, 277 U.S. 438 (1928), overruled by *Katz v. United States*, 389 U.S. 347, 353, (1967). In *Katz*, the Court relied on its own knowledge and experience to conclude that there is a reasonable expectation of privacy in a telephone booth. See *id.*, at 360–361, (Harlan, J., concurring). It is not so clear that courts at present are on so sure a ground. Prudence counsels caution before the facts in the instant case are used to establish far-reaching premises that define the existence, and extent, of privacy expectations enjoyed by employees when using employer-provided communication devices.

Rapid changes in the dynamics of communication and information transmission are evident not just in the

(continued)

(continued)

technology itself but in what society accepts as proper behavior. As one amici brief notes, many employers expect or at least tolerate personal use of such equipment by employees because it often increases worker efficiency.

Even if the Court were certain that the *O'Connor* plurality's approach were the right one, the Court would have difficulty predicting how employees' privacy expectations will be shaped by those changes or the degree to which society will be prepared to recognize those expectations as reasonable. See 480 U.S., at 715. Cell phone and text message communications are so pervasive that some persons may consider them to be essential means or necessary instruments for self-expression, even self-identification. That might strengthen the case for an expectation of privacy. On the other hand, the ubiquity of those devices has made them generally affordable, so one could counter that employees who need cell phones or similar devices for personal matters can purchase and pay for their own. And employer policies concerning communications will of course shape the reasonable expectations of their employees, especially to the extent that such policies are clearly communicated.

A broad holding concerning employees' privacy expectations vis-a-vis employer-provided technological equipment might have implications for future cases that cannot be predicted. It is preferable to dispose of this case on narrower grounds. For present purposes we assume several propositions arguendo: First, Quon had a reasonable expectation of privacy in the text messages sent on the pager provided to him by the City; second, petitioners' review of the transcript constituted a search within the meaning of the Fourth Amendment; and third, the principles applicable to a government employer's search of an employee's physical office apply with at least the same force when the employer intrudes on the employee's privacy in the electronic sphere.

Even if Quon had a reasonable expectation of privacy in his text messages, petitioners did not necessarily violate the Fourth Amendment by obtaining and reviewing the transcripts. Although as a general matter, warrantless searches "are per se unreasonable under the Fourth Amendment," there are "a few specifically established and well-delineated exceptions" to that general rule. *Katz, supra,* at 357. The Court has held that the "special needs" of the workplace justify one such exception. *O'Connor,* 480 U.S., at 725.

Under the approach of the *O'Connor* plurality, when conducted for a "noninvestigatory, work-related purpos[e]"

or for the "investigatio[n] of work-related misconduct," a government employer's warrantless search is reasonable if it is "justified at its inception" and if "the measures adopted are reasonably related to the objectives of the search and not excessively intrusive in light of" the circumstances giving rise to the search. 480 U.S., at 725–726. The search here satisfied the standard of the *O'Connor* plurality and was reasonable under that approach.

The search was justified at its inception because there were "reasonable grounds for suspecting that the search [was] necessary for a noninvestigatory work-related purpose." *Id.,* at 726. As a jury found, Chief Scharf ordered the search in order to determine whether the character limit on the City's contract with Arch Wireless was sufficient to meet the City's needs. The City and OPD had a legitimate interest in ensuring that employees were not being forced to pay out of their own pockets for work-related expenses, or, on the other hand, that the City was not paying for extensive personal communications.

As for the scope of the search, reviewing the transcripts was reasonable because it was an efficient and expedient way to determine whether Quon's overages were the result of work-related messaging or personal use.

Furthermore, and again on the assumption that Quon had a reasonable expectation of privacy in the contents of his messages, the extent of an expectation is relevant to assessing whether the search was too intrusive. See *Von Raab, supra,* at 671. Even if he could assume some level of privacy would inhere in his messages, it would not have been reasonable for Quon to conclude that his messages were in all circumstances immune from scrutiny. Quon was told that his messages were subject to auditing. As a law enforcement officer, he would or should have known that his actions were likely to come under legal scrutiny and that this might entail an analysis of his on-the-job communications. Under the circumstances, a reasonable employee would be aware that sound management principles might require the audit of messages to determine whether the pager was being appropriately used.

Because the search was motivated by a legitimate work-related purpose and because it was not excessive in scope, the search was reasonable under the approach of the *O'Connor* plurality. 480 U.S., at 726. The search was reasonable, and the Court of Appeals erred by holding to the contrary. Petitioners did not violate Quon's Fourth Amendment rights. Because the search was reasonable, petitioners did not violate respondents' Fourth

(continued)

(continued)

Amendment rights, and the court below erred by concluding otherwise. The judgment of the Court of Appeals for the Ninth Circuit is reversed, and the case is remanded for further proceedings consistent with this opinion.

It is so ordered.

JUSTICE KENNEDY, concurring.

Although I join the Court's opinion in full, I write separately to highlight that the Court has sensibly declined to resolve whether the plurality opinion in *O'Connor v. Ortega*, 480 U.S. 709 (1987), provides the correct approach to determining an employee's reasonable expectation of privacy. See ante, at 9. Justice Blackmun, writing for the four dissenting Justices in *O'Connor*, agreed with JUSTICE SCALIA that an employee enjoys a reasonable expectation of privacy in his office. 480 U.S., at 737. But he advocated a third approach to the reasonable expectation of privacy inquiry, separate from those proposed by the *O'Connor* plurality and by JUSTICE SCALIA, see ante, at 8. Recognizing that it is particularly important to safeguard "a public employee's expectation of privacy in the workplace" in light of the "reality of work in modern time," 480 U.S., at 739, which lacks "tidy distinctions" between workplace and private activities, ibid., Justice Blackmun argued that "the precise extent of an employee's expectation of privacy often turns on the nature of the search," *id.*, at 738. And he emphasized that courts should determine this expectation in light of the specific facts of each particular search, rather than by announcing a categorical standard. See *id.*, at 741.

For the reasons stated at page 13 of the Court's opinion, it is clear that respondent Jeff Quon, as a law enforcement officer who served on a SWAT team, should have understood that all of his work-related actions—including all of his communications on his official pager—were likely to be subject to public and legal scrutiny. He therefore had only a limited expectation of privacy in relation to this particular audit of his pager messages. Whether one applies the reasoning from Justice O'Connor's opinion, Justice Scalia's concurrence, or Justice Blackmun's dissent in *O'Connor*, the result is the same: The judgment of the Court of Appeals in this case must be reversed.

The Constitution and Other Sources of U.S. Law

IN THE U.S. LEGAL SYSTEM, laws come from three primary sources: the Constitution, statutes, and case law. Federal law is found in the U.S. Constitution, U.S. Codes, and federal cases. State law comes from state constitutions, state codes, and state cases. In addition to the three primary sources of laws, the legal system also includes administrative regulations from both federal and state administrative agencies.

U.S. Codes are laws passed by the U.S. Congress and are approved by the president. Occasionally, codes are enacted without presidential approval, but this practice requires that the president's veto be overridden by a two-thirds majority of Congress. Federal case law comes from federal appellate courts and from the U.S. Supreme Court. Federal administrative regulations come from federal agencies (e.g., the Social Security Administration). The federal agencies derive their power to make regulations from Congress. On a state level, each state has its own state constitution, state codes (that come from the state legislatures), and state cases (that come from state appellate and supreme courts). State administrative agencies also enact state administrative regulations.

Of all the sources of laws, state and federal, the U.S. Constitution is supreme. As Article VI, Section 2, of the Constitution provides:

> This Constitution, and the Laws of the United States which shall be made in Pursuance thereof; and all treaties made, under the Authority of the United States, shall be the supreme Law of the Land; and the judges in every State shall be bound thereby, any Thing in the Constitution or Laws of any State to the Contrary notwithstanding.

If there is any conflict between the U.S. Constitution and any other law, the Constitution controls. The relationship between statutory law, case law, and the Constitution goes deeper, however.

Statutory Law

Handwritten margin note: Although a law is unconstitutional it doesn't mean it's immorally wrong

The power of the U.S. Congress to enact a law is found in the Constitution. Congress cannot make a law if it does not have the express or implied power to do so by the Constitution. Occasionally, laws that Congress makes are questioned in the courts, and the Supreme Court occasionally decides that a law is outside the power of Congress and is therefore unconstitutional.

Review the case scenarios given earlier in this chapter. Do you think that Congress has the power to ban guns near schools? In the past, Congress did enact a law that made it a federal crime to have a gun near a school. The U.S. Supreme Court ruled that such a law exceeded the power of Congress, however, and declared the law unconstitutional. All federal statutory law must be based on a power given to Congress by the U.S. Constitution.

State statutory law is influenced by the U.S. Constitution. The Constitution sets some limits on the types of laws that states can enact. The Constitution grants certain powers to the federal government and makes that power exclusive. For example, the Constitution grants to the federal government the exclusive right to coin money. States cannot make any law resulting in the creation of its own monetary system. If a power is not exclusively granted to the federal government, then the states are free to enact laws in that area as long as the law is not otherwise contrary to the Constitution. For example, states have the right to enact laws regarding criminal conduct. Yet consider the second hypothetical from the beginning of the chapter. Can a state make it a crime to burn the American flag? Can you think of any constitutional provision that might conflict with that law? If you think that the law might conflict with the First Amendment, you are correct. The Supreme Court said that if burning the flag is an act of political expression, then it is protected by the First Amendment (free speech) to the U.S. Constitution. Making such an act a crime would be against the Constitution, and any such law would therefore be unconstitutional.

State Constitutions

Each state has its own state constitution. These documents, which are often patterned after the U.S. Constitution, establish the state government and its powers and protect the rights and liberties of those who live in the state. State constitutions, like other state laws, are subordinate to the U.S. Constitution. Any time a state constitution conflicts with the Constitution, the U.S. Constitution controls. Many state constitutions contain provisions granting its citizens certain basic rights or freedoms in that state. Such rights must, of course, be consistent with the U.S. Constitution that provides that states must give their citizens certain basic rights. As the Fourteenth Amendment to the U.S. Constitution provides in part:

> No state shall make or enforce any law which shall abridge the privileges or immunities of citizens of the United States; nor shall any State deprive any person of life, liberty, or property, without due process of law; nor deny to any person within its jurisdiction the equal protection of the law.

The Fourteenth Amendment does not prohibit states from granting persons greater rights than those required by the U.S. Constitution. Many of these rights relate to rights that defendants have in criminal cases, and some states do grant greater rights than those

Did You Know?

The U.S. Constitution does not define the number of U.S. Supreme Court judges. In 1869, the number of justices was set at nine. Originally, there were only six members of the Supreme Court.

Supreme Court Building
© Hisham Ibrahim/Photodisc/Getty Images

🏛 **stare decisis**

[pronounce: star-e de-si-sis] (Latin) "Let the decision stand." The rule that when a court has decided a case by applying a legal principle to a set of facts, the court should stick by the principle and apply it to all later cases with clearly similar facts unless there is a strong reason not to, and that courts below must apply the principle in similar cases. These rules help promote fairness and reliability in judicial decision making.

required by the U.S. Constitution. For this reason, state constitutions often play an important role in the area of criminal procedure.

Case Law

Courts, as well as legislatures, are bound to follow the U.S. Constitution. When a constitutional question is presented in a case, then the courts must resolve the case in such a way as to uphold the provisions of the Constitution. The courts must interpret specific articles or amendments to the Constitution and then apply that interpretation to the facts of the case. When interpreting provisions of the Constitution, all trial and appellate courts look to decisions of the U.S. Supreme Court. If the Supreme Court has interpreted a constitutional provision, then the trial and appellate courts must follow that interpretation because of the rule of **stare decisis**. One Supreme Court, however, is not bound by the prior decisions of other Supreme Courts, although the prior decisions are considered and given great deference.

❧ Ethical Decisions—Everyday Choices ❧

The Facts: Brooke is arguing a case in court. Before the argument, each side is required to submit legal memoranda discussing existing law to the judge. In doing research for the memoranda, Brooke finds a published case that strongly supports the opposing side's position.

The Choices: Should Brooke include this case in her legal memoranda or should she omit it, assuming that it is the opposing side's responsibility to mention the case? If the other side does not mention the case to the judge, should Brooke do so, even if it results in a ruling against her client?

Guiding Principles: Attorneys are bound by ethical rules adopted by their states. If they violate the rules, then they can be disciplined (including being disbarred). Most state ethical rules are based on Model Rules of Professional Conduct established by the American Bar Association (ABA), which can be found on the ABA's Web site (<http://www.abanet .org>). Included in those rules is a duty to be honest with the court. Also included is a duty to represent a client diligently. Underlying many of the ethical rules is that attorneys owe a fiduciary duty to their clients. A fiduciary duty means that they owe their client the utmost loyalty and responsibility.

Chapter Summary

The U.S. Constitution, the supreme law of the land, relates to the organization, operation, and powers of the federal government. It was written in 1787 and ratified by the states in 1789. The Constitution was influenced by many prior documents, including the Magna Carta, the English Bill of Rights, the Declaration of Independence, and the Articles of Confederation. The Articles of Confederation, the first document to attempt to establish a national government for the United States, proved to be unworkable because it did not grant sufficient powers to the new government.

The U.S. Constitution consists of a preamble that sets the purpose of the document, seven articles dealing with the organization and powers of the federal government, and twenty-seven amendments, including the Bill of Rights, the first ten amendments. Constitutional law includes not only the Constitution itself but the numerous U.S. Supreme Court cases that interpret various provisions of the Constitution. In addition to the Constitution, U.S. law consists of federal statutes and cases and state constitutions, statutes, and cases. The U.S. Constitution is the supreme law, and all other law must be consistent with the Constitution.

Key Terms

Articles of Confederation
Declaration of Independence
bicameral
federalists
antifederalists
ratified
case law

opinion
published
case brief
syllabus
parallel citation
headnotes
majority opinion

plurality opinion
concurring opinion
dissenting opinion
per curiam opinion
stare decisis

Questions for Review

1. How does the U.S. Constitution affect the federal government?
2. Describe the relevance of the Magna Carta and the English Bill of Rights to the U.S. Constitution.
3. What relevance does the Declaration of Independence have to the U.S. Constitution?
4. What are the Articles of Confederation and why were they unsuccessful?
5. Describe the organization of the U.S. Constitution.
6. What is the Bill of Rights?
7. What is the difference between the Constitution and constitutional law?
8. What is case law and why is it important to constitutional law?
9. List the sources of U.S. law.
10. Describe the relationship of both federal and state statutory law to the U.S. Constitution.

Questions for Analysis

1. Read the Articles of Confederation found in Appendix B and answer the following questions. For each question, state which specific article(s) controls.
   a. What do the Articles of Confederation provide regarding extradition of criminals from one state to another?
   b. What limit was placed on the right of the federal government to enter into treaties?
   c. How many states had to agree for the Committee of the States to take action?
   d. What do the Articles of Confederation state regarding the power of the federal government to tax?
2. Review the summary of the English Bill of Rights (Exhibit 1-2) and the Declaration of Independence (Exhibit 1-3 and Appendix B). What do they have in common?
3. Review Article VI of the Constitution found in Appendix A. Do you think that Dr. Bruce Springer (see Living with the Constitution at the beginning of this chapter) could be forced to sign a loyalty oath? Read the U.S. Supreme Court case of *Cole v. Richardson*, 405 U.S. 676 (1972). Write a short summary of the case. This case can be found in print or on the Internet. (Try searching legal opinions on Google Scholar.)
4. In the case of *Ontario v. Quon*, the Court decided the case without determining if Quon had a reasonable expectation of privacy in his text messages. Why did the Court not want to address this issue?

Assignments and Projects

1. The following is a partial brief of a case found in the chapter. Fill in the missing parts.

Ontario v. Quon
560 U.S. ____(2010)

Judicial History:

Facts:

Issue: Does a government employer violate the Fourth Amendment when a it reads text messages sent and received on a pager the employer owned and issued to an employee in an effort to determine if an appropriate usage plan was in effect and when the employee, a police officer, was advised that text messages were not private?

Holding: A government employer does not violate the Fourth Amendment when a it reads text messages sent and received on a pager the employer owned and issued to an employee in an effort to determine if an appropriate usage plan was in effect and when the employee, a police officer, was advised that text messages were not private.

Rationale: Under the circumstances of this case, the government employer acted reasonably in reading respondent Quon's text messages. The employer had a legitimate business reason for determining how many work-related messages were sent and received. The employer conducted a limited search to make this determination. The respondent was a police officer and should have known that his employer could read text messages if it acted reasonably.

Putting It into Practice

1. Attorneys and their support staff are often required to research factual as well as legal matters. One of the issues at trial in the *Quon* matter was whether Quon had a reasonable expectation that his text messages would be private. In part, this could depend on the "security" of alphanumeric pager transmissions. Using the Internet or any other resources, find information about this topic and write a brief memo describing your findings.

2. All states have state constitutions. Locate a copy of your state constitution and check to see if it contains any provisions similar to the Fourth Amendment of the U.S. Constitution.

Group Activity

Form a group according to your instructor's directions. Review the Bill of Rights to the U.S. Constitution. Assume that you are all members of a committee responsible for drafting a Constitution for a small country that has recently transitioned from a dictatorship into a democracy. Which, if any, of the rights listed in the Bill of Rights would you recommend for this new Constitution? Discuss the advantages and disadvantages of each.

2 The Constitution and the Federal Government: An Overview

The only maxim of a free government ought to be to trust no man living with power to endanger the public liberty.

John Adams

Chapter Outline

Chapter Objectives

When you complete this chapter, you should be able to

1. explain the concept of federalism.
2. describe how the concept of separation of powers relates to the U.S. government.
3. list the provisions of Article I of the U.S. Constitution related to the organization of the U.S. Congress.
4. describe the qualifications and election process for membership in the U.S. Congress.
5. list the provisions of Article II of the U.S. Constitution related to the executive branch of government.
6. explain the concepts of executive privilege and executive immunity.
7. describe the impeachment process as related to the president.
8. summarize the provisions of Article III of the U.S. Constitution related to the federal judiciary.
9. explain the importance of the Judiciary Act of 1789.
10. explain the current structure of the federal court system and the role of each court.

Looking Back

Before reading this chapter, review the following terms and concepts from the previous chapter:

Syllabus A summary of a Supreme Court case prepared by the Court and released with the Court's opinion.

Nominative reporter Early Supreme Court cases were originally published in these reporters, which are named after court reporters of the time.

Dissenting opinions Court opinions written by justices who disagree with the decision of the court. A dissenting opinion is not case law.

Living with the Constitution

Tomas Vierra recently graduated from college with a degree in political science. From the time he was young, his parents stressed how lucky they were to live in the United States, and Tomas grew up with a strong sense of patriotism. Tomas and his parents immigrated to the United States when Tomas was an infant. Several years later they all became citizens.

Tomas's dream is to hold national political office. Soon he will enter law school, thinking that this education will be good preparation for any office.

federalism

A system of political organization with several different levels of government (e.g., city, state, and national) coexisting in the same area, with the lower levels having some independent powers.

separation of powers

The division of the federal government (and state governments) into legislative (lawmaking), judicial (law-interpreting), and executive (law-carrying-on) branches. Each acts to prevent the others from becoming too powerful.

checks and balances

A restraint.

concurrent

Running together; having the same authority at the same time. As examples, courts have concurrent jurisdiction when each one has the power to deal with the same case; concurrent sentences are prison terms that run at the same time; and federal and state governments have concurrent power to govern in many areas.

exclusive

Shutting out all others; sole; one only. For example, if a court has exclusive jurisdiction over a subject, no other court in the area can decide a lawsuit on that subject.

ALTHOUGH THE FOUNDING FATHERS AGREED that a national or federal government was needed, they did not agree about the form this government should take. The result was a compromise intended to prevent the abuses that could result from a powerful central government. The compromise was also intended to satisfy the concerns of both the small and large states. The newly formed government was based on three important concepts: federalism, separation of powers, and checks and balances, and consisted of three branches: the legislative, the judicial, and the executive. This chapter explores the concepts on which this government is based and provides an overview of its structure. Subsequent chapters deal with the various powers granted to each of the branches of government.

Federalism

THE U.S. CONSTITUTION CREATED A national government that was intended to coexist with the existing state governments. Thus, citizens of the United States would be subject to two governments, state and national. The term *federalism* is applied to this system of dual governments (although it is interesting to note that the national government is usually referred to as the *federal* government).

The national government created under the Constitution was not a government of unlimited power. Under Article I, Section 8 of the Constitution, it has *express* power in certain specified areas, such as minting coins and regulating the post office. It has *implied* powers to do whatever is necessary and proper to carry out its express powers. In an attempt to further clarify the powers of state and federal government, the Tenth Amendment to the Constitution was added. This amendment provides that all powers not given to the national government are reserved for the states.

Although state and federal governments are separate, in some areas their respective powers coexist or are **concurrent**. For example, Article 1, Section 8 gives the federal government the right to tax. This power is shared by both federal and state governments. In other areas, the powers of each government are **exclusive**. For example, the federal government is given the exclusive power to coin money. States cannot produce their own currency. Sometimes the Constitution is silent as to whether specific powers are exclusive or concurrent, and disputes arise concerning this issue. Eventually, a court may be asked to determine the matter.

In the case of *Gregory v. Ashcroft*, which follows, the U.S. Supreme Court had to decide if the state of Missouri had the power to require that judges retire at the age of seventy. Several judges claimed that the state did not have this power and that the state law violated a federal law prohibiting employment discrimination. In the decision, affirming the power of the state to have such a law, the Court discusses at length the concept of federalism.

Gregory v. Ashcroft

501 U.S. 452 (1991)

This case deals with the Age Discrimination in Employment Act, abbreviated ADEA in the Court's opinion. This act is federal law created by Congress and found in Title 29 of the United States Code. The Court cites it as 29 U.S.C. *followed by the specific section discussed. The Court also refers to early Supreme Court cases, giving the citation to the nominative reporter, for example,* Texas v. White, 7 Wall. 700, 725 (1869).

(continued)

(continued)

JUSTICE O'CONNOR delivered the opinion of the Court.

Article V, § 26 of the Missouri Constitution provides that "all judges other than municipal judges shall retire at the age of seventy years." We consider whether this mandatory retirement provision violates the federal Age Discrimination in Employment Act (ADEA).

The ADEA makes it unlawful for an "employer" "to discharge any individual" who is at least 40 years old "because of such individual's age." 29 U.S.C. 623(a), 631(a). The term "employer" is defined to include "a State or political subdivision of a State." 29 U.S.C. 630(b)(2). Petitioners work for the State of Missouri. They contend that the Missouri mandatory retirement requirement for judges violates the ADEA.

As every schoolchild learns, our Constitution establishes a system of dual sovereignty between the States and the Federal Government. Over 120 years ago, the Court described the constitutional scheme of dual sovereigns:

> "The people of each State compose a State, having its own government, and endowed with all the functions essential to separate and independent existence . . . Without the States in union, there could be no such political body as the United States. . . . The Constitution, in all its provisions, looks to an indestructible Union, composed of indestructible States." *Texas v. White*, 7 Wall. 700, 725 (1869), quoting *Lane County v. Oregon*, 7 Wall. 71, 76 (1869).

The Constitution created a Federal Government of limited powers. "The powers not delegated to the United States by the Constitution, nor prohibited by it to the States, are reserved to the States respectively, or to the people." U.S. Const., Amdt. 10. The States thus retain substantial sovereign authority under our constitutional system.

This federalist structure of joint sovereigns preserves to the people numerous advantages. It assures a decentralized government that will be more sensitive to the diverse needs of a heterogeneous society; it increases opportunity for citizen involvement in democratic processes; it allows for more innovation and experimentation in government; and it makes government more responsive by putting the States in competition for a mobile citizenry.

Perhaps the principal benefit of the federalist system is a check on abuses of government power. The constitutionally mandated balance of power between the States and the Federal Government was adopted by the Framers to ensure the protection of our fundamental liberties. Just as the separation and independence of the coordinate Branches of the Federal Government serve to prevent the accumulation of excessive power in any one Branch, a healthy balance of power between the States and the Federal Government will reduce the risk of tyranny and abuse from either front.

One fairly can dispute whether our federalist system has been successful in checking government abuse, but there is no doubt about the design. If this "double security" is to be effective, there must be a proper balance between the States and the Federal Government. These twin powers will act as mutual restraints only if both are credible. In the tension between federal and state power lies the promise of liberty.

The Federal Government holds a decided advantage in this delicate balance: the Supremacy Clause. U.S. Const., Art. VI. As long as it is acting within the powers granted it under the Constitution, Congress may impose its will on the States. Congress may legislate in areas traditionally regulated by the States. This is an extraordinary power in a federalist system. It is a power that we must assume Congress does not exercise lightly.

The present case concerns a state constitutional provision through which the people of Missouri establish a qualification for those who sit as their judges. This provision goes beyond an area traditionally regulated by the States; it is a decision of the most fundamental sort for a sovereign entity. Through the structure of its government, and the character of those who exercise government authority, a State defines itself as a sovereign.

In 1974, Congress extended the substantive provisions of the ADEA to include the States as employers. At the same time, Congress amended the definition of "employee" to exclude all elected and most high-ranking government officials. Under the Act, as amended:

> "The term 'employee' means an individual employed by any employer except that the term 'employee' shall not include any person elected to public office in any State or political subdivision of any State by the qualified voters thereof,

(continued)

(continued)

or any person chosen by such officer to be on such officer's personal staff, or an appointee on the policymaking level or an immediate adviser with respect to the exercise of the constitutional or legal powers of the office." 29 U.S.C. 630(f).

Governor Ashcroft contends that the 630(f) exclusion of certain public officials also excludes judges, like petitioners, who are appointed to office by the Governor and are then subject to retention election. Governor Ashcroft relies on the plain language of the statute: it exempts persons appointed "at the policymaking level." The Governor argues that state judges, in fashioning and applying the common law, make policy.

We will not read the ADEA to cover state judges unless Congress has made it clear that judges are included. In the context of a statute that plainly excludes most important state public officials, "appointee on the policymaking level" is sufficiently broad that we cannot conclude that the statute plainly covers appointed state judges. Therefore, it does not.

The people of Missouri have a legitimate, indeed compelling, interest in maintaining a judiciary fully capable of performing the demanding tasks that judges must perform. It is an unfortunate fact of life that physical and mental capacity sometimes diminish with age. The people may therefore wish to replace some older judges. The people of Missouri rationally could conclude that the threat of deterioration at age 70 is sufficiently great, and the alternatives for removal sufficiently inadequate, that they will require all judges to step aside at age 70. This classification does not violate the Equal Protection Clause.

The people of Missouri have established a qualification for those who would be their judges. It is their prerogative as citizens of a sovereign State to do so. Accordingly, the judgment of the Court of Appeals is
AFFIRMED.

Something to Consider

In its decision, the Supreme Court says: "In the tension between federal and state power lies the promise of liberty." What does this statement mean? Do you agree?

Separation of Powers and Checks and Balances

THE CONSTITUTION PROVIDES FOR A national government with three separate and distinct branches: the executive, the legislative, and the judicial branches. Each branch is given a different role. In general, the legislative branch makes laws, the executive branch enforces laws, and the judicial branch interprets laws and applies them to factual disputes. This division of power is referred to as the separation of powers. A benefit of this concept is that no one branch is clothed with too much power because each branch exercises some "check" over the other branches. For example, the legislative branch has the power to make laws. The president, the chief executive, however, has the power to veto legislation. The president's veto can be overridden by a two-thirds majority of Congress. Even if a president approves legislation, that law is still subject to interpretation by the courts, which have the power to determine if the law violates any provision of the Constitution. If a court does so, the law is struck down. This system is called checks and balances. The concepts of separation of powers and checks and balances help ensure that no one group or individual achieves too much power. See Exhibit 2-1 for examples of how the system of checks and balances works with an important power, the power to enact laws.

The concepts of separation of powers and checks and balances played an important role in the Supreme Court's 1998 decision regarding the right of the president to use a line item veto. A line item veto is a veto of only part of a law. It gives the president the right to strike out part of a law, usually a single item of expense in a larger appropriations bill. The majority of the Court found that this practice was the same as "amending" or "repealing" the law and that such a procedure violated the separation of powers. Some of the justices disagreed. The reasons are found in the Court's opinion in *Clinton v. City of New York*.

Exhibit 2-1 Checks and Balances: The Lawmaking Power

Legislature makes the laws.

- President (executive) can veto laws.
- Courts (judicial) can declare laws unconstitutional.

President can veto laws.

- Legislature (Congress) can override veto.

Courts can declare laws unconstitutional.

- Legislature (Congress) can amend or change the law to make it constitutional.
- Legislature (Congress) can introduce a constitutional amendment.
- President (executive) appoints judges subject to Senate approval.

© Cengage Learning 2013

Clinton v. City of New York

524 U.S. 417 (1998)

JUSTICE STEVENS delivered the opinion of the Court.

The Line Item Veto Act gives the President the power to "cancel in whole" three types of provisions that have been signed into law: "(1) any dollar amount of discretionary budget authority; (2) any item of new direct spending; or (3) any limited tax benefit." 2 U.S.C. § 691(a) (1994 ed., Supp. II). In both legal and practical effect, the President has amended two Acts of Congress by repealing a portion of each. There is no provision in the Constitution that authorizes the President to enact, to amend, or to repeal statutes. Both Article I and Article II assign responsibilities to the President that directly relate to the lawmaking process but neither addresses the issue presented by these cases. The President "shall from time to time give to the Congress Information on the State of the Union, and recommend to their Consideration such Measures as he shall judge necessary and expedient . . . " Art. II, §3. Thus, he may initiate and influence legislative proposals. Moreover, after a bill has passed both Houses of Congress, but "before it becomes a Law," it must be presented to the President. If he approves it, "he shall sign it, but if not he shall return it, with his Objections to that House in which it shall have originated, who shall enter the Objections at large on their Journal, and proceed to reconsider it." Art. I, §7, cl. 2. 28.

His "return" of a bill, which is usually described as a "veto," is subject to being overridden by a two-thirds vote in each House.

There are important differences between the President's "return" of a bill pursuant to Article I, §7, and the exercise of the President's cancellation authority pursuant to the Line Item Veto Act. The constitutional return takes place before the bill becomes law; the statutory cancellation occurs after the bill becomes law. The constitutional return is of the entire bill; the statutory cancellation is of only a part. Although the Constitution expressly authorizes the President to play a role in the process of enacting statutes, it is silent on the subject of unilateral Presidential action that either repeals or amends parts of duly enacted statutes.

What has emerged in these cases from the President's exercise of his statutory cancellation powers, however, are truncated versions of two bills that passed both Houses of Congress. They are not the product of the "finely wrought" procedure that the Framers designed.

The Line Item Veto Act authorizes the President himself to effect the repeal of laws, for his own policy reasons, without observing the procedures set out in Article I, §7. The fact that Congress intended such a result is of no moment. Although Congress presumably anticipated that the President might cancel some of the items in the Balanced Budget Act and in the Taxpayer Relief Act, Congress cannot alter the procedures set out in Article I, §7, without amending the Constitution. It is so ordered.

(continued)

(continued)

JUSTICE BREYER, with whom JUSTICE O'CONNOR and JUSTICE SCALIA join dissenting.

In my view the Line Item Veto Act does not violate any specific textual constitutional command, nor does it violate any implicit Separation of Powers principle. Consequently, I believe that the Act is constitutional.

I approach the constitutional question before us with three general considerations in mind. First, the Act represents a legislative effort to provide the President with the power to give effect to some, but not to all, of the expenditure and revenue-diminishing provisions contained in a single massive appropriations bill. And this objective is constitutionally proper.

When our Nation was founded, Congress could easily have provided the President with this kind of power. In that time period, our population was less than four million, federal employees numbered fewer than 5,000, annual federal budget outlays totaled approximately $4 million.

At that time, a Congress, wishing to give a President the power to select among appropriations, could simply have embodied each appropriation in a separate bill, each bill subject to a separate Presidential veto.

Today, however, our population is about 250 million, the Federal Government employs more than four million people, the annual federal budget is $1.5 trillion, and a typical budget appropriations bill may have a dozen titles, hundreds of sections, and spread across more than 500 pages of the Statutes at Large. Congress cannot divide such a bill into thousands, or tens of thousands, of separate appropriations bills, each one of which the President would have to sign, or to veto, separately. Thus, the question is whether the Constitution permits Congress to choose a particular novel means to achieve this same, constitutionally legitimate, end.

I must consider whether the Act nonetheless violates Separation of Powers principles—principles that arise out of the Constitution's vesting of the "executive Power" in "a President," U.S. Const., Art. II, §1, and "all legislative Powers" in "a Congress," Art. I, §1., I recognize that the Act before us is novel. The means chosen do not amount literally to the enactment, repeal, or amendment of a law. Nor, for that matter, do they amount literally to the "line item veto" that the Act's title announces. Those means do not violate any basic Separation of Powers principle. They do not improperly shift the constitutionally foreseen balance of power from Congress to the President. Nor, since they comply with Separation of Powers principles, do they threaten the liberties of individual citizens. They represent an experiment that may, or may not, help representative government work better. The Constitution, in my view, authorizes Congress and the President to try novel methods in this way. Consequently, with respect, I dissent.

For the foregoing reasons, I respectfully dissent.

The Legislative Branch (Article I)

ARTICLE I ESTABLISHES AND SETS forth the powers of the legislative branch of the federal government. Section 1 states: "All legislative Powers herein granted shall be vested in a Congress of the United States, which shall consist of a Senate and House of Representatives." Various sections of Article I cover matters concerning the House of Representatives and the Senate, including:

- qualifications and selection of members
- the compensation of legislators
- legislative protections
- the legislative process
- the powers of Congress to make laws
- impeachment of public officials

Qualification and Selection of Legislators

Membership in the House of Representatives is limited to individuals who (1) are at least twenty-five years of age, (2) have been U.S. citizens for at least seven years, and (3) are inhabitants of the state they represent. They are elected and serve two-year terms.

The number of representatives from each state is determined by state population. The House of Representatives is led by the Speaker of the House, who is elected by the members.

Membership in the Senate is limited to individuals who (1) are at least thirty years of age, (2) have been U.S. citizens for at least nine years, and (3) are inhabitants of the state they represent. Each state has two elected senators who serve six-year terms. Article I specifies that representatives be elected at popular elections, whereas senators are to be selected by state legislators. The selection process of senators was changed with the Seventeenth Amendment in 1913, and senators are now chosen through popular elections. Although senators serve six-year terms, Senate elections are held every two years, with one third of the membership being elected. The Vice President presides as the president of the Senate, although he or she does not vote on issues unless there is a tie vote. See Table 2-1.

Table 2-1 Senators and Representatives	
Senators	**Representatives**
At least thirty years old	At least twenty-five years old
Citizens for nine years	Citizens for seven years
Inhabitants of state they represent	Inhabitants of state they represent
Elected by popular vote	Elected by popular vote
Serve six-year terms	Serve two-year terms
Each state has two senators	Number for each state based on population
Led by Vice President	Led by Speaker of the House

© Cengage Learning 2013

Other than age, citizenship, and residency, the Constitution imposes no limitations on congressional membership. In recent years, some groups have advocated imposing limits on the number of terms that legislators could serve. The Supreme Court case of *U.S. Term Limits, Inc. v. Thornton* addresses the constitutionality of this limit. In *Thornton*, the citizens of Arkansas voted to amend the Arkansas state constitution. The amendment imposed term limits upon the individuals it elected to the House of Representatives and the Senate. The amendment was challenged, and the U.S. Supreme Court agreed with the Arkansas courts that this amendment was unconstitutional. An excerpt from the Court Syllabus for this case is included here.

U.S. Term Limits, Inc. v. Thornton
514 U.S. 779 (1995)

Syllabus:

Respondent Hill filed this suit in Arkansas state court challenging the constitutionality of § 3 of Amendment 73 to the Arkansas Constitution, which prohibits the name of an otherwise-eligible candidate for Congress from appearing on the general election ballot if that candidate has already served three terms in the House of Representatives or two terms in the Senate. The trial court held that § 3 violated Article I of the Federal Constitution, and the Arkansas Supreme Court affirmed. A plurality of the latter court concluded that the States have no authority "to change, add to, or diminish" the age, citizenship, and residency requirements for congressional service enumerated in the Qualifications Clauses, U.S. Const., Art. I, § 2, cl. 2, and Art. I, § 3, cl. 3, and rejected the argument that Amendment 73 is constitutional because it is formulated

(continued)

(continued)

as a ballot access restriction rather than an outright disqualification of congressional incumbents.

Held: Section 3 of Amendment 73 to the Arkansas Constitution violates the Federal Constitution. Pp. 787–838.

(a) The power granted to each House of Congress to judge the "Qualifications of its own Members," Art. I, § 5, cl. 1, does not include the power to alter or add to the qualifications set forth in the Constitution's text. This Court reaffirms that the constitutional qualifications for congressional service are "fixed," at least in the sense that they may not be supplemented by Congress.

(b) So too, the Constitution prohibits States from imposing congressional qualifications additional to those specifically enumerated in its text. Petitioners' argument that States possess control over qualifications as part of the original powers reserved to them by the Tenth Amendment is rejected.

(c) A state congressional term limits measure is unconstitutional when it has the likely effect of handicapping a class of candidates and has the sole purpose of creating additional qualifications indirectly. The Court rejects petitioners' argument that Amendment 73 is valid because it merely precludes certain congressional candidates from being certified and having their names appear on the ballot, and allows them to run as write-in candidates and serve if elected. Even if petitioners' narrow understanding of qualifications is correct, Amendment 73 must fall because it is an indirect attempt to evade the Qualifications Clauses' requirements and trivializes the basic democratic principles underlying those Clauses.

(d) State imposition of term limits for congressional service would effect such a fundamental change in the constitutional framework that it must come through a constitutional amendment properly passed under the procedures set forth in Article V. Absent such an amendment, allowing individual States to craft their own congressional qualifications would erode the structure designed by the Framers to form a "more perfect Union."

Compensation of Legislators

Article I provides that legislators be compensated. It does not, however, fix an amount for this compensation. That amount is determined by Congress itself. To limit a self-serving authorization of excessive compensation, the Twenty-seventh Amendment to the Constitution was adopted providing that any increase in legislative compensation not take effect until at least one election of representatives has intervened.

Legislative Protections

immunity
The freedom of national, state, and local government officials from prosecution for, or arrest during, most official acts, and their freedom from most tort lawsuits resulting from their official duties.

In addition to detailing the organization of the federal Congress, Article I also creates special protection for legislators by creating civil and criminal **immunity** for any "speech or debate" in either house. Legislators cannot be sued for anything they say as long as it is part of the legislative process. The purpose of this immunity is to preserve the integrity of the legislative process. It applies not only to spoken words, but also to written reports and resolutions prepared as part of the legislative process. The immunity also extends to legislative assistants.

The Legislative Process

Enacting federal law is often a long and cumbersome process. Bills are discussed, reviewed by committees, and amended and done so in each house. If the president vetoes the bill, it can go back to Congress, and if then approved by a two-thirds majority of each house, it becomes law despite the presidential veto. If the president does not sign or veto, then the bill becomes law after ten days (excepting Sundays) unless Congress adjourns within that time. Article I sets forth a very brief description of how a bill becomes law:

> All Bills for raising Revenue shall originate in the House of Representatives; but the Senate may propose or concur with amendments as on other Bills.

> Every Bill which shall have passed the House of Representatives and the Senate, shall, before it becomes a law, be presented to the president of the United States: If he approves he shall sign it, but if not he shall return it, with his Objections to that House in which it shall have originated, who shall enter the Objections at large on their Journal, and proceed to reconsider it. If after such Reconsideration two-thirds of that House shall agree to pass the Bill, it shall be sent, together with the Objections, to the other House, by which it shall likewise be reconsidered, and if approved by two-thirds of that House, it shall become a Law. But in all such Cases the Votes of both Houses shall be determined by Yeas and Nays, and the Names of the Persons voting for and against the Bill shall be entered on the Journal of each House respectively. If any Bill shall not be returned by the president within ten Days (Sundays excepted) after it shall have been presented to him, the Same shall be a Law, in like Manner as if he had signed it, unless the Congress by their Adjournment prevent its Return, in which Case it shall not be a Law.

> Every Order, Resolution, or Vote to which the Concurrence of the Senate and House of Representatives may be necessary (except on a question of Adjournment) shall be presented to the president of the United States; and before the Same shall take Effect, shall be approved by him, or being disapproved by him, shall be repassed by two-thirds of the Senate and House of Representatives, according to the Rules and Limitations prescribed in the Case of a Bill.

> (Article I, § 7).

Today, other steps in the process have been added by the legislature. When bills become law, they are generally added to the **United States Code,** which is the topical compilation of laws enacted by Congress and approved by the president (or adopted by Congress overriding a presidential veto).

Powers of Congress

The power of the U.S. Congress is defined by the Constitution. In general, Congress has the power

- to make laws
- to approve presidential appointments, including federal judges, cabinet members, and ambassadors
- to impeach the president, vice president, and other national officers, including judges

In exercising its lawmaking powers, Congress is limited by the Constitution, which lists or enumerates those areas that the legislature can regulate. Article I Section 8 lists many of the powers and expressly gives Congress the right to: lay and collect taxes, borrow money, regulate international and interstate commerce, establish a uniform rule of naturalization and bankruptcies, coin money, punish counterfeiting, establish post offices, provide copyright and patent protection for limited times, and establish tribunals inferior to the Supreme Court. Congress is also given exclusive lawmaking power over the seat of government as well as several described war and military powers.

In addition to the **enumerated powers,** Section 8 further empowers Congress to "make all laws which shall be necessary and proper for carrying into Execution the foregoing

🏛 **United States Code**
The official law books containing federal laws organized by subject. They are recompiled every six years, and supplements are published when needed.

🏛 **enumerated powers**
Mentioned specifically; listed one by one.

🏛 **Necessary and Proper Clause**

The clause (Article I, Section 8, Clause 18) of the U.S. Constitution that gives Congress the power to pass all laws appropriate to carry out its functions.

Powers, and all other Powers vested by this Constitution in the Government of the United States, or in any Department or Officer thereof." This right is known as the **Necessary and Proper Clause.** Unfortunately, questions as to the interpretation of the legislative powers have arisen often. As a result, numerous Supreme Court cases provide interpretations of the various lawmaking powers of Congress.

Another important power of Congress is its power to **impeach** the president, vice president, judges, and other national officers. This process allows Congress to remove these officials from office for misconduct. (See Appendix A for a copy of the entire U.S. Constitution.)

Specific powers of Congress are discussed further in Chapter 4.

The Executive Branch (Article II)

The office of president is created by Article II which states, "The Executive Power shall be vested in a President of the United States of America." Article II describes the qualifications, the election process, and specific powers of the president.

Presidential Qualifications

🏛 **electoral college**

A name for the persons chosen by voters to elect the president and vice president of the United States. The electoral college is now almost a formality, since the electoral college generally votes in accordance with the popular vote of a state. Theoretically, however, some electors might decide to vote differently, a choice that could change the result of a close election.

The president must be a natural-born citizen and be at least thirty-five years old. According to Article II, "No Person except a natural born Citizen, or a Citizen of the United States, at the time of the Adoption of this Constitution, shall be eligible to the Office of President; neither shall any Person be eligible to that Office who shall not have attained to the Age of thirty five Years, and been fourteen Years a Resident within the United States." It is clear that the constitutional founders placed great weight on U.S. citizenship.

Presidential Election Process

In the 2000 election, Albert Gore received more popular votes than did George W. Bush. Nevertheless, Bush became the forty-third president of the United States because the president is not directly elected by popular vote but by an **electoral college.** The number of electors for each state is set by the Twelfth Amendment to the Constitution and allows each state a number equal to the number of senators and representatives. The number of electors for the District of Columbia is set by the Twenty-third Amendment.

🏛 **impeach (impeachment)**

The first step in the removal from public office of a high public official, such as a governor, judge, or the president. In the case of the president of the United States, the House of Representatives makes an accusation by drawing up articles of impeachment, voting on them, and presenting them to the Senate. This process makes up impeachment. Impeachment, however, is popularly thought to include the process that may take place after impeachment: the trial of the president in the Senate and conviction by two-thirds of the senators.

At the popular election, voters usually select a block of electors who support one of the presidential candidates. Thus, when the electors meet to select the president, they usually vote as a block for one candidate rather than in proportion to the way the popular votes are cast within the state. An individual must receive a majority of the electoral votes to become president. In a two-party system, which prevails in the United States, that is usually not a problem. Should any candidate fail to receive a majority of electoral votes, the House of Representatives selects the president. Such was the case in the early years of the United States.

Because of the Twenty-second Amendment, a president can be elected only to two four-year terms of office. See Exhibit 2-2.

Impeachment of the President

Congress has the power TO remove or **impeach** the president from office for "treason, bribery, or other high crimes and misdemeanors." Removing the president from office involves two steps. The first step is impeachment by the U.S. House of Representatives. The term impeachment refers to an accusation of malfeasance; it does not refer to actual removal from office. After the House has impeached or accused the official of some offense, a trial

Exhibit 2-2 The White House: Home of Every President Since John Adams

Courtesy of Photodisc/Getty Images

on the accusations takes place in the U.S. Senate. If the accusation is against the president, then the Chief Justice of the Supreme Court presides over the trial. The president is not removed from office unless two-thirds of all senators present vote to convict. Impeachment of a president has occurred only twice in U.S. history. President Andrew Johnson and President Clinton faced impeachment and trial, although both were acquitted. See Exhibit 2-3 for the Articles of Impeachment (the accusation) that were issued by the House of Representatives against President Clinton.

Exhibit 2-3 Articles of Impeachment against William Clinton

HOUSE RESOLUTION 611

Impeaching William Jefferson Clinton, President of the United States, for high crimes and misdemeanors.

IN THE HOUSE OF REPRESENTATIVES
DECEMBER 15, 1998

Mr. HYDE submitted the following resolution; which was referred to the House Calendar and ordered to be printed.

RESOLUTION
Impeaching William Jefferson Clinton, President of the United States, for high crimes and misdemeanors.

(continued)

(continued)

Resolved, That William Jefferson Clinton, President of the United States, is impeached for high crimes and misdemeanors, and that the following articles of impeachment be exhibited to the United States Senate:

Articles of impeachment exhibited by the House of Representatives of the United States of America in the name of itself and of the people of the United States of America, against William Jefferson Clinton, President of the United States of America, in maintenance and support of its impeachment against him for high crimes and misdemeanors.

Article I

In his conduct while President of the United States, William Jefferson Clinton, in violation of his constitutional oath faithfully to execute the office of President of the United States and, to the best of his ability, preserve, protect, and defend the Constitution of the United States, and in violation of his constitutional duty to take care that the laws be faithfully executed, has willfully corrupted and manipulated the judicial process of the United States for his personal gain and exoneration, impeding the administration of justice, in that:

On August 17, 1998, William Jefferson Clinton swore to tell the truth, the whole truth, and nothing but the truth before a Federal grand jury of the United States. Contrary to that oath, William Jefferson Clinton willfully provided perjurious, false and misleading testimony to the grand jury concerning one or more of the following: (1) the nature and details of his relationship with a subordinate Government employee; (2) prior perjurious, false and misleading testimony he gave in a Federal civil rights action brought against him; (3) prior false and misleading statements he allowed his attorney to make to a Federal judge in that civil rights action; and (4) his corrupt efforts to influence the testimony of witnesses and to impede the discovery of evidence in that civil rights action.

In doing this, William Jefferson Clinton has undermined the integrity of his office, has brought disrepute on the Presidency, has betrayed his trust as President, and has acted in a manner subversive of the rule of law and justice, to the manifest injury of the people of the United States.

Wherefore, William Jefferson Clinton, by such conduct, warrants impeachment and trial, and removal from office and disqualification to hold and enjoy any office of honor, trust, or profit under the United States.

Article II

In his conduct while President of the United States, William Jefferson Clinton, in violation of his constitutional oath faithfully to execute the office of President of the United States and, to the best of his ability, preserve, protect, and defend the Constitution of the United States, and in violation of his constitutional duty to take care that the laws be faithfully executed, has willfully corrupted and manipulated the judicial process of the United States for his personal gain and exoneration, impeding the administration of justice, in that:

(1) On December 23, 1997, William Jefferson Clinton, in sworn answers to written questions asked as part of a Federal civil rights action brought against him, willfully provided perjurious, false and misleading testimony in response to questions deemed relevant by a Federal judge concerning conduct and proposed conduct with subordinate employees.

(2) On January 17, 1998, William Jefferson Clinton swore under oath to tell the truth, the whole truth, and nothing but the truth in a deposition given as part of a Federal civil rights action brought against him. Contrary to that oath, William Jefferson Clinton willfully provided perjurious, false and misleading testimony in response to questions deemed relevant by a Federal judge concerning the nature and details of his relationship with a subordinate Government employee, his knowledge of that employee's involvement and participation in the civil rights action brought against him, and his corrupt efforts to influence the testimony of that employee.

In all of this, William Jefferson Clinton has undermined the integrity of his office, has brought disrepute on the Presidency, has betrayed his trust as President, and has acted in a manner subversive of the rule of law and justice, to the manifest injury of the people of the United States.

Wherefore, William Jefferson Clinton, by such conduct, warrants impeachment and trial, and removal from office and disqualification to hold and enjoy any office of honor, trust, or profit under the United States.

Executive Privilege

The president meets often with cabinet heads to discuss important matters of both domestic and foreign concern. The need for confidentiality during these discussions is obvious. Yet the Constitution is silent as to any privilege or right to keep such communications private and confidential. Not until 1974 was such a privilege formally recognized by the Supreme Court when it decided a case stemming from the famous Watergate scandal.

The Watergate scandal involved a burglary of the Democratic National Committee headquarters during the presidential election. The perpetrators of the break-in were eventually connected to President Nixon's staff, and some evidence indicated that the president was involved in a "cover-up." During investigations of the Watergate break-in, Congress learned that President Nixon secretly made audiotapes of many conversations in the Oval Office. A special prosecutor pursuing criminal indictments against several individuals who were aides and advisors to the president obtained a subpoena duces tecum to get these tapes. The president resisted the subpoena, claiming **executive privilege**. The case soon reached the Supreme Court, which decided that there is a constitutional basis for an executive privilege but that the privilege is not absolute. President Nixon claimed that there was a general privilege applying to all situations. The Court disagreed, indicating that the claim of privilege must be balanced against other interests. In this instance, the Court balanced the privilege with the need for achieving justice in a criminal case and found that the privilege did not exist. The Court did mention, however, that in matters of national security, the result might be the opposite. All the justices concurred in the opinion, except for Justice William Rehnquist, who did not take part. An excerpt from the decision is included here.

 executive privilege

The right of the president and subordinates to keep some information (primarily documents) from public disclosure. The privilege is used most often for military and diplomatic secrets.

United States v. Nixon
418 U.S. 683 (1974)

MR. CHIEF JUSTICE BURGER delivered the opinion of the Court.

The Claim of Privilege

Neither the doctrine of separation of powers, nor the need for confidentiality of high-level communications, without more, can sustain an absolute, unqualified Presidential privilege of immunity from judicial process under all circumstances. The President's need for complete candor and objectivity from advisers calls for great deference from the courts. However, when the privilege depends solely on the broad, undifferentiated claim of public interest in the confidentiality of such conversations, a confrontation with other values arises. Absent a claim of need to protect military, diplomatic, or sensitive national security secrets, we find it difficult to accept the argument that even the very important interest in confidentiality of Presidential communications is significantly diminished by production of such material for in camera inspection with all the protection that a district court will be obliged to provide. The impediment that an absolute, unqualified privilege would place in the way of the primary constitutional duty of the Judicial Branch to do justice in criminal prosecutions would plainly conflict with the function of the courts under Art. III. In designing the structure of our Government and dividing and allocating the sovereign power among three co-equal branches, the Framers of the Constitution sought to provide a comprehensive system, but the separate powers were not intended to operate with absolute independence.

Since we conclude that the legitimate needs of the judicial process may outweigh Presidential privilege, it is necessary to resolve those competing interests in a manner that preserves the essential functions of each branch. The right and indeed the duty to resolve that question does not free the Judiciary from according high respect to the representations made on behalf of the President. The expectation of a President to the confidentiality of his conversations and correspondence, like the claim of confidentiality of judicial deliberations, for example, has all the values to which we accord deference for the privacy of all citizens and, added to those values, is the necessity for protection of the public interest in candid, objective, and even blunt or harsh opinions in Presidential decision-making. A President and those who assist him must be free to explore alternatives in the process of shaping policies and making decisions and to do so in a way many would be unwilling to express except privately. These are the considerations justifying a presumptive privilege for Presidential communications. The privilege is

(continued)

(continued)

fundamental to the operation of Government and inextricably rooted in the separation of powers under the Constitution. But this presumptive privilege must be considered in light of our historic commitment to the rule of law. This is nowhere more profoundly manifest than in our view that "the twofold aim of criminal justice is that guilt shall not escape or innocence suffer." *Berger v. United States*, 295 U.S., at 88. The very integrity of the judicial system and public confidence in the system depend on full disclosure of all the facts, within the framework of the rules of evidence. To ensure that justice is done, it is imperative to the function of courts that compulsory process be available for the production of evidence needed either by the prosecution or by the defense.

In this case we must weigh the importance of the general privilege of confidentiality of Presidential communications in performance of the President's responsibilities against the inroads of such a privilege on the fair administration of criminal justice. The interest in preserving confidentiality is weighty indeed and entitled to great respect. However, we cannot conclude that advisers will be moved to temper the candor of their remarks by the infrequent occasions of disclosure because of the possibility that such conversations will be called for in the context of a criminal prosecution.

Without access to specific facts a criminal prosecution may be totally frustrated. The President's broad interest in confidentiality of communications will not be vitiated by disclosure of a limited number of conversations preliminarily shown to have some bearing on the pending criminal cases.

We conclude that when the ground for asserting privilege as to subpoenaed materials sought for use in a criminal trial is based only on the generalized interest in confidentiality, it cannot prevail over the fundamental demands of due process of law in the fair administration of criminal justice. The generalized assertion of privilege must yield to the demonstrated, specific need for evidence in a pending criminal trial.

Since this matter came before the Court during the pendency of a criminal prosecution, and on representations that time is of the essence, the mandate shall issue forthwith.

MR. JUSTICE REHNQUIST took no part in the consideration or decision of these cases.

Something to Consider

The Court suggests that one reason for its decision was that the president made a general claim that confidentiality was important, but did not claim a "need to protect military, diplomatic, or sensitive national security secrets." Could a president defeat any subpoena by claiming national security? Should a president be able to do so?

Executive Immunity

🏛 executive immunity

The freedom of the president from arrest, criminal prosecution, or civil lawsuits for official acts.

The constitution is silent about whether the president enjoys **executive immunity** in civil or criminal actions. The president is certainly subject to impeachment for the commission of any serious crime, but whether he or she could be prosecuted in a court of law is an unanswered question. The question of immunity in civil lawsuits, on the other hand, has been addressed by the Supreme Court in two major cases: *Nixon v. Fitzgerald*, 457 U.S. 731 (1982), and *Clinton v. Jones*, 520 U.S. 681 (1997). In the *Nixon* case, former President Nixon was sued for money damages by an individual, Fitzgerald, who claimed that he was unjustly fired from his government job. President Nixon was sued for actions that occurred while he was in office, even though at the time of the lawsuit he had already left the presidency. The Court held that President Nixon enjoyed absolute immunity for actions that were part of his official duties as president. He could not be sued during or after his term of office for these acts. The Court said:

> Applying the principles of our cases to claims of this kind, we hold that petitioner, as a former President of the United States, is entitled to absolute immunity from damages liability predicated on his official acts. We consider this immunity a functionally mandated

incident of the President's unique office, rooted in the constitutional tradition of the separation of powers and supported by our history. . . . Because of the singular importance of the President's duties, diversion of his energies by concern with private lawsuits would raise unique risks to the effective functioning of government.

Fifteen years later, in the case of *Clinton v. Jones*, the Supreme Court again considered the question of presidential immunity. President William Clinton was sued while he was in office for actions that occurred before he became president. In this case, the Court did not believe that diversion of the president's energies by concern for the lawsuit justified the grant of immunity. The Court held that the president was not immune from liability for civil actions based on conduct that occurred prior to his taking office. The decision is included here.

Clinton v. Jones
520 U.S. 681 (1997)

JUSTICE STEVENS delivered the opinion of the Court.

This case raises a constitutional and a prudential question concerning the Office of the President of the United States. Respondent, a private citizen, seeks to recover damages from the current occupant of that office based on actions allegedly taken before his term began. The President submits that in all but the most exceptional cases the Constitution requires federal courts to defer such litigation until his term ends and that, in any event, respect for the office warrants such a stay. Despite the force of the arguments supporting the President's submissions, we conclude that they must be rejected.

Petitioner's principal submission—that "in all but the most exceptional cases," the Constitution affords the President temporary immunity from civil damages litigation arising out of events that occurred before he took office—cannot be sustained on the basis of precedent.

The principal rationale for affording certain public servants immunity from suits for money damages arising out of their official acts is inapplicable to unofficial conduct. In cases involving prosecutors, legislators, and judges we have repeatedly explained that the immunity serves the public interest in enabling such officials to perform their designated functions effectively without fear that a particular decision may give rise to personal liability.

That rationale provided the principal basis for our holding that a former President of the United States was "entitled to absolute immunity from damages liability predicated on his official acts," *Fitzgerald*, 457 U.S., at 749. Our central concern was to avoid rendering the

President "unduly cautious in the discharge of his official duties." 457 U.S., at 752, n. 32.

This reasoning provides no support for an immunity for unofficial conduct. As we explained in *Fitzgerald*, "the sphere of protected action must be related closely to the immunity's justifying purposes." *Id.*, at 755. But we have never suggested that the President, or any other official, has an immunity that extends beyond the scope of any action taken in an official capacity.

Petitioner's strongest argument supporting his immunity claim is based on the text and structure of the Constitution. He does not contend that the occupant of the Office of the President is "above the law," in the sense that his conduct is entirely immune from judicial scrutiny. The President argues merely for a postponement of the judicial proceedings that will determine whether he violated any law. His argument is grounded in the character of the office that was created by Article II of the Constitution, and relies on separation of powers principles that have structured our constitutional arrangement since the founding.

As a starting premise, petitioner contends that he occupies a unique office with powers and responsibilities so vast and important that the public interest demands that he devote his undivided time and attention to his public duties.

Petitioner also contends that—as a by product of an otherwise traditional exercise of judicial power—burdens will be placed on the President that will hamper the performance of his official duties. As a factual matter, petitioner contends that this particular case—as well as the

(continued)

(continued)

potential additional litigation that an affirmance of the Court of Appeals judgment might spawn—may impose an unacceptable burden on the President's time and energy, and thereby impair the effective performance of his office.

Petitioner's predictive judgment finds little support in either history or the relatively narrow compass of the issues raised in this particular case. As for the case at hand, if properly managed by the District Court, it appears to us highly unlikely to occupy any substantial amount of petitioner's time.

Of greater significance, petitioner errs by presuming that interactions between the Judicial Branch and the Executive, even quite burdensome interactions, necessarily rise to the level of constitutionally forbidden impairment of the Executive's ability to perform its constitutionally mandated functions. The fact that a federal court's exercise of its traditional Article III jurisdiction may significantly burden the time and attention of the Chief Executive is not sufficient to establish a violation of the Constitution.

President Nixon—as noted above—produced tapes in response to a subpoena duces tecum, see *United States v. Nixon*, President Ford complied with an order to give a deposition in a criminal trial, *United States v. Fromme*, 405 F. Supp. 578 (E.D. Cal. 1975), and President Clinton has twice given videotaped testimony in criminal proceedings, see *United States v. McDougal*, 934 F. Supp. 296 (E.D. Ark. 1996). If the Judiciary may severely burden the Executive Branch by reviewing the legality of the President's official conduct, and if it may direct appropriate process to the President himself, it must follow that the federal courts have power to determine the legality of his unofficial conduct. The burden on the President's time and energy that is a mere by product of such review surely cannot be considered as onerous as the direct burden imposed by judicial review and the occasional invalidation of his official actions. We therefore hold that the doctrine of separation of powers does not require federal courts to stay all private actions against the President until he leaves office.

A Point of Law

Nixon v. Fitzgerald, 457 U.S. 731 (1982)

Clinton v. Jones, 520 U.S. 681 (1997)

A president is absolutely immune from liability for actions that were part of the official duties as president, but not for actions that took place before he became president.

Executive Orders and Presidential Proclamations

executive order

A rule or procedure created by the president or a governor that does not need to be passed by the legislature.

presidential proclamation

A type of a formal government statement meant for immediate widespread announcement.

Congress fulfills its legislative function by enacting laws. The courts fulfill their judicial function by deciding cases. The president also has ways of carrying out presidential duties. An important way is by issuing **executive orders**, which compel some action and are often directed to an administrative agency. Exhibit 2-4 is an example of an executive order issued by President George W. Bush following the terrorist attacks of September 11, 2001.

In addition to executive orders, the president also issues **presidential proclamations**. Such proclamations do not generally deal with substantive issues, although they can (i.e., President Abraham Lincoln's Emancipation Proclamation). Proclamations often recognize important events or causes. Exhibit 2-5 contains two examples of presidential proclamation; one recognizes National Oceans Month, and the other is the Emancipation Proclamation.

Exhibit 2-4 Example of Executive Order

EXPEDITED NATURALIZATION EXECUTIVE ORDER

EXECUTIVE ORDER EXPEDITED NATURALIZATION OF ALIENS AND NONCITIZEN NATIONALS SERVING IN AN ACTIVE-DUTY STATUS DURING THE WAR ON TERRORISM

By the authority vested in me as President by the Constitution and the laws of the United States of America, including section 329 of the Immigration and Nationality Act (8 U.S.C. 1440) (the "Act"), and solely in order to provide expedited naturalization for aliens and noncitizen nationals serving in an active-duty status in the Armed Forces of the United States during the period of the war against terrorists of global reach, it is hereby ordered as follows:

For the purpose of determining qualification for the exception from the usual requirements for naturalization, I designate as a period in which the Armed Forces of the United States were engaged in armed conflict with a hostile foreign force the period beginning on September 11, 2001. Such period will be deemed to terminate on a date designated by future Executive Order. Those persons serving honorably in active-duty status in the Armed Forces of the United States, during the period beginning on September 11, 2001, and terminating on the date to be so designated, are eligible for naturalization in accordance with the statutory exception to the naturalization requirements, as provided in section 329 of the Act. Nothing contained in this order is intended to affect, nor does it affect, any other power, right, or obligation of the United States, its agencies, officers, employees, or any other person under Federal law or the law of nations.

GEORGE W. BUSH
THE WHITE HOUSE

© Cengage Learning 2013

Exhibit 2-5 Examples of Presidential Proclamations

By the President of the United States of America: A Proclamation

During National Oceans Month, we celebrate the value of our oceans to American life and recognize the critical role they continue to play in our economic progress, national security, and natural heritage. Waterborne commerce, sustainable commercial fisheries, recreational fishing, boating, tourism, and energy production are all able to contribute to job growth and strengthen our economy because of the bounty of our oceans, coasts, and Great Lakes.

Last year, I signed an Executive Order directing my Administration to implement our Nation's first comprehensive National Policy for the Stewardship of the Ocean, Our Coasts, and the Great Lakes. This policy makes more effective use of Federal resources by addressing the most critical issues facing our oceans. It establishes a new approach to bringing together Federal, State, local, and tribal governments and all of the ocean's users—from recreational and commercial fishermen, boaters, and industry, to environmental groups, scientists, and the public—to better plan for, manage, and sustain the myriad human uses that healthy oceans, coasts, and the Great Lakes support.

One year after the devastating BP Deepwater Horizon oil spill in the Gulf of Mexico, we remain committed to the full environmental and economic recovery of the region. My Administration is assessing and mitigating the damage that was caused by this tragedy, and restoring and strengthening the Gulf Coast and its communities. These efforts remind us of the responsibility we all share for our oceans and coasts, and the strong connection between the health of our natural resources and that of our communities and economy. While we embrace our oceans as crucial catalysts for trade, bountiful sources of food, and frontiers for renewable energy, we must also recommit to ensuring their safety and sustainability, and to being vigilant guardians of our coastal communities.

NOW, THEREFORE, I, BARACK OBAMA, President of the United States of America, by virtue of the authority vested in me by the Constitution and the laws of the United States, do hereby proclaim June 2011 as National Oceans Month. I call upon Americans to take action to protect, conserve, and restore our oceans, coasts, and Great Lakes.

IN WITNESS WHEREOF, I have hereunto set my hand this second day of June, in the year of our Lord two thousand eleven, and of the Independence of the United States of America the two hundred and thirty-fifth.

BARACK OBAMA

THE EMANCIPATION PROCLAMATION
JANUARY 1, 1863

By the President of the United States of America: A Proclamation.

Whereas, on the twenty-second day of September, in the year of our Lord one thousand eight hundred and sixty-two, a proclamation was issued by the President of the United States, containing, among other things, the following, to wit:

(continued)

(continued)

"That on the first day of January, in the year of our Lord one thousand eight hundred and sixty-three, all persons held as slaves within any State or designated part of a State, the people whereof shall then be in rebellion against the United States, shall be then, thenceforward, and forever free; and the Executive Government of the United States, including the military and naval authority thereof, will recognize and maintain the freedom of such persons, and will do no act or acts to repress such persons, or any of them, in any efforts they may make for their actual freedom.

"That the Executive will, on the first day of January aforesaid, by proclamation, designate the States and parts of States, if any, in which the people thereof, respectively, shall then be in rebellion against the United States; and the fact that any State, or the people thereof, shall on that day be, in good faith, represented in the Congress of the United States by members chosen thereto at elections wherein a majority of the qualified voters of such State shall have participated, shall, in the absence of strong countervailing testimony, be deemed conclusive evidence that such State, and the people thereof, are not then in rebellion against the United States."

Now, therefore I, Abraham Lincoln, President of the United States, by virtue of the power in me vested as Commander-in-Chief, of the Army and Navy of the United States in time of actual armed rebellion against the authority and government of the United States, and as a fit and necessary war measure for suppressing said rebellion, do, on this first day of January, in the year of our Lord one thousand eight hundred and sixty-three, and in accordance with my purpose so to do publicly proclaimed for the full period of one hundred days, from the day first above mentioned, order and designate as the States and parts of States wherein the people thereof respectively, are this day in rebellion against the United States, the following, to wit:

Arkansas, Texas, Louisiana, (except the Parishes of St. Bernard, Plaquemines, Jefferson, St. John, St. Charles, St. James Ascension, Assumption, Terrebonne, Lafourche, St. Mary, St. Martin, and Orleans, including the City of New Orleans) Mississippi, Alabama, Florida, Georgia, South Carolina, North Carolina, and Virginia, (except the forty-eight counties designated as West Virginia, and also the counties of Berkley, Accomac, Northampton, Elizabeth City, York, Princess Ann, and Norfolk, including the cities of Norfolk and Portsmouth[)], and which excepted parts, are for the present, left precisely as if this proclamation were not issued.

And by virtue of the power, and for the purpose aforesaid, I do order and declare that all persons held as slaves within said designated States, and parts of States, are, and henceforward shall be free; and that the Executive government of the United States, including the military and naval authorities thereof, will recognize and maintain the freedom of said persons.

And I hereby enjoin upon the people so declared to be free to abstain from all violence, unless in necessary self-defence; and I recommend to them that, in all cases when allowed, they labor faithfully for reasonable wages.

And I further declare and make known, that such persons of suitable condition, will be received into the armed service of the United States to garrison forts, positions, stations, and other places, and to man vessels of all sorts in said service.

And upon this act, sincerely believed to be an act of justice, warranted by the Constitution, upon military necessity, I invoke the considerate judgment of mankind, and the gracious favor of Almighty God.

In witness whereof, I have hereunto set my hand and caused the seal of the United States to be affixed.

Done at the City of Washington, this first day of January, in the year of our Lord one thousand eight hundred and sixty three, and of the Independence of the United States of America the eighty-seventh.

By the President: ABRAHAM LINCOLN
WILLIAM H. SEWARD, Secretary of State.

Executive Powers

Article II enumerates the executive powers as follows:

- the power to appoint federal judges, ambassadors, and other public consuls and ministers
- the power to serve as the commander in chief
- the power to grant pardons
- the power to call Congress in special session
- the power to veto laws
- general responsibility for enforcing laws

🏛 **inherent power**

The powers a government must have to govern, even if not explicitly stated in its governing documents; for example, the constitutional power of the federal government to conduct foreign affairs or the power of the federal courts to protect constitutional rights.

In addition to these enumerated powers, the president also has **inherent powers**. Inherent powers are those that the president has by virtue of the office. The scope of presidential power has long been subject to debate, beginning with Alexander Hamilton and James Madison. Hamilton argued that the opening line of Article II was a broad grant of power in its own right and that the president had inherent powers, powers not listed in the Constitution. Madison argued that the enumerated powers, the powers actually listed in Article II, are the only powers specifically granted to the president. Constitutional theorists continue to argue over whether Article II was intended to grant to the president inherent powers. Despite what may or may not have been intended by the original framers of the Constitution, American presidential power has expanded over the years. Presidents used various crises, such as wars and the Great Depression, to expand presidential authority. Presidential powers are discussed in more detail in Chapter 5. See Table 2-2.

Table 2-2 Summary of Case Decisions

Case	Issue	Decision
Gregory v. Ashcroft, 501 U.S. 452 (1991)	Federalism	A state has the right to set a minimum retirement age for judges because the federal employment law does not include state employees on a "policy-making level." Through the character of those who exercise government authority, a state defines itself as a sovereign.
Clinton v. City of New York, 524 U.S. 417 (1998)	Separation of powers	The right of the president to exercise a line-item veto interferes with the constitutionally established legislative process.
U.S. Term Limits, Inc. v. Thornton, 514 U.S. 779 (1995)	Legislative qualifications (Article I)	Article I of the Constitution establishes qualifications for U.S. legislators that cannot be changed by state law. Thus, a state law imposing term limits was unconstitutional.
United States v. Nixon, 418 U.S. 683 (1974)	Executive Privilege	The president does not have an unqualified privilege for matters related to the presidency. Any privilege may be outweighed by legitimate needs of the judicial process.
Nixon v. Fitzgerald, 457 U.S. 731 (1982)	Executive Immunity	A President is absolutely immune from liability for actions that were part of the official duties as President
Clinton v. Jones, 520 U.S. 681 (1997)	Executive Immunity	The president is not immune for actions that took place before he became president.

© Cengage Learning 2013

The Judicial Branch (Article III)

Federal Courts and Judges

Article III creates a judicial branch of the federal government, although it did not create the federal court system as we know it today. "The judicial Power of the United States, shall be vested in one supreme Court, and in such inferior Courts as the Congress may from time to time ordain and establish . . . ."

Unlike legislators and the president, federal judges are appointed rather than elected and have life tenure. This is intended to result in a federal judiciary assured of independence. In the majority of states, state court judges face electoral accountability. Unpopular decisions, even if legally correct, can result in losing a subsequent election. Some argue that the independence created in Article III places federal judges in the best position to rule on constitutional issues.

Judicial Powers

Section 2 of Article III also defines federal judicial power in terms of "cases" and "controversies." Hence, courts do not serve as an advisory board. An actual dispute or case must exist before the courts can act. This section authorizes the federal courts to decide all cases "arising under this Constitution, the Laws of the United States, and Treaties made, or which shall be made, under their Authority . . . ." When the United States is a party in a case, the federal courts also have the authority to hear the case. Section 2 authorizes the federal courts to resolve disputes between states and their citizens.

Article III sets up the allocation of power between the lower federal courts and the U.S. Supreme Court. The Supreme Court has original jurisdiction "[I]n all cases affecting Ambassadors, other public Ministers and consuls, and those in which a State shall be Party . . . . In all other Cases before mentioned, the supreme court shall have appellate Jurisdiction." In creating the judicial branch of government, Article III addresses two matters of great concern to the founders of the Constitution. Section 2 of Article III states, "The Trial of all Crimes, except in Cases of Impeachment, shall be by Jury; and such Trial shall be held in the State where the said Crimes shall have been committed; but when not committed within any State, the Trial shall be at such Place or Places as the Congress may by Law have directed." The inclusion of the jury trial was very important to the original framers of the Constitution. This requirement of a jury trial in a criminal matter is at the very core of the concept of a fair trial. Section 3 of Article III states in part; "Treason against the United States, shall consist only in levying War against them, or in adhering to their Enemies, giving them Aid and Comfort." In addition, Section 3 states that "[n]o person shall be convicted of Treason unless on the Testimony of two Witnesses to the same overt Act, or on confession in open Court." The last phrase in Section 3 makes it clear that the descendants of a traitor may only be punished for their own acts of treason.

One judicial power not expressly stated in the Constitution is the power of the Supreme Court to review the constitutionality of state and federal laws. Even so, by the early 1800s the Supreme Court used its power to review constitutional questions involving state and federal laws. Over time, there has been significant debate over the issue of why Article III does not specifically grant to the federal courts the authority to review executive actions and the constitutionality of state and federal laws. There are interesting historical observations and many conflicting opinions. Whatever the historical perspective may be, the power of judicial review exists and is an important part of U.S. government. Federal judicial power is discussed in more detail in Chapter 3.

The Constitution provides little detail regarding the structure that the judicial branch of the government was to take. Although the Constitution specifically created the Supreme Court, it left it up to Congress to establish the lower courts. Furthermore, the Constitution did not fix a number of justices who would sit on the Supreme Court. It did, however, try to ensure the independence of the judiciary by guaranteeing that judges could not be removed without cause and by prohibiting Congress from reducing the

Did You Know?

Chief Justice John Marshall, in *Marbury v. Madison* (1803), declared the Judiciary Act of 1789 unconstitutional. This case marks the first time the United States Supreme Court overturned a law.

Courtesy of the Stapleton Collection/ Historical Picture Library/CORBIS salaries of judges who were in office. Recognizing the importance of the creation of a federal court system, Congress acted quickly to give some structure to the judicial branch. Shortly after the ratification of the Constitution, the Judiciary Act of 1789 was enacted by Congress and approved by the president. This Act accomplished two goals: creation of the first lower federal courts and determination of the number of justices to sit on the Supreme Court.

The Judiciary Act of 1789

inferior court

Any court but the highest one in a court system; a court with special, limited responsibilities, such as a probate court.

admiralty

A court that handles most maritime (seagoing) matters, such as collisions between ships and shipping claims.

diversity of citizenship

The situation that occurs when persons on one side of a case in federal court come from a different state than persons on the other side.

The Judiciary Act of 1789, also known as "An Act to Establish the Federal Courts of the United States," created a court system that is somewhat different from the one that exists today. It included two types of **inferior courts**: district courts and circuit courts that would coexist with the state courts. Both the district courts and circuit courts were trial courts. Thirteen district courts served the eleven states that ratified the Constitution. In addition, district courts were established in Maine and Kentucky, which were not yet states. The original district courts heard limited types of cases: **admiralty**, petty criminal offenses, and minor civil cases in which the United States was a plaintiff. Congress authorized one judge for each of the districts. In addition to fixing boundaries for the district courts (which for the most part paralleled state lines), Congress also created three larger geographical circuits designated as the Eastern, Middle, and Southern circuits.

Each circuit included several districts. Although the circuit courts heard appeals from district courts, they were also trial courts. They conducted trials involving major federal crimes, large civil cases brought by the United States, and cases involving **diversity of citizenship** (cases in which a citizen of one state sues a citizen of another state). In creating the circuit courts, Congress did not authorize any judgeships for these courts. Instead, two Supreme Court justices were to serve in each circuit. In addition to creating the lower court, the first Judiciary Act set the number of justices on the Supreme Court at six. The federal court system created under the Judiciary Act of 1789 was intended to coexist with the state court systems that continued to play an important role in the U.S. justice system.

Subsequent Legislation

Over the years, Congress modified the structure of the lower federal courts several times. The number of district courts and district court judges greatly increased. The power of the district courts broadened, and today they are the primary trial courts in the federal system. In addition to the district courts, Congress also created several special trial courts that hear disputes involving specific areas of law. The concept of circuits has survived. The circuit courts as trial courts were abolished, however. In their place, Congress created courts of appeals, most of which serve geographical circuits. The number of Supreme Court justices is now nine. Most laws detailing the specific organization and operation of the federal judiciary are now found in various sections of Title 28 of the United States Code.

Constitutional versus Legislative Courts

In establishing the lower or "inferior" courts, Congress is not restricted to the authority granted under Article III. Congress also has authority to create courts under Article I of the Constitution. Article III *expressly* authorizes Congress to create courts, whereas Article I *impliedly* authorizes Congress to do so. Article I gives Congress certain stated powers and allows Congress to make laws necessary to carry out these powers. At times, Congress thought it necessary to create special courts that deal with disputes arising under one or more of these powers. Courts that are created pursuant to Article III of the Constitution are

🏛 **constitutional courts**

Courts created pursuant to the U.S. Constitution.

🏛 **legislative courts**

Courts that have been set up by legislatures (Congress, state legislatures, etc.) rather than those set up originally by the U.S. Constitution or by state constitutions.

sometimes called **constitutional courts**, whereas courts created pursuant to Article I are sometimes called **legislative courts**. The primary importance of this distinction is the constitutional protection given to the judges. Article III of the Constitution provides that judges on the federal courts are to be appointed by the president and confirmed by the Senate. They then serve lifetime tenure during "good behavior," and they can be removed only through the impeachment process. According to Article II, Section 4, impeachment is only proper when judges have committed "treason, bribery, or other high crimes and misdemeanors." Furthermore, Article III prohibits Congress from lowering the salary of any judge in office. These protections are to protect the independence of the judiciary and keep the judges free from congressional reprisal for unpopular opinions. Judges serving on legislative courts do not have these protections. These judges are generally appointed for a specific term of years. On the other hand, because of laws passed by Congress, these judges are generally selected in the same way as other judges; that is, they are nominated by the president, subject to confirmation by the Senate. These laws give them the same salary protections as other judges.

The Federal Court System

TODAY, A THREE-TIER SYSTEM of courts makes up the federal court system. This system includes trial courts, intermediate courts of appeals, and the Supreme Court.

Federal Trial Courts

The federal trial courts include the district courts, which are the general trial courts in the federal system, as well as several courts that hear special types of cases.

🏛 *et seq.*

(Latin) Abbreviation for *et sequentes* ("and the following"). For example, "page 27 et seq." means "page twenty-seven and the following pages." Used with a code citation, it means "and the following code sections."

U.S. DISTRICT COURTS (28 U.S.C. § 1330 *et seq.*)

The primary trial court in the federal court system is the U.S. district court. Currently, there are ninety-four different district courts serving not only the states but also the District of Columbia, Puerto Rico, the Virgin Islands, Guam, and the Northern Mariana Islands. Each state has at least one district court, and many have more. The district courts are trial courts that hear federal civil and criminal cases. The number of judges assigned to any district court is fixed by Congress and varies according to the population. In most cases, matters in the district court are presided over by one judge. When the constitutionality of a state law is at issue, however, a three-judge panel conducts the trial. In some cases, trials in the district court are before juries. District court judges are appointed or nominated by the president subject to confirmation by the Senate. They have lifetime tenure, subject to impeachment.

🏛 **magistrate judges**

[pronounce: maj-eh-strate] A judge, usually with limited functions and powers. U.S. magistrates conduct pretrial proceedings, try minor criminal matters, and so forth.

Assisting the district court judges with their duties are **magistrate judges**. Magistrate judges are authorized under federal law and must have at least five years' membership in a state bar. These judges, who are appointed by the district court judges, often hear preliminary matters in both civil and criminal cases. With the consent of the parties, a magistrate judge can preside over any matter. Magistrate judges serve eight-year terms and can be removed by the district court judges.

BANKRUPTCY COURTS AND JUDGES (28 U.S.C. § 151 *et seq.*)

Bankruptcy courts are special units of the district courts, and each district court has a bankruptcy court that handles all bankruptcy matters. Bankruptcy judges are appointed by the justices from the court of appeals for the circuit in which the district court is located. A bankruptcy judge is appointed for a term of fourteen years.

U.S. COURT OF INTERNATIONAL TRADE (28 U.S.C. § 251 *et seq.*)

The Court of International Trade (formerly known as the U.S. Customs Court) handles controversies involving international trade agreements and tariffs. In handling these cases, the court has the same power as the district courts. In establishing the Court of International Trade, Congress made it clear that this court is created pursuant to Article III of the Constitution. As such, the judges are appointed by the president, confirmed by the Senate, and serve lifetime terms. This court is located in New York City.

U.S. COURT OF FEDERAL CLAIMS (28 U.S.C. § 171 *et seq.*)

The Court of Federal Claims hears cases where parties are seeking money damages against the United States for claims based on the Constitution, federal statutes, executive regulations, or contracts with the United States. The following are examples of some of the types of cases heard by this court:

🏛 **eminent domain**
The government's right and power to take private land for public use by paying for it.

- cases dealing with the value of property taken by the government under **eminent domain**
- cases involving a party's right to a tax refund
- cases involving intellectual property
- cases involving civilian and military pay issues
- cases involving public contracts

In some instances, cases can be heard either in this court or in the district court. This court was created pursuant to Article I of the Constitution rather than Article III. Its sixteen judges are appointed by the president and confirmed by the Senate. Because this court is not an Article III court, however, the judges do not have lifetime terms. Instead, they serve fifteen-year terms.

MISCELLANEOUS TRIAL COURTS

Acting under authority found in Article I of the Constitution, Congress has also created the United States Tax Court and the United States Court of Appeals for Veterans Claims. The U.S. Tax Court hears tax disputes involving taxpayers and the Internal Revenue Service. The U.S. Court of Appeals for Veterans Claims hears appeals from the Bureau of Veterans' Appeals. A special court for military proceedings, the Court of Military Review, also exists. After the terrorist attacks of September 11, 2001, military tribunals received substantial attention. These courts can hear cases involving acts committed by enemy combatants. Also receiving attention after the terrorist attacks is the special court created under the Foreign Intelligence Surveillance Act of 1978 (FISA courts) and modified under the U.S.A. Patriot Act of 2001. This court, comprised of eleven federal district court judges appointed by the Chief Justice of the U.S. Supreme Court, reviews the attorney general's application for search warrants for electronic surveillance aimed at obtaining foreign intelligence information. Their decisions are subject to review by a three-judge panel of appellate court justices also appointed by the Chief Justice.

Table 2-3 is a chart of the various federal trial courts.

Table 2-3 Federal Trial Courts		
Court	**Type**	**Function**
U.S. District Courts	Constitutional	Primary trial courts in federal court system; judges and/or juries hear civil and criminal cases
Bankruptcy Court	Adjunct to district court	Hears bankruptcy matters

Table 2-3 Federal Trial Courts *(continued)*

Court	Type	Function
U.S. Court of International Trade	Constitutional	Handles controversies involving international trade agreements and tariffs
U.S. Court of Federal Claims	Legislative	Hears cases seeking money damages against the United States
U.S. Tax Court	Legislative	Hears cases involving tax disputes
U.S. Court of Appeals for Veterans Claims	Legislative	Hears appeals from administrative hearings of the Bureau of Veterans' Appeals
Court of Military Review	Legislative	Handles military proceedings

© Cengage Learning 2013

U.S. Courts of Appeals (28 U.S.C. § 41 *et seq.*)

The second tier of the federal court system consists of courts of appeals. The term *circuit* is used to refer to the geographical area included in the court of appeals jurisdiction. The U.S. Courts of Appeals include the following:

- The courts of appeals for the eleven circuits hears appeals from several district courts located within a circuit. Congress divided the states and territories into eleven circuits. The courts of appeals also hear appeals from tax courts and from several administrative agencies.
- The Court of Appeals for the District of Columbia hears appeals from the district court in Washington, DC.
- The Court of Appeals for the Federal Circuit has nationwide jurisdiction and hears all appeals from the Court of International Trade and the Court of Claims as well as appeals related to patent cases.

Judges serving on the courts of appeals are nominated by the president, confirmed by the Senate; they serve for life, subject to removal by impeachment. The number of judges assigned to each circuit varies depending on need, and the number is fixed by Congress. Cases heard in the court of appeals are normally heard before a three-judge panel. See Exhibit 2-6.

Court of Appeals for the Armed Forces (Article I Court)

In addition to the courts of appeals that were created under Article III of the Constitution, Congress created a Court of Appeals for the Armed Forces. This court is created under Article I of the Constitution and hears appeals from military courts. Although this court is not usually considered to be part of the judiciary, the U.S. Supreme Court can grant discretionary review of its decisions.

U.S. Supreme Court

The only court expressly provided for in the Constitution is the U.S. Supreme Court. The first Supreme Court was actually created under the Judiciary Act of 1789, which fixed the number of justices at six. Today, the Supreme Court, located in Washington, DC, consists of a total of nine justices: the Chief Justice and eight Associate Justices. It begins a new term each year on the first Monday in October. It currently receives more than 7,000 petitions a year. Supreme Court justices are nominated by the president, confirmed by the Senate; they serve for life, subject to impeachment. See Exhibit 2-7.

Exhibit 2-6 Federal Appellate Court Circuits

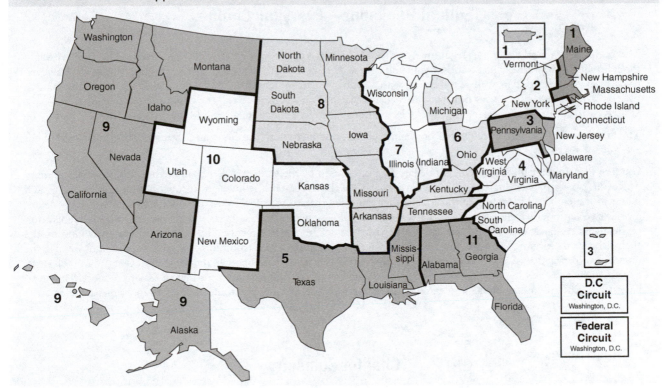

© Cengage Learning 2013

Exhibit 2-7 The United States Federal Courts

Supreme Court	**United States Supreme Court**
Appellate Courts	**U.S. Courts of Appeals** 12 Regional Circuit Courts of Appeals 1 U.S. Court of Appeals for the Federal Circuit
Trial Courts	**U.S. District courts** 94 judicial districts U.S. Bankruptcy Courts **U.S. Court of International Trade** **U.S. Court of Federal Claims**
Federal Courts and other entities outside the Judicial Branch	**Military Courts (Trial and Appellate)** **Court of Veterans Appeals** **U.S. Tax Court** **Federal administrative agencies and boards**

© Cengage Learning 2013

❧ Ethical Decisions—Everyday Choices ❧

The Facts: Alicia works as a paralegal for Attorney Matthews. A wealthy client invited Matthews to play golf with him the following day at an exclusive and private golf course. Matthews wants to accept the invitation. Matthews, however, has a brief court hearing as well as a meeting with a local city council member. The meeting with the city council member concerns some zoning issues dealing with a client. Matthews asks Alicia to call the court and tell them that he is sick and needs to continue the hearing. He also asks her to call the city council member and do the same.

The Problem: Should Alicia follow her boss's instructions and lie to both the court and the city council member? What are Alicia's alternatives?

Guiding Principles: Unlike lawyers, paralegals are not licensed by the state and therefore are not subject to disciplinary proceedings by any licensing board. State bar associations, however, require lawyers to supervise all staff properly, and if any staff member violates any of the state bar ethical rules, the attorney faces possible disciplinary proceedings. In addition, two national paralegal organizations, the National Association of Legal Assistants and the National Federation of Paralegal Associations, publish ethical standards or guidelines for paralegals. These standards can be found on the Web sites for the organizations. In general, these rules prohibit a paralegal from doing anything that might involve the unauthorized practice of law. They also require that paralegals know and observe the same ethical standards of attorneys. Attorneys generally have an ethical duty to not make any untrue statement of fact or law to a court. They also have an ethical duty not to make any material misstatement of fact to anyone in the course of representing a client.

Chapter Summary

The framers of the Constitution formed a government based on federalism, separation of powers, and checks and balances. With the creation of a national government, citizens of the United States became subject to two governments: state and national. These two governments were intended to coexist. Under the U.S. Constitution, the federal government has specific powers. All other powers belong to the states.

The national government created by the Constitution consists of three separate branches: the legislative, the judiciary, and the executive. Each branch has separate powers that serve as a check on the power of the other branches. The legislative branch makes laws, the executive branch enforces laws, and the judicial branch interprets laws and applies them to factual disputes.

The Constitution sets forth various provisions concerning the legislative branch of government. Both senators and representatives must meet age requirements (thirty years old for senators, twenty-five for representatives), be U.S. citizens for at least seven years, and be inhabitants of the states they represent. Senators serve six-year terms, and representatives serve two-year terms. While engaged in speech and debate in either house, they enjoy immunity. The Constitution briefly sets forth the legislative process and lists the powers over which Congress has authority. The Constitution gives the legislature the right to impeach public officials. All executive power in the government is vested in the president, who must be a natural-born citizen and at least thirty-five years of age. The president is selected by the electoral college. The Supreme Court recognized that the president has limited executive privilege not to disclose communications with advisors. Furthermore, the president has civil immunity with regard to acts committed while in office. The president has no immunity for acts committed prior to taking office. If the president commits treason, bribery, or other high crimes or misdemeanors, then he or she can be impeached and eventually removed from office. Impeachment occurs when the president is accused by the House of Representatives. The impeachment or accusation is followed by a trial in the Senate. The president is removed from office only if two-thirds of all senators present vote to convict the president of the charges.

The judicial branch of the government is created in Article III of the Constitution that provides for a Supreme Court and other courts that Congress may create. Using its authority under Article III, the legislature established a federal court system consisting of courts of appeals and trial courts in addition to the Supreme Court. Because these courts are created pursuant to the Constitution, they are known as constitutional courts. The most common trial courts are district courts. These courts hear civil and criminal trials. Under Article III, Congress also established the Court of International Trade, which handles controversies involving international trade agreements and tariffs. Courts of appeals review decisions from the trial courts. The Supreme Court is primarily a court of review but in some cases does have original jurisdiction. All federal judges serving on constitutional courts are appointed by the resident, are approved by the Senate, and serve for life. They can be removed from office through impeachment. In addition to the courts created pursuant to constitutional authority, Congress used its legislative power to create special courts, known as legislative courts. These courts include Bankruptcy Courts, the Court of Federal Claims, United States Tax Court, the U.S. Court of Appeals for Veterans Claims, and the Court of Military Review.

Key Terms

federalism
separation of powers
checks and balances
concurrent
exclusive
immunity
United States Code
enumerated power

Necessary and Proper Clause
electoral college
impeach
executive privilege
executive immunity
executive order
presidential proclamation
inherent power

inferior court
admiralty
diversity of citizenship
constitutional courts
legislative courts
et seq.
magistrate judges
eminent domain

Questions for Review

1. What does it mean to say that the U.S. system of government is based on the concept of federalism?
2. What is meant by "separation of powers"?
3. Discuss the checks and balances system.
4. Where in the Constitution is the Necessary and Proper Clause found? What authority stems from this clause?
5. Describe the power and privileges of the U.S. president.
6. Outline the impeachment process of the president.
7. What is the importance of the Judiciary Act of 1789?
8. What constitutional protections do judges on constitutional courts receive that judges in legislative courts do not?
9. Compare and contrast a constitutional court with a legislative court.
10. List and describe the functions of the various trial courts in the federal court system.

Questions for Analysis

1. Refer to the situation described in Living with the Constitution at the beginning of the chapter.
   a. If Tomas wanted to run for election to the U.S. House of Representatives, could he do so? If so, when?
   b. If Tomas wanted to run for election to the U.S. Senate, could he do so? If so, when?
   c. Could Tomas eventually run for president of the United States?
   d. Could Tomas become a federal judge? If so, when?
   e. Does the Constitution limit Tomas's ability to run for any state office?

2. Answer the following questions regarding the *Clinton v. City of New York* case.
   a. Why did the U.S. Supreme Court hold that the cancellation procedures authorized by the Act were not authorized by the Constitution?
   b. Discuss the two related government arguments that were rejected by the Court.
3. Answer the following questions regarding the *Thornton* case:
   a. On what grounds did the respondent seek to challenge the Arkansas amendment?
   b. According to the *Thornton* court, how may changes with respect to term limits be made?
4. Why were there different results in *Nixon v. Fitzgerald* and *Clinton v. Jones*?
5. The electoral college generally works with a two-party system. What happens if a powerful third party develops?

Assignments and Projects

1. In a recent case, *Free Enterprise Fund v. Public Company Accounting Oversight Bd.*, 561 U.S. ____ (2010), the Supreme Court discussed the issue of separation of powers as it relates to the power of the president to remove members of a board created in response to the national financial crisis. Locate the case in print or on the Internet and briefly summarize why the Court believed that the doctrine of separation of powers was violated.
2. Find and access the Web site for the Supreme Court. Search the site for information about the traditions of the court. Summarize.
3. Complete the missing parts of the following case brief.

Gregory v. Ashcroft
501 U.S. 452 (1991)

Judicial History [not provided]

Facts: The Missouri constitution mandated that all state judges retire at age seventy. Several judges filed a lawsuit claiming that this rule violated the federal age discrimination laws as well as the Equal Protection Clause of the U.S. Constitution. The Age Discrimination in Employment Act excluded employees who worked as government employees on a policy-making level.

Issue:

Holding: Missouri law requiring that judges retire at age seventy did not violate the ADEA because the judges came within an exclusion applying to government employees who worked on a policy-making level.

Rationale:

Putting It into Practice

1. Assume that you want to file a civil lawsuit in your local U.S. district court. Locate the address and telephone number for the court.

2. Locate the name and address of your U.S. senators and representatives.

Group Activity

1. Discuss the following in small groups: Which branch of government is the most powerful and why? Select one member of your group to summarize your conclusion to the entire class.

3 Federal Judicial Power

The greatest dangers to liberty lurk in insidious encroachment by men of zeal—well-meaning but without understanding.

Louis Brandeis, Supreme Court Justice, 1928

Chapter Outline

Chapter Objectives

When you complete this chapter you should be able to

1. explain the concept of jurisdiction.
2. list the types of cases over which the federal judicial branch has subject matter jurisdiction.
3. compare the original and appellate jurisdiction of the Supreme Court.
4. explain the difference between a direct appeal and a petition for writ of certiorari.
5. discuss the concept of justiciability.
6. describe the effect of mootness, ripeness, lack of standing, and political questions on the power of courts to hear cases.

7. explain the doctrine of judicial review.
8. discuss the importance of the Eleventh Amendment to the Constitution to the federal judicial branch.
9. describe the relationship between federal courts and state courts.
10. explain the importance of the Supremacy Clause to court decisions.

Looking Back

Before reading this chapter, review the following terms and concepts from the previous chapters:

federal court system This system includes three levels of courts: district courts that are primarily trial courts, courts of appeals that are primarily courts of review, and one Supreme Court that is the court of last resort and hears only selected cases. (Chapter 2)

Article III of the Constitution This section of the Constitution created a judicial branch of the federal government.

executive order A law put out by the president or a governor that does not need to be passed by the legislature.

Living with the Constitution

Amanda Wilson owns and operates a bar. Recently, the state enacted a law allowing women to buy 3.2 percent beer at age eighteen but denying men that privilege until age twenty-one. Wilson wanted to challenge the law as discriminatory. She knew that the challenge would have to be made in court, but she was not sure which court was the proper one. She believed that if she filed the case in a state court, the judges would be too inclined to side with the state. She hoped there was some alternative.

ONE OF THE MANY WEAKNESSES of the Articles of Confederation was the lack of a national court system. This defect was cured with the inclusion of Article III in the Constitution, which created a judicial branch of the federal government and granted the judicial branch jurisdiction and powers over certain matters. Through a series of cases interpreting Article III, the Supreme Court further defined and explained the jurisdiction and power of the federal courts. Chapter 2 discussed the organization of the federal courts. This chapter discusses the jurisdiction and powers of these courts.

Jurisdiction of the Federal Courts

THE TERM *JURISDICTION* REFERS TO the power or authority that a court has to hear a particular case. The extent of federal court jurisdiction was a concern to many of the framers of the Constitution. How the newly created federal courts would relate to the existing state courts presented questions. In *Federalist Paper 82*, Alexander Hamilton described the issue by raising the following questions: (1) Would the federal courts possess exclusive jurisdiction over cases having federal subject-matter jurisdiction? (2) Would state courts have concurrent jurisdiction over such cases? (3) If jurisdiction were to be concurrent, what would be the relationship between state and federal courts? For the most part, these questions are answered by congressional legislation or by decisions of the Supreme Court.

Recall from Chapter 2 that district courts have the power or jurisdiction to hear trials, whereas the courts of appeals have the power or jurisdiction to hear appeals or reviews of trials. Every federal court has some limits regarding the cases that can be heard in the court, not only in terms of trials or appeals, but also in terms of the types of cases that the court can hear. The jurisdiction of the Supreme Court is also limited.

Subject Matter Jurisdiction

According to the Constitution, only certain kinds of cases can be brought in federal courts. This requirement is known as *subject matter jurisdiction*. Under the Constitution (Article III), the subject matter jurisdiction of federal courts is limited to the following:

🏛 federal question

A legal issue directly involving the U.S. Constitution, statutes, or treaties. Federal courts have jurisdiction in cases involving a federal question.

- cases arising under the Constitution (sometimes called **federal question**)
- cases arising under federal laws (also called federal question)
- cases arising under treaties
- cases affecting ambassadors, other public ministers, and consuls
- admiralty and maritime cases
- controversies to which the United States is a party
- controversies between two or more states
- controversies between a state and citizens of another state
- controversies between citizens of different states (known as *diversity of citizenship*)
- controversies between citizens of the same state claiming lands under grants of different states
- controversies between a state or citizens and foreign states, citizens, or subjects (also known as diversity of citizenship)

For the federal court to have jurisdiction over a case, the case must fall into one of the listed categories. If such a case *also* includes a claim based on state law, however, the federal courts are allowed to hear all related claims rather than being limited solely to the federal issues. The power to do so is referred to as *supplemental* jurisdiction. It is also called *pendent* or *ancillary* jurisdiction.

The jurisdiction of the federal courts is a constitutional limitation, and Congress has no power to grant additional jurisdiction. Congress can, however, further limit the constitutional grant of power. One example of doing so is the congressional imposition of a monetary limit when a court exercises jurisdiction based on diversity of citizenship. Federal law requires that if the dispute is based on money damages, then the amount in controversy must exceed $75,000. The Constitution is silent about any monetary limits.

Diversity of citizenship is a common and important basis for federal subject-matter. It applies to individuals and businesses. Traditionally, a corporation has been considered a citizen of the state in which it is incorporated as well as in the state of its principal place of business. In today's economic environment, complicated questions regarding the principal place of business. In the past, courts applied two tests, one based on the "nerve center" of the company (its headquarters) and the other based on the extent of its business activity. In 2010, the Supreme Court addressed the issue in *Hertz v. Friend*. Hertz (a corporation) was sued in state court in California and sought to have the case heard in federal court claiming it was not a citizen of California. The California courts found that the principal place of business was California because of the extent of its business activity within the state, even though its headquarters was not located in the state. The Supreme Court, however, held that the proper test to determine the principal place of business was the nerve center. Read the following excerpt from the Court's opinion.

Hertz v. Friend
559 U.S. ___ (2010)

JUSTICE BREYER delivered the opinion of the Court

The phrase "principal place of business" has proved more difficult to apply than its originators likely expected. If a corporation's headquarters and executive offices were in the same State in which it did most of its business, the test seemed straightforward. The "principal place of business" was located in that State. But suppose those corporate headquarters, including executive offices, are in one State, while the corporation's plants or other centers of business activity are located in other States? In 1959 a distinguished federal district judge, Edward Weinfeld, relied on the Second Circuit's interpretation of the Bankruptcy Act to answer this question in part:

"Where a corporation is engaged in far-flung and varied activities which are carried on in different states, its principal place of business is the nerve center from which it radiates out to its constituent parts and from which its officers direct, control and coordinate all activities without regard to locale, in the furtherance of the corporate objective." *Scot Typewriter Co.*, 170 F. Supp., at 865.

Scot's analysis, however, did not go far enough. For it did not answer what courts should do when the operations of the corporation are not "far-flung" but rather limited to only a few States. When faced with this question, various courts have focused more heavily on where a corporation's actual business activities are located. Perhaps because corporations come in many different forms, involve many different kinds of business activities, and locate offices and plants for different reasons in different ways in different regions, a general "business activities" approach has proved unusually difficult to apply. Courts must decide which factors are more important than others: for example, plant location, sales or servicing centers; transactions, payrolls, or revenue generation.

We conclude that "principal place of business" is best read as referring to the place where a corporation's officers direct, control, and coordinate the corporation's activities. It is the place that Courts of Appeals have called the corporation's "nerve center." And in practice it should normally be the place where the corporation maintains its headquarters—provided that the headquarters is the actual center of direction, control, and coordination, *i.e.*, the "nerve center," and not simply an office where the corporation holds its board meetings (for example, attended

(continued)

(continued)

by directors and officers who have traveled there for the occasion). We recognize that there may be no perfect test that satisfies all administrative and purposive criteria. We recognize as well that, under the "nerve center" test we adopt today, there will be hard cases. For example, in this era of telecommuting, some corporations may divide their command and coordinating functions among officers who work at several different locations, perhaps communicating over the Internet. That said, our test nonetheless points courts in a single direction, towards the center of overall direction, control, and coordination. Courts do not have to try to weigh corporate functions, assets, or revenues different in kind, one from the other. Our approach provides a sensible test that is relatively easier to apply, not a test that will, in all instances, automatically generate a result.

We also recognize that the use of a "nerve center" test may in some cases produce results that seem to cut against the basic rationale for 28 U.S.C. §1332. For example, if the bulk of a company's business activities visible to the public take place in New Jersey, while its top officers direct those activities just across the river in New York, the "principal place of business" is New York. One could argue that members of the public in New Jersey would be *less* likely to be prejudiced against the corporation than persons in New York—yet the corporation will still be entitled to remove a New Jersey state case to federal court. And note too that the same corporation would

be unable to remove a New York state case to federal court, despite the New York public's presumed prejudice against the corporation.

We understand that such seeming anomalies will arise. However, in view of the necessity of having a clearer rule, we must accept them. Accepting occasionally counterintuitive results is the price the legal system must pay to avoid overly complex jurisdictional administration while producing the benefits that accompany a more uniform legal system.

The burden of persuasion for establishing diversity jurisdiction, of course, remains on the party asserting it. Indeed, if the record reveals attempts at manipulation—for example, that the alleged "nerve center" is nothing more than a mail drop box, a bare office with a computer, or the location of an annual executive retreat—the courts should instead take as the "nerve center" the place of actual direction, control, and coordination, in the absence of such manipulation.

Petitioner's unchallenged declaration suggests that Hertz's center of direction, control, and coordination, its "nerve center," and its corporate headquarters are one and the same, and they are located in New Jersey, not in California. Because respondents should have a fair opportunity to litigate their case in light of our holding, however, we vacate the Ninth Circuit's judgment and remand the case for further proceedings consistent with this opinion.

It is so ordered.

Original versus Appellate Jurisdiction

original jurisdiction
The power of a court to take a case, try it, and decide it (as opposed to appellate jurisdiction, which is the power of a court to hear and decide an appeal).

Original jurisdiction refers to the power that a court has to hear a trial and resolve the factual dispute between the parties. *Appellate jurisdiction* refers to the power to hear an appeal or other review of a proceeding that occurred in a lower court. For the most part, district courts are courts of original jurisdiction and courts of appeals and the Supreme Court are courts of appellate jurisdiction. Under the Constitution, however, the U.S. Supreme Court has limited original jurisdiction.

Supreme Court Original Jurisdiction

The Constitution confers the Supreme Court with original jurisdiction in cases involving ambassadors, public ministers, and consuls, and cases in which a state is a party. The Constitution, however, is silent as to whether the Supreme Court is the *only* court that can hear these cases. This issue was addressed by Congress when it enacted laws specifying those cases over which the Supreme Court has *exclusive jurisdiction* and those cases over which the Supreme Court has *concurrent jurisdiction* with the district courts. The Supreme Court has exclusive original jurisdiction over cases between states. As in all other cases, the original jurisdiction is concurrent or shared with the district courts. As a practical matter, the Supreme Court would rarely agree to take original jurisdiction when a case could be heard at the district court level. The Supreme Court's workload does not allow for it.

A practical problem arises when the Supreme Court exercises original jurisdiction, as it must when one state sues another state. In such a situation, it is impractical for all the justices on the Court to preside over a trial that could take weeks or months. Instead, the Court normally appoints a special master to preside over the actual trial. A **special master** is an individual with legal expertise who acts as a judge and reports his or her findings to the Court. The Court then acts on the findings and enters a judgment based on the findings.

Supreme Court Appellate Jurisdiction

🏛 **special master**
An individual appointed by the court to preside over a case in place of a judge.

Appellate jurisdiction of the Supreme Court is exercised in two ways: through a *direct appeal* and through a writ, the most common of which is a **writ of certiorari.** A direct appeal, sometimes called an appeal of right, *requires* the Supreme Court to review a matter. A writ of certiorari is a discretionary review. Whether a party can file a direct appeal or must file a petition for a writ of certiorari is a matter of statutory law. The United States Code (§§1253 through 1259) sets out the rules. A party can file a direct appeal from a district court decision when the decision is one that must be determined by a three-judge panel (i.e., a case challenging the constitutionality of a state law). In other cases, appellate review is generally obtained by the Supreme Court's granting a writ of certiorari. Such cases include reviews from decisions of the federal court of appeals and reviews from state supreme courts or the supreme court of Puerto Rico where there is a federal question. Decisions from the Court of Appeals for the Armed Forces are also reviewable through a writ of certiorari. See Tables 3-1 and 3-2.

🏛 **writ of certiorari**
[pronounce: sir-sho-rare-ee] A request for certiorari (or "cert." for short) is similar to an appeal, but it is one that the higher court is not required to take for decision. It is literally a writ from the higher court asking the lower court for the record of the case.

Writ of Certiorari

A party seeking Supreme Court review through certiorari files a *petition for a writ of certiorari* with the Supreme Court. The petition for the writ of certiorari sets forth the legal issues in the case and reasons for the Court to grant a hearing. Because the Court can only hear a very small percentage of the cases seeking discretionary review, the petition must set forth a compelling argument for the request being granted. After the petition is filed, the justices vote on whether to grant the writ. The petition is granted if four of the nine justices vote to hear the case, which is referred to as the **Rule of Four.** The granting of a petition for writ of certiorari is no guarantee that the justices will ultimately vote in favor of the petitioner. The denial of a petition for writ of certiorari is not to be considered an agreement or affirmation of the lower court decision. See Appendix D for an excerpt from one of the petitions for writ of certiorari filed in the Bush–Gore presidential litigation.

🏛 **Rule of Four**
The principle that if at least four of the nine U.S. Supreme Court justices vote to take a case, the Court will hear the case. The Court uses the Rule of Four for cases that reach the Court by certiorari.

Table 3-1 Types of Jurisdiction

Jurisdiction	Power
Subject matter jurisdiction	Power to hear the type of case
Supplemental/pendent/ancillary jurisdiction	Power of a federal court to hear a case within state jurisdiction if it is associated with a case within federal court subject matter jurisdiction
Original jurisdiction	Power of a court to try a case or to be the first to resolve the dispute
Appellate jurisdiction	Power of a court to review a lower court decision
Exclusive jurisdiction	Power to hear a case is vested in only one court
Concurrent jurisdiction	Power to hear a case is shared by different courts (i.e., both federal and state)

Table 3-2 Supreme Court Jurisdiction		
Original Jurisdiction	Exclusive	State v. State
	Concurrent (with district courts)	Cases involving ambassadors, public ministers, and consuls
Appellate Jurisdiction	Direct appeal	Review of district court case requiring a three-judge panel
	Writ of certiorari	Review of state supreme court and federal appellate court cases

© Cengage Learning 2013

Case or Controversy: Justiciability

THE CONSTITUTION GIVES THE FEDERAL courts jurisdiction over *cases* or *controversies*. There must be an actual controversy or dispute before the court can act because without a dispute the court is rendering an advisory opinion rather than resolving a controversy. The term **justiciable** is sometimes used to describe the concept that before the Supreme Court will hear a matter, the matter must present an actual controversy, which generally means that there must be some real harm immediately threatening the plaintiff. The Supreme Court will not hear a case in which the threatened harm no longer exists (**mootness**), in which no harm is yet really threatened (**ripeness**), or in which the party bringing the action is not the one who is threatened (**standing**). In addition, even though a real dispute may exist, the Supreme Court will not hear a matter where the issue is a **political question**.

Mootness

The constitutional requirement of a case or controversy means that there must be a *current* dispute before the case. If, for example, the case settles before the Supreme Court has an opportunity to hear the matter, then the Court is generally powerless to act on the case. The Court will not engage in "what-ifs." This rule was established by the Supreme Court in early cases such as *Mills v. Green*, 159 U.S. 651, decided in 1895. In that case, the plaintiff, who was a citizen of the state of South Carolina, tried to register to vote in an election to take place on the third Tuesday of August 1895. The registrar of voters would not allow the plaintiff to register because he lacked certain qualifications that were required of all voters under South Carolina law. The plaintiff sued, asking the court to order the registrar to allow him to vote in the August election. The plaintiff won at the trial level but lost on appeal. He then appealed to the U.S. Supreme Court, filing the appeal on September 4, 1895, after the election had taken place. The Supreme Court refused to hear the appeal, stating that because the date of the election had passed, the issue was moot:

> The duty of this court, as of every other judicial tribunal, is to decide actual controversies by a judgment which can be carried into effect, and not to give opinions upon moot questions or abstract propositions, or to declare principles or rules of law which cannot affect the matter in issue in the case before it.

Sometimes the Supreme Court hears a case when the particular issue no longer affects the parties to the case but does affect others in a similar situation. The case of *Roe v. Wade*, 410 U.S. 113 (1973), is an example. In *Roe v. Wade*, the plaintiff sued to enjoin the state of Texas from enforcing antiabortion laws that imposed criminal penalties on doctors who performed abortions. By the time the case reached the Supreme Court, the plaintiff had already given birth. Thus, as to her, the issue was moot. The Court, however, reasoned that if it refused to hear the case, then the abortion issue would never be decided by the Court because getting a case before the Supreme Court always takes longer than a pregnancy.

justiciable

[pronounce: justish-able]
Proper to be decided by a particular court. For example, a "justiciable controversy" is a real, rather than hypothetical, dispute. Federal courts may handle only cases that present a justiciable controversy.

mootness

No longer important or no longer needing a decision because it has already been decided.

ripeness

A case is ripe for selection and decision by the U.S. Supreme Court if the legal issues involved are clear enough, well enough evolved and presented so that a clear decision can come out of the case.

standing

A person's right to bring (start) or join a lawsuit because he or she is directly affected by the issues raised. This right is called "standing to sue."

political question

An issue that a court may refuse to decide because it concerns a decision properly made by the executive or legislative branch of government and because the court has no adequate standards of review or no adequate way to enforce the court's judgment.

The Supreme Court will not refuse to hear a case based on mootness when the type of conduct is subject to being repeated. Similarly, the Court will not refuse to hear a case based on mootness when there can be collateral consequences, even though the main relief sought can no longer be granted by the Court. Consider the case of a criminal defendant who is found guilty of a felony but has served the entire sentence prior to the case reaching the Supreme Court. The Court can do nothing about the jail time. A convicted felon, however, suffers loss other than incarceration. For example, he or she loses many civil liberties. A successful decision in the Supreme Court will give such persons more than just the satisfaction of knowing they were right.

Ripeness

Under the doctrine of mootness, the Supreme Court will not hear a case when a controversy no longer exists. Under the doctrine of ripeness, the Court will not hear a case when a controversy does not *yet* exist. This issue has arisen in many cases in which local municipalities, states, or administrative agencies have passed laws or regulations whose constitutionality is seriously questionable but when no one has yet been punished or damaged by the law. For example, in the case of *Poe v. Ullman,* 367 U.S. 497 (1961), the plaintiffs, two married women, sued because of a Connecticut statute that prohibited the use of contraceptives as well as the dissemination of information about contraceptives by medical personnel. The statutes in question were enacted in 1879 but had only been used one time to prosecute anyone, and, in that case, the matter was eventually dismissed. The Supreme Court held that the matter was not "ripe" because there was no real harm threatened to the plaintiffs. The Court said:

> This Court cannot be umpire to debates concerning harmless, empty shadows. To find it necessary to pass on these statutes now, in order to protect appellants from the hazards of prosecution would be to close our eyes to reality.

Standing

One of the most litigated issues regarding justiciability is the question of standing. To have standing to sue, the plaintiff must personally be an aggrieved party. That is, the plaintiff must be the one suffering some harm or incurring some damage. The Supreme Court has established three criteria that must be met before standing exists:

1. The plaintiff must suffer a specific and actual injury (injury is not limited to physical harm).
2. A causal relationship between the injury and the challenged conduct of the defendant must exist.
3. There must be a likelihood that a favorable decision in the case will end the injury or compensate for it.

Problems with standing arise when the plaintiff is not suing for an injury that is personal and limited to the plaintiff. A common situation arises when a threatened harm affects the public or a group of people and an individual or association brings a lawsuit on behalf of the group. The Supreme Court is clear that, for this type of suit to go forward, the plaintiff must have a personal stake in the outcome. Two cases illustrate. In *Sierra Club v. Morton*, 405 U.S. 727 (1972), the petitioner, a membership corporation with "a special interest in the conservation and sound maintenance of the national parks, game refuges, and forests of the country," brought a suit to restrain federal officials from approving an extensive skiing development in the Mineral King Valley in the Sequoia National Forest. The petitioner did not allege that the challenged development would affect the club or its members in their activities or that they used Mineral King, but maintained that the project would adversely change the area's aesthetics and ecology. The Supreme Court held that a person has standing to seek judicial review *only* if the person can show that he or she, individually, has suffered or will suffer injury, whether economic or otherwise. In this case, in which the petitioner asserted no individual harm, standing was lacking.

On the other hand, the Court found the necessary harm in the case of *Pierce v. Society of Sisters*, 268 U.S. 510 (1925). In this case, the state of Oregon enacted legislation requiring children to attend public schools. The respondents, Society of Sisters, owned property used in connection with their goal of providing religious education to children. They alleged that as a result of the Oregon legislation, their property and business would suffer a loss. Because they had a personal stake, the Supreme Court agreed with the lower courts in finding that they had standing to bring the suit.

A Point of Law

Sierra Club v. Morton, 405 U.S. 727 (1972)

Pierce v. Society of Sisters, 268 U.S. 510 (1925)

A party cannot bring an action in court unless that party has some personal stake in the outcome. A conservation group lacked standing to sue a business that was interfering with an area's aesthetics and ecology because the club members were not personally affected. A group of nuns who operated a private school, however, did have standing to sue over a state law requiring public school attendance because their business was adversely affected.

In 2004 the Supreme Court considered the standing issue in connection with one of the most publicized cases to come before the Court, the case in which the constitutionality of the pledge of allegiance was challenged. In *Elk Grove Unified School Dist. v. Newdow*, 542 U.S. 1 (2004), a school requirement that the pledge of allegiance be recited was challenged by a father of a student. The student's parents were divorced and the mother had sole legal custody, including the right to make decisions about the welfare of the child. After hearings in the lower courts, the mother filed a petition in court on behalf of her child asking that the case be dismissed. The Supreme Court reasoned that California law gave the mother the exclusive right to make decisions regarding the child. Based on this, the father had no standing to challenge the recitation of the pledge of allegiance. This right belonged exclusively to the parent having custody.

In 2007, in *Massachusetts v. E.P.A.*, 549 U.S. 497, the Supreme Court considered the standing issue in connection with one of the most important issues of the times, the environment. Massachusetts and several other states sued the Environmental Protection Action for refusing to regulate the emission of certain pollutants by motor vehicles as required by the Clean Air Act. Before addressing the substantive issues in the case, the Court addressed the question of whether a state suffered any personal harm and had standing to pursue such a suit. The Court referred to prior decisions affirming the requirement that "a litigant must demonstrate that it has suffered a concrete and particularized injury that is either actual or imminent, that the injury is fairly traceable to the defendant." In this case, the Court found standing stating that "the State has an interest independent of and behind the titles of its citizens, in all the earth and air within its domain. It has the last word as to whether its mountains shall be stripped of their forests and its inhabitants shall breathe pure air." A second and important factor in the Court's decision was that Congress expressly granted states the right to bring lawsuits pursuant to the Clean Air Act.

Other standing issues arise in cases brought by taxpayers trying to establish standing by claiming that their tax dollars are being misspent. An important preliminary question in these cases is whether the taxpayer is challenging a local tax or a federal tax. The Supreme Court is much less likely to find standing when federal taxes are involved because the taxpayer has such a small personal interest. In any event, before the Court will find standing, the taxpayer must show (1) that the expense in question must be an exercise of the taxing and spending power of the government and not an incidental expense of government and (2) that the spending program must violate a specific provision of the Constitution. Both of these criteria were met by the plaintiff in *Flast* v. *Cohen*, 392 U.S. 83 (1968). In *Flast*, plaintiff taxpayers alleged that federal funds were disbursed by federal officials under the Elementary and Secondary Education Act of 1965 to finance instruction and the purchase of educational materials for use in religious and sectarian schools, in violation of the Establishment and Free Exercise Clauses of the First Amendment. The Court found that the plaintiffs met the standing requirement because (1) the expenditure was pursuant to the taxing and spending power of the government under Article I, Section 8, and (2) the plaintiffs claimed that the expenditure was in violation of a specific constitutional provision, that is, the **Establishment** and **Free Exercise Clauses** of the First Amendment. Recently, however, the Court has affirmed its reluctance to find standing based solely on taxpayer status. Following is an excerpt from the case of *Hein v. Freedom From Religion Foundation, Inc.*, a 2007 decision, finding no standing. The facts leading to the lawsuit are set out in the case excerpt.

🏛 **Establishment Clause**

That part of the First Amendment to the U.S. Constitution that states "Congress shall make no law respecting an *establishment* of religion."

🏛 **Free Exercise Clause**

That part of the First Amendment to the U.S. Constitution that states, "Congress shall make no law . . . prohibiting the *free exercise* [*of religion*]."

Hein v. Freedom From Religion Foundation, Inc.,
551 U.S. 587 (2007)

JUSTICE ALITO announced the judgment of the Court and delivered an opinion in which THE CHIEF JUSTICE and Justice KENNEDY join.

This is a lawsuit in which it was claimed that conferences held as part of the President's Faith-Based and Community Initiatives program violated the Establishment Clause of the First Amendment because, among other things, President Bush and former Secretary of Education Paige gave speeches that used "religious imagery" and praised the efficacy of faith-based programs in delivering social services. The plaintiffs contend that they meet the standing requirements of Article III of the Constitution because they pay federal taxes.

In *Flast v. Cohen,* 392 U.S. 83 (1968), we recognized a narrow exception to the general rule against federal taxpayer standing. Under *Flast,* a plaintiff asserting an Establishment Clause claim has standing to challenge a law authorizing the use of federal funds in a way that allegedly violates the Establishment Clause. In the present case, Congress did not specifically authorize the use of federal funds to pay for the conferences or speeches that the plaintiffs challenged. Instead, the conferences and speeches were paid for out of general Executive Branch appropriations. The Court of Appeals, however, held that the plaintiffs have standing as taxpayers because the conferences were paid for with money appropriated by Congress.

The question that is presented here is whether this broad reading of *Flast* is correct. We hold that it is not. We therefore reverse the decision of the Court of Appeals.

In 2001, the President issued an executive order creating the White House Office of Faith-Based and Community Initiatives within the Executive Office of the President. The purpose of this new office was to ensure that "private and charitable community groups, including religious ones . . . have the fullest opportunity permitted by law to compete on a level playing field, so long as they achieve valid public purposes" and adhere to "the bedrock principles of pluralism, nondiscrimination, evenhandedness, and neutrality." By separate executive orders, the President also created Executive Department Centers for Faith-Based and Community Initiatives within several federal agencies and departments. No congressional legislation specifically authorized the creation of the White House Office or the Executive Department Centers. Rather, they were "created entirely within the executive branch . . . by Presidential executive order." Nor has Congress enacted any law specifically appropriating money for these entities' activities. Instead, their activities are funded through general Executive Branch appropriations.

The respondents are Freedom From Religion Foundation, Inc., a nonstock corporation "opposed to government endorsement of religion," and three of its members. Respondents brought suit in the United States District Court for the Western District of Wisconsin, alleging that petitioners violated the Establishment Clause by organizing conferences at which faith-based organizations allegedly "are singled out as being particularly worthy of federal funding . . . , and the belief in God is extolled as distinguishing the claimed effectiveness of faith-based social services." In short, respondents alleged that the conferences were designed to promote, and had the effect of promoting, religious community groups over secular ones.

The only asserted basis for standing was that the individual respondents are federal taxpayers who are "opposed to the use of Congressional taxpayer appropriations to advance and promote religion."

The District Court dismissed the claims against petitioners for lack of standing. Because petitioners in this case acted "at the President's request and on the President's behalf" and were not "charged with the administration of a congressional program," the District Court concluded that the challenged activities were "not 'exercises of congressional power'" sufficient to provide a basis for taxpayer standing under *Flast.*

A divided panel of the United States Court of Appeals for the Seventh Circuit reversed. The majority read *Flast* as granting federal taxpayers standing to challenge Executive Branch programs on Establishment Clause grounds so long as the activities are "financed by a congressional appropriation." We granted certiorari and we now reverse.

Article III of the Constitution limits the judicial power of the United States to the resolution of "Cases" and "Controversies," and "Article III standing . . . enforces the Constitution's case-or-controversy requirement.'" *DaimlerChrysler Corp. v. Cuno,* 547 U.S. (2006) (quoting *Elk Grove Unified School Dist. v. Newdow,* 542 U.S. 1, 11 (2004)).

The constitutionally mandated standing inquiry is especially important in a case like this one, in which taxpayers seek "to challenge laws of general application where their own injury is not distinct from that suffered in

(continued)

(continued)

general by other taxpayers or citizens." *ASARCO, supra,* at 613 (opinion of KENNEDY, J.). This is because "[t]he judicial power of the United States defined by Art. III is not an unconditioned authority to determine the constitutionality of legislative or executive acts." *Valley Forge Christian College v. Americans United for Separation of Church and State, Inc.,* 454 U.S. 464, 471 (1982). The federal courts are not empowered to seek out and strike down any governmental act that they deem to be repugnant to the Constitution. Rather, federal courts sit "solely, to decide on the rights of individuals," *Marbury v. Madison,* 1 Cranch 137, 170, 2 L.Ed. 60 (1803), and must "refrai[n] from passing upon the constitutionality of an act . . . unless obliged to do so in the proper performance of our judicial function, when the question is raised by a party whose interests entitle him to raise it.'" *Valley Forge, supra,* at 474.

In *Flast,* the Court carved out a narrow exception to the general constitutional prohibition against taxpayer standing. Respondents argue that this case falls within the *Flast* exception, which they read to cover any "expenditure of government funds in violation of the Establishment Clause." But this broad reading fails to observe "the rigor with which the *Flast* exception to the *Frothingham* principle ought to be applied." *Valley Forge,* 454 U.S., at 481.

The expenditures challenged in *Flast* were funded by a specific congressional appropriation and were disbursed to private schools (including religiously affiliated schools) pursuant to a direct and unambiguous congressional mandate. Given that the alleged Establishment Clause violation in *Flast* was funded by a specific congressional appropriation and was undertaken pursuant to an express congressional mandate, the Court concluded that the taxpayer-plaintiffs had established the requisite "logical link between [their taxpayer] status and the type of legislative enactment attacked."

The link between congressional action and constitutional violation that supported taxpayer standing in *Flast* is missing here. Respondents do not challenge any specific congressional action or appropriation; nor do they ask the Court to invalidate any congressional enactment or legislatively created program as unconstitutional. That is because the expenditures at issue here were not made pursuant to any Act of Congress. Rather, Congress provided general appropriations to the Executive Branch to fund its day-to-day activities. These appropriations did not expressly authorize, direct, or even mention the expenditures of which respondents complain. Those expenditures resulted from executive discretion, not congressional action.

We have never found taxpayer standing under such circumstances. It is significant that, in the four decades since its creation, the *Flast* exception has largely been confined to its facts. We have declined to lower the taxpayer standing bar in suits alleging violations of any constitutional provision apart from the Establishment Clause. We have similarly refused to extend *Flast* to permit taxpayer standing for Establishment Clause challenges that do not implicate Congress' taxing and spending power.

While respondents argue that Executive Branch expenditures in support of religion are no different from legislative extractions, *Flast* itself rejected this equivalence: "It will not be sufficient to allege an incidental expenditure of tax funds in the administration of an essentially regulatory statute." 392 U.S., at 102. The constitutional requirements for federal-court jurisdiction—including the standing requirements and Article III—"are an essential ingredient of separation and equilibration of powers." *Steel Co. v. Citizens for Better Environment,* 523 U.S. 83, 101 (1998). "Relaxation of standing requirements is directly related to the expansion of judicial power," and lowering the taxpayer standing bar to permit challenges of purely executive actions "would significantly alter the allocation of power at the national level, with a shift away from a democratic form of government." *Richardson,* 418 U.S., at 188 (Powell, J., concurring).

Over the years, *Flast* has been defended by some and criticized by others. But the present case does not require us to reconsider that precedent. The Court of Appeals did not apply *Flast*; it extended *Flast*. It is a necessary concomitant of the doctrine of *stare decisis* that a precedent is not always expanded to the limit of its logic. That was the approach that then-Justice Rehnquist took in his opinion for the Court in *Valley Forge,* and it is the approach we take here. We do not extend *Flast,* but we also do not overrule it. We leave *Flast* as we found it.

For these reasons, the judgment of the Court of Appeals for the Seventh Circuit is reversed.

It is so ordered.

··

Something to Consider

The Court based its decision in *Hein* on the fact that the taxpayer expenditure was made by the executive branch rather than the legislative branch. Is this a logical distinction in relationship to the question of standing?

Political Question

The Supreme Court also refuses to hear cases on the grounds of lack of justiciability when the case presents a political question. As the term is used here, a political question is not the same as a political issue. In fact, the Court hears and decides many cases relating to politics. The cases stemming from the 2000 presidential election are clear examples of political issues decided by the courts. The Supreme Court, however, refuses to hear cases when it believes that deciding an issue would be a violation of the separation of powers doctrine. If the Constitution clearly gives power over an area to either the executive or legislative branch, then the Court will not interfere.

A leading case in this area is *Nixon v. United States*, 506 U.S. 224 (1993). In this case, plaintiff Nixon (a federal court judge, not the president) challenged an impeachment trial in the Senate. The Court refused to decide the case, saying that it presented a political question because the Senate clearly has all responsibility for an impeachment trial.

An example of a case in which the Court found that there was no political question is *Baker v. Carr*, 369 U.S. 186 (1962), a case dealing with **reapportionment**. In this case, the plaintiffs alleged that a 1901 Tennessee statute apportioning the members of the General Assembly among the state's ninety-five counties denied the equal protection of the laws accorded them by the Fourteenth Amendment to the Constitution of the United States by virtue of the debasement of their votes. The trial court held that it lacked jurisdiction because it was a political question. The Supreme Court reversed and remanded the case to the district court for trial and further proceedings. In reaching its decision, the Court emphasized that whether a case presented a political question depended on the separation of powers doctrine and had to be decided on a case-by-case basis. In analyzing this case, the Court listed the types of cases in which political questions were likely to be found, including the following:

1. foreign relations (such as whether a treaty was terminated or whether to recognize a foreign government)
2. validity of enactments (e.g., how long a constitutional amendment remains open for ratification)
3. status of an Indian tribe

The Court also explained the criteria by which it decides whether a case presents a political question:

> Prominent on the surface of any case held to involve a political question is found a textually demonstrable constitutional commitment of the issue to a coordinate political department; or a lack of judicially discoverable and manageable standards for resolving it; or the impossibility of deciding without an initial policy determination of a kind clearly for nonjudicial discretion; or the impossibility of a court's undertaking independent resolution without expressing lack of the respect due coordinate branches of government; or an unusual need for unquestioning adherence to a political decision already made; or the potentiality of embarrassment from multifarious pronouncements by various departments on one question.

The Court needs to be certain that it is not interfering in an area reserved to another branch of government and that it can impose a workable standard to resolve the issue. In *Baker v. Carr*, the Court found that there was no political question because in deciding the case it was not intruding into a power reserved to the executive or legislative branch of government. The only thing in question was the constitutionality of a state law, and it is the job of the judiciary to interpret the Constitution. See Exhibit 3-1 and Table 3-3.

reapportionment

Changing the boundaries of legislative districts to reflect changes in population and ensure that each person's vote for representatives carries roughly equal weight.

A Point of Law

Nixon v. United States, 506 U.S. 224 (1993)

Baker v. Carr, 369 U.S. 186 (1962)

The Court refuses to hear cases raising political questions that are more appropriately handled by either the executive or legislative branch of the government. The Court refused to hear a case challenging a senate impeachment proceeding (*Nixon*) because impeachment is the responsibility of Congress. On the other hand, the Court agreed to hear a case concerning a state reapportionment law (*Baker*) because the issue was the constitutionality of a law, which is not a question to be decided by either the legislative or executive branch.

Exhibit 3-1 Justiciability

A CASE OR CONTROVERSY DOES NOT EXIST WHERE:

The issue is ***moot***. →	The dispute is already resolved.
The issue is ***not ripe***. →	No issue has yet arisen.
The plaintiff ***lacks standing***. →	The plaintiff has suffered no real harm.
The case involves a ***political question***. →	Power belongs to another branch of government.

© Cengage Learning 2013

Table 3-3 Case Summaries: Justiciability

Case	Issue	Decision
Mills v. Green, 159 U.S. 651 (1895)	Mootness	A challenge of voting requirements for a special election is moot once the election has taken place.
Roe v. Wade, 410 U.S. 113 (1973)	Mootness	An issue will be heard even though it is moot as to the petitioner if it is not moot as to others in a similar situation.
Poe v. Ullman, 367 U.S. 497 (1961)	Ripeness	A statute that is never enforced is not ripe for hearing because it poses no real harm to the plaintiffs.
Sierra Club v. Morton, 405 U.S. 727 (1972)	Standing	For a club to have standing, its members must be personally affected. Members of the Sierra Club were not personally affected by a business that interfered with the ecology; thus, the club lacked standing to sue.
Pierce v. Society of Sisters, 268 U.S. 510 (1925)	Standing	A group of nuns operating a private school had standing to sue over a state law requiring public school attendance because their business was adversely affected; thus, they were personally affected.
Elk Grove Unified Sch. Dist. v. Newdow, 542 U.S. 1 (2004)	Standing	A father who does not have legal custody has no standing to challenge a requirement that his child recite the pledge of allegiance in school.
Massachusetts v. E.P.A., 549 U.S. 497 (2007)	Standing	A state has standing to sue the E.P.A. for not enforcing an environmental law because it has an interest in protecting the natural resources of the state and because Congress specifically gives the state the right to sue.

(continued)

Table 3-3   Case Summaries: Justiciability *(continued)*

Flast v. Cohen, 392 U.S. 83 (1968)	Standing	Taxpayers have standing to sue over an expenditure of tax money only when the tax is imposed pursuant to its taxing and spending power and the tax violates a specific provision of the Constitution.
Hein v. Freedom From Religion Foundation, Inc., 551 U.S. 587 (2007)	Standing	Taxpayers do not have standing to sue over expenditures of money by the executive branch, even when the First Amendment is an issue.
Nixon v. United States, 506 U.S. 224 (1993)	Political question	A case challenging a Senate impeachment proceeding will not be heard by the Court because an impeachment trial is the responsibility of the Senate, making it a political question.
Baker v. Carr, 369 U.S. 186 (1962)	Political question	The constitutionality of a state reapportionment law is not a political question; thus, the Court will hear such cases.

© Cengage Learning 2013

The Nature of Judicial Power

ALTHOUGH THE CONSTITUTION CONFERS JUDICIAL power on the Supreme Court and such inferior courts as Congress creates, it does not spell out what judicial power means. The Constitution lists the cases coming under federal jurisdiction, but it does not state what the courts can do with these cases. The power that any court has depends on whether the court is one of original jurisdiction (a trial court) or one of appellate jurisdiction.

Historically, in courts of original jurisdiction, judicial power always included the right to decide disputes between parties by providing a remedy to the prevailing party. In a civil case, it is usually a judgment for money, although it may be some form of equitable relief such as an **injunction**. In criminal cases, the guilt or innocence of a defendant is determined. If found guilty, a sentence is imposed. Another power that courts have is the power to issue writs. A **writ** is an order from the court directed to a lower court, some government official, or a government agency requiring it to take some action. Common writs include the writ of mandamus, writ of habeas corpus, and writ of certiorari. A **writ of mandamus** is an order to a lower court or an agency requiring that it do something or refrain from doing something. This writ is usually issued when the court or agency refuses to do something that it is required to do. A **writ of habeas corpus** is an order that can be issued when a party is in custody (often prison), directing the custodian to explain why the person should not be released. In reality, it is often a type of appeal from a criminal conviction. A writ of certiorari is used by the Supreme Court in exercise of its appellate jurisdiction. This writ is directed to a court of appeals and orders the court to send to the Supreme Court its record in a particular case in which one party is seeking Supreme Court review.

A court of appellate jurisdiction has the power to affirm the lower court decision, reverse the decision, or reverse and **remand** the decision. When a court remands a case, it sends it back to the trial court for a retrial in accordance with the court's appellate decision. Courts of appellate jurisdiction also have power to issue writs.

Sometimes the resolution of a civil or criminal dispute depends on the meaning of a provision of the Constitution and whether that constitutional provision conflicts with a federal or state law or a state court decision. The Constitution says nothing about the power of a court to interpret the Constitution or the power to invalidate federal or state laws or overturn state court decisions if they conflict with the Constitution. Through a

Glossary sidebar

🏛 **injunction**

A court order to do or to stop doing a particular thing.

🏛 **writ**

A judge's order requiring that something be done outside the courtroom or authorizing it to be done.

🏛 **writ of mandamus**

[pronounce: man-day-mus] A writ of mandamus is a court order that directs a public official or government department to do something. It may be sent to the executive branch, the legislative branch, or a lower court.

🏛 **writ of habeas corpus**

[pronounce: hay-bee-as core-pus] A judicial order to someone holding a person to bring that person to court. It is most often used to get a person out of unlawful imprisonment by forcing the captor and the person being held to come to court for a decision on the legality of the imprisonment or other holding (such as keeping a child when someone else claims custody).

🏛 **remand**

Send back. For example, a higher court may remand (send back) a case to a lower court, directing the lower court to take some action.

series of cases, however, the Supreme Court has affirmed the power of the courts to interpret the Constitution and to invalidate federal and state laws that conflict with this interpretation. This power is known as the power of judicial review.

Judicial Review

🏛 judicial review
A court's power to declare a statute unconstitutional and to interpret laws.

🏛 commission
A written grant of authority to do a particular thing, given by the government to one of its branches or to an individual or organization.

THE POWER OF THE COURTS to interpret the Constitution and invalidate conflicting laws, known as the power of **judicial review**, was first affirmed in the landmark case of *Marbury v. Madison*, decided in 1803. In this era, American politics was dominated by two parties, the Federalists and the Republicans. In the presidential election of 1800, Republican Thomas Jefferson defeated incumbent Federalist John Adams. To preserve the power and influence of the Federalist party, before leaving office President Adams and a Federalist Congress created many new judicial positions and filled them with men sympathetic to the Federalist position. Senate confirmation of these individuals occurred only one day prior to Jefferson's inauguration. According to the procedures of the time, after Senate confirmation, a written document called a **commission** was prepared and signed by the president. The commission authorized the candidate to take office. Again, according to the procedures of the time, the commissions for all Adams's appointees were sent to the Secretary of State. The Secretary of State was supposed to deliver the commission to the candidate, who would then take office. Unfortunately, because of the time constraints, four of Adams's last-minute appointees did not receive their commissions before Jefferson took office. Upon taking office, Jefferson ordered his Secretary of State, James Madison, not to deliver the commissions. (See Exhibit 3-2.) Believing that he needed the commission to take office, one appointee, William Marbury, sued James Madison as Secretary of State, asking that the court force him to deliver the commission. The nature of the action filed by Marbury was a petition for writ of mandamus. The action was filed in the Supreme Court under the Court's original jurisdiction. As a side note, the chief justice of the U.S. Supreme Court, who also authored the Court's opinion, was John Marshall, Secretary of State under John Adams.

In the opinion, Marshall lists three questions or issues that the Court must decide:

1. Did Marbury have the right to the commission he demanded?
2. If he had the right and the right was violated, do the laws of the country afford him a remedy?
3. If they do afford a remedy, is it mandamus issuing from the Supreme Court?

The Court answered the first two questions in the affirmative. In analyzing the last question, the Court had to determine if the Supreme Court had the power to issue a writ of mandamus against an officeholder of the federal government as an exercise of its *original* jurisdiction. To make this decision, it would be necessary for the Supreme Court to interpret Article III of the Constitution and determine if the Constitution conflicted with the legislative act that created the federal courts and, if it did, whether the Court could invalidate such legislation.

In the Judiciary Act of 1789, Congress gave the Supreme Court the right to issue writs of mandamus to any person holding office under the authority of the United States in exercise of its original jurisdiction. Looking at the language of Article III, Section 2, however, the Court noted that the original jurisdiction of the Supreme Court applied to "cases affecting Ambassadors, other public Ministers and Consuls, and those in which a State shall be Party." Article III does not mention cases affecting those holding public office.

In deciding *Marbury v. Madison*, the Supreme Court held that although Congress could regulate the appellate jurisdiction of the Supreme Court, its original jurisdiction came exclusively from the Constitution. Any law trying to expand or change the original jurisdiction of the Supreme Court was thus in conflict with the Constitution and could not be enforced by the Court. In explaining the Court's decision, Chief Justice Marshall justifies the right of the Court to invalidate legislative action by making the following points:

1. The U.S. Constitution created a legislative branch with limited power. It would be inconceivable to say that Congress could pass any law, even one repugnant to the Constitution, and have it enforced. To do so would mean that the Constitution was not the supreme law of the land but, rather, was on the same level as any legislative act.
2. It is and always has been the duty of the judicial branch to say what the law is.
3. Under the Constitution, the judicial power is given to all cases arising under the Constitution. It would be ludicrous to believe that the Court could not interpret the Constitution in carrying out this power.
4. Why do judges take an oath to support the Constitution if it is not their job to enforce and interpret it?

Within a few years, the Supreme Court affirmed that the power of judicial review—that is, the power to review laws to determine if they conflict with the Constitution—extended not only to federal laws but also to state legislation and to decisions of state courts. Today, the power of judicial review is one of the most important powers of the Court. An excerpt from the Court's opinion in *Marbury v. Madison* is included here.

Marbury v. Madison
5 U.S. 137 (1803)

In the opinion, the Court addressed three issues: (1) Was Marbury entitled to the commission appointing him as a justice of the peace? (2) Do the laws afford him a remedy? (3) Is the remedy a writ of mandamus issued by the Supreme Court? In answering the last question, the Court considered both a law passed by Congress giving the Court the right to issue a writ and the Constitution, which did not.

Opinion:

It is the opinion of the court,

1st. That by signing the commission of Mr. Marbury, the president of the United States appointed him a justice of peace, for the county of Washington in the district of Columbia; and that the seal of the United States, affixed thereto by the secretary of state, is conclusive testimony of the verity of the signature, and of the completion of the appointment; and that the appointment conferred on him a legal right to the office for the space of five years.

2dly. That, having this legal title to the office, he has a consequent right to the commission; a refusal to deliver which, is a plain violation of that right, for which the laws of his country afford him a remedy.

It remains to be enquired whether,

He is entitled to the remedy for which he applies. This depends on,

1st. The nature of the writ applied for, and,

2dly. The power of this court.

Blackstone, in the 3d volume of his commentaries, page 110, defines a mandamus to be, "a command issued in the King's name from the court of King's Bench, and directed to any person, corporation, or inferior court of judicature within the King's dominions, requiring them to do some particular thing therein specified, which appertains to their office and duty, and which the court of King's Bench has previously determined, or at least supposed, to be consonant to right and justice."

This writ, if awarded, would be directed to an officer of government, and its mandate to him would be, to use the words of Blackstone, "to do a particular thing therein specified, which appertains to his office and duty and which the court has previously determined, or at least supposes, to be consonant to right and justice."

This is a plain case for a mandamus, either to deliver the commission, or a copy of it from the record; and it only remains to be enquired,

Whether it can issue from this court.

(continued)

(continued)

The act to establish the judicial courts of the United States authorizes the supreme court "to issue writs of mandamus, in cases warranted by the principles and usages of law, to any courts appointed, or persons." The secretary of state, being a person holding an office under the authority of the United States, is precisely within the letter of the description; and if this court is not authorized to issue a writ of mandamus to such an officer, it must be because the law is unconstitutional, and therefore absolutely incapable of conferring the authority, and assigning the duties which its words purport to confer and assign.

The constitution vests the whole judicial power of the United States in one supreme court, and such inferior courts as congress shall, from time to time, ordain and establish. This power is expressly extended to all cases arising under the laws of the United States; and consequently, in some form, may be exercised over the present case; because the right claimed is given by a law of the United States.

In the distribution of this power it is declared that "the supreme court shall have original jurisdiction in all cases affecting ambassadors, other public ministers and consuls, and those in which a state shall be a party. In all other cases, the supreme court shall have appellate jurisdiction."

It has been insisted, at the bar, that as the original grant of jurisdiction, to the supreme and inferior courts, is general, and the clause, assigning original jurisdiction to the supreme court, contains no negative or restrictive words; the power remains to the legislature, to assign original jurisdiction to that court in other cases than those specified in the article which has been recited; provided those cases belong to the judicial power of the United States.

If it had been intended to leave it to the discretion of the legislature to apportion the judicial power between the supreme and inferior courts according to the will of that body, it would certainly have been useless to have proceeded further than to have defined the judicial powers, and the tribunals in which it should be vested. The subsequent part of the section is mere surplusage, is entirely without meaning, if such is to be the construction. If congress remains at liberty to give this court appellate jurisdiction, where the constitution has declared their jurisdiction shall be original; and original jurisdiction where the constitution has declared it shall be appellate; the distribution of jurisdiction, made in the constitution, is form without substance.

Affirmative words are often, in their operation, negative of other objects than those affirmed; and in this case, a negative or exclusive sense must be given to them or they have no operation at all.

It cannot be presumed that any clause in the constitution is intended to be without effect; and therefore such a construction is inadmissible, unless the words require it.

When an instrument organizing fundamentally a judicial system, divides it into one supreme, and so many inferior courts as the legislature may ordain and establish; then enumerates its powers, and proceeds so far to distribute them, as to define the jurisdiction of the supreme court by declaring the cases in which it shall take original jurisdiction, and that in others it shall take appellate jurisdiction; the plain import of the words seems to be, that in one class of cases its jurisdiction is original, and not appellate; in the other it is appellate, and not original. If any other construction would render the clause inoperative, that is an additional reason for rejecting such other construction, and for adhering to their obvious meaning.

To enable this court then to issue a mandamus, it must be shown to be an exercise of appellate jurisdiction, or to be necessary to enable them to exercise appellate jurisdiction.

It is the essential criterion of appellate jurisdiction, that it revises and corrects the proceedings in a cause already instituted, and does not create that cause. Although, therefore, a mandamus may be directed to courts, yet to issue such a writ to an officer for the delivery of a paper, is in effect the same as to sustain an original action for that paper, and therefore seems not to belong to appellate, but to original jurisdiction. Neither is it necessary in such a case as this, to enable the court to exercise its appellate jurisdiction.

The authority, therefore, given to the supreme court, by the act establishing the judicial courts of the United States, to issue writs of mandamus to public officers, appears not to be warranted by the constitution; and it becomes necessary to enquire whether a jurisdiction, so conferred, can be exercised.

The question, whether an act, repugnant to the constitution, can become the law of the land, is a question deeply interesting to the United States; but, happily, not of an intricacy proportioned to its interest. It seems only necessary to recognize certain principles, supposed to have been long and well established, to decide it.

That the people have an original right to establish, for their future government, such principles as, in their opinion, shall most conduce to their own happiness, is the basis, on which the whole American fabric has been erected. The exercise of this original right is a very great exertion;

(continued)

(continued)

nor can it, nor ought it to be frequently repeated. The principles, therefore, so established, are deemed fundamental. And as the authority, from which they proceed, is supreme, and can seldom act, they are designed to be permanent.

This original and supreme will organizes the government, and assigns, to different departments, their respective powers. It may either stop here; or establish certain limits not to be transcended by those departments.

The government of the United States is of the latter description. The powers of the legislature are defined, and limited; and that those limits may not be mistaken, or forgotten, the constitution is written. To what purpose are powers limited, and to what purpose is that limitation committed to writing, if these limits may, at any time, be passed by those intended to be restrained? The distinction, between a government with limited and unlimited powers, is abolished, if those limits do not confine the persons on whom they are imposed, and if acts prohibited and acts allowed, are of equal obligation. It is a proposition too plain to be contested, that the constitution controls any legislative act repugnant to it; or, that the legislature may alter the constitution by an ordinary act.

Between these alternatives there is no middle ground. The constitution is either a superior, paramount law, unchangeable by ordinary means, or it is on a level with ordinary legislative acts, and like other acts, is alterable when the legislature shall please to alter it.

If the former part of the alternative be true, then a legislative act contrary to the constitution is not law: if the latter part be true, then written constitutions are absurd attempts, on the part of the people, to limit a power, in its own nature illimitable.

Certainly all those who have framed written constitutions contemplate them as forming the fundamental and paramount law of the nation, and consequently the theory of every such government must be, that an act of the legislature, repugnant to the constitution, is void.

This theory is essentially attached to a written constitution, and is consequently to be considered, by this court, as one of the fundamental principles of our society. It is not therefore to be lost sight of in the further consideration of this subject.

If an act of the legislature, repugnant to the constitution, is void, does it, notwithstanding its invalidity, bind the courts, and oblige them to give it effect? Or, in other words, though it be not law, does it constitute a rule as operative as if it was a law? This would be to overthrow in fact what was established in theory; and would seem, at first view, an absurdity too gross to be insisted on. It shall, however, receive a more attentive consideration.

It is emphatically the province and duty of the judicial department to say what the law is. Those who apply the rule to particular cases, must of necessity expound and interpret that rule. If two laws conflict with each other, the courts must decide on the operation of each.

So if a law be in opposition to the constitution; if both the law and the constitution apply to a particular case, so that the court must either decide that case conformably to the law, disregarding the constitution; or conformably to the constitution, disregarding the law; the court must determine which of these conflicting rules governs the case. This is of the very essence of judicial duty.

If then the courts are to regard the constitution; and the constitution is superior to any ordinary act of the legislature; the constitution, and not such ordinary act, must govern the case to which they both apply.

Those then who controvert the principle that the constitution is to be considered, in court, as a paramount law, are reduced to the necessity of maintaining that courts must close their eyes on the constitution, and see only the law.

This doctrine would subvert the very foundation of all written constitutions. It would declare that an act, which, according to the principles and theory of our government, is entirely void; is yet, in practice, completely obligatory. It would declare, that if the legislature shall do what is expressly forbidden, such act, notwithstanding the express prohibition, is in reality effectual. It would be giving to the legislature a practical and real omnipotence, with the same breath which professes to restrict their powers within narrow limits. It is prescribing limits, and declaring that those limits may be passed at pleasure.

That it thus reduces to nothing what we have deemed the greatest improvement on political institutions—a written constitution—would of itself be sufficient, in America, where written constitutions have been viewed with so much reverence, for rejecting the construction. But the peculiar expressions of the constitution of the United States furnish additional arguments in favor of its rejection.

Thus, the particular phraseology of the constitution of the United States confirms and strengthens the principle, supposed to be essential to all written constitutions, that a law repugnant to the constitution is void; and that courts, as well as other departments, are bound by that instrument.

The rule must be discharged.

Exhibit 3-2 James Madison and Thomas Jefferson played important roles in *Marbury v. Madison*. Both became U.S. Presidents. Madison is also known as the Father of the Constitution.

Courtesy of Bettmann/CORBIS

Courtesy of Philip Gendreau/Bettmann/Corbis

Sovereign Immunity and the Eleventh Amendment

ALTHOUGH THE CONSTITUTION CREATES FEDERAL court jurisdiction when the United States is a party, that does not mean that citizens have unlimited rights to sue the government. In fact, the doctrine of *sovereign immunity* limits the types of lawsuits that can be brought against federal and state governments. The doctrine of sovereign immunity dates back to English common law, which provided that the King could not be sued. Today, that doctrine carries over and, to a limited extent, applies to federal and state governments. Lawsuits against the federal and state governments are not allowed without the consent of the government. This consent is found in both the federal and state statutes or codes listing circumstances under which the government can and cannot be sued.

The doctrine of sovereign immunity as applied to state governments was not always recognized under the Constitution. Article III gave the federal courts power over actions between a state and citizens of another state. In 1793, in the case of *Chisholm v. Georgia*, 2 U.S. 419, the Supreme Court held that Article III allowed a state to be sued by a citizen of another state in federal court. States acted immediately to reaffirm their right of sovereign immunity. Because the Supreme Court held that the Constitution allowed suits against states, the only way it could be changed was through a constitutional amendment. The Eleventh Amendment resulted.

A Point of Law

Chisholm v. Georgia, 2 U.S. 419 (1793)

Article III of the Constitution allows citizens of one state to sue another state in federal court. (The rule was changed by the Eleventh Amendment.)

The Eleventh Amendment provides that

> [t]he Judicial power of the United States shall not be construed to extend to any suit in law or equity, commenced or prosecuted against one of the United States by Citizens of another State or by Citizens or Subjects of any Foreign State.

This amendment has also been interpreted by the Supreme Court to prohibit suits in federal court brought against a state by a citizen of that same state. On the other hand, according to various decisions by the Supreme Court, this amendment does *not* prohibit the following types of suits in federal court:

- suits brought by the federal government rather than a citizen
- suits brought against a state for violating a statute enacted pursuant to the Fourteenth Amendment in which there has been a history of the state's violating the due process or equal protection of its citizens
- Supreme Court review (usually through a writ of certiorari) of state court decisions
- lawsuits brought against a state subdivision (such as a city or county)
- lawsuits against state officials in which they are accused of violating the U.S. Constitution, as long as the lawsuits do not seek money damages from a state treasury
- lawsuits originally filed in a state court and removed to federal court at the request of the state.

In *Board of Trs. of the Univ. of Ala. v. Garrett*, 531 U.S. 356 (2001), the Supreme Court held that states could not be sued for damages in federal court for violations of the Americans with Disabilities Act. The Court's opinion focused on the rule that the Eleventh Amendment provides sovereign immunity to states unless Congress enacts legislation to remedy past violations of the Fourteenth Amendment by the states. Furthermore, the legislation must clearly indicate a congressional intention to abrogate the sovereign immunity of the Eleventh Amendment. The Court found that the Americans with Disabilities Act did not result in an abrogation of sovereign immunity.

A Point of Law

Board of Trs. of the Univ. of Ala. v. Garrett, 531 U.S. 356 (2001)

The Eleventh Amendment provides sovereign immunity to states in lawsuits filed in federal court based on the Americans with Disabilities Act. A private individual cannot sue a state in federal court for violating this act.

The Relationship between Federal and State Courts

THE CREATION OF A FEDERAL judiciary was never intended to supplant state court systems. In fact, in the early days of the new nation, the state court systems played a much larger role than the federal courts in administering justice. Although the relationship between the federal and state courts is not defined in the Constitution, both case law and statutory law have established certain principles.

Concurrent Jurisdiction

The Constitution lists several types of cases over which the federal courts
have subject-matter jurisdiction. It does not say that this jurisdiction is
exclusive to the federal courts, and in most cases, the jurisdiction is not
exclusive but rather *concurrent*. Unless a federal statute specifically provides otherwise, state courts have concurrent jurisdiction over all cases
and controversies listed in Article III, except suits between states, those to
which the United States is a party, those to which a foreign state is a
party, and those within the traditional admiralty jurisdiction. Thus, even
cases involving a federal question can often be brought in either federal
or state court.

A party bringing a lawsuit in which both the federal and state courts
have jurisdiction chooses the court in which to file the case. Should the
plaintiff file in state court, however, the defendant in such an action generally has the right to have the case removed to the federal court. The reverse is not true. If a case is initially filed in federal court, then it cannot
be removed to state court.

Abstention Doctrine

In most cases of concurrent jurisdiction, if either party chooses the federal court, that decision stands. However, in cases in which the issues involve matters that have traditionally
been handled in state court (such as divorce cases and probate matters) or in which the interpretation of a state law is in question the federal courts often abstain from hearing the
case. The Court has often described these cases by saying they create "exceptions" to
the federal court's subject-matter jurisdiction. Furthermore, in criminal cases, the Supreme
Court has invoked the abstention doctrine to make it clear that the federal courts are not to
enjoin state criminal proceedings unless great irreparable harm is shown, even when the
defendant is alleging that state law violates the Constitution.

🏛 **enjoin**

Require or command. A court's
issuing of an injunction
directing someone to do or,
more likely, to refrain from
doing certain acts.

In a recent case, *Marshall v. Marshall*, the Supreme Court addressed this doctrine in relationship to an involved probate matter. In this case, the Court recognized that although the
federal courts usually abstained from hearing domestic disputes or probate matters, no constitutional or statutory basis requires the federal courts to do so. Where appropriate, the federal
courts could hear domestic or probate matters. An excerpt from the opinion follows.

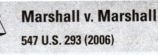

Marshall v. Marshall
547 U.S. 293 (2006)

Marshall v. Marshall resulted from the competing court
claims filed by the surviving spouse and son of J. Howard Marshall regarding their interests in his estate. While
son E. Pierce Marshall was probating his father's estate
in Texas state court, his spouse, Vickie Marshall (also
known as Anna Nicole Smith) filed for bankruptcy in federal court in California. The bankruptcy case became con-
tentious and when J. Howard Marshall II contested the

*dischargeability of a debt, Vicki Marshall countered with
a claim against him alleging that he tortiously interfered
with his father's desire to create a trust on behalf of Vicki.
Eventually, based on findings from the bankruptcy court, a
federal district court awarded Vicki several million dollars.
This award was reversed by the Court of Appeals for the
Ninth Circuit on the basis that the federal courts lacked
jurisdiction because of the "probate exception" to its*

(continued)

(continued)

jurisdictional authority. The U.S. Supreme Court granted certiorari. The following is an excerpt of its opinion.

JUSTICE GINSBURG delivered the opinion of the Court.

In *Cohens* v. *Virginia*, Chief Justice Marshall famously cautioned: "It is most true that this Court will not take jurisdiction if it should not: but it is equally true, that it must take jurisdiction, if it should . . . . We have no more right to decline the exercise of jurisdiction which is given, than to usurp that which is not given." 6 Wheat. 264, 404 (1821).

Among longstanding limitations on federal jurisdiction otherwise properly exercised are the so-called "domestic relations" and "probate" exceptions. Neither is compelled by the text of the Constitution or federal statute. Both are judicially created doctrines stemming in large measure from misty understandings of English legal history. Nevertheless, the Ninth Circuit in the instant case read the probate exception broadly to exclude from the federal courts' adjudicatory authority "not only direct challenges to a will or trust, but also questions which would ordinarily be decided by a probate court in determining the validity of the decedent's estate planning instrument." 392 F. 3d 1118, 1133 (2004). The Court of Appeals further held that a State's vesting of exclusive jurisdiction over probate matters in a special court strips federal courts of jurisdiction to entertain any "probate related matter," including claims respecting "tax liability, debt, gift, [or] tort." *Id.*, at 1136. We hold that the Ninth Circuit had no warrant from Congress, or from decisions of this Court, for its sweeping extension of the probate exception.

Petitioner, Vickie Lynn Marshall (Vickie), also known as Anna Nicole Smith, is the surviving widow of J. Howard Marshall II (J. Howard). Vickie and J. Howard met in October 1991. After a courtship lasting more than two years, they were married on June 27, 1994. J. Howard died on August 4, 1995. Although he lavished gifts and significant sums of money on Vickie during their courtship and marriage, J. Howard did not include anything for Vickie in his will. According to Vickie, J. Howard intended to provide for her financial security through a gift in the form of a "catch-all" trust.

Respondent, E. Pierce Marshall (Pierce), one of J. Howard's sons, was the ultimate beneficiary of J. Howard's estate plan, which consisted of a living trust and a "pourover" will. Under the terms of the will, all of J. Howard's assets not already included in the trust were to be transferred to the trust upon his death.

Competing claims regarding J. Howard's fortune ignited proceedings in both state and federal courts.

We granted certiorari, 545 U. S. ___ (2005), to resolve the apparent confusion among federal courts concerning the scope of the probate exception. Satisfied that the instant case does not fall within the ambit of the narrow exception recognized by our decisions, we reverse the Ninth Circuit's judgment.

Federal jurisdiction in this case is premised on 28 U. S. C. §1334, the statute vesting in federal district courts jurisdiction in bankruptcy cases and related proceedings. Decisions of this Court have recognized a "probate exception," kin to the domestic relations exception, to otherwise proper federal jurisdiction. See *Markham* v. *Allen*, 326 U. S., at 494; see also *Sutton* v. *English*, 246 U. S. 199 (1918); *Waterman* v. *Canal-Louisiana Bank & Trust Co.*, 215 U. S. 33 (1909). Like the domestic relations exception, the probate exception has been linked to language contained in the Judiciary Act of 1789.

In *Markham*, the plaintiff Alien Property Custodian commenced suit in Federal District Court against an executor and resident heirs to determine the Custodian's asserted rights regarding a decedent's estate. 326 U. S., at 491–492. Jurisdiction was predicated on §24(1) of the Judicial Code, now 28 U. S. C. §1345, which provides for federal jurisdiction over suits brought by an officer of the United States. At the time the federal suit commenced, the estate was undergoing probate administration in a state court. The Custodian had issued an order vesting in himself all right, title, and interest of German legatees. He sought and gained in the District Court a judgment determining that the resident heirs had no interest in the estate, and that the Custodian, substituting himself for the German legatees, was entitled to the entire net estate, including specified real estate passing under the will.

Reversing the Ninth Circuit, which had ordered the case dismissed for want of federal subject-matter jurisdiction, this Court held that federal jurisdiction was properly invoked. The Court first stated:

"It is true that a federal court has no jurisdiction to probate a will or administer an estate . . . . But it has been established by a long series of decisions of this Court that federal courts of equity have jurisdiction to entertain suits 'in favor of creditors, legatees and heirs' and other claimants against a decedent's estate 'to establish their claims'

(continued)

(continued)

so long as the federal court does not interfere with the probate proceedings or assume general jurisdiction of the probate or control of the property in the custody of the state court." 326 U. S., at 494 (quoting *Waterman*, 215 U. S., at 43).

Next, the Court described a probate exception of distinctly limited scope:

"[W]hile a federal court may not exercise its jurisdiction to disturb or affect the possession of property in the custody of a state court, . . . it may exercise its jurisdiction to adjudicate rights in such property where the final judgment does not undertake to interfere with the state court's possession save to the extent that the state court is bound by the judgment to recognize the right adjudicated by the federal court." 326 U. S., at 494.

The first of the above-quoted passages from *Markham* is not a model of clear statement. The Court observed that federal courts have jurisdiction to entertain suits to determine the rights of creditors, legatees, heirs, and other claimants against a decedent's estate, "so long as the federal court does not *interfere with the probate proceedings.*" *Ibid.* (emphasis added). Lower federal courts have puzzled over the meaning of the words "interfere with the probate proceedings," and some have read those words to block federal jurisdiction over a range of matters well beyond probate of a will or administration of a decedent's estate.

We read *Markham*'s enigmatic words, to proscribe "disturb[ing] or affect[ing] the possession of property in the custody of a state court." 326 U. S., at 494. In short, we comprehend the "interference" language in *Markham* as essentially a reiteration of the general principle that, when one court is exercising *in rem* jurisdiction over a *res*, a second court will not assume *in rem* jurisdiction over the same *res*. See, *e.g., Penn General Casualty Co. v. Pennsylvania ex rel. Schnader*, 294 U. S. 189, 195–196 (1935) ; *Waterman*, 215 U. S., at 45–46. Thus, the probate exception reserves to state probate courts the probate or annulment of a will and the administration of a decedent's estate; it also precludes federal courts from endeavoring to dispose of property that is in the custody of a state probate court. But it does not bar federal courts from adjudicating matters outside those confines and otherwise within federal jurisdiction.

As the Court of Appeals correctly observed, Vickie's claim does not "involve the administration of an estate, the probate of a will, or any other purely probate matter." 392 F. 3d, at 1133. Provoked by Pierce's claim in the bankruptcy proceedings, Vickie's claim alleges a widely recognized tort. Vickie seeks an *in personam* judgment against Pierce, not the probate or annulment of a will. Nor does she seek to reach a *res* in the custody of a state court. See *Markham*, 326 U. S., at 494.

Furthermore, no "sound policy considerations" militate in favor of extending the probate exception to cover the case at hand. Trial courts, both federal and state, often address conduct of the kind Vickie alleges. State probate courts possess no "special proficiency . . . in handling [such] issues."

We therefore hold that the District Court properly asserted jurisdiction over Vickie's counterclaim against Pierce. For the reasons stated, the judgment of the Court of Appeals for the Ninth Circuit is reversed, and the case is remanded for further proceedings consistent with this opinion.

It is so ordered.

❧ Ethical Decisions—Everyday Choices ❧

The Facts: Judge Harry Townsend sits as a federal appellate court judge. The law school from which the judge graduated (more than thirty years ago) is the appellant in a case set for hearing before the appellate court. Although the judge makes small annual contributions to an alumni fund, he is not active in any of the school's activities.

The Problem: Can Judge Townsend sit on the panel of judges who hear this case or must he recuse (disqualify) himself?

Guiding Principles: All federal judges are bound by a Code of Conduct for U.S. judges. This code requires judges to uphold the integrity and independence of the judiciary, to avoid impropriety or the appearance of impropriety, to perform duties of the office impartially and diligently, to regulate outside activities so as to minimize the risk of conflicts with judicial duties, to file reports of compensation received for law-related and extrajudicial activities, and to refrain from political activity. A judge may engage in extrajudicial activities that improve the law, the legal system, and the administration of justice. More details about the Judicial Code of Conduct can be found on the government Web site for U.S. courts and the federal judiciary. (Search for "code of conduct for federal judges.")

Supreme Court Review of State Court Decisions

For the most part, state and federal courts operate independently. The Supreme Court does, however, have the right to review certain decisions or judgments of state courts through a writ of certiorari. The Supreme Court can exercise this right in any of the following circumstances:

1. when the state decision involves the validity of a treaty or a U.S. statute
2. when the state decision involves a state statute that is claimed to be in violation of the U.S. Constitution, treaties, or laws of the United States
3. when the state decision involves a claim based on any right under the U.S. Constitution, U.S. statutes, or treaties

Before the Supreme Court will grant certiorari, which is discretionary, the party seeking review must first seek review in the highest state court.

Supremacy Clause

Under Article VI, Section 2, the Constitution is made the supreme law of the land. This section specifically applies to state courts. Because the Supreme Court has the right to interpret the Constitution, any cases involving constitutional interpretation are binding on the states.

Chapter Summary

According to the Constitution, the federal courts have jurisdiction to hear cases arising under the Constitution, federal laws, or treaties; cases affecting ambassadors, other public ministers, and consuls; admiralty and maritime cases; and controversies to which the United States is a party or controversies between two or more states, between a state and citizens of another state, between citizens of different states (known as diversity of citizenship), and between citizens of the same state claiming lands under grants of different states. The Constitution also gives the Supreme Court original jurisdiction in cases involving ambassadors, public ministers, and consuls, and in cases in which a state is a party. Congress cannot extend or take away this jurisdiction. Appellate jurisdiction of the Supreme Court is exercised in two ways, through a direct appeal or through a writ, most often a writ of certiorari. A direct appeal, sometimes called an appeal of right, *requires* the Supreme Court to review a matter. A writ of certiorari, is a discretionary review. A writ of certiorari is granted only if four justices agree to hear the case (the Rule of Four).

Before the federal courts can hear a case, the case must present an actual and current dispute or controversy, which is sometimes referred to as the doctrine of justiciability. The courts will not hear cases in which a controversy no longer exists (mootness) or in which the controversy has not yet arisen (ripeness). The courts will not hear cases in which the party bringing the action is not the aggrieved party or does not have a sufficient interest in the outcome of the case (standing). Furthermore, if the case presents a political question and a court believes that the area of controversy is within the realm of another branch of government, it will also refuse to hear the case.

One of the most important powers that the federal courts have is the power of judicial review. This power gives the courts the right to interpret the Constitution and declare invalid any federal or state law or case decision that is contrary to the Constitution. This right was affirmed by the Supreme Court in the landmark case of *Marbury v. Madison*.

Shortly after the federal courts were created, the Eleventh Amendment to the Constitution was passed, which prohibits the federal court from hearing cases brought against states by citizens of another state. The Supreme Court later held this amendment to include actions brought by citizens of the same state. The Eleventh Amendment does not prohibit actions brought against a state by the federal government nor actions based on laws passed pursuant to the Fourteenth Amendment. It also does not apply to actions against local municipalities, political subdivisions, or government officials who are accused of violating the Constitution. The Eleventh Amendment does not affect the right of the Supreme Court to review state court decisions.

The federal court system exists along with state court systems, and, in many instances, the different court systems have concurrent jurisdiction. When concurrent jurisdiction exists and a party has chosen to file a case in state court, the defendant can usually remove the case to federal court. Sometimes, the abstention doctrine applies, and the federal courts will refuse to hear a case. The abstention doctrine means that federal courts can refuse to hear cases that are traditionally based on state law, such as some family law and probate matters. On constitutional questions, the Supreme Court's decisions are binding on all other courts.

Key Terms

federal question	ripeness	writ
original jurisdiction	standing	writ of mandamus
special master	political question	writ of habeas corpus
writ of certiorari	Establishment Clause	remand
Rule of Four	Free Exercise Clause	judicial review
justiciable	reapportionment	commission
mootness	injunction	enjoin

Questions for Review

1. Describe the types of cases within the subject-matter jurisdiction of the federal courts.
2. Compare the Supreme Court's original jurisdiction with the Supreme Court's appellate jurisdiction.
3. Explain the difference between a direct appeal and a petition for writ of certiorari.
4. What does justiciability mean?
5. Compare and contrast the concepts of mootness and ripeness and explain their relevance to the constitutional requirement that the courts have jurisdiction only when there is a case or controversy.
6. Describe two situations under which a plaintiff might have problems with standing to bring a lawsuit.
7. Explain the abstention doctrine.
8. What is the doctrine of judicial review?
9. Explain the concept of sovereign immunity. How does it relate to the Eleventh Amendment to the Constitution?
10. How does the Supremacy Clause of the Constitution affect the relationship between federal and state courts?

Questions for Analysis

1. Review the case scenario described in Living with the Constitution at the beginning of the chapter. Discuss problems that Wilson might face with standing and ripeness. Does the federal court have subject-matter jurisdiction over this type of case?
2. Why can courts not give advisory opinions?
3. Review the Court's decision in *Hertz v. Friend*. Is the "nerve center" approach to determining diversity of citizenship really practical in today's world of telecommuting and online conferences?
4. Why do taxpayers generally lack standing to file court actions attacking the way that taxes are spent? Why did the Court allow such a lawsuit in *Flast v. Cohen,* 392 U.S. 83 (1968)?

Assignments and Projects

1. Complete the missing sections of the following brief for *Marbury v. Madison*.

Marbury v. Madison
5 U.S. 137 (1803)

Judicial History: This is a petition for writ of mandate filed by Petitioner Marbury against Respondent Secretary of State James Madison. It was filed as a case of original jurisdiction in the U.S. Supreme Court.

Facts: In the presidential election of 1800, incumbent John Adams was defeated by Thomas Jefferson. Before leaving office, President Adams nominated several individuals, including petitioner Marbury, for judicial positions. Senate confirmation of these individuals occurred only one day prior to Jefferson's inauguration. After Senate confirmation, commissions for these individuals were prepared and signed by the president. The commissions authorized the candidates to take office. The commissions for all of Adams's appointees were sent to the secretary of state for delivery to the candidates, who would then take office. Unfortunately, because of the time constraints, four of Adams's last-minute appointees did not receive their commissions before Jefferson took office. Upon taking office, Jefferson ordered his secretary of state, James Madison, not to deliver the commissions. Believing that he needed the commission to take office, one appointee, William Marbury, filed this petition for writ of mandate, asking the Court to order Secretary of State James Madison to deliver the commission.

Issues:
1. Did Marbury have the right to the commission he demanded?
2. If he had the right and the right was violated, do the laws of the country afford him a remedy?
3. If they do afford a remedy, is it mandamus issuing from the Supreme Court?

Holding:
1. Yes. Marbury did have the right to the commission he demanded.
2. Yes. The laws of the country afford him a remedy.
3. No. Mandamus issuing from the Supreme Court as an exercise of its original jurisdiction is not proper when directed against an officer of the federal government.

Rationale:

2. Access the Supreme Court Web site at <http://www.supremecourtus.gov>. Identify the current members of the Supreme Court.

Putting It into Practice

1. By the time a case reaches the Supreme Court, there has been extensive litigation in trial and appellate courts. Before parties file lawsuits, they usually try to resolve their disputes informally. Assume that you work for the state of Massachusetts in the case of *Massachusetts v. E.P.A.* described in the chapter. Draft a letter to be sent to the E.P.A. requesting that it enforce the provisions of the Clean Air Act relating to pollutants emitted by motor vehicles. Before writing the letter, search the Internet for some general information regarding the harmful effects of various motor vehicle emissions. Also search the Internet for some general information about the Clean Air Act. Use relevant information in your letter.

Group Activity

Form small groups according to directions from your instructor. Discuss both sides of the following questions: Does a nonminority defendant in a criminal case have standing to challenge the exclusion of minority defendants from juries? List arguments on both sides of the issue. Compare your arguments with those in *Powers v. Ohio*, 499 U.S. 400 (1991) and *Campbell v. Louisiana*, 523 U.S. 392 (1998).

4 Federal Legislative Powers

The natural progress of things is for liberty to yield and government to gain ground.

Thomas Jefferson

Chapter Outline

Chapter Objectives

When you complete this chapter you should be able to

1. list the general areas that Congress can regulate.

2. identify the constitutional articles and amendments that enumerate the powers of Congress.

3. explain what is meant by the Necessary and Proper Clause.

4. summarize the taxation and spending power of the federal government.

5. explain why the Supreme Court once held the income tax unconstitutional, and describe the constitutional basis for the income tax today.

6. describe the difference between interstate and intrastate commerce.

7. summarize the various tests used by the Supreme Court to determine if an activity can be regulated by Congress under the Interstate Commerce Clause.

8. describe the types of laws passed by Congress pursuant to the Interstate Commerce Clause.

9. describe the war powers and fiscal powers of Congress.

10. explain the situations under which Congress can conduct investigations and delegate authority to administrative agencies.

Looking Back

Before reading this chapter, review the following terms and concepts from the previous chapter:

Separation of powers Each branch of the U.S. government has a function. The function of the legislature is to make laws. (Chapter 2)

Checks and balances As part of the checks and balances system, the Supreme Court has the power to review laws to determine their constitutionality. (Chapter 2)

Federalism National and state governments operate concurrently in the United States. Each has the power to make and enforce laws, subject to constitutional limitations. (Chapter 2)

Political question The Supreme Court refuses to hear cases that involve political questions, that is, issues totally within the realm of another branch of government. (Chapter 3)

Living with the Constitution

In a recent television interview, Marcia Hsu, a first-time candidate for the U.S. House of Representatives, was asked why she was seeking this office. She responded that she wanted to make a difference. Public education needs improvement, drug use is too high, Internet pornography is too available, and taxes are too high, she believes. Specifically, if elected, she intends to introduce the following legislation: a bill mandating continuing education for all teachers in elementary and secondary schools, a bill making possession of marijuana on school grounds a federal crime, a bill requiring that all public libraries install Internet filters on computers available to the public, and a bill limiting both federal and state income tax.

UNDOUBTEDLY, MARCIA HSU HOPES TO make a difference by participating in the lawmaking process. As a member of Congress, Ms. Hsu would play an important role in that process. Under the system of government in place in the United States, the main function of the legislature is to make laws. Because of the system of **federalism**, lawmaking power is shared by federal and state legislatures. The Constitution specifically sets forth or **enumerates** the lawmaking powers of the federal legislature. These powers are not unlimited, and all powers that are not granted to the federal government belong to the states. This chapter focuses on several important powers of the U.S. Congress, including the powers to tax and spend, the power to regulate interstate commerce, the war powers, and the money powers. This chapter also discusses the power of Congress to hold investigations and the power to delegate its lawmaking authority to administrative agencies. (The state's power to legislate is discussed in Chapter 6.)

🏛 **federalism**

A system of political organization with several different levels of government (e.g., city, state, and national) coexisting in the same area, with the lower levels having some independent powers.

🏛 **enumerated**

Mentioned specifically; listed one by one.

The Legislative Power in General

UNDER THE CONSTITUTION, THE FEDERAL government is given the power to regulate all matters dealing with foreign relations and limited matters of domestic concern. Some areas of foreign relations are within the power of the president, but most are within the realm of Congress. For example, the president is given the power to negotiate treaties, but Congress must approve them. The lawmaking power of Congress is found primarily in Article I, Section 8 of the Constitution. Under Section 8, Congress has the power

- to tax and borrow money
- to regulate interstate and foreign commerce
- to regulate immigration
- to regulate bankruptcies
- to coin money and punish counterfeiting
- to establish post offices
- to regulate patents and copyrights
- to establish lower federal courts
- to regulate maritime matters
- to declare war
- to provide for and regulate an army and navy
- to regulate a militia
- to make all laws for the nation's capital

In addition to the powers enumerated in Article I, Congress is also given the power to make all laws necessary and proper for carrying out all powers granted to it in the Constitution. The **Necessary and Proper Clause** is an important source of congressional power.

Various amendments to the Constitution confer additional powers by granting Congress the right to enact laws necessary to enforce the terms of the amendment. Those amendments include the following:

🏛 **Necessary and Proper Clause**

Article I, Section 8, Clause 18, of the U.S. Constitution gives Congress the power to pass all laws appropriate to carry out its functions.

- the Thirteenth Amendment, which expressly outlaws slavery and involuntary servitude
- the Fourteenth Amendment, which prohibits any state from denying a person due process or equal protection
- the Fifteenth Amendment, which prohibits any state from denying the right to vote to any citizen because of race or color
- the Nineteenth Amendment, which gives women the right to vote
- the Twenty-third Amendment, which deals with the right of Washington, D.C. to cast electoral votes for the president
- the Twenty-fourth Amendment, which outlaws poll taxes
- the Twenty-sixth Amendment, which lowered the age of the right to vote to eighteen.

Exhibit 4-1   Power to Enact Laws

THE FEDERAL LEGISLATURE IS ALLOWED TO ENACT A LAW WHEN:

1. The law involves one of the enumerated powers of Article I, Section 8, *or*
2. The law is enacted to enforce the provisions of one of the amendments allowing Congress to do so, *or*
3. The law is necessary and proper to carry out the provisions of the enumerated powers.

An early important case dealing with the nature and extent of the federal legislative power is *McCulloch v. Maryland*, 17 U.S. 316 (1819). This case addressed two major issues: the interpretation to be given the Necessary and Proper Clause and the supremacy of federal laws when a state law conflicts. This case arose after the U.S. Congress chartered a national bank that was to be located in the state of Maryland. Maryland subsequently enacted a tax against all banks not chartered by the state. The federal bank refused to pay the tax, and the case resulted. In deciding the case, the Supreme Court gave a broad interpretation to the phrase *necessary and proper*, stating that it includes all reasonable means. The Court also affirmed the supremacy of federal laws over state laws. The opinion, written by John Marshall, follows.

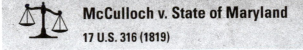

McCulloch v. State of Maryland
17 U.S. 316 (1819)

MARSHALL, CH. J., delivered the opinion of the court.

The first question made in the cause is—has Congress power to incorporate a bank?

This government is acknowledged by all, to be one of enumerated powers. That principle is now universally admitted. But the question respecting the extent of the powers actually granted, is perpetually arising, and will probably continue to arise, so long as our system shall exist. In discussing these questions, the conflicting powers of the general and state governments must be brought into view, and the supremacy of their respective laws, when they are in opposition, must be settled.

Among the enumerated powers, we do not find that of establishing a bank or creating a corporation. But there is no phrase in the instrument which, like the articles of confederation, excludes incidental or implied powers; and which requires that everything granted shall be expressly and minutely described.

Although, among the enumerated powers of government, we do not find the word "bank" or "incorporation," we find the great powers, to lay and collect taxes; to borrow money; to regulate commerce; to declare and conduct a war; and to raise and support armies and navies. The sword and the purse, all the external relations, and no inconsiderable portion of the industry of the nation, are intrusted to its government.

The government which has a right to do an act, and has imposed on it, the duty of performing that act, must, according to the dictates of reason, be allowed to select the means.

But the argument on which most reliance is placed, is drawn from that peculiar language of this clause. Congress is not empowered by it to make all laws, which may have relation to the powers conferred on the government, but such only as may be "necessary and proper" for carrying them into execution. The word "necessary" is considered as controlling the whole sentence, and as limiting the right to pass laws for the execution of the granted powers, to such as are indispensable, and without which the power would be nugatory. That it excludes the choice of means, and leaves to Congress, in each case, that only which is most direct and simple.

Is it true, that this is the sense in which the word "necessary" is always used? Does it always import an absolute physical necessity, so strong, that one thing to which another may be termed necessary, cannot exist without that other? We think it does not. If reference be had to its use, in the common affairs of the world, or in approved authors, we find that it frequently imports no more than that one thing is convenient, or useful, or essential to another. To employ the means necessary to an end, is generally understood as employing any means calculated to produce the end, and not as being confined

(continued)

(continued)

to those single means, without which the end would be entirely unattainable. Such is the character of human language, that no word conveys to the mind, in all situations, one single definite idea; and nothing is more common than to use words in a figurative sense. Almost all compositions contain words, which, taken in their rigorous sense, would convey a meaning different from that which is obviously intended.

But the argument which most conclusively demonstrates the error of the construction contended for by the counsel for the state of Maryland, is founded on the intention of the convention, as manifested in the whole clause. This clause, as construed by the state of Maryland, would abridge, and almost annihilate, this useful and necessary right of the legislature to select its means. That this could not be intended, is, we should think, had it not been already controverted, too apparent for controversy.

We think so for the following reasons: 1st. The clause is placed among the powers of Congress, not among the limitations on those powers. Its terms purport to enlarge, not to diminish the powers vested in the government. It purports to be an additional power, not a restriction on those already granted. No reason has been, or can be assigned, for thus concealing an intention to narrow the discretion of the national legislature, under words which purport to enlarge it. The framers of the constitution wished its adoption, and well knew that it would be endangered by its strength, not by its weakness. Had they been capable of using language which would convey to the eye one idea, and, after deep reflection, impress on the mind, another, they would rather have disguised the grant of power, than its limitation. If, then, their intention had been, by this clause, to restrain the free use of means which might otherwise have been implied, that intention would have been inserted in another place, and would have been expressed in terms resembling these. "In carrying into execution the foregoing powers, and all others, no laws shall be passed but such as are necessary and proper." Had the intention been to make this clause restrictive, it would unquestionably have been so in form as well as in effect.

That a corporation must be considered as a means not less usual, not of higher dignity, not more requiring a particular specification than other means, has been sufficiently proved.

If a corporation may be employed, indiscriminately with other means, to carry into execution the powers of the government, no particular reason can be assigned for excluding the use of a bank, if required for its fiscal operations. To use one, must be within the discretion of Congress, if it be an appropriate mode of executing the powers of government. That it is a convenient, a useful, and essential instrument in the prosecution of its fiscal operations, is not now a subject of controversy. All those who have been concerned in the administration of our finances, have concurred in representing its importance and necessity; and so strongly have they been felt, that statesmen of the first class, whose previous opinions against it had been confirmed by every circumstance which can fix the human judgment, have yielded those opinions to the exigencies of the nation.

It being the opinion of the court, that the act incorporating the bank is constitutional; and that the power of establishing a branch in the state of Maryland might be properly exercised by the bank itself, we proceed to inquire—

Whether the state of Maryland may, without violating the constitution, tax that branch?

On this ground, the counsel for the bank place its claim to be exempted from the power of a state to tax its operations. There is no express provision for the case, but the claim has been sustained on a principle which so entirely pervades the constitution, is so intermixed with the materials which compose it, so interwoven with its web, so blended with its texture, as to be incapable of being separated from it, without rending it into shreds. This great principle is, that the constitution and the laws made in pursuance thereof are supreme; that they control the constitution and laws of the respective states, and cannot be controlled by them.

But, waiving this theory for the present, let us resume the inquiry, whether this power can be exercised by the respective states, consistently with a fair construction of the constitution? That the power to tax involves the power to destroy; that the power to destroy may defeat and render useless the power to create; that there is a plain repugnance in conferring on one government a power to control the constitutional measures of another, which other, with respect to those very measures, is declared to be supreme over that which exerts the control, are propositions not to be denied. The American people have declared their

(continued)

(continued)

constitution and the laws made in pursuance thereof, to be supreme; but this principle would transfer the supremacy, in fact, to the states. If the states may tax one instrument, employed by the government in the execution of its powers, they may tax any and every other instrument. They may tax the mail; they may tax the mint; they may tax patent-rights; they may tax the papers of the custom-house; they may tax judicial process; they may tax all the means employed by the government, to an excess which would defeat all the ends of government. This was not intended by the American people. They did not design to make their government dependent on the states.

The court has bestowed on this subject its most deliberate consideration. The result is a conviction that the states have no power, by taxation or otherwise, to retard, impede, burden, or in any manner control, the operations of the constitutional laws enacted by Congress to carry into execution the powers vested in the general government. This is, we think, the unavoidable consequence of that supremacy which the constitution has declared. We are unanimously of opinion, that the law passed by the legislature of Maryland, imposing a tax on the Bank of the United States, is unconstitutional and void.

In *McCulloch,* the federal government's incorporation of a bank was directly related to a power clearly enumerated in the Constitution, the power to regulate money. Recently, the Supreme Court was faced with a case questioning the power of Congress to enact a law that provides for civil commitment of violent sex offenders. The Court stated that the civil commitment law was certainly "necessary and proper" to laws criminalizing the underlying criminal conduct. A question arose, however, because the underlying criminal acts are not themselves the subject of an enumerated power. Rather the criminal acts are justified as "necessary and proper" to non-criminal enumerated powers. In a divided opinion, the Court held that the Necessary and Proper Clause justified the law. The dissent maintained that such an interpretation of the Necessary and Proper Clause conferred too much power on the federal government. An excerpt from that case follows.

United States v. Comstock
560 U.S. ___ (2010)

Justice Breyer delivered the opinion of the Court.

A federal civil-commitment statute authorizes the Department of Justice to detain a mentally ill, sexually dangerous federal prisoner beyond the date the prisoner would otherwise be released. 18 U. S. C. §4248. We have previously examined similar statutes enacted under state law to determine whether they violate the Due Process Clause. But this case presents a different question. Here we ask whether the Federal Government has the authority under Article I of the Constitution to enact this federal civil-commitment program or whether its doing so falls beyond the reach of a government "of enumerated powers." *McCulloch v. Maryland* , 4 Wheat. 316, 405 (1819). We conclude that the Constitution grants Congress the

authority to enact §4248 as "necessary and proper for carrying into Execution" the powers "vested by" the "Constitution in the Government of the United States." Art. I, §8, cl. 18.

Indeed even the dissent acknowledges that Congress has the implied power to criminalize any conduct that might interfere with the exercise of an enumerated power, and also the additional power to imprison people who violate those (inferentially authorized) laws, and the additional power to provide for the safe and reasonable management of those prisons, and the additional power to regulate the prisoners' behavior even after their release. Of course, each of those powers, like the powers addressed in *Sabri, Hall,* and *McCulloch,* is ultimately

(continued)

(continued)

"derived from" an enumerated power. And, as the dissent agrees, that enumerated power is "the enumerated power that justifies the defendant's statute of conviction." Neither we nor the dissent can point to a single specific enumerated power "that justifies a criminal defendant's arrest or conviction," in *all* cases because Congress relies on different enumerated powers (often, but not exclusively, its Commerce Clause power) to enact its various federal criminal statutes. But every such statute must itself be legitimately predicated on an enumerated power. And the same enumerated power that justifies the creation of a federal criminal statute, and that justifies the additional implied federal powers that the dissent considers legitimate, justifies civil commitment under §4248 as well. Thus, we must reject respondents' argument that the Necessary and Proper Clause permits no more than a single step between an enumerated power and an Act of Congress.

Nor need we fear that our holding today confers on Congress a general "police power, which the Founders denied the National Government and reposed in the States." *Morrison* , 529 U. S., at 618. As the Solicitor General repeatedly confirmed at oral argument, §4248 is narrow in scope. It has been applied to only a small fraction of federal prisoners. See Tr. of Oral Arg. 24-25 (105 individuals have been subject to §4248 out of over 188,000 federal inmates); see also Dept. of Justice, Bureau of Justice Statistics, W. Sabol, H. West, & M. Cooper, Prisoners in 2008, p. 8 (rev. Apr. 2010) (Table 8), online at http://bjs .ojp.usdoj.gov/content/pub/pdf/p08.pdf/ (as visited May 4, 2010, and available in Clerk of Court's case file). And its reach is limited to individuals already "in the custody of the" Federal Government. §4248(a); Tr. of Oral Arg. 7 ("[Federal authority for §4248] has always depended on the fact of Federal custody, on the fact that this person has entered the criminal justice system . . ."). Indeed, the Solicitor General argues that "the Federal Government would not have . . . the power to commit a person who . . . has been released from prison and whose period of supervised release is also completed." *Id.,* at 9. Thus, far from a "general police power," §4248 is a reasonably adapted and narrowly tailored means of pursuing the Government's legitimate interest as a federal custodian in the responsible administration of its prison system.

To be sure, as we have previously acknowledged,

"The Federal Government undertakes activities today that would have been unimaginable to the Framers in two senses; first, because the Framers would not have conceived that *any* government would conduct such activities; and second, because the Framers would not have believed that the *Federal* Government, rather than the States, would assume such responsibilities. Yet the powers conferred upon the Federal Government by the Constitution were phrased in language broad enough to allow for the expansion of the Federal Government's role." *New York*, 505 U. S., at 157.

The Framers demonstrated considerable foresight in drafting a Constitution capable of such resilience through time. As Chief Justice Marshall observed nearly 200 years ago, the Necessary and Proper Clause is part of "a constitution intended to endure for ages to come, and, consequently, to be adapted to the various crises of human affairs." *McCulloch* , 4 Wheat., at 415 (emphasis deleted).

We take five considerations together. They include: (1) the breadth of the Necessary and Proper Clause, (2) the long history of federal involvement in this arena, (3) the sound reasons for the statute's enactment in light of the Government's custodial interest in safeguarding the public from dangers posed by those in federal custody, (4) the statute's accommodation of state interests, and (5) the statute's narrow scope. Taken together, these considerations lead us to conclude that the statute is a "necessary and proper" means of exercising the federal authority that permits Congress to create federal criminal laws, to punish their violation, to imprison violators, to provide appropriately for those imprisoned, and to maintain the security of those who are not imprisoned but who may be affected by the federal imprisonment of others. The Constitution consequently authorizes Congress to enact the statute.

We do not reach or decide any claim that the statute or its application denies equal protection of the laws, procedural or substantive due process, or any other rights guaranteed by the Constitution. Respondents are free to pursue those claims on remand, and any others they have preserved.

The judgment of the Court of Appeals for the Fourth Circuit with respect to Congress' power to enact this statute is reversed, and the case is remanded for further proceedings consistent with this opinion.

It is so ordered.

JUSTICE THOMAS, with whom JUSTICE SCALIA joins, dissenting.

(continued)

(continued)

Absent congressional action that is in accordance with, or necessary and proper to, an enumerated power, the duty to protect citizens from violent crime, including acts of sexual violence, belongs solely to the States. *Morrison,* ("[W]e can think of no better example of the police power, which the Founders denied the National Government and reposed in the States, than the suppression of violent crime"); see *Cohens v. Virginia,* 6 Wheat. 264, 426, 5 L.Ed. 257 (1821) (Marshall, C.J.) (stating that Congress has "no general right to punish murder committed within any of the States").

Not long ago, this Court described the Necessary and Proper Clause as "the last, best hope of those who defend ultra vires congressional action." *Printz, supra,* at 923. Regrettably, today's opinion breathes new life into that Clause, and-the Court's protestations to the contrary notwithstanding, comes perilously close to transforming the Necessary and Proper Clause into a basis for the federal police power that "we *always* have rejected," *Lopez,* 514 U.S., at 584, (THOMAS, J., concurring) (citing *Gregory, supra,* at 457; *Wirtz,* 392 U.S., at 196; *Jones & Laughlin Steel Corp.,* 301 U.S., at 37). In so doing, the Court endorses the precise abuse of power Article I is designed to prevent-the use of a limited grant of authority as a "pretext . . . for the accomplishment of objects not intrusted to the government." *McCulloch, supra,* at 423.

I respectfully dissent.

Something to Consider
Do you find the majority opinion or the dissent to be more persuasive? Why?

Taxation and Spending Powers

A MAJOR PROBLEM WITH THE Articles of Confederation was the inability of the national government to tax. Without this ability, the government was powerless to function. This problem was corrected in the Constitution. The first power given to Congress under Article I, Section 8 was the "Power To lay and collect Taxes." The Constitution refers to the following types of taxes, although it does not define them: duty, impost, excise, direct tax, and capitation tax. The meanings of a duty, impost, excise, and capitation tax are well established. A duty is a tax on imports or exports. An impost is an import tax. An excise is a tax on the manufacture, sale, or use of goods or on the carrying on of an occupation or activity. A capitation tax is a tax on a person at a fixed rate, such as a **poll tax.** The meaning of direct tax, however, is not clear and presented several problems for Congress as well as the Supreme Court.

🏛 **poll tax**

A tax, now illegal, paid to vote or for the right to vote.

The meaning of direct tax was considered by the Supreme Court as early as 1796 in the case of *Hylton v. United States,* 3 U.S. 171 (1796), a case challenging the imposition of a tax on carriages. The tax was a uniform tax on anyone who owned a carriage, and it was challenged as being in violation of the direct tax because the tax was not assessed in proportion to state population. In its opinion, the Court presented the following hypothetical situation. Assume that the tax is a direct tax. Suppose that two states with equal population were taxed on carriages. Because the tax would have to be based on population and because each state has the same population, the tax would have to be the same. Now, the Court continued, assume that each state is taxed $80,000, but that in state A there are 100 carriages and in state B, 1,000 carriages. The Court reasoned that if this tax were a direct tax, the owners of carriages in state A would pay ten times as much as carriage owners in state B. After deciding that such a result did not make sense, the Court found this tax to be an indirect tax and stated that it believed that the only direct taxes were land and poll taxes. The Court did not believe that a tax on personal property was a direct tax. In the late 1800s, the Supreme Court changed its interpretation of the direct tax, saying that it did apply to personal property. This issue is discussed further in the section on income tax.

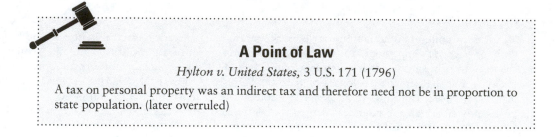

A Point of Law

Hylton v. United States, 3 U.S. 171 (1796)

A tax on personal property was an indirect tax and therefore need not be in proportion to state population. (later overruled)

Limitations on the Power to Tax

The power to tax is not unqualified. Article I sets forth the following requirements for taxes:

1. All duties, imposts, and excises must be uniform throughout the United States (Article I § 8).
2. Capitation and other direct taxes must be imposed according to state population. (Article I § 9). (This requirement has been modified by the Sixteenth Amendment, which allows the imposition of an income tax without regard to state population.)
3. Taxes on goods exported from a state were prohibited (Article I § 9).

Over time, Congress enacted numerous tax laws. Many of these laws were challenged by taxpayers who claimed that the laws exceeded the constitutional tax power. Challenges are commonly based on the following arguments:

1. The tax was a direct, rather than indirect, tax and was not based on congressional representation as required under Article I § 9.
2. The tax was imposed to regulate rather than raise revenue and is not within the constitutional right to regulate.
3. The tax violates another provision of the Constitution.

As a result of the challenges, several Supreme Court decisions explain and clarify the right of the federal government to tax. In addition, as an indirect result of the challenges, two constitutional amendments dealing with taxes, the Sixteenth and Twenty-fourth Amendments, were adopted. The Sixteenth Amendment specifically permitted the income tax, which had been declared unconstitutional by the Supreme Court. The Twenty-fourth Amendment eliminated the poll tax.

Income Tax: Direct or Indirect

Today, no reasonable American doubts the right of the federal government to impose an income tax. On April 15 of each year, lines at the post office attest to the obligation to pay these taxes. The right of the federal government to impose an income tax, however, was not clearly granted in the original Constitution. The Constitution does not specifically mention "income tax." It does, however, give Congress the general right to "tax." A uniform income tax, with each person in the country paying the same rate, would violate Article I, Section 9 if it were considered a direct tax because it would not be in proportion to state population. On the other hand, it would be constitutional if it were an indirect tax. Whether the income tax was a direct tax or an indirect tax presented a controversy. Congress believed that it was an indirect tax and passed laws creating income taxes. These laws were challenged by various taxpayers and were eventually considered by the

Supreme Court in the case of *Pollock v. Farmers' Loan & Trust Co.*, 157 U.S. 429 (1895). *Pollock* involved a challenge to an 1894 congressional Act creating an income tax. Pollock claimed that an income tax was a direct tax that was not related to state population, but to individual income. The Supreme Court agreed and held that the income tax was unconstitutional. The Court reasoned that the income tax included a tax on rents and revenue from real property. Because a tax on real property was a direct tax, so also was a tax on the proceeds of property. The Court then reasoned that it could not distinguish between real property and personal property. If a tax on real property was a direct tax, so also was a tax on personal property.

A Point of Law

Pollock v. Farmers' Loan & Trust Co., 157 U.S. 429 (1895)

The income tax was a direct tax and because it was not in proportion to state population, it was unconstitutional. (later changed by constitutional amendment)

After the *Pollock* case, the Constitution was amended to authorize an income tax. The Sixteenth Amendment to the Constitution provides:

> The Congress shall have power to lay and collect taxes on incomes, from whatever source derived, without apportionment among the several States, and without regard to any census or enumeration.

As a result of the Sixteenth Amendment, the distinction between direct and indirect taxes has no relevance in connection with income taxes.

Regulation versus Revenue

The primary purpose of the power to tax is to be able to raise revenue necessary to run the government. Occasionally, Congress has other motivations in imposing a tax, usually to discourage certain activities, such as drugs or gambling. Although some early cases from the Supreme Court invalidated taxes that were intended to destroy a business rather than raise revenue, later cases indicate that the Court will not base its decision on the subjective intent of Congress in enacting a tax.

Taxes in Conflict with Other Constitutional Provisions

The imposition of a tax cannot result in the abridgement of other constitutional rights. The 1969 Supreme Court case of *Leary v. United States*, 395 U.S. 6 (1969), provides one example. The *Leary* case involved famous activist Timothy Leary, who was convicted of violating the "Marihuana Tax Act," a federal law imposing a tax on the transfer of marijuana. Leary failed to file forms required of anyone who dealt in marijuana. On its face, the law taxed legal sellers of marijuana. It required, however, that everyone who transferred the drug file a form. Leary argued successfully that the filing requirements of this tax law violated his Fifth Amendment privilege against self-incrimination.

A Point of Law

Leary v. United States, 395 U.S. 6 (1969)

Income tax requirements cannot deprive a person of his or her Fifth Amendment rights against self-incrimination. Thus, a tax law requiring an individual to file a form indicating that the person illegally sold marijuana was unconstitutional.

Tax conflicts also arise when the federal government attempts to tax a state or employees of a state acting in their official capacity. Although the Constitution does not expressly prohibit federal taxation of state governments, the Supreme Court held that this taxation violates the notion of federalism as set forth in the Tenth Amendment. However, a tax on a state is not in violation of the Constitution, if the activity taxed is not one normally associated with state government. Such was the case in *New York v. United States* when the federal government sought to enforce a tax against the state of New York for the sale of mineral water from Saratoga Springs. In this case, the state opposed the tax, claiming that the tax was unconstitutional because it violated its rights under the Tenth Amendment. Eventually, the case reached the Supreme Court. The Court recognized state immunity from taxation, but only when the state was involved in a government activity:

> But the fact that ours is a federal constitutional system, as expressly recognized in the Tenth Amendment, carries with it implications regarding the taxing power as in other aspects of government . . . .Thus, for Congress to tax State activities while leaving untaxed the same activities pursued by private persons would do violence to the presuppositions derived from the fact that we are a Nation composed of States.

When a state is involved in a nongovernmental activity, such as bottling water, however, the immunity does not exist:

> When a state enters the market place seeking customers it divests itself of its quasi sovereignty pro tanto, and takes on the character of a trader, so far, at least, as the taxing power of the federal government is concerned.

A Point of Law

New York v. United States, 326 U.S. 572 (1946)

Normally, the federal government cannot tax a state because doing so violates the concept of federalism. When a state is engaged in a commercial, nongovernmental enterprise, such as selling bottled water, however, a federal tax on the commercial enterprise is constitutional.

Spending Power

Along with the power to tax, the federal government has the power to spend for the "general welfare." This provision has been broadly interpreted by the Supreme Court, which has upheld numerous federal spending projects, even though not related to any other power of government. The Court has said that it is up to Congress, not the Court, to determine what constitutes the general welfare.

Interstate Commerce Power

ONE OF THE MOST IMPORTANT powers given to Congress is the power to regulate commerce. Included in the commerce power is the right to regulate foreign commerce, commerce among the states (interstate commerce), and commerce with the Indian tribes. Not included in the commerce power is the right to regulate commerce that is totally intrastate. Regulation of commerce with foreign nations and Indian tribes presented little difficulty for Congress. Regulation of interstate commerce did, however, create many problems and resulted in numerous Supreme Court cases concerning the meaning of commerce and the meaning of interstate. Because of the broad interpretations given to both these terms, the Interstate Commerce Clause forms the basis of many of the laws enacted by Congress.

Commerce and the Supreme Court

The meaning of interstate commerce came into question early in U.S. history. In 1824, the Supreme Court, headed by John Marshall, was presented with the famous case of *Gibbons v. Ogden*, 22 U.S. 1. This case resulted from a conflict concerning the right to navigate seaways in New York. The state of New York granted an exclusive license to Robert Fulton and Robert Livingston to operate steamboats in New York waters. This right was then legally transferred to Aaron Ogden. As a result, Ogden claimed that any boat traveling in New York waterways needed his permission. Thomas Gibbons, the petitioner in the case, was engaged in ferrying passengers from New Jersey to New York and therefore was traveling in New York waters. He did not have permission from Ogden to do so. Gibbons, though, claimed that he had the right to navigate the waters pursuant to a federal law passed in 1793 entitled "An act for enrolling and licensing ships and vessels to be employed in the coasting trade and fisheries, and for regulating the same." This law was enacted under the power to regulate interstate commerce. Ogden filed a lawsuit to *enjoin* or stop Gibbons from using New York waterways, claiming that the federal law did not apply because transporting people was not commerce. Gibbons claimed that he was engaged in interstate commerce and therefore the law of Congress applied. The trial court found in favor of Ogden, and Gibbons appealed to the U.S. Supreme Court. In ruling in favor of Gibbons, the Supreme Court decided that transporting passengers was commerce. In its decision, the Supreme Court discussed in detail the meaning of the phrase *interstate commerce*, stating that it should be broadly interpreted and that it includes all "intercourse" between states. The Court's decision in *Gibbons v. Ogden* is included here.

Gibbons v. Ogden
22 U.S. 1 (1824)

The Court refers to the parties as follows:
Gibbons (claiming under federal law) = appellant
Ogden (claiming under state law) = appellee

MR. CHIEF JUSTICE MARSHALL delivered the opinion of the Court, and, after stating the case, proceeded as follows:

The appellant contends that this decree is erroneous, because the laws which purport to give the exclusive privilege it sustains, are repugnant to the constitution and laws of the United States. They are said to be repugnant to that clause in the constitution which authorizes Congress to regulate commerce.

(continued)

(continued)

The subject to be regulated is commerce; and to ascertain the extent of the power, it becomes necessary to settle the meaning of the word. The counsel for the appellee would limit it to traffic, to buying and selling, or the interchange of commodities, and do not admit that it comprehends navigation. Commerce, undoubtedly, is traffic, but it is something more: it is intercourse. It describes the commercial intercourse between nations, and parts of nations and is regulated by prescribing rules for carrying on that intercourse. The mind can scarcely conceive a system for regulating commerce between nations, which shall exclude all laws concerning navigation, which shall be silent on the admission of the vessels of the one nation into the ports of the other, and be confined to prescribing rules for the conduct of individuals, in the actual employment of buying and selling, or of barter.

If commerce does not include navigation, the government of the Union has no direct power over that subject, and can make no law prescribing what shall constitute American vessels, or requiring that they shall be navigated by American seamen. Yet this power has been exercised from the commencement of the government, has been exercised with the consent of all, and has been understood by all to be a commercial regulation. The power over commerce, including navigation, was one of the primary objects for which the people of America adopted their government, and must have been contemplated in forming it.

To what commerce does this power extend? The constitution informs us, to commerce "with foreign nations, and among the several States, and with the Indian tribes." The subject to which the power is next applied, is to commerce "among the several States." The word "among" means intermingled with. A thing which is among others, is intermingled with them. Commerce among the States, cannot stop at the external boundary line of each State, but may be introduced into the interior.

It is not intended to say that these words comprehend that commerce, which is completely internal, which is carried on between man and man in a State, or between different parts of the same State, and which does not extend to or affect other States. Such a power would be inconvenient, and is certainly unnecessary.

Comprehensive as the word "among" is, it may very properly be restricted to that commerce which concerns more States than one. The phrase is not one which would probably have been selected to indicate the completely interior traffic of a State, because it is not an apt phrase for that purpose. The completely internal commerce of a State, then, may be considered as reserved for the State itself.

We are now arrived at the inquiry—What is this power?

It is the power to regulate; that is, to prescribe the rule by which commerce is to be governed. This power, like all others vested in Congress, is complete in itself, may be exercised to its utmost extent, and acknowledges no limitations, other than are prescribed in the constitution. These are expressed in plain terms, and do not affect the questions which arise in this case. The power of Congress, then, comprehends navigation, within the limits of every State in the Union; so far as that navigation may be, in any manner, connected with "commerce with foreign nations, or among the several States, or with the Indian tribes." It may, of consequence, pass the jurisdictional line of New York, and act upon the very waters to which the prohibition now under consideration applies.

But it has been urged with great earnestness, that, although the power of Congress to regulate commerce with foreign nations, and among the several States, be co-extensive with the subject itself, and have no other limits than are prescribed in the constitution, yet the States may severally exercise the same power, within their respective jurisdictions. In support of this argument, it is said, that they possessed it as an inseparable attribute of sovereignty, before the formation of the constitution, and still retain it, except so far as they have surrendered it by that instrument; that this principle results from the nature of the government, and is secured by the tenth amendment; that an affirmative grant of power is not exclusive, unless in its own nature it be such that the continued exercise of it by the former possessor is inconsistent with the grant, and that this is not of that description.

The sole question is, can a State regulate commerce among the States while Congress is regulating it? In exercising the power of regulating their own purely internal affairs, whether of trading or police, the States may sometimes enact laws, the validity of which depends on their interfering with, and being contrary to, an act of Congress passed in pursuance of the constitution, the Court will enter upon the inquiry, whether the laws of New-York, as expounded by the highest tribunal of that

(continued)

(continued)

State, have, in their application to this case, come into collision with an act of Congress, and deprived a citizen of a right to which that act entitles him. Should this collision exist, it will be immaterial whether those laws were passed in virtue of a concurrent power "to regulate commerce with foreign nations and among the several States," or, in virtue of a power to regulate their domestic trade and police.

The framers of our constitution foresaw this state of things, and provided for it, by declaring the supremacy not only of itself, but of the laws made in pursuance of it. All inquiry into this subject seems to the Court to be put completely at rest, by the act already mentioned, entitled, "An act for the enrolling and licensing of steam boats." This act authorizes a steam boat employed, or intended to be employed, only in a river or bay of the United States, owned wholly or in part by an alien, resident within the United States, to be enrolled and licensed as if the same belonged to a citizen of the United States.

DECREE. This Court is, therefore, of opinion, that the decree of the Court of New York affirming the decree of the Chancellor of that State, which perpetually enjoins the said Thomas Gibbons, the appellant, from navigating the waters of the State of New York with the steam boats the Stoudinger and the Bellona, by steam or fire, is erroneous, and ought to be reversed, and the same is hereby reversed and annulled.

🏛 **intrastate**

"Within." For example, intrastate commerce is business carried out entirely within one state, as opposed to interstate commerce. Intra is usually contrasted with inter (meaning either between or among).

Despite the broad analysis of interstate commerce in *Gibbons v. Ogden*, subsequent Supreme Courts struggled with the meanings of both commerce and interstate. Prior to the late 1930s, the Supreme Court applied a narrow interpretation to the phrase, striking down several federal laws. Unlike the Court in *Gibbons*, the Supreme Court in the late 1800s and early 1900s took a very restrictive view of commerce, distinguishing commerce from other aspects of business. The Court held that Congress had no power to regulate such activities as manufacturing, mining, or production because they were not really part of commerce.

The term *interstate* also created problems, especially when the regulated activity took place totally within one state (**intrastate**) but had some effect on interstate commerce. Unfortunately, the Court did not have a specific standard by which to judge whether an activity occurring totally within one state could come under the interstate commerce power. In some cases, the Court considered whether the activity had a direct rather than indirect effect on interstate commerce. If the effect was indirect, then the law was likely to be declared unconstitutional. This standard was described and used in the case of *A.L.A. Schechter Poultry Corp. v. United States*. The issue in this case concerned the constitutionality of a federal law that created criminal penalties for violating stated trade practices in the poultry business, including wage requirements and selling restrictions. A.L.A. Schechter Poultry Corporation was prosecuted under the statute. Schechter operated a poultry slaughterhouse in New York and then sold the poultry to local retailers who in turn sold to the consumer. Even though Schechter's activities took place totally within New York, the government maintained that it was involved in interstate commerce because 96 percent of all poultry sold in New York came from out of state and, in fact, the poultry eventually slaughtered and sold by Schechter came from out of state. Schechter claimed that there was no interstate connection because it did not purchase the poultry directly from out-of-state companies. The out-of-state companies sold the poultry to middlemen, who in turn sold to Schechter. This latter sale occurred totally within the state of New York. Schechter thus claimed it had no *direct* connection to interstate commerce. It bought, sold, and slaughtered the poultry totally within the state of New York. In agreeing with Schechter, the Supreme Court discussed the requirement that to be regulated an activity had to directly affect interstate commerce:

In determining how far the federal government may go in controlling intrastate transactions upon the ground that they "affect" interstate commerce, there is a necessary and well-established distinction between direct and indirect effects. The precise line can be drawn only as individual cases arise, but the distinction is clear in principle. Direct effects are illustrated by the railroad cases we have cited, as, e.g., the effect of failure to use prescribed safety appliances on railroads which are the highways of both interstate and intrastate commerce, injury to an employee engaged in interstate transportation by the negligence of an employee engaged in an intrastate movement, the fixing of rates for intrastate transportation which unjustly discriminate against interstate commerce. But where the effect of intrastate transactions upon interstate commerce is merely indirect, such transactions remain within the domain of state power. If the Commerce Clause were construed to reach all enterprises and transactions which could be said to have an indirect effect upon interstate commerce, the federal authority would embrace practically all the activities of the people, and the authority of the state over its domestic concerns would exist only by sufferance of the federal government.

A Point of Law

A.L.A. Schechter Poultry Corp. v. United States, 295 U.S. 495 (1935)

A federal law regulating a poultry business that was conducted entirely within one state was not a proper exercise of the power under the Interstate Commerce Clause. Although intrastate activities can sometimes be regulated under the Interstate Commerce Clause, the activities must have a direct impact on interstate commerce. Given that the only connection was that the poultry initially came from out of state, the only impact on interstate commerce was indirect. (This test is no longer used.)

Another test used by early Supreme Courts in judging whether an activity came under interstate commerce was the "stream of commerce" test. If the activity was an essential part of an interstate transaction, then it could be regulated. This doctrine appeared in the case of *Swift & Co. v. United States*, 196 U.S. 375 (1905), a case involving the prosecution of individuals under a federal law prohibiting activities that are in restraint of trade. In *Swift*, a group of meatpackers agreed not to bid against one another in buying cattle, thus limiting the bidding that took place. Such conduct restrained or limited the ability of the sellers to obtain a fair price. The bidding took place totally within the state, although the meat was eventually shipped to places outside the state. The Court held that the meatpackers' activity did come within the federal law because it was part of the stream of interstate commerce:

> When cattle are sent for sale from a place in one state, with the expectation that they will end their transit, after purchase, in another, and when in effect they do so, with only the interruption necessary to find a purchaser at the stock yards, and when this is a typical, constantly recurring course, the current thus existing is a current of commerce among the states, and the purchase of the cattle is a part and incident of such commerce.

In the late 1930s, the view of the Supreme Court toward interstate commerce changed. The Court abandoned its narrow view of commerce, overruling many of its prior decisions, and developed new criteria for determining whether the activity was interstate. Most of the cases stemmed from legislation passed as a result of Franklin Roosevelt's New Deal policies, which were intended to restore economic stability during the Great Depression. One of the most important cases decided in this era was the case of *Wickard v. Filburn*. In this case, the U.S. Supreme Court was asked to decide whether a federal law, the Agricultural Adjustment Act of 1938, could be used to impose penalties on wheat farmers who exceeded an imposed quota of wheat available for marketing, even if the wheat was intended for a farmer's own use. In its opinion, the Supreme Court restated the view that the Interstate Commerce Clause has broad applicability. The opinion is included here.

Wickard v. Filburn
317 U.S. 111 (1942)

In this case, Wickard, who was the Secretary of Agriculture, is the appellant and Filburn, the wheat farmer, is the appellee.

On Appeal from the District Court of the United States for the Southern District of Ohio.

MR. JUSTICE JACKSON delivered the opinion of the Court.

In July of 1940, pursuant to the Agricultural Adjustment Act of 1938, as then amended, there were established for the appellee's 1941 crop a wheat acreage allotment of 11.1 acres and a normal yield of 20.1 bushels of wheat an acre. He sowed, however, 23 acres, and harvested from his 11.9 acres of excess acreage 239 bushels, which under the terms of the Act as amended on May 26, 1941, constituted marketing excess, subject to a penalty of 49 cents a bushel, or $117.11 in all. The appellee has not paid the penalty.

The general scheme of the Agricultural Adjustment Act of 1938 as related to wheat is to control the volume moving in interstate and foreign commerce in order to avoid surpluses and shortages and the consequent abnormally low or high wheat prices and obstructions to commerce. It is urged that under the Commerce Clause of the Constitution, Article I, 8, clause 3, Congress does not possess the power it has in this instance sought to exercise. The Act includes a definition of "market" and its derivatives so that as related to wheat in addition to its conventional meaning it also means to dispose of "by feeding (in any form) to poultry or livestock which, or the products of which, are sold, bartered, or exchanged, or to be so disposed of." Hence, marketing quotas not only embrace all that may be sold without penalty but also what may be consumed on the premises. Penalties do not depend upon whether any part of the wheat either within or without the quota is sold or intended to be sold.

Appellee says that this is a regulation of production and consumption of wheat. Such activities are, he urges, beyond the reach of Congressional power under the Commerce Clause, since they are local in character, and their effects upon interstate commerce are at most "indirect." In answer the Government argues that the statute regulates neither production nor consumption, but only marketing; and, in the alternative, that if the Act does go beyond the regulation of marketing it is sustainable as a "necessary and proper" implementation of the power of Congress over interstate commerce.

The Government's concern lest the Act be held to be a regulation of production or consumption rather than of marketing is attributable to a few dicta and decisions of this Court which might be understood to lay it down that activities such as "production," "manufacturing," and "mining" are strictly "local" and, except in special circumstances which are not present here, cannot be regulated under the commerce power because their effects upon interstate commerce are, as matter of law, only "indirect." Even today, when this power has been held to have great latitude, there is no decision of this Court that such activities may be regulated where no part of the product is intended for interstate commerce or intermingled with the subjects thereof. We believe that a review of the course of decision under the Commerce Clause will make plain, however, that questions of the power of Congress are not to be decided by reference to any formula which would give controlling force to nomenclature such as "production" and "indirect" and foreclose consideration of the actual effects of the activity in question upon interstate commerce.

(continued)

(continued)

At the beginning Chief Justice Marshall described the Federal commerce power with a breadth never yet exceeded. *Gibbons v. Ogden*, 9 Wheat. 1, 194, 195. It was not until 1887 with the enactment of the Interstate Commerce Act that the interstate commerce power began to exert positive influence in American law and life. This first important federal resort to the commerce power was followed in 1890 by the Sherman Anti-Trust Act and, thereafter, mainly after 1903, by many others. These statutes ushered in new phases of adjudication, which required the Court to approach the interpretation of the Commerce Clause in the light of an actual exercise by Congress of its power thereunder.

When it first dealt with this new legislation, the Court adhered to its earlier pronouncements, and allowed but little scope to the power of Congress. These earlier pronouncements also played an important part in several of the five cases in which this Court later held that Acts of Congress under the Commerce Clause were in excess of its power.

Even while important opinions in this line of restrictive authority were being written, however, other cases called forth broader interpretations of the Commerce Clause destined to supersede the earlier ones, and to bring about a return to the principles first enunciated by Chief Justice Marshall in *Gibbons v. Ogden, supra*.

Mr. Justice Holmes, in sustaining the exercise of national power over intrastate activity, stated for the Court that "commerce among the states is not a technical legal conception, but a practical one, drawn from the course of business." *Swift & Co. v. United States*, 196 U.S. 375, 398, 25 S. Ct. 276, 280. It was soon demonstrated that the effects of many kinds of intrastate activity upon interstate commerce were such as to make them a proper subject of federal regulation. In the *Shreveport Rate* Cases (*Houston, E. & W.T.R. Co. v. United States*), 234 U.S. 342, 34 S. Ct. 833, the Court held that railroad rates of an admittedly intrastate character and fixed by authority of the state might, nevertheless, be revised by the Federal Government because of the economic effects which they had upon interstate commerce. The opinion of Mr. Justice Hughes found federal intervention constitutionally authorized because of "matters having such a close and substantial relation to interstate traffic that the control is essential or appropriate to the security of that traffic, to the efficiency of the interstate service, and to

the maintenance of the conditions under which interstate commerce may be conducted upon fair terms and without molestation or hindrance." 234 U.S. at page 351, 34 S. Ct. at page 836.

The Court's recognition of the relevance of the economic effects in the application of the Commerce Clause exemplified by this statement has made the mechanical application of legal formulas no longer feasible. Once an economic measure of the reach of the power granted to Congress in the Commerce Clause is accepted, questions of federal power cannot be decided simply by finding the activity in question to be "production" nor can consideration of its economic effects be foreclosed by calling them "indirect." The present Chief Justice has said in summary of the present state of the law: "The commerce power is not confined in its exercise to the regulation of commerce among the states. It extends to those activities intrastate which so affect interstate commerce, or the exertion of the power of Congress over it, as to make regulation of them appropriate means to the attainment of a legitimate end, the effective execution of the granted power to regulate interstate commerce .... The power of Congress over interstate commerce is plenary and complete in itself, may be exercised to its utmost extent, and acknowledges no limitations other than are prescribed in the Constitution .... It follows that no form of state activity can constitutionally thwart the regulatory power granted by the commerce clause to Congress. Hence the reach of that power extends to those intrastate activities which in a substantial way interfere with or obstruct the exercise of the granted power." *United States v. Wrightwood Dairy Co.*, 315 U.S. 110, 119, 62 S. Ct. 523, 526.

Whether the subject of the regulation in question was "production," "consumption," or "marketing" is, therefore, not material for purposes of deciding the question of federal power before us. That an activity is of local character may help in a doubtful case to determine whether Congress intended to reach it. But even if appellee's activity be local and though it may not be regarded as commerce, it may still, whatever its nature, be reached by Congress if it exerts a substantial economic effect on interstate commerce and this irrespective of whether such effect is what might at some earlier time have been defined as "direct" or "indirect."

The parties have stipulated a summary of the economics of the wheat industry. Commerce among the

(continued)

(continued)

states in wheat is large and important. Although wheat is raised in every state but one, production in most states is not equal to consumption. Sixteen states on average have had a surplus of wheat above their own requirements for feed, seed, and food. Thirty-two states and the District of Columbia, where production has been below consumption, have looked to these surplus-producing states for their supply as well as for wheat for export and carryover.

The wheat industry has been a problem industry for some years. The decline in the export trade has left a large surplus in production which in connection with an abnormally large supply of wheat and other grains in recent years caused congestion in a number of markets; tied up railroad cars; and caused elevators in some instances to turn away grains, and railroads to institute embargoes to prevent further congestion.

In the absence of regulation the price of wheat in the United States would be much affected by world conditions. During 1941 producers who cooperated with the Agricultural Adjustment program received an average price on the farm of about $1.16 a bushel as compared with the world market price of 40 cents a bushel.

The effect of consumption of homegrown wheat on interstate commerce is due to the fact that it constitutes the most variable factor in the disappearance of the wheat crop. Consumption on the farm where grown appears to vary in an amount greater than 20 per cent of average production. The total amount of wheat consumed as food varies but relatively little, and use as seed is relatively constant.

It is said, however, that this Act, forcing some farmers into the market to buy what they could provide for themselves, is an unfair promotion of the markets and prices of specializing wheat growers. It is of the essence of regulation that it lays a restraining hand on the self-interest of the regulated and that advantages from the regulation commonly fall to others. The conflicts of economic interest between the regulated and those who advantage by it are wisely left under our system to resolution by the Congress under its more flexible and responsible legislative process. Such conflicts rarely lend themselves to judicial determination. And with the wisdom, workability, or fairness, of the plan of regulation we have nothing to do.

REVERSED.

As a result of numerous cases decided since the 1930s, the Supreme Court today recognizes three criteria for determining whether congressional legislation is consistent with the power to regulate interstate commerce. If any *one* of the following criterion is present, then the Court will probably uphold the law, unless it violates some other provision of the Constitution:

1. Does the law regulate the use of a channel of interstate commerce?
2. Does the law regulate or protect an instrumentality of interstate commerce or persons or things in interstate commerce?
3. Does the law regulate an activity that has a substantial impact on interstate commerce?

The first two criteria are fairly straightforward. A channel of interstate commerce includes such things as waterways, highways, and airways. An instrumentality of interstate commerce includes such items as the telephone, radio, television, and the Internet. The wording for persons or things traveling in interstate commerce is self-evident. The third criteria, however, has presented more difficulty. Specifically, it concerns how much of an impact an activity must have on interstate commerce. See Exhibits 4-2 and 4-3. In a 1995 case, *United States v. Lopez*, 514 U.S. 549, the Supreme Court decided that the impact must be substantial. Otherwise, the Court reasoned, the power of the legislature would be unchecked.

Until the *Lopez* case, many thought that the Supreme Court would uphold any law as long as some connection to interstate commerce could be shown. In *Lopez*, the Supreme Court was asked to decide the constitutionality of a federal statute making it a crime to

Exhibit 4-2 Supreme Court Tests

SUPREME COURT TESTS FOR INTERSTATE COMMERCE

Before the late 1930s
- Did the regulated activity have a *direct* rather than *indirect* impact on interstate commerce?
- Did the regulated activity concern something that was in the *stream of commerce*?

Current Tests:
- Does the regulation affect a *channel* of interstate commerce?
- Does the regulation affect an *instrumentality* of interstate commerce?
- Does the regulated activity have a *substantial impact* on interstate commerce?

© Cengage Learning 2013

Exhibit 4-3 Is It Interstate Commerce?

IS IT INTERSTATE COMMERCE?

Over the years, the Supreme Court considered numerous cases deciding whether an activity can be regulated under the Interstate Commerce Clause. The Court said yes in the following situations:
1. carrying lottery tickets from state to state
2. transporting a woman from one state to another in a common carrier
3. carrying whiskey across a state line in a private automobile where the whiskey is intended for personal consumption
4. driving a stolen automobile between two states
5. transmitting an electrical impulse over a telegraph line between two states
6. intrastate coal mining
7. intrastate extortionate credit transactions
8. restaurants using substantial interstate supplies
9. hotels catering to interstate guests
10. production of home-grown wheat

© Cengage Learning 2013

possess a gun near a school. In a landmark decision, the Court struck down the law, stating that any connection between gun possession near schools and interstate commerce was too slight to satisfy constitutional requirements. Four of the nine justices disagreed with the decision, however. A few years later, in 2000, the Court reaffirmed its interpretation of interstate commerce in the case of *United States v. Morrison*, 529 U.S. 598. In *Morrison*, Petitioner Brzonkala filed a civil lawsuit alleging that she was raped by respondents while the three were students at the Virginia Polytechnic Institute and that this attack violated 42 U.S.C. 13981, which provides a federal civil remedy for the victims of gender-motivated violence. The Supreme Court, in a five-to-four decision, held the law unconstitutional, relying heavily on its decision in the *Lopez* case:

> The Constitution requires a distinction between what is truly national and what is truly local, and there is no better example of the police power, which the Founders undeniably left reposed in the States and denied the central government, than the suppression of violent crime and vindication of its victims. Congress therefore may not regulate noneconomic, violent criminal conduct based solely on the conduct's aggregate effect on interstate commerce.

Excerpts from the majority and dissenting opinions in *Lopez* are included here.

United States v. Lopez
514 U.S. 549 (1995)

CHIEF JUSTICE REHNQUIST delivered the opinion of the Court.

In the Gun-Free School Zones Act of 1990, Congress made it a federal offense "for any individual knowingly to possess a firearm at a place that the individual knows, or has reasonable cause to believe, is a school zone." 18 U.S.C. § 922(q)(1)(A) (1988 ed., Supp. V). On March 10, 1992, respondent, who was then a 12th-grade student, arrived at Edison High School in San Antonio, Texas, carrying a concealed .38 caliber handgun and five bullets.

On appeal, respondent challenged his conviction based on his claim that 922(q) exceeded Congress' power to legislate under the Commerce Clause. We start with first principles. The Constitution creates a Federal Government of enumerated powers. This constitutionally mandated division of authority "was adopted by the Framers to ensure protection of our fundamental liberties."

The Constitution delegates to Congress the power "to regulate Commerce with foreign Nations, and among the several States, and with the Indian Tribes." U.S. Const., Art. I, 8, cl. 3. The Court, through Chief Justice Marshall, first defined the nature of Congress' commerce power in *Gibbons v. Ogden*, 9 Wheat. 1, 189-190 (1824):

> Commerce, undoubtedly, is traffic, but it is something more: it is intercourse. It describes the commercial intercourse between nations, and parts of nations, in all its branches, and is regulated by prescribing rules for carrying on that intercourse.

But modern-era precedents which have expanded congressional power under the Commerce Clause confirm that this power is subject to outer limits. In *Jones & Laughlin Steel*, the Court warned that the scope of the interstate commerce power "must be considered in the light of our dual system of government and may not be extended so as to embrace effects upon interstate commerce so indirect and remote that to embrace them, in view of our complex society, would effectually obliterate the distinction between what is national and what is local and create a completely centralized government." 301 U.S., at 37.

Consistent with this structure, we have identified three broad categories of activity that Congress may regulate under its commerce power. First, Congress may regulate the use of the channels of interstate commerce.

Second, Congress is empowered to regulate and protect the instrumentalities of interstate commerce, or persons or things in interstate commerce, even though the threat may come only from intrastate activities. Finally, Congress' commerce authority includes the power to regulate those activities having a substantial relation to interstate commerce, *Jones & Laughlin Steel*, 301 U.S., at 37, i.e., those activities that substantially affect interstate commerce.

Within this final category, admittedly, our case law has not been clear whether an activity must "affect" or "substantially affect" interstate commerce in order to be within Congress' power to regulate it under the Commerce Clause. We conclude, consistent with the great weight of our case law, that the proper test requires an analysis of whether the regulated activity "substantially affects" interstate commerce.

We now turn to consider the power of Congress, in the light of this framework, to enact 922(q). The first two categories of authority may be quickly disposed of: 922(q) is not a regulation of the use of the channels of interstate commerce, nor is it an attempt to prohibit the interstate transportation of a commodity through the channels of commerce; nor can 922(q) be justified as a regulation by which Congress has sought to protect an instrumentality of interstate commerce or a thing in interstate commerce. Thus, if 922(q) is to be sustained, it must be under the third category as a regulation of an activity that substantially affects interstate commerce.

First, we have upheld a wide variety of congressional Acts regulating intrastate economic activity where we have concluded that the activity substantially affected interstate commerce. Examples include the regulation of intrastate coal mining, intrastate extortionate credit transactions, restaurants utilizing substantial interstate supplies, inns and hotels catering to interstate guests, and production and consumption of home-grown wheat. These examples are by no means exhaustive, but the pattern is clear. Where economic activity substantially affects interstate commerce, legislation regulating that activity will be sustained.

Section 922(q) is a criminal statute that by its terms has nothing to do with "commerce" or any sort of economic enterprise, however broadly one might define those terms. Section 922(q) is not an essential part of a larger

(continued)

(continued)

regulation of economic activity, in which the regulatory scheme could be undercut unless the intrastate activity were regulated. It cannot, therefore, be sustained under our cases upholding regulations of activities that arise out of or are connected with a commercial transaction, which viewed in the aggregate, substantially affects interstate commerce.

Second, 922(q) contains no jurisdictional element which would ensure, through case-by-case inquiry, that the firearm possession in question affects interstate commerce. For example, in *United States v. Bass*, 404 U.S. 336 (1971), the Court interpreted former 18 U.S.C. § 1202(a), which made it a crime for a felon to "receive, possess or transport in commerce or affecting commerce . . . any firearm." 404 U.S., at 337. The Court interpreted the possession component of 1202(a) to require an additional nexus to interstate commerce both because the statute was ambiguous and because "unless Congress conveys its purpose clearly, it will not be deemed to have significantly changed the federal-state balance." *Id.*, at 349. Unlike the statute in Bass, 922(q) has no express jurisdictional element which might limit its reach to a discrete set of firearm possessions that additionally have an explicit connection with or effect on interstate commerce.

The Government's essential contention, in fine, is that we may determine here that 922(q) is valid because possession of a firearm in a local school zone does indeed substantially affect interstate commerce. The Government argues that possession of a firearm in a school zone may result in violent crime and that violent crime can be expected to affect the functioning of the national economy in two ways. First, the costs of violent crime are substantial, and, through the mechanism of insurance, those costs are spread throughout the population. Second, violent crime reduces the willingness of individuals to travel to areas within the country that are perceived to be unsafe. The Government also argues that the presence of guns in schools poses a substantial threat to the educational process by threatening the learning environment. A handicapped educational process, in turn, will result in a less productive citizenry. That, in turn, would have an adverse effect on the Nation's economic well-being. As a result, the Government argues that Congress could rationally have concluded that 922(q) substantially affects interstate commerce.

We pause to consider the implications of the Government's arguments. Under the theories that the Government presents in support of 922(q), it is difficult to perceive any limitation on federal power, even in areas such as criminal law enforcement or education where States historically have been sovereign. Thus, if we were to accept the Government's arguments, we are hard-pressed to posit any activity by an individual that Congress is without power to regulate.

For the foregoing reasons the judgment of the Court of Appeals is

Affirmed.

Justice Breyer, with whom Justice Stevens, Justice Souter, and Justice Ginsburg join, dissenting.

The issue in this case is whether the Commerce Clause authorizes Congress to enact a statute that makes it a crime to possess a gun in, or near, a school. 18 U.S.C. § 922(q)(1)(A) (1988 ed., Supp. V). In my view, the statute falls well within the scope of the commerce power as this Court has understood that power over the last half-century.

In reaching this conclusion, I apply three basic principles of Commerce Clause interpretation. First, the power to "regulate Commerce . . . among the several States," U.S. Const., Art. I, 8, cl. 3, encompasses the power to regulate local activities insofar as they significantly affect interstate commerce. See, e.g., *Gibbons v. Ogden*, 9 Wheat. 1, 194-195 (1824) (Marshall, C. J.); *Wickard v. Filburn*, 317 U.S. 111, 125 (1942).

Second, in determining whether a local activity will likely have a significant effect upon interstate commerce, a court must consider, not the effect of an individual act (a single instance of gun possession), but rather the cumulative effect of all similar instances (i.e., the effect of all guns possessed in or near schools).

Third, the Constitution requires us to judge the connection between a regulated activity and interstate commerce, not directly, but at one remove. Courts must give Congress a degree of leeway in determining the existence of a significant factual connection between the regulated activity and interstate commerce—both because the Constitution delegates the commerce power directly to Congress and because the determination requires an empirical judgment of a kind that a legislature is more likely than a court to make with accuracy. The traditional words "rational basis" capture this leeway. Thus, the specific question before us, as the Court recognizes, is not whether the "regulated activity sufficiently affected

(continued)

(continued)

interstate commerce," but, rather, whether Congress could have had "a rational basis" for so concluding.

Applying these principles to the case at hand, we must ask whether Congress could have had a rational basis for finding a significant (or substantial) connection between gun-related school violence and interstate commerce. Or, to put the question in the language of the explicit finding that Congress made when it amended this law in 1994: Could Congress rationally have found that "violent crime in school zones," through its effect on the "quality of education," significantly (or substantially) affects "interstate" or "foreign commerce"? 18 U.S.C.A. § 922(q)(1)(F), (G) (Nov. 1994 Supp.). As long as one views the commerce connection, not as a "technical legal conception," but as "a practical one," the answer to this question must be yes. Numerous reports and studies—generated both inside and outside government—make clear that Congress could reasonably have found the empirical connection that its law, implicitly or explicitly, asserts.

For one thing, reports, hearings, and other readily available literature make clear that the problem of guns in and around schools is widespread and extremely serious. These materials report, for example, that four percent of American high school students (and six percent of inner-city high school students) carry a gun to school at least occasionally,

Having found that guns in schools significantly undermine the quality of education in our Nation's classrooms, Congress could also have found, given the effect of education upon interstate and foreign commerce, that gun-related violence in and around schools is a commercial, as well as a human, problem. Education, although far more than a matter of economics, has long been inextricably intertwined with the Nation's economy.

Increasing global competition also has made primary and secondary education economically more important. The portion of the American economy attributable to international trade nearly tripled between 1950 and 1980, and more than 70 percent of American-made goods now compete with imports. Yet, lagging worker productivity has contributed to negative trade balances and to real hourly compensation that has fallen below wages in 10 other industrialized nations.

Finally, there is evidence that, today more than ever, many firms base their location decisions upon the presence, or absence, of a work force with a basic education. The economic links I have just sketched seem fairly obvious. Why then is it not equally obvious, in light of those links, that a widespread, serious, and substantial physical threat to teaching and learning also substantially threatens the commerce to which that teaching and learning is inextricably tied? That is to say, guns in the hands of six percent of inner-city high school students and gun-related violence throughout a city's schools must threaten the trade and commerce that those schools support. The only question, then, is whether the latter threat is (to use the majority's terminology) "substantial." And, the evidence of (1) the extent of the gun-related violence problem, (2) the extent of the resulting negative effect on classroom learning, and (3) the extent of the consequent negative commercial effects, see supra, at 6-9, when taken together, indicate a threat to trade and commerce that is "substantial." At the very least, Congress could rationally have concluded that the links are "substantial."

In sum, a holding that the particular statute before us falls within the commerce power would not expand the scope of that Clause. Rather, it simply would apply pre-existing law to changing economic circumstances. Respectfully, I dissent.

Something to Consider

Do you find the majority opinion or the dissent to be more persuasive? Why?

🏛 **police powers**

The government's right and power to set up and enforce laws to provide for the safety, health, and general welfare of the people; for example, police power includes the power to license occupations, such as haircutting.

Interstate Commerce and Congress

Congress uses the Interstate Commerce Clause to enact legislation affecting a variety of areas, including civil rights, business, the environment, criminal justice, and communication (including the Internet). In each of these areas, the law passed must include some connection to interstate commerce. Often, states also have the right to legislate in these areas because the states have general **police powers**. Police power is the power to make laws to provide for the general welfare of the population. Because Congress does not have general police powers, it must base its right to make any law on the powers granted in the Constitution. Because of the Supreme Court interpretation of interstate commerce, Congress has wide latitude in the subjects it can regulate. Some important areas include business legislation, criminal laws, the environment, communications and the Internet, and civil rights legislation.

BUSINESS LEGISLATION

Congress has used the Interstate Commerce Clause to enact different types of laws affecting businesses. The Sherman Antitrust Act and the Clayton Act provide criminal and civil penalties for businesses engaging in activities that are in restraint of trade. The Microsoft antitrust lawsuit is an example of a case resulting from these laws. The Securities Exchange Acts of 1933 and 1934, which regulate the stock market, are also based on the Interstate Commerce Clause. Labor and minimum-wage laws as well as some federal employment discrimination laws are also based on the Interstate Commerce Clause. These laws only apply to businesses that are engaged in interstate commerce and often contain language such as that found in the employment discrimination statutes:

> (b)The term "employer" means a person engaged in an industry affecting commerce who has fifteen or more employees for each working day in each of twenty or more calendar weeks in the current or preceding calendar year. (42 U.S.C. § 2000e)

CRIMINAL LAWS

Congress does not have an express power to enact laws that create crimes. It makes such laws incidental to other express powers. For example, because Congress is given the right to regulate the post office, it can make it a crime to perpetrate a fraud through the use of the mail. Congress also uses the Interstate Commerce Clause to enact numerous criminal laws. Using this power, Congress has outlawed such behavior as arson, failure to pay child support, racketeering, and transportation of drugs. Of course, each statute creating a crime must somehow be related to interstate commerce. The code section dealing with failure to pay child support illustrates:

> a) Offense.—Any person who—
>
> (1) willfully fails to pay a support obligation with respect to a child who resides in another State, if such obligation has remained unpaid for a period longer than 1 year, or is greater than $5,000;
>
> (2) travels in interstate or foreign commerce with the intent to evade a support obligation, if such obligation has remained unpaid for a period longer than 1 year, or is greater than $5,000;
>
> or
>
> (3) willfully fails to pay a support obligation with respect to a child who resides in another State, if such obligation has remained unpaid for a period longer than 2 years, or is greater than $10,000; shall be punished as provided in subsection (c). (11 U.S.C. § 228)

THE ENVIRONMENT

Protection of the environment is a concern to Congress, but it does not have express power to regulate this area. For many years, Congress used the Interstate Commerce Clause to regulate the environment. Today, there are laws dealing with air, water, solid waste disposal, asbestos, tropical forests, and oil pollution, in addition to governmental agencies, such as the Environmental Protection Agency. Many of the environmental laws are based on the Interstate Commerce Clause.

COMMUNICATIONS AND THE INTERNET

Another important area regulated by the Interstate Commerce Clause is the communications media, including the Internet. Congress created the Federal Communications Commission (FCC) by the Communications Act of 1934 and charged it with regulating interstate and international communications by radio, television, wire, satellite, and cable. Today, the FCC also regulates cell phones, pagers, and two-way radios. In 1996, Congress passed the Telecommunications Act of 1996, which was the first major overhaul of telecommunications law in almost sixty-two years. The Telecommunications Act of 1996 affects telephone service, local and long distance, cable programming and other video services, broadcast services, and services provided to schools. The wide use of the Internet has raised important public concerns, and Congress was prompted to confront the issue of pornography. In response, Congress enacted the Child Pornography Prevention Act of 1996 (CPPA). Parts of this act, however, did not withstand constitutional scrutiny by the Supreme Court. The case is discussed below.

CIVIL RIGHTS LEGISLATION

Congress does not have any general *express* power to legislate against discrimination. The Thirteenth, Fourteenth, and Fifteenth Amendments give Congress *limited* rights to enact civil rights legislation but it does not give it the same broad power that it has under the Commerce Clause. Thus, Congress frequently uses the Interstate Commerce Clause as its basis for civil rights laws, at least when these laws seek to regulate individuals or businesses. These laws, however, only apply to individuals or businesses that affect interstate commerce. In two famous cases, *Heart of Atlanta Hotel* and *McClung v. Katzenbach*, the Supreme Court affirmed the right of Congress to do so. Civil rights legislation and the *Heart of Atlanta Hotel* case are discussed in more detail in Chapter 7.

UNIVERSAL HEALTHCARE REFORM

A basis for Congress enacting universal health care is the Commerce Clause. To date, several lower federal courts have ruled on whether this law is authorized under the Commerce Clause and the decisions are not uniform. The Supreme Court has yet to rule, but will inevitably do so.

Limits on the Power to Regulate Interstate Commerce

Although the power to regulate interstate commerce gives Congress wide latitude in enacting laws, it is not without limits. See Table 4-1. The *Lopez* and *Morrison* cases demonstrate that the current Supreme Court will not find an interstate commerce connection in every activity. The long-term effect of these five-to-four decisions is not clear, yet one clear limit is the Supreme Court's willingness to strike down a law if it violates some other right granted under the Constitution. This willingness is illustrated by a recent Supreme Court case invalidating a law that prohibited the dissemination of "virtual" child pornography. This law defined child pornography as including computer-generated images. In the case of *Ashcroft v. Free Speech Coalition*, decided in 2002, the Supreme Court held that such a law violated the First Amendment rights to free speech without addressing the Commerce Clause.

Table 4-1 Interstate Commerce and Congress

Areas Legislated under the Commerce Clause	Examples of Laws Enacted	Connection to Interstate Commerce
Business legislation	• Antitrust laws • Laws regarding the stock market • Creation of the Securities and Exchange Commission • Labor and minimum wage laws • Employment discrimination	Generally applied to business engaged in interstate commerce
Criminal laws	• Arson • Failure to pay child support • Racketeering • Transportation of drugs	Generally required that someone cross state lines
Environment	• Laws dealing with air, water, solid waste disposal, asbestos, tropical forests, and oil pollution • Creation of the Environmental Protection Agency	Often affects channels of interstate commerce (i.e., navigable waters, air); may also affect economic, political, and social matters among various states
Communications and the Internet	• Creation of the Federal Communications Commission • Telecommunications Act • Internet pornography	Modes of communication cross state lines
Civil rights	• Various civil rights acts	Generally applies to business engaged in interstate commerce

© Cengage Learning 2013

Something to Consider

The Court struck down the Child Pornography Protection Act because it violated the First Amendment. If the statute were more narrowly drawn so as not to violate the First Amendment, do you think that the Court would uphold the power of Congress to make the law under the Interstate Commerce Clause?

War Powers

ARTICLE I, SECTION 8 ENUMERATES several powers related to the ability of the nation to engage in war. Congress is authorized to declare war and to raise and support an army and navy. The president, however, is made the commander in chief of the armed forces under Article II. Historically, this division of power between the president and Congress has created controversies over the power of the president to act without congressional approval. Although the Constitution gives Congress the right to declare war, it does not make this power an exclusive one. There have been many instances in U.S. history when a president ordered the use of troops without congressional approval. It is generally agreed that the president has the

🏛 **political question**

An issue that a court may refuse to decide because it concerns a decision properly made by the executive or legislative branch of government and because the court has no adequate standards of review or no adequate way to enforce the court's judgment. Most political questions are international diplomatic issues (e.g., whether or not a foreign country is an independent nation) that are considered by the federal courts to be best left to the president of the United States.

right to do so to defend the country if there is an attack. How long the president can act without congressional approval or whether the president can act in the absence of attack remain controversial issues, however. This controversy reached a peak during the Vietnam War. In the late 1960s and early 1970s, the United States was engaged in a military conflict in Vietnam without a congressional declaration of war. The controversy over the Vietnam War was monumental. Although lawsuits were filed claiming that the president exceeded his power, the courts refused to hear these cases, calling the issue a **political question**. In response to presidential acts in this conflict, Congress, using its war powers, enacted the War Powers Resolution. This Act recognizes the power of the president to commit troops in a military emergency, but requires that the president consult with Congress as soon as possible. It also limits the right of the president to commit to the use of military without congressional approval after sixty days. Subsequent presidents questioned the constitutionality of this law, but no court has ruled on it.

The terrorist attacks of September 11, 2001, created greater interest in the war powers of Congress, and the "War on Terror" continues to create difficulties for both Congress and the president. Immediately after the events of September 11, Congress enacted the "Authorization to Use Military Force Against Terrorists," and the "USA Patriot Act." Both enactments afford the president express authority (1) in the fight against terrorists in the use of military force, (2) in the the handling of "enemy combatants," and (3) in the power of the intelligence community to gather information on suspected foreign and domestic terrorists. The president's use of these powers, and the resulting Supreme Court action, is discussed in Chapter 5.

Fiscal Powers

UNDER THE CONSTITUTION, CONGRESS IS given the exclusive power to regulate the money system in the United States. This power expressly carries with it the rights to coin money and to punish counterfeiters. It was also held to impliedly give Congress the right to charter a national bank.

Congress also has exclusive power over bankruptcy. Using this power, Congress enacted laws and created courts that govern bankruptcy proceedings. The bankruptcy courts are adjuncts to the federal district courts throughout the United States.

🏛 **subpoena**

[pronounce: suh-pee-na] A court's order to a person that he or she appear in court to testify (give evidence) in a case. Some administrative agencies may also issue subpoenas.

🏛 **contempt**

A willful disobeying of a judge's command or official court order. It is also possible to be in contempt of a legislature or an administrative agency.

Power to Investigate

As PART OF ITS FUNCTION, Congress has the power to conduct investigations. Investigations take place when one or both houses of Congress determine a need for further inquiry. Normally, a committee is appointed to handle the investigation. The power to investigate, however, is not unlimited. It must be related to the constitutional powers of Congress; it cannot be conducted merely to look into individual affairs. Commonly, investigations are related to proposed legislation, to the conduct of the president or other national officers, or to qualifications of individuals appointed to federal positions, such as judges and cabinet heads. Congressional investigations have played an important role in U.S. history. For example, the Watergate scandal, which eventually resulted in the resignation of President Richard M. Nixon, was fueled by information revealed by witnesses during congressional hearings.

The primary tool of the investigation is the ability to **subpoena** witnesses to appear before the committee and answer questions. To enforce this ability, Congress has **contempt** power. Contempt power is the power to punish any individual who unlawfully refuses to answer questions, although individuals have the right to refuse to answer questions when one of their constitutional rights would be violated. The most common basis for lawfully refusing to answer a question is the Fifth Amendment privilege against self-incrimination.

Delegation of Congressional Powers

IN EXERCISING ITS CONSTITUTIONAL POWERS, Congress regulates many areas of domestic and foreign concern. This regulation often requires continued monitoring as well as detailed regulations for day-to-day implementation. Practically, Congress cannot assume these responsibilities and has therefore created numerous administrative agencies and commissions to regulate specific areas. For example, after the stock market crash of 1929, Congress outlawed the use of false and fraudulent practices in connection with the sale of corporate stock. To determine exactly how that was to be done and to monitor the rules, Congress created the Securities and Exchange Commission (SEC), an independent administrative agency. Congress gave the SEC the power to make and enforce rules, today known as administrative regulations. In addition to administrative agencies, Congress has occasionally empowered the president to make executive orders implementing general legislation.

At times, the power of Congress to delegate its power to administrative agencies or to the president has been questioned. In the 1930s, the Supreme Court ruled that delegation of congressional duties was unconstitutional in several situations. Since that time, the Court has upheld congressional delegation, at least where Congress sets some standards for the administrative regulations. A 1996 case, *Loving v. United States*, 517 U.S. 748, demonstrates the Court's view on this topic. Petitioner Loving, a member of the military, was convicted of murder in a military court under the Uniform Code of Military Justice (U.C.M.J.) and was sentenced to die. The death sentence resulted because the court found "aggravating circumstances" surrounding the murder. Although the crime of murder is defined in the U.C.M.J., the nature of "aggravating circumstances" is not. Relying on a section of the U.C.M.J. that allows the president to set limits for punishment of offenses, the president issued an executive order defining aggravating circumstances. As one basis for challenging the death sentence, Loving claimed that Congress had no power to delegate the right to make this determination. That was an essential part of the law, Loving claimed, and must be exercised by Congress. The Supreme Court disagreed and found that it was a legitimate delegation:

> The fundamental precept of the delegation doctrine is that the lawmaking function belongs to Congress, U.S. Const., Art. I, Section 1, and may not be conveyed to another branch or entity. *Field v. Clark*, 143 U.S. 649, 692 (1892). This principle does not mean, however, that only Congress can make a rule of prospective force. To burden Congress with all federal rulemaking would divert that branch from more pressing issues, and defeat the Framers' design of a workable National Government.

The Supreme Court did recognize some limits to this power, however:

> Congress as a general rule must also "lay down by legislative act an intelligible principle to which the person or body authorized to act is directed to conform." *J. W. Hampton, Jr., & Co. v. United States*, 276 U.S. 394, 409 (1928); *Touby*, 500 U.S., at 165. The intelligible-principle rule seeks to enforce the understanding that Congress may not delegate the power to make laws and so may delegate no more than the authority to make policies and rules that implement its statutes.

This standard need not be very specific. For example, the Court has upheld the delegation to the Federal Power Commission of authority to determine rates using "just and reasonable" as a standard.

A Point of Law

Loving v. United States, 517 U.S. 748 (1996)

It was not an improper delegation of legislative power to allow the president to define the term "aggravating circumstances" as used in the Uniform Code of Military Justice's rules regarding punishment for the crime of murder.

☙ Ethical Decisions—Everyday Choices ☙

The Facts: Rene works as a legislative aide to a U.S. senator. Recently, a group of the senator's constituents had an appointment to see the senator regarding some proposed legislation of interest to them. Because of travel delays, the constituents were unable to keep the appointment. When they tried to reschedule the appointment, they were initially told that the senator was unavailable until the following week. Unfortunately, they were leaving Washington, DC, before that time. Sympathizing with their dilemma, Rene rescheduled some of the senator's appointments and managed to arrange a meeting between the constituents and the senator. In appreciation, the constituents later mailed Rene a gift certificate at a local restaurant in the amount of $200. Incidentally, one of the constituents was Rene's cousin.

The Problem: What should Rene do with the gift certificate?

Guiding Principles: Both the U.S. House of Representatives and the U.S. Senate have adopted ethical standards for their members and their staff. Information about these ethical standards can be found on the Web sites of both the U.S. House of Representatives and the U.S. Senate. Important standards of both the House and the Senate include limits on gifts and reimbursement for travel expenses, prohibition on the use of government space and equipment for campaign purposes, and a ban on conflicting interests. Both the House and the Senate prohibit gifts in excess of $100 unless the gift is from a relative or close personal friend.

Chapter Summary

Legislative powers include the power to make laws, approve certain presidential appointments, and conduct impeachment proceedings. In carrying out these powers, the legislature is allowed to conduct investigations and delegate certain responsibilities to administrative agencies. The lawmaking power of Congress is limited by the Constitution to certain enumerated powers, most of which are found in Article I, Section 8. Various amendments also confer some legislative powers on Congress. Among the enumerated powers of Congress are the powers to impose taxes, spend money for the general welfare, regulate interstate and foreign commerce, declare war, and regulate several fiscal areas. The lawmaking power of Congress is subject to the principle of federalism. All powers not given to the federal government are reserved to the states. In the event of a conflict between federal and state law, the Supremacy Clause of the Constitution requires that federal law control.

Under Article I, Section 8, Congress can impose import, export, and excise taxes as long as they are uniform throughout the states. The Constitution also provides that any direct tax must be in proportion to state population. At one point, the Supreme Court held that the income tax violated this section. The Sixteenth Amendment was then passed, specifically allowing Congress to impose an income tax. One of the most important powers of Congress is the power to regulate interstate commerce. Whether a particular activity can be regulated under the Interstate Commerce Clause is the subject of numerous Supreme Court cases. Today, the Court says that an activity can be regulated if it is a channel of interstate commerce, is an instrumentality of interstate commerce, or has a substantial impact on interstate commerce. Congress uses the Interstate Commerce Clause to enact legislation in the areas of business, criminal law, environment, communications and the Internet, and civil rights.

Congress also has the power to declare war and to regulate many fiscal areas. The division of war powers between Congress and the president has resulted in many disagreements, leading Congress to enact the War Powers Resolution, which limits the right of the president to engage in military actions without congressional approval. In fiscal areas, Congress has the right to coin money and regulate bankruptcy. To carry out its duties, Congress can conduct investigations and delegate certain tasks to administrative agencies.

Key Terms

federalism	poll tax	political question
enumerated	intrastate	subpoena
Necessary and Proper Clause	police powers	contempt

Questions for Review

1. List the enumerated powers of Congress.
2. What parts of the Constitution contain the enumerated powers of Congress?
3. What is the Necessary and Proper Clause, and where is it found?
4. Describe the taxing and spending powers of the federal government.
5. Why did the Supreme Court once hold the income tax unconstitutional? Is it still unconstitutional? Explain.
6. What is the difference between interstate and intrastate commerce?
7. List and explain the various tests used by the Supreme Court to determine if an activity can be regulated by Congress under the Interstate Commerce Clause.
8. What types of laws have been passed by Congress pursuant to the Interstate Commerce Clause?
9. Describe the war powers and fiscal powers of Congress.
10. Under what situations can Congress conduct investigations and delegate authority to administrative agencies?

Questions for Analysis

1. Reread Living with the Constitution at the beginning of the chapter. Marcia Hsu wants to introduce several bills. As a member of Congress, which, if any, of the bills deals with an area within federal legislative power? Specify which federal power justifies each bill.
2. Answer the following questions regarding the case *McCulloch v. Maryland*.
   a. Why did Maryland claim that the federal government could not establish a national bank?
   b. Why did the federal government claim that the Maryland tax was unconstitutional?
3. Answer the following questions regarding the case *Gibbons v. Ogden*.
   a. How did the Supreme Court define interstate commerce?
   b. Did the Court believe that states could also regulate interstate commerce?
4. Answer the following questions regarding the case *Wickard v. Filburn*.
   a. Why did Filburn believe that he was not involved in interstate commerce and that therefore the federal law should not apply to him?
   b. What argument did the government make supporting the belief that the quota should apply to Filburn?

5. Answer the following questions regarding the case *United States v. Lopez*.
   a. Why does Justice Rehnquist believe that before an activity can be regulated by Congress it must *substantially affect* interstate commerce, rather than just *affect* it?
   b. Why did Justices Breyer, Stevens, Souter, and Ginsburg disagree with Chief Justice Rehnquist?

Assignments and Projects

1. Using basic research skills, determine how many bills in the latest congressional session refer to interstate commerce? Describe five different types of bills.
2. Complete the following case brief.

Wickard v. Fillburn
317 U.S. 111 (1942)

Judicial History
[Not provided]

Facts: Pursuant to a federal law, the Agricultural Adjustment Act of 1938, a quota was imposed on the appellee, Filburn, a farmer, limiting the amount of wheat he could grow even though the wheat was grown entirely for his own use. Filburn exceeded the quota and a fine was imposed. He refused to pay the fine.

Issue: Is Congress validly using its power to regulate interstate commerce when it enacts a law that allows quotas to be placed on the amount of wheat that can be grown when the wheat is entirely for the farmer's own use?

Holding:

Rationale:

Putting It into Practice

1. In the *Lopez* case, the Supreme Court held that the federal law making it a crime to possess a gun near a school was not a proper exercise of the interstate commerce power. After the decision, Congress amended the section. The following paragraph was added to the code sections: "(2) (A) It shall be unlawful for any individual knowingly to possess a firearm that has moved in or that otherwise affects interstate or foreign commerce at a place that the individual knows, or has reasonable cause to believe, is a school zone." Assume that you work for a criminal defense attorney who now represents a defendant charged with the commission of the amended law. The defendant purchased the gun from a local gun store and has never traveled outside the state in which it was purchased. The prosecutor claims that the gun affects interstate commerce because the gun was manufactured in a different state. Write a short memo to the attorney describing the amendment and analyzing the constitutionality of the amended law in view of the *Lopez* case.

Group Activity

1. Working in small groups, discuss areas in which you think a federal law is needed. Be sure to identify the power allowing such laws.

5 Federal Executive Power

The Buck Stops Here

Sign on the desk of President Harry Truman

Chapter Outline

Chapter Objectives

....

When you complete this chapter you should be able to

1. identify the various sources of presidential powers.

2. outline the constitutionally enumerated presidential powers.

3. distinguish express presidential powers from inherent presidential powers.

4. summarize the powers of the president as commander in chief.

5. explain the main features of the War Powers Act.

6. explain the provisions of the Suspension Clause.

7. discuss various situations in which the president has the power to suspend the writ of habeas corpus.

8. compare and contrast a treaty with an executive agreement.

9. describe how a presidential appointment works and explain the relevance of the term *inferior officer*.

10. describe the types of offenses subject to presidential pardon and the effect of a pardon.

Looking Back

....

Before reading this chapter, review the following terms and concepts from previous chapters:

Inherent power The powers a government must have to govern, even if not explicitly stated in its governing documents; for example, the constitutional power of the federal government to conduct foreign affairs or the power of the federal courts to protect constitutional rights. (Chapter 2)

Enumerated power Mentioned specifically; listed one by one. (Chapter 2)

Political question An issue or question that the Supreme Court will not decide because it is within the realm of the legislative or executive branch of government and to hear such a case violates the notion of separation of powers. (Chapter 3)

Living with the Constitution

....

Jordan Maguire just graduated from high school and will start college in the fall, majoring in political science. While in high school, Jordan was involved in numerous service organizations and served as student body president. When Jordan expressed an interest in learning more about the political system, a counselor suggested that Jordan apply for a position as a White House intern. At the very least, Jordan would learn more about the U.S. presidency.

THE UNITED STATES CONSTITUTION VESTS executive power in one person, the president. Although the president represents only one branch of the federal government, this person is undoubtedly the most important individual in the government of the United States. The president represents the United States in dealings with all foreign countries and leads the nation in domestic matters. Presidential powers stem from three sources: the Constitution, Congress, and the nature of the presidency itself. Although the Constitution does not *define* executive power, it does *enumerate* several specific powers given to the president, most of which are found in Article II, Section 2. Under this section, the president is made commander in chief of the armed forces and is given the power to grant pardons, to make treaties, and to appoint various federal officers including ambassadors and federal judges as well as the power to call special sessions of Congress. Under Article I, Section 7, known as the **Presentment Clause,** the president has the right to veto legislation. Additional presidential powers stem from two other sources. Recall from Chapter 4 that under some circumstances, Congress has the right to delegate some of its powers to the president. When the president acts pursuant to such authority, the Supreme Court usually upholds the action. Other powers—called inherent powers—are derived from the very nature of the presidency and are not expressly stated in the Constitution. Inherent powers are generally limited to foreign matters. This chapter discusses the various presidential powers.

🏛 **Presentment clause**

Clause in the Constitution requiring that bills passed by both the Senate and the House of Representatives be presented to the President for signature; basis of presidential veto power.

Express versus Inherent Powers

A SLIGHT DIFFERENCE IN THE WORDING OF ARTICLE I AND ARTICLE II of the Constitution has led to arguments that, unlike Congress, the president is not limited to constitutionally enumerated powers. Because Article I refers to "legislative powers *herein granted*" and Article II refers simply to "executive powers," the argument is that executive powers are not limited to those actually granted in the constitution. There is very little law regarding the limits of the president's power, but the existing law suggests that the president has considerable inherent powers in international dealings but little, if any, inherent powers in domestic matters.

The philosophy behind this distinction is explained by the Court in two cases: *United States v. Curtiss-Wright Export Corp.*, 299 U.S. 304 (1936) and *Youngstown Sheet & Tube Co. v. Sawyer*, 343 U.S. 579 (1952). *Curtiss-Wright* involved the legality of a 1934 presidential proclamation in which the president prohibited Americans from selling weapons to either Bolivia or Paraguay, countries involved in an undeclared war. The proclamation followed a joint resolution of Congress authorizing the president to take this action. Curtiss-Wright, along with others, was charged with a crime for violating the proclamation. The defendants claimed that the presidential proclamation was illegal because it exceeded the powers of the president. The trial court agreed and dismissed the case. The government appealed to the Supreme Court.

In reversing the trial court, the Supreme Court stressed the broad powers that the president has in foreign matters as opposed to domestic concerns. According to the Court, this distinction is based on historical reasons. When the nation was formed, the federal government was given two distinct powers: powers over domestic matters and powers over international matters. Power over domestic issues is shared with the states. The Constitution grants to the federal government specific powers in this field, leaving all others to the states. On the other hand, international matters are not within the realm of the states. In a sense, in the area of international matters, the new nation assumed all powers previously held by the Crown. As a result, in dealing with foreign matters, the president has more power than in dealing with domestic matters. In the *Curtiss-Wright* case, one other fact contributed to the Court's decision. Prior to taking action, Congress issued a joint resolution authorizing the president to take such action. It is impossible to say how the Court would have ruled if the president acted without congressional approval, although the opinion certainly implies that the Court would recognize broad presidential powers in foreign matters. An excerpt from the case in which the Court discusses the general powers of the president is included here.

United States v. Curtiss-Wright Export Corp.

299 U.S. 304 (1936)

As Marshall said in his great argument of March 7, 1800, in the House of Representatives, "The President is the sole organ of the nation in its external relations, and its sole representative with foreign nations." The Senate Committee on Foreign Relations at a very early day in our history (February 15, 1816), reported to the Senate, among other things, as follows:

> The President is the constitutional representative of the United States with regard to foreign nations. He manages our concerns with foreign nations and must necessarily be most competent to determine when, how, and upon what subjects negotiation may be urged with the greatest prospect of success.

It is important to bear in mind that we are here dealing not alone with an authority vested in the President by an exertion of legislative power, but with such an authority plus the very delicate, plenary and exclusive power of the President as the sole organ of the federal government in the field of international relations—a power which does not require as a basis for its exercise an act of Congress, but which, of course, like every other governmental power, must be exercised in subordination to the applicable provisions of the Constitution. It is quite apparent that if, in the maintenance of our international relations, embarrassment—perhaps serious embarrassment—is to be avoided and success for our aims achieved, congressional legislation which is to be made effective through negotiation and inquiry within the international field must often accord to the President a degree of discretion and freedom from statutory restriction which would not be admissible were domestic affairs alone involved. Moreover, he, not Congress, has the better opportunity of knowing the conditions which prevail in foreign countries, and especially is this true in time of war. He has his confidential sources of information. He has his agents in the form of diplomatic, consular and other officials. Secrecy in respect of information gathered by them may be highly necessary, and the premature disclosure of it productive of harmful results. Indeed, so clearly is this true that the first President refused to accede to a request to lay before the House of Representatives the instructions, correspondence and documents relating to the negotiation of the Jay Treaty—a refusal the wisdom of which was recognized by the House itself and has never since been doubted. In his reply to the request, President Washington said:

> The nature of foreign negotiations requires caution, and their success must often depend on secrecy; and even when brought to a conclusion a full disclosure of all the measures, demands, or eventual concessions which may have been proposed or contemplated would be extremely impolitic; for this might have a pernicious influence on future negotiations, or produce immediate inconveniences, perhaps danger and mischief, in relation to other powers. The necessity of such caution and secrecy was one cogent reason for vesting the power of making treaties in the President, with the advice and consent of the Senate, the principle on which that body was formed confining it to a small number of members. To admit, then, a right in the House of Representatives to demand and to have as a matter of course all the papers respecting a negotiation with a foreign power would be to establish a dangerous precedent. Messages and Papers of the Presidents, p. 194.

When the President is to be authorized by legislation to act in respect of a matter intended to affect a situation in foreign territory, the legislator properly bears in mind the important consideration that the form of the President's action—or, indeed, whether he shall act at all—may well depend, among other things, upon the nature of the confidential information which he has or may thereafter receive, or upon the effect which his action may have upon our foreign relations. In the light of the foregoing observations, it is evident that this court should not be in haste to apply a general rule which will have the effect of condemning legislation like that under review as constituting an unlawful delegation of legislative power. The principles which justify such legislation find overwhelming support in the unbroken legislative practice which has prevailed almost from the inception of the national government to the present day.

The question of inherent powers in domestic matters was considered by the Supreme Court in the case of *Youngstown Sheet & Tube Co. v. Sawyer*, 343 U.S. 579 (1952). After a nationwide steel strike was called by the steelworkers' union, the president issued a proclamation ordering the secretary of commerce to take over the steel mills to avoid a national catastrophe. The Court held that the president had *no* inherent power to do so. (An excerpt from the opinion in *Youngstown* follows.)

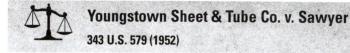

Youngstown Sheet & Tube Co. v. Sawyer
343 U.S. 579 (1952)

MR. JUSTICE BLACK delivered the opinion of the Court.

We are asked to decide whether the President was acting within his constitutional power when he issued an order directing the Secretary of Commerce to take possession of and operate most of the Nation's steel mills. The mill owners argue that the President's order amounts to lawmaking, a legislative function which the Constitution has expressly confided to the Congress and not to the President. The Government's position is that the order was made on findings of the President that his action was necessary to avert a national catastrophe which would inevitably result from a stoppage of steel production, and that in meeting this grave emergency the President was acting within the aggregate of his constitutional powers as the Nation's Chief Executive and the Commander in Chief of the Armed Forces of the United States.

The President's power, if any, to issue the order must stem either from an act of Congress or from the Constitution itself. There is no statute that expressly authorizes the President to take possession of property as he did here. It is clear that if the President had authority to issue the order he did, it must be found in some provision of the Constitution. And it is not claimed that express constitutional language grants this power to the President. The contention is that presidential power should be implied from the aggregate of his powers under the Constitution. Particular reliance is placed on provisions in Article II which say that "The executive Power shall be vested in a President . . ."; that "he shall take Care that the Laws be faithfully executed"; and that he "shall be Commander in Chief of the Army and Navy of the United States."

The order cannot properly be sustained as an exercise of the President's military power as Commander in Chief of the Armed Forces. Even though "theater of war" be an expanding concept, we cannot with faithfulness to our constitutional system hold that the Commander in Chief of the Armed Forces has the ultimate power as such to take possession of private property in order to keep labor disputes from stopping production. This is a job for the Nation's lawmakers, not for its military authorities.

Nor can the seizure order be sustained because of the several constitutional provisions that grant executive power to the President. In the framework of our Constitution, the President's power to see that the laws are faithfully executed refutes the idea that he is to be a lawmaker. The Constitution limits his functions in the lawmaking process to the recommending of laws he thinks wise and the vetoing of laws he thinks bad. And the Constitution is neither silent nor equivocal about who shall make laws which the President is to execute. The first section of the first article says that "All legislative Powers herein granted shall be vested in a Congress of the United States . . . ." After granting many powers to the Congress, Article I goes on to provide that Congress may "make all Laws which shall be necessary and proper for carrying into Execution the foregoing Powers, and all other Powers vested by this Constitution in the Government of the United States, or in any Department or Officer thereof."

The Founders of this Nation entrusted the lawmaking power to the Congress alone in both good and bad times. It would do no good to recall the historical events, the fears of power and the hopes for freedom that lay behind their choice. Such a review would but confirm our holding that this seizure order cannot stand.

The judgment of the District Court is AFFIRMED.

The President as Commander in Chief

THE CONSTITUTION GIVES CONGRESS THE power to declare war, and Article II makes the president the commander in chief of the armed forces. The Constitution does not explain the nature and extent of these powers nor how the powers of Congress and the president relate to each other. Various questions have therefore arisen regarding both the congressional war powers and the powers of the president as commander in chief. Chapter 4 discussed the congressional war powers. This chapter discusses two issues regarding presidential powers as commander in chief:

1. the right of the President to use military force in the absence of a congressional declaration of war, and
2. the nature and limits of the presidential power aside from ordering the use of military action

Military Action in the Absence of Congressional Declaration of War

History repeatedly shows that the president's powers as commander in chief are not limited to times when Congress formally declares war. Presidents have ordered military action in numerous, and often controversial, situations. One situation that is not generally controversial, however, is the right of the president to use military force when the country is attacked by foreign enemies. The right of the president to use military force in such a case was recognized by the Supreme Court in a famous Civil War case known as "The Prize Cases." These cases, consisting of several similar cases heard together by the Court, dealt with actions taken by President Lincoln prior to any congressional declaration of war. President Lincoln used his power as commander in chief to impose a blockade on the southern states. Ships ignoring the blockade were taken as war "prizes," a practice allowed under international laws of war. The seizure of the ships would be unlawful if no war existed. In discussing the issues in the case, the Court, including the dissent, recognized the power of a president to use force when the country is attacked. Excerpts from the majority decision and dissent are included here.

The Prize Cases: Brig Amy Warwick
67 U.S. 635 (1862)

At the beginning of the Civil War, before Congress actually declared war, President Lincoln ordered a blockade of southern ports. Several ships disregarded the blockade and pursuant to international laws of war were taken as war "prizes." Lawsuits were filed to contest this taking on the basis that the international rules of war should not apply because Congress had not declared war and because the President did not have the power to do so. The Court consolidated the cases and they became known as "The Prize Cases." The ultimate question before the Court was whether war existed at the time the ships were taken, even though war had not been formally declared by Congress.

MR. JUSTICE GRIER.

There are certain propositions of law which must necessarily affect the ultimate decision of these cases, and many others, which it will be proper to discuss and decide before we notice the special facts peculiar to each.

They are,

1st. Had the President a right to institute a blockade of ports in possession of persons in armed rebellion against the Government, on the principles of international law, as known and acknowledged among civilized States?

(continued)

(continued)

2d. Was the property of persons domiciled or residing within those States a proper subject of capture on the sea as "enemies' property?"

I. Let us enquire whether, at the time this blockade was instituted, a state of war existed which would justify a resort to these means of subduing the hostile force.

War has been well defined to be, "That state in which a nation prosecutes its right by force." The parties belligerent in a public war are independent nations. But it is not necessary to constitute war, that both parties should be acknowledged as independent nations or sovereign States. A war may exist where one of the belligerents, claims sovereign rights as against the other.

Insurrection against a government may or may not culminate in an organized rebellion, but a civil war always begins by insurrection against the lawful authority of the Government. A civil war is never solemnly declared; it becomes such by its accidents—the number, power, and organization of the persons who originate and carry it on. When the party in rebellion occupy and hold in a hostile manner a certain portion of territory; have declared their independence; have cast off their allegiance; have organized armies; have commenced hostilities against their former sovereign, the world acknowledges them as belligerents, and the contest a war. They claim to be in arms to establish their liberty and independence, in order to become a sovereign State, while the sovereign party treats them as insurgents and rebels who owe allegiance, and who should be punished with death for their treason. As a civil war is never publicly proclaimed, against insurgents, its actual existence is a fact in our domestic history which the Court is bound to notice and to know.

If a war be made by invasion of a foreign nation, the President is not only authorized but bound to resist force by force. He does not initiate the war, but is bound to accept the challenge without waiting for any special legislative authority. And whether the hostile party be a foreign invader, or States organized in rebellion, it is none the less a war, although the declaration of it be "unilateral."

Whether the President in fulfilling his duties, as Commander-in-chief, in suppressing an insurrection, has met with such armed hostile resistance, and a civil war of such alarming proportions as will compel him to accord to them the character of belligerents, is a question to be decided by him, and this Court must be governed by the decisions and acts of the political department of the Government to which this power was entrusted. He must determine what degree of force the crisis demands. The proclamation of blockade is itself official and conclusive evidence to the Court that a state of war existed which demanded and authorized a recourse to such a measure, under the circumstances peculiar to the case.

On this first question therefore we are of the opinion that the President had a right, jure belli, to institute a blockade of ports in possession of the States in rebellion, which neutrals are bound to regard.

II. We come now to the consideration of the second question. What is included in the term "enemies' property?"

Is the property of all persons residing within the territory of the States now in rebellion, captured on the high seas, to be treated as "enemies' property" whether the owner be in arms against the Government or not?

Whether property be liable to capture as "enemies' property" does not in any manner depend on the personal allegiance of the owner. "It is the illegal traffic that stamps it as 'enemies' property.' It is of no consequence whether it belongs to an ally or a citizen." 8 Cr., 384.

The produce of the soil of the hostile territory, as well as other property engaged in the commerce of the hostile power, as the source of its wealth and strength, are always regarded as legitimate prize, without regard to the domicile of the owner, and much more so if he reside and trade within their territory.

Mr. Justice Nelson, dissenting.

It will be seen, therefore, that ample provision has been made under the Constitution and laws against any sudden and unexpected disturbance of the public peace from insurrection at home or invasion from abroad. The whole military and naval power of the country is put under the control of the President to meet the emergency. He may call out a force in proportion to its necessities, one regiment or fifty, one ship-of-war or any number at his discretion. If, like the insurrection in the State of Pennsylvania in 1793, the disturbance is confined to a small district of country, a few regiments of the militia may be sufficient to suppress it. If of the dimension of the present, when it first broke out, a much larger force would be required. But whatever its numbers, whether great or small, that may be required, ample provision is here made; and whether great or small, the nature of the

(continued)

(continued)

power is the same. It is the exercise of a power under the municipal laws of the country and not under the law of nations; and, as we see, furnishes the most ample means of repelling attacks from abroad or suppressing disturbances at home until the assembling of Congress, who can, if it be deemed necessary, bring into operation the war power, and thus change the nature and character of the contest.

Upon the whole, after the most careful consideration of this case which the pressure of other duties has admitted, I am compelled to the conclusion that no civil war existed between this Government and the States in insurrection till recognized by the Act of Congress 13th of July, 1861; that the President does not possess the power under the Constitution to declare war or recognize its existence within the meaning of the law of nations, which carries with it belligerent rights, and thus change the country and all its citizens from a state of peace to a state of war; that this power belongs exclusively to the Congress of the United States, and, consequently, that the President had no power to set on foot a blockade under the law of nations, and that the capture of the vessel and cargo in this case, and in all cases before us in which the capture occurred before the 13th of July, 1861, for breach of blockade, or as enemies' property, are illegal and void, and that the decrees of condemnation should be reversed and the vessel and cargo restored.

MR. CHIEF JUSTICE TANEY, MR. JUSTICE CARTON and MR. JUSTICE CLIFFORD, concurred in the dissenting opinion of Mr. Justice Nelson.

Since the Civil War, several presidents used their power as commander in chief to use military force in situations where the United States was actually attacked and where Congress did not declare war. Military conflicts in Korea and Vietnam are two examples. Although several constitutional challenges were made during the Vietnam War, the Court refused to consider the question, calling it a political question. As a result of opposition to U.S. involvement in Vietnam, in 1973 Congress enacted the War Powers Resolution. This Act seeks to limit the power of the president to engage in hostile military action without congressional approval. The War Powers Resolution contains the following major provisions:

- The power of the president as commander in chief to use military force can only be used if (a) Congress has declared war, (b) there is specific statutory authorization, or (c) a national emergency is created by attack on the United States, its territories, possessions, or armed forces.
- If possible, the president should consult with Congress prior to using military action.
- If there is no prior consultation, the president must report to Congress within forty-eight hours of using force and make periodic reports thereafter.
- Use of force is limited to sixty days unless certain conditions exist.
- Congress has the power the order the removal of armed forces from hostile situations.

Since its enactment, several presidents have questioned the constitutionality of the act, claiming that it deprives the president of powers implied under the Constitution.

Limits of Powers as Commander in Chief

As the commander in chief, the president is charged with the defense and protection of the United States, which has included more than the use of military action. For example, during World War II, in *Korematsu v. United States*, 323 U.S. 214 (1944), the Supreme Court affirmed the right of the president to issue an executive order regarding "the removal, relocation, maintenance and supervision" of persons of Japanese ancestry. (Such a practice is highly unlikely to be approved by the Court today.)

The president's position as commander in chief, however, does not carry with it unlimited powers. Among the first questions the Supreme Court considered regarding this subject

martial law

Government completely by the military; control of the domestic civilian population by the military in wartime or during a breakdown of civilian control.

Suspension Clause

Article I, Section 9 of the U.S. Constitution authorizing the president to suspend the writ of habeas corpus only in times of rebellion or invasion and when required for public safety.

were the rights of the president to declare **martial law**, suspend the **writ of habeas corpus**, and require military rather than civilian trials. The writ of habeas corpus is a procedure used by those who are confined, giving them access to our courts. When the writ is suspended, individuals have no right to court trials. Article I, Section 9 of the Constitution, the **Suspension Clause**, allows the president to suspend the writ of habeas corpus only in the case of "rebellion or invasion" and when required for public safety. In the case of *Ex parte Milligan*, the Supreme Court acknowledged that the president did have power to suspend the writ of habeas corpus, but it was not unlimited. The facts of the case are as follows. At the beginning of the Civil War, President Lincoln issued a proclamation subjecting any person who was disloyal to the Union to martial law. The proclamation made such individuals subject to trial by military commissions, suspending their right to the writ of habeas corpus. The proclamation was ratified by Congress, which authorized the president to suspend the writ of habeas corpus. Milligan, a citizen of Indiana, was arrested for violating the president's edict and was tried before a military commission. He maintained that the president had no right to suspend the writ of habeas corpus or to deny him the right to a trial by jury. Although the Court affirmed the right of the president to declare martial law during an emergency, here the Supreme Court agreed with Milligan. An excerpt from the Court's opinions explaining its reasoning is included here.

Ex parte Milligan
71 U.S. 2 (1866)

It is claimed that martial law covers with its broad mantle the proceedings of this military commission. The proposition is this: that in a time of war the commander of an armed force (if in his opinion the exigencies of the country demand it, and of which he is to judge), has the power, within the lines of his military district, to suspend all civil rights and their remedies, and subject citizens as well as soldiers to the rule of his will; and in the exercise of his lawful authority cannot be restrained, except by his superior officer or the President of the United States.

If this position is sound to the extent claimed, then when war exists, foreign or domestic, and the country is subdivided into military departments for mere convenience, the commander of one of them can, if he chooses, within his limits, on the plea of necessity, with the approval of the Executive, substitute military force for and to the exclusion of the laws, and punish all persons, as he thinks right and proper, without fixed or certain rules.

The statement of this proposition shows its importance; for, if true, republican government is a failure, and there is an end of liberty regulated by law. Martial law, established on such a basis, destroys every guarantee of the Constitution, and effectually renders the "military independent of and superior to the civil power"—the attempt to do which by the King of Great Britain was deemed by

our fathers such an offence, that they assigned it to the world as one of the causes which impelled them to declare their independence. Civil liberty and this kind of martial law cannot endure together; the antagonism is irreconcilable; and, in the conflict, one or the other must perish.

It is essential to the safety of every government that, in a great crisis, like the one we have just passed through, there should be a power somewhere of suspending the writ of habeas corpus. In every war, there are men of previously good character, wicked enough to counsel their fellow-citizens to resist the measures deemed necessary by a good government to sustain its just authority and overthrow its enemies; and their influence may lead to dangerous combinations. In the emergency of the times, an immediate public investigation according to law may not be possible; and yet, the period to the country may be too imminent to suffer such persons to go at large. Unquestionably, there is then an exigency which demands that the government, if it should see fit in the exercise of a proper discretion to make arrests, should not be required to produce the persons arrested in answer to a writ of habeas corpus.

It follows, from what has been said on this subject, that there are occasions when martial rule can be properly applied. If, in foreign invasion or civil war, the courts are actually closed, and it is impossible to administer criminal

(continued)

(continued)

justice according to law, then, on the theatre of active military operations, where war really prevails, there is a necessity to furnish a substitute for the civil authority, thus overthrown, to preserve the safety of the army and society; and as no power is left but the military, it is allowed to govern by martial rule until the laws can have their free course. As necessity creates the rule, so it limits its duration; for, if this government is continued after the courts are reinstated, it is a gross usurpation of power. Martial rule can never exist where the courts are open, and in the proper and unobstructed exercise of their jurisdiction. It is also confined to the locality of actual war. Because, during the late Rebellion it could have been enforced in Virginia, where the national authority was overturned and the courts driven out, it does not follow that it should obtain in Indiana, where that authority was never disputed, and justice was always administered. And so in the case of a foreign invasion, martial rule may become a necessity in one state, when, in another, it would be "mere lawless violence." We are not without precedents in English and American history illustrating our views of this question; but it is hardly necessary to make particular reference to them.

Something to Consider

Assume that Jones, a U.S. citizen, is arrested in the United States and is incarcerated. Can he be denied a right to file a petition for writ of habeas corpus? Can he be tried by a military tribunal? Suppose that the USA Patriot Act of 2001 authorizes the president to suspend the writ of habeas corpus and order trial by military tribunal for all suspected terrorists working as agents of foreign powers, would your answer change?

writ of habeas corpus (Latin) "You have the body." A judicial order to someone holding a person to bring that person to court. It is most often used to get a person out of unlawful imprisonment by forcing the captor and the person being held to come to court for a decision on the legality of the imprisonment or other holding (such as keeping a child when someone else claims custody). [pronounce: Hay-bee-as cor-pus]

The *Milligan* case demonstrated the Court's belief that national security alone does not justify a president's suspension or termination of basic constitutional rights. In *Milligan*, the Court stressed that Milligan was not a foreign enemy and that his arrest took place in a state within the Union when the courts were open and functioning. On the other hand, in the case of *Ex parte Quirin*, the Court addressed a similar issue in relationship to enemy saboteurs who were apprehended on U.S. soil during World War II. The power to order military tribunals was affirmed by the Supreme Court in the case of *Ex parte Quirin*, 317 U.S. 1 (1942). The petitioners in this case were born in Germany but lived in the United States. All returned to Germany between 1933 and 1941. After the declaration of war between the United States and Germany, petitioners received training at a sabotage school near Berlin, Germany, where they were instructed in the use of explosives and in methods of secret writing. Thereafter, petitioners boarded a German submarine that proceeded across the Atlantic to Long Island, New York. The four were put ashore, carrying with them a supply of explosives, fuses, and incendiary and timing devices. While landing, they wore German Marine Infantry uniforms or parts of uniforms. Immediately after landing, they buried their uniforms and the other articles mentioned and proceeded in civilian dress to New York City. When they were caught, the president ordered that they be tried in a military tribunal. The Supreme Court upheld the order that they be tried in a military tribunal rather than a court of law, saying that the president had the right to order the militairy trials. The Court gave two reasons: (1) Congress had enacted laws authorizing the president to do so, and (2) this right was included in the president's constitutional powers as commander in chief. (Military tribunals are not only used for enemy agents. Using its power to regulate the armed forces, Congress enacted the Uniform Code of Military Justice in 1951. This law established standards of justice that apply to anyone who is in the military.)

In two other cases, the Court limited the power of a president who claimed to be acting in the interest of national security. In *United States v. United States Dist. Court*, 407 U.S. 297 (1972), the Court decided that the president could not order a wiretap without a warrant against members of a domestic organization suspected of subversive activities. The Court believed that the freedoms of the Fourth Amendment could not be guaranteed if domestic security surveillance was conducted solely within the discretion of the president without the detached judgment of a neutral magistrate. In reaching its decision, the Court emphasized that it was not describing presidential powers in relationship to foreign groups, saying: "The instant case requires no judgment on the scope of the president's surveillance power with respect to the activities of foreign powers, within or without this country." This question has not been decided by the Court. Whether the Court would continue to limit the president's power in connection with wiretapping is also unknown in light of the war on terror and the USA Patriot Act. The Patriot Act was enacted by Congress following the events of September 11, 2001, in an effort to fight terrorism. This Act recognizes "domestic terrorists" and gives the government greater powers over activities such as wiretapping.

In another case, *New York Times Co. v. United States*, 403 U.S. 713 (1971), the Court made it clear that the president could not stop newspapers from publishing a sensitive document regarding the war in Vietnam (the "Pentagon Papers"). The president argued that an injunction was necessary for national security. In a concurring opinion, Justice Hugo Black explains: "To find that the President has 'inherent power' to halt the publication of news by resort to the courts would wipe out the First Amendment and destroy the fundamental liberty and security of the very people the Government hopes to make 'secure.'" See Exhibit 5-1.

A Point of Law

Ex parte Quirin, 317 U.S. 1 (1942)

United States v. United States Dist. Court, 407 U.S. 297 (1972)

New York Times Co. v. United States, 403 U.S. 713 (1971)

The president has the power to protect the national security of the country. Using such power, the president can order military trials for enemy saboteurs apprehended on U.S. soil during war. The president does not, however, have the power to order a wiretap without a search warrant against a domestic organization suspected of subversive actions. Nor does the president have the power to stop the press from publishing sensitive information.

Exhibit 5-1   Presidential Powers as Commander in Chief

According to the Supreme Court, as commander in chief the President could:

- use military force to defend the country against foreign attack
- order a blockade of ports without a congressional declaration of war
- issue executive orders during World War II regarding relocation of persons of Japanese ancestry
- order military trials for enemy saboteurs arrested on U.S. soil

According to the Supreme Court, as commander in chief the President could *not*:

- order the government take over of the nation's steel mills
- order military trials for nonmilitary U.S. citizens
- conduct warrantless searches of domestic organizations suspected of subversive activities
- order a newspaper not to publish sensitive material

Executive Power and the War on Terror

The executive power of the president plays an important role in the "war on terror" and has led to several Supreme Court cases in an attempt to define the extent and limits of the president's powers. Soon after the attacks of September 11, 2001, Congress passed an Act entitled "Authorization to Use Military Force" giving the president the power to "use all necessary and appropriate force against those nations, organizations, or persons he determines planned, authorized, committed, or aided the terrorist attacks that occurred on September 11, 2001, or harbored such organizations or persons, in order to prevent any future acts of international terrorism against the United States by such nations, organizations or persons."

The president soon used that power to order troops into Afghanistan for the purpose of tracking down those responsible for the September 11 attacks. The president referred to these hostiles as "unlawful enemy combatants," a phrase that referred to hostile enemies who were not technically "prisoners of war" and therefore not entitled to the protections of established treaties. Since the attacks of September 11 and the initial powers given to the president under the Authorization to Use Military Force, the president has exercised power to create military tribunals to review the status of those designated as enemy combatants. Access to U.S. courts through the writ of habeas corpus was denied to detainees who were to be limited to the military tribunals. An important question in connection with these actions concerned the right of the government to invoke the "Suspension Clause" of the Constitution—the clause that allows the government to suspend the right of habeas corpus. Some of the important cases decided by the Supreme Court dealing with these issues are the following:

- *Hamdi v. Rumsfeld*, 542 U.S. 507 (2004)
- *Rasul v. Rumsfeld*, 542 U.S. 466 (2004)
- *Hamdan v. Rumsfeld*, 548 U.S. 557 (2006)
- *Boumediene v. Bush*, 553 U.S. 723 (2008)

Hamdi v. Rumsfeld

During the course of the Afghan invasion, U.S. forces captured an individual, Yasef Hamdi, who was a U.S. citizen. He was eventually imprisoned within the United States. Because he was designated as an enemy combatant, the president argued that he could be held without the basic constitutional rights of an accused criminal. A petition for writ of habeas corpus was filed on his behalf, challenging his status as an enemy combatant. The appellate court eventually held that the court had no right to intervene in the government's actions. The Supreme Court reversed and found that as a U.S. citizen being held on American soil, Hamdi was entitled to due process and judicial review. (This case is discussed in more detail in Chapter 9.)

Rasul v. Rumsfeld

In this case, the Court extended due process rights to non-U.S. citizens detained at Guantanamo Bay by holding that they had access to U.S. courts to challenge whether they were being legally held as enemy combatants. (It did not give them the right to a court trial on the underlying issue as to whether they were terrorists.)

Hamdan v. Rumsfeld

In *Hamdan v. Rumsfeld,* petitioner Hamdan, a foreign national held in Guantanamo Bay, filed a petition for writ of habeas corpus challenging the administration's procedures for trying him. Hamden asserted that the military commissions established by the president to try enemy combatants were not legal. He claimed that the president did not have the power to create them and that, in any event, the commissions violated basic tenets of military and international law. The Supreme Court ultimately agreed with Hamdan. The Court held that the commissions had to be authorized either by Congress or by the Uniform Code of Military Justice. Furthermore, the commissions as established violated the rules of international law, in particular the Geneva Convention.

Boumediene v. Bush

After the Supreme Court in *Hamdan* restricted the right of the administration to rely entirely on military tribunals, in 2006 Congress passed the Military Commisson Act, stating that captives were not entitled to the U.S. justice system and staying all petitions for writ of habeas corpus. This Act gave the president the power to order military trials for all detainees. In *Boumediene v. Bush*, 553 U.S. 723 (2008), provisions of this Act were challenged as unconstitutional. In this case, the government made two arguments. First, the government argued that even though the United States maintained a military base on Guantanamo Bay, the territory was a Cuban sovereignty and therefore the Constitution did not apply. Second, the government argued that various congressional enactments provided sufficient constitutional safeguards as alternatives to the writ of habeas corpus. A majority of the Supreme Court rejected the government arguments, finding that the Constitution did apply to detainees on Guantanamo Bay and that the president could not order military trials under the current legislation because adequate safeguards were not in place. In finding that the Constitution did apply, the Court noted: "The detainees, moreover, are held in a territory that, while technically not part of the United States, is under the complete and total control of our Government." Excerpts from the Court's opinion related to the sufficiency of the alternative safeguards to the writ of habeas corpus follow.

Boumediene v. Bush
553 U.S. 723 (2008)

In light of this holding the question becomes whether the statute stripping jurisdiction to issue the writ avoids the Suspension Clause mandate because Congress has provided adequate substitute procedures for habeas corpus.

We do not endeavor to offer a comprehensive summary of the requisites for an adequate substitute for habeas corpus. We do consider it uncontroversial, however, that the privilege of habeas corpus entitles the prisoner to a meaningful opportunity to demonstrate that he is being held pursuant to "the erroneous application or interpretation" of relevant law. And the habeas court must have the power to order the conditional release of an individual unlawfully detained—though release need not be the exclusive remedy and is not the appropriate one in every case in which the writ is granted.

Where a person is detained by executive order, rather than, say, after being tried and convicted in a court, the need for collateral review is most pressing. A criminal conviction in the usual course occurs after a judicial hearing before a tribunal disinterested in the outcome and committed to procedures designed to ensure its own independence. These dynamics are not inherent in executive detention orders or executive review procedures. In this context the need for habeas corpus is more urgent. The intended duration of the detention and the reasons for it bear upon the precise scope of the inquiry. Habeas corpus proceedings need not resemble a criminal trial, even when the detention is by executive order. But the writ must be effective. The habeas court must have sufficient authority to conduct a meaningful review of both the cause for detention and the Executive's power to detain.

(continued)

(continued)

For the writ of habeas corpus, or its substitute, to function as an effective and proper remedy in this context, the court that conducts the habeas proceeding must have the means to correct errors that occurred during the proceedings. This includes some authority to assess the sufficiency of the Government's evidence against the detainee. It also must have the authority to admit and consider relevant exculpatory evidence that was not introduced during the earlier proceeding. Federal habeas petitioners long have had the means to supplement the record on review, even in the postconviction habeas setting. Here that opportunity is constitutionally required.

It suffices that the Government has not established that the detainees' access to the statutory review provisions at issue is an adequate substitute for the writ of habeas corpus. MCA §7 thus effects an unconstitutional suspension of the writ. In view of our holding we need not discuss the reach of the writ with respect to claims of unlawful conditions of treatment or confinement.

Treaties and Executive Agreements

🏛 **treaty**

A formal agreement between countries on a major political subject. The treaty clause of the U.S. Constitution requires the approval of two-thirds of the Senate for any treaty made by the president.

🏛 **executive agreement**

A document, similar to a treaty, that is signed by the president but does not require the approval of the Senate (as a treaty does).

THE PRESIDENT HAS THE POWER to negotiate and enter into **treaties** with foreign nations subject to ratification by two-thirds of the Senate. Treaties cover a broad range of subjects, although they cannot contain any provision that violates provisions of the Constitution. In addition to treaties, presidents often negotiate and enter into agreements, known as **executive agreements**, with heads of other nations. In substance, there is little difference between an executive agreement and a treaty, although the Court has continually ruled that executive agreements do not need Senate approval.

Even though Congress approves a treaty, however, does not mean that the terms of the treaty will always be enforced by the courts. In a recent case, *Medellin v. Texas*, 552 U.S. 491 (2008), the Supreme Court refused to enforce a provision of a treaty known as the Vienna Convention. Pursuant to this treaty, Mexican nationals accused of serious crimes were entitled to be advised that they could notify their consul to ask for help. Medellin, a Mexican national, was accused of murder in Texas, but the state did not advise Medellin of this right. Medellin was convicted and sentenced to death. In ruling on his challenge to the state's refusal to comply with the terms of the treaty, the U.S. Supreme Court held that the terms of the treaty were not binding on domestic law. The Court's reasoning emphasizes the role of the president and the role of Congress regarding the effect of a treaty. The president has the right to negotiate, but treaties are subject to congressional approval. Furthermore, congressional approval of the treaty does not necessarily mean that all the provisions become binding as domestic U.S. law. This depends on the terms of the treaty. The Court held that the state of Texas was not obligated to comply with the provisions of the treaty requiring that Medellin be advised of his right to notify the Mexican consul.

Appointment Power

THE POWER OF THE PRESIDENT to appoint various officials is found in the following language in Article II, Section 2:

by and with the Advice and Consent of the Senate, he shall appoint Ambassadors, other public Ministers and Consuls, Judges of the supreme Court, and all other Officers of the United States....,

The President shall have Power to fill up all Vacancies that may happen during the Recess of the Senate, by granting Commissions which shall expire at the End of their next Session.

In addition to the positions listed in the Constitution, federal law allows the president to appoint all federal district court and court of appeals justices.

The appointment process requires two separate steps. An individual is nominated by the president and then approved by the Senate, which has no say in who is nominated. The power to appoint officials also carries with it the power to remove them from office, unless, like judges, they are subject to removal only by impeachment.

Not all government officials are appointed by the president. The Constitution allows *inferior officers* to be appointed by the courts or by heads of departments. Which government officers are inferior officers is sometimes not clear. In a 1988 case, the Supreme Court considered whether a **special prosecutor** was an inferior officer and could be appointed by the court rather than by the president. A second important issue in the case was whether a special prosecutor authorized by Congress and appointed by the court violated the separation of powers doctrine because the special prosecutor was charged with enforcing the law, an executive function. The majority of the Supreme Court ruled that the special prosecutor was an inferior officer and did not violate the doctrine of separation of powers. Justice Antonin Scalia dissented primarily because he believed that the appointment method of the special prosecutor violated the separation of powers doctrine. The Constitution says that all executive power is vested in the president, Justice Scalia argued, and allowing Congress and the courts to authorize and appoint an individual exercising executive functions violates the clear language of the Constitution. The opinion and dissent are included here.

🏛 **special prosecutor**

A prosecutor appointed specially to investigate and, if appropriate, prosecute a particular case.

⚖ Morrison v. Olson
487 U.S. 654 (1988)

This case deals with constitutionality of a law (18 U.S.C. § 49) authorizing the appointment of independent counsel to investigate certain high officials for violation of federal criminal laws. Independent counsel is appointed by the Special Division of the district court when the Attorney General indicates a need. He or she is removable by the Attorney General only for cause. Removal is subject to judicial review.

CHIEF JUSTICE REHNQUIST delivered the opinion of the Court.

This case presents us with a challenge to the independent counsel provisions of the Ethics in Government Act of 1978, 28 U.S.C. §49, 591 et seq. (1982 ed., Supp. V). We hold today that these provisions of the Act do not violate the Appointments Clause of the Constitution, Art. II, 2, cl. 2, or the limitations of Article III, nor do they impermissibly interfere with the President's authority under Article II in violation of the constitutional principle of separation of powers.

A divided Court of Appeals ruled first that an independent counsel is not an "inferior Officer" of the United States for purposes of the Appointments Clause. We now reverse.

We turn to consider the merits of appellees' constitutional claims.

Principal officers are selected by the President with the advice and consent of the Senate. Inferior officers Congress may allow to be appointed by the President alone, by the heads of departments, or by the Judiciary. The initial question is, accordingly, whether appellant is an "inferior" or a "principal" officer. If she is the latter, as the Court of Appeals concluded, then the Act is in violation of the Appointments Clause.

The line between "inferior" and "principal" officers is one that is far from clear, and the Framers provided little guidance into where it should be drawn. We need not attempt here to decide exactly where the line falls between the two types of officers, because in our view appellant clearly falls on the "inferior officer" side of that line. Several factors lead to this conclusion.

First, appellant is subject to removal by a higher Executive Branch official. Although appellant may not be "subordinate" to the Attorney General (and the President) insofar as she possesses a degree of independent discretion to exercise the powers delegated to her under the

(continued)

(continued)

Act, the fact that she can be removed by the Attorney General indicates that she is to some degree "inferior" in rank and authority. Second, appellant is empowered by the Act to perform only certain, limited duties. An independent counsel's role is restricted primarily to investigation and, if appropriate, prosecution for certain federal crimes. Third, appellant's office is limited in jurisdiction. Finally, appellant's office is limited in tenure. There is concededly no time limit on the appointment of a particular counsel. Nonetheless, the office of independent counsel is "temporary" in the sense that an independent counsel is appointed essentially to accomplish a single task, and when that task is over the office is terminated, either by the counsel herself or by action of the Special Division.

We now turn to consider whether the Act is invalid under the constitutional principle of separation of powers.

We observe first that this case does not involve an attempt by Congress to increase its own powers at the expense of the Executive Branch. The Act does empower certain Members of Congress to request the Attorney General to apply for the appointment of an independent counsel, but the Attorney General has no duty to comply with the request, although he must respond within a certain time limit. §592(g). Other than that, Congress' role under the Act is limited to receiving reports or other information and oversight of the independent counsel's activities, §595(a), functions that we have recognized generally as being incidental to the legislative function of Congress.

Similarly, we do not think that the Act works any judicial usurpation of properly executive functions. No independent counsel may be appointed without a specific request by the Attorney General, and the Attorney General's decision not to request appointment if he finds "no reasonable grounds to believe that further investigation is warranted" is committed to his unreviewable discretion. The Act thus gives the Executive a degree of control over the power to initiate an investigation by the independent counsel. Notwithstanding the fact that the counsel is to some degree "independent" and free from executive supervision to a greater extent than other federal prosecutors, in our view these features of the Act give the Executive Branch sufficient control over the independent counsel to ensure that the President is able to perform his constitutionally assigned duties.

Reversed.

Justice Scalia, dissenting.

This suit is about power. The allocation of power among Congress, the President, and the courts in such fashion as to preserve the equilibrium the Constitution sought to establish—so that "a gradual concentration of the several powers in the same department," can effectively be resisted. The present case began when the Legislative and Executive Branches became "embroiled in a dispute concerning the scope of the congressional investigatory power." By the application of this statute in the present case, Congress has effectively compelled a criminal investigation of a high-level appointee of the President in connection with his actions arising out of a bitter power dispute between the President and the Legislative Branch. The decisions regarding the scope of that further investigation, its duration, and, finally, whether or not prosecution should ensue, are likewise beyond the control of the President and his subordinates.

The independent counsel is not an inferior officer because she is not subordinate to any officer in the Executive Branch (indeed, not even to the President). Dictionaries in use at the time of the Constitutional Convention gave the word "inferiour" two meanings which it still bears today: (1) "lower in place,... station,... rank of life,... value or excellency," and (2) "subordinate." S. Johnson, Dictionary of the English Language (6th ed. 1785). That "inferior" means "subordinate" is also consistent with what little we know about the evolution of the Appointments Clause. Of course one is not a "superior officer" without some supervisory responsibility, just as, I suggest, one is not an "inferior officer" within the meaning of the provision under discussion unless one is subject to supervision by a "superior officer." To be sure, it is not a sufficient condition for "inferior" officer status that one be subordinate to a principal officer. Even an officer who is subordinate to a department head can be a principal officer.

Because appellant is not subordinate to another officer, she is not an "inferior" officer and her appointment other than by the President with the advice and consent of the Senate is unconstitutional. A government of laws means a government of rules. Today's decision on the basic issue of fragmentation of executive power is ungoverned by rule, and hence ungoverned by law. And it fails to explain why it is not true that—as the text of the Constitution seems to require, as the Founders seemed to expect, and as our past cases have uniformly assumed—all purely executive power must be under the control of the President.

pardon

A president's or governor's release of a person from punishment for a crime.

Power to Pardon

THE CONSTITUTION EMPOWERS THE PRESIDENT to "Grant Reprieves and Pardons for Offences against the United States, except in Cases of Impeachment." The power of the president to **pardon** extends only to federal crimes. Pardons for state crimes are within the power of the state governor. Pardons, which eliminate the consequences of the criminal act, can be granted before or after a person is formally charged with a crime. One of the most famous pardons, that granted to former President Richard Nixon by his successor Gerald Ford (see Exhibit 5-2), was granted before President Nixon was charged with any crime. Included in the power to pardon is the power to **commute** a sentence, which includes commuting a death penalty to life in prison. Also included in the power to pardon is the power to grant **amnesty** to a group of people.

To facilitate the numerous requests for pardon that are made each year, the Office of Pardons was created and several procedural rules were made part of the Code of Federal Regulations. Because the president has absolute discretion in issuing a pardon, these rules are advisory only. If an individual desires a pardon, then that person usually files a petition with the Office of Pardons. The petition is reviewed by the attorney for the Office of Pardons and often by the U.S. attorney for the district in which the individual was

Did You Know?

George Washington was the president to appoint the most justices to the U.S. Supreme Court. He appointed eleven justices during a time when the Supreme Court consisted of only six justices. President Washington was elected the first president of the United States in 1789.

Courtesy of the Collection of The Corcoran Gallery of Art/CORBIS

Exhibit 5-2   Richard Nixon Pardon

PRESIDENT GERALD R. FORD'S PROCLAMATION 4311, GRANTING A PARDON TO RICHARD NIXON
SEPTEMBER 8, 1974

By the President of the United States of America a Proclamation

Richard Nixon became the thirty-seventh President of the United States on January 20, 1969 and was reelected in 1972 for a second term by the electors of forty-nine of the fifty states. His term in office continued until his resignation on August 9, 1974.

Pursuant to resolutions of the House of Representatives, its Committee on the Judiciary conducted an inquiry and investigation on the impeachment of the President extending over more than eight months. The hearings of the Committee and its deliberations, which received wide national publicity over television, radio, and in printed media, resulted in votes adverse to Richard Nixon on recommended Articles of Impeachment.

As a result of certain acts or omissions occurring before his resignation from the Office of President, Richard Nixon has become liable to possible indictment and trial for offenses against the United States. Whether or not he shall be so prosecuted depends on findings of the appropriate grand jury and on the discretion of the authorized prosecutor. Should an indictment ensue, the accused shall then be entitled to a fair trial by an impartial jury, as guaranteed to every individual by the Constitution.

It is believed that a trial of Richard Nixon, if it became necessary, could not fairly begin until a year or more has elapsed. In the meantime, the tranquility to which this nation has been restored by the events of recent weeks could be irreparably lost by the prospects of bringing to trial a former President of the United States. The prospects of such trial will cause prolonged and divisive debate over the propriety of exposing to further punishment and degradation a man who has already paid the unprecedented penalty of relinquishing the highest elective office of the United States.

Now, THEREFORE, I, GERALD R. FORD, President of the United States, pursuant to the pardon power conferred upon me by Article II, Section 2, of the Constitution, have granted and by these presents do grant a full, free, and absolute pardon unto Richard Nixon for all offenses against the United States which he, Richard Nixon, has committed or may have committed or taken part in during the period from January 20, 1969 through August 9, 1974.

IN WITNESS WHEREOF, I have hereunto set my hand this eighth day of September, in the year of our Lord nineteen hundred and seventy-four, and of the Independence of the United States of America the one hundred and ninety-ninth.

GERALD R. FORD

🏛 **commute**
Changing a criminal punishment to one less severe.

🏛 **amnesty**
A wiping out, by the government, of guilt for persons guilty of a crime; a general governmental forgiving; a general pardon.

originally convicted of a crime. In general, a pardon is granted on the basis of the petitioner's demonstrated good conduct for at least five years after conviction and release from prison. In lieu of this procedure, parties can make direct application to the president. This procedure may be used in high-profile cases or cases involving friends of the president. Along with the power to pardon an individual, the president also has the power to commute a sentence. This results in a reduction of a person's sentence. See Appendix C for a petition for a commutation.

≈ Ethical Decisions—Everyday Choices ≈

The Facts: Martin worked as a case manager for the Social Security Administration. Martin, who was also a paralegal, agreed to represent Chris, his neighbor, in a Social Security Administration appeal hearing regarding the denial of some benefits. The hearing was to take place in a different branch office from the one in which Martin worked.

The Problem: Can Martin represent a neighbor before the Social Security Administration regarding the denial of the neighbor's benefits?

Guiding Principles: State laws generally make the unauthorized practice of law a crime. The ethical guidelines from the National Association of Legal Assistants and the National Federation of Paralegal Associations require that paralegals not engage in the unauthorized practice of law. Representing others in court or before a tribunal is normally considered the practice of law. Some administrative agencies, such as the Social Security Administration, however, allow nonlawyers to represent others. In addition to these rules, all government employees are governed by certain ethical rules, one of which is to avoid conflicts of interest. The Office of Government Ethics is part of the executive branch of government and enforces these rules. This office seeks to ensure that the government's business is conducted with impartiality and integrity.

Chapter Summary

The Constitution vests executive power in one person, the president. The Constitution confers on the president the power to grant pardons, make treaties, appoint various federal officers, call special sessions of Congress, and veto legislation. The Constitution also makes the president the commander in chief of the armed forces. In addition to those powers enunciated in the Constitution, presidential powers also stem from authorization of Congress and from the very nature of the presidency itself (inherent powers.) Inherent powers are generally limited to foreign matters. The president carries out many of these powers through proclamations and executive orders.

As commander in chief, the president's power extends beyond formally declared war. The president can use military force to defend the country against foreign attack. To limit the power of the president when war has not been declared, Congress enacted the War Powers Resolution. According to the Supreme Court, in addition to power over the armed forces, as commander in chief the president could order military trials for enemy saboteurs, order a blockade of southern ports during the Civil War, and order the relocation of persons of Japanese ancestry during World War II. The president could not, however, take over the nation's steel mills in the name of national security, order military trials for nonmilitary U.S. citizens, conduct warrantless searches of domestic organizations suspected of subversive activities, or order a newspaper not to publish sensitive material.

The president has the power to negotiate treaties with foreign nations. Treaties must be approved by the Senate. Presidents also enter into executive agreements with heads of foreign nations. Such agreements do not need Senate approval. In substance, there is sometimes little difference between treaties and executive agreements. The president has the power to appoint ambassadors, consuls, foreign ministers, and most federal judges. He does not have the power to appoint inferior officers. The president can grant pardons for federal crimes. Pardons eliminate the consequences of the criminal act.

Key Terms

Presentment Clause	treaty	commute
martial law	executive agreement	amnesty
Suspension Clause	special prosecutor	
writ of habeas corpus	pardon	

Questions for Review

1. List the sources of presidential powers.
2. What presidential powers are enumerated in the Constitution?
3. Compare and contrast express presidential powers and inherent presidential powers.
4. What powers does the president have as commander in chief?
5. List the main features of the War Powers Act.
6. What is the Suspension Clause?
7. Discuss the power of the president to order military trials for unlawful enemy combatants.
8. What is the difference between a treaty and an executive agreement?
9. Describe how a presidential appointment works, and explain the relevance of the term inferior officer.
10. What does the power to pardon allow the president to do?

Questions for Analysis

1. Would the decision in the *Curtiss-Wright* case be the same if the president's acts were not authorized by Congress? Quote language from the case to support your answer.
2. Do you think that the War Powers Resolution is constitutional? Why or why not?
3. Why were there different results in *Ex parte Milligan* and *Ex parte Quirin*?
4. Answer the following questions regarding the *Morrison* case:
   a. Why did the Court find that the special prosecutor was an inferior officer?
   b. Why did Justice Scalia disagree?
5. According to *Bush v. Boumediene,* in the case of an "enemy combatant," what procedural safeguards must be in place to justify the suspension of the right to a writ of habeas corpus?

Assignments and Projects

1. Brief the case of *Youngstown Sheet & Tube Co. v. Sawyer*, 343 U.S. 579 (1952), using the format in previous chapters.
2. Using a legal dictionary (many are available on the Internet), define the following terms found in the cases in this chapter: appellee, plenary power, UCMJ, and ex parte.
3. The cases described in this chapter often involved members of the president's cabinet, including the secretary of commerce, and the attorney general. Who currently holds those positions?

4. The confinement and trial of enemy combatants in the War on Terror has been a difficult situation. Research this issue and write a short paper on the current status.
5. Review the facts in Living with the Constitution at the beginning of this chapter. Information about White House interns can be found on the White House Web site. Read that information and answer the following:
   a. Could Jordan Maguire qualify to be an intern? Explain.
   b. List the various departments in the White House in which interns might work.

Putting It into Practice

Using any general Internet search engine, find an application for a presidential pardon for use after an individual has completed his or her sentence. Read the complete form. Assume that you will be interviewing a client who wishes to apply for a pardon. Draft a questionnaire you could use in the interview to obtain relevant information.

Group Activity

Discuss the following in small groups: Should detainees labeled as "unlawful enemy combatants" in the war on terror have constitutional rights? Should it matter whether they are U.S. citizens? Select one member of your group to summarize your reasons and conclusion to the entire class.

6 State Powers and the Constitution

Every government is in some respects a problem for every other government.

George Frost Kennan

Chapter Outline

Federal Preemption
- Express Preemption
- Field Preemption
- Conflict Preemption

Dormant Commerce Clause
- Discriminatory State Laws
- Market Participant Exception

Burden on Interstate Commerce versus Local Benefit

State Tax Laws and Commerce

State Laws and Immigration

Other Constitutional Challenges to State Laws

Chapter Objectives

When you complete this chapter you should be able to

1. describe the principles used by the Supreme Court in evaluating the constitutionality of a state law.

2. explain the terms *express preemption*, *field preemption*, and *conflict preemption*.

3. define the Dormant Commerce Clause.

4. explain how the Interstate Commerce Clause limits the right of states to enact laws.

5. define the term *market participant*, and explain how this concept affects the right of states to discriminate against out-of-state businesses.

6. describe the criteria used by the Court to determine if a state law violates the Dormant Commerce Clause.

7. explain why states may have constitutional problems when they tax out-of-state businesses.

8. list the criteria used by the Court to determine the constitutionality of a tax on an out-of-state business.

9. identify the provisions of the U.S. Constitution that limit the powers of the state to enact laws or impose taxes.

10. explain how the Equal Protection Clause and the Due Process Clause affect the constitutionality of laws dealing with interstate commerce.

Looking Back

Before reading this chapter, review the following terms and concepts from the previous chapters:

Federalism The system of government in the United States in which its citizens are subject to the laws of both the federal government and state government. (Chapter 2)

Power of judicial review The power of the Supreme Court to review federal and state laws and to declare invalid any law that violates the U.S. Constitution. (Chapter 2)

Commerce Clause The provision in Article I, Section 8 of the Constitution giving the U.S. legislature the right to regulate foreign and interstate commerce. It includes the right to regulate instrumentalities of commerce and anything that substantially affects interstate commerce. (Chapter 4)

Gibbons v. Ogden A Supreme Court case dealing with the power of the federal government to regulate interstate commerce. Gibbons transported passengers via steamboat between New Jersey and New York and was authorized to do so under a federal law. In doing this transporting, Gibbons violated a state law giving the respondent exclusive use of the waterway. The Supreme Court held that (1) this action was commerce and the federal government had the right to regulate it, and (2) the state law conflicted with the federal law, and, because of the Supremacy Clause, the federal law controlled regulation of the waterway. (Chapters 2 and 4)

Syllabus The summary of a case; most Supreme Court cases are published with an official syllabus that comes from the Supreme Court but is not part of the actual Court opinion. (Chapter 1)

Living with the Constitution

Rhonda Berk is a creative individual who uses her talents to make one-of-a-kind knitted sweaters. She sells these sweaters using an "auction" type Web site. She collects and pays sales tax on items sold to residents of her state, but not on those sold to residents of other states.

Recently, Berk read a news article stating that a neighboring state was considering taking action to force all Internet businesses to collect and pay sales tax on items sold within that state. In the past, approximately 15 percent of her total sales have come from this state. She wonders if a state can do that.

UNDER THE SYSTEM OF FEDERALISM, Americans are governed by both federal laws and state laws. The federal legislative power, which is limited to powers granted by the Constitution, was discussed in Chapter 4. The power of states to enact laws is much broader. States have general **police power**, which means that they can enact any law or impose any tax that promotes the general welfare of the people, *unless* those laws violate some provision of the U.S. Constitution. The Tenth Amendment to the U.S. Constitution contains a provision affirming the powers of states to enact laws:

> The powers not delegated to the United States by the Constitution, nor prohibited by it to the States, are reserved to the States respectively, or to the people.

Sometimes a state law or tax affects an area also regulated or taxed by the federal government. For example, recall the 1824 case of *Gibbons v. Ogden,* 22 U.S. 1, in which both federal and state laws regulated the waterways between New Jersey and New York. In this case, the Supreme Court decided that the New York state law was unconstitutional because the Commerce Clause prohibited New York from enacting this law. On the other hand, consider the government's action against Microsoft for antitrust violations stemming from its marketing practices. This action was initiated by the U.S. Department of Justice based on federal law. States, however, also have antitrust laws, and many pursued actions against Microsoft under their state laws.

Gibbons v. Ogden and the *Microsoft* case illustrate important aspects of the states' lawmaking power. The existence of a federal law does not necessarily prohibit a state from enacting similar laws or imposing taxes. At times, however, the Constitution imposes limits or restrictions on state laws and taxes. In general, a state law is unconstitutional

- if a federal law **preempts** the state law,
- if a state law or tax violates the Commerce Clause, even though there is no federal law on the subject (**Dormant Commerce Clause**), or
- if the state law violates some other provision of the Constitution.

This chapter discusses these limitations on a state's power to legislate and impose taxes.

police power
The government's right and power to set up and enforce laws to provide for the safety, health, and general welfare of the people; for example, police power includes the power to license occupations such as haircutting.

preempts
Supersedes.

Dormant Commerce Clause
The principle that the Commerce Clause prevents state regulation of interstate commerce even if the specific regulated activity is not covered by federal laws.

Federal Preemption

THE SUPREMACY CLAUSE MAKES IT clear that the Constitution and laws enacted pursuant to the Constitution are the supreme law of the land. Thus, any state law or local ordinance that conflicts or interferes with federal laws is unconstitutional and therefore unenforceable. In such a case, the federal law *preempts* the state law. This same principle applies to regulations of federal and state agencies. Ultimately, the determination of the constitutionality of state laws is up to the U.S. Supreme Court, which has been presented with numerous cases dealing with this issue. Although the members of the Court usually agree about the criteria to be used in making a decision, they just as often disagree about how to apply those criteria to the facts of the case.

A federal law preempts or supersedes a state law whenever the state law is inconsistent with the federal law. In a 1992 case, *Gade v. National Solid Wastes Management Assn.*, 505 U.S. 88, Justice Sandra Day O'Connor, writing for the majority, states: "Our ultimate task in any preemption case is to determine whether state regulation is consistent with the structure and purpose of the statute as a whole." The Court then identifies three types of preemption: express preemption, field preemption, and conflict preemption.

express preemption

The principle that a state law is unconstitutional because a federal law expressly supersedes it.

Express preemption occurs when the federal law actually contains a provision that the federal law preempts any state laws on the same subject. **Field preemption** refers to situations in which the Court implies that Congress intended to preempt the field (subject area) because the federal law is so extensive or pervasive that no room is left for state laws. **Conflict preemption** refers to situations in which the state and federal laws are in conflict so that compliance with both state and federal law is impossible.

field preemption

The principle that a state law is unconstitutional because Congress impliedly usurped total control over the subject matter by enacting federal legislation.

Express Preemption

Federal statutes and regulations expressly preempt state laws when a provision in the federal law indicates that to be the intent of Congress. Sometimes, determining this intent is a challenge for the Court. Consider the following provision found in a federal law regarding cigarette warning labels:

conflict preemption

The principle that a state law is unconstitutional because it conflicts with a federal law.

> (b) No requirement or prohibition based on smoking and health shall be imposed under State law with respect to the advertising or promotion of any cigarettes the packages of which are labeled in conformity with the provisions of this Act.

Clearly, this provision tells us that any state law requiring cigarette manufacturers to include different or additional warnings on their packages or in their advertising would be preempted and unconstitutional. Yet does it mean more than that? In one case, *Cippoloni v. Liggett*, cigarette manufacturers argued that it also preempted a state's common-law tort liability for injuries caused by smoking. They argued that their tort liability was a requirement imposed by state law related to smoking and therefore was within the language of the express preemption provision. In other words, because they had complied with the federal warning labels required of cigarettes, they should have no other liability.

Ultimately, this case reached the Supreme Court. In reaching its decision, the Court carefully analyzed the exact language of the provision and closely examined each of the plaintiff's claims. The plaintiff's original lawsuit contained several theories of liability, including allegations that (1) the cigarette companies were negligent in not warning of all the dangers of smoking, that (2) they had expressly warranted that smoking was safe, and that (3) they fraudulently concealed information. The Court could not come to a majority opinion on all the claims. The Court concluded that some of the claims were preempted and some were not. The Court stated that it must give the preemption clause a very narrow meaning and that because of the historic police powers of the state a federal law should not preempt unless it is the clear intent of Congress. The Court could only find this intent in relationship to a few of the causes of action. The claim based on the failure to warn of the dangers of smoking was preempted because it stemmed from a state requirement or duty based on smoking and health. The Court refused to find that the action for breach of express warranty was preempted because such an action does not stem from a duty imposed by the state but by the manufacturer. It also refused to find preemption on the concealment claim because that was based on a duty not to deceive, not a requirement based on smoking or health. Two justices believed that all claims should be preempted, believing that to be the clear intent of Congress as indicated from the words of the statute. On the other hand, three justices believed that none of the claims was preempted, finding no clear indication of congressional intent to preempt any state law. Although all the justices seemed to agree that the intent of Congress should be the determining factor, there was obviously strong disagreement as to what that intent was.

A Point of Law

Cipollone v. Liggett Group, 505 U.S. 504 (1992)

A federal law can preempt not only a state legislative enactment but also a state common-law right to sue. Whether express preemption exists depends on congressional intent. The Supreme Court closely examines the words of a federal law to determine that intent, but often disagrees in that determination. In *Cipollone,* a majority of the justices agreed that a cigarette manufacturer who complied with federal labeling requirements could not be sued under state law for failing to adequately warn of the dangers of cigarette smoking. This was because a federal law expressly prohibited states from imposing duties in addition to the labeling requirements.

Several justices disagreed.

🏛 common law

Legal principles and obligations developed through court cases rather than legislative action.

  Cipollone was decided in 1992. In 2000, the Court decided a case with a similar issue, *Geier v. American Honda Motor Co.* This case involved a lawsuit for damages resulting from an automobile accident. The plaintiff claimed that the defendant automobile manufacturer was liable because it had failed to install air bags and that under the state's **common law,** not doing so constituted both negligence and strict liability. The car manufacturer claimed that the state's common law was preempted by a federal law that required it to install seat belts but not air bags in the car in question. The federal law contained the following express preemption provision:

> Whenever a Federal motor vehicle safety standard established under this subchapter is in effect, no State or political subdivision of a State shall have any authority either to establish, or to continue in effect, with respect to any motor vehicle or item of motor vehicle equipment, any safety standard applicable to the same aspect of performance of such vehicle or item of equipment which is not identical to the Federal standard. 15 U.S.C. §1392(d) (1988 ed.)

🏛 saving clause

A clause in a statute (or a contract) that states that if part of the statute (or contract) is declared void, the remainder stays in effect; a clause in a statute that preserves certain rights, responsibilities, or liabilities that are in existence as of the adoption of the statute but would otherwise be lost upon its adoption.

In addition to the preemption clause, the federal law also had a **saving clause.** A saving clause is one that creates exceptions to the types of laws that are preempted. In other words, it authorizes state laws consistent with the language of the saving clause. In the *Geier* case, the saving clause provided that compliance with the federal standard "does not exempt any person from any liability under common law."

  The Supreme Court unanimously agreed that the plain meaning of the saving clause was that the federal law did not expressly preempt the state action, yet that did not totally resolve the issue. Even though there was no express preemption here, the Court considered whether the state common law was preempted because of an actual conflict between the state and federal laws. (In *Geier,* the Court did find a conflict, as discussed later in the chapter.) Today, the key factor in determining if a federal law preempts a state law (or common law right to sue) is the intent of Congress in enacting the federal law. Unfortunately, congressional intent is sometimes viewed differently by different justices. For example, in the 2011 case, *Bruesewitz v. Wyeth LLC,* 562 U.S. ___ (2011), the Court disagreed over the "clear intent" of the following provision in the National Childhood Vaccine Injury Act:

> No vaccine manufacturer shall be liable in a civil action for damages arising from a vaccine-related injury or death associated with the administration of a vaccine

after October 1, 1988, if the injury or death resulted from side effects that were unavoidable even though the vaccine was properly prepared and was accompanied by proper directions and warnings.

The justices disagreed as to whether this preempted a lawsuit based on a design defect of the drug. The majority held that it did. These justices focused on the phrase "even though," finding that the intent was to eliminate liability when drugs were properly prepared and contained proper directions. The dissent focused on the word "unavoidable," stating that design defects could be avoided. (The majority observed that all side effects could be avoided in one way or another.)

To summarize, some federal laws contain clauses limiting or prohibiting state laws on the same subject. Any state law (common law or statutory law) that violates these limitations or prohibitions is unconstitutional and expressly preempted by federal law. The Supreme Court, however, gives a narrow interpretation to preemption clauses because of the historic police powers of states. An express preemption clause in a federal law can be modified by a saving clause that expressly allows certain state laws. Even when the Court finds that there is no *express* preemption, it still considers if the state law is otherwise preempted.

Field Preemption

The failure to include an express preemption clause in a federal law does not mean that a similar state law is constitutional. The Supreme Court also considers whether Congress intended to usurp total control over the subject matter of the law. If so, the federal law *implicitly* preempts any state law. The Courts use the term *field preemption* to explain this concept. The key factor in deciding if field preemption applies is the intent of Congress in passing the federal law. Did Congress intend for the federal law to preempt any state or local rules? In the case of *Rice v. Santa Fe Elevator Corp.*, 331 U.S. 218 (1947), the Court acknowledged that it was difficult to determine congressional intent, saying, "It is often a perplexing question whether Congress has precluded state action or by the choice of selective regulatory measures has left the police power of the States undisturbed except if the state and federal regulations collide." In this case, the Court considered whether extensive federal regulations governing grain warehouses preempted the area so that a state law also regulating grain warehouses was unconstitutional. The state argued that the state law supplemented rather than conflicted with the federal law and therefore should be constitutional. The Supreme Court recognized that the laws did not necessarily conflict but stated that it still had to consider whether the federal law was intended to preempt the area. It set out various criteria to be used in making this determination:

1. Is the scheme of federal regulation so pervasive as to make reasonable the inference that Congress left no room for the states to supplement it?
2. Does the Act of Congress touch a field in which the federal interest is so dominant that the federal system will be assumed to preclude enforcement of state laws on the same subject?
3. What is the object sought to be obtained by the federal law and the character of obligations imposed by it?
4. Does the state policy produce a result inconsistent with the objective of the federal statute?

In deciding that the Federal Warehouse Act did preempt most of the provisions of state law, the Court considered these criteria along with information from committee reports issued when an amendment to the Act was under consideration. These reports helped the

Court determine the intent of Congress. In this case, the committee reports contained language indicating that the federal law was intended to preempt the field:

> While a warehouseman need not operate under the Act, if he chose to be licensed under it, he would then "be authorized to operate without regard to State acts and be solely responsible to the Federal act." [11 S. Rep. No. 1775, 71st Cong., 3d Sess., p. 2.] Warehousemen, having made their choice to operate under state or federal law, should "then be permitted to operate without interference on the part of any agency." *Id.*, pp. 2–3. Or, as stated by the House Committee, the purpose of the amendment to 29 was to make the Act "independent of any State legislation on the subject." H.R. Rep. No. 2314, 70th Cong., 2d Sess., p. 4

The Court found this language to be persuasive as to the intent of Congress to preempt the field.

In 1985, the Court again considered the issue of field preemption in the case of *Hillsborough County v. Automated Medical Laboratories*, 471 U.S. 707, where the legal issue concerned the constitutionality of local ordinances regulating the collection of blood plasma by medical labs. In this case, the respondent, Automated Medical Labs, operated blood plasma centers, one of which was located in Hillsborough County, Florida. Collection of blood plasma is extensively regulated by the Food and Drug Administration. Hillsborough County imposed a license fee on the center and imposed additional requirements. The Court's opinion is included here.

Hillsborough County v. Automated Medical Laboratories
471 U.S. 707 (1985)

MARSHALL, J., delivered the opinion for a unanimous Court.

The question presented is whether the federal regulations governing the collection of blood plasma from paid donors pre-empt certain local ordinances.

Pursuant to 351 of the Act, the Food and Drug Administration (FDA) established standards for the collection of plasma. 21 CFR 640.60–640.76 (1984). The regulations require that a licensed physician determine the suitability of a donor before the first donation and thereafter at subsequent intervals of no longer than one year. A physician must also inform the donor of the hazards of the procedure and obtain the donor's consent, and must be on the premises when the procedure is performed. In addition, the regulations establish minimum standards for donor eligibility, specify procedures that must be followed in performing plasmapheresis, and impose labeling requirements.

In 1980, Hillsborough County adopted Ordinances 80-11 and 80-12. Ordinance 80-11 imposes a $225 license fee on plasmapheresis centers within the county. It also requires such centers to allow the County Health Department "reasonable and continuing access" to their premises for inspection purposes, and to furnish information deemed relevant by the Department.

Ordinance 80-12 establishes a countywide identification system, which requires all potential donors to obtain from the County Health Department an identification card, valid for six months, that may be used only at the plasmapheresis center specified on the card. The ordinance incorporates by reference the FDA's blood plasma regulations, but also imposes donor testing and recordkeeping requirements beyond those contained in the federal regulations. In December 1981, appellee filed suit challenging the constitutionality of the ordinances and their implementing regulations. It is a familiar and well-established principle that the Supremacy Clause, U.S. Const., Art. VI, cl. 2, invalidates state laws that "interfere with, or are contrary to," federal law. *Gibbons v. Ogden*, 9 Wheat. 1, 211 (1824). Under the Supremacy Clause, federal law may supersede state law in several different ways. First, when acting within constitutional limits, Congress is empowered to pre-empt state law by so stating in express terms. In the absence of express pre-emptive language, Congress' intent to preempt all state law in a particular

(continued)

(continued)

area may be inferred where the scheme of federal regulation is sufficiently comprehensive to make reasonable the inference that Congress "left no room" for supplementary state regulation. *Rice v. Santa Fe Elevator Corp.*, 331 U.S. 218, 230 (1947). Pre-emption of a whole field also will be inferred where the field is one in which "the federal interest is so dominant that the federal system will be assumed to preclude enforcement of state laws on the same subject." *See Hines v. Davidowitz*, 312 U.S. 52 (1941).

Even where Congress has not completely displaced state regulation in a specific area, state law is nullified to the extent that it actually conflicts with federal law. Such a conflict arises when "compliance with both federal and state regulations is a physical impossibility," *Florida Lime & Avocado Growers, Inc. v. Paul*, 373 U.S. 132, 142–143 (1963), or when state law "stands as an obstacle to the accomplishment and execution of the full purposes and objectives of Congress." *Hines v. Davidowitz, supra*, at 67.

In arguing that the Hillsborough County ordinances and regulations are pre-empted, appellee faces an uphill battle. The first hurdle that appellee must overcome is the FDA's statement, when it promulgated the plasmapheresis regulations in 1973, that it did not intend its regulations to be exclusive. The FDA explained in a statement accompanying the regulations that "these regulations are not intended to usurp the powers of State or local authorities to regulate plasmapheresis procedures in their localities." 38 Fed. Reg. 19365 (1973).

The question whether the regulation of an entire field has been reserved by the Federal Government is, essentially, a question of ascertaining the intent underlying the federal scheme. In this case, appellee concedes that neither Congress nor the FDA expressly pre-empted state and local regulation of plasmapheresis. Thus, if the county ordinances challenged here are to fail they must do so either because Congress or the FDA implicitly pre-empted the whole field of plasmapheresis regulation, or because particular provisions in the local ordinances conflict with the federal scheme.

The FDA's statement is dispositive on the question of implicit intent to pre-empt. Given the clear indication of the FDA's intention not to pre-empt and the deference with which we must review the challenged ordinances, we conclude that these ordinances are not pre-empted by the federal scheme.

We reject the argument that an intent to pre-empt may be inferred from the comprehensiveness of the FDA's regulations at issue here. As a result of their specialized functions, agencies normally deal with problems in far more detail than does Congress. To infer pre-emption whenever an agency deals with a problem comprehensively is virtually tantamount to saying that whenever a federal agency decides to step into a field, its regulations will be exclusive. Such a rule, of course, would be inconsistent with the federal-state balance embodied in our Supremacy Clause jurisprudence.

We hold that Hillsborough County Ordinances 80-11 and 80-12, and their implementing regulations, are not pre-empted by the scheme for federal regulation of plasmapheresis.

Conflict Preemption

As explained in *Hillsborough*, if both the federal and state governments enact regulations and these laws conflict, the Supremacy Clause of the Constitution (Article VI) controls. The federal law preempts the state law. This principle was recognized by the Supreme Court as early as 1824 in the case of *Gibbons v. Ogden*, in which the Court struck down a New York law conflicting with a federal law concerning navigation. (See the case excerpt in Chapter 4.) Although the supremacy of federal law is unquestioned, courts are still called to determine if a conflict exists. Two common criteria are used by the Court to make this decision:

1. Is compliance with both federal and state regulations a physical impossibility?
2. Does state law stand as an obstacle to the accomplishment and execution of the full purposes and objectives of Congress?

Examples of conflicts between state and federal laws are found in several cases following *Gibbons v. Ogden*. One example is the 1996 case of *Barnett Bank, N.A. v. Nelson*, 517 U.S. 25. This case involved a 1916 federal law that gave national banks the right to sell insurance in small towns (less than 5,000 population) and a 1974 Florida law that prohibited banks from selling insurance. A unanimous Court held that the laws obviously conflicted. The federal law provided that the bank could sell insurance and the state law said it could not. In 2000, the issue of conflict between state and federal law arose in *Geier v. American Honda Motor Co.* Recall from earlier in this chapter, the Court did not find express preemption in this case because of the saving clause. However, the majority found a conflict between the federal safety standard and the state common-law principle. The safety standard made air bags optional. The state common-law principle would have required that air bags be installed. An excerpt from the Court's opinion follows. This case illustrates how the Court analyzes the concept of conflict preemption along with field and express preemption. The Court uses the phrase "ordinary preemption principles" to refer to field preemption. See Table 6-1.

Table 6-1 Federal Preemption

Federal Preemption	State Law Is Unconstitutional If . . .
• Express preemption	The federal law contains a provision superseding all state laws.
• Field preemption	It can be implied from various factors, such as the scope of the federal law, that Congress intended to preempt the field.
• Conflict preemption	The federal and state laws actually conflict.

© Cengage Learning 2013

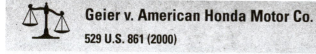

Geier v. American Honda Motor Co.
529 U.S. 861 (2000)

JUSTICE BREYER delivered the opinion of the Court.

This case focuses on the 1984 version of a Federal Motor Vehicle Safety Standard promulgated by the Department of Transportation under the authority of the National Traffic and Motor Vehicle Safety Act of 1966. The standard, FMVSS 208, required auto manufacturers to equip some but not all of their 1987 vehicles with passive restraints. We ask whether the Act pre-empts a state common-law tort action in which the plaintiff claims that the defendant auto manufacturer, who was in compliance with the standard, should nonetheless have equipped a 1987 automobile with airbags. We conclude that the Act, taken together with FMVSS 208, pre-empts the lawsuit.

In 1992, petitioner Alexis Geier, driving a 1987 Honda Accord, collided with a tree and was seriously injured. The car was equipped with manual shoulder and lap belts which Geier had buckled up at the time. The car was not equipped with airbags or other passive restraint devices.

Geier and her parents, also petitioners, sued the car's manufacturer, American Honda Motor Company, Inc., and its affiliates (hereinafter American Honda), under District of Columbia tort law. They claimed, among other things, that American Honda had designed its car negligently and defectively because it lacked a driver's side airbag.

In reaching our conclusion, we consider three subsidiary questions. First, does the Act's express preemption provision pre-empt this lawsuit? We think not. Second, do ordinary pre-emption principles nonetheless apply? We hold that they do. Third, does this lawsuit actually conflict with FMVSS 208, hence with the Act itself? We hold that it does.

We first ask whether the Safety Act's express preemption provision pre-empts this tort action. The provision reads as follows:

> Whenever a Federal motor vehicle safety standard established under this subchapter is in effect, no State or political subdivision of a State shall have any authority either to establish, or to continue in effect, with respect to any motor vehicle or item of motor vehicle equipment, any safety standard applicable to the same aspect of performance of such vehicle or item of equipment which is not identical to the Federal standard. 15 U.S.C. § 1392(d) (1988 ed.).

The Act contains another provision. That provision, a "saving" clause, says that "compliance with" a federal safety standard "does not exempt any person from any liability under common law." 15 U.S.C. § 1397(k) (1988 ed.).

(continued)

(continued)

Without the saving clause, a broad reading of the express pre-emption provision arguably might pre-empt those actions, for it is possible to read the pre-emption provision, standing alone, as applying to standards imposed in common-law tort actions, as well as standards contained in state legislation or regulations. And if so, it would pre-empt all nonidentical state standards established in tort actions covering the same aspect of performance as an applicable federal standard, even if the federal standard merely established a minimum standard. On that broad reading of the preemption clause little, if any, potential "liability at common law" would remain. And few, if any, state tort actions would remain for the saving clause to save. Hence the broad reading cannot be correct. The language of the pre-emption provision permits a narrow reading that excludes common-law actions. Given the presence of the saving clause, we conclude that the pre-emption clause must be so read.

We have just said that the saving clause *at least* removes tort actions from the scope of the express pre-emption clause. Does it do more? In particular, does it foreclose or limit the operation of ordinary pre-emption principles insofar as those principles instruct us to read statutes as pre-empting state laws (including common-law rules) that "actually conflict" with the statute or federal standards promulgated thereunder.

We now conclude that the saving clause (like the express pre-emption provision) does *not* bar the ordinary working of conflict pre-emption principles. The basic question, then, is whether a common-law "no airbag" action like the one before us actually conflicts with FMVSS 208. We hold that it does.

The 1984 FMVSS 208 standard deliberately sought a *gradual* phase-in of passive restraints. And it explained that the phased-in requirement would allow more time for manufacturers to develop airbags or other, better, safer passive restraint systems. It would help develop information about the comparative effectiveness of different systems, would lead to a mix in which airbags and other nonseatbelt passive restraint systems played a more prominent role than would otherwise result, and would promote public acceptance.

In effect, petitioners' tort action depends upon its claim that manufacturers had a duty to install an airbag when they manufactured the 1987 Honda Accord. Such a state law—*i.e.*, a rule of state tort law imposing such a duty—by its terms would have required manufacturers of all similar cars to install airbags rather than other passive restraint systems, such as automatic belts or passive interiors. It would have required all manufacturers to have installed airbags in respect to the entire District-of-Columbia-related portion of their 1987 new car fleet, even though FMVSS 208 at that time required only that 10% of a manufacturer's nationwide fleet be equipped with any passive restraint device at all. It thereby also would have stood as an obstacle to the gradual passive restraint phase-in that the federal regulation deliberately imposed. Because the rule of law for which petitioners contend would have stood "as an obstacle to the accomplishment and execution of " the important means-related federal objectives that we have just discussed, it is pre-empted.

The judgment of the Court of Appeals is affirmed.

JUSTICE STEVENS, with whom JUSTICE SOUTER, JUSTICE THOMAS, and JUSTICE GINSBURG join, dissenting "This is a case about federalism," *Coleman v. Thompson*, 501 U.S. 722, 726 (1991), that is, about respect for "the constitutional role of the States as sovereign entities." *Alden v Maine*, 527 U.S. 706, 713 (1999). It raises important questions concerning the way in which the Federal Government may exercise its undoubted power to oust state courts of their traditional jurisdiction over common-law tort actions. The rule the Court enforces today was not enacted by Congress and is not to be found in the text of any Executive Order or regulation. It has a unique origin: it is the product of the Court's interpretation of the final commentary accompanying an interim administrative regulation and the history of airbag regulation generally. Like many other judge-made rules, its contours are not precisely defined.

Because of the role of States as separate sovereigns in our federal system, we have long presumed that state laws—particularly those, such as the provision of tort remedies to compensate for personal injuries, that are within the scope of the States' historic police powers—are not to be pre-empted by a federal statute unless it is the clear and manifest purpose of Congress to do so. The Safety Act contains both an express pre-emption provision, 15 U.S.C. § 1392(d), and a saving clause that expressly preserves common-law claims, § 1397(k).

Despite its acknowledgement that the saving clause "preserves those actions that seek to establish greater safety than the minimum safety achieved by a federal regulation intended to provide a floor," *ante*, at 7, the Court completely ignores the important fact that by definition all of the standards established under

(continued)

(continued)

the Safety Act—like the British regulations that governed the number and capacity of lifeboats aboard the *Titanic*—impose minimum, rather than fixed or maximum, requirements. 15 U.S.C. § 1391(2); ("federal *minimum* safety standards should not pre-empt a state tort action"); *Hillsborough County v. Automated Medical Laboratories, Inc.*, 471 U.S. 707, 721 (1985). The phase-in program authorized by Standard 208 thus set minimum percentage requirements for the installation of passive restraints, increasing in annual stages of 10, 25, 40, and 100%. Those requirements were not ceilings, and it is obvious that the Secretary favored a more rapid increase. The possibility that exposure to potential tort liability might accelerate the rate of increase would actually further the only goal explicitly mentioned in the standard itself: reducing the number of deaths and severity of injuries of vehicle occupants.

Because neither the text of the statute nor the text of the regulation contains any indication of an intent to pre-empt petitioners' cause of action, and because I cannot agree with the Court's unprecedented use of inferences from regulatory history and commentary as a basis for implied pre-emption, I am convinced that Honda has not overcome the presumption against pre-emption in this case. I therefore respectfully dissent.

Just a few years after *Geier*, the Supreme Court addressed almost an identical factual situation involving the same general regulations as in *Geier*. The case, *Williamson v. Mazda Motor of America*, 562 U.S. ___ (2011), involved a regulation giving auto manufacturers the option of installing either lap seat belts or shoulder-lap belts in the rear inner seat. As with *Geier*, a lawsuit was filed against a manufacturer who chose the lesser safety device. Here, however, the Court did not find the case preempted. Again, the Court based its decision on the federal agency's reason for the safety regulations. Looking at various documents from the agency, the Court decided that the reasons for the law in *Williamson* were sufficiently different from those in *Geier* to warrant a different decision. The Court's Syllabus explains.

Williamson v. Mazda Motor of America Inc.
562 U.S. ___ (2011)

The 1989 version of Federal Motor Vehicle Safety Standard 208 (FMVSS 208) requires, as relevant here, auto manufacturers to install seatbelts on the rear seats of passenger vehicles. They must install lap-and-shoulder belts on seats next to a vehicle's doors or frames, but may install either those belts or simple lap belts on rearinner seats, *e.g.*, those next to a minivan's aisle.

The Williamson family and Thanh Williamson's estate brought this California tort suit, claiming that Thanh died in an accident because the rear aisle seat of the Mazda minivan in which she was riding had a lap belt instead of lap-and-shoulder belts. The state trial court dismissed their claim on the pleadings. The State Court of Appeal affirmed, relying on *Geier v. American Honda*

Motor Co., 529 U.S. 861, in which this Court found that an earlier (1984) version of FMVSS 208—which required installation of passive restraint devices—preempted a state tort suit against an auto manufacturer on a failure to install airbags.

Held: FMVSS 208 does not pre-empt state tort suits claiming that manufacturers should have installed lap-and-shoulder belts, instead of lap belts, on rear inner seats.

(a) Because this case involves (1) the same statute as *Geier*, (2) a later version of the same regulation, and (3) a somewhat similar claim that a state tort action conflicts with the federal regulation, the answers to two of the subsidiary questions posed in *Geier* apply directly here. Thus, the statute's express pre-emption

(continued)

(continued)

clause cannot pre-empt the common-law tort action here; but neither can its saving clause foreclose or limit the operation of ordinary conflict pre-emption principles. The Court consequently turns to *Geier*'s third subsidiary question, whether, in fact, the state tort action conflicts with the federal regulation.

(b) Under ordinary conflict pre-emption principles a state law that "stands as an obstacle to the accomplishment" of a federal law is preempted. *Hines v. Davidowitz*, 312 U. S. 52, 67. In *Geier*, the state law stood as an obstacle to the accomplishment of a significant federal regulatory objective, namely, giving manufacturers a choice among different kinds of passive restraint systems. This conclusion was supported by the regulation's history, the agency's contemporaneous explanation, and the Government's current understanding of the regulation. The history showed that the Department of Transportation (DOT) had long thought it important to leave manufacturers with a choice of systems. DOT's contemporaneous explanation of the regulation made clear that manufacturer choice was an important means for achieving DOT's basic objectives. It phased in passive restraint requirements to give manufacturers time to improve airbag technology and develop better systems; it worried that requiring airbags would cause a public backlash; and it was concerned about airbag safety and cost. Finally, the Government's current understanding was that a tort suit insisting upon airbag use would "stan[d] as an obstacle to the accomplishment and execution of these objectives." 529 U. S., at 883.

(c) Like the regulation in *Geier*, the instant regulation leaves the manufacturer with a choice, and the tort suit here would restrict that choice. But in contrast to *Geier*, the choice here is not a significant regulatory objective. The regulation's history resembles the history of airbags to some degree. DOT rejected a regulation requiring lap-and-shoulder belts in rear seats in 1984. But by 1989, changed circumstances led DOT to require manufacturers to install lap-and-shoulder belts for rear outer seats but to retain a manufacturer choice for rear inner seats. Its reasons for doing so differed considerably from its 1984 reasons for permitting a choice of passive restraint. It was not concerned about consumer acceptance; it thought that lap-and-shoulder belts would increase safety and did not pose additional safety risks; and it was not seeking to use the regulation to spur development of alternative safety devices. Instead, DOT thought that the requirement would not be cost effective. That fact alone cannot show that DOT sought to forbid common-law tort suits. For one thing, DOT did not believe that costs would remain frozen. For another, many federal safety regulations embody a cost effectiveness judgment. To infer pre-emptive intent from the mere existence of such a cost-effectiveness judgment would eliminate the possibility that the agency seeks only to set forth a minimum standard. Finally, the Solicitor General represents that DOT's regulation does not pre-empt this tort suit. As in *Geier*, "the agency's own views should make a difference," 529 U. S., at 883, and DOT has not expressed inconsistent views on this subject.

Dormant Commerce Clause

IN ADDITION TO THE PRINCIPLES of federal preemption, whenever a state enacts a law that impacts interstate commerce, the Commerce Clause can also affect the constitutionality of the state law. Recall from Chapter 4 that the Commerce Clause of the Constitution gives Congress the power to make laws regarding interstate commerce. Using this power, Congress enacted numerous laws touching on a variety of subjects, yet it did not pass laws controlling every area of interstate commerce. In these areas, its lawmaking power is said to lay "dormant." The question arises, then, whether states have the right to make laws controlling those areas in which the federal government's power lies dormant, or, in other words, in which Congress has not acted. The Constitution does not say. The Supreme Court, however, decided that the Interstate Commerce Clause imposes limits on the right of states to make laws affecting interstate commerce even if those laws regulate areas where Congress did not act. The Court's position is that the Interstate Commerce Clause has both a positive and negative aspect. The positive aspect is that it gives power to the federal government to regulate. The negative aspect is that it limits the rights of states to regulate. The negative aspect is referred to as the Dormant Commerce Clause. This concept was explained by Justice Clarence Thomas in the 1994 case of *Oregon Waste Sys. v. Department of Envtl. Quality*, 511 U.S. 93:

> The Commerce Clause provides that "the Congress shall have Power . . . to regulate Commerce . . . among the several States." Art. I, 8, cl. 3. Though phrased as a grant of regulatory power to Congress, the Clause has long been understood to have a "negative" aspect that denies the States the power unjustifiably to discriminate against or burden the interstate flow of articles of commerce.

The Dormant Commerce Clause is not a *total* prohibition on the right of states to make laws affecting interstate commerce. Rather, it imposes limits. If a state enacts a law that exceeds those limits, then the Court will find the law to be unconstitutional. One of the first cases to discuss the nature of the dormant commerce power is the 1851 case *Cooley v. Board of Wardens*, 53 U.S. 299. This case involved the constitutionality of a state law that required vessels to use local pilots when entering a state harbor. If they failed to use a local pilot, a fine was imposed. The Court believed that regulation of pilots on vessels did come under the Interstate Commerce Clause. In fact, in 1789, Congress had enacted some federal laws regulating pilots, but these laws did not regulate the specific area covered by the Philadelphia law. At issue was whether a state (or local government) had the right to make *any* law affecting this subject. In its decision, the Court decided that the Commerce Clause prohibits some state laws but not all. In *Cooley*, the Court decided that states have the right to regulate their harbors and ports and that, for this subject, local rules would be better than one national rule. The *Cooley* opinion is included here.

Cooley v. Board of Wardens
53 U.S. 299 (1851)

It becomes necessary to consider whether this law of Pennsylvania, being a regulation of commerce, is valid.

We are brought directly and unavoidably to the consideration of the question, whether the grant of the commercial power to Congress, did per se deprive the states of all power to regulate pilots. This question has never been decided by this court, nor, in our judgment, has any case depending upon all the considerations which must govern this one, come before this court. The grant of commercial power to Congress does not contain any terms which expressly exclude the states from exercising an authority over its subject-matter.

The diversities of opinion which have existed on this subject, have arisen from the different views taken of the nature of this power. Now the power to regulate commerce, embraces a vast field, containing not only many, but exceedingly various subjects, quite unlike in their nature; some imperatively demanding a single uniform rule, operating equally on the commerce of the United States in every port; and some, like the subject now in question, as imperatively demanding that diversity, which alone can meet the local necessities of navigation.

Whatever subjects of this power are in their nature national, or admit only of one uniform system, or plan of regulation, may justly be said to be of such a nature as to require exclusive legislation by Congress. That this cannot be affirmed of laws for the regulation of pilots and pilotage is plain. The act of 1789 contains a clear and authoritative declaration by the first Congress, that the nature of this subject is such, that until Congress should find it necessary to exert its power, it should be left to the legislation of the states; that it is local and not national; that it is likely to be the best provided for, not by one system, or plan of regulations, but by as many as the legislative discretion of the several states should deem applicable to the local peculiarities of the ports within their limits.

Viewed in this light, so much of this act of 1789 as declares that pilots shall continue to be regulated "by such laws as the states may respectively hereafter enact for that purpose," manifests the understanding of

(continued)

(continued)

Congress, at the outset of the government, that the nature of this subject is not such as to require its exclusive legislation. The practice of the states, and of the national government, has been in conformity with this declaration, from the origin of the national government to this time; and the nature of the subject when examined, is such as to leave no doubt of the superior fitness and propriety, not to say the absolute necessity, of different systems of regulation, drawn from local knowledge and experience, and conformed to local wants.

We are of opinion that this state law was enacted by virtue of a power, residing in the state to legislate; that it is not in conflict with any law of Congress; that it does not interfere with any system which Congress has established by making regulations, or by intentionally leaving individuals to their own unrestricted action; that this law is therefore valid, and the judgment of the Supreme Court of Pennsylvania in each case must be affirmed.

Something to Consider

Cooley was decided more than 150 years ago. Do you think it still applies in today's commercial climate?

After *Cooley*, the Court considered the constitutionality of many state laws that affect commerce and developed criteria for making this decision. Generally, the Court considers two factors:

1. Does the state law discriminate against out-of-state interests?
2. How great is the burden on interstate commerce in relationship to the local necessity for the law?

If the state law discriminates, then the Court will probably find it unconstitutional. If the law does not unfairly discriminate, then the Court balances the burden it puts on interstate commerce with the local necessity. If the burden is too great, then the law is probably unconstitutional. This standard was expressed in the *Oregon Waste* case mentioned earlier:

> Consistent with these principles, we have held that the first step in analyzing any law subject to judicial scrutiny under the negative Commerce Clause is to determine whether it "regulates evenhandedly with only 'incidental' effects on interstate commerce, or discriminates against interstate commerce." As we use the term here, "discrimination" simply means differential treatment of in-state and out-of-state economic interests that benefits the former and burdens the latter. If a restriction on commerce is discriminatory, it is virtually per se invalid. By contrast, nondiscriminatory regulations that have only incidental effects on interstate commerce are valid unless the burden imposed on such commerce is clearly excessive in relation to the putative local benefits.

Discriminatory State Laws

Before the Constitution was adopted, commerce among the states was a problem. States were interested in their own financial concerns and often obstructed commercial interests of other states by imposing unfair taxes and regulations. This practice was one of the reasons for the inclusion of the Interstate Commerce Clause in the Constitution. Therefore, it is not surprising that in reviewing a state law, the Court gives great weight to whether the law discriminates against out-of-state interests. If it does, then the Court is likely to strike the law down. The following are examples of laws the Court found discriminatory:

1. An Oregon law that imposed a surcharge on solid waste. The amount was $2.50 per ton if the waste was generated out of state, but only $0.85 if generated within the state. *Oregon Waste Sys. v. Department of Envtl. Quality*, 511 U.S. 93 (1994).

2. A state law requiring trash haulers to deliver waste to a specific private waste facility, charging more than other out-of-state centers. *C & A Carbone v. Town of Clarkstown*, 511 U.S. 383 (1994).
3. A Maine property tax exemption for charitable institutions that excluded organizations operated principally for the benefit of nonresidents. *Camps Newfound/ Owatonna, Inc. v. Town of Harrison*, 520 U.S. 564 (1997).
4. A state law that "tolled" the statute of limitations for a breach of contract case for times that the defendant was out of state. *Bendix Autolite Corp. v. Midwesco Enterprises, Inc.*, 486 U.S. 888 (1988).

The following are examples of cases the Court found *not* discriminatory:

1. A Maryland statute prohibiting oil producers or refiners from operating retail service stations within the state and requiring them to extend all temporary price reductions uniformly to all stations they supply. Although this law greatly favored local businesses, the Court found it not discriminatory because it applied to all oil producers and refiners, both in-state and out-of-state; it did not impede the flow of any goods through interstate commerce; and it did not create a barrier against interstate independent dealers, only producers or refiners. *Exxon Corp. v. Governor of Maryland*, 437 U.S. 117 (1978).
2. A Minnesota law prohibiting milk from being packaged in plastic containers. The law was passed for environmental reasons, although the result was a benefit to the large paper industry of Minnesota. The Court found the law not discriminatory because it was even-handed, covered all milk producers under the law, and created only an incidental burden on interstate commerce. *Minnesota v. Clover Leaf Creamery Co.*, 449 U.S. 456 (1981).
3. A state law requiring trash haulers to deliver waste to a local public processing facility did not violate the Commerce Clause because the state has an interest in protecting the health and welfare of its citizens, and, in this case, the benefit outweighed any minimal burden on commerce. *United Haulers Assoc. Inc. v. Oneida-Herkimer Solid Waste Mgmt. Auth.*, 550 U.S. 330 (2007).

Market Participant Exception

The Court allows state discriminatory practices when the state is a "market participant" rather than just a lawmaker. The Court recognizes that states do not always act solely as governing bodies. They can actually be participants in the commercial activity. When they act in this capacity, they are no different than any other participant. The case of *Reeves, Inc. v. Stake*, 447 U.S. 429 (1980), illustrates. For more than fifty years, South Dakota operated a cement plant that produced cement for both state residents and out-of-state buyers. In 1978, because of a cement shortage, the State Cement Commission announced a policy to confine the sale of cement by the state plant to residents of South Dakota. This policy forced the petitioner, a ready-mix concrete distributor and one of the out-of-state buyers, to cut its production severely. The Court held that the program did not violate the Dormant Commerce Clause because there is no constitutional plan to limit the ability of the states to operate freely in the free market. See Exhibit 6-1 and Table 6-2.

Exhibit 6-1   Dormant Commerce Clause

DORMANT COMMERCE CLAUSE
State laws affecting interstate commerce are unconstitutional even though not preempted if
  the state laws discriminate against out-of-state interests, *or*
  they place an excessive burden on interstate commerce and do not serve any great local need.

Table 6-2 State Laws and the Dormant Commerce Clause

Case	Facts	*Un*constitutional: Violates the Dormant Commerce Clause Because:	Constitutional: Does *Not* Violate the Dormant Commerce Clause Because:
Oregon Waste Sys. v. Department of Envtl. Quality, 511 U.S. 93 (1994)	A state law, imposing a surcharge on solid waste, charged more for waste produced out of the state.	Law unfairly discriminated against out-of-state interests.	
C & A Carbone v. Town of Clarkstown, 511 U.S. 383 (1994)	A state law required trash haulers to deliver waste to a specific *private* waste facility, charging more than other out-of-state centers.	Law unfairly discriminated against out-of-state interests.	
Camps Newfound/Owatonna, Inc. v. Town of Harrison, 520 U.S. 564 (1997)	A property tax exemption for charitable institutions excluded organizations operating principally for the benefit of nonresidents.	Law unfairly discriminated against out-of-state interests.	
Bendix Autolite Corp. v. Midwesco Enterprises, Inc., 486 U.S. 888 (1988)	A state law tolled the statute of limitations when the defendant was out of state.	Law unfairly discriminated against out-of-state interests.	
Exxon Corp. v. Governor of Maryland, 437 U.S. 117 (1978)	A statute prohibited oil producers or refiners from operating retail service stations within the state and required them to extend all temporary price reductions uniformly to all stations they supply.		No discrimination because the law applied to all oil producers and refiners; it was not too great a burden on interstate commerce because it did not impede the flow of products among states.
Minnesota v. Clover Leaf Creamery Co., 449 U.S. 456 (1981)	A law prohibited milk from being packaged in plastic containers in a state with a large paper industry.		No discrimination because the law was even-handed, covered all milk producers, and created only an incidental burden on interstate commerce.
United Haulers Assoc. Inc. v. Oneida-Herkimer Solid Waste Mgmt. Auth., 550 U.S. 330 (2007)	A state law required trash haulers to deliver waste to a local *public* processing facility.		Did not violate the Commerce Clause because the state has an interest in protecting the health and welfare of its citizens, and, in this case, the benefit outweighed any minimal burden on commerce.
Reeves, Inc. v. Stake, 447 U.S. 429 (1980)	A state operated a cement plant selling to both state and out-of-state buyers for many years. Because of a cement shortage, sales were confined to residents of the state.		The state was a market participant and thus discrimination against out-of-state interests was permissible.
Southern. Pac. Co. v. Arizona, 325 U.S. 761 (1945)	A state law limited the length of trains that could pass through the state.	No discrimination, but the free flow of commerce greatly outweighed any local concern.	

Burden on Interstate Commerce versus Local Benefit

Even if a state law does not discriminate against out-of-state interests, the Court still examines the effect of the law on interstate commerce. It also considers the benefit to the local area. If the law places too great a burden on commerce and does not serve any great, overriding local interest, then the Court finds it unconstitutional. This subjective determination by the Court often leads to disagreement among the justices. The case of *Southern Pac. Co. v. Arizona*, 325 U.S. 761 (1945), illustrates how the Court applies these criteria. This case involved an Arizona law limiting the length of trains that could pass through the state. The law was enacted as a health-and-safety measure. The Court reviewed the facts that showed that only two states had this type of maximum train length, that the train traveled extensively in interstate commerce, and that, despite the law, the accident rate in Arizona was higher than elsewhere in the United States. The Court found that the free flow of commerce here greatly outweighed any local concern and held the law to be unconstitutional. The Court's opinion is included here.

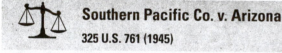

Southern Pacific Co. v. Arizona
325 U.S. 761 (1945)

MR. CHIEF JUSTICE STONE delivered the opinion of the Court.

The Arizona Train Limit Law of May 16, 1912, Arizona Code Ann., 1939, 69–119, makes it unlawful for any person or corporation to operate within the state a railroad train of more than fourteen passenger or seventy freight cars, and authorizes the state to recover a money penalty for each violation of the Act.

After an extended trial, without a jury, the court made detailed findings of fact on the basis of which it gave judgment for the railroad company. The Supreme Court of Arizona reversed and directed judgment for the state. The case comes here on appeal, appellant raising by its assignments of error the questions presented here for decision.

We are brought to appellant's principal contention, that the state statute contravenes the commerce clause of the Federal Constitution.

Although the commerce clause conferred on the national government power to regulate commerce, its possession of the power does not exclude all state power of regulation. Ever since *Willson v. Black-Bird Creek Marsh Co.*, 2 Pet. 245, and *Cooley v. Board of Wardens*, 12 How. 299, it has been recognized that, in the absence of conflicting legislation by Congress, there is a residuum of power in the state to make laws governing matters of local concern which

nevertheless in some measure affect interstate commerce or even, to some extent, regulate it. When the regulation of matters of local concern is local in character and effect, and its impact on the national commerce does not seriously interfere with its operation, and the consequent incentive to deal with them nationally is slight, such regulation has been generally held to be within state authority. But ever since *Gibbons v. Ogden*, 9 Wheat. 1, the states have not been deemed to have authority to impede substantially the free flow of commerce from state to state, or to regulate those phases of the national commerce which, because of the need of national uniformity, demand that their regulation, if any, be prescribed by a single authority. Whether or not this long recognized distribution of power between the national and the state governments is predicated upon the implications of the commerce clause itself or upon the presumed intention of Congress, where Congress has not spoken, the result is the same.

Congress has undoubted power to redefine the distribution of power over interstate commerce. It may permit the states to regulate the commerce in a manner which would otherwise not be permissible. But in general Congress has left it to the courts to formulate the rules thus interpreting the commerce clause in its application, doubtless because it has appreciated the destructive consequences to the commerce of the nation if their protection were withdrawn, and

(continued)

(continued)

has been aware that in their application state laws will not be invalidated without the support of relevant factual material which will "afford a sure basis" for an informed judgment.

Hence the matters for ultimate determination here are the nature and extent of the burden which the state regulation of interstate trains, adopted as a safety measure, imposes on interstate commerce, and whether the relative weights of the state and national interests involved are such as to make inapplicable the rule, generally observed, that the free flow of interstate commerce and its freedom from local restraints in matters requiring uniformity of regulation are interests safeguarded by the commerce clause from state interference.

The findings show that the operation of long trains, that is trains of more than fourteen passenger and more than seventy freight cars, is standard practice over the main lines of the railroads of the United States, and that, if the length of trains is to be regulated at all, national uniformity in the regulation adopted, such as only Congress can prescribe, is practically indispensable to the operation of an efficient and economical national railway system. On many railroads passenger trains of more than fourteen cars and freight trains of more than seventy cars are operated, and on some systems freight trains are run ranging from one hundred and twenty-five to one hundred and sixty cars in length. Outside of Arizona, where the length of trains is not restricted, appellant runs a substantial proportion of long trains. In Arizona, approximately 93% of the freight traffic and 95% of the passenger traffic is interstate. The additional cost of operation of trains complying with the Train Limit Law in Arizona amounts for the two railroads traversing that state to about $1,000,000 a year. The reduction in train lengths also impedes efficient operation. More locomotives and more manpower are required; the necessary conversion and reconversion of train lengths at terminals and the delay caused by breaking up and remaking long trains upon entering and leaving the state in order to comply with the law, delays the traffic and diminishes its volume moved in a given time, especially when traffic is heavy.

The unchallenged findings leave no doubt that the Arizona Train Limit Law imposes a serious burden on the interstate commerce conducted by appellant. It materially impedes the movement of appellant's interstate trains through that state and interposes a substantial obstruction to the national policy proclaimed by Congress, to promote adequate, economical and efficient railway transportation service. The serious impediment to the free flow of commerce by the local regulation of train

lengths and the practical necessity that such regulation, if any, must be prescribed by a single body having a nation-wide authority are apparent.

The trial court found that the Arizona law had no reasonable relation to safety, and made train operation more dangerous. We think, as the trial court found, that the Arizona Train Limit Law, viewed as a safety measure, affords at most slight and dubious advantage, if any, over unregulated train lengths, because it results in an increase in the number of trains and train operations and the consequent increase in train accidents of a character generally more severe than those due to slack action. Here we conclude that the state does go too far. Its regulation of train lengths, admittedly obstructive to interstate train operation, and having a seriously adverse effect on transportation efficiency and economy, passes beyond what is plainly essential for safety since it does not appear that it will lessen rather than increase the danger of accident. Its attempted regulation of the operation of interstate trains cannot establish nation-wide control such as is essential to the maintenance of an efficient transportation system, which Congress alone can prescribe. The state interest cannot be preserved at the expense of the national interest by an enactment which regulates interstate train lengths without securing such control, which is a matter of national concern. To this the interest of the state here asserted is subordinate.

REVERSED.

MR. JUSTICE DOUGLAS, DISSENTING.

I have expressed my doubts whether the courts should intervene in situations like the present and strike down state legislation on the grounds that it burdens interstate commerce. [W]e are dealing here with state legislation in the field of safety where the propriety of local regulation has long been recognized. Whether the question arises under the Commerce Clause or the Fourteenth Amendment, I think the legislation is entitled to a presumption of validity. If a State passed a law prohibiting the hauling of more than one freight car at a time, we would have a situation comparable in effect to a state law requiring all railroads within its borders to operate on narrow gauge tracks. The question is one of degree and calls for a close appraisal of the facts. I am not persuaded that the evidence adduced by the railroads overcomes the presumption of validity to which this train limit law is entitled. Arizona's train-limit law should stand as an allowable regulation enacted to protect the lives and limbs of the men who operate the trains.

State Tax Laws and Commerce

ONE OF THE POWERS SHARED by state and federal governments is the power to tax. All states impose taxes of some type, taxes that often have some impact on interstate commerce. Common state taxes include the following:

income tax: a tax on the income of an individual or business
sales tax: a tax imposed on goods that are sold
real property tax: a tax on the ownership of real property
franchise tax: a tax on the right of a company to do business; it may be a percentage of income or assets or may be a fixed fee
use tax: a tax on products brought into a state in lieu of a sales tax
ad valorem: a tax on real or personal property assessed according to the value of the property
excise tax: a tax on the manufacture, sale, or use of goods or on the carrying on of an occupation or activity

As long as a state tax is imposed on a resident of the state and is related to the resident's property or activities within the state, there is usually no problem. When a state seeks to tax an out-of-state resident or an activity taking place out of the state, however, the Interstate Commerce Clause affects the constitutionality of the tax.

The Supreme Court addressed the right of states to tax interstate commerce in 1873 in two cases, referred to as the *State Freight Cases*, decided on the same day. The decisions in these cases demonstrated the difficult and confusing nature of the issue. In one case, the Court struck down a state tax assessed on every ton of freight transported in the state. In the other case, the Court upheld a tax on the income of a railway, the income of which was based on freight that it carried. The difference, the Court said, was that in the first case the tax was a direct assessment against interstate commerce because the transportation of freight was interstate commerce, whereas in the second case it was not a direct tax on interstate commerce because income is not commerce.

In deciding these and subsequent cases, the Court considered two important policies, the right of businesses to engage in interstate commerce without unfair state interference and the right of states to make businesses pay a fair share of services they use (i.e., fire, police). The Court recognized that the Interstate Commerce Clause was never intended to allow businesses to escape paying their fair share of state taxes just because they are engaged in interstate commerce.

For more than one hundred years following the *State Freight Cases*, the Supreme Court focused on the name given to the tax assessed by the state. Any tax that seemed to be a direct tax on commerce, such as that in the first *State Freight Case,* was held unconstitutional. Included were taxes referred to as taxes for "the privilege of doing business" in a state. On the other hand, income taxes and sales taxes were often upheld. Finally, in 1977, in the case of *Complete Auto Transit, Inc. v. Brady*, 430 U.S. 274, the Court recognized the artificial distinction in this analysis and ruled that the name of the tax was irrelevant. In *Complete Auto*, the tax in question was based on a percentage of goods sold and was, in substance, a sales tax. The tax was challenged, however, because it was called a tax for the privilege of doing business, and, based on prior case law, this language indicated that it was intended to be a tax impeding interstate commerce. In *Complete Auto*, a unanimous Supreme Court rejected earlier decisions that looked to the form rather than the substance of the tax and held that a state tax is valid when four criteria are met:

1. **The tax must be on an activity that has a substantial nexus with the taxing state.** A state can only tax a person, property, or activity that has some connection with the state. Many cases involve taxes on mail-order businesses in which the Court has upheld taxes when the business has some outlet, sales personnel, or property within the state, but has not upheld taxes when the only connection is a sales catalog distributed in the state.
2. **The tax must be fairly apportioned.** This requirement is intended to eliminate double taxes. The Court here asks the question: If a second state imposes an identical tax, will the business face a double tax?
3. **The tax does not discriminate against interstate commerce.** States cannot impose taxes that favor local businesses.
4. **The tax is fairly related to the services provided by the state.** This requirement is generally met if the business has some presence in the state. It is assumed that the business shares in government services (i.e., fire, police) in the same way as every other business in the state.

The opinion in this case follows.

Complete Auto Transit, Inc. v. Brad
430 U.S. 274 (1977)

BLACKMUN, J., delivered the opinion for a unanimous Court.

Once again we are presented with "'the perennial problem of the validity of a state tax for the privilege of carrying on, within a state, certain activities' related to a corporation's operation of an interstate business." *Colonial Pipeline Co. v. Traigle*, 421 U.S. 100, 101 (1975), quoting *Memphis Gas Co. v. Stone*, 335 U.S. 80, 85 (1948). The Supreme Court of Mississippi unanimously sustained the tax against appellant's constitutional challenge. We noted probable jurisdiction in order to consider anew the applicable principles in this troublesome area.

The taxes in question are sales taxes assessed by the Mississippi State Tax Commission against the appellant, Complete Auto Transit, Inc. The assessments were made pursuant to the following Mississippi statutes:

There is hereby levied and assessed and shall be collected, privilege taxes for the privilege of engaging or continuing in business or doing business within this state to be determined by the application of rates against gross proceeds of sales or gross

income or values, as the case may be, as provided in the following sections." Miss. Code Ann., 1942, 10105 (1972 Supp.), as amended.

Upon every person operating a pipeline, railroad, airplane, bus, truck, or any other transportation business for the transportation of persons or property for compensation or hire between points within this State, there is hereby levied, assessed, and shall be collected, a tax equal to five per cent of the gross income of such business. . . . 10109(2), as amended.

Any person liable for the tax is required to add it to the gross sales price and, "insofar as practicable," to collect it at the time the sales price is collected.

Appellant is a Michigan corporation engaged in the business of transporting motor vehicles by motor carrier for General Motors Corporation. General Motors assembles outside Mississippi vehicles that are destined for dealers within the State. The vehicles are then shipped by rail to Jackson, Miss., where, usually within 48 hours, they are loaded onto appellant's trucks and transported by appellant

(continued)

(continued)

to the Mississippi dealers. Appellant is paid on a contract basis for the transportation from the railhead to the dealers.

By letter dated October 5, 1971, the Mississippi Tax Commission informed appellant that it was being assessed taxes and interest totaling $122,160.59 for the sales of transportation services during the three-year period from August 1, 1968, through July 31, 1971. Remittance within 10 days was requested. By similar letter dated December 28, 1972, the Commission advised appellant of an assessment of $42,990.89 for the period from August 1, 1971, through July 31, 1972. Appellant paid the assessments under protest and, in April 1973, instituted the present refund action in the Chancery Court of the First Judicial District of Hinds County.

Appellant claimed that its transportation was but one part of an interstate movement, and that the taxes assessed and paid were unconstitutional as applied to operations in interstate commerce. The Chancery Court, in an unreported opinion, sustained the assessments.

The Mississippi Supreme Court affirmed. It concluded:

> It will be noted that Taxpayer has a large operation in this State. It is dependent upon the State for police protection and other State services the same as other citizens. It should pay its fair share of taxes so long, but only so long, as the tax does not discriminate against interstate commerce, and there is no danger of interstate commerce being smothered by cumulative taxes of several states. There is no possibility of any other state duplicating the tax involved in this case.

Appellant, in its complaint in Chancery Court, did not allege that its activity which Mississippi taxes does not have a sufficient nexus with the State; or that the tax discriminates against interstate commerce; or that the tax is unfairly apportioned; or that it is unrelated to services provided by the State.

Appellant's attack is based solely on decisions of this Court holding that a tax on the "privilege" of engaging in an activity in the State may not be applied to an activity that is part of interstate commerce. *See*, e.g., *Spector Motor Service v. O'Connor*, 340 U.S. 602 (1951); *Freeman v. Hewit*, 329 U.S. 249 (1946). This rule looks only to the fact that the incidence of the tax is the "privilege of doing business"; it deems irrelevant any consideration of the practical effect of the tax. The rule reflects an underlying philosophy that interstate commerce should enjoy a sort of "free trade" immunity from state taxation.

Appellee, in its turn, relies on decisions of this Court stating that "it was not the purpose of the commerce clause to relieve those engaged in interstate commerce from their just share of state tax burden even though it increases the cost of doing the business." *Western Live Stock v. Bureau of Revenue*, 303 U.S. 250, 254 (1938). These decisions have considered not the formal language of the tax statute but rather its practical effect, and have sustained a tax against Commerce Clause challenge when the tax is applied to an activity with a substantial nexus with the taxing State, is fairly apportioned, does not discriminate against interstate commerce, and is fairly related to the services provided by the State.

Over the years, the Court has applied this practical analysis in approving many types of tax that avoided running afoul of the prohibition against taxing the "privilege of doing business," but in each instance it has refused to overrule the prohibition. Under the present state of the law, the *Spector* rule, as it has come to be known, has no relationship to economic realities. Rather it stands only as a trap for the unwary draftsman.

In this case, of course, we are confronted with a situation like that presented in *Spector*. The tax is labeled a privilege tax "for the privilege of ... doing business" in Mississippi, 10105 of the State's 1942 Code, as amended, and the activity taxed is, or has been assumed to be, interstate commerce. We note again that no claim is made that the activity is not sufficiently connected to the State to justify a tax, or that the tax is not fairly related to benefits provided the taxpayer, or that the tax discriminates against interstate commerce, or that the tax is not fairly apportioned.

The view of the Commerce Clause that gave rise to the rule of *Spector* perhaps was not without some substance. Nonetheless, the possibility of defending it in the abstract does not alter the fact that the Court has rejected the proposition that interstate commerce is immune from state taxation:

> It is a truism that the mere act of carrying on business in interstate commerce does not exempt a corporation from state taxation. "It was not the purpose of the commerce clause to relieve those engaged in interstate commerce from their just share of state tax burden even though it increases the cost of doing business." *Western Live Stock v. Bureau of Revenue*, 303 U.S. 250, 254 (1938). *Colonial Pipeline Co. v. Traigle*, 421 U.S., at 108.

(continued)

(continued)

Not only has the philosophy underlying the rule been rejected, but the rule itself has been stripped of any practical significance. If Mississippi had called its tax one on "net income" or on the "going concern value" of appellant's business, the *Spector* rule could not invalidate it. There is no economic consequence that follows necessarily from the use of the particular words, "privilege of doing business," and a focus on that formalism merely obscures the question whether the tax produces a forbidden effect. Simply put, the *Spector* rule does not address the problems with which the Commerce Clause is concerned. Accordingly, we now reject the rule of *Spector Motor Service, Inc. v. O'Connor,* that a state tax on the "privilege of doing business" is per se unconstitutional when it is applied to interstate commerce, and that case is overruled.

There being no objection to Mississippi's tax on appellant except that it was imposed on nothing other than the "privilege of doing business" that is interstate, the judgment of the Supreme Court of Mississippi is affirmed.

It is so ordered.

With the growing economic problems experienced by many states and the need to increase tax revenue, states have begun to examine and question the loss of sales taxes due to Internet sales where no sales tax is collected or paid. Internet businesses have relied on a 1992 case in which the Court held that a mail-order business was not required to collect or pay sales taxes unless it had a physical presence in the state. Read the syllabus of the case and consider if Internet businesses are correct in their reliance on this case. Before reading the syllabus, consider this more detailed description of the facts from the actual opinion:

"Quill is a Delaware corporation with offices and warehouses in Illinois, California, and Georgia. None of its employees work or reside in North Dakota and its ownership of tangible property in that State is either insignificant or nonexistent. Quill sells office equipment and supplies; it solicits business through catalogs and flyers, advertisements in national periodicals, and telephone calls. Its annual national sales exceed $200,000,000, of which almost $1,000,000 are made to about 3,000 customers in North Dakota. It is the sixth largest vendor of office supplies in the State. It delivers all of its merchandise to its North Dakota customers by mail or common carrier from out of state locations."

Quill v. North Dakota
504 U.S. 298 (1992)

Respondent North Dakota filed an action in state court to require petitioner Quill Corporation—an out of state mail order house with neither outlets nor sales representatives in the State—to collect and pay a use tax on goods purchased for use in the State. The trial court ruled in Quill's favor. It found the case indistinguishable from *National Bellas Hess, Inc. v. Department of Revenue of Ill.,* 386 U.S. 753, which, in holding that a similar Illinois statute violated the Fourteenth Amendment's Due Process Clause and created an unconstitutional burden on interstate commerce, concluded that a "seller whose only connection with customers in the State is by common carrier or the . . . mail" lacked the requisite minimum contacts with the State. *Id.,* at 758. The State Supreme Court reversed, concluding, *inter alia,* that, pursuant to *Complete Auto Transit, Inc. v. Brady,* 430 U.S. 274, and its progeny, the Commerce Clause no longer mandated the sort of physical presence nexus suggested in *Bellas Hess;* and that, with respect to the Due Process Clause, cases following *Bellas Hess* had not construed minimum contacts to require physical presence within a State as a prerequisite to the legitimate exercise of state power.

(continued)

(continued)

Held:

1. The Due Process Clause does not bar enforcement of the State's use tax against Quill. This Court's due process jurisprudence has evolved substantially since *Bellas Hess,* abandoning formalistic tests focused on a defendant's presence within a State in favor of a more flexible inquiry into whether a defendant's contacts with the forum made it reasonable, in the context of the federal system of government, to require it to defend the suit in that State. See, *Shaffer v. Heitner,* 433 U.S. 186, 212. Thus, to the extent that this Court's decisions have indicated that the clause requires a physical presence in a State, they are overruled. In this case, Quill has purposefully directed its activities at North Dakota residents, the magnitude of those contacts are more than sufficient for due process purposes, and the tax is related to the benefits Quill receives from access to the State.

2. The State's enforcement of the use tax against Quill places an unconstitutional burden on interstate commerce.

    (a) *Bellas Hess* was not rendered obsolete by this Court's subsequent decision in *Complete Auto, supra,* which set forth the four part test that continues to govern the validity of state taxes under the Commerce Clause. Although *Complete Auto* renounced an analytical approach that looked to a statute's formal language rather than its practical effect in determining a state tax statute's validity, the *Bellas Hess* decision did not rely on such formalism. Nor is *Bellas Hess* inconsistent with *Complete Auto.* It concerns the first part of the *Complete Auto* test and stands for the proposition that a vendor whose only contacts with the taxing State are by mail or common carrier lacks the "substantial nexus" required by the Commerce Clause.

    (b) Contrary to the State's argument, a mail order house may have the "minimum contacts" with a taxing State as required by the Due Process Clause, and yet lack the "substantial nexus" with the State required by the Commerce Clause. These requirements are not identical and are animated by different constitutional concerns and policies. Due process concerns the fundamental fairness of governmental activity, and the touchstone of due process nexus analysis is often identified as "notice" or "fair warning." In contrast, the Commerce Clause and its nexus requirement are informed by structural concerns about the effects of state regulation on the national economy. pp. 12–13.

    (c) The evolution of this Court's Commerce Clause jurisprudence does not indicate repudiation of the *Bellas Hess* rule. While cases subsequent to *Bellas Hess* and concerning other types of taxes have not adopted a bright line, physical presence requirement similar to that in *Bellas Hess,* see, *e. g., Standard Pressed Steel Co. v. Department of Revenue of Wash.,* 419 U.S. 560, their reasoning does not compel rejection of the *Bellas Hess* rule regarding sales and use taxes. To the contrary, the continuing value of a bright line rule in this area and the doctrine and principles of *stare decisis* indicate that the rule remains good law.

    (d) The underlying issue here is one that Congress may be better qualified to resolve and one that it has the ultimate power to resolve.

    470 N. W. 2d 203, reversed and remanded.

....

Something to Consider

Based on the principles discussed in *Complete Auto* and *Quill,* under what circumstances do you think a state could impose a tax on goods sold over the Internet? In today's commercial world, is maintaining a Web site accessible for making purchases the same as maintaining a physical store within the state?

State Laws and Immigration

ONE area in which recent state laws threaten to conflict with federal laws is immigration. The ability to regulate immigration is clearly within the enumerated powers of Congress. In recent years, however, several border states have experienced problems with undocumented individuals and have expressed dissatisfaction with federal laws and enforcement. In 2011, the Supreme Court decided one case concerning an Arizona state law (similar to laws in other states) that imposed licensing sanctions on employers who knowingly employ illegal aliens. The Court decided that this law was not preempted because a federal law expressly allowed such laws. The Court also noted that the state law was not impliedly preempted nor in conflict with the federal law. The following excerpts from the Court Syllabus outline the Court's reasoning.

Chamber of Commerce of the United States of America v . Whiting

563 U.S. ___ (2011)

The Immigration Reform and Control Act (IRCA) makes it "unlawful for a person or other entity . . . to hire, or to recruit or refer for a fee, for employment in the United States an alien knowing the alien is an unauthorized alien." 8 U. S. C. §1324a(a)(1)(A). Employers that violate that prohibition may be subjected to federal civil and criminal sanctions. IRCA also restricts the ability of States to combat employment of unauthorized workers; the Act expressly preempts "any State or local law imposing civil or criminal sanctions (other than through licensing and similar laws) upon those who employ, or recruit or refer for a fee for employment, unauthorized aliens." §1324a(h)(2).

IRCA also requires employers to take steps to verify an employee's eligibility for employment. In an attempt to improve that verification process in the Illegal Immigration Reform and Immigrant Responsibility Act (IIRIRA), Congress created E-Verify—an internet-based system employers can use to check the work authorization status of employees.

The District Court found that the plain language of IRCA's preemption clause did not invalidate the Arizona law because the law did no more than impose licensing conditions on businesses operating within the State. Nor was the state law preempted with respect to E-Verify, the court concluded, because although Congress had made the program voluntary at the national level, it had expressed no intent to prevent States from mandating participation. The Ninth Circuit affirmed.

Held: The judgment is affirmed.

Arizona's licensing law falls well within the confines of the authority Congress chose to leave to the States and therefore is not expressly preempted. While IRCA prohibits States from imposing "civil or criminal sanctions" on those who employ unauthorized aliens, it preserves state authority to impose sanctions "through licensing and similar laws." §1324a(h)(2). That is what the Arizona law does—it instructs courts to suspend or revoke the business licenses of in-state employers that employ unauthorized aliens. The definition of "license" contained in the Arizona statute largely parrots the definition of "license" that Congress codified in the Administrative Procedure Act (APA).

The Arizona licensing law is not impliedly preempted by federal law. At its broadest, the Chamber's argument is that Congress intended the federal system to be exclusive. But Arizona's procedures simply implement the sanctions that Congress expressly allowed the States to pursue through licensing laws. Given that Congress specifically preserved such authority for the States, it stands to reason that Congress did not intend to prevent the States from using appropriate tools to exercise that authority.

Arizona's requirement that employers use E-Verify is not impliedly preempted. The IIRIRA provision setting up E-Verify contains no language circumscribing state action. Moreover, Arizona's use of E-Verify does not conflict with the federal scheme. The state law requires no more than that an employer, after hiring an employee, "verify the employment eligibility of the employee" through E-Verify. Ariz. Rev. Stat. Ann. §23–214(A). And the consequences of not using E-Verify are the same under the state and federal law—an employer forfeits an otherwise available rebuttable presumption of Arizona's requirement that employers use E-Verify in no way obstructs achieving the aims of the federal program. In fact, the Government has consistently expanded and encouraged the use of E-Verify, and Congress has directed that E-Verify be made available in all 50 States.

Another Arizona law continues to present questions, however. In part this law gives state law enforcement officers the right to determine immigration status anytime a lawful stop is made. The U.S. Department of Justice challenged the law in court. Included in its Complaint is the following allegation, explaining briefly the reason for the challenge:

> Although states may exercise their police power in a manner that has an incidental or indirect effect on aliens, a state may *not* establish its own immigration policy or enforce state laws in a manner that interferes with the federal immigration laws. The Constitution and the federal immigration laws do not permit the development of a patchwork of state and local immigration policies throughout the country.

It is likely that the Supreme Court will eventually rule on this issue.

Other Constitutional Challenges to State Laws

A STATE LAW OR TAX is unconstitutional whenever it violates any provision of the Constitution. See Exhibit 6-2. The doctrines of preemption and the Dormant Commerce Clause are only two instances in which this violation occurs. Several other provisions in the Constitution impose limits or prohibitions on state power to legislate and tax.

🏛 **bill of attainder**

The wiping out of civil rights that may occur when a person is found guilty of a felony or receives a death sentence. It usually includes the government's taking of all the person's property. This practice is no longer done in the United States. A bill of attainder was a legislative Act pronouncing a person guilty (usually of treason) without a trial and sentencing the person to death and attainder. This practice is now prohibited by the U.S. Constitution (Article I, Section 9).

Exhibit 6-2   Analyzing a State Law

ANALYZING A STATE LAW

In upholding the tax in *Complete Auto,* the Court obviously believed that the four criteria were satisfied. An examination of the facts shows why.

1. **The nexus requirement is met.** The state was taxing an activity that took place in the state, that is, the sale of services in the state.
2. **The fair apportionment requirement is met.** The state was taxing services within the state, so there would be no double tax with another state because another state would not have the right to tax the same thing. Thus, the tax was fairly apportioned.
3. **There is no discrimination.** There is nothing to indicate that services by local businesses paid any different sales tax.
4. **There is a reasonable relationship to services provided.** Complete Auto sells services in the state and must therefore be in a position where it might need local government services. A 5 percent sales tax is certainly reasonable enough to justify the belief that the tax is reasonably related to normal services provided by local governments.

© Cengage Learning 2013

🏛 **ex post facto law**

(Latin) After the fact. An ex post facto law is one that retroactively attempts to make an action a crime that was not a crime at the time it was done or a law that attempts to reduce a person's rights based on a past act that was not subject to the law when it was done. Ex post facto laws are prohibited by the U.S. Constitution (Article I, Section 9).

Article I, Section 10 is entitled "Powers Denied to the States" and prohibits states from the following:

- entering into treaties or alliances
- coining money
- passing a bill of attainder, ex post facto law, or law impairing the obligation of contracts
- granting a title of nobility

A **bill of attainder** is a law that punishes a specific individual or individuals for some act. It is a legislative determination that an individual has done something for which he or she should be punished. The effect of this type of act is to deny the accused the right to a trial. An **ex post facto** imposes criminal punishment for an act that was not a crime at the time the act occurred or a law that increases the punishment for a crime. Laws impairing the obligation of contract are laws that interfere with existing contractual duties that parties owe one another. Such a law operates to eliminate the obligation of one of the parties to the contract, resulting in a deprivation of some property interest to the other party.

Intending to preserve the power of the federal government to regulate foreign commerce and other foreign matters, Article I, Section 10 also prohibits states from the following *unless* they have the consent of Congress:

- lay any **imposts** or **duties** on imports or exports, except what may be absolutely necessary for executing its inspection laws (import and export clause)
- lay any **duty of tonnage**, keep troops, or ships of war in time of peace, enter into any agreement or compact with another state, or with a foreign power, or engage in war, unless actually invaded, or in such imminent danger as will not admit of delay

Article IV deals with the relations among the various states. To promote harmony and unity among the states, this article requires that states

- give **full faith and credit** to laws of other states
- extend the privileges and immunities of the state to citizens of all states (privileges and immunities clause)
- **extradite** criminals who are wanted in another state

Various Amendments to the Constitution also limit the powers of the states by prohibiting them from making laws that

- abridge the privileges or immunities of citizens of the United States or violate notions of due process or equal protection (Fourteenth Amendment)
- deny or abridge the right to vote because of race (Fifteenth Amendment), gender (Nineteenth Amendment), failure to pay a poll tax (Twenty-fourth Amendment), or age if eighteen years or older (Twenty-sixth Amendment)

These amendments deal primarily with laws that interfere with a party's basic civil liberties and are discussed in detail in subsequent chapters. In some instances, however, the Equal Protection Clause, Privileges and Immunities Clause, and the Due Process Clause are also used in conjunction with the Dormant Commerce Clause to challenge state laws.

The Equal Protection Clause arises whenever a state law is claimed to be discriminatory. If out-of-state businesses are treated differently than in-state businesses, then the Equal Protection Clause is often violated along with the Commerce Clause. In this kind of case, the Privileges and Immunities Clause might also apply. This clause requires that states extend the same privileges and immunities to state citizens and noncitizens. If the state is not giving out-of-state businesses the same privileges and immunities as it does its own citizens, then this clause might well be violated.

The Due Process Clause often arises whenever the state law involves a tax. Due process requires that a business or individual must have minimum contacts with a state before being taxed by that state. See Exhibit 6-3.

🏛 imposts

Taxes; import taxes.

🏛 duty

A tax on imports or exports.

🏛 duty of tonnage

Governmental port charges or port taxes on a boat.

🏛 full faith and credit

The constitutional requirement that each state must treat as valid, and enforce where appropriate, the laws and court decisions of other states. There are exceptions to this rule, especially those cases in which the other state lacked proper jurisdiction.

🏛 extradite

Extradition; one country (or state) giving up a person to a second country (or state) when the second requests the person for a trial or for punishment after trial.

Exhibit 6-3 Managing Shared Powers

MANAGING SHARED POWERS

Federal and state governments share many powers, such as the power to regulate antitrust activities. As with any shared power, the potential exists for placing an excessive burden on a regulated business. The following is taken from the settlement agreement entered into among Microsoft, the U.S. government, and selected states in connection with the antitrust lawsuit against Microsoft. Note how it handles the overlap in federal and state powers and tries to minimize the extra burden to Microsoft:

IV. Compliance and Enforcement Procedures

A. Enforcement Authority

1. The Plaintiffs shall have exclusive responsibility for enforcing this Final Judgment. Without in any way limiting the sovereign enforcement authority of each of the plaintiff States, the plaintiff States shall form a committee to coordinate their enforcement of this Final Judgment. A plaintiff State shall take no action to enforce this Final Judgment without first consulting with the United States and with the plaintiff States' enforcement committee.

2. To determine and enforce compliance with this Final Judgment, duly authorized representatives of the United States and the plaintiff States, on reasonable notice to Microsoft and subject to any lawful privilege, shall be permitted the following:

   a. Access during normal office hours to inspect any and all source code, books, ledgers, accounts, correspondence, memoranda and other documents and records in the possession, custody, or control of Microsoft, which may have counsel present, regarding any matters contained in this Final Judgment.

   b. Subject to the reasonable convenience of Microsoft and without restraint or interference from it, to interview, informally or on the record, officers, employees, or agents of Microsoft, who may have counsel present, regarding any matters contained in this Final Judgment.

   c. Upon written request of the United States or a duly designated representative of a plaintiff State, on reasonable notice given to Microsoft, Microsoft shall submit such written reports under oath as requested regarding any matters contained in this Final Judgment.

   Individual plaintiff States will consult with the plaintiff States' enforcement committee to minimize the duplication and burden of the exercise of the foregoing powers, where practicable.

© Cengage Learning 2013

≈ **Ethical Decisions—Everyday Choices** ≈

The Facts: Cooper is an attorney who is a member of the New York Bar. Cooper's brother-in-law, who lives in California, recently found himself in trouble with the law and wants Cooper to represent him in court. In preparing for the case, Cooper sent his paralegal, Davis, to California to interview witnesses and to check and summarize court documents. Davis received a paralegal certificate from a New York school.

The Problem: Can Cooper appear in a California court on behalf of a client even though he is not a member of the California Bar? Can Davis, who knows nothing about California law, act as a paralegal in California?

Guiding Principles: Attorneys are licensed to practice by individual states. Generally, to be licensed, the attorney must take a bar exam in the state. Many states allow attorneys to appear in cases even though they are not members of the state bar as long as they associate with local counsel and as long as the number of cases handled is limited. All ethical guidelines require that the attorney act competently, which means knowing the appropriate law. Paralegals are governed by different rules. Because they are not licensed by any state, no laws prohibit them from moving or working in different states. Like attorneys, however, they must act competently and ethically.

Chapter Summary

Under the system of federalism, Americans are subject to both federal and state laws. States have general police power to enact laws and impose taxes that promote the general welfare. The power of the states is not without constitutional limits. Using the power of judicial review, the Supreme Court ultimately determines the constitutionality of any state law or tax. The Supreme Court usually employs the following principles in judging a state law:

1. When both a federal law and state law regulate the same area, the state law is preempted by the federal law and is therefore unconstitutional if
   a. the federal law expresses the intent that it alone controls (express preemption).
   b. the federal law impliedly suggests that it alone controls (field preemption).
   c. the state law conflicts with the federal law (conflict preemption).
2. Even if there is no federal legislation on the same subject, a state law affecting interstate commerce may prohibit such a law because the Court has ruled that the Interstate Commerce Clause has a negative aspect that sometimes limits the rights of states to make laws affecting interstate commerce. Known as the Dormant Commerce Clause, this generally prohibits state laws when
   a. The state law discriminates against out-of-state businesses.
   b. It places too great a burden on interstate commerce in relationship to the local benefit.
3. A state tax on a business engaged in interstate commerce is unconstitutional if
   a. There is no connection between the state and the activity taxed.
   b. The tax is not fairly apportioned and may result in double taxation.
   c. The tax discriminates against out-of-state businesses.
   d. There is no relationship to services rendered by the state.
4. A state law is unconstitutional if a specific provision in the Constitution prohibits it. Included here are provisions prohibiting such laws as bills of attainder, ex post facto laws, laws affecting the obligations of contracts, and laws imposing certain export and import taxes. The Constitution also prohibits any laws that violate the Equal Protection Clause or the Due Process Clause.

Key Terms

police power	conflict preemption	imposts
preempts	common law	duty
Dormant Commerce Clause	saving clause	duty of tonnage
express preemption	bill of attainder	full faith and credit
field preemption	ex post facto law	extradite

Questions for Review

1. In general, what does the Supreme Court consider when faced with the constitutionality of a state law?
2. Define the terms express preemption, field preemption, and conflict preemption.
3. What is the Dormant Commerce Clause?
4. How does the Interstate Commerce Clause limit the right of states to enact laws?
5. How does being a market participant affect the right of a state to discriminate against out-of-state businesses?
6. What criteria does the Court use to determine if a state law violates the Dormant Commerce Clause?
7. Why do states have constitutional problems when they tax out-of-state businesses?

8. List the criteria used by the Court to determine the constitutionality of a tax on an out-of-state business.
9. What provisions of the Constitution limit the powers of the state to enact laws or impose taxes?
10. How can the Equal Protection Clause and the Due Process Clause affect the constitutionality of laws dealing with interstate commerce?

Questions for Analysis

1. Review the Living with the Constitution situation presented at the beginning of this chapter. Do you think that a state can tax all goods sold to its residents over the Internet? Is there a difference between an Internet Web site where the owner of the site sells items to the public and an Internet Web site that provides a forum for individuals to sell items to the public?
2. Answer the following regarding the case of *Hillsborough County v. Automated Medical Laboratories*.
   a. In arguing that the Hillsborough County ordinances and regulations are preempted, the Court said that the appellee faced an uphill battle. What was this battle, and did the appellee succeed in its argument?
   b. Why did the Court think that the extensiveness of the federal rules did not result in preemption?
   c. What was the Court's holding in this case?
3. Answer the following regarding *Geier v. American Honda Motor Co.*
   a. Why did the Court believe that there was no express preemption?
   b. What was the language of the saving clause?
   c. Why did the Court believe that there was a conflict between state and federal law?
4. What are the factual differences between the *Geier* and *Williamson* cases? Why were those differences important?
5. Answer the following regarding the case of *Cooley v. Board of Wardens*.
   a. According to the Court, when should states be allowed to regulate interstate commerce?
   b. How did the Act of 1789 impact the Court's decision?
6. Answer the following regarding the case of *Southern Pac. Co. v. Arizona*.
   a. What factors did this case ultimately depend on? Quote language from the Court.
   b. Why did Justice Douglas disagree with the majority?

Assignments and Projects

1. Using the format shown in previous chapters, brief the case of *Complete Auto Transit, Inc. v. Brady*.
2. In *Rice v. Santa Fe Elevator Corp.*, the Court set forth several criteria for determining if field preemption exists. Using these criteria and following the format in Exhibit 6-2, show how the Court came to the conclusion in the *Hillsborough* case that field preemption did not exist.

Putting It into Practice

Assume that your law office represents Rhonda Berk (see Living with the Constitution) who sells individually made handcrafted items on an "auction" type Web site. Berk, who is a resident of Idaho, received a letter from a neighboring state (State A) demanding that she pay sales tax on all the sales she made for the past year. Berk sold some items to residents of the neighboring state, but they constituted only about 15 percent of her total sales. All her sales are shipped by ground, and all the shippers travel through State A to reach their destination. Draft a letter to be sent to the Tax Board of State A refuting its claim for taxes.

Group Activities

1. Assume the following: State A is experiencing high unemployment and in an effort to help with this enacts a law giving all businesses that have over five hundred employees a tax credit if at least 75 percent of the total number of employees are residents of State A. The law further imposes a tax surcharge if more than 20 percent of the employees are not residents of the United States. Form small groups and discuss the constitutionality of the tax credit and the tax surcharge. List arguments for and against its constitutionality. Select one member of the group to present your conclusions to the entire class.

2. Review the syllabus for *Williamson v. Mazda Motors of America, Inc.* Assume that you were on the Supreme Court and about to hear oral arguments in this case. Draft a list of questions that you would ask attorneys for each side. When you finish, listen to the actual oral arguments in the case. (The oral arguments are easily located on the Internet.) Compare your list of questions to those asked by the Supreme Court.

7 Constitutional Protections of Civil Rights and Liberties

Where Slavery is, there Liberty cannot be;
and where Liberty is, there Slavery cannot be.

Charles Sumner

Chapter Outline

Chapter Objectives

When you complete this chapter you should be able to

1. explain the importance of the Ninth Amendment to the protection of civil rights and liberties.

2. summarize the Court's various descriptions of the terms *civil rights* and *liberties*.

3. list the various sources of the protection of civil rights and liberties.

4. define writ of habeas corpus, bill of attainder, and ex post facto laws.

5. summarize the rights and liberties found in the Bill of Rights.

6. describe the rights afforded by the Second Amendment.

7. explain how the Constitution provides protection against the infringement of civil rights and liberties by state and local governments.

8. describe the protections afforded by the Fourteenth Amendment.

9. describe the constitutional provisions that give Congress the power to enact civil rights legislation.

10. explain what is meant by the *state action doctrine*.

Looking Back

Before reading this chapter, review the following terms and concepts from the previous chapters:

Interstate Commerce Clause/civil rights legislation Congress used the Interstate Commerce Clause to enact several civil rights bills. These laws prohibit discrimination by individuals or businesses involved in interstate commerce. (Chapter 4)

Supreme Court jurisdiction The Supreme Court does not have unlimited jurisdiction. It has the power to hear cases from state courts only when a federal law or the U.S. Constitution is an issue. (Chapter 3)

***Lopez* case** A Supreme Court case invalidating a federal law making it a crime to possess a gun near a school; Court held that the Interstate Commerce Clause gives Congress wide latitude, but it does have limits and this is one. (Chapter 4)

Suspension Clause in the Constitution giving the president the right to "suspend" or eliminate the right to petition for a writ of habeas corpus. (Chapter 5)

Living with the Constitution

Robert Orland was taken into custody by city police who suspected him of terrorist activities. In part, this suspicion was based on information provided to the police by an acquaintance of Orland. Orland was held in custody for thirty days during which time he was not allowed to speak to anyone, including a lawyer. He was not taken to court and no bail was set. After discovering that the acquaintance had lied to them, the police eventually freed Orland.

THE PREAMBLE TO THE CONSTITUTION states that the Constitution was established to "secure the Blessings of Liberty to ourselves and our posterity." Yet, as important as the concept of liberty was to the framers of the Constitution, the original seven articles contain little mention of individual rights and freedoms. With a few exceptions, provisions in the original seven articles deal with the creation and powers of the new government rather than the protection of civil rights. However, many of the amendments, especially the Bill of Rights, prevent government from interfering with numerous basic rights and liberties. The full nature and extent of these rights and liberties are found in Supreme Court decisions interpreting the various constitutional provisions. This chapter presents an overview of how the Constitution protects our basic civil rights and liberties. Subsequent chapters deal with specific rights related to equal protection, due process, economic freedoms, freedom of expression, freedom of religion, privacy, and rights of criminal defendants.

Civil Rights and Liberties: Sources of Protections

EVEN THOUGH THE TERMS ARE widely used, there is no universally agreed definition for the terms *civil rights* or *liberties*. The framers of the Constitution certainly believed that all men possessed certain fundamental rights and freedoms, a belief clearly reflected in the Declaration of Independence: "We hold these truths to be self-evident, that all men are created equal, that they are endowed by their Creator with certain unalienable Rights, that among these are Life, Liberty, and the pursuit of Happiness."

History, however, proves that the exact nature of these "unalienable rights" is anything but self-evident. Although the Constitution, especially the Bill of Rights, expressly sets forth a list of basic rights, the framers of the Constitution recognized that a complete list of rights was not only impossible, but also inadvisable, and included in the Bill of Rights a statement that "The enumeration in the Constitution, of certain rights, shall not be construed to deny or disparage others retained by the people" (Ninth Amendment). One Court has described the concept of liberty as follows: "Although the Court has not assumed to define 'liberty' with any great precision, that term is not confined to mere freedom from bodily restraint. Liberty under law extends to the full range of conduct which the individual is free to pursue, and it cannot be restricted except for a proper governmental objective." *Bolling v. Sharpe,* 347 U.S. 497 (1954).

Today, the concept of civil rights and liberties includes protection from laws that discriminate because of such factors as race, color, religion, sex, age, disability, or national origin. It includes the right to fair and just proceedings in both criminal and civil cases. It also includes freedom from unwarranted government control in our personal, political, and economic lives.

The protection of civil rights and liberties comes from various sources, including the U.S. Constitution, federal legislation, state constitutions, and state legislation. Various articles and amendments to the U.S. Constitution provide protections against infringement of rights by federal and state governments. Using the Interstate Commerce Clause and various constitutional amendments, Congress enacted legislation broadening those protections. State constitutions and state laws provide additional protections for civil rights and liberties. The Constitution and federal laws are subject to interpretation and review by the Supreme Court. State constitutions and laws are subject to review by state and sometimes federal courts.

Original Constitutional Protections

The original Constitution contains only a few provisions relating to individual rights and liberties, most of which relate to criminal prosecutions. The following guarantees are found:

1. The federal government cannot suspend the privilege of the writ of habeas corpus unless public safety demands it because of rebellion or invasion (Article I, § 9)

2. Neither the federal nor state government can pass a bill of attainder
3. Neither the federal nor a state government can pass an ex post facto law
4. Trials for federal crimes should be jury trials in the state where the crime was committed (Article III, § 2); this right is also found in the Sixth Amendment
5. Conviction of treason requires two witnesses or a confession in open court (Article III, § 3)

PETITION FOR WRIT OF HABEAS CORPUS

writ of habeas corpus (habeas corpus)

(Latin) "You have the body." A judicial order to someone holding a person to bring that person to court. It is most often used to get a person out of unlawful imprisonment by forcing the captor and the person being held to come to court for a decision on the legality of the imprisonment or other holding (such as keeping a child when someone else claims custody). (pronounce: hay-bee-as core-pus)

A petition for a **writ of habeas corpus** is a document filed in court in which a prisoner (or other person in custody) requests that he or she be released from custody. It was a fundamental English right and was used when individuals claimed they were unjustly imprisoned. The Constitution guarantees the continuation of this right by limiting the power of the federal government to suspend it. Today, the petition is commonly used to challenge a state criminal conviction in federal court. If an individual was convicted of a state crime and unsuccessfully appealed the conviction in the state courts, that person can file a petition for a writ of habeas corpus in federal court *if* he or she claims that any federal laws or constitutional rights were violated. This petition asks the federal court to review the state court proceedings. Although the Constitution demands that this right not be eliminated, it does not prevent Congress from imposing limitations and strict procedures. Detailed rules about the necessary procedures and limitations on the number of petitions that can be filed are found in the United States Code (28 U.S.C., § 2241). Appendix C contains an example of the petition.

Petitions for writs of habeas corpus have also become an important procedure for individuals confined as enemy combatants in the war on terror. As discussed in Chapter 5, the president's suspension of this right for enemy combatants has led to various Supreme Court cases.

BILL OF ATTAINDER

bill of attainder

The wiping out of civil rights that may occur when a person is found guilty of a felony or receives a death sentence. It usually includes the government's taking of all the person's property. This is no longer done in the United States. A *bill of attainder* was a legislative act pronouncing a person guilty (usually of treason) without a trial and sentencing the person to death and *attainder*. This is now prohibited by the U.S. Constitution.

The Constitution prohibits both federal and state governments from enacting a bill of attainder. A **bill of attainder** is a law that punishes a *specific* individual or individuals for some act. It is a legislative determination that an individual did something for which he or she should be punished. The effect of this type of act is to deny the accused the right to a trial. Once the law is passed, punishment is automatic. A bill of attainder violates two basic constitutional principles: the separation of power between the legislative and the judicial branch and the right to a jury trial in a criminal case.

Sometimes disputes arise concerning the nature of a legislative act. A law that says anyone who commits a murder should be sentenced to life in prison is certainly *not* a bill of attainder. On the other hand, a law that says John Smith should be imprisoned for life because he committed a murder is clearly a bill of attainder. But what about a law making it a crime for a member of the Communist Party to serve as an officer or employee of a labor union? In a case with those facts, *United States v. Brown*, 381 U.S. 437 (1965), a divided Court found that the law was a bill of attainder. The majority felt that the statute was a legislative determination that all members of the Communist Party had certain characteristics that made them unfit to work for the labor union. As such, it punished that group. The punishment here was not imprisonment, but the loss of labor union employment.

A Point of Law

United States v. Brown, 381 U.S. 437 (1965)

A legislative enactment that punishes an individual or a specific group of people is a bill of attainder and unconstitutional. Thus, a law prohibiting any member of the Communist Party from serving as an officer of a labor union was found to be a bill of attainder.

EX POST FACTO LAWS

🏛 **ex post facto laws**

(Latin) After the fact. An *ex post facto law* is one that retroactively attempts to make an action a crime that was not a crime at the time it was done or a law that attempts to reduce a person's rights based on a past act that was not subject to the law when it was done. Ex post facto laws are prohibited by the U.S. Constitution (Article I, Section 9).

Both federal and state governments are prohibited from enacting **ex post facto laws**. These are laws that impose criminal punishment for an act that was not a crime at the time the act occurred or that increase the punishment for a crime. For example, suppose that Smith holds a party in a public park and serves alcohol at the party. The next week, the city enacts an ordinance making it a crime to have possessed, in the last ninety days, alcohol at the park. Such a law would be unconstitutional. The Courts also hold that laws increasing the sentence for a crime cannot be applied retroactively. However, in *Dobbert v. Florida*, 432 U.S. 282 (1977), the Supreme Court allowed a retroactive application of a Florida law imposing the death penalty where a prior death penalty law was declared unconstitutional. The defendant was initially convicted of torturing and murdering his children and was sentenced to die. Subsequently, the death penalty law was declared unconstitutional. Florida then enacted a new death penalty law. The new law created new procedures for the way the death penalty was to be imposed, and these procedures actually afforded the defendant more protection than the prior law. After a sentencing hearing under the new law, the defendant was again sentenced to die. He asked the Supreme Court to overturn the sentence because of a violation of the ex post facto rule. The Court disagreed, although several justices dissented. An excerpt from the decision in that case, along with an excerpt from the dissenting opinion, follows.

⚖ Dobbert v. Florida

432 U.S. 282 (1977)

MR. JUSTICE REHNQUIST delivered the opinion of the Court.

It is well settled, however, that "[t]he inhibition upon the passage of ex post facto laws does not give a criminal a right to be tried, in all respects, by the law in force when the crime charged was committed." *Gibson v. Mississippi*, 162 U.S. 565, 590 (1896).

Even though it may work to the disadvantage of a defendant, a procedural change is not ex post facto. For example, in *Hopt v. Utah*, 110 U.S. 574 (1884), as of the date of the alleged homicide a convicted felon could not have been called as a witness. Subsequent to that date, but prior to the trial of the case, this law was changed; a convicted felon was called to the stand and testified, implicating Hopt in the crime charged against him. Even

though this change in the law obviously had a detrimental impact upon the defendant, the Court found that the law was not ex post facto because it neither made criminal a theretofore innocent act, nor aggravated a crime previously committed, nor provided greater punishment, nor changed the proof necessary to convict. *Id.*, at 589.

In the case at hand, the change in the statute was clearly procedural. The new statute simply altered the methods employed in determining whether the death penalty was to be imposed; there was no change in the quantum of punishment attached to the crime.

In this case, not only was the change in the law procedural, it was ameliorative. Under the old procedure, the death penalty was "presumed" unless the jury, in its unbridled discretion, made a recommendation for mercy.

(continued)

(continued)

The Florida Legislature enacted the new procedure specifically to provide the constitutional procedural protections required by *Furman*, thus providing capital defendants with more, rather than less, judicial protection. Finally, in what may be termed a tripartite review, the Florida Supreme Court is required to review each sentence of death. This crucial protection demonstrates that the new statute affords significantly more safeguards to the defendant than did the old. Death is not automatic, absent a jury recommendation of mercy, as it was under the old procedure.

Petitioner's second ex post facto claim is based on the contention that at the time he murdered his children there was no death penalty "in effect" in Florida. [T]his sophistic argument mocks the substance of the Ex Post Facto Clause. Whether or not the old statute would, in the future, withstand constitutional attack, it clearly indicated Florida's view of the severity of murder and of the degree of punishment which the legislature wished to impose upon murderers. The statute was intended to provide maximum deterrence, and its existence on the statute books provided fair warning as to the degree of culpability which the State ascribed to the act of murder.

Here the existence of the statute served as an "operative fact" to warn the petitioner of the penalty which Florida would seek to impose on him if he were convicted of first-degree murder. This was sufficient compliance with the ex post facto provision of the United States Constitution. The judgment of the Supreme Court of Florida is therefore

Affirmed.

MR. JUSTICE STEVENS, with whom MR. JUSTICE BRENNAN and MR. JUSTICE MARSHALL join, dissenting.

This conclusion represents a clear departure from the test the Court has applied in past cases construing the Ex Post Facto Clause. That test was stated in *Lindsey v. Washington*, 301 U.S. 397, 401, in language that might have been written with the present case in mind:

"The Constitution forbids the application of any new punitive measure to a crime already consummated, to the detriment or material disadvantage of the wrongdoer."

We should adhere to the *Lindsey* test. Fair warning cannot be the touchstone, for two reasons. First, "fair warning" does not provide a workable test for deciding particular cases. Second, as Mr. Justice Harlan has explained, fair notice is not the only important value underlying the constitutional prohibition; the Ex Post Facto Clause also provides a basic protection against improperly motivated or capricious legislation. It ensures that the sovereign will govern impartially and that it will be perceived as doing so. The Court's "fair warning" test, if it extends beyond this case, would allow government action that is just the opposite of impartial. If that be so, the "fair warning" rationale will defeat the very purpose of the Clause.

If I am correct that the Ex Post Facto Clause was intended as a barrier to capricious government action, today's holding is actually perverse. For when human life is at stake, the need to prevent capricious punishment is greatest, as our decisions in *Furman* and *Proffitt* establish.

I respectfully dissent.

Something to Consider

What is the purpose of an ex post facto law? Was that purpose served or defeated by the decision in this case?

Protections Found in the Bill of Rights

When the Constitution was originally drafted and submitted to the states for ratification, the failure of the document to guarantee individual rights and liberties caused considerable dissatisfaction. Supporters of the Constitution as drafted argued that the limited powers given the central government would act as a limit on the ability of the government to infringe individual rights. Others believed that any expression of individual rights should be in state constitutions. Still, the fear of a tyrannical government was strong, and ratification of the Constitution might not have occurred without the promise of adding a bill of rights. The first ten amendments to the Constitution, known as the Bill of Rights, were ratified in 1791.

The Bill of Rights serves as a protection for rights and liberties affecting all aspects of American life. The First Amendment lists rights guaranteeing freedom of religion, speech, press, assembly, and rights to petition the government. The Second Amendment deals with the right to bear arms. The Third Amendment, which has little if any application today, prohibits soldiers from being quartered in private homes. The Fourth, Fifth, Sixth, and Eighth Amendments all deal with the rights of those suspected of or accused of crimes. The Fifth Amendment also contains a general guarantee of due process from the federal government and a prohibition on the taking of property for public use without just compensation. The Seventh Amendment guarantees the right to a jury trial in civil cases when the amount in controversy exceeds $20. The Ninth and Tenth Amendments are general statements. The Ninth Amendment makes it clear that the rights listed in the Constitution do not constitute an exclusive list. The Tenth Amendment is a reaffirmation of states rights to exercise power. See Exhibit 7-1 for the complete text of the Bill of Rights.

Exhibit 7-1   The Bill of Rights

AMENDMENT I

Congress shall make no law respecting an establishment of religion, or prohibiting the free exercise thereof; or abridging the freedom of speech, or of the press; or the right of the people peaceably to assemble, and to petition the Government for a redress of grievances.

AMENDMENT II

A well regulated Militia, being necessary to the security of a free State, the right of the people to keep and bear Arms, shall not be infringed.

AMENDMENT III

No Soldier shall, in time of peace be quartered in any house, without the consent of the Owner, nor in time of war, but in a manner to be prescribed by law.

AMENDMENT IV

The right of the people to be secure in their persons, houses, papers, and effects, against unreasonable searches and seizures, shall not be violated, and no Warrants shall issue, but upon probable cause, supported by Oath or affirmation, and particularly describing the place to be searched, and the persons or things to be seized.

AMENDMENT V

No person shall be held to answer for a capital, or otherwise infamous crime, unless on a presentment or indictment of a Grand Jury, except in cases arising in the land or naval forces, or in the Militia, when in actual service in time of War or public danger; nor shall any person be subject for the same offence to be twice put in jeopardy of life or limb; nor shall be compelled in any criminal case to be a witness against himself, nor be deprived of life, liberty, or property, without due process of law; nor shall private property be taken for public use, without just compensation.

AMENDMENT VI

In all criminal prosecutions, the accused shall enjoy the right to a speedy and public trial, by an impartial jury of the State and district wherein the crime shall have been committed, which district shall have been previously ascertained by law, and to be informed of the nature and cause of the accusation; to be confronted with the witnesses against him; to have compulsory process for obtaining witnesses in his favor, and to have the Assistance of Counsel for his defence.

AMENDMENT VII

In suits at common law, where the value in controversy shall exceed twenty dollars, the right of trial by jury shall be preserved, and no fact tried by a jury, shall be otherwise reexamined in any Court of the United States, than according to the rules of the common law.

AMENDMENT VIII

Excessive bail shall not be required, nor excessive fines imposed, nor cruel and unusual punishments inflicted.

AMENDMENT IX

The enumeration in the Constitution, of certain rights, shall not be construed to deny or disparage others retained by the people.

AMENDMENT X

The powers not delegated to the United States by the Constitution, nor prohibited by it to the States, are reserved to the States respectively, or to the people.

Protections of the Second Amendment

For many years, the exact nature of the right to bear arms has been debated. The introductory clause, "A well regulated Militia, being necessary to the security of a free State," led some to argue that the right existed only in relationship to a national or state military service. However, in two recent cases, the Supreme Court affirmed the right of individuals to "bear arms." In the first case, *District of Columbia v. Heller*, the Court decided that the federal government could not violate an individual's Second Amendment right, and, in the second case, *McDonald v. City of Chicago*, the Court decided that the amendment also applied to the states. Excerpts from the Court Syllabus for each case follow and summarize the Court's reasoning.

District of Columbia v. Heller
554 U.S. 570 (2008)

District of Columbia law bans handgun possession by making it a crime to carry an unregistered firearm and prohibiting the registration of handguns; provides separately that no person may carry an unlicensed handgun, but authorizes the police chief to issue 1-year licenses; and requires residents to keep lawfully owned firearms unloaded and dissembled or bound by a trigger lock or similar device. Respondent Heller, a D. C. special policeman, applied to register a handgun he wished to keep at home, but the District refused. He filed this suit seeking, on Second Amendment grounds, to enjoin the city from enforcing the bar on handgun registration, the licensing requirement insofar as it prohibits carrying an unlicensed firearm in the home, and the trigger-lock requirement insofar as it prohibits the use of functional firearms in the home. The District Court dismissed the suit, but the D. C. Circuit reversed, holding that the Second Amendment protects an individual's right to possess firearms and that the city's total ban on handguns, as well as its requirement that firearms in the home be kept nonfunctional even when necessary for self-defense, violated that right.

Held:

1. The Second Amendment protects an individual right to possess a firearm unconnected with service in a militia, and to use that arm for traditionally lawful purposes, such as self-defense within the home.

   (a) The Amendment's prefatory clause announces a purpose, but does not limit or expand the scope of the second part, the operative clause. The operative clause's text and history demonstrate

that it connotes an individual right to keep and bear arms.

   (b) The prefatory clause comports with the Court's interpretation of the operative clause. The "militia" comprised all males physically capable of acting in concert for the common defense. The Antifederalists feared that the Federal Government would disarm the people in order to disable this citizens' militia, enabling a politicized standing army or a select militia to rule. The response was to deny Congress power to abridge the ancient right of individuals to keep and bear arms, so that the ideal of a citizens' militia would be preserved.

   (c) The Court's interpretation is confirmed by analogous arms-bearing rights in state constitutions that preceded and immediately followed the Second Amendment.

   (d) The Second Amendment's drafting history, while of dubious interpretive worth, reveals three state Second Amendment proposals that unequivocally referred to an individual right to bear arms.

   (e) Interpretation of the Second Amendment by scholars, courts and legislators, from immediately after its ratification through the late 19th century also supports the Court's conclusion.

   (f) None of the Court's precedents forecloses the Court's interpretation. Neither *United States v. Cruikshank*, 92 U.S. 542, nor *Presser v. Illinois*, 116 U.S. 252, refutes the individual-rights interpretation. *United States v. Miller*, 307 U.S. 174,

(continued)

(continued)

does not limit the right to keep and bear arms to militia purposes, but rather limits the type of weapon to which the right applies to those used by the militia, i.e., those in common use for lawful purposes.

2. Like most rights, the Second Amendment right is not unlimited. It is not a right to keep and carry any weapon whatsoever in any manner whatsoever and for whatever purpose: For example, concealed weapons prohibitions have been upheld under the Amendment or state analogues. The Court's opinion should not be taken to cast doubt on longstanding prohibitions on the possession of firearms by felons and the mentally ill, or laws forbidding the carrying of firearms in sensitive places such as schools and government buildings, or laws imposing conditions and qualifications on the commercial sale of arms. *Miller*'s holding that the sorts of weapons protected are those "in common use at the time" finds support in the historical tradition of prohibiting the carrying of dangerous and unusual weapons.

3. The handgun ban and the trigger-lock requirement (as applied to self-defense) violate the Second Amendment. The District's total ban on handgun possession in the home amounts to a prohibition on an entire class of "arms" that Americans overwhelmingly choose for the lawful purpose of self-defense. Under any of the standards of scrutiny the Court has applied to enumerated constitutional rights, this prohibition—in the place where the importance of the lawful defense of self, family, and property is most acute—would fail constitutional muster. Similarly, the requirement that any lawful firearm in the home be disassembled or bound by a trigger lock makes it impossible for citizens to use arms for the core lawful purpose of self-defense and is hence unconstitutional. Because Heller conceded at oral argument that the D.C. licensing law is permissible if it is not enforced arbitrarily and capriciously, the Court assumes that a license will satisfy his prayer for relief and does not address the licensing requirement. Assuming he is not disqualified from exercising Second Amendment rights, the District must permit Heller to register his handgun and must issue him a license to carry it in the home.

McDonald v. City of Chicago
561 U.S. ___ (2010)

Two years ago, in *District of Columbia v. Heller*, 554 U.S. 570, this Court held that the Second Amendment protects the right to keep and bear arms for the purpose of self-defense and struck down a District of Columbia law that banned the possession of handguns in the home. Chicago (hereinafter City) and the village of Oak Park, a Chicago suburb, have laws effectively banning handgun possession by almost all private citizens. After *Heller,* petitioners filed this federal suit against the City, which was consolidated with two related actions, alleging that the City's handgun ban has left them vulnerable to criminals. They sought a declaration that the ban and several related City ordinances violate the Second and Fourteenth Amendments. Rejecting petitioners' argument that the ordinances are unconstitutional, the court noted that the Seventh Circuit previously had upheld the

constitutionality of a handgun ban, that *Heller* had explicitly refrained from opining on whether the Second Amendment applied to the States, and that the court had a duty to follow established Circuit precedent. The Seventh Circuit affirmed, relying on three 19th-century cases—*United States v. Cruikshank*, 92 U.S. 542, *Presser v. Illinois*, 116 U.S. 252, and *Miller v. Texas*, 153 U.S. 535—which were decided in the wake of this Court's interpretation of the Fourteenth Amendments Privileges or Immunities Clause in the *Slaughter-House Cases*, 16 Wall. 36.

Held: The judgment is reversed, and the case is remanded. Justice Alito delivered the opinion of the Court concluding that the Fourteenth Amendment incorporates the Second Amendment right, recognized in *Heller,* to keep and bear arms for the purpose of self-defense.

(continued)

(continued)

(a) Petitioners base their case on two submissions. Primarily, they argue that the right to keep and bear arms is protected by the Privileges or Immunities Clause of the Fourteenth Amendment and that the *Slaughter-House Cases'* narrow interpretation of the Clause should now be rejected. As a secondary argument, they contend that the Fourteenth Amendment's Due Process Clause incorporates the Second Amendment right. Chicago and Oak Park (municipal respondents) maintain that a right set out in the Bill of Rights applies to the States only when it is an indispensable attribute of *any* "'civilized'" legal system. If it is possible to imagine a civilized country that does not recognize the right, municipal respondents assert, that right is not protected by due process. And since there are civilized countries that ban or strictly regulate the private possession of handguns, they maintain that due process does not preclude such measures.

...

(b) Whether the Second Amendment right to keep and bear arms applies to the States is considered in light of the Court's precedents applying the Bill of Rights' protections to the States.

(1) In the late 19th century, the Court began to hold that the Due Process Clause prohibits the States from infringing Bill of Rights protections. See, *e.g., Hurtado v. California*, 110 U.S. 516.

(2) Justice Black championed the alternative theory that §1 of the Fourteenth Amendment totally incorporated all of the Bill of Rights' provisions, see, *e.g., Adamson v. California*, 332 U.S. 46 (Black, J., dissenting), but the Court never has embraced that theory.

(3) The Court eventually moved in the direction advocated by Justice Black, by adopting a theory of selective incorporation by which the Due Process Clause incorporates particular rights contained in the first eight Amendments. See, *e.g., Gideon v. Wainright*, 372 U.S. 335. The Court clarified that the governing standard is whether a particular Bill of Rights protection is fundamental to our Nation's particular scheme of ordered liberty and system of justice. *Duncan, supra*, at 149, n. 14. The Court eventually held that almost all of the Bill of Rights' guarantees met the requirements for protection under the Due Process Clause.

(c) The Fourteenth Amendment makes the Second Amendment right to keep and bear arms fully applicable to the States.

(1) The Court must decide whether that right is fundamental to the Nation's scheme of ordered liberty, *Duncan v. Louisiana*, 391 U.S. 145, or, as the Court has said in a related context, whether it is "deeply rooted in this Nation's history and tradition," *Washington v. Glucksberg*, 521 U.S. 702. *Heller* points unmistakably to the answer. Self-defense is a basic right, recognized by many legal systems from ancient times to the present, and the *Heller* Court held that individual self-defense is "the central component" of the Second Amendment right. 554 U.S., at ___. Explaining that "the need for defense of self, family, and property is most acute" in the home, *ibid.*, the Court found that this right applies to handguns because they are "the most preferred firearm in the nation to 'keep' and use for protection of one's home and family," *id.*, at ___. It thus concluded that citizens must be permitted "to use [handguns] for the core lawful purpose of self-defense." *Id.*, at ___. *Heller* also clarifies that this right is "deeply rooted in this Nation's history and traditions," *Glucksberg, supra*, at 721. *Heller* explored the right's origins in English law and noted the esteem with which the right was regarded during the colonial era and at the time of the ratification of the Bill of Rights. This is powerful evidence that the right was regarded as fundamental in the sense relevant here. That understanding persisted in the years immediately following the Bill of Rights' ratification and is confirmed by the state constitutions of that era, which protected the right to keep and bear arms.

(2) A survey of the contemporaneous history also demonstrates clearly that the Fourteenth Amendment's Framers and ratifiers counted the right to keep and bear arms among those fundamental rights necessary to the Nation's system of ordered liberty.

(i) By the 1850's, the fear that the National Government would disarm the universal militia had largely faded, but the right to keep and bear arms was highly valued for self-defense. In Congressional debates on the proposed

(continued)

(continued)

Amendment, its legislative proponents in the 39th Congress referred to the right to keep and bear arms as a fundamental right deserving of protection. Evidence from the period immediately following the Amendment's ratification confirms that that right was considered fundamental.

Justice Alito, joined by The Chief Justice, Justice Scalia, and Justice Kennedy, concluded, in Parts II–C, IV, and V, that the Fourteenth Amendment's Due Process

Clause incorporates the Second Amendment right recognized in *Heller*.

(a) Petitioners argue that that the Second Amendment right is one of the "privileges or immunities of citizens of the United States." There is no need to reconsider the Court's interpretation of the Privileges or Immunities Clause in the *Slaughter-House Cases* because, for many decades, the Court has analyzed the question whether particular rights are protected against state infringement under the Fourteenth Amendment's Due Process Clause.

Protections Found in Other Amendments

🏛 **Reconstruction Amendments**

The Thirteenth, Fourteenth, and Fifteenth Amendments that were enacted after the Civil War and meant to provide constitutional protection to the newly freed slaves

In addition to the Bill of Rights, other amendments guarantee important civil rights and liberties. The Thirteenth, Fourteenth, and Fifteenth Amendments, also known as the **Reconstruction Amendments**, were enacted after the Civil War and were meant to provide constitutional protection to the newly freed slaves. The Thirteenth Amendment outlawed slavery and involuntary servitude anywhere in the United States, and the Fifteenth Amendment prohibited both federal and state governments from interfering with the right to vote on account of race or color. The Fourteenth Amendment prohibits states from denying individuals due process of law, equal protection of the law, or the privileges and immunities of a citizen. The term *state* as used in the Fourteenth Amendment includes not only state governments, but also local governments. The Fourteenth Amendment is discussed in more detail later in the chapter.

🏛 **poll tax**

A fee required of an individual in order to vote.

One of the most fundamental rights of American citizens is the right to vote. This right is protected by several amendments in addition to the Fifteenth Amendment described above. The Nineteenth Amendment extended the right to vote to women; and the Twenty-sixth extended it to eighteen-year-olds. The Twenty-fourth Amendment prohibits **poll taxes**. These amendments apply to both federal and state governments and prohibit any activity by federal or state governments that interferes with the rights guaranteed in the amendments.

The Bill of Rights and State Government

Whether the Bill of Rights was intended to act as a limit on the power of only the federal government or whether it was also meant to apply to state and local governments is not clear from the Constitution itself. The First Amendment specifically mentions Congress (i.e., Congress shall make no law ...), but the other amendments are not this specific. For example, the Fourth Amendment refers to the "right of the people" and the Fifth Amendment refers to "no person." Thus, it was up to the Supreme Court to determine the extent of the applicability of these amendments. This was done in 1833 in the case of *Barron v. Baltimore*. In this case, the City of Baltimore took the plaintiff's property for public purposes without compensating him for it. Plaintiff Barron claimed that the Fifth Amendment was violated. The defendant did not contest the facts. Instead, it argued that the Fifth Amendment applied only to the federal government. As a local government, it was not bound by the Bill of Rights. The Supreme Court agreed. The opinion follows. In the opinion, federal government is referred to as the "general government."

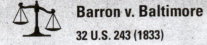

Barron v. Baltimore
32 U.S. 243 (1833)

MR. CHIEF JUSTICE MARSHALL delivered the opinion of the Court.

The plaintiff contends, that it comes within that clause in the fifth amendment to the constitution, which inhibits the taking of private property for public use, without just compensation. He insists, that this amendment being in favor of the liberty of the citizen, ought to be so construed as to restrain the legislative power of a state, as well as that of the United States. If this proposition be untrue, the court can take no jurisdiction of the cause.

The question thus presented is, we think, of great importance, but not of much difficulty. The constitution was ordained and established by the people of the United States for themselves, for their own government, and not for the government of the individual states. Each state established a constitution for itself, and in that constitution, provided such limitations and restrictions on the powers of its particular government, as its judgment dictated. The people of the United States framed such a government for the United States as they supposed best adapted to their situation and best calculated to promote their interests. If these propositions be correct, the fifth amendment must be understood as restraining the power of the general government, not as applicable to the states. In their several constitutions, they have imposed such restrictions on their respective governments, as their own wisdom suggested; such as they deemed most proper for themselves. It is a subject on which they judge exclusively, and with which others interfere no further than they are supposed to have a common interest.

Had the people of the several states, or any of them, required changes in their constitutions; had they required additional safe-guards to liberty from the apprehended encroachments of their particular governments; the remedy was in their own hands, and could have been applied by themselves. A convention could have been assembled by the discontented state, and the required improvements could have been made by itself.

But it is universally understood, it is a part of the history of the day, that the great revolution which established the constitution of the United States, was not effected without immense opposition. Serious fears were extensively entertained, that those powers which the patriot statesmen, who then watched over the interests of our country, deemed essential to union, and to the attainment of those unvaluable objects for which union was sought, might be exercised in a manner dangerous to liberty. In almost every convention by which the constitution was adopted, amendments to guard against the abuse of power were recommended. These amendments demanded security against the apprehended encroachments of the general government—not against those of the local governments. In compliance with a sentiment thus generally expressed, to quiet fears thus extensively entertained, amendments were proposed by the required majority in congress, and adopted by the states. These amendments contain no expression indicating an intention to apply them to the state governments. This court cannot so apply them.

We are of opinion, that the provision in the fifth amendment to the constitution, declaring that private property shall not be taken for public use, without just compensation, is intended solely as a limitation on the exercise of power by the government of the United States, and is not applicable to the legislation of the states. This court, therefore, has no jurisdiction of the cause, and it is dismissed.

The *Barron* decision made it clear that other than the protections found in the Articles, the U.S. Constitution did not afford any protection against infringement of civil rights and liberties by state or local government. The practical effect of this rule was that the federal courts, including the Supreme Court, were powerless to act in cases where parties claimed that a state violated their rights. The sole remedies for such claims had to come from state courts. After the Civil War, it was apparent that this was not an adequate way to protect the rights of ex-slaves. As a result, the Thirteenth, Fourteenth, and Fifteenth Amendments were added to the Constitution, extending federal protection to state infringement of civil rights in some situations. The Fourteenth Amendment, which is the most important of the three, contains provisions that have become instrumental in the development of federal protection against state deprivation of civil rights.

The Fourteenth Amendment

The Fourteenth Amendment set forth four basic concepts:

1. All persons born in the United States or naturalized are citizens.
2. No state can make or enforce laws that abridge the privilege or immunities of citizens.
3. No state can deprive a person of life, liberty, or property without due process.
4. No state can deny a person equal protection of the laws.

The first provision, making all persons citizens, was necessary because of an earlier Supreme Court case, the *Dred Scott* decision, in which the Court held that slaves were not citizens and therefore not entitled to constitutional protections. *Scott v. Sandford*, 60 U.S. 393 (1857). The other rights listed in the Fourteenth Amendment to the Constitution cannot be defined with textbook precision, a fact that was recognized by the Supreme Court in various decisions dealing with the Fourteenth Amendment. Consider the Court's early attempts to explain the key terms: "privileges and immunities," "due process," and "equal protection."

Privileges and Immunities

"The inquiry, he says, is, what are the privileges and immunities of citizens of the several States? We feel no hesitation in confining these expressions to those privileges and immunities which are fundamental; which belong of right to the citizens of all free governments, and which have at all times been enjoyed by citizens of the several States which compose this Union, from the time of their becoming free, independent, and sovereign. What these fundamental principles are, it would be more tedious than difficult to enumerate. They may all, however, be comprehended under the following general heads: protection by the government, with the right to acquire and possess property of every kind, and to pursue and obtain happiness and safety, subject, nevertheless, to such restraints as the government may prescribe for the general good of the whole." *Slaughter-House Cases*, 83 U.S. 36 (1872) (quoting *Corfield v. Coryell*, decided by Mr. Justice Washington in the Circuit Court for the District of Pennsylvania in 1823).

Due Process

"Is it a fundamental principle of liberty and justice which inheres in the very idea of free government and is the inalienable right of a citizen of such a government? If it is, and if it is of a nature that pertains to process of law, this court has declared it to be essential to due process of law." *Twining v. New Jersey*, 211 U.S. 78 (1908).

Equal Protection

"While the equal protection clause does not require a legislature to achieve 'abstract symmetry' or to classify with 'mathematical nicety', that clause does require lawmakers to refrain from invidious distinctions of the sort drawn by the statute challenged in this case." *Reed v. Reed*, 404 U.S. 71 (1971).

The Incorporation Doctrine

Shortly after the Fourteenth Amendment was adopted in 1868, parties argued that the Fourteenth Amendment extended the Bill of Rights to state as well as federal action. This concept is sometimes referred to as the **Incorporation Doctrine**. The Supreme Court, however, never accepted the argument that the Bill of Rights was totally incorporated. Instead, over many years, it selectively incorporated specific rights.

The Supreme Court first considered the issue of incorporation in the *Slaughter-House Cases*, 83 U.S. 36 (1872). The plaintiff in this case argued that the Privileges and Immunities Clause of the Fourteenth Amendment incorporated at least some provisions of the Bill of Rights. The *Slaughter-House Cases* resulted from a number of different lawsuits that challenged a Louisiana law giving one corporation a monopoly on operating animal

Incorporation Doctrine
The legal theory used by the Supreme Court to apply the rights found in the Bill of Rights to the states by using the Fourteenth Amendment requirement that states provide due process to all their citizens.

slaughterhouses. Supposedly this was done as a sanitation measure. As a result of the law, several businesses were forced to close. These businesses sued in state courts claiming, among other things, that the Louisiana law violated the Privileges and Immunities Clause of the Fourteenth Amendment. After losing at the state level, they petitioned for a hearing before the Supreme Court asking the Court to declare the Louisiana law unconstitutional. In a divided opinion, the Court held that the Privileges and Immunities Clause of the Fourteenth Amendment did not incorporate any of the Bill of Rights.

A few years after the *Slaughter-House Cases*, the Supreme Court considered if the Due Process Clause of the Fourteenth Amendment applied any of the Bill of Rights to states. In the case of *Hurtado v. California*, 110 U.S. 516 (1884), the Court reviewed a death penalty case in a state that did not hold grand jury hearings, a right guaranteed in the Bill of Rights. Hurtado claimed that this violated the Fourteenth Amendment Due Process Clause. The Court disagreed saying:

> "The fourteenth amendment," as was said by Mr. Justice Bradley in *Missouri v. Lewis*, 101 U.S. 22-31, "does not profess to secure to all persons in the United States the benefit of the same laws and the same remedies. Great diversities in these respects may exist in two states separated only by an imaginary line. On one side of this line there may be a right of trial by jury, and on the other side no such right. Each state prescribes its own modes of judicial proceeding."

In *Hurtado*, the Supreme Court held that due process did not require a grand jury hearing. However, the decision in *Hurtado* did not rule out the possibility that some of the Bill of Rights might be included in the concept of due process. In the 1908 case *Twining v. New Jersey*, the Supreme Court stated that the Due Process Clause might incorporate some of the rights found in the Bill of Rights. In *Twining* the Supreme Court decided whether the Fifth Amendment protection against self-incrimination was a requirement of due process. Although the Court decided that it was not, it admitted that some of the rights in the Bill of Rights might be incorporated. The Court also explained how it determines if any specific right is required of due process. The following is an excerpt from the opinion.

Twining v. New Jersey
211 U.S. 78 (1908)

It is possible that some of the personal rights safeguarded by the first eight Amendments against national action may also be safeguarded against state action, because a denial of them would be a denial of due process of law. If this is so, it is not because those rights are enumerated in the first eight Amendments, but because they are of such a nature that they are included in the conception of due process of law. Few phrases of the law are so elusive of exact apprehension as this. Doubtless the difficulties of ascertaining its connotation have been increased in American jurisprudence, where it has been embodied in constitutions and put to new uses as a limit on legislative power. This court has always declined to give a comprehensive definition of it, and has preferred that its full meaning should be gradually ascertained by the process of inclusion and exclusion in the course of the decisions of cases as they arise. There are certain general principles, well settled, however, which narrow the field of discussion, and may serve as helps to correct conclusions. These principles grow out of the proposition universally accepted by American courts that the words "due process of law" are equivalent in meaning to the words "law of the land," contained in that chapter of Magna Charta which provides that "no freeman shall be taken, or imprisoned, or disseised, or outlawed, or exiled, or any wise destroyed; nor shall we go upon him, nor send upon

(continued)

(continued)

him, but by the lawful judgment of his peers or by the law of the land." From the consideration of the meaning of the words in the light of their historical origin this court has drawn the following conclusions:

First. What is due process of law may be ascertained by an examination of those settled usages and modes of proceedings existing in the common and statute law of England before the emigration of our ancestors, and shown not to have been unsuited to their civil and political condition by having been acted on by them after the settlement of this country.

Second. It does not follow, however, that a procedure settled in English law at the time of the emigration, and brought to this country and practised by our ancestors, is an essential element of due process of law. If that were so, the procedure of the first half of the seventeenth century would be fastened upon the American jurisprudence like a straight jacket, only to be unloosed by constitutional amendment.

Third. But, consistently with the requirements of due process, no change in ancient procedure can be made which disregards those fundamental principles, to be ascertained from time to time by judicial action, which have relation to process of law, and protect the citizen in his private right, and guard him against the arbitrary action of government. This idea has been many times expressed in differing words by this court, and it seems well to cite some expressions of it. The words "due process of law" were intended to secure the individual from the arbitrary exercise of the powers of government, unrestrained by the established principles of private rights and distributive justice. This court has never attempted to define with precision the words "due process of law." It is sufficient to say that there are certain immutable principles of justice which inhere in the very idea of free government which no member of the Union may disregard.

We prefer to rest our decision on broader grounds, and inquire whether the exemption from self-incrimination is of such a nature that it must be included in the conception of due process. Is it a fundamental principle of liberty and justice which inheres in the very idea of free government and is the inalienable right of a citizen of such a government? If it is, and if it is of a nature that pertains to process of law, this court has declared it to be essential to due process of law. In approaching such a question it must not be forgotten that in a free representative government nothing is more fundamental than the right of the people, through their appointed servants, to govern themselves in accordance with their own will, except so far as they have restrained themselves by constitutional limits specifically established, and that, in our peculiar dual form of government, nothing is more fundamental than the full power of the state to order its own affairs and govern its own people, except so far as the Federal Constitution, expressly or by fair implication, has withdrawn that power. The power of the people of the states to make and alter their laws at pleasure is the greatest security for liberty and justice, this court has said in *Hurtado v. California*, 110 U.S. 516, 527. We are not invested with the jurisdiction to pass upon the expediency, wisdom, or justice of the laws of the states as declared by their courts, but only to determine their conformity with the Federal Constitution and the paramount laws enacted pursuant to it. Under the guise of interpreting the Constitution we must take care that we do not import into the discussion our own personal views of what would be wise, just, and fitting rules of government to be adopted by a free people, and confound them with constitutional limitations.

In *Twining*, the Court concluded that the right against self-incrimination was not a requirement of due process. This decision was overruled by subsequent cases and the right against self-incrimination is now considered to be part of due process.

After *Twining*, the Supreme Court continued to hear cases where state action was claimed to be in violation of the Due Process Clause. In the 1960s, under Chief Justice Earl Warren, the number of such cases grew. During this era, such famous cases as *Miranda v. Arizona* and *Gideon v. Wainwright* were decided and almost all of the rights spelled out in the Bill of Rights were incorporated into the Fourteenth Amendment provision on due process. Today, only a few of the rights found in the first ten amendments do not pertain to state action. The Supreme Court ruled that the Fifth Amendment right to a grand jury hearing and the Seventh Amendment right to a civil jury trial are not incorporated. The Court has not ruled on whether the Third Amendment rights regarding quartering of soldiers or the Eighth Amendment prohibition on excessive fines are incorporated. See Table 7-1.

Table 7-1	A Historical Look at the Development of the Incorporation Doctrine	
1833	The Bill of Rights did not apply to state and local governments.	*Barron v. Baltimore*, 32 U.S. 243
1857	Slaves were not citizens and not entitled to any constitutional protection.	*Dred Scott* decision
1868	States were prohibited from denying its citizens due process, equal protection or privileges and immunities.	Fourteenth Amendment
1872	The Privileges and Immunities Clause of the Fourteenth Amendment did not incorporate any of the Bill of Rights.	*Slaughter-House Cases*, 83 U.S. 36
1884	In holding that due process did not require a grand jury hearing (a requirement of the Fifth Amendment), the Supreme Court did not rule out the possibility that some of the Bill of Rights might be included in the concept of due process.	*Hurtado v. California*, 110 U.S. 516
1908	Rights that are a fundamental principle of liberty and justice, which inhere in the very idea of free government and are the inalienable rights of a citizen of such a government are protected by due process. (Here, due process did not apply to self-incrimination, although this was later changed.)	*Twining v. New Jersey*, 211 U.S. 78
Current View	The Fourteenth Amendment Due Process Clause extends most of the Bill of Rights protections against action by State (the Incorporation Doctrine).	*McDonald v. City of Chicago*, 561 U.S. (2010)

© Cengage Learning 2013

Due Process Clauses of the Fifth and Fourteenth Amendments

ALTHOUGH MOST OF THE RIGHTS listed in the Bill of Rights are incorporated into the Fourteenth Amendment due process requirements, due process is certainly not limited to these rights. Both the Fifth and Fourteenth Amendments contain Due Process Clauses and the Court has used these as a basis for numerous procedural and substantive rights. The federal and state civil and criminal court processes must adhere to due process standards that include proper notice and the opportunity for a fair hearing. In addition, several other economic, personal, and political rights are related to due process. This topic is discussed in detail in Chapters 9 and 10.

The Equal Protection Clause of the Fourteenth Amendment

THE SUPREME COURT USES THE Equal Protection Clause as a basis for invalidating discriminatory state laws. This clause is found only in the Fourteenth Amendment and therefore applies only to state action, not to action by the federal government. However, the relationship between equal protection and due process is so close that the Court applies the notions of equal protection to the federal government through the Fifth Amendment Due Process Clause.

The Fourteenth Amendment and the Equal Protection Clause were originally intended to prevent states from discriminating against African Americans. Its application, however, is not limited to this type of discrimination. On the other hand, it was never intended to be a total ban on all laws that treat people differently. In determining if a law violates the Equal Protection Clause, the Supreme Court considers the type of discrimination and the individuals discriminated against. If the Court determines that a law discriminates on the basis of race or ethnicity, the law will probably be found to be unconstitutional. On the other hand, if the law has a legitimate social or economic goal and does not discriminate on the basis of a physical characteristic, such as race or gender, it will probably be upheld. An example of this type of law is found in California where property taxes are based on the purchase price of a home. The result of this law is that two people owning identical homes pay substantially different property taxes if one purchased the property years before the other when the home values were much lower. The Supreme Court found no equal protection violation here. *Nordlinger v. Hahn*, 505 U.S. 1 (1992).

A Point of Law

Nordlinger v. Hahn, 505 U.S. 1 (1992)

The Equal Protection Cause prohibits certain types of discrimination but does not guarantee that all people are treated equally. Thus, a state law resulting in disparity of real estate taxes was not unconstitutional because it had a legitimate social or economic goal.

One question that faced the nation for years was whether the Equal Protection Clause was violated by the practice of segregation when facilities were "separate but equal." In a landmark decision in 1896, *Plessy v. Ferguson*, 163 U.S. 537, the Supreme Court decided that a law requiring blacks to ride in separate railroad cars did not violate the Equal Protection Clause. In 1954, the Court readdressed this issue in one of the most important cases ever decided, *Brown v. Board of Education*. The plaintiffs in *Brown* asked the Court to abolish the system of segregated public schools, claiming that this violated the Equal Protection Clause. Like prior Supreme Courts, this Court considered the historical basis for the Fourteenth Amendment. Unlike prior Supreme Courts, however, this Court discounted the history of the times and emphasized current social context of public education. The unanimous decision follows.

Brown v. Board of Education

347 U.S. 483 (1954)

Mr. Chief Justice Warren delivered the opinion of the Court.

These cases come to us from the States of Kansas, South Carolina, Virginia, and Delaware. They are premised on different facts and different local conditions, but a common legal question justifies their consideration together in this consolidated opinion.

In each of the cases, minors of the Negro race, through their legal representatives, seek the aid of the courts in obtaining admission to the public schools of their community on a nonsegregated basis. In each instance, they had been denied admission to schools attended by white children under laws requiring or permitting segregation according to race. This segregation was alleged to

(continued)

(continued)

deprive the plaintiffs of the equal protection of the laws under the Fourteenth Amendment. In each of the cases other than the Delaware case, a three-judge federal district court denied relief to the plaintiffs on the so-called "separate but equal" doctrine announced by this Court in *Plessy v. Ferguson*, 163 U.S. 537 (1896). Under that doctrine, equality of treatment is accorded when the races are provided substantially equal facilities, even though these facilities be separate. In the Delaware case, the Supreme Court of Delaware adhered to that doctrine, but ordered that the plaintiffs be admitted to the white schools because of their superiority to the Negro schools.

The plaintiffs contend that segregated public schools are not "equal" and cannot be made "equal," and that hence they are deprived of the equal protection of the laws. Because of the obvious importance of the question presented, the Court took jurisdiction.

In the first cases in this Court construing the Fourteenth Amendment, decided shortly after its adoption, the Court interpreted it as proscribing all state-imposed discriminations against the Negro race. The doctrine of "separate but equal" did not make its appearance in this Court until 1896 in the case of *Plessy v. Ferguson, supra,* involving not education but transportation. American courts have since labored with the doctrine for over half a century. In this Court, there have been six cases involving the "separate but equal" doctrine in the field of public education. In *Cumming v. County Board of Education*, 175 U.S. 528, and *Gong Lum v. Rice*, 275 U.S. 78, the validity of the doctrine itself was not challenged. In more recent cases, all on the graduate school level, inequality was found in that specific benefits enjoyed by white students were denied to Negro students of the same educational qualifications. In none of these cases was it necessary to re-examine the doctrine to grant relief to the Negro plaintiff. And in *Sweatt v. Painter*, 339 U.S. 629, the Court expressly reserved decision on the question whether *Plessy v. Ferguson* should be held inapplicable to public education.

In the instant cases, that question is directly presented. Here, unlike *Sweatt v. Painter*, there are findings below that the Negro and white schools involved have been equalized, or are being equalized, with respect to buildings, curricula, qualifications and salaries of teachers, and other "tangible" factors. Our decision, therefore, cannot turn on merely a comparison of these tangible factors in the Negro and white schools involved in each of the cases. We must look instead to the effect of segregation itself on public education.

In approaching this problem, we cannot turn the clock back to 1868 when the Amendment was adopted, or even to 1896 when *Plessy v. Ferguson* was written. We must consider public education in the light of its full development and its present place in American life throughout the Nation. Only in this way can it be determined if segregation in public schools deprives these plaintiffs of the equal protection of the laws.

Today, education is perhaps the most important function of state and local governments. Compulsory school attendance laws and the great expenditures for education both demonstrate our recognition of the importance of education to our democratic society. It is required in the performance of our most basic public responsibilities, even service in the armed forces. It is the very foundation of good citizenship. Today it is a principal instrument in awakening the child to cultural values, in preparing him for later professional training, and in helping him to adjust normally to his environment. In these days, it is doubtful that any child may reasonably be expected to succeed in life if he is denied the opportunity of an education. Such an opportunity, where the state has undertaken to provide it, is a right which must be made available to all on equal terms.

We come then to the question presented: Does segregation of children in public schools solely on the basis of race, even though the physical facilities and other "tangible" factors may be equal, deprive the children of the minority group of equal educational opportunities? We believe that it does.

To separate children from others of similar age and qualifications solely because of their race generates a feeling of inferiority as to their status in the community that may affect their hearts and minds in a way unlikely ever to be undone. The effect of this separation on their educational opportunities was well stated by a finding in the Kansas case by a court which nevertheless felt compelled to rule against the Negro plaintiffs:

Segregation of white and colored children in public schools has a detrimental effect upon the colored children. The impact is greater when it has the sanction of the law; for the policy of separating the races is usually interpreted as denoting the inferiority of the negro group. A sense of inferiority affects the motivation of a child to learn. Segregation with

(continued)

(continued)

the sanction of law, therefore, has a tendency to [retard] the educational and mental development of negro children and to deprive them of some of the benefits they would receive in a racially integrated school system.

Whatever may have been the extent of psychological knowledge at the time of *Plessy v. Ferguson*, this finding is amply supported by modern authority. Any language in *Plessy v. Ferguson* contrary to this finding is rejected.

We conclude that in the field of public education the doctrine of "separate but equal" has no place. Separate educational facilities are inherently unequal. Therefore, we hold that the plaintiffs and others similarly situated for whom the actions have been brought are, by reason of the segregation complained of, deprived of the equal protection of the laws guaranteed by the Fourteenth Amendment. This disposition makes unnecessary any discussion whether such segregation also violates the Due Process Clause of the Fourteenth Amendment.

It is so ordered.

The Equal Protection Clause of the Fourteenth Amendment provides an important basis for many Supreme Court decisions affecting civil rights and liberties. This is discussed more fully in Chapter 8.

Privileges and Immunities Clause of the Fourteenth Amendment

IN THE *SLAUGHTER-HOUSE CASES*, the Supreme Court gave the Privileges and Immunities Clause of the Fourteenth Amendment a very restrictive interpretation, stating that it related to rights only in relationship to the federal government. After the *Slaughter-House Cases*, parties rarely relied on the Privileges and Immunities Clause as a source of protection against state activity, and, until recently, this clause was not considered to be an important source of civil rights and liberties. In 1999, however, the Court decided a case, *Saenz v. Roe*, 526 U.S. 489, indicating that this clause might become a more important consideration in evaluating violations of civil rights by states. This case arose because of a California law that restricted welfare benefits to individuals who resided in California for less than one year. The Court Syllabus explains.

Saenz v. Roe
526 U.S. 489 (1999)

California, which has the sixth highest welfare benefit levels in the country, sought to amend its Aid to Families with Dependent Children (AFDC) program in 1992 by limiting new residents, for the first year they live in the State, to the benefits they would have received in the State of their prior residence. Cal. Welf. & Inst. Code Ann. §11450.03. Although the Secretary of Health and Human Services approved the change—a requirement for it to go into effect—the Federal District Court enjoined its implementation, finding that, under *Shapiro v. Thompson*, 394 U.S. 618, and *Zobel v. Williams*, 457 U.S. 55, it penalized "the decision of new residents to migrate to California and be treated equally with existing residents," *Green v. Anderson*, 811 F. Supp. 516, 521. After the Ninth Circuit invalidated the Secretary's approval of §11450.03 in a separate proceeding, this Court ordered *Green* to be dismissed. The provision thus remained inoperative until after Congress enacted

(continued)

(continued)

the Personal Responsibility and Work Opportunity Reconciliation Act of 1996 (PRWORA), which replaced AFDC with Temporary Assistance to Needy Families (TANF). PRWORA expressly authorizes any State receiving a TANF grant to pay the benefit amount of another State's TANF program to residents who have lived in the State for less than 12 months. Since the Secretary no longer needed to approve §11450.03, California announced that enforcement would begin on April 1, 1997. On that date, respondents filed this class action, challenging the constitutionality of §11450.03's durational residency requirement and PRWORA's approval of that requirement. In issuing a preliminary injunction, the District Court found that PRWORA's existence did not affect its analysis in *Green*. Without reaching the merits, the Ninth Circuit affirmed the injunction.

Held:

1. Section 11450.03 violates Section 1 of the Fourteenth Amendment.

   (a) In assessing laws denying welfare benefits to newly arrived residents, this Court held in *Shapiro* that a State cannot enact durational residency requirements in order to inhibit the migration of needy persons into the State, and that a classification that has the effect of imposing a penalty on the right to travel violates the Equal Protection Clause absent a compelling governmental interest.

   (b) The right to travel embraces three different components: the right to enter and leave another State; the right to be treated as a welcome visitor while temporarily present in another State; and, for those travelers who elect to become permanent residents, the right to be treated like other citizens of that State.

   (c) The right of newly arrived citizens to the same privileges and immunities enjoyed by other citizens of their new State—the third aspect of the right to travel—is at issue here. That right is protected by the new arrival's status as both a state citizen and a United States citizen, and it is plainly identified in the Fourteenth Amendment's Privileges or Immunities Clause, see *Slaughter-House Cases*, 16 Wall. 36, 80. That newly arrived citizens have both state and federal capacities adds special force to their claim that they have the same rights as others who share their citizenship.

   (d) Since the right to travel embraces a citizen's right to be treated equally in her new State of residence, a discriminatory classification is itself a penalty. California's classifications are defined entirely by the period of residency and the location of the disfavored class members' prior residences. Within the category of new residents, those who lived in another country or in a State that had higher benefits than California are treated like lifetime residents; and within the broad subcategory of new arrivals who are treated less favorably, there are 45 smaller classes whose benefit levels are determined by the law of their former States. California's legitimate interest in saving money does not justify this discriminatory scheme. The Fourteenth Amendment's Citizenship Clause expressly equates citizenship with residence, *Zobel*, 457 U.S., at 69, and does not tolerate a hierarchy of subclasses of similarly situated citizens based on the location of their prior residences.

2. PRWORA's approval of durational residency requirements does not resuscitate §11450.03. This Court has consistently held that Congress may not authorize the States to violate the Fourteenth Amendment. Moreover, the protection afforded to a citizen by that Amendment's Citizenship Clause limits the powers of the National Government as well as the States. Congress' Article I powers to legislate are limited not only by the scope of the Framers' affirmative delegation, but also by the principle that the powers may not be exercised in a way that violates other specific provisions of the Constitution. See *Williams v. Rhodes*, 393 U.S. 23, 29.

134 F.3d 1400, affirmed.

JUSTICE STEVENS delivered the opinion of the Court, in which JUSTICES O'CONNOR, SCALIA, KENNEDY, SOUTER, GINSBURG, and BREYER joined. CHIEF JUSTICE REHNQUIST filed a dissenting opinion, in which JUSTICE THOMAS joined. JUSTICE THOMAS filed a dissenting opinion, in which CHIEF JUSTICE REHNQUIST joined.

Congress and Civil Rights Legislation

CONGRESS HAS THE AUTHORITY TO ENACT civil rights laws through its power to regulate interstate commerce (Chapter 4) and through express power given to Congress in the various reconstruction and voting amendments. In its attempt to guarantee civil rights to all, Congress enacted numerous laws prohibiting certain conduct by federal government, by state government, and by private individuals. Congressional power to enact civil rights laws affecting federal and state governments is generally acknowledged. However, congressional power to regulate private conduct often meets constitutional challenges. See Table 7-2.

Table 7-2 Summary of Civil Rights and Constitutional Amendments

Amendments	Rights Protected
Amendment I	Rights guaranteeing freedom of religion, speech, press, assembly, and right to petition the government
Amendment II	Right to bear arms
Amendment III	Prohibits soldiers from being quartered in private homes
Amendments IV, V, VI, and VIII	Rights of those suspected of or accused of crimes
Amendment V	General guarantee of due process from the federal government and a prohibition on the taking of property for public use without just compensation
Amendment VII	Right to a jury trial in certain civil cases where the amount in controversy exceeds $20
Amendments IX	Rights listed in the Constitution are not an exclusive list
Amendment X	Reaffirmation of states' rights to exercise power
Amendment XIII	Outlawed slavery and involuntary servitude anywhere in the United States
Amendment XIV	Prohibits states from denying individuals due process of law, equal protection of the law, or the privileges and immunities of a citizen
Amendment XV	Prohibits both the federal and state governments from interfering with the right to vote on account of race or color
Amendments XIX, XXIV, and XXVI	Extends the right to vote to women, eliminates poll taxes, and extends the right to vote to eighteen-year-olds

© Cengage Learning 2013

State Action Doctrine

One of the earliest attempts to use the Reconstruction Amendments as a basis for laws prohibiting private conduct occurred in 1875 when Congress enacted a Civil Rights Act prohibiting discrimination in all inns, public conveyances, and places of amusement. Anyone violating the act was guilty of a crime. The constitutionality of this act was questioned in 1883 in a series of cases referred to as the *Civil Rights Cases* (*United States v. Stanley*, 109 U.S. 3 (1883)). In these cases, the Supreme Court found the law unconstitutional because it outlawed private conduct, not state action. The following excerpt from the case explains the Court's interpretation of the Fourteenth Amendment.

Civil Rights Cases: United States v. Stanley
109 U.S. 3 (1883)

It declares that "no state shall make or enforce any law which shall abridge the privileges or immunities of citizens of the United States; nor shall any state deprive any person of life, liberty, or property without due process of law; nor deny to any person within its jurisdiction the equal protection of the laws." It is state action of a particular character that is prohibited. Individual invasion of individual rights is not the subject-matter of the amendment. It has a deeper and broader scope. It nullifies and makes void all state legislation, and state action of every kind, which impairs the privileges and immunities of citizens of the United States, or which injures them in life, liberty, or property without due process of law, or which denies to any of them the equal protection of the laws. It not only does this, but, in order that the national will, thus declared, may not be a mere brutum fulmen, the last section of the amendment invests congress with power to enforce it by appropriate legislation. To enforce what? To enforce the prohibition. To adopt appropriate legislation for correcting the effects of such prohibited state law and state acts, and thus to render them effectually null, void, and innocuous. This is the legislative power conferred upon congress, and this is the whole of it. It does not invest congress with power to legislate upon subjects which are within the domain of state legislation; but to provide modes of relief against state legislation, or state action, of the kind referred to. It does not authorize congress to create a code of municipal law for the regulation of private rights; but to provide modes of redress against the operation of state laws, and the action of state officers, executive or judicial, when these are subversive of the fundamental rights specified in the amendment. Positive rights and privileges are undoubtedly secured by the fourteenth amendment; but they are secured by way of prohibition against state laws and state proceedings affecting those rights and privileges, and by power given to congress to legislate for the purpose of carrying such prohibition into effect; and such legislation must necessarily be predicated upon such supposed state laws or state proceedings, and be directed to the correction of their operation and effect.

And so in the present case, until some state law has been passed, or some state action through its officers or agents has been taken, adverse to the rights of citizens sought to be protected by the fourteenth amendment, no legislation of the United States under said amendment, nor any proceeding under such legislation, can be called into activity, for the prohibitions of the amendment are against state laws and acts done under state authority.

The wrongful act of an individual, unsupported by any such authority, is simply a private wrong, or a crime of that individual; an invasion of the rights of the injured party, it is true, whether they affect his person, his property, or his reputation; but if not sanctioned in some way by the state, or not done under state authority, his rights remain in full force, and may presumably be vindicated by resort to the laws of the state for redress.

In addition to the Fourteenth and Fifteenth Amendments, parties in the *Civil Rights Cases* also argued that the Thirteenth Amendment authorized Congress to enact the law in question. Plaintiffs argued that the legislation outlawing discrimination in public places was justified under this amendment because such discrimination was a badge of slavery and a form of servitude. Unlike the Fourteenth and Fifteenth Amendments, the Thirteenth is not limited to state action. "Neither slavery nor involuntary servitude, except as a punishment for crime whereof the party shall have been duly convicted, shall exist within the United States, or any place subject to their jurisdiction." The Court disagreed with plaintiffs' arguments and stated that the Thirteenth Amendment was limited to slavery.

In recent times, the Supreme Court broadened its interpretation of the Thirteenth Amendment. In the case of *Jones v. Alfred H. Mayer Co.*, 392 U.S. 409 (1968), the Supreme Court ruled on the constitutionality of the part of the Civil Rights Act of 1968 that prohibited all racial discrimination in the sale or rental of property. The Act was based on congressional power under the Thirteenth Amendment. The Court held that this was a legitimate exercise of power. The Thirteenth Amendment did more than outlaw slavery, the Court stated. It also outlawed the vestiges of slavery and Congress has the right to determine what those vestiges are.

A Point of Law

Civil Rights Cases: United States v. Stanley, 109 U.S. 3 (1883)

Jones v. Alfred H. Mayer Co., 392 U.S. 409 (1968)

The Fourteenth and Fifteenth Amendments give Congress the power to enact civil rights laws that regulate the conduct of the states, not conduct of individuals. Although the Thirteenth Amendment is not limited to regulating state action, it was originally limited to outlawing slavery. It is now used as a basis for federal laws that interfere with the "vestiges" of slavery, such as racial discrimination in the sale or rental of property.

Interstate Commerce Clause

Because of the limitations found in the Reconstruction Amendments, Congress looked to other constitutional sources of power to enact civil rights laws that would limit behavior of private individuals or businesses. They turned to the Commerce Clause and enacted a number of laws that prohibited discrimination by businesses involved in interstate commerce. In response to years of civil rights violations, Congress enacted the Civil Rights Act of 1964. The power to enact this law was based on the Interstate Commerce Clause rather than the Reconstruction Amendments. This Act contains the following provisions:

Title II of the Civil Rights Act of 1964 prohibits discrimination in places of public accommodation because of race, color, religion, or national origin. Places of public accommodation are hotels, motels, restaurants, movie theaters, stadiums, and concert halls.

Title III of the Civil Rights Act of 1964 prohibits discrimination in public facilities because of race, color, religion, or national origin. Public facilities are facilities owned, operated, or managed by state or local governments.

Title IV of the Civil Rights Act of 1964 prohibits discrimination in public schools because of race, color, religion, sex, or national origin. Public schools include elementary schools, secondary schools, and public colleges and universities.

Title VII of the Civil Rights Act of 1964 prohibits employment discrimination because of race, color, religion, sex, or national origin.

Other important civil rights legislation provides the following protections:

The Voting Rights Act of 1965 prohibits discrimination in voting practices or procedures because of race and color.

The Fair Housing Act, contained in Title VIII of the Civil Rights Act of 1968, prohibits discrimination in the sale, financing, or rental of housing because of race, color, religion, sex, handicap, familial status, or national origin.

The Civil Rights of Institutionalized Persons Act of 1980 ensures that the rights of persons in institutions are protected against unconstitutional conditions. Those confined in government institutions include persons with disabilities, the elderly in government-run nursing homes, and prisoners.

The Americans with Disabilities Act of 1990 (ADA) prohibits discrimination in employment; in places of public accommodation, including all hotels, restaurants, retail stores, theaters, health-care facilities, convention centers, parks, and places of recreation; in transportation services; and in all activities of state and local governments because a person has a disability.

In cases such as *Heart of Atlanta Motel*, the Supreme Court upheld the power of Congress using the Interstate Commerce Clause as a basis for this legislation. Congress has also used its spending power to justify civil rights protections by requiring recipients of federal aid to follow certain standards of conduct. Following is the opinion from the *Heart of Atlanta Motel* case.

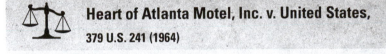

Heart of Atlanta Motel, Inc. v. United States,
379 U.S. 241 (1964)

MR. JUSTICE CLARK delivered the opinion of the Court. This is an action, attacking the constitutionality of Title II of the Civil Rights Act of 1964.

The Factual Background and Contentions of the Parties

Appellant owns and operates the Heart of Atlanta Motel which has 216 rooms available to transient guests. It is readily accessible to interstate highways 75 and 85 and state highways 23 and 41. Appellant solicits patronage from outside the State of Georgia through various national advertising media, including magazines of national circulation; it maintains over 50 billboards and highway signs within the State, soliciting patronage for the motel; it accepts convention trade from outside Georgia and approximately 75% of its registered guests are from out of State. Prior to passage of the Act the motel had followed a practice of refusing to rent rooms to Negroes, and it alleged that it intended to continue to do so. In an effort to perpetuate that policy this suit was filed.

The appellant contends that Congress in passing this Act exceeded its power to regulate commerce under Art. I § 8, cl. 3, of the Constitution of the United States.

The appellees counter that the unavailability to Negroes of adequate accommodations interferes significantly with interstate travel, and that Congress, under the Commerce Clause, has power to remove such obstructions and restraints.

The History of the Act

Congress first evidenced its interest in civil rights legislation in the Civil Rights or Enforcement Act of April 9, 1866. There followed four Acts, with a fifth, the Civil Rights Act of March 1, 1875, culminating the series. In 1883 this Court struck down the public accommodations sections of the 1875 Act in the *Civil Rights Cases*. No major legislation in this field had been enacted by Congress for 82 years when the Civil Rights Act of 1957 became law. It was followed by the Civil Rights Act of 1960. Three years later, on June 19, 1963, the late President Kennedy called for civil rights legislation in a message to Congress to which he attached a proposed bill. However, it was not until July 2, 1964, upon the recommendation of President Johnson, that the Civil Rights Act of 1964, here under attack, was finally passed.

The Act as finally adopted was most comprehensive, undertaking to prevent through peaceful and voluntary

(continued)

(continued)

settlement discrimination in voting, as well as in places of accommodation and public facilities, federally secured programs and in employment. Since Title II is the only portion under attack here, we confine our consideration to those public accommodation provisions.

Application of Title II to Heart of Atlanta Motel

It is admitted that the operation of the motel brings it within the provisions of the Act and that appellant refused to provide lodging for transient Negroes because of their race or color and that it intends to continue that policy unless restrained. The sole question posed is, therefore, the constitutionality of the Civil Rights Act of 1964 as applied to these facts. Our study of the legislative record, made in the light of prior cases, has brought us to the conclusion that Congress possessed ample power in this regard.

The Basis of Congressional Action

While the Act as adopted carried no congressional findings the record of its passage through each house is replete with evidence of the burdens that discrimination by race or color places upon interstate commerce. This testimony included the fact that our people have become increasingly mobile with millions of people of all races traveling from State to State; that Negroes in particular have been the subject of discrimination in transient accommodations, having to travel great distances to secure the same; that often they have been unable to obtain accommodations and have had to call upon friends to put them up overnight, and that these conditions had become so acute as to require the listing of available lodging for Negroes in a special guidebook which was itself "dramatic testimony to the difficulties" Negroes encounter in travel. These exclusionary practices were found to be nationwide. We shall not burden this opinion with further details since the voluminous testimony presents overwhelming evidence that discrimination by hotels and motels impedes interstate travel.

The Power of Congress Over Interstate Travel

The power of Congress to deal with these obstructions depends on the meaning of the Commerce Clause. Its meaning was first enunciated 140 years ago by the great Chief Justice John Marshall in *Gibbons v. Ogden,* 9 Wheat. 1 (1824), in these words: "The subject to be regulated is commerce; and ... to ascertain the extent of the power, it becomes necessary to settle the meaning of the word. The counsel for the appellee would limit it to traffic, to buying and selling, or the interchange of commodities ... but it is something more: it is intercourse ... between nations, and parts of nations, in all its branches, and is regulated by prescribing rules for carrying on that intercourse."

In short, the determinative test of the exercise of power by the Congress under the Commerce Clause is simply whether the activity sought to be regulated is "commerce which concerns more States than one" and has a real and substantial relation to the national interest. Let us now turn to this facet of the problem.

That the "intercourse" of which the Chief Justice spoke included the movement of persons through more States than one was settled as early as 1849, in the *Passenger Cases,* 7 How. 283, where Mr. Justice McLean stated: "That the transportation of passengers is a part of commerce is not now an open question." At 401. Again in 1913 Mr. Justice McKenna, speaking for the Court, said: "Commerce among the States, we have said, consists of intercourse and traffic between their citizens, and includes the transportation of persons and property." *Hoke v. United States,* 227 U.S. 308, 320.

In framing Title II of this Act Congress was also dealing with what it considered a moral problem. But that fact does not detract from the overwhelming evidence of the disruptive effect that racial discrimination has had on commercial intercourse. It was this burden which empowered Congress to enact appropriate legislation, and, given this basis for the exercise of its power, Congress was not restricted by the fact that the particular obstruction to interstate commerce with which it was dealing was also deemed a moral and social wrong. It is said that the operation of the motel here is of a purely local character. But, assuming this to be true, "if it is interstate commerce that feels the pinch, it does not matter how local the operation which applies the squeeze." *United States v. Women's Sportswear Mfrs. Assn.,* 336 U.S. 460, 464 (1949).

Thus the power of Congress to promote interstate commerce also includes the power to regulate the local incidents thereof, including local activities in both the States of origin and destination, which might have a substantial and harmful effect upon that commerce. One need only examine the evidence which we have discussed above to see that Congress may—as it has—prohibit

(continued)

(continued)

racial discrimination by motels serving travelers, however "local" their operations may appear.

We, therefore, conclude that the action of the Congress in the adoption of the Act as applied here to a motel which concededly serves interstate travelers is within the power granted it by the Commerce Clause of the Constitution, as interpreted by this Court for 140 years. It may be argued that Congress could have pursued other methods to eliminate the obstructions it found in interstate commerce caused by racial

discrimination. But this is a matter of policy that rests entirely with the Congress not with the courts. How obstructions in commerce may be removed—what means are to be employed—is within the sound and exclusive discretion of the Congress. It is subject only to one caveat—that the means chosen by it must be reasonably adapted to the end permitted by the Constitution. We cannot say that its choice here was not so adapted. The Constitution requires no more.

Affirmed.

Something to Consider

Using the reasoning of this case, do you think that any motel or hotel would be exempt from the provisions of the Civil Rights Act of 1964?

Over the years, the Supreme Court has liberally interpreted the Commerce Clause and upheld numerous laws. However, recently the Court made it clear that the Commerce Clause does have limits. Recall the *Lopez* case from Chapter 4 when the Supreme Court held that the law banning guns near schools was unconstitutional because the connection with interstate commerce was not sufficient. This decision was recently affirmed by the Supreme Court in the case of *United States v. Morrison*. In *Morrison*, the petitioner filed a lawsuit claiming that the respondent raped her and that as a result she was entitled to monetary damages under a federal law allowing a victim of gender-based violence to sue for civil damages in federal court (42 U.S.C. § 13981). The trial court dismissed the case, holding that the federal law was unconstitutional. The Court of Appeals agreed and the Supreme Court granted a hearing. In enacting section 13981, Congress specifically stated that it based the law on its powers under the Commerce Clause and the Fourteenth Amendment. Based primarily on its decision in the recently decided *Lopez* case, the Court, in a 5-4 decision, holding that no authority under the Commerce Clause existed. Relying on the *Civil Rights Cases*, the Court also refused to find authority for the law under the Fourteenth Amendment. The decision and one dissent follow.

Did You Know?

Roger B. Taney was the first Catholic justice on the U.S. Supreme Court. Did you know Justice Taney wrote the *Dred Scott v. Sanford* (1855) decision?

Courtesy of Bettmann/CORBIS

United States v. Morrison
529 U.S. 598 (2000)

CHIEF JUSTICE REHNQUIST delivered the opinion of the Court.

In these cases we consider the constitutionality of 42 U.S.C. §13981, which provides a federal civil remedy for the victims of gender-motivated violence.

Every law enacted by Congress must be based on one or more of its powers enumerated in the Constitution. Congress explicitly identified the sources of federal authority on which it relied in enacting §13981. It said that a "federal civil rights cause of action" is established

(continued)

(continued)

"[p]ursuant to the affirmative power of Congress ... under section 5 of the Fourteenth Amendment to the Constitution, as well as under section 8 of Article I of the Constitution." 42 U.S.C. §13981(a). We address Congress' authority to enact this remedy under each of these constitutional provisions in turn.

II

As we discussed at length in *Lopez*, our interpretation of the Commerce Clause has changed as our Nation has developed. *See Lopez*, 514 U.S., at 552–557; *Lopez* emphasized, however, that even under our modern, expansive interpretation of the Commerce Clause, Congress' regulatory authority is not without effective bounds. *Id.*, at 557.

With these principles underlying our Commerce Clause jurisprudence as reference points, the proper resolution of the present cases is clear. Gender-motivated crimes of violence are not, in any sense of the phrase, economic activity. While we need not adopt a categorical rule against aggregating the effects of any noneconomic activity in order to decide these cases, thus far in our Nation's history our cases have upheld Commerce Clause regulation of intrastate activity only where that activity is economic in nature.

III

Because we conclude that the Commerce Clause does not provide Congress with authority to enact §13981, we address petitioners' alternative argument that the section's civil remedy should be upheld as an exercise of Congress' remedial power under §5 of the Fourteenth Amendment. As noted above, Congress expressly invoked the Fourteenth Amendment as a source of authority to enact §13981.

Petitioners' §5 argument is founded on an assertion that there is pervasive bias in various state justice systems against victims of gender-motivated violence. This assertion is supported by a voluminous congressional record. Specifically, Congress received evidence that many participants in state justice systems are perpetuating an array of erroneous stereotypes and assumptions. Congress concluded that these discriminatory stereotypes often result in insufficient investigation and prosecution of gender-motivated crime, inappropriate focus on the behavior and credibility of the victims of that crime, and unacceptably lenient punishments for those who are actually convicted

of gender-motivated violence. See H. R. Conf. Rep. No. 103-711, at 385–386; S. Rep. No. 103-138, at 38, 41–55; S. Rep. No. 102-197, at 33–35, 41, 43–47. Petitioners contend that this bias denies victims of gender-motivated violence the equal protection of the laws and that Congress therefore acted appropriately in enacting a private civil remedy against the perpetrators of gender-motivated violence to both remedy the States' bias and deter future instances of discrimination in the state courts.

However, the language and purpose of the Fourteenth Amendment place certain limitations on the manner in which Congress may attack discriminatory conduct. These limitations are necessary to prevent the Fourteenth Amendment from obliterating the Framers' carefully crafted balance of power between the States and the National Government. Foremost among these limitations is the time-honored principle that the Fourteenth Amendment, by its very terms, prohibits only state action. "[T]he principle has become firmly embedded in our constitutional law that the action inhibited by the first section of the Fourteenth Amendment is only such action as may fairly be said to be that of the States. That Amendment erects no shield against merely private conduct, however discriminatory or wrongful." *Shelley v. Kraemer*, 334 U.S. 1, 13, and n. 12 (1948).

Shortly after the Fourteenth Amendment was adopted, we decided two cases interpreting the Amendment's provisions, *United States v. Harris*, 106 U.S. 629 (1883), and the *Civil Rights Cases*, 109 U.S. 3 (1883). In *Harris*, the Court considered a challenge to §2 of the Civil Rights Act of 1871. That section sought to punish "private persons" for "conspiring to deprive any one of the equal protection of the laws enacted by the State." 106 U.S., at 639. We concluded that this law exceeded Congress' §5 power because the law was "directed exclusively against the action of private persons, without reference to the laws of the State, or their administration by her officers." *Id.*, at 640.

We reached a similar conclusion in the *Civil Rights Cases*. In those consolidated cases, we held that the public accommodation provisions of the Civil Rights Act of 1875, which applied to purely private conduct, were beyond the scope of the §5 enforcement power. 109 U.S., at 11.

The force of the doctrine of *stare decisis* behind these decisions stems not only from the length of time they have been on the books, but also from the insight

(continued)

(continued)

attributable to the Members of the Court at that time. Every Member had been appointed by President Lincoln, Grant, Hayes, Garfield, or Arthur—and each of their judicial appointees obviously had intimate knowledge and familiarity with the events surrounding the adoption of the Fourteenth Amendment.

We believe that the description of the §5 power contained in the *Civil Rights Cases* is correct.

For these reasons, we conclude that Congress' power under §5 does not extend to the enactment of §13981.

IV

Petitioner Brzonkala's complaint alleges that she was the victim of a brutal assault. But Congress' effort in §13981 to provide a federal civil remedy can be sustained neither under the Commerce Clause nor under §5 of the Fourteenth Amendment. If the allegations here are true, no civilized system of justice could fail to provide her a remedy for the conduct of respondent Morrison. But under our federal system that remedy must be provided by the Commonwealth of Virginia, and not by the United States. The judgment of the Court of Appeals is

Affirmed.

[Morrison was a 5–4 decision. The four dissenting justices felt the law was a constitutional exercise of the Commerce Power.]

Dissent. The Federal Government's argument, is that Congress used §5 to remedy the actions of *state actors*, namely, those States which, through discriminatory design or the discriminatory conduct of their officials, failed to provide adequate (or any) state remedies for women injured by gender-motivated violence—a failure that the States, and Congress, documented in depth.

The Court responds directly to the relevant "state actor" claim by finding that the present law lacks "congruence and proportionality" to the state discrimination that it purports to remedy. That is because the law, unlike federal laws prohibiting literacy tests for voting, imposing voting rights requirements, or punishing state officials who intentionally discriminated in jury selection,

Katzenbach v. Morgan, 384 U.S. 641 (1966); *South Carolina v. Katzenbach*, 383 U.S. 301 (1966); *Ex parte Virginia*, 100 U.S. 339 (1880), is not "directed ... at any State or state actor." *Ante*, at 26.

But why can Congress not provide a remedy against private actors? Those private actors, of course, did not themselves violate the Constitution. But this Court has held that Congress at least sometimes can enact remedial "legislation ... that prohibits conduct which is not itself unconstitutional." *Flores*, 521 U.S., at 518; *see also Katzenbach v. Morgan, supra*, at 651; *South Carolina v. Katzenbach, supra*, at 308. The statutory remedy does not in any sense purport to "determine what constitutes a constitutional violation." *Flores, supra*, at 519. It intrudes little upon either States or private parties. It may lead state actors to improve their own remedial systems, primarily through example. It restricts private actors only by imposing liability for private conduct that is, in the main, already forbidden by state law. Why is the remedy "disproportionate"? And given the relation between remedy and violation—the creation of a federal remedy to substitute for constitutionally inadequate state remedies—where is the lack of "congruence"?

The majority adds that Congress found that the problem of inadequacy of state remedies "does not exist in all States, or even most States." *Ante*, at 27. But Congress had before it the task force reports of at least 21 States documenting constitutional violations. And it made its own findings about pervasive gender-based stereotypes hampering many state legal systems, sometimes unconstitutionally so. *See*, e.g., S. Rep. No. 103-138, pp. 38, 41–42, 44–47 (1993); S. Rep. No. 102-197, pp. 39, 44–49 (1991); H. R. Conf. Rep. No. 103-711, p. 385 (1994). The record nowhere reveals a congressional finding that the problem "does not exist" elsewhere. Why can Congress not take the evidence before it as evidence of a national problem? This Court has not previously held that Congress must document the existence of a problem in every State prior to proposing a national solution. And the deference this Court gives to Congress' chosen remedy under §5, *Flores, supra*, at 536, suggests that any such requirement would be inappropriate.

Emerging Issues—Same-Sex Marriage

One of the most important civil rights issues of this era is whether same-sex marriages are a civil right protected by the Constitution. Some states addressed this issue through legislative action and some faced it in the courts. To date, however, the Supreme Court has not ruled on this issue. In a recent lower court case, *Perry v. Schwarzenegger*, a district court in California, addressed the issues and ruled that the right to marry is a fundamental right protected by both the Due Process and the Equal Protection Clauses. Therefore, a state constitutional amendment (referred to as Proposition 8) limiting marriage to a man and a woman was found to be in violation of the U.S. Constitution. In its order, the court discussed these issues:

> Plaintiffs challenge Proposition 8 under the Due Process and Equal Protection Clauses of the Fourteenth Amendment. Each challenge is independently meritorious, as Proposition 8 both unconstitutionally burdens the exercise of the fundamental right to marry and creates an irrational classification on the basis of sexual orientation. California does not meet its due process obligation to allow plaintiffs to marry by offering them a substitute and inferior institution that denies marriage to same sex couples. ....

> Many of the purported interests identified by proponents are nothing more than a fear or unarticulated dislike of same-sex couples. Those interests that are legitimate are unrelated to the classification drawn by Proposition 8. The evidence shows that, by every available metric, opposite-sex couples are not better than their same-sex counterparts; instead, as partners, parents and citizens, opposite-sex couples and same-sex couples are equal. Proposition 8 violates the Equal Protection Clause because it does not treat them equally.

Enforcement of Civil Rights

The U.S. Department of Justice established a civil rights division to enforce the wide variety of civil rights laws. Individuals can report alleged violations of civil rights laws and, if appropriate, the civil rights division will investigate and file complaints against those who violate the laws. The civil rights division consists of the following sections: criminal section, disability rights section, educational opportunities section, federal coordination and compliance section, housing and civil enforcement section, office of special counsel for immigration-related employment practices, special litigation section, and voting section.

≈ Ethical Decisions—Everyday Choices ≈

The Facts: Recently, Bradley took his automobile in for some repairs but was very dissatisfied with the work done and wanted the repair company to refund his payment to them. They refused. Bradley, who works as a paralegal for the Department of Justice, then wrote a letter on office stationery demanding the return of his money and threatening legal action should it not be refunded. He signed the letter with his name, but did not indicate his position.

The Problem: Was it proper for Bradley to use office stationery for a personal problem? Was Bradley engaged in the unauthorized practice of law by signing the letter and not indicating his status as a paralegal?

(continued)

(continued)

Guiding Principles: A paralegal working for the government must be aware of ethical rules pertaining to government employees as well as to rules pertaining to paralegals. Various laws and regulations govern the conduct of employees of the Department of Justice. These are found in the Code of Federal Regulations and are administered by the ethics office of the Department of Justice. One of the rules deals with misuse of position and government resources. In addition, paralegals must always use care to avoid creating an impression that they are lawyers rather than paralegals. While paralegals can sign letters, their status should always be indicated.

Chapter Summary

Civil rights and liberties refer to basic rights to be free from unwarranted government control of our personal, political, and economic lives. While no exact definition of these terms exists, civil rights and liberties generally includes prohibition on laws that discriminate because of such factors as race, gender, or disability. It also includes the right to fair and just hearings in civil and criminal cases. Protection of civil rights and liberties was a concern of the founding fathers as indicated by the Preamble to the Constitution. Although the Constitution provides protections for civil rights and liberties, most of the protections are found in the amendments rather than the articles. The articles of the Constitution guarantee the right to a writ of habeas corpus and prohibit bills of attainder and ex post facto laws. Writs of habeas corpus provide a remedy against unjust incarceration. Bills of attainder prohibit the legislature from usurping judicial power, and ex post facto laws prohibit laws that impose criminal penalties for conduct not made criminal until after the fact.

The Bill of Rights, or the first ten amendments, provide protection against laws that infringe on rights of free speech, press, assembly, or free exercise of religion. The Bill of Rights also guarantees the right to individuals to bear arms. Several of the amendments provide safeguards in criminal cases. In addition to the Bill of Rights, civil rights and liberties gain protection from the Reconstruction Amendments (the Thirteenth, Fourteenth, and Fifteenth Amendments). These amendments deal with the problems created in the aftermath of the Civil War. The Fourteenth Amendment has provided the greatest protections against infringement of civil rights and liberties through such clauses as the Due Process Clause, the Equal Protection Clause and, more recently, through the Privileges and Immunities Clause. Other amendments also protect voting rights.

Some of the amendments specifically give protection against both federal and state infringement of rights. However, the Supreme Court said that the Bill of Rights applied only to the federal government and did not grant any protection against state action. Years after the adoption of the Fourteenth Amendment, the Supreme Court decided that many of the rights and liberties found in the Bill of Rights do apply to state action because they are incorporated or included in the concept of due process. Due process applies to state action through the Fourteenth Amendment.

In addition to the Constitution, civil rights protection is found in congressional legislation. Congress has the power to enact civil rights laws through its power to regulate interstate commerce and through power expressly granted to Congress in some of the amendments. Civil rights laws based on the Interstate Commerce Clause are constitutional only if they apply to individuals or businesses engaged in interstate commerce. Civil rights laws based on express power found in the amendments are constitutional only if they apply to government action.

Key Terms

writ of habeas corpus	ex post facto laws	poll tax
bill of attainder	Reconstruction Amendments	Incorporation Doctrine

Questions for Review

1. What is the relevance of the Ninth Amendment to the Constitution to the protection of civil rights and liberties?
2. How has the Supreme Court explained or defined the terms "civil rights" and "liberties"?
3. What sources contain provisions protecting civil rights and liberties?
4. Define the following: writ of habeas corpus, bill of attainder, and ex post facto laws.
5. What are the rights found in the Bill of Rights?
6. Explain the right found in the Second Amendment.
7. How does the Constitution provide protection against infringement of civil rights and liberties by state and local governments?
8. What are the protections afforded by the Fourteenth Amendment?
9. Where does Congress get the power to enact civil rights legislation?
10. What is the "state action doctrine"?

Questions for Analysis

1. Reread the facts in Living with the Constitution at the beginning of the chapter. Orland wishes to sue for damages suffered as a result of a violation of his constitutional rights. Which provisions, if any, of the Constitution were violated by the city police? Which, if any, were violated by Orland's acquaintance?
2. Answer the following questions regarding the *Dobbert v. Florida* case.
   a. Why was the Florida law, under which Dobbert was eventually sentenced to die, not ex post facto?
   b. Why did Justice Stevens dissent?
3. Answer the following questions regarding the *Barron v. Baltimore* case.
   a. According to Chief Justice Marshall, why was the Constitution established?
   b. If citizens want protection from their states, what does the Court say they should do?
4. Answer the following questions regarding *Twining v. New Jersey.*
   a. What is the historical origin of the term "due process"?
   b. According to the opinion, how should the Court determine what due process means in specific cases?
   c. What does the Court say the greatest security for liberty and justice is?
5. Why did the Court find that the Interstate Commerce Clause allowed Congress to enact a law that protected the civil rights of individuals in *Heart of Atlanta Motel, Inc. v. United States*, but did not allow the enactment of the law in *United States v. Morrison*?
6. Why did the Court in *Saenz v. Roe* find that California's welfare laws violated the Privileges and Immunities Clause?

Assignments and Projects

1. Using the format found in previous chapters, write a case brief for *Brown v. Board of Education.*
2. Identify organizations in your state that protect individuals from discrimination. What types of discrimination are prohibited?
3. Using the Internet, trace and summarize the subsequent proceedings in Perry v. Schwarzenneger.
4. Locate a copy of the oral arguments in *United States v. Morrison,* in either written or oral form. (You can find the oral argument for this and many other cases throught the Internet.) Read or listen to the argument. Summarize the petitioner's argument.

Putting It into Practice

1. Read the Petition for Writ of Habeas Corpus found in Appendix E. Write a memorandum summarizing the basis for the defendant's request.
2. Assume that you work for a law firm that has been contacted by Janet Smith who believes she was fired from her job because of her age. You were asked to prepare a draft of a complaint. Locate a copy of a form or sample complaint that you can use as a basis for drafting your complaint.

Group Activities

1. In small groups, discuss the phrase "vestiges of slavery." Make a list of activities or practices that might be included in the phrase. Share your list with the entire class.
2. Read the selection from the petitioner's brief in *United States v. Morrison* found in Appendix G. Compose a list of questions you might ask the petitioner if you were a justice on the Supreme Court hearing arguments in the case. Why do you think the Court did not accept the petitioner's argument?

8 Equal Protection

Democracy arises out of the notion that those who are equal in any respect are equal in all respects....

Aristotle

Chapter Outline

Chapter Objectives

When you complete this chapter you should be able to

1. explain the difference between classification and invidious discrimination.

2. describe the circumstances under which the Equal Protection Clause applies to private conduct.

3. explain why the federal government is subject to the requirements of the Equal Protection Clause.

4. define the terms suspect class, quasi-suspect class, and fundamental rights.

5. compare and contrast the three tests used by the Supreme Court when evaluating laws and practices for equal protection violations.

6. describe examples of laws that violate the Equal Protection Clause.

7. describe examples of laws that do not violate the Equal Protection Clause.

8. explain how the Equal Protection Clause protects voting rights.

9. summarize the "one person, one vote" rule.

10. describe the difficulties stemming from efforts to eliminate equal protection violations.

Looking Back

Before reading this chapter, review the following terms and concepts from the previous chapters:

Brown v. Board of Education The Supreme Court case in which the doctrine of separate but equal facilities for schools was held to be unconstitutional in violation of the Fourteenth Amendment. (Chapter 7)

Judicial review The Supreme Court has the power to review state laws to determine if they are consistent with the Constitution. (Chapter 3)

Supremacy Clause The part of the Constitution that provides that it and federal laws enacted pursuant to the Constitution are the supreme law of the land. Laws that conflict with the Constitution are struck down by the Supreme Court. (Chapter 3)

Congressional legislation and civil rights In addition to the protections found in the Constitution, Congress enacted several laws protecting the rights of citizens. Thus, some rights, not guaranteed by clauses such as equal protection, are protected through legislation. (Chapter 7)

Living with the Constitution

The Ebert family lives in a lower-income neighborhood in a large city. In the fall, their oldest child starts school. For many years, the neighborhood school has struggled. Academically, students at this school perform appreciably lower than students at other schools in the same school district. Also, extracurricular activities are more limited than at other schools. When they registered their child for school, the Eberts asked that the child be assigned to a school located in a more affluent area where children performed better academically and where a variety of outside activities were provided. Their request was denied. The Eberts believe that this is a violation of the Equal Protection Clause and have decided to see a civil rights lawyer.

THE CIVIL WAR ENDED ONE of the most invidious practices in American history. However, it did not eliminate the prejudices that were ingrained in many Americans. Even though slavery was abolished, many southern states enacted laws and enforced practices that denied African Americans many fundamental rights. Recall from the previous chapter that the Thirteenth, Fourteenth, and Fifteenth Amendments were added to the Constitution to abolish these discriminatory laws and practices. The Thirteenth and Fifteenth Amendments are very limited in scope, the Thirteenth abolishing slavery and the Fifteenth dealing only with voting rights. The Fourteenth Amendment is much broader and provides the courts and Congress a constitutional basis for the protection of civil rights. As a result of court decisions and congressional legislation, the Fourteenth Amendment protections extend far beyond discriminatory practices against African-Americans. The previous chapter presented an overview of the Reconstruction Amendments. However, because of their importance, two provisions of the Fourteenth Amendment—the Equal Protection Clause and the Due Process Clause—require a more in-depth analysis. This chapter deals with the Equal Protection Clause. The next chapter covers the Due Process Clause.

Classification versus Invidious Discrimination

LAWS OFTEN DENY PRIVILEGES OR grant rights to limited groups or classifications of individuals. For example, children must be a certain age to enter school. Teenagers must be a certain age to drive. Seniors must be a certain age to receive social security benefits. These age classifications are accepted and are not a violation of the Constitution. Sometimes a government is allowed to treat people differently. However, in some instances, the Equal Protection Clause makes such treatment unconstitutional.

When the Civil War ended, some states enacted laws and engaged in practices where individuals were classified by their race and treated accordingly. This practice was targeted by the Fourteenth Amendment, which, in part, provides that no state shall "deny to any person within its jurisdiction the equal protection of the laws." Another important section of the Fourteenth Amendment is Section 5, which provides: "The Congress shall have power to enforce, by appropriate legislation, the provisions of this article." This clause enables Congress to pass laws and is therefore sometimes referred to as an **enabling clause**.

The Equal Protection Clause applies to laws or governmental practices that treat different classifications of people differently but it does not mean that all such laws or practices *violate* the Equal Protection Clause. The Supreme Court acknowledges that not all laws creating classifications are unconstitutional. "Statutes create many classifications which do not deny equal protection; it is only 'invidious discrimination' which offends the Constitution." *Ferguson v. Skrupa*, 372 U.S. 726 (1963). Today, **invidious discrimination** refers to a type of discrimination or classification based on ill will or prejudice because of characteristics such as race, color, religion, sex, age, legitimacy, disability, or national origin.

A historical look at Supreme Court decisions shows that societal attitudes and changes affect the precise meaning the Court has given to the term *invidious discrimination*. For example, consider the practice of **segregation**, a practice clearly recognized today as invidious discrimination. This was not always the case. In 1896, in the case of *Plessy v. Ferguson*, 163 U.S. 537, the Supreme Court ruled that a Louisiana law requiring separate railroad cars was *not* unconstitutional and did not violate the Fourteenth Amendment Equal Protection Clause. The Court said:

> The object of the amendment was undoubtedly to enforce the absolute equality of
> the two races before the law, but, in the nature of things, it could not have been

---

enabling clause

The section or clause in a constitutional article or amendment that grants Congress the power to make laws to enforce the article or amendment

invidious discrimination

Illegally unequal treatment based on race, color, religion, sex, age, handicap, or national origin.

segregation

1. The separation of property into groups. Segregation of assets involves identifying and setting aside the property belonging to one person from a common fund or pot. 2. The unconstitutional practice of separating persons in housing, schooling, and public accommodation, based on race, color, nationality, etc.

intended to abolish distinctions based upon color, or to enforce social, as distinguished from political, equality, or a commingling of the two races upon terms unsatisfactory to either. Laws permitting, and even requiring, their separation, in places where they are liable to be brought into contact, do not necessarily imply the inferiority of either race to the other, and have been generally, if not universally, recognized as within the competency of the state legislatures in the exercise of their police power.

🏛 **separate but equal doctrine**
The rule, established in the 1896 Supreme Court case *Plessy v. Ferguson* and then rejected as unconstitutional in the 1954 *Brown* decision, that when races are given substantially equal facilities, they may lawfully be segregated.

As a result of *Plessy v. Ferguson*, the **separate but equal doctrine** developed. Segregation was lawful as long as separate facilities were equal. This system continued to be applied in several states until 1954 and the case of *Brown v. Board of Education* (see Chapter 7). In *Brown*, the Court decided that separate but equal had no place in public education and rejected the doctrine of *Plessy v. Ferguson*. In the years following *Brown*, the Court outlawed segregation in other areas of public life.

The Supreme Court has made it clear that a government practice of maintaining separate but equal public facilities is invidious discrimination and a violation of equal protection. In other situations, the Court decides on a case-by-case basis whether a particular classification results in a violation of equal protection.

Exhibit 8-1   Dr. Martin Luther King, Civil Rights March on Washington, D.C., 1963

Courtesy of Bettman/CORBIS

Application of the Equal Protection Clause to State and Federal Government

WITHIN A FEW YEARS OF the Fourteenth Amendment's ratification, the Supreme Court ruled that it applied only to state action and not to private conduct. However, several questions about the exact nature of state action arose, including:

1. Do equal protection rights exist when state employees discriminate?
2. Do equal protection rights exist when the federal government discriminates?
3. Do equal protection rights exist when a private party who has some connection to state government discriminates?

The Supreme Court has considered each of these questions.

State Employees

State action includes actions of individual state authorities, a fact recognized by the Supreme Court in an early decision. Soon after the ratification of the Fourteenth Amendment, Congress enacted legislation making it a crime to violate the provisions of the amendment. In 1879, the Supreme Court considered the appeal of a local judge who was convicted under this law because he refused to allow racial minorities on juries in his court. The Supreme Court considered whether the Fourteenth Amendment controlled the acts of private individuals who worked for the state and decided that it did:

> A State acts by its legislative, its executive, or its judicial authorities. It can act in no other way. The constitutional provision, therefore, must mean that no agency of the State, or of the officers or agents by whom its powers are exerted, shall deny to any person within its jurisdiction the equal protection of the laws. Whoever, by virtue of public position under a State government, deprives another of property, life, or liberty, without due process of law, or denies or takes away the equal protection of the laws, violates the constitutional inhibition; and as he acts in the name and for the State, and is clothed with the State's power, his act is that of the State. This must be so, or the constitutional prohibition has no meaning. Then the State has clothed one of its agents with power to annul or to evade it. *Ex parte Virginia*, 100 U.S. 339 (1879).

Federal Government

No provision in the Constitution prohibits the *federal* government from violating equal protection rights of individuals. Nevertheless, the Supreme Court held that the types of protections required by the Equal Protection Clause of the Fourteenth Amendment apply to the federal government because they are included in the protections afforded by the Due Process Clause of the Fifth Amendment. The Court decided this in a companion case to *Brown v. Board of Education* involving a segregated school in Washington, D.C. and therefore under federal, rather than state, jurisdiction. In deciding that equal protection rights applied to the federal government the Court said:

> We have this day held that the Equal Protection Clause of the Fourteenth Amendment prohibits the states from maintaining racially segregated public schools. The legal problem in the District of Columbia is somewhat different, however. The Fifth Amendment, which is applicable in the District of Columbia, does not contain an equal protection clause as does the Fourteenth Amendment

which applies only to the states. But the concepts of equal protection and due process, both stemming from our American ideal of fairness, are not mutually exclusive. The "equal protection of the laws" is a more explicit safeguard of prohibited unfairness than "due process of law," and, therefore, we do not imply that the two are always interchangeable phrases. But, as this Court has recognized, discrimination may be so unjustifiable as to be violative of due process. *Bolling v. Sharpe,* 347 U.S. 497 (1954).

A Point of Law

Ex parte Virginia, 100 U.S. 339 (1879)

Bolling v. Sharpe, 347 U.S. 497 (1954)

Although the Equal Protection Clause of the Fourteenth Amendment applies only to the states (and the actions of individual state authorities), the Due Process Clause of the Fifth Amendment requires the same protections against actions of the federal government. Thus, it was a constitutional violation for a public school located in Washington, D.C. to segregate.

Private Discrimination and State Action

Racial discrimination is abhorred by the Court whether it is committed by state officials or private parties. However, in early cases the Court acknowledged that it had no constitutional power to use the Fourteenth Amendment to limit the practice by private parties. Nevertheless, if the Court finds a sufficient relationship between the state and discrimination by private parties, it will invoke the Fourteenth Amendment. One of the first cases to do this is the case of *Shelley v. Kraemer*, 334 U.S. 1 (1948). In this case, private property owners signed contracts (restrictive agreements) agreeing not to sell to certain racial minorities. The Shelley family, which was African American, acquired a home subject to this covenant by using an intermediary to make the purchase. Kraemer, one of the other property owners, sued to evict the Shelleys and to enforce the restrictive agreement. The state supreme court ruled in favor of Kraemer, finding that no federal constitutional rights were involved because there was no state action. The U.S. Supreme Court held otherwise. The Court acknowledged that the discrimination was private:

> We conclude, therefore, that the restrictive agreements standing alone cannot be regarded as a violation of any rights guaranteed to petitioners by the Fourteenth Amendment. So long as the purposes of those agreements are effectuated by voluntary adherence to their terms, it would appear clear that there has been no action by the State and the provisions of the Amendment have not been violated.

But the Court emphasized that in this case there was more than private conduct. In filing a lawsuit to evict the Shelleys, the parties asked the state courts to enforce the discriminatory practice. Furthermore, the eviction could not have occurred without state court intervention. The Court felt that this was a sufficient state action to make the Fourteenth Amendment applicable:

> The short of the matter is that from the time of the adoption of the Fourteenth Amendment until the present, it has been the consistent ruling of this Court that

the action of the States to which the Amendment has reference, includes action of state courts and state judicial officials.

> We have no doubt that there has been state action in these cases in the full and complete sense of the phrase. The undisputed facts disclose that petitioners were willing purchasers of properties upon which they desired to establish homes. The owners of the properties were willing sellers; and contracts of sale were accordingly consummated. It is clear that but for the active intervention of the state courts, supported by the full panoply of state power, petitioners would have been free to occupy the properties in question without restraint.

The Supreme Court also found state action in the following situations:

1. A deputy sheriff hired by a private park to provide security where the deputy enforced a discriminatory policy of the park excluding blacks. *Griffin v. Maryland*, 378 U.S. 130 (1964).
2. A privately owned restaurant that refused to serve blacks, when the restaurant leased space from the state in a publicly owned building. *Burton v. Wilmington Parking Authority*, 365 U.S. 715 (1961).

On the other hand, in *Moose Lodge No. 107 v. Irvis*, 407 U.S. 163 (1972), the Court refused to find state action when the discriminatory conduct was by a private club whose only connection to the state was that it had a liquor license. In this case the Court found that the relationship to the state was not enough: "where the impetus for the discrimination is private, the State must have significantly involved itself with invidious discrimination." See Table 8-1.

Table 8-1 Actions by Private Parties and State Action

Court finds state action in discrimination by private parties when:	Court does not find state action in discrimination by private parties when:
1. Private party uses courts to enforce discriminatory practice.	1. The only connection to the state is the purchase of a liquor license.
2. Private party hires a deputy sheriff as security to enforce discriminatory practice.	
3. Private party leases property from the state.	

© Cengage Learning 2013

How the Supreme Court Reviews Laws for Equal Protection Violations

BECAUSE OF THE POWER OF judicial review, the courts, and ultimately the Supreme Court, decide if any state law or practice violates the Equal Protection Clause. In doing this, courts are often asked to void a state law. Under the American system of federalism, this is not something courts do lightly. The Supreme Court gives great deference to the power of the states to enact laws and upholds state laws when possible. On the other hand, when a state law violates a provision of the Constitution, the Supreme Court must strike down the law.

In reviewing laws that are challenged as being in violation of the Equal Protection Clause, the Court recognizes two important facts: (1) not all laws based on classifications should be evaluated the same way, and (2) not all laws based on classifications violate equal protection rules. The Supreme Court believes that it has a greater obligation to individuals who have experienced discrimination over a long period of time; they have little power in the social and political arena and are thus unable to cure problems through the legislative process. The Court also believes that it has a greater obligation when it comes to protecting constitutional rights than in protecting other rights and privileges. As a result, the Supreme Court developed three different tests or standards for determining if state laws violate the Equal Protection Clause. These three tests are referred to as rational basis, strict scrutiny, and intermediate scrutiny. Each of these tests sets forth criteria or standards that the law must meet in order to be constitutional. The strict scrutiny test requires the highest standards and the rational basis test requires the lowest standards. The standard that the Court uses in reviewing a law often affects the outcome of the case. When the Court applies the rational basis test, it is more likely that the state law is upheld. When it applies the strict scrutiny test, it is more likely that the law is found unconstitutional. Although the Court's tests or standards are somewhat subjective and certainly do not offer mathematical precision, they do provide a basis for the Court's analysis of any law that is challenged as being in violation of the Equal Protection Clause.

In determining which test to apply, the Court looks at three questions:

1. Does the law target a suspect class?
2. Does the law affect a fundamental right?
3. Is there purposeful discrimination?

If the Court finds that the law targets a *suspect class* or affects a *fundamental right* and finds that there is also *purposeful discrimination*, then the Court strictly scrutinizes the law. In other situations the Court applies less stringent tests.

Suspect Class

Over the years, the Supreme Court has reviewed laws that classify or discriminate on the basis of many different characteristics including race, ethnicity, national origin, alien status, gender, legitimacy, poverty, age, and mental disability. A **suspect class** is a classification that immediately suggests a prejudicial motive behind the law and includes those groups who were historically the target of discrimination. Sometimes the Court refers to members of a suspect class as members of a "**discrete and insular minority**." A law targets a suspect class when it classifies a group based on race, ethnicity, or national origin. Such a law is subject to the highest degree of scrutiny by the Court. Not as suspect as these are classes based on gender and legitimacy. The Court found that these two categories share some, but not all, of the characteristics of a suspect class. It, therefore, created a second-tier class referred to as a **quasi-suspect class**. Laws that discriminate on the basis of gender or legitimacy are subject to an intermediate level of scrutiny by the Court. Alien status is a problem for the Court; sometimes it considers such status to be a suspect class and other times a quasi-suspect class. Poverty, age, or mental disability do not create a suspect class.

Fundamental Rights

A **fundamental right** is one that is expressly or impliedly found in the Constitution. Thus, such rights as the right to travel, the rights of a defendant in criminal cases, and the right to vote are considered fundamental rights. On the other hand, education is not considered a fundamental right since it is not found in the Constitution. Laws that affect fundamental rights are highly suspect and subject to strict scrutiny regardless of what classification is found in the law. For example, several states enacted laws that required long residency requirements before individuals qualified for welfare assistance. *Shapiro v. Thompson*, 394 U.S. 618 (1969). Such laws discriminate against the poor. If the Court reviewed these laws based on the classification, that is, poverty, the law would be reviewed under the rational

---

🏛 suspect class (suspect classification)

Making choices based on factors such as race or nationality. These choices, only rarely legitimate, must be strongly justified if challenged. (Gender is a quasi-suspect classification that must be justified, but not as strongly if challenged.)

🏛 discrete and insular minority

A phrase used by the Supreme Court to refer to suspect classes of people.

🏛 quasi-suspect class

A classification in the law based on factors such as gender or legitimacy that must be strongly justified if the law is challenged.

🏛 fundamental right

The basic rights, such as the right to vote and the right to travel, most strongly protected by the Constitution.

basis test. However, this law affects the right to travel, to move between states. Since this is a constitutional right, the law was reviewed under strict scrutiny and held to be unconstitutional and in violation of the Equal Protection Clause.

Rational Basis Test

When a law does not target a suspect or quasi-suspect class nor affect a fundamental right, the Court applies the rational basis test. The rational basis test asks the question: "Does a state law have a rational basis for promoting a legitimate state interest?" In other words, does the law serve some legitimate state interest and is the law reasonably related to that end? If the answer is yes, then the law is probably constitutional. A legitimate state interest is generally any of the standard **police powers** possessed by states. This includes the power to enact laws that promote the safety, health, and general welfare of its citizens. For example, consider the case of a state law that banned advertising signs on vehicles unless the vehicle was used in a business. This law allowed some people to put signs on their vehicles while others could not. It does not, however, involve a fundamental right nor does it target a suspect class. Thus, the Court asked two questions: Did the law have a legitimate purpose and was the law rationally related to that purpose? The Court found that the state might have a legitimate state interest— vehicular safety—and that the law was a reasonable way to deal with the problem. The fact that all vehicles were not treated the same was irrelevant. *Railway Express Agency, Inc. v. New York*, 336 U.S. 106 (1949). On the other hand, consider a local law that required a special permit for a group home for mentally retarded individuals but not for most other types of group facilities, such as nursing homes. Since this law did not involve a fundamental right and it did not target a suspect class, the Court asked the same two questions. Here, however, the Court said that the law was based on irrational prejudice against the mentally retarded, not on any legitimate state purpose. It found the law unconstitutional (*City of Cleburne v. Cleburne Living Ctr., Inc.*, 473 U.S. 432 (1985)); the opinion is found later in the chapter.

The rational basis test is used to evaluate many types of state laws, especially those where unequal treatment is related to economic legislation. For example, this standard was applied in challenges against a state constitutional provision that allowed taxation of personal property owned by corporations but not personal property owned by individuals. The Supreme Court upheld this law saying:

> The Equal Protection Clause does not mean that a State may not draw lines that treat one class of individuals or entities differently from the others. The test is whether the difference in treatment is an invidious discrimination. Where taxation is concerned and no specific federal right, apart from equal protection, is imperiled, the States have large leeway in making classifications and drawing lines which in their judgment produce reasonable systems of taxation. *Lehnhausen v. Lake Shore Auto Parts Co.*, 410 U.S. 356 (1973).

The rational basis standard is not limited to laws that have an economic purpose. The Court recently used this test in a case challenging a Colorado law discriminating against homosexuals (*Romer v. Evans*, which is printed later in the chapter). This test was also used to evaluate a law that discriminates because of age.

Strict Scrutiny

Whenever a law targets a suspect class or burdens a fundamental right, the Court reviews the law with the highest degree of scrutiny. There must be some overwhelming necessity or "compelling" governmental interest for the law, as opposed to the "legitimate" government interest required under the rational basis test. As mentioned above, the most common and

---

🏛 **police powers**

The government's right and power to set up and enforce laws to provide for the safety, health, and general welfare of the people; for example, police power includes the power to license occupations such as hair cutting.

obvious suspect class is a class based on race. If a law targets a particular race, it will undoubtedly be closely scrutinized. This principle was stated by the Court in the case of *Korematsu v. United States*, 323 U.S. 214 (1944). The law in this case prohibited individuals of Japanese ancestry from being in certain military areas. In describing the way the Court should evaluate the law, Justice Black stated:

> It should be noted, to begin with, that all legal restrictions which curtail the civil rights of a single racial group are immediately suspect. That is not to say that all such restrictions are unconstitutional. It is to say that courts must subject them to the most rigid scrutiny. Pressing public necessity may sometimes justify the existence of such restrictions; racial antagonism never can.

In *Korematsu* the Court found that the war was a pressing public necessity and that the law did not violate the Constitution. In most cases, the Court holds any law that discriminates against any racial group to be unconstitutional.

In other cases, the Court considered classes based on ethnicity or alienage to be suspect. For example, the Court applied strict scrutiny in striking down a state law requiring recipients of welfare benefits to be citizens or residents for fifteen years. The Court said:

> But the Court's decisions have established that classifications based on alienage, like those based on nationality or race, are inherently suspect and subject to close judicial scrutiny. Aliens as a class are a prime example of a "discrete and insular" minority (*see United States v. Carolene Products Co.*, 304 U.S. 144, 152–53, n. 4 (1938)) for whom such heightened judicial solicitude is appropriate. *Graham v. Richardson*, 403 U.S. 365 (1971).

Even if a court finds that the state law does not target a suspect class, if it takes away a "fundamental" right, the Court reviews the law with strict scrutiny, just as it does with race if there is proof that the state engaged in purposeful discrimination.

Some laws are obviously discriminatory. For example, a law that allows the state to give a hiring preference to men obviously discriminates against women. This law is discriminatory on its face. When a law is discriminatory on its face, the Court implies that there is a discriminatory *purpose*. However, some laws do not appear to be discriminatory. They are "**facially neutral**," that is, the law does not appear to discriminate. For example, consider a rule in criminal cases that allows each attorney to exercise **peremptory challenges** when selecting a jury. A peremptory challenge allows the attorney to excuse any person from the jury without stating a reason. Nothing in the law refers to race. However, what if a prosecutor uses these challenges to excuse all blacks from the jury? In such a case, the law itself is not discriminatory. It is facially neutral. However, when all members of a class are excluded from the jury, this neutral law is *applied* in such a way that it is discriminatory. The individual challenging the law must prove that the discrimination is purposeful, but once that is done, the Court applies the strict scrutiny standard. Sometimes this is a problem, as it was in the case of *McCleskey v. Kemp*, 481 U.S. 279 (1987). In this case, the petitioner challenged the capital punishment laws of the state of Georgia on the grounds they were discriminately applied in violation of the Eighth and Fourteenth Amendments. In support of the claim, the petitioner introduced a statistical study showing a disparity in the imposition of the death sentence in Georgia based on the murder victim's race and, to a lesser extent, the defendant's race. The study was based on over 2,000 murder cases that occurred in Georgia during the 1970s and involves data relating to the victim's race, the defendant's race, and the various combinations of such persons' races. Although the study showed that race played a role in the imposition of the death penalty,

🏛 **facially neutral**
A type of law that does not discriminate by its terms, but may result in discriminatory practices anyway.

🏛 **peremptory challenges**
A peremptory challenge to a potential juror is the automatic elimination of that person from the jury by one side before trial without needing to state the reason for the elimination. Each side has the right to a certain number of peremptory challenges, and all other attempts to eliminate a potential juror must be for a reason (which may or may not be accepted by the judge).

the Court rejected the defendant's appeal because he did not prove *purposeful* discrimination:

> Our analysis begins with the basic principle that a defendant who alleges an equal protection violation has the burden of proving "the existence of purposeful discrimination." *Whitus v. Georgia*, 385 U.S. 545, 550 (1967). A corollary to this principle is that a criminal defendant must prove that the purposeful discrimination "had a discriminatory effect" on him. *Wayte v. United States*, 470 U.S. 598, 608 (1985). Thus, to prevail under the Equal Protection Clause, McCleskey must prove that the decision makers in his case acted with discriminatory purpose.

Intermediate Level of Scrutiny

In recent years, discrimination based on gender has become an important issue in American law. In addressing this type of discrimination, the Court uses a standard somewhere between strict scrutiny and rational basis. Sometimes it is referred to as *heightened scrutiny*. In a pivotal case dealing with the constitutionality of a law allowing women to drink beer at age 18 and men at 21, the Court said:

> To withstand constitutional challenge, previous cases establish that classifications by gender must serve important governmental objectives and must be substantially related to achievement of those objectives. *Craig v. Boren*, 429 U.S. 190 (1976).

The Court was thus looking for a law with a *substantial* relationship to achieving an *important* government interest, as opposed to a rational basis test of requiring a law to have a *reasonable* relationship to achieving a *legitimate* government interest or the strict scrutiny test of requiring a law to be necessary to achieve a *compelling* government interest. In holding the Virginia Military Institute's practice of admitting only male students was unconstitutional, the Supreme Court reaffirmed this standard, saying:

> To summarize the Court's current directions for cases of official classification based on gender: Focusing on the differential treatment or denial of opportunity for which relief is sought, the reviewing court must determine whether the proffered justification is "exceedingly persuasive." The burden of justification is demanding and it rests entirely on the State. The State must show "at least that the challenged classification serves 'important governmental objectives and that the discriminatory means employed' are 'substantially related to the achievement of those objectives'."

The opinion in this case is found later in the chapter.

This intermediate level of scrutiny is also applied when discrimination is based on illegitimacy. Using this standard the Court invalidated laws that denied inheritance rights or support to illegitimate children, while giving these rights to legitimate children. Occasionally this standard, rather than strict scrutiny, is also applied where discrimination is against aliens.

In the case of *City of Cleburne v. Cleburne Living Ctr., Inc.*, 473 U.S. 432 (1985), the Supreme Court discusses the different tests it uses in reviewing the constitutionality of state laws challenged under the Equal Protection Clause. In *Cleburne*, a group home for the mentally retarded was forced to apply for a special zoning permit. The owners of the home challenged the law as being a violation of the Equal Protection Clause. At the trial level, the district court applied a rational basis test and found the law constitutional. On appeal, the court determined that mental retardation was a "quasi-suspect class" and applied an

Table 8-2 Equal Protection: How Challenged Laws Are Reviewed

Rational Basis	Strict Scrutiny	Intermediate Scrutiny
Law is constitutional if:	*Law is constitutional if:*	*Law is constitutional if:*
Law has a *reasonable* relationship to *legitimate* government interest	Law is *necessary* to achieve a *compelling* state interest	Law is *substantially* related to an *important* government interest
Application:	*Application:*	*Application:*
Laws that classify by age or mental retardation; laws that have an economic purpose; laws that do not fall into other categories	Laws that classify by "suspect class" (race, ethnicity, and sometimes alien status) or burden a fundamental right and demonstrate purposeful discrimination	Laws that classify by quasi-suspect class (gender, legitimacy, or sometimes alien status)

© Cengage Learning 2013

intermediate level of scrutiny. The appellate court found the law unconstitutional. An important question for the Supreme Court was which test to apply. In its opinion, the Court discusses the different tests applied to various classifications. See Table 8-2 for a summary of the tests. The *City of Cleburne* case follows.

City of Cleburne v. Cleburne Living Ctr., Inc.

473 U.S. 432 (1985)

JUSTICE WHITE delivered the opinion of the Court.

The Equal Protection Clause of the Fourteenth Amendment commands that no State shall "deny to any person within its jurisdiction the equal protection of the laws," which is essentially a direction that all persons similarly situated should be treated alike. *Plyler v. Doe*, 457 U.S. 202, 216 (1982). The general rule is that legislation is presumed to be valid and will be sustained if the classification drawn by the statute is rationally related to a legitimate state interest. When social or economic legislation is at issue, the Equal Protection Clause allows the States wide latitude, and the Constitution presumes that even improvident decisions will eventually be rectified by the democratic processes.

The general rule gives way, however, when a statute classifies by race, alienage, or national origin. These factors are so seldom relevant to the achievement of any legitimate state interest that laws grounded in such considerations are deemed to reflect prejudice and antipathy—a view that those in the burdened class are not as worthy or deserving as others. For these reasons and

because such discrimination is unlikely to be soon rectified by legislative means, these laws are subjected to strict scrutiny and will be sustained only if they are suitably tailored to serve a compelling state interest. Similar oversight by the courts is due when state laws impinge on personal rights protected by the Constitution.

Legislative classifications based on gender also call for a heightened standard of review. That factor generally provides no sensible ground for differential treatment. "What differentiates sex from such nonsuspect statutes as intelligence or physical disability ... is that the sex characteristic frequently bears no relation to ability to perform or contribute to society." *Frontiero v. Richardson*, 411 U.S. 677, 686 (1973) (plurality opinion). Rather than resting on meaningful considerations, statutes distributing benefits and burdens between the sexes in different ways very likely reflect outmoded notions of the relative capabilities of men and women. A gender classification fails unless it is substantially related to a sufficiently important governmental interest. *Craig v. Boren*, 429 U.S. 190 (1976). Because illegitimacy is

(continued)

(continued)

beyond the individual's control and bears "no relation to the individual's ability to participate in and contribute to society," *Mathews v. Lucas*, 427 U.S. 495, 505 (1976), official discriminations resting on that characteristic are also subject to somewhat heightened review. Those restrictions "will survive equal protection scrutiny to the extent they are substantially related to a legitimate state interest." *Mills v. Habluetzel*, 456 U.S. 91, 99 (1982).

We have declined, however, to extend heightened review to differential treatment based on age:

"While the treatment of the aged in this Nation has not been wholly free of discrimination, such persons, unlike, say, those who have been discriminated against on the basis of race or national origin, have not experienced a 'history of purposeful unequal treatment' or been subjected to unique disabilities on the basis of stereotyped characteristics not truly indicative of their abilities." *Massachusetts Board of Retirement v. Murgia*, 427 U.S. 307, 313 (1976).

Against this background, we conclude for several reasons that the Court of Appeals erred in holding mental retardation a quasi-suspect classification calling for a more exacting standard of judicial review than is normally accorded economic and social legislation. First, it is undeniable, that those who are mentally retarded have a reduced ability to cope with and function in the everyday world. They are thus different, immutably so, in relevant respects, and the States' interest in dealing with and providing for them is plainly a legitimate one. How this large and diversified group is to be treated under the law is a difficult and often a technical matter, very much a task for legislators guided by qualified professionals and not by the perhaps ill-informed opinions of the judiciary.

Second, the distinctive legislative response, both national and state, to the plight of those who are mentally retarded demonstrates not only that they have unique problems, but also that the lawmakers have been addressing their difficulties in a manner that belies a continuing antipathy or prejudice and a corresponding need for more intrusive oversight by the judiciary. Especially given the wide variation in the abilities and needs of the retarded themselves, governmental bodies must have a certain amount of flexibility and freedom from judicial oversight in shaping and limiting their remedial efforts.

Third, the legislative response, which could hardly have occurred and survived without public support, negates any claim that the mentally retarded are politically powerless in the sense that they have no ability to attract the attention of the lawmakers. Any minority can be said to be powerless to assert direct control over the legislature, but if that were a criterion for higher level scrutiny by the courts, much economic and social legislation would now be suspect.

Fourth, if the large and amorphous class of the mentally retarded were deemed quasi-suspect for the reasons given by the Court of Appeals, it would be difficult to find a principled way to distinguish a variety of other groups who have perhaps immutable disabilities setting them off from others, who cannot themselves mandate the desired legislative responses, and who can claim some degree of prejudice from at least part of the public at large. One need mention in this respect only the aging, the disabled, the mentally ill, and the infirm. We are reluctant to set out on that course, and we decline to do so.

Our refusal to recognize the retarded as a quasi-suspect class does not leave them entirely unprotected from invidious discrimination. To withstand equal protection review, legislation that distinguishes between the mentally retarded and others must be rationally related to a legitimate governmental purpose. This standard, we believe, affords government the latitude necessary both to pursue policies designed to assist the retarded in realizing their full potential, and to freely and efficiently engage in activities that burden the retarded in what is essentially an incidental manner. The State may not rely on a classification whose relationship to an asserted goal is so attenuated as to render the distinction arbitrary or irrational.

We turn to the issue of the validity of the zoning ordinance insofar as it requires a special use permit for homes for the mentally retarded. We inquire first whether requiring a special use permit in the circumstances here deprives respondents of the equal protection of the laws.

The constitutional issue is clearly posed. The city does not require a special use permit in an R-3 zone for apartment houses, multiple dwellings, boarding and lodging houses, fraternity or sorority houses, dormitories, apartment hotels, hospitals, sanitariums, nursing homes for convalescents or the aged (other than for the insane or feebleminded or alcoholics or drug addicts), private

(continued)

(continued)

clubs or fraternal orders, and other specified uses. It does, however, insist on a special permit for the Featherston home, and it does so, as the District Court found, because it would be a facility for the mentally retarded.

It is true, as already pointed out, that the mentally retarded as a group are indeed different from others not sharing their misfortune, and in this respect they may be different from those who would occupy other facilities that would be permitted in an R-3 zone without a special permit. But this difference is largely irrelevant. Because in

our view the record does not reveal any rational basis for believing that the Featherston home would pose any special threat to the city's legitimate interests, we affirm the judgment below insofar as it holds the ordinance invalid as applied in this case.

The judgment of the Court of Appeals is affirmed insofar as it invalidates the zoning ordinance as applied to the Featherston home. The judgment is otherwise vacated, and the case is remanded.

It is so ordered.

Something to Consider

In this case, the Court mentions that discrimination based on race, alienage, or national origin "is unlikely to be soon rectified by legislative means." What does the Court mean by this? Do you agree? The Court also says that laws that discriminate because of these factors might be upheld if the state shows a "compelling state interest." Can you identify any such needs?

Violations of Equal Protection: Applying the Tests

VIOLATIONS OF EQUAL PROTECTION OCCUR when rights are denied to individuals based on some classifications. The type of classification often determines the test or standard used by the Court in reviewing an alleged violation. Several cases illustrate how the Supreme Court evaluates classifications for equal protection violations.

Race, Ethnicity, and National Origin (Strict Scrutiny)

Any law or government practice that purposefully discriminates because of race, ethnicity, or national origin violates the Equal Protection Clause unless the government can show a *compelling* reason for its existence. In the last fifty years, the only compelling reason recognized by the Court was national security in a time of war. During World War II, the Court upheld laws and practices that targeted Japanese Americans. Aside from this situation, laws that discriminate because of race are almost always found unconstitutional.

In applying the strict scrutiny test, the Court not only looks at the language of the law, but also how the law is enforced. If the law is enforced in such a way as to discriminate against a racial group, it will probably be found unconstitutional. This principle applied as early as 1886 in the case of *Yick Wo v. Hopkins*, 118 U.S. 356. Here, a San Francisco ordinance made it a crime to carry on a laundry within city limits without permission of the Board of Supervisors. The law did not mention race. However, it was enforced solely against Chinese. In overturning a criminal conviction resulting from a violation of the law, the Court said:

Though the law itself be fair on its face, and impartial in appearance, yet, if it is applied and administered by public authority with an evil eye and an unequal hand, so as practically to make unjust and illegal discriminations between persons in similar circumstances, material to their rights, the denial of equal justice is still within the prohibition of the constitution.

Gender (Intermediate Scrutiny)

At the time the Constitution was adopted, laws did not treat men and women equally. Women had few rights and, if married, had no legal existence separate from their husbands. It is not surprising, then, that the Court had a difficult time applying the Equal Protection Clause to laws that discriminated because of gender. In 1872, the Court addressed the issue in reviewing a state law that prohibited women from becoming lawyers. The Court upheld the law. In a concurring opinion, one justice expressed the attitude of the Court:

> The natural and proper timidity and delicacy which belongs to the female sex evidently unfits it for many of the occupations of civil life. The constitution of the family organization, which is founded in the divine ordinance, as well as in the nature of things, indicates the domestic sphere as that which properly belongs to the domain and functions of womanhood. The harmony, not to say identity, of interest and views which belong, or should belong, to the family institution is repugnant to the idea of a woman adopting a distinct and independent career from that of her husband. *Bradwell v. State of Illinois*, 83 U.S. 130 (1872).

This attitude prevailed well into the twentieth century. In 1948, the Court was asked to invalidate a state law that prohibited women from working as bartenders unless their father or husband owned the liquor license. *Goesaert v. Cleary*, 335 U.S. 464 (1948). The Court refused to do this, holding that the law was a valid exercise of state police power and not a violation of equal protection. Consider the following excerpt from the Court's opinion:

> Michigan could, beyond question, forbid all women from working behind a bar. This is so despite the vast changes in the social and legal position of women. The fact that women may now have achieved the virtues that men have long claimed as their prerogatives and now indulge in vices that men have long practiced, does not preclude the States from drawing a sharp line between the sexes, certainly, in such matters as the regulation of the liquor traffic. See the Twenty-First Amendment and *Carter v. Virginia*, 321 U.S. 131. The Constitution does not require legislatures to reflect sociological insight, or shifting social standards, any more than it requires them to keep abreast of the latest scientific standards.

On the other hand, a growing minority of judges were shifting attitudes about gender equality. Three justices dissented in the *Goesaert* case with the following language:

> While the equal protection clause does not require a legislature to achieve "abstract symmetry" or to classify with "mathematical nicety," that clause does require lawmakers to refrain from invidious distinctions of the sort drawn by the statute challenged in this case.
>
> The statute arbitrarily discriminates between male and female owners of liquor establishments. A male owner, although he himself is always absent from his bar, may employ his wife and daughter as barmaids. A female owner may neither work as a barmaid herself nor employ her daughter in that position, even if a man is always present in the establishment to keep order. This inevitable result of the classification belies the assumption that the statute was motivated by a legislative solicitude for the moral and physical well-being of women who, but for the law, would be employed as barmaids. Since there could be no other conceivable justification for such discrimination against women owners of liquor establishments, the statute should be held invalid as a denial of equal protection.

In the 1970s, the Court considered the changing social standards, and it struck down a law that set the age of majority for women at eighteen and for men at twenty-one. The law required that a divorced father support a daughter until age eighteen, while he was required to support a son until age twenty-one. The Court said:

> Notwithstanding the "old notions" to which the Utah court referred, we perceive nothing rational in the distinction which, when related to the divorce decree, results in the appellee's liability for support for Sherri only to age 18 but for Rick to age 21. This imposes "criteria wholly unrelated to the objective of that statute." A child, male or female, is still a child. No longer is the female destined solely for the home and the rearing of the family, and only the male for the marketplace and the world of ideas. *See Taylor v. Louisiana*, 419 U.S. 522, 535 (1975). Women's activities and responsibilities are increasing and expanding. Coeducation is a fact, not a rarity. The presence of women in business, in the professions, in government and, indeed, in all walks of life where education is a desirable, if not always a necessary, antecedent is apparent and a proper subject of judicial notice. If a specified age of minority is required for the boy in order to assure him parental support while he attains his education and training, so, too, is it for the girl. *Stanton v. Stanton*, 421 U.S. 7 (1975).

Since the 1970s, the Court also struck down many gender-based laws including ones that:

1. Give a preference to a man in deciding who should be the executor of an estate, all other factors being equal. *Reed v. Reed*, 404 U.S. 71 (1971).
2. Allow eighteen-year-old women to buy beer, but require men to be twenty-one. *Craig v. Boren*, 429 U.S. 190 (1976).
3. Permit the state to operate an all-male military academy, the Virginia Military Institute. *United States v. Virginia*, 518 U.S. 515 (1996). (The opinion in this case is found later in the chapter.)

A few cases decided by the Supreme Court relate to gender bias against men. In these cases, the Court applies the same rules and logic. In one case the Court held that a state-run nursing school admitting only women was in violation of the Equal Protection Clause. *Mississippi Univ. for Women v. Hogan*, 458 U.S. 718 (1982). It also struck down a law that gave unwed mothers the right to consent to an adoption of the child, but did not give the same right to the unwed father. *Caban v. Mohammed*, 441 U.S. 380 (1979).

Nevertheless, the Court still recognizes that some situations justify classification by gender. In the case of *Michael M. v. Superior Court of Sonoma County*, 450 U.S. 464 (1981), the Court upheld a state law on statutory rape involving minors that applied to men only. In this case, both the male and female were under eighteen. In a 6–3 decision, the majority applied an intermediate level of scrutiny and found that the state had an important governmental interest in enacting this law—to prevent teenage pregnancies—and that the law had a substantial relationship to achieve this goal.

In modern times, gender bias has been most apparent in employment situations. Since the Fourteenth Amendment applies to government only, most private employers are not subject to the Equal Protection Clause. Congress has dealt with this by enacting legislation that does guarantee equal treatment in a work environment.

Following is the case *United States v. Virginia*, setting forth the Court's current position on gender bias.

United States v. Virginia
518 U.S. 515 (1996)

The cross-petitions in this case present two ultimate issues. First, does Virginia's exclusion of women from the educational opportunities provided by VMI—extraordinary opportunities for military training and civilian leadership development—deny to women the equal protection of the laws guaranteed by the Fourteenth Amendment? Second, if VMI's "unique" situation, as Virginia's sole single-sex public institution of higher education—offends the Constitution's equal protection principle, what is the remedial requirement?

Parties who seek to defend gender-based government action must demonstrate an "exceedingly persuasive justification" for that action.

Today's skeptical scrutiny of official action denying rights or opportunities based on sex responds to volumes of history. In 1971, for the first time in our Nation's history, this Court ruled in favor of a woman who complained that her State had denied her the equal protection of its laws. *Reed v. Reed*. Since *Reed*, the Court has repeatedly recognized that neither federal nor state government acts compatibly with the equal protection principle when a law or official policy denies to women, simply because they are women, full citizenship stature—equal opportunity to aspire, achieve, participate in and contribute to society based on their individual talents and capacities.

Without equating gender classifications, for all purposes, to classifications based on race or national origin, the Court, in post-*Reed* decisions, has carefully inspected official action that closes a door or denies opportunity to women (or to men). To summarize the Court's current directions for cases of official classification based on gender: Focusing on the differential treatment or denial of opportunity for which relief is sought, the reviewing court must determine whether the proffered justification is "exceedingly persuasive." The burden of justification is demanding and it rests entirely on the State. The State must show "at least that the challenged classification serves 'important governmental objectives and that the discriminatory means employed' are 'substantially related to the achievement of those objectives'." The justification must be genuine, not hypothesized or invented in response to litigation. And it must not rely on overbroad generalizations about the different talents, capacities, or preferences of males and females.

The heightened review standard our precedent establishes does not make sex a proscribed classification. Supposed "inherent differences" are no longer accepted as a ground for race or national origin classifications. See *Loving v. Virginia*, 388 U.S. 1 (1967). Physical differences between men and women, however, are enduring: "The two sexes are not fungible; a community made up exclusively of one sex is different from a community composed of both." *Ballard v. United States*, 329 U.S. 187, 193 (1946).

Measuring the record in this case against the review standard just described, we conclude that Virginia has shown no "exceedingly persuasive justification" for excluding all women from the citizen-soldier training afforded by VMI. We therefore affirm the Fourth Circuit's initial judgment, which held that Virginia had violated the Fourteenth Amendment's Equal Protection Clause. Because the remedy proffered by Virginia—the Mary Baldwin VWIL program—does not cure the constitutional violation, i.e., it does not provide equal opportunity, we reverse the Fourth Circuit's final judgment in this case.

Virginia argues that VMI's adversative method of training provides educational benefits that cannot be made available, unmodified, to women. Alterations to accommodate women would necessarily be "radical," so "drastic," Virginia asserts, as to transform, indeed "destroy," VMI's program.

It is uncontested that women's admission would require accommodations, primarily in arranging housing assignments and physical training programs for female cadets. It is also undisputed, however, that "the VMI methodology could be used to educate women." 852 F. Supp., at 481. The District Court even allowed that some women may prefer it to the methodology a women's college might pursue.

Education, to be sure, is not a "one size fits all" business. The issue, however, is not whether "women—or men—should be forced to attend VMI"; rather, the question is whether the State can constitutionally deny to women who have the will and capacity, the training and attendant opportunities that VMI uniquely affords.

The notion that admission of women would downgrade VMI's stature, destroy the adversative system and, with it, even the school, is a judgment hardly proved, a

(continued)

(continued)

prediction hardly different from other "self-fulfilling prophecies," once routinely used to deny rights or opportunities.

Women's successful entry into the federal military academies, and their participation in the Nation's military forces, indicate that Virginia's fears for the future of VMI may not be solidly grounded. The State's justification for excluding all women from "citizen-soldier" training for which some are qualified, in any event, cannot rank as "exceedingly persuasive," as we have explained and applied that standard.

In the second phase of the litigation, Virginia presented its remedial plan—maintain VMI as a male-only college and create VWIL as a separate program for women. The United States challenges this "remedial" ruling as pervasively misguided. A remedial decree, this Court has said, must closely fit the constitutional violation; it must be shaped to place persons unconstitutionally denied an opportunity or advantage in "the position they would have occupied in the absence of discrimination." (*See Milliken v. Bradley*, 433 U.S. 267, 280 (1977). The constitutional violation in this case is the categorical exclusion of women from an extraordinary educational opportunity afforded men. A proper remedy for an unconstitutional exclusion, we have explained, aims to "eliminate so far as possible the discriminatory effects of the past" and to "bar like discrimination in the future." *Louisiana v. United States*, 380 U.S. 145, 154 (1965).

Virginia chose not to eliminate, but to leave untouched, VMI's exclusionary policy. For women only, however, Virginia proposed a separate program, different in kind from VMI and unequal in tangible and intangible facilities. Having violated the Constitution's equal protection requirement, Virginia was obliged to show that its remedial proposal "directly addressed and related to" the violation. Virginia described VWIL as a "parallel program," and asserted that VWIL shares VMI's mission of producing "citizen-soldiers" and VMI's goals of providing "education, military training, mental and physical discipline, character … and leadership development." In exposing the character of, and differences in, the VMI and VWIL programs, we recapitulate facts earlier presented.

VWIL affords women no opportunity to experience the rigorous military training for which VMI is famed. Instead, the VWIL program "deemphasizes" military

education, and uses a "cooperative method" of education "which reinforces self-esteem."

VWIL students participate in ROTC and a "largely ceremonial" Virginia Corps of Cadets, but Virginia deliberately did not make VWIL a military institute. The VWIL House is not a military-style residence and VWIL students need not live together throughout the 4-year program, eat meals together, or wear uniforms during the school day. VWIL students thus do not experience the "barracks" life "crucial to the VMI experience," the spartan living arrangements designed to foster an "egalitarian ethic."

VWIL students receive their "leadership training" in seminars, externships, and speaker series, episodes and encounters lacking the "physical rigor, mental stress, … minute regulation of behavior, and indoctrination in desirable values" made hallmarks of VMI's citizen-soldier training, kept away from the pressures, hazards, and psychological bonding characteristic of VMI's adversative training, VWIL students will not know the "feeling of tremendous accomplishment" commonly experienced by VMI's successful cadets.

As earlier stated, generalizations about "the way women are," estimates of what is appropriate for most women, no longer justify denying opportunity to women whose talent and capacity place them outside the average description.

In myriad respects other than military training, VWIL does not qualify as VMI's equal. VWIL's student body, faculty, course offerings, and facilities hardly match VMI's. Nor can the VWIL graduate anticipate the benefits associated with VMI's 157-year history, the school's prestige, and its influential alumni network.

VMI offers an educational opportunity no other Virginia institution provides, and the school's "prestige"—associated with its success in developing "citizen-soldiers"—is unequaled. Virginia has closed this facility to its daughters and, instead, has devised for them a "parallel program," with a faculty less impressively credentialed and less well paid, more limited course offerings, fewer opportunities for military training and for scientific specialization. VMI, beyond question, "possesses to a far greater degree" than the VWIL program "those qualities which are incapable of objective measurement but which make for greatness in a … school," including "position and influence of the alumni, standing in the community, traditions and prestige." Women seeking and fit for a

(continued)

(continued)

VMI-quality education cannot be offered anything less, under the State's obligation to afford them genuinely equal protection.

For the reasons stated, the final judgment of the Court of Appeals is reversed, and the case is remanded for further proceedings consistent with this opinion.

It is so ordered.

JUSTICE THOMAS took no part in the consideration or decision of this case.

Justice Scalia wrote a strong dissent criticizing the majority for creating a higher standard of review for gender discrimination cases and for ignoring the historical tradition of military and same-sex education. Justice Scalia says that by requiring the state to show, "extremely persuasive justification" for the school, the majority is in essence requiring strict scrutiny.

Something to Consider

The entire opinion for the VMI case can be found on numerous Web sites or in printed versions of Supreme Court cases. Read the entirety of the Scalia dissent. Do you find his argument or the argument of the majority to be more persuasive?

Alien Status (Strict or Intermediate Scrutiny)

The Fourteenth Amendment protects "persons," not "citizens." Thus, the Court extended constitutional protections, including equal protection, to both legal and illegal aliens. Included in laws that were held unconstitutional are the following:

1. Laws that deny welfare benefits to resident aliens. *Graham v. Richardson*, 403 U.S. 365 (1971).
2. State laws that deny an alien the right to obtain a fishing license that is necessary to the alien's business as a commercial fisherman. *Takahashi v. Fish & Game Com.*, 334 U.S. 410 (1948).
3. State laws that deny a resident alien the right to take the bar examination. *In re Griffiths*, 413 U.S. 717 (1973).
4. State laws withholding funds from local school districts that enroll undocumented aliens. *Plyler v. Doe*, 457 U.S. 202 (1982).

On the other hand, the Court upheld laws denying aliens the right to hold certain government jobs. Requiring citizenship for teachers and police officers is not a denial of equal protection, according to the Court, because "some state functions are so bound up with the operation of the State as a governmental entity as to permit exclusion from those functions of all persons who have not become part of the process of self-government."

Other Classifications

Discrimination is not limited to race or gender. Laws single out individuals for a number of personal characteristics, and some of these laws have been attacked as being in violation of the Equal Protection Clause. Other characteristics considered by the Supreme Court include illegitimacy, poverty, age, sexual orientation, and developmental disabilities. In some cases the Court found the challenged laws violated the Equal Protection Clause and in others the Court found the classifications met the proper test for constitutionality. In the case of legitimacy, the Court favored the intermediate scrutiny test. In reviewing the other classifications, unless a fundamental right was involved, the Court used the rational basis test. The following are examples of the Court's rulings:

1. The Court upheld a state policy of funding schools through property taxes even though poorer neighborhoods had less money for education. *San Antonio Indep. Sch. Dist. v. Rodriguez*, 411 U.S. 1 (1973).
2. The Court struck down a state law requiring convicted indigent defendants to pay for a copy of the transcript they needed for an appeal. *Griffin v. Illinois*, 351 U.S. 12 (1956).

In the first case, the Court applied a rational basis test saying that poverty was not a suspect class and education was not a fundamental right. In the second case, the Court applied the strict scrutiny test because the rights of a criminal defendant are fundamental rights.

In another case, the Court upheld a state law that required police to retire at age fifty. *Massachusetts Bd. of Retirement v. Murgia*, 427 U.S. 307 (1976). In discussing age discrimination, the Court said:

> While the treatment of the aged in this Nation has not been wholly free of discrimination, such persons, unlike, say, those who have been discriminated against on the basis of race or national origin, have not experienced a "history of purposeful unequal treatment" or been subjected to unique disabilities on the basis of stereotyped characteristics not truly indicative of their abilities.

As a result, the Court applied a rational basis test finding that requiring retirement at age fifty was reasonable in light of the job that police do.

Although the Court refuses to find equal protection violations in some disability and age classifications, legislation prohibits similar discrimination today. The Americans with Disabilities Act and The Age Discrimination in Employment Act provide remedies in addition to the Equal Protection Clause of the Constitution.

In *Romer v. Evans*, 517 U.S. 620 (1996), the Supreme Court considered a state law that classified individuals by their sexual preference. Reacting to local ordinances that banned discrimination based on sexual orientation, Colorado voters adopted by statewide referendum "Amendment 2" to their state constitution. This amendment prohibited all legislative, executive, or judicial action at any level of state or local government designed to protect the status of persons based on their "homosexual, lesbian or bisexual orientation, conduct, practices or relationships." The constitutional amendment was challenged in court. The state courts applied a standard of strict scrutiny and found the law unconstitutional. The Supreme Court granted certiorari. In its decision, the Court applies the rational basis test, but comes to the same conclusion as the state courts. Justice Scalia wrote a strong dissenting opinion, also applying the rational basis test. The following excerpts summarize the positions of each side:

> From the Court's opinion written by Justice Kennedy:
>
> The Fourteenth Amendment's promise that no person shall be denied the equal protection of the laws must co-exist with the practical necessity that most legislation classifies for one purpose or another, with resulting disadvantage to various groups or persons. We have attempted to reconcile the principle with the reality by stating that, if a law neither burdens a fundamental right nor targets a suspect class, we will uphold the legislative classification so long as it bears a rational relation to some legitimate end. Amendment 2 fails, indeed defies, even this conventional inquiry. Amendment 2 confounds this normal process of judicial review. It is at once too narrow and too broad. It identifies persons by a single trait and then denies them protection across the board. The resulting disqualification of a class of persons from the right to seek specific protection from the law is unprecedented in our jurisprudence.

The primary rationale the State offers for Amendment 2 is respect for other citizens' freedom of association, and in particular the liberties of landlords or employers who have personal or religious objections to homosexuality. Colorado also cites its interest in conserving resources to fight discrimination against other groups. The breadth of the Amendment is so far removed from these particular justifications that we find it impossible to credit them. We must conclude that Amendment 2 classifies homosexuals not to further a proper legislative end but to make them unequal to everyone else. This Colorado cannot do. A State cannot so deem a class of persons a stranger to its laws. Amendment 2 violates the Equal Protection Clause, and the judgment of the Supreme Court of Colorado is affirmed.

JUSTICE SCALIA, with whom the CHIEF JUSTICE and JUSTICE THOMAS join, dissenting.

The Court has mistaken a Kulturkampf for a fit of spite. The constitutional amendment before us here is not the manifestation of a "bare desire to harm" homosexuals, but is rather a modest attempt by seemingly tolerant Coloradans to preserve traditional sexual mores against the efforts of a politically powerful minority to revise those mores through use of the laws. That objective, and the means chosen to achieve it, are not only unimpeachable under any constitutional doctrine hitherto pronounced (hence the opinion's heavy reliance upon principles of righteousness rather than judicial holdings); they have been specifically approved by the Congress of the United States and by this Court.

Something to Consider

Does the majority opinion in this case support an argument that banning same-sex marriages is unconstitutional?

Table 8-3 Equal Protection Case Summaries

Case	Classification	Facts	Holding
Yick Wo v. Hopkins, 118 U.S. 356 (1886)	Race, Ethnicity, or National Origin	An ordinance making it a crime to carry on a laundry within city limits was enforced solely against Chinese, even though it did not mention race.	Unconstitutional
Korematsu v. United States, 323 U.S. 214 (1944)	Race, Ethnicity, or National Origin	During World War II, a law prohibited individuals of Japanese ancestry from being in certain military areas.	Constitutional (the war was a compelling reason)
McCleskey v. Kemp, 481 U.S. 279 (1987)	Race, Ethnicity, or National Origin	Defendant challenged the state's death penalty claiming statistical studies showed its imposition was based on race.	Constitutional (no showing of purposeful discrimination)
City of Cleburne v. Cleburne Living Ctr., Inc., 473 U.S. 432 (1985)	Mental disability	A group home for the mentally disabled was forced to apply for a special zoning permit.	Unconstitutional
Craig v. Boren, 429 U.S. 190 (1976)	Gender	A law allowed eighteen-year-old women to buy beer, but required men to be twenty-one.	Unconstitutional
Stanton v. Stanton, 421 U.S. 7 (1975)	Gender	A law set the age of majority for women at eighteen and for men at twenty-one.	Unconstitutional
Reed v. Reed, 404 U.S. 71 (1971)	Gender	A law gave preference to a man in deciding who should be the executor of an estate, all other factors being equal.	Unconstitutional
United States v. Virginia, 518 U.S. 515 (1996)	Gender	State operated a military institute exclusively for men.	Unconstitutional

Table 8-3 *(continued)*

Case	Classification	Facts	Holding
Mississippi Univ. for Women v. Hogan, 458 U.S. 718 (1982)	Gender	A state-run nursing school admitted only women.	Unconstitutional
Caban v. Mohammed, 441 U.S. 380 (1979)	Gender	A law gave unwed mothers the right to consent to an adoption of the child, but not the unwed father.	Unconstitutional
Michael M. v. Superior Court of Sonoma County, 450 U.S. 464 (1981)	Gender	A law criminalized statutory rape for a male, but not a female.	Constitutional
Graham v. Richardson, 403 U.S. 365 (1971)	Alienage	A law denied welfare benefits to resident aliens.	Unconstitutional
Takahashi v. Fish & Game Com., 334 U.S. 410 (1948)	Alienage	A state law denied the right to obtain a fishing license necessary to the alien's business as a commercial fisherman.	Unconstitutional
In re Griffiths, 413 U.S. 717 (1973)	Alienage	A state law denied a resident alien the right to take the bar examination.	Unconstitutional
Plyler v. Doe, 457 U.S. 202 (1982)	Alienage	A state law withheld funds from local school districts enrolling undocumented aliens.	Unconstitutional
San Antonio Indep. Sch. Dist. v. Rodriguez, 411 U.S. 1 (1973)	Poverty	A state funded schools through property taxes even though poorer neighborhoods had less money for education.	Constitutional
Griffin v. Illinois, 351 U.S. 12 (1956)	Poverty/ Fundamental right to fair trial	A state law required convicted indigent defendants to pay for a copy of the transcript needed for an appeal.	Unconstitutional
Massachusetts Bd. of Retirement v. Murgia, 427 U.S. 307 (1976)	Age	A state law required police to retire at age fifty.	Constitutional
Romer v. Evans, 517 U.S. 620 (1996)	Sexual Preference	A state constitution prohibited all legislative, executive, or judicial action designed to protect the status of persons based on their sexual preference.	Unconstitutional

Equal Protection and Voting Rights

ARTICLE II SECTION 2 OF the Constitution provides the manner of electing the president who is not chosen by popular vote but rather by electors from each state. The selection of electors is to be determined by the state legislatures. Even though the Constitution does not provide for presidential selection by popular vote, the right to vote is one of the most cherished and fundamental rights Americans possess. "The right of suffrage is a fundamental matter in a free and democratic society.... The right to exercise the franchise in a free and unimpaired manner is preservative of other basic civil and political rights." *Reynolds v. Sims*, 377 U.S. 533 (1964). Because this is a fundamental right, the Court closely scrutinizes any law that attempts to restrict or limit that right.

A state law that abridges the right to vote because of race violates the Fifteenth Amendment to the Constitution, which provides "the right of citizens of the United States to vote shall not be denied or abridged by the United States or by any State on account of race, color, or previous condition of servitude." In most cases, such a law also violates the Equal Protection Clause of the Constitution. Laws that abridge the right to vote for reasons other than race do not violate the Fifteenth Amendment but may violate the Equal Protection Clause. The Supreme Court has reviewed various laws and practices that present equal protection issues including laws that impose qualifications for voters and laws that restrict a candidate's access to the ballot. Another major issue for the Court is reapportionment or redistricting for elections. In the 2000 presidential election, the Court also considered if Florida's vote recount process violated the Equal Protection Clause.

Voter Qualifications

Many states impose conditions or qualifications for voters. For example, some states require that in order to vote a person have no felony convictions. A state might also require reasonable residency and registration requirements. Under these laws, some individuals lose the right to vote. However, the Supreme Court said such a result does not necessarily constitute an equal protection violation. On the other hand, the Supreme Court held that requiring a *lengthy* state residence as a prerequisite to being allowed to vote is a denial of equal protection. The Court reasoned that such a law deprived a group of people of a fundamental right without any compelling reason, especially in light of the fact that the state exercised general criminal and taxing authorities over the individuals.

In other cases, the Court considered whether a state or local government could limit the right to vote to property owners, a practice favored by local municipalities, especially in school elections. In most cases, the Court held that such laws violate the Equal Protection Clause. Denying non-property owners the right to vote was without justification especially when they, too, have an interest in the outcome of the election. However, in one case dealing with an election of a water storage district, the Court upheld the property ownership limitation because the cost fell disproportionately on landowners.

On the other hand, recently, the Supreme Court, *Crawford v. Marion County Election Bd.*, 553 U.S. 181 (2008), upheld a state law requiring that an individual produce a government issued photo I.D. The official Court Syllabus explains:

⚖ Crawford v. Marion County
553 U.S. 181 (2008)

After Indiana enacted an election law (SEA 483) requiring citizens voting in person to present government-issued photo identification, petitioners filed separate suits challenging the law's constitutionality. Following discovery, the District Court granted respondents summary judgment, finding the evidence in the record insufficient to support a facial attack on the statute's validity. In affirming, the Seventh Circuit declined to judge the law by the strict standard set for poll taxes in *Harper v. Virginia Bd. of Elections*, 383 U.S. 663, finding the burden on voters offset by the benefit of reducing the risk of fraud.

Held: The judgment is affirmed.

Justice Stevens, joined by The Chief Justice and Justice Kennedy, concluded that the evidence in the record does not support a facial attack on SEA 483's validity.

(a) Under *Harper*, even rational restrictions on the right to vote are invidious if they are unrelated to voter qualifications. However, "even handed restrictions" protecting the "integrity and reliability of the electoral process itself" satisfy *Harper*'s standard. *Anderson v. Celebrezze*, 460 U.S. 780, n. 9. A state law's burden on a political party, an individual voter, or a discrete class of voters must be justified by relevant and legitimate state interests "sufficiently weighty to justify the limitation." *Norman v. Reed*, 502 U.S. 279.

(b) Each of Indiana's asserted interests is unquestionably relevant to its interest in protecting the integrity and reliability of the electoral process. The first

(continued)

(continued)

is the interest in deterring and detecting voter fraud. Indiana has a valid interest in participating in a nationwide effort to improve and modernize election procedures criticized as antiquated and inefficient. Indiana also claims a particular interest in preventing voter fraud in response to the problem of voter registration rolls with a large number of names of persons who are either deceased or no longer live in Indiana. While the record contains no evidence that the fraud SEA 483 addresses—in-person voter impersonation at polling places—has actually occurred in Indiana, such fraud has occurred in other parts of the country, and Indiana's own experience with voter fraud in a 2003 mayoral primary demonstrates a real risk that voter fraud could affect a close election's outcome. There is no question about the legitimacy or importance of a State's interest in counting only eligible voters' votes. Finally, Indiana's interest in protecting public confidence in elections, while closely related to its interest in preventing voter fraud, has independent significance, because such confidence encourages citizen participation in the democratic process.

(c) The relevant burdens here are those imposed on eligible voters who lack photo identification cards that comply with SEA 483. Because Indiana's cards are free, the inconvenience of going to the Bureau of Motor Vehicles, gathering required documents, and posing for a photograph does not qualify as a substantial burden on most voters' right to vote, or represent a significant increase over the usual burdens of voting. The severity of the somewhat heavier burden that may be placed on a limited number of persons—*e.g.*, elderly persons born out-of-state, who may have difficulty obtaining a birth certificate—is mitigated by the fact that eligible voters without photo identification may cast provisional ballots that will be counted if they execute the required affidavit at the circuit court clerk's office. Even assuming that the burden may not be justified as to a few voters, that conclusion is by no means sufficient to establish petitioners' right to the relief they seek.

(d) Petitioners argue that Indiana's interests do not justify the burden imposed on voters who cannot afford or obtain a birth certificate and who must make a second trip to the circuit court clerk's office, but it is not possible to quantify, based on the evidence in the record, either that burden's magnitude or the portion of the burden that is fully justified. A facial challenge must fail where the statute has a " 'plainly legitimate sweep.' " *Id.*, at ___. When considering SEA 483's broad application to all Indiana voters, it "imposes only a limited burden on voters' rights." *Burdick v. Takushi*, 504 U.S. 428. The "precise interests" advanced by Indiana are therefore sufficient to defeat petitioners' facial challenge. *Id.*, at 434. Pp. 16–20.

(e) Valid neutral justifications for a nondiscriminatory law, such as SEA 483, should not be disregarded simply because partisan interests may have provided one motivation for the votes of individual legislators.

JUSTICE SCALIA, joined by JUSTICE THOMAS and JUSTICE ALITO, was of the view that petitioners' premise that the voter-identification law might have imposed a special burden on some voters is irrelevant. The law should be upheld because its overall burden is minimal and justified. A law respecting the right to vote should be evaluated under the approach in *Burdick v. Takushi*, 504 U.S. 428, which calls for application of a deferential, "important regulatory interests" standard for nonsevere, nondiscriminatory restrictions, reserving strict scrutiny for laws that severely restrict the right to vote, *id.*, at 433–434. The different ways in which Indiana's law affects different voters are no more than different impacts of the single burden that the law uniformly imposes on all voters: To vote in person, everyone must have and present a photo identification that can be obtained for free. This is a generally applicable, nondiscriminatory voting regulation. The law's universally applicable requirements are eminently reasonable because the burden of acquiring, possessing, and showing a free photo identification is not a significant increase over the usual voting burdens, and the State's stated interests are sufficient to sustain that minimal burden. Pp. 1–6.

STEVENS, J., announced the judgment of the Court and delivered an opinion, in which ROBERTS, C. J., and KENNEDY, J., joined. SCALIA, J., filed an opinion concurring in the judgment, in which THOMAS and ALITO, JJ., joined. SOUTER, J., filed a dissenting opinion, in which GINSBURG, J., joined. BREYER, J., filed a dissenting opinion.

Something to Consider

The Court mentioned that the benefits of the law outweighed the burdens it might impose, but acknowledged that for some, the burden might be greater. Are equal protection violations related to the number of people suffering discrimination?

Access to Ballot

The right to vote requires that all interested candidates have equal access to the ballot. If a special-interest candidate cannot get his or her name on the ballot, the voter's right to choose is limited. Thus, imposing filing fees for candidates is unconstitutional if no alternative exists for indigent candidates. Likewise, laws that limit the right of independent candidates to get their names on the ballot are highly suspect. In one case, the Court struck down a law that allowed only the major party candidates to appear on the ballot. However, the Court recognizes that states have a legitimate interest in keeping ballots to a reasonable length and has upheld restrictions requiring that a candidate obtain a minimum number of signatures before qualifying for the ballot.

One Person, One Vote: Apportionment and Districting

One of the most fundamental principles in a democratic society is that each person has an equal say in an election. One person's vote should not count more than another's just because that person is richer or more educated or belongs to a specific racial group.

> How then can one person be given twice or ten times the voting power of another person in a state-wide election merely because he lives in a rural area or because he lives in the smallest rural county? Once the geographical unit for which a representative is to be chosen is designated, all who participate in the election are to have an equal vote—whatever their race, whatever their sex, whatever their occupation, whatever their income, and wherever their home may be in that geographical unit. This is required by the Equal Protection Clause of the Fourteenth Amendment. The concept of "we the people" under the Constitution visualizes no preferred class of voters but equality among those who meet the basic qualifications. The idea that every voter is equal to every other voter in his State, when he casts his ballot in favor of one of several competing candidates, underlies many of our decisions.
>
> The conception of political equality from the Declaration of Independence, to Lincoln's Gettysburg Address, to the Fifteenth, Seventeenth, and Nineteenth Amendments can mean only one thing—one person, one vote. *Gray v. Sanders*, 372 U.S. 368 (1963).

Unfortunately, "one person, one vote" does not occur when the number of elected officials from different districts or geographical areas is not in proportion to the population of each district or if districts are configured in such a way as to defeat the interests of minority groups. For example, consider the following situations:

1. State X creates four congressional districts within the state. One district has a population of one million, another district has a population of two million, a third district has a population of three million, and the last has a population of four million. Each district selects one representative to Congress.
2. State Y creates eight congressional districts within the state. The state has a population of twelve million. Included in the population are approximately four million individuals belonging to a racial minority. Each district has approximately one-and-one-half million people. No district has more than 40 percent respresenting the racial minority.

The first example presents a problem of apportionment. The second example presents a problem in the way that districting lines are drawn. Both examples result in "diluted" votes for some of the voters. In the first example, each vote in the smaller district counts four times as much as each vote in the largest district. In the second example, the ability of a minority group to elect any official is greatly reduced because they do not have a majority of any district. (If district lines are intentionally drawn this way, the practice is called **gerrymandering**.)

🏛 **gerrymandering**
Creating geographical voting districts in such a way that one group is favored over another.

In most cases, the Court requires that elections be based on fair apportionment. The "one person, one vote" generally controls. This rule applies to local as well as national elections. Apportionment for federal congressional elections depends on figures resulting from the official census. The accuracy of the census is therefore important.

Drawing proper geographical district lines to achieve fair representation is a difficult problem. This issue is addressed in Supreme Court cases and legislation, specifically the Voters Registration Act of 1965. The Supreme Court said that the practice of creating congressional districts along racial lines is highly suspect, even when the lines are drawn to give minorities more rather than less voting power. In one case, *Shaw v. Reno*, 509 U.S. 630 (1993), the Court reviewed a South Carolina plan for newly created districts. The districts were drawn in extremely irregular shapes that managed to include many minority neighborhoods. In commenting on the plan, the Court said:

> We believe that reapportionment is one area in which appearances do matter. A reapportionment plan that includes in one district individuals who belong to the same race, but who are otherwise widely separated by geographical and political boundaries, and who may have little in common with one another but the color of their skin, bears an uncomfortable resemblance to political apartheid. It reinforces the perception that members of the same racial group—regardless of their age, education, economic status, or the community in which they live—think alike, share the same political interests, and will prefer the same candidates at the polls. We have rejected such perceptions elsewhere as impermissible racial stereotypes.

In *Shaw*, the plaintiffs, a group of South Carolina voters, filed a lawsuit challenging the redistricting plan but the lawsuit was dismissed. The Supreme Court granted a hearing and ruled that the case should not be dismissed because the plaintiffs might have an equal protection claim.

Uncounted Votes

After the 2000 presidential election, the Court faced a new voting rights issue dealing with votes that went uncounted. Presidential votes on over 9,000 Florida ballots remained uncounted in an election when President Bush won by under 1,800 votes. The Florida Supreme Court ordered a manual recount with instructions that the intent of the voter should be determined in the recount. Unfortunately, the Court did not set any standards as to how to accomplish this. President Bush asked the Supreme Court to reverse the order of the Florida Supreme Court ordering the recount. The president claimed that because the order to recount was void of any discernible standards, some ballots with partially punched "chads" were counted while others with similar "chads" were not. This, the president claimed, was a violation of equal protection. Candidate Gore, of course, contended that there was no equal protection violation. Following is an excerpt from the Supreme Court opinion.

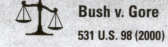

Bush v. Gore

531 U.S. 98 (2000)

PER CURIAM.

The right to vote is protected in more than the initial allocation of the franchise. Equal protection applies as well to the manner of its exercise. Having once granted the right to vote on equal terms, the State may not, by later arbitrary and disparate treatment, value one person's vote over that of another.

The question before us is whether the recount procedures the Florida Supreme Court has adopted are consistent with its obligation to avoid arbitrary and disparate treatment of the members of its electorate.

Much of the controversy seems to revolve around ballot cards designed to be perforated by a stylus but which, either through error or deliberate omission, have not been perforated with sufficient precision for a machine to count them. In some cases a piece of the card—a chad—is hanging, say by two corners. In other cases there is no separation at all, just an indentation.

The Florida Supreme Court has ordered that the intent of the voter be discerned from such ballots. The recount mechanisms implemented in response to the decisions of the Florida Supreme Court do not satisfy the minimum requirement for non-arbitrary treatment of voters necessary to secure the fundamental right. Florida's basic command for the count of legally cast votes is to consider the "intent of the voter." This is unobjectionable as an abstract proposition and a starting principle. The problem inheres in the absence of specific standards to ensure its equal application. The formulation of uniform rules to determine intent based on these recurring circumstances is practicable and, we conclude, necessary.

In this instance the question is how to interpret the marks or holes or scratches on an inanimate object, a piece of cardboard or paper which, it is said, might not have registered as a vote during the machine count. The factfinder confronts a thing, not a person. The search for intent can be confined by specific rules designed to ensure uniform treatment.

The want of those rules here has led to unequal evaluation of ballots in various respects. As seems to have been acknowledged at oral argument, the standards for accepting or rejecting contested ballots might vary not only from county to county but indeed within a single county from one recount team to another.

The record provides some examples. A monitor in Miami-Dade County testified at trial that he observed that three members of the county canvassing board applied different standards in defining a legal vote.

In addition to these difficulties the actual process by which the votes were to be counted under the Florida Supreme Court's decision raises further concerns. That order did not specify who would recount the ballots. The county canvassing boards were forced to pull together ad hoc teams comprised of judges from various Circuits who had no previous training in handling and interpreting ballots. Furthermore, while others were permitted to observe, they were prohibited from objecting during the recount.

The recount process, in its features here described, is inconsistent with the minimum procedures necessary to protect the fundamental right of each voter in the special instance of a statewide recount under the authority of a single state judicial officer. Our consideration is limited to the present circumstances, for the problem of equal protection in election processes generally presents many complexities.

Upon due consideration of the difficulties identified to this point, it is obvious that the recount cannot be conducted in compliance with the requirements of equal protection and due process without substantial additional work.

The Supreme Court of Florida has said that the legislature intended the State's electors to "participate fully in the federal electoral process," as provided in 3 U.S.C. § 5. That statute, in turn, requires that any controversy or contest that is designed to lead to a conclusive selection of electors be completed by December 12. That date is upon us, and there is no recount procedure in place under the State Supreme Court's order that comports with minimal constitutional standards. Because it is evident that any recount seeking to meet the December 12 date will be unconstitutional for the reasons we have discussed, we reverse the judgment of the Supreme Court of Florida ordering a recount to proceed.

It is so ordered.

Remedies for Violations of Equal Protection

IN 1954, IN THE CASE of *Brown v. Board of Education* (Chapter 7), the Supreme Court found that segregation in public schools violated the Equal Protection Clause. The next question it addressed was what to do about it. When the Court finds that a law violates the Equal Protection Clause, it may or may not suggest some remedy. Often the Court leaves it to the appropriate legislatures to enact new laws to eliminate the constitutional violations. Sometimes a proposed remedy to a problem presents even more legal issues. This is certainly true in the case of proposed remedies for school segregation (plans such as busing), school admission and employment discrimination (affirmative action plans), and voter discrimination (redistricting plans).

Desegregation and Schools

In *Brown*, the Court declared that segregation was illegal, but then it had to decide how integration was to be achieved. A second Supreme Court case, usually referred to as *Brown II*, resulted. *Brown II* reflects the difficulty the Court has in actually providing a remedy for an equal protection violation. The Court, in this case, referred the problem back to the local school districts, which were to be supervised by local courts. The opinion follows.

Brown v. Board of Education
349 U.S. 294 (1955) (Brown II)

MR. CHIEF JUSTICE WARREN delivered the opinion of the Court.

These cases were decided on May 17, 1954. The opinions of that date, declaring the fundamental principle that racial discrimination in public education is unconstitutional, are incorporated herein by reference. All provisions of federal, state, or local law requiring or permitting such discrimination must yield to this principle. There remains for consideration the manner in which relief is to be accorded.

The defendants in the cases coming to us from South Carolina and Virginia are awaiting the decision of this Court concerning relief.

Full implementation of these constitutional principles may require solution of varied local school problems. School authorities have the primary responsibility for elucidating, assessing, and solving these problems; courts will have to consider whether the action of school authorities constitutes good faith implementation of the governing constitutional principles. Because of their proximity to local conditions and the possible need for further hearings, the courts which originally heard these cases can best perform this judicial appraisal.

Accordingly, we believe it appropriate to remand the cases to those courts.

In fashioning and effectuating the decrees, the courts will be guided by equitable principles. Traditionally, equity has been characterized by a practical flexibility in shaping its remedies and by a facility for adjusting and reconciling public and private needs. These cases call for the exercise of these traditional attributes of equity power. At stake is the personal interest of the plaintiffs in admission to public schools as soon as practicable on a nondiscriminatory basis. To effectuate this interest may call for elimination of a variety of obstacles in making the transition to school systems operated in accordance with the constitutional principles set forth in our May 17, 1954, decision. Courts of equity may properly take into account the public interest in the elimination of such obstacles in a systematic and effective manner. But it should go without saying that the vitality of these constitutional principles cannot be allowed to yield simply because of disagreement with them.

While giving weight to these public and private considerations, the courts will require that the defendants make a prompt and reasonable start toward full

(continued)

(continued)

compliance with our May 17, 1954, ruling. Once such a start has been made, the courts may find that additional time is necessary to carry out the ruling in an effective manner. The burden rests upon the defendants to establish that such time is necessary in the public interest and is consistent with good faith compliance at the earliest practicable date. To that end, the courts may consider problems related to administration, arising from the physical condition of the school plant, the school transportation system, personnel, revision of school districts and attendance areas into compact units to achieve a system of determining admission to the public schools on a nonracial basis, and revision of local laws and regulations which may be necessary in solving the foregoing problems. They will also consider the adequacy of any plans the defendants may propose to meet these problems and to effectuate a transition to a racially nondiscriminatory school system. During this period of transition, the courts will retain jurisdiction of these cases.

The judgments below, except that in the Delaware case, are accordingly reversed and the cases are remanded to the District Courts to take such proceedings and enter such orders and decrees consistent with this opinion as are necessary and proper to admit to public schools on a racially nondiscriminatory basis with all deliberate speed the parties to these cases. The judgment in the Delaware case—ordering the immediate admission of the plaintiffs to schools previously attended only by white children—is affirmed on the basis of the principles stated in our May 17, 1954, opinion, but the case is remanded to the Supreme Court of Delaware for such further proceedings as that Court may deem necessary in light of this opinion.

It is so ordered.

Brown v. Board of Education and the follow-up case were decided over fifty years ago. During this time, school districts and courts struggled with the problem of achieving integrated school systems. Schools developed a number of programs including rezoning school boundaries, instituting magnet schools, and giving students freedom to choose a school. None of these methods was completely successful and all led to various court decisions, including cases from the Supreme Court. Probably the most controversial remedy instituted by school districts and supported by the Supreme Court was busing. After fifty years, and numerous attempts to achieve the result demanded by the Court in *Brown v. Board of Education*, the district and state courts still hear cases trying to eliminate racial segregation in school systems.

Affirmative Action

In an effort to eliminate the effects of years of race and gender bias, many states adopted "affirmative action" programs, sometimes referred to by the courts as "benign" or "reverse discrimination." Like the practices they seek to remedy, affirmative action laws, which are generally based on race or gender, are challenged as being in violation of the Equal Protection Clause. If an affirmative action law is based on race or gender, the law is suspect regardless of the motivation.

Equal protection challenges to affirmative action laws occur primarily in two areas: (1) school admissions policies and (2) government employment. The Court considered affirmative action in relationship to medical school admissions in the case of *Regents of University of California v. Bakke*, 438 U.S. 265 (1978). The University of California medical school had two admissions programs for the entering class of one hundred students— the regular admissions program and the special admissions program reserved for sixteen minorities. Minority applicants were admitted with significantly lower scores than Bakke's. Consequently, he filed suit alleging that the special admissions program operated to exclude him on the basis of his race in violation of the Equal Protection Clause of the

Fourteenth Amendment. A majority of the Court ruled in Bakke's favor, even though a majority could not agree on the reasons for the decision. The result, however, is a general consensus that minority admission policies cannot be based on a quota system.

Although the Supreme Court held that the University of California's admission policy violated equal protection principles, it did not outlaw the practice of considering race in admissions. This issue arose in 2003 in two cases from the University of Michigan: *Gratz v. Bollinger*, 539 U.S. 244 (2003) and *Grutter v. Bollinger*, 539 U.S. 306 (2003). The undergraduate admission policy, which was the subject of *Gratz*, was based on a total of one hundred points that were determined by such factors as school grades, standardized test scores, high school quality, curriculum strength, geography, alumni relationships, leadership, and race. Underrepresented minorities were automatically given twenty points. The petitioners in the case claimed they were denied equal protection of the law because the university denied them the opportunity to compete for admission on an equal basis. In fact, one petitioner showed that minority students with similar qualifications were admitted. In *Gratz,* the Court affirmed that diversity is a legitimate state interest. However, laws enacted to promote diversity must be very narrowly drawn. The University of Michigan undergraduate admissions policy did not meet this test and was therefore unconstitutional. The following language from the Court Syllabus explains the Court's reasoning:

[T]he Court finds that the University's current policy, which automatically distributes 20 points, or one-fifth of the points needed to guarantee admission, to every single "underrepresented minority" applicant solely because of race, is not narrowly tailored to achieve educational diversity. In *Bakke*, Justice Powell explained his view that it would be permissible for a university to employ an admissions program in which "race or ethnic background may be deemed a 'plus' in a particular applicant's file." 438 U.S., at 317. He emphasized, however, the importance of considering each particular applicant as an individual, assessing all of the qualities that individual possesses, and in turn, evaluating that individual's ability to contribute to the unique setting of higher education. The admissions program Justice Powell described did not contemplate that any single characteristic automatically ensured a specific and identifiable contribution to a university's diversity. The current LSA policy does not provide the individualized consideration Justice Powell contemplated. The only consideration that accompanies the 20-point automatic distribution to all applicants from underrepresented minorities is a factual review to determine whether an individual is a member of one of these minority groups. Moreover, unlike Justice Powell's example, where the race of a "particular black applicant" could be considered without being decisive, see *id.*, at 317, the LSA's 20-point distribution has the effect of making "the factor of race ... decisive" for virtually every minimally qualified underrepresented minority applicant, *ibid*. Nothing in Justice Powell's *Bakke* opinion signaled that a university may employ whatever means it desires to achieve diversity without regard to the limits imposed by strict scrutiny.

In the *Grutter* case, the Court noted that the law school admission policy was considerably different from the undergraduate admission policy. The law school did not assign set points to minority status. Admission was determined by a number of variables, including grades, academic ability, potential, and a personal essay describing how the applicant will contribute to law school life and diversity. The policy did not define diversity solely in terms of racial and ethnic status and did not restrict the types of diversity contributions eligible for consideration in admissions. However, the admission policy expressed the school's commitment to certain underrepresented minorities. In upholding the constitutionality of the law school's admission policies, the Supreme Court reaffirmed the basic concept from *Bakke*—diversity in college admissions is a legitimate state interest and is a factor that can be considered in the admission policy. Key factors in the Court's decision were the facts that the admission policy was individualized, something that did not happen with the undergraduate admission procedure, and that there was no undue harm to nonminority students. The following excerpt from the Court's decision explains this holding.

Grutter v. Bollinger
539 U.S. 306 (2003)

That a race-conscious admissions program does not operate as a quota does not, by itself, satisfy the requirement of individualized consideration. When using race as a "plus" factor in university admissions, a university's admissions program must remain flexible enough to ensure that each applicant is evaluated as an individual and not in a way that makes an applicant's race or ethnicity the defining feature of his or her application. The importance of this individualized consideration in the context of a race-conscious admissions program is paramount.

Here, the Law School engages in a highly individualized, holistic review of each applicant's file, giving serious consideration to all the ways an applicant might contribute to a diverse educational environment. The Law School affords this individualized consideration to applicants of all races. Unlike the program at issue in *Gratz v. Bollinger, ante,* the Law School awards no mechanical, predetermined diversity "bonuses" based on race or ethnicity. The Law School's admissions policy "is flexible enough to consider all pertinent elements of diversity in light of the particular qualifications of each applicant, and to place them on the same footing for consideration, although not necessarily according them the same weight." *Bakke, supra,* at 317 (opinion of Powell, J.).

We also find that the Law School's race-conscious admissions program adequately ensures that all factors that may contribute to student body diversity are meaningfully considered alongside race in admissions decisions. With respect to the use of race itself, all underrepresented minority students admitted by the Law School have been deemed qualified.

The Law School does not, however, limit in any way the broad range of qualities and experiences that may be considered valuable contributions to student body diversity. To the contrary, the 1992 policy makes clear there are many possible bases for diversity admissions, and provides examples of admittees who have lived or traveled widely abroad, are fluent in several languages, have overcome personal adversity and family hardship, have exceptional records of extensive community service, and have had successful careers in other fields. All applicants have the opportunity to highlight their own potential diversity contributions through the submission of a personal statement, letters of recommendation, and an essay describing the ways in which the applicant will contribute to the life and diversity of the Law School.

Petitioner and the United States argue that the Law School's plan is not narrowly tailored because race-neutral means exist to obtain the educational benefits of student body diversity that the Law School seeks. We disagree. Narrow tailoring does not require exhaustion of every conceivable race-neutral alternative. Nor does it require a university to choose between maintaining a reputation for excellence or fulfilling a commitment to provide educational opportunities to members of all racial groups. Narrow tailoring does, however, require serious, good faith consideration of workable race-neutral alternatives that will achieve the diversity the university seeks.

We agree with the Court of Appeals that the Law School sufficiently considered workable race-neutral alternatives.

We acknowledge that "there are serious problems of justice connected with the idea of preference itself." *Bakke,* 438 U.S., at 298 (opinion of Powell, J.). Narrow

(continued)

(continued)

tailoring, therefore, requires that a race-conscious admissions program not unduly harm members of any racial group. Even remedial race-based governmental action generally "remains subject to continuing oversight to assure that it will work the least harm possible to other innocent persons competing for the benefit." *Id.*, at 308. To be narrowly tailored, a race-conscious admissions program must not "unduly burden individuals who are not members of the favored racial and ethnic groups." *Metro Broadcasting, Inc. v. FCC*, 497 U.S. 547, 630 (1990) (O'Connor, J., dissenting).

We are satisfied that the Law School's admissions program does not. Because the Law School considers "all pertinent elements of diversity," it can (and does) select nonminority applicants who have greater potential to enhance student body diversity over underrepresented minority applicants. We agree that, in the context of its individualized inquiry into the possible diversity contributions of all applicants, the Law School's race-conscious admissions program does not unduly harm nonminority applicants.

In *Grutter*, the Court also makes an important observation that may have an impact on future decisions regarding this issue. The Court stated that even if a minority admission procedure is narrowly drawn so as to be constitutional, it must have an endpoint. The Court suggests that "sunset provisions" be included in any policy:

> Race-conscious admissions policies must be limited in time. This requirement reflects that racial classifications, however compelling their goals, are potentially so dangerous that they may be employed no more broadly than the interest demands. Enshrining a permanent justification for racial preferences would offend this fundamental equal protection principle. We see no reason to exempt race-conscious admissions programs from the requirement that all governmental use of race must have a logical end point.... We expect that 25 years from now, the use of racial preferences will no longer be necessary to further the interest approved today.

The Court continues to closely scrutinize cases in which race is a factor in admissions. For example, in 2007, in *Parents Involved in Community Schools v. Seattle School*, the Court held that a policy using race as an admission criteria was unconstitutional when it was the sole factor in the decision process. The Syllabus summarizes the reasoning.

Parents Involved In Community Schools v. Seattle School
551 U.S. 701 (2007)

Respondent school districts voluntarily adopted student assignment plans that rely on race to determine which schools certain children may attend. The Seattle district, which has never operated legally segregated schools or been subject to court-ordered desegregation, classified children as white or nonwhite, and used the racial classifications as a "tiebreaker" to allocate slots in particular high schools. The Jefferson County, Ky., district was subject to a desegregation decree until 2000, when the District Court dissolved the decree after finding that the district had eliminated the vestiges of prior segregation to the greatest extent practicable. In 2001, the district adopted its plan classifying students as black or "other" in order to make certain elementary school assignments and to rule on transfer requests.

Petitioners, an organization of Seattle parents (Parents Involved) and the mother of a Jefferson County student (Joshua), whose children were or could be

(continued)

(continued)

assigned under the foregoing plans, filed these suits contending, *inter alia,* that allocating children to different public schools based solely on their race violates the Fourteenth Amendment's equal protection guarantee. In the Seattle case, the District Court granted the school district summary judgment, finding, *inter alia,* that its plan survived strict scrutiny on the federal constitutional claim because it was narrowly tailored to serve a compelling government interest. The Ninth Circuit affirmed. In the Jefferson County case, the District Court found that the school district had asserted a compelling interest in maintaining racially diverse schools, and that its plan was, in all relevant respects, narrowly tailored to serve that interest. The Sixth Circuit affirmed.

Held: The judgments are reversed, and the cases are remanded.

The Chief Justice delivered the opinion of the Court with respect to Parts I, II, III–A, and III–C, concluding:

The school districts have not carried their heavy burden of showing that the interest they seek to achieve justifies the extreme means they have chosen—discriminating among individual students based on race by relying upon racial classifications in making school assignments

(a) Because "racial classifications are simply too pernicious to permit any but the most exact connection between justification and classification," *Fullilove* v. *Klutznick,* 448 U.S. 448 (Stevens, J., dissenting), governmental distributions of burdens or benefits based on individual racial classifications are reviewed under strict scrutiny, *e.g., Johnson* v. *California,* 543 U.S. 499. Thus, the school districts must demonstrate that their use of such classifications is "narrowly tailored" to achieve a "compelling" government interest. *Adarand, supra,* at 227.

Although remedying the effects of past intentional discrimination is a compelling interest under the strict scrutiny test, see *Freeman* v. *Pitts,* 503 U.S. 467, that interest is not involved here because the Seattle schools were never segregated by law nor subject to court-ordered desegregation, and the desegregation decree to which the Jefferson County schools were previously subject has been dissolved. Moreover, these cases are not governed by *Grutter* v. *Bollinger,* 539 U.S. 306, in which the Court held that, for strict scrutiny purposes, a government interest in student body diversity "in the context of higher education" is compelling. That interest was not focused on race alone but encompassed "all factors that may

contribute to student body diversity," *id.,* at 337, including, *e.g.,* having "overcome personal adversity and family hardship," *id.,* at 338. Quoting Justice Powell's articulation of diversity in *Regents of the University of California* v. *Bakke,* 438 U.S. 265, the *Grutter* Court noted that "'it is not an interest in simple ethnic diversity, in which a specified percentage of the student body is in effect guaranteed to be members of selected ethnic groups,' that can justify the use of race," 539 U.S., at 324–325, but "'a far broader array of qualifications and characteristics of which racial or ethnic origin is but a single though important element, '" *id.,* at 325. In the present cases, by contrast, race is not considered as part of a broader effort to achieve "exposure to widely diverse people, cultures, ideas, and viewpoints," *id.,* at 330; race, for some students, is determinative standing alone. The districts argue that other factors, such as student preferences, affect assignment decisions under their plans, but under each plan when race comes into play, it is decisive by itself. It is not simply one factor weighed with others in reaching a decision, as in *Grutter*; it is *the* factor. See *Gratz* v. *Bollinger,* 539 U.S. 244. Even as to race, the plans here employ only a limited notion of diversity, viewing race exclusively in white/nonwhite terms in Seattle and black/"other" terms in Jefferson County.

(b) Despite the districts' assertion that they employed individual racial classifications in a way necessary to achieve their stated ends, the minimal effect these classifications have on student assignments suggests that other means would be effective. Seattle's racial tiebreaker results, in the end, only in shifting a small number of students between schools. Similarly, Jefferson County admits that its use of racial classifications has had a minimal effect, and claims only that its guidelines provide a firm definition of the goal of racially integrated schools, thereby providing administrators with authority to collaborate with principals and staff to maintain schools within the desired range. Classifying and assigning schoolchildren according to a binary conception of race is an extreme approach in light of this Court's precedents and the Nation's history of using race in public schools, and requires more than such an amorphous end to justify it. In *Grutter*, in contrast, the consideration of race was viewed as indispensable in more than tripling minority representation at the law school there at issue. See 539 U.S., at 320. While the Court does not suggest that *greater* use of race would be preferable, the

(continued)

(continued)

minimal impact of the districts' racial classifications on school enrollment casts doubt on the necessity of using such classifications. The districts have also failed to show they considered methods other than explicit racial classifications to achieve their stated goals. Narrow tailoring requires "serious, good faith consideration of workable race-neutral alternatives," *id.,* at 339, and yet in Seattle several alternative assignment plans—many of which would not have used express racial classifications—were rejected with little or no consideration. Jefferson County has failed to present any evidence that it considered alternatives, even though the district already claims that its goals are achieved primarily through means other than the racial classifications.

A second area where affirmative action laws are challenged is in the workplace. In a 1980 case, *Fullilove v. Klutznick*, 448 U.S. 448, the Supreme Court upheld a federal law requiring that when states received federal funds granted for local public works programs, 10 percent of all funds must go to minority businesses. The Court held that Congress had the right to enact such remedial legislation. However, when faced with the question as to whether a state could enact a similar law, the Court reached a different result. In *Richmond v. J. A. Croson Co.*, 488 U.S. 469 (1989), the Court reviewed a state law similar to the federal law that had already been found to be constitutional. However, the Court emphasized the point that Section 5 of the Fourteenth Amendment gave Congress (and not the states) the right to enact legislation to enforce the provisions of the Fourteenth Amendment. As a result, the Court reviewed the state law using the same standard it used to review any law that was classified by race and found the law to be unconstitutional:

> While there is no doubt that the sorry history of both private and public discrimination in this country has contributed to a lack of opportunities for black entrepreneurs, this observation, standing alone, cannot justify a rigid racial quota in the awarding of public contracts in Richmond, Virginia. Like the claim that discrimination in primary and secondary schooling justifies a rigid racial preference in medical school admissions, an amorphous claim that there has been past discrimination in a particular industry cannot justify the use of an unyielding racial quota.

Workplace discrimination and affirmative action policies are not limited to race and gender. Affirmative action policies are intended to protect those who have suffered a history of discrimination and include those with disabilities and veterans. In 2010, President Obama signed an executive order (13548) ordering federal agencies to adopt policies promoting employment for the disabled. The Supreme Court has not ruled on all issues related to this topic.

Nonlegislative Remedies

Not all remedies for equal protection violations are new laws. In some instances, such as the executive order of President Obama described above, executive action is taken. For example, the internment of the Japanese during World War II has always been a controversial and highly criticized act. To help remedy the result of this action against the Japanese, on August 10, 1988, President Ronald Reagan signed the Civil Liberties Act of 1988. The Act was passed by Congress to provide a presidential apology and symbolic payment of $20,000 to the internees, evacuees, and persons of Japanese ancestry who lost liberty or property because of the discriminatory action by the federal government during World War II. The Act also created the Civil Liberties Public Education Fund to help teach children and the public about the internment period.

Additionally, many equal protection violations are not the result of laws that violate the Constitution, but rather practices that violate the law. Monitoring violations of such practices is a duty of the Civil Rights Division of the U.S. Department of Justice. They file civil and criminal cases where appropriate. Exhibit 8-2 is an example of a complaint filed by the Department of Justice.

Exhibit 8-2   Civil Complaint

IN THE UNITED STATES DISTRICT COURT
FOR THE DISTRICT OF NEW JERSEY

UNITED STATES OF AMERICA, Plaintiff
v.
STATE OF NEW JERSEY, AND
DIVISION OF STATE POLICE OF THE
NEW JERSEY DEPARTMENT OF LAW AND PUBLIC SAFETY, Defendants.

CIVIL NO. 99-5970 (MLC)
COMPLAINT

The United States brings this action under 42 U.S.C.§ 14141, and the Omnibus Crime Control and Safe Streets Act, as amended, 42 U.S.C.§ 3789d(c)(3), to remedy a pattern or practice of racially discriminatory conduct by law enforcement officers of the Division of State Police, New Jersey Department of Public Safety, that deprives persons of rights, privileges, or immunities secured or protected by the Constitution or laws of the United States, including the Fourteenth Amendment and rights protected by the anti-discrimination provisions and implementing regulations of the Omnibus Crime Control and Safe Streets Act, as amended, 42 U.S.C.§ 3789d(c).

The United States of America alleges:

DEFENDANTS

1. Defendant State of New Jersey is legally responsible for the operation of the Division of State Police, New Jersey Department of Public Safety, and for the activities of the troopers, employees, and agents of the Division of State Police.

2. Defendant Division of State Police, New Jersey Department of Law and Public Safety ("New Jersey State Police"), is responsible for highway enforcement of motor vehicle and criminal laws of the State of New Jersey, for providing police coverage in various areas of the State, and for providing other law enforcement services throughout the State.

JURISDICTION AND VENUE

3. This Court has jurisdiction of this action under 28 U.S.C.§§ 1331 and 1345.

4. The United States is authorized to initiate this action pursuant to 42 U.S.C.§ 14141 and 42 U.S.C.§ 3789d(c)(3).

5. Venue is proper in the District of New Jersey pursuant to 28 U.S.C.§ 1391 because the claims set forth in this Complaint all arose in this District and defendants reside in this District.

FACTUAL ALLEGATIONS

6. The New Jersey State Police is a program or activity of the State of New Jersey funded, in part, by funds made available under the Omnibus Crime Control and Safe Streets Act, as amended ("Safe Streets Act").

7. Defendants have engaged in and continue to engage in a pattern or practice of performing vehicle stops and post-stop enforcement actions and procedures, including searches, of African American motorists traveling on New Jersey roadways, including the New Jersey Turnpike, that:
a. have the intent of discriminating on the basis of race; and
b. use criteria or methods of administration that have the effect of discriminating on the basis of race.

8. Defendants, through their acts or omissions, have tolerated and continue to tolerate racially discriminatory law enforcement by New Jersey State troopers, described in ¶ 7 above. These acts or omissions include, but are not limited to:
a. failing to implement and enforce policies related to vehicle stops that appropriately guide and limit the discretion of individual troopers;
b. failing to train troopers adequately to prevent racially discriminatory conduct related to vehicle stops;

(continued)

(continued)

    c. failing to supervise troopers adequately to prevent racially discriminatory conduct related to vehicle stops;

    d. failing to monitor troopers adequately who engage in or may be likely to engage in racially discriminatory conduct related to vehicle stops;

    e. failing to establish a procedure whereby all civilian complaints are documented, and are investigated and adjudicated adequately; and

    f. failing to discipline adequately troopers who engage in racially discriminatory conduct related to vehicle stops.

9. The pattern or practice, described in ¶¶ 7–8 above, constitutes intentional racial discrimination by defendants in performing vehicle stops and post-stop enforcement actions and procedures, including searches, of African American motorists traveling on New Jersey highways, including the New Jersey Turnpike.

CAUSES OF ACTION

10. Through the actions described in ¶¶ 7–9 above, defendants have engaged in and continue to engage in a pattern or practice of conduct by law enforcement officers that deprives persons traveling in New Jersey of rights, privileges, or immunities secured or protected by the Constitution or the laws of the United States, in violation of 42 U.S.C. § 14141.

11. Through the actions described in ¶¶ 7–9 above, defendants have engaged in and continue to engage in a pattern or practice of conduct that subjects persons traveling in New Jersey to discrimination on the basis of race in violation of the anti-discrimination provisions and implementing regulations of the Omnibus Crime Control and Safe Streets Act, as amended, 42 U.S.C. § 3789d(c).

PRAYER FOR RELIEF

12. The Attorney General is authorized under 42 U.S.C. § 14141 and 42 U.S.C. § 3789d(c)(3) to seek declaratory and equitable relief to eliminate a pattern or practice of law enforcement conduct that deprives persons of rights, privileges, or immunities secured or protected by the Constitution or laws of the United States, including the Fourteenth Amendment, and rights protected by the anti-discrimination provisions and implementing regulations of the Safe Streets Act.

WHEREFORE, the United States prays that the Court:

    a. declare that defendants have engaged in a pattern or practice by New Jersey State troopers of depriving persons of rights, privileges, or immunities secured or protected by the Constitution or laws of the United States, in violation of 42 U.S.C. § 14141 and the anti-discrimination provisions and implementing regulations of the Omnibus Crime Control and Safe Streets Act, as amended, 42 U.S.C. § 3789d(c), as described in ¶¶ 7–9 above;

    b. order defendants to refrain from engaging in any of the predicate acts forming the basis of the pattern or practice of conduct as described in ¶¶ 7–9 above;

    c. order defendants to adopt and implement policies and procedures to remedy the pattern or practice of conduct described in ¶¶ 7–9 above, and to prevent troopers of the New Jersey State Police from depriving persons of rights, privileges, or immunities secured or protected by the Constitution or laws of the United States, including rights protected by the anti-discrimination provisions and implementing regulations of the Omnibus Crime Control and Safe Streets Act, as amended, 42 U.S.C. § 3789d(c); and

    d. order such other appropriate relief as the interests of justice may require.

> Respectfully submitted,
> JANET RENO
> Attorney General of the United States

⤳ **Ethical Decisions—Everyday Choices** ⤳

The Facts: Lisa, a paralegal in a large litigation law firm, was asked to draft a civil rights complaint on behalf of new clients. In doing this, she finds she must contact the client to obtain some factual information. Lisa has several questions.

The Problem: Can Lisa, a paralegal, talk to the client without the attorney being present? If so, how should she identify herself? After she drafts the complaint, can she sign the document?

Guiding Principles: Paralegals cannot engage in the unauthorized practice of law. They must also carefully identify themselves and their status. The unauthorized practice of law includes giving legal advice, appearing in court, and signing documents that are filed in court.

Chapter Summary

The Equal Protection Clause of the Fourteenth Amendment provides that no state shall "deny to any person within its jurisdiction the equal protection of the laws." This provision prohibits laws and practices that invidiously discriminate against one or more groups. It does not require that all laws treat all persons the same. The Equal Protection Clause is found only in the Fourteenth Amendment, which applies to state rather than federal governments. However, the Supreme Court said that equal protection of the laws applies to the federal government through the Due Process Clause of the Fifth Amendment. Neither the Fourteenth nor the Fifth Amendments apply to private conduct. However, if the Court finds a substantial relationship between private conduct and government action, it finds that the Equal Protection Clause applies.

The Supreme Court is responsible for ultimately determining if any law or practice violates the Equal Protection Clause. In doing this, the Court developed three tests: the rational basis test, strict scrutiny, and intermediate scrutiny. In determining which test to use, the Court considers if the law or practice targets a suspect class or deals with a fundamental right. A suspect class includes classification by race, ethnicity, or national origin. Sometimes it includes alien status. The Court also identified quasi-suspect classes, including classes based on gender, legitimacy, and sometimes alien status. A fundamental right is one found expressly or impliedly in the Constitution. If a law targets a suspect class or deals with a fundamental right, the Court applies the strict scrutiny test. Under this test, a law is constitutional only if it is necessary to achieve a compelling government interest. If a quasi-suspect class is targeted, the Court applies intermediate scrutiny. Under this test, a law is constitutional if it is substantially related to an important government interest. Other laws and practices are reviewed under a rational basis test. Under this test, laws are constitutional if they are reasonably related to a legitimate state purpose. When laws discriminate because of race, ethnicity, or national origin, they are almost always found to be unconstitutional. On the other hand, laws subject to the rational basis test are more likely to be found constitutional.

The Equal Protection Clause applies to laws and practices that result in certain classes of individuals losing the right to vote or losing the right to have their votes properly counted. Laws that impose unreasonable qualifications on voters, deny certain candidates access to the ballot, or result in unequal voting power (the one person, one vote rule) generally violate the Equal Protection Clause.

The Equal Protection Clause applies to all laws that invidiously discriminate, even if the discrimination is an attempt to remedy a past violation. Thus, affirmative action laws and redistricting are sometimes found to be violations of the Equal Protection Clause. However, the Court reaffirmed that race can be used as a factor in school admissions, as long as the admission policy is narrowly tailored.

Key Terms

enabling clause	suspect class	police powers
invidious discrimination	discrete and insular minority	facially neutral
segregation	quasi-suspect class	peremptory challenges
separate but equal doctrine	fundamental rights	gerrymandering

Questions for Review

1. What is the difference between laws based on classifications and laws that invidiously discriminate?
2. Under what, if any, circumstances does the Equal Protection Clause apply to private conduct?
3. Is the federal government bound by the provisions of the Equal Protection Clause? Explain.
4. Define the terms *suspect class*, *quasi-suspect class*, and *fundamental rights*, and explain how each term affects the Equal Protection Clause.
5. Compare and contrast the three tests used by the Supreme Court when evaluating laws and practices for equal protection violations.

6. Summarize three Supreme Court cases when the Court found violations of the Equal Protection Clause.
7. Summarize three Supreme Court cases when the Court found no violation of the Equal Protection Clause.
8. In what ways does the Equal Protection Clause protect voting rights?
9. What is the "one person, one vote" rule?
10. What are some of the problems stemming from efforts to eliminate equal protection violations by such means as affirmative action?

Questions for Analysis

1. Refer to the facts in Living with the Constitution, where parents challenge the way in which school assignments are made.
   a. Is the school assignment based on any classification? If so, what?
   b. Is any fundamental right involved?
   c. If this case were to be heard by the Supreme Court, which test would they use to analyze the practice?
2. Refer to case *City of Cleburne v. Cleburne Living Ctr., Inc.*
   a. Why does the Supreme Court feel justified in departing from the general rule that state laws are presumed to be valid when laws classify by factors such as race, alienage, and national origin?
   b. Why do laws that classify by gender require heightened scrutiny?
   c. Why do laws that classify by age require only the rational basis test?
   d. Which test did the Court apply in this case and why?
3. Refer to the case *Bush v. Gore*.
   a. Why did the Court find an equal protection violation in the recount?
4. Refer to the *Brown II* case.
   a. According to the Supreme Court, who has primary responsibility for desegregating the schools?
   b. What practical problems could a court consider in deciding if a school district is integrating with proper speed?
5. Refer to *Grutter v. Bollinger*.
   a. Why did the Court find race-conscious policy to be constitutional for the law school?
   b. How did the Court explain the concept of "narrow tailoring"?
   c. Why does the decision in this case differ from the decision in *Parents Involved In Community Schools v. Seattle School*?

Assignments and Projects

1. Following the format provided in previous chapters, brief the case *United States v. Virginia*.
2. Summarize the factual allegations of the Complaint filed by the Department of Justice against the State of New Jersey.
3. A leader in the civil rights movement was Dr. Martin Luther King, Jr. Research his life and write a short paper summarizing his accomplishments.

Putting It into Practice

1. Assume that you work for a law firm representing the Ebert family.
   a. Identify any local, state, or federal agencies that might investigate their claim of discrimination.
   b. Write a letter to the Westside School District explaining the Ebert's concerns.

Group Activities

1. Review Table 8-3. For each case, list the standard of review the Court used to decide the case

2. Obtain a copy of Dr. King's "I Have a Dream" speech. Has his dream come true? Discuss.

9 Due Process

*I know not what course others may take; but as for me, give
me liberty, or give me death.*

Patrick Henry

Chapter Outline

Due Process—An Overview
    Who Is Considered a Person?
    What Constitutes Government Action?
    How Liberty and Property Are Interpreted

Substantive Due Process
    Standard for Determining Substantive
    Due Process Violations
    Substantive Due Process and Liberty
    Substantive Due Process and Property

Procedural Due Process
    Standards for Determining Procedural
    Due Process Violations
    Procedural Due Process and
    Criminal Cases
    Procedural Due Process and Civil Lawsuits
    Procedural Due Process and Government
    Agencies

Chapter Objectives

When you complete this chapter you should be able to

1. explain the relationship of the Magna Carta and the English Bill of Rights to the concept of due process.

2. distinguish substantive due process from procedural due process.

3. explain the terms *person, liberty,* and *property,* as they are used in the Fifth and Fourteenth Amendments.

4. determine if private conduct is regulated by the Due Process Clauses.

5. explain the standards used by the Supreme Court when it reviews a law for substantive due process violations.

6. describe some of the liberty interests protected by substantive due process.

7. describe the property interests protected by substantive due process.

8. explain the relationship of the Due Process Clause to criminal cases.

9. explain the relationship of the Due Process Clause to civil lawsuits.

10. describe the basic requirements for due process whenever the government deprives a person of life, liberty, or property.

Looking Back

Before reading this chapter, review the following terms and concepts from the previous chapters:

Magna Carta A document written in 1215 by the nobles of England and presented to King John in response to his many abuses. It contained provisions limiting the right of the king to tax and provisions protecting property rights of the barons. It also limited the right of the government to punish alleged criminals, providing that no freeman should be imprisoned "except by lawful judgment of his peers or by the law of the land." (Chapter 1)

English Bill of Rights A list of rights demanded by English lords from the monarch in 1689. (Chapter 1)

Incorporation Doctrine The term "due process" as used in the Fourteenth Amendment incorporates most of the specific rights spelled out in the Bill of Rights and makes them applicable to state government. (Chapter 7)

Equal Protection Clause The provision of the Fourteenth Amendment limiting the right of the states to enact laws that create classifications and either grant or deny rights based on these classifications. The concept of equal protection applies to the federal government through the Fifth Amendment due process clause. (Chapter 8)

Fundamental Rights Rights that are expressed or implied in the Constitution. Any attempt by state or federal government to take away or limit these rights requires a compelling government need. (Chapter 8)

Living with the Constitution

Michael was planning a lengthy vacation to visit several European countries. In planning the trip, he did extensive surfing of the Internet. One Web site of particular interest was the site maintained by the U.S. Department of State, where he found the following warning about being arrested in a foreign country:

- few countries provide a jury trial
- many countries do not permit pre-trial release on bail
- pre-trial detention, often in solitary confinement, can last several months
- prisons may lack even minimal comforts, such as beds, toilets, and washbasins
- diets are often inadequate and require supplements from relatives and friends
- officials may not speak English
- physical abuse, confiscation of property, degrading treatment, and extortion are possible
- persons convicted may face sentences ranging from fines and jail time to years of hard labor and even the death penalty
- penalties for drug possession and penalties for drug trafficking are often the same, so possession of one ounce of marijuana could result in years in a foreign jail

Michael knew he better be very careful when traveling abroad. If he found himself in trouble, he might not find a legal system based on the concept of due process.

THE AMERICAN LEGAL SYSTEM IS based on a concept of fairness. As a result, the government cannot imprison individuals or take away their property without justification and without following established procedures. This concept of fairness is firmly established in the Constitution in the Due Process Clauses of the Fifth and Fourteenth Amendments to the Constitution that prohibit the federal and the state government from depriving a person of "life, liberty, or property, without due process of law...." The concept of due process did not originate with the framers of the Constitution. Due process was an important part of the Magna Carta, where it is referred to as "the law of the land" and was later affirmed in the subsequent English document, the English Bill of Rights. Both of these documents contain provisions limiting the right of the king to imprison individuals or to seize property. (The Magna Carta is found in Appendix B.) This chapter discusses the constitutional aspects and requirements of due process. Subsequent chapters cover specific applications of due process.

Due Process—An Overview

THE FIFTH AMENDMENT, WHICH APPLIES to the federal government, provides in part: "no person shall be ... deprived of life, liberty, or property, without due process of law...." The Fourteenth Amendment, which applies to state governments, contains almost identical language: "nor shall any state deprive any person of life, liberty, or property, without due process of law."

The Constitution contains no definition of due process, although one Supreme Court justice, Felix Frankfurter, described it as follows:

> It is now the settled doctrine of this Court that the Due Process Clause embodies a system of rights based on moral principles so deeply embedded in the traditions and feelings of our people as to be deemed fundamental to a civilized society as conceived by our whole history. Due process is that which comports with the deepest notions of what is fair and right and just. *Solesbee v. Balkcom*, 339 U.S. 9 (1950) (dissenting opinion).

The term "*due process*" is not limited to procedural rules. The Supreme Court gives this constitutional term a much broader meaning. The Court states that the Due Process Clauses provide two types of protections: substantive and procedural. **Substantive due process** limits the right of federal and state governments to enact laws that interfere with life, property, or liberty. **Procedural due process** deals with the procedures that government uses whenever it actually deprives a person of life, liberty, or property. The differences between substantive and procedural due process can be seen in the following examples.

Suppose a state enacts a law prohibiting any business from allowing minors to work more than ten hours a week during the school year. Jones, who owns a fast-food restaurant, claims that this law deprives him of his right to carry on his business and interferes with his property and liberty. Jones argues that if an employee wants to work more than ten hours and Jones agrees, the employee should be free (or have the liberty) to do so. The state, on the other hand, maintains the restrictive law is necessary to assure that a minor's education is not jeopardized. Whether the law is a valid exercise of state **police powers** is a question of substantive due process. Does the state have the right to enact a law that deprives Jones of his freedom or liberty to hire minors? Now, suppose that Jones has his sixteen-year-old son working at his business fifteen hours a week. The proper authorities find out about this, and without any notice or warning they appear at the business and close it down, seizing all personal property on the premises. Even if a court decided that the state could enact a law

---

🏛 **substantive due process**

No law or government procedure should be arbitrary or unfair.

🏛 **procedural due process**

What constitutes due process of law varies from situation to situation, but the core of the idea is that a person should always have notice and a real chance to present his or her side in a legal dispute.

🏛 **police powers**

The government's right and power to set up and enforce laws to provide for the safety, health, and general welfare of the people; for example, police power includes the power to license occupations such as hair cutting.

limiting the hours minors could work, a second issue arises in *how* the law is enforced. This is procedural due process.

Who Is Considered a Person?

Both substantive and procedural due process rights are granted to "persons." Over the years, the Supreme Court had to decide if "person" includes corporations, noncitizens, or states.

CORPORATIONS

Several Supreme Court cases involved corporations claiming their due process rights were violated. Whether a corporation is considered a "person" depends on the specific type of interest the corporation seeks to protect. When the right is personal in nature, such as the rights of criminal defendants, the Court usually says that a corporation is not a person. "The liberty referred to in that Amendment is the liberty of natural, not artificial, persons." *Northwestern Natl. Life Ins. Co. v. Riggs*, 203 U.S. 243 (1906). Thus, in criminal cases, corporations have no right under the Due Process Clause to claim the privilege against self-incrimination. On the other hand, when the interest is a property interest, such as the operation of a business, the Court generally holds that a corporation is a person. Thus, a corporation operating a private school could challenge a state law requiring that children attend a public school. The corporation maintained that this deprived them of property without due process. In agreeing with them, the Court said:

> Appellees are corporations, and therefore, it is said, they cannot claim for themselves the liberty which the 14th Amendment guarantees. Accepted in the proper sense, this is true. *Northwestern Life Ins. Co. v. Riggs*, 203 U.S. 243, 255.... But they have business and property for which they claim protection. These are threatened with destruction through the unwarranted compulsion which appellants are exercising over present and prospective patrons of their schools. And this court has gone very far to protect against loss threatened by such action. *Pierce v. Society of Sisters*, 268 U.S. 510 (1925).

The Court also held that a newspaper corporation was a person in a case involving freedom of the press:

> Appellant contends that the Fourteenth Amendment does not apply to corporations; but this is only partly true. A corporation, we have held, is not a "citizen" within the meaning of the privileges and immunities clause ... But a corporation is a "person" within the meaning of the equal protection and due process of law clauses, which are the clauses involved here. *Grosjean v. American Press Co.*, 297 U.S. 233 (1936).

NONCITIZENS

Both the Fifth and Fourteenth Amendments use the word *person* rather than *citizen*. It is not surprising, therefore, that due process claims are made by those who are not citizens. In an early case, *Yick Wo v. Hopkins*, 118 U.S. 356 (1886), the Court described the Fourteenth Amendment in this way: "These provisions are universal in their application, to all persons within the territorial jurisdiction, without regard to any differences of race, of color, or of nationality." Later cases clarified that this statement was limited to persons residing within the United States, even if they were in the country illegally.

Since the events of September 11, 2001, and the following war on terror, the question of due process rights of those designated as "enemy combatants" has received serious consideration. Prior to 2001, the Court had considered only a few cases dealing with this issue. One such case is *Johnson v. Eisentrager*, 339 U.S. 763 (1950). This case involved due process claims by nonresident enemy aliens, who were tried for war crimes by a military tribunal rather than in a court of law. They claimed that denial of a court trial violated their constitutional due process rights. The Court made it clear that the Constitution did not apply to them because they were not apprehended on American soil.

After the events of September 11, the Supreme Court again addressed the issue of due process rights of U.S. citizens held in custody as enemy combatants. In *Hamdi v. Rumsfeld*, 542 U.S. 507 (2004), decided in 2004, the Court found that, although citizens designated as enemy combatants could be detained, such individuals do have due process rights. Therefore the president could not hold Hamdi without affording him basic constitutional rights of due process. (See Chapter 5 for a discussion of the president's authority.) In reaching its conclusion, the Court stressed the fact that Hamdi was not a citizen of nations with whom the United States was at war and he was not seized on a traditional battlefield. On the other hand, the Court also emphasized that the procedures required by due process may differ from procedures required in other custodial situations. The following language summarizes the Court's position:

> We hold that a citizen-detainee seeking to challenge his classification as an enemy combatant must receive notice of the factual basis for his classification, and a fair opportunity to rebut the Government's factual assertions before a neutral decisionmaker. *See Cleveland Bd. of Ed. v. Loudermill*, 470 U.S. 532, 542 (1985) "An essential principle of due process is that a deprivation of life, liberty, or property 'be preceded by notice and opportunity for hearing appropriate to the nature of the case.'"

> At the same time, the exigencies of the circumstances may demand that, aside from these core elements, enemy combatant proceedings may be tailored to alleviate their uncommon potential to burden the Executive at a time of ongoing military conflict. Hearsay, for example, may need to be accepted as the most reliable available evidence from the Government in such a proceeding. Likewise, the Constitution would not be offended by a presumption in favor of the Government's evidence, so long as that presumption remained a rebuttable one and fair opportunity for rebuttal were provided. In sum, while the full protections that accompany challenges to detentions in other settings may prove unworkable and inappropriate in the enemy-combatant setting, the threats to military operations posed by a basic system of independent review are not so weighty as to trump a citizen's core rights to challenge meaningfully the Government's case and to be heard by an impartial adjudicator.

STATES

One category definitely not included in "person" is the state. In the case of *South Carolina v. Katzenbach*, 383 U.S. 301 (1966), South Carolina challenged a federal law (the Voting Act of 1965) claiming that it violated the state's due process rights. The Court disagreed saying, "the word 'person' in the context of the Due Process Clause of the Fifth Amendment cannot, by any reasonable mode of interpretation, be expanded to encompass the States of the Union, and to our knowledge this has never been done by any court."

A Point of Law

Supreme Court Definitions of "Person"

Through a series of cases, the Supreme Court has held that the term "person" includes more than individuals. It includes corporations if a property interest is involved [*Pierce v. Society of Sisters*, 268 U.S. 510 (1925), as well as resident aliens, even if illegally in the country [*Yick Wo v. Hopkins*, 118 U.S. 356 (1886)]. It also includes citizens who are detained and accused of being enemy combatants as a result of the events of September 11 [*Hamdi v. Rumsfeld*]. However the term "person" does not include corporations if the interest is a personal one such as the right against self-incrimination [*Northwestern Natl. Life Ins. Co. v. Riggs*, 203 U.S. 243 (1906)]; it does not include enemy aliens who are citizens of nations with whom the United States is at war [*Johnson v. Eisentrager*, 339 U.S. 763 (1950)]; and does not include the states [*South Carolina v. Katzenbach*, 383 U.S. 301 (1966)].

What Constitutes Government Action?

Due process, like equal protection, applies only to actions by government. However, the Court finds government action in private conduct where a strong connection between the state and a private party exists. In *Brentwood Acad. v. Tennessee Sch. Ath. Assn.*, 531 U.S. 288 (2002), a statewide private association that regulated interscholastic athletic competition among public and private schools was held subject to due process requirements. The facts indicated that most of the state's public high schools were members of the association, representing 84 percent of the association's membership. School officials made up the voting membership of the association's governing council and control board that typically held meetings during regular school hours. The association staff, although not state employees, could join the state retirement system. The association set membership standards and student eligibility rules and had the power to penalize any member school that violated those rules. The State Board of Education acknowledged the association's role in regulating interscholastic competition in public schools, and its members sat as nonvoting members of the association's governing bodies. When the association penalized Brentwood Academy for violating a recruiting rule, Brentwood sued the association and its executive director claiming the rule's enforcement was state action that violated the Fourteenth Amendment. In upholding the right of Brentwood to pursue their claim the Court said:

> Our cases try to plot a line between state action subject to Fourteenth Amendment scrutiny and private conduct (however exceptionable) that is not. The judicial obligation is not only to preserve an area of individual freedom by limiting the reach of federal law and avoid the imposition of responsibility on a State for conduct it could not control, but also to assure that constitutional standards are invoked when it can be said that the State is *responsible* for the specific conduct of which the plaintiff complains. Thus, we say that state action may be found if, though only if, there is such a close nexus between the State and the challenged action that seemingly private behavior may be fairly treated as that of the State itself.

In this case the Court found the action of the board to be state action:

> The entwinement down from the State Board is therefore unmistakable, just as the entwinement up from the member public schools is overwhelming. Entwinement will support a conclusion that an ostensibly private organization ought to be charged with a public character and judged by constitutional standards; entwinement to the degree shown here requires it.

A Point of Law

Brentwood Acad. v. Tennessee Secondary Sch. Ath. Assn., 531 U.S. 288 (2002)

Actions by private parties are considered government action under the Fifth and Fourteenth Amendments when the private parties have a strong connection to a governmental entity. Thus, the actions of a private interscholastic athletic organization were held to be government action and subject to due process when the association regulated athletics at public schools and the officials and members of the organization were public school officials or employees.

How Liberty and Property Are Interpreted

The Fifth and Fourteenth Amendments protect interests that are included in the terms "life, liberty, or property." Sometimes determining if a specific interest is included in these terms is difficult. For example, is the right to choose an abortion a type of liberty? Is a driver's license a type of property? Is the right to employment a type of property? The Supreme Court, in interpreting the Due Process Clauses, has held that the terms *liberty* and *property* include many different interests. In early cases, the Supreme Court held that liberty includes the right or freedom to enter into contracts or agreements. This became known as liberty of contract.

Like the term *liberty*, the term *property* is given a broad interpretation by the Supreme Court. Not only does it include traditional real and personal property, but under some circumstances includes such interests as employment rights, government benefits, driver's licenses, and the right to attend school.

Substantive Due Process

SUBSTANTIVE DUE PROCESS REFERS TO the concept that the Fifth and Fourteenth Amendments prevent both federal and state governments from enacting laws that deprive a person of life, liberty, or property, unless those laws meet due process requirements. The concept is controversial and has many critics who believe the Supreme Court uses this concept to protect rights that should not be constitutionally protected. In spite of the criticism, substantive due process plays an important role in the Supreme Court's protection of economic and personal freedoms. Although the concept no longer has much significance in the protection of economic interests, it continues to play an important role in the protection of personal freedoms.

Standard for Determining Substantive Due Process Violations

Not all laws that deprive a person of life, liberty, or property violate substantive due process. Neither the Constitution nor the Court requires this. Ultimately, whether any specific law violates substantive due process is determined by the courts. To make the decision, the Supreme Court developed various tests. In determining if any state or federal law violates substantive due process, the Court first addresses two questions:

1. Does the law actually deprive a person of life, liberty, or property?
2. If it does, is the law a proper exercise of government power?

fundamental right

The basic rights, such as the right to vote and the right to travel. These are most strongly protected by the Constitution.

In answering the second question, the Court analyzes the law in the same way as it does when a law is claimed to be a violation of equal protection. It evaluates the law by weighing the right that is affected with the government interest. As long as the law does not interfere with a **fundamental right**, it is generally upheld if the law is not arbitrary and it is reasonably related to the purpose of the law. When a fundamental right is involved, the Court closely scrutinizes the law and requires that the government show a compelling government need for the law. Fundamental rights include those rights that are expressed or implied by some constitutional provision. The difference between fundamental and non-fundamental rights was discussed in more detail in the previous chapter.

Exhibit 9-1 Violation of Substantive Due Process

A Law Violates Substantive Due Process If It Involves:

    A non-fundamental right and is arbitrary and irrational
    A fundamental right and there is no compelling government purpose

© Cengage Learning 2013

Substantive Due Process and Liberty

Substantive due process issues arise most often with laws that deprive a person of rights that come within the term *liberty*. In fact, the development of the doctrine of substantive due process originated with cases dealing with economic liberty, in particular, the freedom or liberty to contract. Today, most cases deal with laws that interfere with personal liberties, such as the right to abortion or the right to die, or with laws that allow incarceration or commitment of individuals because they pose a threat to society.

ECONOMIC LIBERTIES

"liberty" to contract

The constitutionally protected right to make and enforce contracts, as limited only by reasonable laws about health, safety, and consumer protection.

In 1905, in the case of *Lochner v. New York*, 198 U.S. 45, the Supreme Court struck down a New York law limiting the number of hours that bakers could work, stating that the law violated the Due Process Clause of the Constitution because it deprived business owners and employees of their freedom or **"liberty" to contract**. The Court recognized the state's right to enact laws regulating businesses even if those laws interfere with the freedom of parties to enter contracts. However, since the term *liberty* included "economic" freedom, any economic legislation had to meet due process requirements. In the *Lochner* decision, the Court held that due process required that the law have a rational basis in achieving a legitimate state interest. Since the law limiting the number of hours that bakers could work did not meet this test, it was held to be unconstitutional. Today, the Court holds that laws affecting economic interests are constitutional as long as they serve a legitimate state interest and are not arbitrary or irrational. The Court has applied this standard to numerous laws involving economic liberty interests such as:

- minimum wage requirements
- child employment restrictions
- workers' compensation laws
- collective bargaining requirements
- price controls

All of these laws interfered in one way or another with the freedom of employers and employees to contract. However, because the laws served a legitimate government purpose and because they were not arbitrary, they were upheld by the Court. In modern times, it is rare for the Court to hold that laws having an economic purpose violate due process. On the other hand, the Court has struck down many laws that interfere with personal liberties, often because it applies a different standard of review. See Table 9-1.

Table 9-1 Supreme Court Tests for Reviewing Economic Laws for Substantive Due Process Violations

Older View [*Lochner v. New York* (1905)]	Current View
1. Law must serve legitimate state interest and	1. Law must serve legitimate state interest and
2. Have a *rational basis* for serving that interest	2. Not be *arbitrary* or *irrational*

© Cengage Learning 2013

PERSONAL LIBERTIES

Since the 1960s, personal freedoms, such as the right to use contraceptives, the right to an abortion, and the right to withdraw medical care, have all been included in the concept of liberty. In a 1999 case, *Connecticut v. Gabbert*, 526 U.S. 286, the Supreme Court summarized its interpretation of liberty as follows:

> The liberty guaranteed by the Fourteenth Amendment denotes not merely freedom from bodily restraint but also the right of the individual to contract, to engage in any of the common occupations of life, to acquire useful knowledge, to marry, establish a home and bring up children, to worship God according to the dictates of his own conscience, and generally to enjoy those privileges long recognized ... as essential to the orderly pursuit of happiness by free men.

The following is a list of some of the notable cases affording the protection of substantive due process to personal liberties:

- Freedom to marry; *Loving v. Virginia*, 388 U.S. 1 (1967)
- Contraception; *Griswold v. Connecticut*, 381 U.S. 479 (1965)
- Abortion; *Roe v. Wade*, 410 U.S. 113 (1973)
- Right to reject medical care; *Cruzan v. Director, Missouri Dept. of Health*, 497 U.S. 261 (1990)

In recent years, the right to an abortion has been limited, but not abolished. This subject is discussed in more detail in Chapter 13. Although the Court allowed a party to refuse medical treatment in *Cruzan*, no Supreme Court case has actually found that the right to commit suicide is a personal liberty. A few states, including Oregon, have laws allowing physician assisted suicide. After the Oregon law was enacted, the federal government attempted to stop the practice of physician assisted suicide by preventing doctors from prescribing federally regulated drugs used in physician assisted suicide. Although the drugs were federally regulated, they were not prohibited. The issue before the Supreme Court was whether the federal government had the right to prevent physicians from prescribing the drugs for the purpose of suicide. In *Gonzales v. Oregon*, 546 U.S. 243 (2006), the Supreme Court held that the federal government did not have such a power, and the Court upheld the state law. It is important to note that the Supreme Court did not find that individuals have a "liberty" interest in committing suicide. Thus, at this point, the right is dependent on state law. Many of the rights considered to be "personal liberties" are also included in the concept of privacy and are discussed in Chapter 13.

In recent years the Court was asked to rule on laws that allow states to confine the mentally ill and developmentally disabled. All parties seem to recognize that in some cases an individual must be committed for his own safety and the safety of others. Acting on that principle, several states enacted laws that allow commitment of "sexually violent predators." This commitment is not imprisonment for the commission of a particular offense, but rather for the possibility that the individual will commit crimes in the future. In *Kansas v. Hendricks*, 521 U.S. 346 (1997), the Court upheld a Kansas law that established procedures for the civil commitment of persons who, due to a "mental abnormality" or a "personality disorder," are likely to engage in "predatory acts of sexual violence." Hendricks had a long history of sexually molesting children and was scheduled for release from prison when the state filed a petition to have him civilly committed. Hendricks conceded that he could not control the urge to molest children. The Court concluded that Hendricks' admitted lack of control coupled with a prediction of future danger provided a compelling government interest and the law satisfied substance due process requirements. In a case decided a few years later, *Kansas v. Crane*, 534 U.S. 407 (2002), the Court clarified this decision by stating that proof of serious, but not absolute, difficulty in controlling behavior was a requirement of substantive due process. The mere fact that an individual committed sex crimes was not enough to justify a civil commitment.

A more recent expression of the Court's approach to personal liberty is found in the 2003 case of *Lawrence v. Texas*, 539 U.S. 558. In this case, the Supreme Court held that sexual conduct between consenting adults of the same sex was protected by the Fourteenth Amendment. Justice Kennedy began the majority opinion with the following statement:

> Liberty protects the person from unwarranted government intrusions into a dwelling or other private places. In our tradition the State is not omnipresent in the home. And there are other spheres of our lives and existence, outside the home, where the State should not be a dominant presence. Freedom extends beyond spatial bounds. Liberty presumes an autonomy of self that includes freedom of thought, belief, expression, and certain intimate conduct. The instant case involves liberty of the person both in its spatial and more transcendent dimensions.

See Table 9-2 for an overview of the development of the concept of liberty.

Table 9-2 Liberty—An Historical Perspective

1872	Liberty includes only protection against vestiges of slavery (*Slaughter-House Cases*)
1905	Liberty includes economic freedoms such as the freedom to contract (*Lochner v. New York*)
1960s and 1970s	Liberty includes personal freedoms such as freedom to marry (*Loving v. Virginia*), contraception (*Griswold v. Connecticut*), and abortion (*Roe v. Wade*)
1990	Liberty includes the right to reject medical treatment (*Cruzan v. Director, Missouri Dept. of Health*)
2002	Liberty includes civil commitments (*Kansas v. Crane*)
2003	Liberty includes intimate sexual conduct between consenting adults of the same sex (*Lawrence v. Texas*)

Substantive Due Process and Property

Due process applies to deprivations of property as well as to deprivations of liberty. In most cases, when a state deprives a person of property, procedural rather than substantive due process is the issue. However, three cases dealing with damages in civil lawsuits illustrate how substantive due process can be a concern. The first case, *Duke Power Co. v. Carolina Envtl. Study Group*, 438 U.S. 59 (1978), involved the constitutionality of a 1957 federal law that limited the amount of damages that could be claimed from private companies in the event of a nuclear power accident. Fearing potential future injuries, a group of people living near a power plant filed a lawsuit challenging the statute as being in violation of substantive due process. In this case, the Supreme Court upheld the law saying there was a legitimate government interest in encouraging the development of nuclear power, and the law was a rational way to achieve that goal. The Court stated its rationale as follows:

> The record before us fully supports the need for the imposition of a statutory limit on liability to encourage private industry participation and hence bears a rational relationship to Congress' concern for stimulating the involvement of private enterprise in the production of electric energy through the use of atomic power.

The second case, *BMW of N. Am. v. Gore*, 517 U.S. 559 (1996), involved the constitutionality of a large jury award of punitive damages. In 1990, Dr. Ira Gore, Jr., purchased a BMW sports sedan for $40,750.88 from an authorized BMW dealer in Birmingham, Alabama. After a while, he became aware that the car had been repainted. Convinced that he was cheated, Dr. Gore brought suit for fraud against petitioner BMW of North America (BMW), the American distributor of BMW automobiles. The complaint prayed for $500,000 in compensatory and punitive damages and costs. A jury awarded Dr. Gore $4 million in punitive damages but this amount was reduced to $2 million by the Alabama courts. BMW filed a petition for writ of certiorari with the Supreme Court.

Punitive damages are often allowed in civil cases when a defendant engaged in extremely egregious conduct resulting in damage. This type of damage is meant to punish a defendant rather than to compensate an injured plaintiff. In *BMW v. Gore* the Supreme Court held that the Due Process Clause allows such damages but not when the damages are "grossly excessive." A majority of the Court felt that, under these circumstances, $2 million was excessive and that it violated both substantive and procedural due process. The procedural due process violation occurred because the defendant did not receive notice of the magnitude of the potential punitive damage award. The Court said:

> Elementary notions of fairness enshrined in our constitutional jurisprudence dictate that a person receive fair notice not only of the conduct that will subject him to punishment but also of the severity of the penalty that a State may impose. Three guideposts, each of which indicates that BMW did not receive adequate notice of the magnitude of the sanction that Alabama might impose for adhering to the nondisclosure policy adopted in 1983, lead us to the conclusion that the $2 million award against BMW is grossly excessive: the degree of reprehensibility of the nondisclosure; the disparity between the harm or potential harm suffered by Dr. Gore and his punitive damages award; and the difference between this remedy and the civil penalties authorized or imposed in comparable cases.

In 2003, the Supreme Court again addressed the issue of punitive damages and the Due Process Clause in *State Farm Mut. Auto. Ins. Co. v. Campbell*, 538 U.S. 408 (2003). In this case, State Farm was ordered to pay punitive damages in the amount of $145 million and compensatory damages of $1 million. At trial, the plaintiffs were allowed to present evidence of questionable conduct by State Farm in several states. In finding the award of damages unconstitutional and a violation of the Fourteenth Amendment, the Court stated that one state cannot base a punitive damage award on conduct in other states. "A state cannot punish a defendant for conduct that may have been lawful where it occurred.... Nor, as a general rule, does a State have a legitimate concern in imposing punitive damages to punish a defendant for unlawful acts committed outside of the State's jurisdiction." Furthermore, the Court found the disparity between the compensatory damages and the punitive damages to be too great. The Court refused to set any absolute guideline, but did mention that any disparity greater than a single-digit ratio would be highly questionable.

In 2008, in *Exxon Shipping v. Baker*, 554 U.S. 471, the Supreme Court addressed the issue of punitive damages in connection with the huge oil spill caused by the negligence of the captain of the Exxon Valdez off the Alaskan coast. Evidence indicated that the captain had a known problem with alcohol and had been drinking at the time of the incident. Ultimately, in addition to compensatory damages, a judgment of over 2 billion dollars was entered against Exxon, an amount that was several times the amount of actual compensatory damages. This case was heard by the Supreme Court, but not as a "due process" case. Because of the nature of the incident, the punitive damages were evaluated under federal maritime common law rather than the Constitution. As with other civil actions, though, federal maritime common law did not specify a precise amount that could be awarded as punitive damages. In this case the Court found that punitive damages should not exceed the amount of the compensatory damages. Although the decision is not binding on cases coming under the Due Process Clause, the decision may signal a formula to be imposed in all cases. Consider the following statement of the Court:

> Whatever may be the constitutional significance of the unpredictability of high punitive awards, this feature of happenstance is in tension with the function of the awards as punitive, just because of the implication of unfairness that an eccentrically high punitive verdict carries in a system whose commonly held notion of law rests on a sense of fairness in dealing with one another. Thus, a penalty should be reasonably predictable in its severity, so that even Justice Holmes's "bad man" can look ahead with some ability to know what the stakes are in choosing one course of action or another.

See Exhibit 9-2 for an example of allegations in a civil complaint requesting punitive damages.

Exhibit 9-2 Sample Punitive Damage Allegations

THE CONSTITUTION AND PUNITIVE DAMAGES
Because punitive damages raise several constitutional issues, when parties ask for them in a complaint filed in a civil lawsuit, the answer to the complaint usually raises the Constitution as an affirmative defense. The following paragraphs may appear in an answer:

64. Plaintiffs' claim for punitive damages against defendant cannot be sustained, because an award of punitive damages under _____ [state] law without proof of every element beyond a reasonable doubt would violate defendant's due process rights under the Fourteenth Amendment to the United States Constitution and under Article _____, Section _____ of the Constitution of _____ [state].

65. Alternatively, unless both defendant's liability for punitive damages and the appropriate amount of punitive damages are required to be established by clear and convincing evidence, any award of punitive damages would violate defendant's due process rights guaranteed by the Fourteenth Amendment to the United States Constitution and under Article _____, Section _____ of the Constitution of _____ [state].

(continued)

(continued)

66. Plaintiffs' claim for punitive damages against defendant cannot be sustained, because any award of punitive damages under _____ [state] law without bifurcating the trial of all punitive damages issues would violate defendant's due process rights guaranteed by the Fourteenth Amendment to the United States Constitution and under Article _____, Section _____ of the Constitution of _____ [state].

69. Plaintiffs' claim for punitive damages against defendant cannot be sustained, because an award of punitive damages under _____ [state] law for the purpose of compensating plaintiffs for elements of damage not otherwise recognized by _____ [state] law would violate defendant's due process rights guaranteed by the Fourteenth Amendment to the United States Constitution and under Article _____, Section _____ of the Constitution of _____ [state].

72. Plaintiffs' claim for punitive damages against defendant cannot be sustained because it calls for the court to make an award of punitive damages based on defendant's lawful but irrelevant conduct outside _____ [state] and thereby places unreasonable, state imposed limitations on interstate commerce in violation of the Commerce Clause of the United States Constitution.

Courtesy of Delmar, a Cengage Learning business   3B AMJUR PP AUTO § 1181.1

© Cengage Learning 2013

Procedural Due Process

SUBSTANTIVE DUE PROCESS DEALS WITH the government's right to enact laws that deprive a person of life, liberty, or property. Procedural due process assumes that the government has the right but questions *how* the right is exercised in a particular case.

Standards for Determining Procedural Due Process Violations

Although the specific dictates of procedural due process depend on whether the proceeding is a criminal case, a civil lawsuit, or some other government taking; general requirements exist in all cases. Usually, before a person is deprived of life, liberty, or property, that person must receive proper notice and the opportunity for a fair hearing, although sometimes action can be taken prior to a hearing. In rare instances, no hearing is required. Due process also requires that a hearing be conducted by an impartial panel, affording the opportunity for cross examination of witnesses. See Exhibit 9-3.

Exhibit 9-3   Procedural Due Process Requirements

Procedural Due Process Usually Requires

1. Notice of proposed taking *and*
2. Opportunity for fair hearing conducted by impartial panel with opportunity for cross-examination of witnesses.

© Cengage Learning 2013

Procedural Due Process and Criminal Cases

All aspects of a criminal case, beginning with the police investigation, must comply with procedural due process. Some of the procedural due process requirements are expressly set out in the Bill of Rights, and in the Fourth, Fifth, Sixth, and Eighth Amendments. Most of these requirements are incorporated in the Fourteenth Amendment. The constitutional rules for criminal procedure are discussed in detail in Chapter 14. In summary, however, the following procedures are required by the Bill of Rights:

1. Searches, arrests, and seizures of property must be reasonable. (Fourth Amendment)
2. Search and arrest warrants must be specific and based on probable cause. (Fourth Amendment)

3. Physical or psychological force cannot be used to compel a confession. (Fifth Amendment)
4. A defendant cannot be subject to double jeopardy. (Fifth Amendment)
5. In serious federal offenses, the defendant is entitled to a grand jury hearing. (Fifth Amendment)
6. A defendant is entitled to be notified of the charges against him. (Sixth Amendment)
7. A defendant is entitled to a public trial before a jury in the district in which the crime occurred. (Sixth Amendment)
8. A defendant is entitled to the assistance of counsel. (Sixth Amendment)
9. The defendant has the right to compel witnesses to attend the trial and the right to cross-examine witnesses against him. (Sixth Amendment)
10. A defendant cannot be subject to cruel and unusual punishment. (Eighth Amendment)
11. If bail is set, it must be reasonable. (Eighth Amendment)

Due process in criminal cases, however, is not limited to the specific rights in the Bill of Rights. Any procedure that interferes with the right of a criminal defendant to notice and a fair trial creates a potential violation of procedural due process. For example, the notice requirement of procedural due process requires that criminal laws be sufficiently specific so that a defendant knows what type of behavior is illegal. Laws that are too vague fail to give notice to individuals of the type of behavior expected of them and are therefore unconstitutional. Local ordinances are especially prone to attack on this basis, and laws that prohibit vagrancy, loitering, and cruising often come under attack. In *City of Chicago v. Morales*, a 1999 case, the Supreme Court reviewed a Chicago ordinance prohibiting gangs from loitering. The Court's opinion, finding that the law was too vague, is printed below along with a dissent filed by Justice Scalia.

City of Chicago v. Morales
527 U.S. 41 (1999)

JUSTICE STEVENS announced the judgment of the Court.

In 1992, the Chicago City Council enacted the Gang Congregation Ordinance, which prohibits "criminal street gang members" from "loitering" with one another or with other persons in any public place. The question presented is whether the Supreme Court of Illinois correctly held that the ordinance violates the Due Process Clause of the Fourteenth Amendment to the Federal Constitution. The ordinance creates a criminal offense punishable by a fine of up to $500, imprisonment for not more than six months, and a requirement to perform up to 120 hours of community service. Commission of the offense involves four predicates. First, the police officer must reasonably believe that at least one of the two or more persons present in a "public place" is a "criminal street gang member." Second, the persons must be "loitering," which the ordinance defines as "remaining in any one place with no apparent purpose." Third, the officer must then order "all" of the persons to disperse and remove themselves "from the area." Fourth, a person must

disobey the officer's order. If any person, whether a gang member or not, disobeys the officer's order, that person is guilty of violating the ordinance.

The basic factual predicate for the city's ordinance is not in dispute. As the city argues in its brief, "the very presence of a large collection of obviously brazen, insistent, and lawless gang members and hangers-on on the public ways intimidates residents, who become afraid even to leave their homes and go about their business. That, in turn, imperils community residents' sense of safety and security, detracts from property values, and can ultimately destabilize entire neighborhoods." The findings in the ordinance explain that it was motivated by these concerns. We have no doubt that a law that directly prohibited such intimidating conduct would be constitutional, but this ordinance broadly covers a significant amount of additional activity. Uncertainty about the scope of that additional coverage provides the basis for respondents' claim that the ordinance is too vague.

(continued)

(continued)

We, like the Illinois courts, conclude that the ordinance is invalid on its face. The freedom to loiter for innocent purposes is part of the "liberty" protected by the Due Process Clause of the Fourteenth Amendment. We have expressly identified this "right to remove from one place to another according to inclination" as "an attribute of personal liberty" protected by the Constitution. *Williams v. Fears*, 179 U.S. 270, 274 (1900). Indeed, it is apparent that an individual's decision to remain in a public place of his choice is as much a part of his liberty as the freedom of movement inside frontiers that is "a part of our heritage" *Kent v. Dulles*, 357 U.S. 116, 126 (1958), or the right to move "to whatsoever place one's own inclination may direct" identified in Blackstone's Commentaries. 1 W. Blackstone, *Commentaries on the Laws of England* 130 (1765).

Vagueness may invalidate a criminal law for either of two independent reasons. First, it may fail to provide the kind of notice that will enable ordinary people to understand what conduct it prohibits; second, it may authorize and even encourage arbitrary and discriminatory enforcement. Accordingly, we first consider whether the ordinance provides fair notice to the citizen and then discuss its potential for arbitrary enforcement.

Since the city cannot conceivably have meant to criminalize each instance a citizen stands in public with a gang member, the vagueness that dooms this ordinance is not the product of uncertainty about the normal meaning of "loitering," but rather about what loitering is covered by the ordinance and what is not. [T]he purpose of the fair notice requirement is to enable the ordinary citizen to conform his or her conduct to the law. "No one may be required at peril of life, liberty or property to speculate as to the meaning of penal statutes." *Lanzetta v. New Jersey*, 306 U.S. 451, 453 (1939).

The broad sweep of the ordinance also violates "the requirement that a legislature establish minimal guidelines to govern law enforcement." *Kolender v. Lawson*, 461 U.S., at 358. The mandatory language in the enactment directs the police to issue an order without first making any inquiry about their possible purposes. It matters not whether the reason that a gang member and his father, for example, might loiter near Wrigley Field is to rob an unsuspecting fan or just to get a glimpse of Sammy Sosa leaving the ballpark; in either event, if their purpose is not apparent to a nearby police officer, she may—indeed, she "shall"—order them to disperse.

Accordingly, the judgment of the Supreme Court of Illinois is affirmed.

JUSTICE SCALIA, dissenting.

Until the ordinance that is before us today was adopted, the citizens of Chicago were free to stand about in public places with no apparent purpose—to engage, that is, in conduct that appeared to be loitering. In recent years, however, the city has been afflicted with criminal street gangs. Many residents of the inner city felt that they were prisoners in their own homes. Once again, Chicagoans decided that to eliminate the problem it was worth restricting some of the freedom that they once enjoyed. The minor limitation upon the free state of nature that this prophylactic arrangement imposed upon all Chicagoans seemed to them (and it seems to me) a small price to pay for liberation of their streets.

The majority today invalidates this perfectly reasonable measure by ignoring our rules governing facial challenges, by elevating loitering to a constitutionally guaranteed right, and by discerning vagueness where, according to our usual standards, none exists.

When our normal criteria for facial challenges are applied, it is clear that the Justices in the majority have transposed the burden of proof. Instead of requiring the respondents, who are challenging the Ordinance, to show that it is invalid in all its applications, they have required the petitioner to show that it is valid in all its applications. Both the plurality opinion and the concurrences display a lively imagination, creating hypothetical situations in which the law's application would (in their view) be ambiguous. But that creative role has been usurped from the petitioner, who can defeat the respondents' facial challenge by conjuring up *a single valid application* of the law. My contribution would go something like this: Tony, a member of the Jets criminal street gang, is standing alongside and chatting with fellow gang members while staking out their turf at Promontory Point on the South Side of Chicago; the group is flashing gang signs and displaying their distinctive tattoos to passersby. Officer Krupke, applying the Ordinance at issue here, orders the group to disperse. After some speculative discussion (probably irrelevant here) over whether the Jets are

(continued)

(continued)

depraved because they are deprived, Tony and the other gang members break off further conversation with the statement—not entirely coherent, but evidently intended to be rude—"Gee, Officer Krupke, krup you." A tense standoff ensues until Officer Krupke arrests the group for failing to obey his dispersal order. Even assuming (as the Justices in the majority do, but I do not) that a law requiring obedience to a dispersal order is impermissibly vague unless it is clear to the objects of the order, before its issuance, that their conduct justifies it, I find it hard to believe that the Jets would not have known they had it coming. That should settle the matter of respondents' facial challenge to the Ordinance's vagueness.

The fact is that the present ordinance is entirely clear in its application, cannot be violated except with full knowledge and intent, and vests no more discretion in the police than innumerable other measures authorizing police orders to preserve the public peace and safety. The majority's real quarrel with the Chicago Ordinance is simply that it permits (or indeed requires) too much harmless conduct by innocent citizens to be proscribed.

But in our democratic system, how much harmless conduct to proscribe is not a judgment to be made by the courts. So long as constitutionally guaranteed rights are not affected, and so long as the proscription has a rational basis, *all sorts* of perfectly harmless activity by millions of perfectly innocent people can be forbidden—riding a motorcycle without a safety helmet, for example, starting a campfire in a national forest, or selling a safe and effective drug not yet approved by the FDA. All of these acts are entirely innocent and harmless in themselves, but because of the *risk* of harm that they entail, the freedom to engage in them has been abridged. The citizens of Chicago have decided that depriving themselves of the freedom to "hang out" with a gang member is necessary to eliminate pervasive gang crime and intimidation—and that the elimination of the one is worth the deprivation of the other. This Court has no business second-guessing either the degree of necessity or the fairness of the trade.

I dissent from the judgment of the Court.

Something to Consider

The Court states that "the purpose of the fair notice requirement is to enable the ordinary citizen to conform his or her conduct to the law." Why did the majority feel the Chicago ordinance did not do this? Why did Justice Scalia believe that it did?

The vagueness concept played an important role a few years later in a case involving Jeffrey Skilling and the Enron financial disaster. Skilling, the CEO of Enron, was convicted of conspiracy to violate several different criminal laws. One of these crimes related to the United States Code, section 1346, defining the term "scheme or artifice to defraud" to include a scheme "to deprive another of the intangible right of honest services." Unfortunately "honest services" was not defined. However, over the years, a variety of cases decided that this section prohibited bribes and kickbacks. The government did not allege that Skilling took a bribe or kickback. Rather they contended that section 1346 included various financial schemes. The excerpt from the Court's opinion explains why the Court found this to be unconstitutionally vague.

Due process violations can also occur in post-conviction proceedings, especially attempts to revoke probation or parole. The Court has said that revoking probation or parole deprives an individual of liberty and is therefore subject to due process. In these instances, the defendant is entitled to a hearing before the government takes action.

Skilling v. United States

561 U.S. ___ (2010)

It has long been our practice, before striking a federal statute as impermissibly vague, to consider whether the prescription is amenable to a limiting construction. See, e.g., *Hooper* v. *California,* 155 U.S. 648, 657 (1895) "The elementary rule is that *every reasonable construction* must be resorted to, in order to save a statute from unconstitutionality."

Although some applications of the honest-services doctrine occasioned disagreement among the Courts of Appeals, these cases do not cloud the doctrine's solid core: The "vast majority" of the honest-services cases involved offenders who, in violation of a fiduciary duty, participated in bribery or kickback schemes. *United States* v. *Runnels,* 833 F. 2d 1183, 1187 (CA6 1987).

In view of this history, there is no doubt that Congress intended §1346 to reach *at least* bribes and kickbacks. Reading the statute to proscribe a wider range of offensive conduct, we acknowledge, would raise the due process concerns underlying the vagueness doctrine. To preserve the statute without transgressing constitutional limitations, we now hold that §1346 criminalizes *only* the bribe-and-kickback.

The Government urges us to go further by locating within §1346's compass another category of proscribed conduct: "undisclosed self-dealing by a public official or private employee— *i.e.,* the taking of official action by the employee that furthers his own undisclosed financial interests while purporting to act in the interests of those to whom he owes a fiduciary duty."

Interpreted to encompass only bribery and kickback schemes, §1346 is not unconstitutionally vague. Recall that the void-for-vagueness doctrine addresses concerns about (1) fair notice and (2) arbitrary and discriminatory prosecutions. See *Kolender,* 461 U.S., at 357. A prohibition on fraudulently depriving another of one's honest services by accepting bribes or kickbacks does not present a problem on either score.

As to fair notice, "whatever the school of thought concerning the scope and meaning of " §1346, it has always been "as plain as a pikestaff that" bribes and kickbacks constitute honest-services fraud, *Williams*

v. *United States,* 341 U.S. 97, 101 (1951), and the statute's *mens rea* requirement further blunts any notice concern, see, *e.g., Screws* v. *United States,* 325 U.S. 91, 101–104 (1945) (plurality opinion). See also *Broadrick* v. *Oklahoma,* 413 U.S. 601, 608 (1973) ("[E]ven if the outermost boundaries of [a statute are] imprecise, any such uncertainty has little relevance … where appellants' conduct falls squarely within the 'hard core' of the statute's proscriptions."). Today's decision clarifies that no other misconduct falls within §1346's province. See *United States* v. *Lanier,* 520 U.S. 259, 266 (1997).

It remains to determine whether Skilling's conduct violated §1346. Skilling's honest-services prosecution, the Government concedes, was not "prototypical." The Government charged Skilling with conspiring to defraud Enron's shareholders by misrepresenting the company's fiscal health, thereby artificially inflating its stock price. It was the Government's theory at trial that Skilling "profited from the fraudulent scheme … through the receipt of salary and bonuses, … and through the sale of approximately $200 million in Enron stock, which netted him $89 million." *Id.,* at 51.

The Government did not, at any time, allege that Skilling solicited or accepted side payments from a third party in exchange for making these misrepresentations. It is therefore clear that, as we read §1346, Skilling did not commit honest-services fraud.

Whether potential reversal on the conspiracy count touches any of Skilling's other convictions is also an open question. All of his convictions, Skilling contends, hinged on the conspiracy count and, like dominoes, must fall if it falls. The District Court, deciding Skilling's motion for bail pending appeal, found this argument dubious, App. 1141a–1142a, but the Fifth Circuit had no occasion to rule on it. That court may do so on remand.

*   *   *

For the foregoing reasons, we affirm the Fifth Circuit's ruling on Skilling's fair-trial argument, vacate its ruling on his conspiracy conviction, and remand the case for proceedings consistent with this opinion.

It is so ordered.

Something to Consider

In *City of Chicago v. Morales,* the Court stated that the law in question was invalid on its face. Was the law in *Skilling* invalid on its face? If *Skilling* were the first case to come before the Court asking for an interpretation of Section 1346, would the result have been the same?

JUVENILE PROCEEDINGS

Although they are not technically considered criminal proceedings, juvenile proceedings can result in a similar loss of personal liberty. For many years, states did not grant many procedural safeguards to juveniles who were accused of crimes, even though the juvenile faced substantial loss of freedom. In 1967 the Supreme Court addressed this problem in the landmark case, *In re Gault.*, 387 U.S. 1 (1967). In this case, Gerald Gault, a fifteen-year-old, was taken into custody for making lewd remarks to a neighbor. The following excerpt from the case details the procedures followed by the state court:

In re Gault
387 U.S. 1 (1967)

At the time Gerald was picked up, his mother and father were both at work. No notice that Gerald was being taken into custody was left at the home. No other steps were taken to advise them that their son had, in effect, been arrested. Gerald was taken to the Children's Detention Home. When his mother arrived home at about 6 o'clock, Gerald was not there. Gerald's older brother was sent to look for him at the trailer home of the Lewis family. He apparently learned then that Gerald was in custody. He so informed his mother. The two of them went to the Detention Home. The deputy probation officer, Flagg, who was also superintendent of the Detention Home, told Mrs. Gault "why Jerry was there" and said that a hearing would be held in Juvenile Court at 3 o' clock the following day, June 9.

Officer Flagg filed a petition with the court on the hearing day, June 9, 1964. It was not served on the Gaults. Indeed, none of them saw this petition until the habeas corpus hearing on August 17, 1964. The petition was entirely formal. It made no reference to any factual basis for the judicial action which it initiated. It recited only that "said minor is under the age of eighteen years, and is in need of the protection of this Honorable Court; and that said minor is a delinquent minor." It prayed for a hearing and an order regarding "the care and custody of said minor." Officer Flagg executed a formal affidavit in support of the petition.

On June 9, Gerald, his mother, his older brother, and Probation Officers Flagg and Henderson appeared before the Juvenile Judge in chambers. Gerald's father was not there. He was at work out of the city. Mrs. Cook, the complainant, was not there. No one was sworn at this hearing. No transcript or recording was made. No memorandum or record of the substance of the proceedings was prepared. Our information about the proceeding and

the subsequent hearing on June 15, derives entirely from the testimony of the Juvenile Court Judge, Mr. and Mrs. Gault and Officer Flagg at the habeas corpus proceeding conducted two months later. From this, it appears that at the June 9 hearing Gerald was questioned by the judge about the telephone call. There was conflict as to what he said. His mother recalled that Gerald said he only dialed Mrs. Cook's number and handed the telephone to his friend, Ronald. Officer Flagg recalled that Gerald had admitted making the lewd remarks. Judge McGhee testified that Gerald "admitted making one of these lewd statements." At the conclusion of the hearing, the judge said he would "think about it." Gerald was taken back to the Detention Home. He was not sent to his own home with his parents. On June 11 or 12, after having been detained since June 8, Gerald was released and driven home. There is no explanation in the record as to why he was kept in the Detention Home or why he was released. At 5 p. m. on the day of Gerald's release, Mrs. Gault received a note signed by Officer Flagg. It was on plain paper, not letterhead. Its entire text was as follows:

Mrs. Gault:

Judge McGHEE has set Monday June 15, 1964 at 11:00 A. M. as the date and time for further Hearings on Gerald's delinquency

/s/ Flagg

At the appointed time on Monday, June 15, Gerald, his father and mother, Ronald Lewis and his father, and Officers Flagg and Henderson were present before Judge McGhee. Witnesses at the habeas corpus proceeding differed in their recollections of Gerald's testimony at the June 15 hearing. Mr. and Mrs. Gault recalled that Gerald again testified that he had only dialed the number and

(continued)

(continued)

that the other boy had made the remarks. Officer Flagg agreed that at this hearing Gerald did not admit making the lewd remarks. But Judge McGhee recalled that "there was some admission again of some of the lewd statements. He didn't admit any of the more serious lewd statements." Again, the complainant, Mrs. Cook, was not present. Mrs. Gault asked that Mrs. Cook be present "so she could see which boy that done the talking, the dirty talking over the phone." The Juvenile Judge said "she didn't have to be present at that hearing." The judge did not speak to Mrs. Cook or communicate with her at any time. Probation Officer Flagg had talked to her once over the telephone on June 9.

At this June 15 hearing a "referral report" made by the probation officers was filed with the court, although not disclosed to Gerald or his parents. This listed the charge as "Lewd Phone Calls." At the conclusion of the hearing, the judge committed Gerald as a juvenile delinquent to the State Industrial School "for the period of his minority that is, until 21, unless sooner discharged by due process of law." An order to that effect was entered. It recites that "after a full hearing and due deliberation the Court finds that said minor is a delinquent child, and that said minor is of the age of 15 years."

No appeal is permitted by Arizona law in juvenile cases. On August 3, 1964, a petition for a writ of habeas corpus was filed with the Supreme Court of Arizona and referred by it to the Superior Court for hearing.

In the *Gault* decision, the Supreme Court summarized the development of the juvenile justice system. This system developed with the intent of protecting youthful offenders from the harshness of the adult criminal justice system. The lack of procedural safeguards was rationalized by the idea that juveniles had a right not to liberty but to custody. The state, in operating the juvenile justice system, was simply acting in the place of the parents, who have custodial rights over the child. In *Gault*, the Supreme Court rejected this notion, holding that a juvenile is entitled to procedural safeguards under due process. The Court concluded:

> Ultimately, however, we confront the reality of that portion of the Juvenile Court process with which we deal in this case. A boy is charged with misconduct. The boy is committed to an institution where he may be restrained of liberty for years. It is of no constitutional consequence and of limited practical meaning that the institution to which he is committed is called an Industrial School. The fact of the matter is that, however euphemistic the title, a "receiving home" or an "industrial school" for juveniles is an institution of confinement in which the child is incarcerated for a greater or lesser time. His world becomes "a building with whitewashed walls, regimented routine and institutional hours...." Instead of mother and father and sisters and brothers and friends and classmates, his world is peopled by guards, custodians, state employees, and "delinquents" confined with him for anything from waywardness to rape and homicide.
>
> In view of this, it would be extraordinary if our Constitution did not require the procedural regularity and the exercise of care implied in the phrase "due process." Under our Constitution, the condition of being a boy does not justify a kangaroo court.

In particular, the Supreme Court decided that juveniles are entitled to the following procedural safeguards:

1. Sufficient notice of the charges given in time to prepare for a hearing
2. Right to counsel, which includes being advised of the right and being provided counsel without cost if unable to afford an attorney

3. Constitutional protection against self-incrimination, which is granted to adults

4. Opportunity to cross-examine witnesses

The *Gault* case did not give juveniles all of the rights given to adult offenders. The Court held that due process for a juvenile does not require a jury trial or the right to bail. Two recent cases, however, apply the Eighth Amendment prohibition of cruel and unusual punishment to juvenile proceedings. In the first case, *Roper v. Simmons*, the Court held that the death penalty could not be imposed on any person who was under 18 at the time the crime was committed. In reaching this decision, the Court relied heavily on national consensus against the death penalty in relationship to juveniles as well as the immaturity of juveniles. In the second case, *Graham v. Florida* 560 U.S. __ (2010), the Court applied a rationale similar to that applied in *Roper* and held that life imprisonment without the possibility of parole for non-homicide cases was unconstitutional when applied to anyone under the age of 18 at the time the crime was committed. An excerpt from the Syllabus in Roper and from the dissenting opinions of Justice Scalia follows.

Roper v. Simmons
543 U.S. 551 (2005)

At age 17, respondent Simmons planned and committed a capital murder. After he had turned 18, he was sentenced to death. His direct appeal and subsequent petitions for state and federal postconviction relief were rejected. This Court then held, in *Atkins v. Virginia,* 536 U.S. 304, that the Eighth Amendment, applicable to the States through the Fourteenth Amendment, prohibits the execution of a mentally retarded person. Simmons filed a new petition for state postconviction relief, arguing that *Atkins'* reasoning established that the Constitution prohibits the execution of a juvenile who was under 18 when he committed his crime. The Missouri Supreme Court agreed and set aside Simmons' death sentence in favor of life imprisonment without eligibility for release. It held that a national consensus has developed against the execution of those offenders.

Held: The Eighth and Fourteenth Amendments forbid imposition of the death penalty on offenders who were under the age of 18 when their crimes were committed.

(a) The Eighth Amendment's prohibition against "cruel and unusual punishments" must be interpreted according to its text, by considering history, tradition, and precedent, and with due regard for its purpose and function in the constitutional design. To implement this framework this Court has established the propriety and affirmed the necessity of referring to "the evolving standards of decency that mark the progress of a maturing society" to determine which punishments are so disproportionate as to be "cruel and unusual." *Trop v. Dulles,* 356 U.S. 86, 100—101. In 1988, in *Thompson v. Oklahoma,* 487 U.S. 815, 818—838, a plurality determined that national standards of decency did not permit the execution of any offender under age 16 at the time of the crime. The next year, in *Stanford,* a 5-to-4 Court referred to contemporary standards of decency, but concluded the Eighth and Fourteenth Amendments did not proscribe the execution of offenders over 15 but under 18 because 22 of 37 death penalty States permitted that penalty for 16-year-old offenders, and 25 permitted it for 17-year-olds, thereby indicating there was no national consensus. 492 U.S., at 370—371. That same day the Court held, in *Penry v. Lynaugh,* 492 U.S. 302, 334, that the Eighth Amendment did not mandate a categorical exemption from the death penalty for mentally retarded persons because only two States had enacted laws banning such executions. Three terms ago in *Atkins,* however, the Court held that standards of decency had evolved since *Penry* and now demonstrated that the execution of the mentally retarded is cruel and unusual punishment. The *Atkins* Court noted that objective indicia of society's standards, as expressed in pertinent legislative enactments and state practice, demonstrated that such executions had become so truly unusual that it was fair to say that a national consensus has developed against them. 536 U.S., at 314—315. After observing that mental retardation diminishes

(continued)

(continued)

personal culpability even if the offender can distinguish right from wrong, *id.,* at 318, and that mentally retarded offenders' impairments make it less defensible to impose the death penalty as retribution for past crimes or as a real deterrent to future crimes, *id.,* at 319—320, the Court ruled that the death penalty constitutes an excessive sanction for the entire category of mentally retarded offenders, and that the Eighth Amendment places a substantive restriction on the State's power to take such an offender's life, *id.,* at 321. Just as the *Atkins* Court reconsidered the issue decided in *Penry,* the Court now reconsiders the issue decided in *Stanford.*

(b) Both objective indicia of consensus, as expressed in particular by the enactments of legislatures that have addressed the question, and the Court's own determination in the exercise of its independent judgment, demonstrate that the death penalty is a disproportionate punishment for juveniles.

(1) As in *Atkins,* the objective indicia of national consensus here–the rejection of the juvenile death penalty in the majority of States; the infrequency of its use even where it remains on the books; and the consistency in the trend toward abolition of the practice–provide sufficient evidence that today society views juveniles, in the words *Atkins* used respecting the mentally retarded, as "categorically less culpable than the average criminal," 536 U.S., at 316. The evidence of such consensus is similar, and in some respects parallel, to the evidence in *Atkins:* 30 States prohibit the juvenile death penalty, including 12 that have rejected it altogether and 18 that maintain it but, by express provision or judicial interpretation, exclude juveniles from its reach. Moreover, even in the 20 States without a formal prohibition, the execution of juveniles is infrequent. Although, by contrast to *Atkins,* the rate of change in reducing the incidence of the juvenile death penalty, or in taking specific steps to abolish it, has been less dramatic, the difference between this case and *Atkins* in that respect is counterbalanced by the consistent direction of the change toward abolition. Indeed, the slower pace here may be explained by the simple fact that the impropriety of executing juveniles between 16 and 18 years old gained wide recognition earlier than the impropriety of executing the mentally retarded.

(2) Three general differences between juveniles under 18 and adults demonstrate that juvenile offenders cannot with reliability be classified among the worst offenders.

Juveniles' susceptibility to immature and irresponsible behavior means "their irresponsible conduct is not as morally reprehensible as that of an adult." *Thompson v. Oklahoma,* 487 U.S. 815, 835. Their own vulnerability and comparative lack of control over their immediate surroundings mean juveniles have a greater claim than adults to be forgiven for failing to escape negative influences in their whole environment. See *Stanford, supra,* at 395. The reality that juveniles still struggle to define their identity means it is less supportable to conclude that even a heinous crime committed by a juvenile is evidence of irretrievably depraved character. The Thompson plurality recognized the import of these characteristics with respect to juveniles under 16. The same reasoning applies to all juvenile offenders under 18. Although the Court cannot deny or overlook the brutal crimes too many juvenile offenders have committed, it disagrees with petitioner's contention that, given the Court's own insistence on individualized consideration in capital sentencing, it is arbitrary and unnecessary to adopt a categorical rule barring imposition of the death penalty on an offender under 18. An unacceptable likelihood exists that the brutality or cold-blooded nature of any particular crime would overpower mitigating arguments based on youth as a matter of course, even where the juvenile offender's objective immaturity, vulnerability, and lack of true depravity should require a sentence less severe than death.

The following is an excerpt from the dissenting opinion of Justice Scalia:

In urging approval of a constitution that gave life-tenured judges the power to nullify laws enacted by the people's representatives, Alexander Hamilton assured the citizens of New York that there was little risk in this, since "[t]he judiciary ... ha[s] neither FORCE nor WILL but merely judgment." The Federalist No. 78, p. 465 (C. Rossiter ed. 1961). But Hamilton had in mind a traditional judiciary, "bound down by strict rules and precedents which serve to define and point out their duty in every particular case that comes before them." *Id.,* at 471. Bound down, indeed. What a mockery today's opinion makes of Hamilton's expectation, announcing the Court's conclusion that the meaning of our Constitution has changed over the past 15 years–not, mind you, that this Court's decision 15 years ago was *wrong,* but that the Constitution *has changed.* The Court reaches this implausible result by purporting to advert, not to the original

(continued)

(continued)

meaning of the Eighth Amendment, but to "the evolving standards of decency," *ante*, at 6 (internal quotation marks omitted), of our national society. It then finds, on the flimsiest of grounds, that a national consensus which could not be perceived in our people's laws barely 15 years ago now solidly exists. Worse still, the Court says in so many words that what our people's laws say about the issue does not, in the last analysis, matter: "[I]n the end our own judgment will be brought to bear on the question of the acceptability of the death penalty under the Eighth Amendment." *Ante*, at 9 (internal quotation marks omitted). The Court thus proclaims itself sole arbiter of our Nation's moral standards–and in the course of discharging that awesome responsibility purports to take guidance from the views of foreign courts and legislatures. Because I do not believe that the meaning of our Eighth Amendment, any more than the meaning of other provisions of our Constitution, should be determined by the subjective views of five Members of this Court and like-minded foreigners, I dissent.

Something to Consider

Is it fair to treat an intelligent 17-year-old the same way as a person who qualifies as mentally retarded?

Constitutional protection of criminal defendants is discussed in more detail in Chapter 14.

Procedural Due Process and Civil Lawsuits

A successful civil lawsuit usually deprives a defendant of property (money damages) or liberty (such as an injunction). Therefore, as long as there is some government involvement, due process requirements apply. Although many civil lawsuits are between private parties, the parties must use state or federal courts and procedures to pursue the litigation and collect any judgment or seize property. This is sufficient government action to bring all civil lawsuits within the due process requirements of the Fifth and Fourteenth Amendments.

Procedural due process requirements for civil cases are different from those in criminal cases. The Bill of Rights contains only one provision related to civil cases—the requirement of a jury in all cases where the dispute exceeds $20—and this provision has *not* been applied to the states through the Fourteenth Amendment. In addition to the question of jury trials, procedural due process issues in civil lawsuits concern notice, jurisdiction of a state over non-resident defendants, prejudgment attachment of property, burden of proof required at trial, and the rights of indigent parties. As discussed previously in this chapter, punitive damages presents both substantive and procedural due process issues.

NOTICE

service of process

The delivery (or its legal equivalent, such as publication in a newspaper in some cases) of a legal paper, such as a writ, by an authorized person in a way that meets certain formal requirements. It is the way to notify a person of a lawsuit.

Assume that the check for your car payment bounced and when you contact the bank you find that the money was seized by court order. You discover that you were named in a lawsuit and instead of being personally served with papers, notice was published in a legal newspaper. A subsequent trial took place that you knew nothing about. Does it seem fair? Of course not. Giving proper notice of a civil lawsuit is a requirement of procedural due process. Property cannot be taken to satisfy a judgment if the defendant was not properly notified of the lawsuit and given an opportunity to appear at trial. Giving notice of a pending civil lawsuit is sometimes referred to as **service of process**. All states have rules specifying how service can be done. The Due Process Clause does not dictate any specific method as long as the method is reasonably calculated to give the defendant actual notice of the suit. Service can be made by publication, but only when the defendant's whereabouts are unknown.

In addition to the type of notice that must be given, in some cases due process requires that notice be given to those who are not actually parties to the case, but who have an interest in the outcome. One issue that arises concerns the right of biological fathers to receive notice of adoption proceedings. Once the father establishes a parental relationship, notice is required, but when the biological father makes no effort to establish a relationship with the child, notice is not required. *Lehr v. Robertson*, 527 U.S. 41 (1983).

JURISDICTION OVER NON-RESIDENT DEFENDANTS

Assume you are in an auto accident caused by a driver who lives in another state. Two months later you are sued in the home state of the other driver. You have never been to that state and have no connection with the state. Is it fair to require you to go to the other state to defend yourself in its courts for something that happened in your state? Basic fairness, due process, is a question that arises whenever a state tries to exercise jurisdiction over a non-resident defendant. The Due Process Clause limits a state's right to exercise jurisdiction over non-residents. However, the Supreme Court acknowledged this limitation even before the Fourteenth Amendment in *Pennoyer v. Neff*, 95 U.S. 714 (1877), a case challenging ownership of real property located in the state of Oregon. Neff, who was not a resident of Oregon, had been sued in Oregon in a prior action for breach of an agreement. Pursuant to Oregon law, he was served by publication. He defaulted and judgment was entered against him. His land was seized and sold to Pennoyer at a sheriff's sale to satisfy the judgment. Neff then filed a lawsuit claiming that because he was not a resident of Oregon, that state's courts had no jurisdiction over him and the original judgment and subsequent sale of his property were therefore void. The Supreme Court agreed saying:

> The authority of every tribunal is necessarily restricted by the territorial limits of the State in which it is established. Any attempt to exercise authority beyond those limits would be deemed in every other forum, as has been said by this court, in illegitimate assumption of power, and be resisted as mere abuse.

State courts are not totally prohibited from exercising jurisdiction over non-resident defendants. The Fourteenth Amendment does, however, impose limits on this jurisdiction. In *International Shoe Co. v. Washington*, 326 U.S. 310 (1945), the Supreme Court set forth the rule that continues to be followed. For a court to exercise jurisdiction over a non-resident defendant, that defendant must have sufficient contacts with the state to satisfy traditional notions of fair play and substantial justice. The Court said:

> Historically the jurisdiction of courts to render judgment in personam is grounded on their de facto power over the defendant's person. Hence his presence within the territorial jurisdiction of court was prerequisite to its rendition of a judgment personally binding him. *Pennoyer v. Neff*, 95 U.S. 714, 733. But now ... due process requires only that in order to subject a defendant to a judgment in personam, if he be not present within the territory of the forum, he have certain minimum contacts with it such that the maintenance of the suit does not offend traditional notions of fair play and substantial justice.
>
> To the extent that a corporation exercises the privilege of conducting activities within a state, it enjoys the benefits and protection of the laws of that state. The exercise of that privilege may give rise to obligations; and, so far as those obligations arise out of or are connected with the activities within the state, a procedure which requires the corporation to respond to a suit brought to enforce them can, in most instances, hardly be said to be undue....

In *Pennoyer* and *International Shoe*, the Court discusses jurisdiction "in personam." Jurisdiction is sometimes categorized as *in personam, in rem*, or *quasi in rem*. **In personam jurisdiction** means jurisdiction over the person. A court needs this type of jurisdiction when it imposes an order or judgment that requires the defendant to do something or pay money. Historically, courts have been allowed to exercise jurisdiction in cases where the title to property was in question and the property was located within the state, even though the defendant resided outside the state. This is known as **in rem jurisdiction**. Courts also exercise jurisdiction over non-resident defendants when they owned any property in the state even though the subject of the lawsuit is unrelated to the property. Acquiring this type of jurisdiction, known as **quasi in rem jurisdiction**, requires that the property be **attached** prior to the action. Any judgment is limited to the value of the property. In cases following *International Shoe Co.*, the Court made it clear that both in rem and quasi in rem jurisdiction require the same standards as in personam jurisdiction. There must be minimum contacts that satisfy the Due Process Clause. The following language illustrates the Court's position:

> The case for applying to jurisdiction in rem the same test of "fair play and substantial justice" as governs assertions of jurisdiction in personam is simple and straightforward. It is premised on recognition that "the phrase, 'judicial jurisdiction over a thing,' is a customary elliptical way of referring to jurisdiction over the interests of persons in a thing." *Restatement (Second) of Conflict of Laws* 56, Introductory Note (1971). This recognition leads to the conclusion that in order to justify an exercise of jurisdiction in rem, the basis for jurisdiction must be sufficient to justify exercising "jurisdiction over the interests of persons in a thing." The standard for determining whether an exercise of jurisdiction over the interests of persons is consistent with the Due Process Clause is the minimum-contacts standard elucidated in *International Shoe. Shaffer v. Heitner*, 433 U.S. 186 (1977).

PREJUDGMENT ATTACHMENT OF PROPERTY

After a **party** obtains a judgment, it can be collected by seizing property or wages of the **judgment debtor**, usually by obtaining a writ of execution or attachment from the court. There is no due process problem with this taking because the parties had the opportunity to be heard (a trial) and present defenses. However, some laws allow the taking of property before trial. This practice does present due process problems. In *Sniadach v. Family Finance Corp.*, 395 U.S. 337 (1969), the Supreme Court found that a Wisconsin law allowing a creditor to garnish the debtor's wages before any notice or hearing was unconstitutional. Condemning the unfairness of the practice, the Court said: "The result is that a prejudgment garnishment of the Wisconsin type may as a practical matter drive a wage-earning family to the wall. Where the taking of one's property is so obvious, it needs no extended argument to conclude that absent notice and a prior hearing this prejudgment garnishment procedure violates the fundamental principles of due process." Not all prejudgment attachments violate procedural due process, however. If a law allows for proper notice and a hearing, the law will probably be valid.

BURDEN OF PROOF

Most civil cases are decided by a burden of proof known as the *preponderance of evidence*, meaning that there is more evidence that supports the plaintiff's case than supports the defendant's case. However, the Supreme Court held that due process requires that civil cases resulting in termination of parental rights or civil commitment (i.e., mental institution)

🏛 **in personam jurisdiction**

(Latin) Describes a lawsuit brought to enforce rights against another person.

🏛 **in rem jurisdiction**

(Latin) Describes a lawsuit brought to enforce rights in a "thing" or property located as opposed to one brought to enforce rights against another person.

🏛 **quasi in rem jurisdiction**

A type of lawsuit "in between" in rem and in personam called "quasi in rem" or "sort of concerning a thing." Quasi in rem actions are really directed against a person, but are formally directed only against property (or vice versa); for example, a mortgage foreclosure.

🏛 **attach**

Formally seizing property (or a person) in order to bring it under the control of the court. This is usually done by getting a court order to have a law enforcement officer take control of the property.

🏛 **party**

A person who is either a plaintiff or a defendant in a lawsuit.

🏛 **judgment debtor**

A person owing money as a result of a judgment in court.

clear and convincing evidence

Stronger evidence than a preponderance of the evidence (evidence that something is more likely to be true than false) but not as strong as beyond a reasonable doubt. Clear and convincing evidence is required for a few civil lawsuits, such as those involving the reformation of a contract.

must be determined by "**clear and convincing evidence**" rather than a mere preponderance. Clear and convincing evidence is more than a preponderance but less than the reasonable doubt standard required in criminal cases.

RIGHTS OF INDIGENT PARTIES

Due process in criminal cases requires that indigent defendants be provided with attorneys and support services at state expense. Such a general rule does not apply in civil cases. In some situations, however, the Court does require court-appointed counsel. One such case is *Turner v. Rogers*, involving a civil contempt proceeding in a child support case. An excerpt from the Court Syllabus is found below. Other rights in civil cases include waiver of filing fees and blood tests. For example, in *Boddie v. Connecticut*, 401 U.S. 371 (1971), a divorce case, due process of law required that a court waive filing fees and costs for indigents. In *Little v. Streater*, 452 U.S. 1 (1981), the Court held that an indigent defendant in a paternity case was also entitled to blood tests at state expense. Refusal to supply this testing resulted in a lack of "a meaningful opportunity to be heard."

Turner v. Rogers
564 U.S. ___ (2011)

After a South Carolina family court ordered petitioner Turner to pay $51.73 per week to respondent Rogers to help support their child, Turner repeatedly failed to pay the amount due and was held in contempt five times. The fifth time he did not pay but completed a 6-month sentence. After his release, the family court clerk issued a new "show cause" order against Turner because he was $5728.76 in arrears. Both he and Rogers were unrepresented by counsel at his brief civil contempt hearing. The judge found Turner in willful contempt and sentenced him to 12 months in prison without making any finding as to his ability to pay or indicating on the contempt order form whether he was able to make support payments.

Held:

The Fourteenth Amendment's Due Process Clause does not *automatically* require the State to provide counsel at civil contempt proceedings to an indigent noncustodial parent who is subject to a child support order, even if that individual faces incarceration. In particular, that Clause does not require that counsel be provided where the opposing parent or other custodian is not represented by counsel and the State provides alternative procedural safeguards equivalent to adequate notice of the importance of the ability to pay, a fair opportunity to present, and to dispute, relevant information, and express court

findings as to the supporting parent's ability to comply with the support order.

Because a contempt proceeding to compel support payments is civil, the question whether the "specific dictates of due process" require appointed counsel is determined by examining the "distinct factors" this Court has used to decide what specific safeguards are needed to make a civil proceeding fundamentally fair. *Mathews v. Eldridge*, 424 U.S. 319. As relevant here those factors include (1) the nature of "the private interest that will be affected," (2) the comparative "risk" of an "erroneous deprivation" of that interest with and without "additional or substitute procedural safeguards," and (3) the nature and magnitude of any countervailing interest in not providing "additional or substitute procedural requirement[s]." Ibid.

Under the circumstances, Turner's incarceration violated due process because he received neither counsel nor the benefit of alternative procedures like those the Court describes. He did not have clear notice that his ability to pay would constitute the critical question in his civil contempt proceeding. No one provided him with a form (or the equivalent) designed to elicit information about his financial circumstances. And the trial court did not find that he was able to pay his arrearage, but nonetheless found him in civil contempt and ordered him incarcerated.

Procedural Due Process and Government Agencies

🏛 **administrative agency**
A sub-branch of the government set up to carry out the laws. For example, the police department is a local administrative agency and the IRS is a national one.

Due process applies *any time* the government deprives a person of liberty or property. Oftentimes the deprivation is a result of action by an **administrative agency** and may involve an administrative hearing. An administrative agency is an agency created by government (such as a department of motor vehicles) to handle a specific governmental function. Administrative agencies often take away or deprive persons of interests that could be considered property or liberty interests. For example, a department of motor vehicles might take away a driver's license or an unemployment office might terminate unemployment benefits. In such cases, individuals often claim that they are entitled to due process rights before the agency takes any action. The procedures required by due process vary depending on the specific facts. In a frequently cited case, *Mathews v. Eldridge*, 424 U.S. 319, a 1976 case dealing with the termination of social security benefits, the Court said that due process is not a "technical conception with a fixed content unrelated to time, place and circumstances." Furthermore, due process requires "such procedural protections as the particular situation demands." The Court then set forth three factors that must be considered in determining specific dictates of due process:

1. The nature of the private interest that will be affected by official action,
2. The risk of an erroneous deprivation of that interest, and
3. The government's interest and burden in providing additional or different procedures.

SITUATIONS REQUIRING DUE PROCESS

Many cases involving action by a government or by an administrative agency involve the deprivation of some intangible interest such as the right to drive, the right to receive unemployment benefits, or even the right to a job. A key issue in many cases is whether a property or liberty interest is involved. The following are brief descriptions of some of the situations decided by the Supreme Court.

1. Termination of employment

The Court considered several cases dealing with termination of employment. If the individual has a *right* to continued employment, such as a tenured college instructor, the Court finds a property interest entitling the person to a hearing before termination. On the other hand, when an employee can be terminated at will, there is no property right. The Court explained its reasoning in a case involving a college teacher who was not rehired after one year. The college policy awarded tenure after four years. The Court said there was no property interest here because the teacher had no right to continued employment. Since there was no property right, there was no right to a hearing regarding the failure to rehire. The Court also found that there was no liberty interest here. "It stretches the concept too far to suggest that a person is deprived of 'liberty' when he simply is not rehired in one job but remains as free as before to seek another. To have a property interest in a benefit, a person clearly must have more than an abstract need or desire for it. He must have more than a unilateral expectation of it. He must, instead, have a legitimate claim of entitlement to it." *Board of Regents v. Roth*, 408 U.S. 564 (1972).

2. Termination of government benefits

In looking at government benefits, the Court applies similar reasoning. When a person is receiving benefits and the government terminates these benefits, due process must be followed. However, in two cases the Court differentiated what due process required.

In *Goldberg v. Kelly*, 397 U.S. 254 (1970), the Court reviewed the termination of *welfare* benefits and found that the recipient was entitled to notice and a hearing before the benefits could be terminated. "The interest of the eligible recipient in uninterrupted receipt of public assistance, coupled with the State's interest that his payments not be erroneously terminated, clearly outweighs the State's competing concern to prevent any increase in its fiscal and administrative burdens."

In a similar case, *Mathews v. Eldridge*, dealing with social security *disability* benefits, the Court found that such benefits were a property right but due process did not require a *prior* hearing. The Court compared the case with *Goldberg*, finding that a crucial element in *Goldberg* was that welfare benefits are paid to those who are barely subsisting. The Court did not feel that this element was present in the case of disability benefits. "Eligibility for disability benefits, in contrast, is not based upon financial need. Indeed, it is wholly unrelated to the worker's income or support from many other sources, such as earnings of other family members, workmen's compensation awards, tort claims awards, savings, private insurance, public or private pensions, veterans' benefits, food stamps, public assistance, or the many other important programs, both public and private, which contain provisions for disability payments affecting a substantial portion of the work force...." The Court decided that a hearing after the fact satisfied due process. In reaching its decision, the Court applied a similar analysis to that applied in *Goldberg*. It weighed the effect of the loss with the necessity for taking prompt government action. It just reached a different conclusion. Interestingly, however, language from the *Mathews* case is frequently cited by parties claiming the right to a pre-termination hearing.

3. Suspension of driving privileges

According to the Supreme Court, the right to drive is a property interest, although sometimes it is characterized as a liberty interest. Thus, due process must be followed in suspending a license. Although a hearing *prior* to the suspension is not always required, a fair hearing is required. Two cases illustrate. In the first case, *Mackey v. Montrym*, 443 U.S. 1 (1979), the Court upheld a state law allowing immediate suspension of a driver's license of a suspected drunk driver for failure to take a chemical test. The driver was entitled to a hearing after the suspension. In the second case, *Bell v. Burson*, 402 U.S. 535 (1971), the Court struck down a law that required the license suspension of uninsured drivers involved in an accident. The law permitted a hearing, but denied the driver the opportunity to produce evidence at the hearing regarding fault. The Court found that this denied the driver a fair hearing:

> In cases where there is no reasonable possibility of a judgment being rendered against a licensee, Georgia's interest in protecting a claimant from the possibility of an unrecoverable judgment is not, within the context of the State's fault-oriented scheme, a justification for denying the process due its citizens. Nor is additional expense occasioned by the expanded hearing sufficient to withstand the constitutional requirement. While the problem of additional expense must be kept in mind, it does not justify denying a hearing meeting the ordinary standards of due process.

4. School suspension and corporal punishment

The right of students to attend school has been viewed as both a property and a liberty right subject to procedural due process. In *Goss v. Lopez*, 419 U.S. 565 (1975), the Court held that a student facing disciplinary suspension from school was entitled to a notice of the charges and a hearing. The Court said that normally this should precede the suspension.

However, when suspension results from a student's dangerous conduct, a hearing *after* the suspension was allowed. The Court has also addressed the issue of corporal punishment of students. Students have a liberty interest in being free from corporal punishment. In *Ingraham v. Wright*, 430 U.S. 651 (1977), the Supreme Court held that procedural safeguards are required for corporal punishment. However, procedural safeguards did not require a hearing because punishment was administered only after the principal and the teacher conferred. More importantly, the student had an adequate remedy should the punishment be unwarranted or excessive, because tort law allowed the student to sue for damages under those circumstances.

5. Interruption of utility service

When utilities are provided by a governmental entity, there may be a due process property interest in uninterrupted service. In one case, *Memphis Light, Gas & Water Div. v. Craft*, 436 U.S. 1 (1978), the Court was asked to decide if government-provided utilities could be terminated without a prior hearing. The utility service was subject to a local law allowing the utilities to be terminated for cause but not terminated at will. The Court decided that the law created an entitlement to services and that therefore the right to utility service was a property interest protected by due process. In this case a hearing was required before utilities could be disconnected:

> Under the balancing approach outlined in *Mathews*, some administrative procedure for entertaining customer complaints prior to termination is required to afford reasonable assurance against erroneous or arbitrary withholding of essential services. The customer's interest is self-evident. Utility service is a necessity of modern life; indeed, the discontinuance of water or heating for even short periods of time may threaten health and safety. And the risk of an erroneous deprivation, given the necessary reliance on computers, is not insubstantial.

6. Injury to reputation

When individuals are fired from jobs or suspended from school, their reputation also suffers. In several cases dealing with such issues the Court often referred to the person's reputation as creating a liberty interest. However, in the case of *Paul v. Davis*, 424 U.S. 693 (1976), the Court stated that reputation alone, without some other recognized property or liberty interest, did not create a situation requiring due process. In *Paul*, an individual's name was erroneously included on a published list of active shoplifters. The list was distributed to various businesses. The Court held that the petitioner had no right to procedural due process:

> While we have in a number of our prior cases pointed out the frequently drastic effect of the "stigma" which may result from defamation by the government in a variety of contexts, this line of cases does not establish the proposition that reputation alone, apart from some more tangible interests such as employment, is either "liberty" or "property" by itself sufficient to invoke the procedural protection of the Due Process Clause.

7. Injuries caused by negligent conduct of government officials

In recent times, some parties have argued that due process applies to intentional, negligent, and reckless conduct of government agents resulting in injuries. The argument that this conduct constitutes a deprivation of due process rights was explained by the Court in

Daniels v. Williams, 474 U.S. 327 (1986), a case involving a prisoner who was injured when he slipped and fell:

> He claims that, while an inmate at the city jail in Richmond, Virginia, he slipped on a pillow negligently left on the stairs by respondent, a correctional deputy stationed at the jail. Respondent's negligence, the argument runs, "deprived" petitioner of his "liberty" interest in freedom from bodily injury, *see Ingraham v. Wright*, 430 U.S. 651, 673 (1977); because respondent maintains that he is entitled to the defense of sovereign immunity in a state tort suit, petitioner is without an "adequate" state remedy, *cf. Hudson v. Palmer*, 468 U.S. 517, 534–536 (1984). Accordingly, the deprivation of liberty was without "due process of law."

These cases usually involve mistreatment of prisoners or high-speed police chases resulting in an accident. While parties are generally successful when they can show harm resulting from intentional misconduct, they are generally unsuccessful when the conduct is negligent or even reckless.

The reason for these arguments is found in 42 U.S.C. section 1983, which allows parties to sue a governmental agency for money damages if they are injured because a governmental entity deprived them of a constitutional right. By alleging a due process violation, parties hope to pursue a civil lawsuit for money damages. However, the Supreme Court made it clear in the *Daniels* case that it did not accept such an interpretation of "deprive." "We conclude that the Due Process Clause is simply not implicated by a negligent act of an official causing unintended loss of or injury to life, liberty, or property." The Court also refused to find a deprivation of due process in a case involving reckless indifference—a high-speed police chase resulting in injuries to an innocent person. *County of Sacramento v. Lewis*, 523 U.S. 833 (1998).

However, the Court did say that a person committed in a mental institution who is injured through the negligence of the custodians was deprived of due process. "The combination of a patient's involuntary commitment and his total dependence on his custodians obliges the government to take thought and make reasonable provision for the patient's welfare." *Lewis* quoting *Youngberg v. Romeo*, 457 U.S. 307 (1982).

Did You Know?

Thurgood Marshall was the first African American justice on the U.S. Supreme Court. Did you know he was chief counsel in the *Brown v. Board of Education* cases? President John F. Kennedy appointed Marshall to the U.S. Court of Appeals for the Second Circuit. President Lyndon Johnson appointed him to the U.S. Supreme Court in 1967.

Courtesy of Historical/CORBIS

A Point of Law

Deprivations of Liberty or Property: Due Process Required

When the government deprives a person of life, liberty, or property, due process must be followed. In the following situations, the Court held that a deprivation of liberty or property required due process:

1. Termination of government employment when there is a right to continued employment—*Board of Regents v. Roth*, 408 U.S. 564 (1972)
2. Termination of government benefits—*Goldberg v. Kelly*, 397 U.S. 254 (1970)
3. Suspension of driving privileges—*Bell v. Burson*, 402 U.S. 535 (1971)
4. School suspension and corporal punishment—*Goss v. Lopez*, 419 U.S. 565 (1975) and *Ingraham v. Wright*, 430 U.S. 651 (1977)

(continued)

A Point of Law *(continued)*

5. Interruption of government provided utility service—*Memphis Light, Gas & Water Div. v. Craft*, 436 U.S. 1 (1978)
6. Injuries caused by negligent conduct of government to mentally disabled who were committed to an institution—*Youngberg v. Romeo*, 457 U.S. 307 (1982)

No Deprivation of Liberty or Property

In the following situations, the Court found no liberty or property interest requiring due process:

1. Actions that injure reputations—*Paul v. Davis*, 424 U.S. 693 (1976)
2. Injuries caused by negligent conduct of government officials—*Daniels v. Williams*, 474 U.S. 327 (1986)
3. Injuries caused by reckless conduct of government officials in high-speed police chases—*County of Sacramento v. Lewis*, 523 U.S. 833 (1998)

Due Process Hearing Not Required

Normally, due process requires a hearing before the government deprives a person of life, liberty, or property. However, in the following situations, the Court has held that a prior hearing is not necessary:

1. Social Security disability payments—*Mathews v. Eldridge*, 424 U.S. 319 (1976)
2. Suspension of driver's license for failure to submit to a chemical test—*Mackey v. Montrym*, 443 U.S. 1 (1979)
3. School suspension for dangerous conduct and imposition of corporal punishment—*Ingraham v. Wright*, 430 U.S. 651 (1977)

≈ Ethical Decisions—Everyday Choices ≈

The Facts: Marisa works as a paralegal in a litigation law firm where one of her duties is interviewing clients. Richard Rios, a client of the firm, is a plaintiff in a large civil lawsuit in which punitive damages have been requested. During an interview with Marisa, he asked that she explain what punitive damages were and how much he could expect in his case. Marisa recently read both the *BMW* and *State Farm* cases dealing with punitive damages.

The Problem: What can Marisa tell Rios about punitive damages? Can she summarize these two cases for Rios?

Guiding Principles: Paralegals cannot give legal advice. To do so is an unauthorized practice of law. However, they can answer simple factual questions that may involve the law, but do not involve giving legal advice. What constitutes legal advice is sometimes unclear, but generally advising a person of their legal rights or obligations under a particular factual situation is considered legal advice. Providing factual information such as the amount of a filing fee is not considered legal advice.

Chapter Summary

The Fifth and Fourteenth Amendments prohibit federal and state government from depriving a person of life, liberty, or property without due process of law. The Due Process Clauses provide two types of protections: substantive due process, which limits the types of laws that government can enact, and procedural due process, which limits the procedures that government uses when it actually deprives a person of life, liberty, or property. Whether the Court is faced with issues of substantive due process or procedural due process, the same preliminary determinations must be made. The Court must determine that the interest that is lost comes within the meaning of "life, liberty, and property," that the party claiming a due process violation is a "person," and that government has caused the deprivation. The term *liberty* includes not only freedom from physical restraint but also freedom to enter into contracts and freedom to make many personal choices. Many of the "liberties" are part of the constitutional right to privacy. The term *property* includes not only real and personal property but such interests as employment rights and government benefits. The term *person* includes individuals residing in the United States, whether they are citizens or not. It includes corporations when an economic interest is involved, but not when a personal freedom is involved. The Fifth and Fourteenth Amendments apply only to conduct by government. However, if a private party has a close tie to government, the conduct of such a party may come within the Due Process Clauses.

Substantive due process prevents government from enacting laws that interfere with life, liberty, or property unless those laws meet certain requirements. If the law interferes with a fundamental right, the government must show a compelling need for the law. If the law interferes with an interest that is not fundamental, it is lawful as long as it serves a legitimate state interest and is not arbitrary. Substantive due process often involves laws that deprive a person of a "liberty" interest. In addition to the right to be free from physical restraint, liberty also includes the right to be free to enter into contracts and the right to be free to make many personal choices. Many of the personal choices, such as the right to choose an abortion or the right to refuse medical care, are part of the right to privacy. Although it is not expressly stated, the right to privacy is implied by many constitutional provisions and is thus a fundamental right. Substantive due process also limits the right of a government to enact laws that deprive a person of property, such as laws that allow punitive damages in civil lawsuits.

Procedural due process deals with the way in which the government takes away life, liberty, or property. It applies to any government taking including proceedings in criminal cases, civil cases, and administrative actions. In criminal cases, many of the due process requirements are found in the Bill of Rights. Civil cases also require due process, which includes proper notice and sufficient state contacts with a non-resident defendant. Due process in civil cases also limits prejudgment attachments and the imposition of punitive damages. When government deprives a person of a Fifth or Fourteenth Amendment interest outside a criminal or civil case, it must also follow due process requirements, although the precise requirements vary with the situation. In general, government must provide notice and a fair hearing before depriving a person of life, liberty, or property.

Key Terms

substantive due process	service of process	party
procedural due process	in personam jurisdiction	judgment debtor
police powers	in rem jurisdiction	clear and convincing evidence
fundamental right	quasi in rem jurisdiction	administrative agency
"liberty" to contract	attach	

Questions for Review

1. In general, what does the Due Process Clause provide, and what is meant by due process?
2. Compare and contrast substantive due process and procedural due process.
3. Explain the terms *liberty*, *property*, and *person* as those terms are used in the Fifth and Fourteenth Amendments.
4. When do the Fifth and Fourteenth Amendments apply to private conduct?

5. What standards are used by the Supreme Court when it reviews a law for substantive due process violations?
6. What are some of the liberty interests protected by substantive due process?
7. What property interests are protected by substantive due process?
8. Briefly summarize the procedures required by the Due Process Clause in criminal cases.
9. What aspects of a civil case are governed by the Due Process Clause?
10. What are the basic requirements for due process whenever the government deprives a person of life, liberty, or property?

Questions for Analysis

1. The Supreme Court upheld laws that regulate the following:
   - minimum wage requirements
   - child employment restrictions
   - workers' compensation laws
   - collective bargaining requirements
   - price controls

   How does each of these restrict an individual's liberty? What is the state interest to be protected by such laws?
2. Because of health costs, Congress proposes to limit the amount of damages recoverable in a medical malpractice case. In fact, some states have such laws now. In light of the holding in *Duke Power Co. v. Carolina Envtl. Study Group*, do you think laws limiting damages in medical malpractice cases are constitutional? Explain your answer.
3. Answer the following questions based on *City of Chicago v. Morales*, 527 U.S. 41 (1999):
   a. Did Chicago have a legitimate government interest in passing the loitering ordinance?
   b. What was the constitutional due process problem with the ordinance?
4. Why did Justice Scalia dissent in *Roper v. Simmons*?

Assignments and Projects

1. Using the format found in previous chapters, write a case brief for *City of Chicago v. Morales*. Include a section in the brief summarizing the rationale in the dissent.
2. The Supreme Court reversed the conviction of Jeffrey Skilling, the notable figure in the Enron financial crisis, but remanded it for further proceedings. Using the Internet or other research tools, find out what eventually happened in the "further proceedings."
3. Using the Internet or other research tools, locate and listen to or read the oral arguments in *Roper v. Simmons*. Summarize the argument you believe is most forceful.

Putting It into Practice

1. Assume that you work for a law firm that represents an individual whose driver's license was suspended because of too many speeding tickets. Check the Web site for your state's department of motor vehicles for procedures and/or forms to be used to request a hearing regarding the suspension. If you cannot find the information online, contact a local motor vehicle office to obtain the information. Write a letter to the client explaining the procedures he should follow to challenge the suspension.

Group Activity

In groups of nine students, discuss the *Roper v. Simmons* case. After discussing the case, vote on how you would decide the case. Compare your results with other groups in the class.

10 Economic Freedom and Property Rights

If you make a living, if you earn your own money, you're free—however free one can be on this planet.

Theodore White

Chapter Outline

Chapter Objectives

When you complete this chapter you should be able to

1. identify provisions of the Constitution that protect property rights and economic interests, and briefly describe the protections granted by each provision.

2. describe how substantive due process protects property interests.

3. explain how the Supreme Court used the Due Process Clause to strike down labor laws and business regulations.

4. describe the different ways government takes property so as to require compensation under the Fifth Amendment.

5. list the criteria used by the Supreme Court to determine if a law or regulation results in a *taking* for Fifth Amendment purposes.

6. describe examples of laws or regulations that resulted in a *taking* for Fifth Amendment purposes.

7. compare and contrast a *taking* with a *forfeiture*.

8. identify the type of law that comes under the provisions of the Contract Clause.

9. explain what is meant by the *obligation of contracts*.

10. explain how state police power affects the Contract Clause.

Looking Back

Before reading this chapter, review the following terms and concepts from the previous chapters:

State police power Every state has the right to enact laws that promote the health, welfare, safety, and morals of its residents. In exercising this power, states cannot violate any provision of the U.S. Constitution. (Chapter 6)

Substantive due process The concept derived from the Fifth and Fourteenth Amendment Due Process Clauses limiting the right of government to enact laws that deprive a person of life, liberty, or property. (Chapter 9)

Living with the Constitution

Rebecca Walters owns several apartment buildings, and the rent from these is her sole source of income. Two months ago, the city where the apartments are located passed a rent control ordinance limiting the amount of rent that could be charged. The ordinance also provides that tenants cannot be evicted unless there is cause. Walters does not believe that the government should have the right to enact a law that controls her agreements with tenants. She also feels that the law is taking away her property. She plans to consult a lawyer.

PROPERTY AND ECONOMIC INTERESTS, SUCH as the right to own a home, to choose a career or business, and to enter into contracts, are important freedoms in American society. Like other freedoms, property and economic interests enjoy some protection in the Constitution. The previous chapter briefly discussed how Due Process Clauses of the Fifth and Fourteenth Amendments protect property and economic interests. Other provisions of the Constitution providing protection of economic and property interests include:

- The Fifth Amendment Takings Clause: "nor shall private property be taken for public use, without just compensation."
- Article 1, Section 10: "No State shall . . . pass any . . . Law impairing the Obligation of Contracts."

This chapter discusses how the Constitution protects property interests and guarantees certain economic liberties.

Economic Due Process

THE FIFTH AND FOURTEENTH AMENDMENTS prohibit government from depriving a person of life, liberty, or property without due process. Recall from the previous chapter that the Due Process Clause provides two types of protections: procedural and substantive. Economic due process is a concept based primarily on the notion of substantive due process. That is, the government should not enact laws that interfere with economic interests or liberties unless the laws are related to a legitimate state purpose and are not arbitrary or irrational.

The concept of economic due process developed soon after the enactment of the Fourteenth Amendment when parties argued that due process protections extended beyond traditional **real property** and **personal property** and also applied to economic interests, such as the right to enter into contracts. This right, it was argued, was a type of freedom or "liberty" and, as such, was also protected by the Fifth and Fourteenth Amendments. The Supreme Court, however, was not ready to accept this interpretation of liberty. Initially, the Supreme Court refused to apply the Fourteenth Amendment to any general economic concerns, indicating that the Fourteenth Amendment was intended to give protection against the vestiges of slavery. This belief is expressed in the famous *Slaughter-House Cases*, 83 U.S. 36, decided in 1872, just a few years after the adoption of the Fourteenth Amendment. These cases involved the constitutionality of a Louisiana law granting a **monopoly** to certain individuals to operate slaughterhouses within the city of New Orleans and other cities. As a result, many others were denied the right to engage in the business of operating slaughterhouses, and they challenged the Louisiana law, claiming among other things that the law violated the Due Process Clause because it took away their property and their economic liberty without due process of law. Among their arguments was the claim that the right to engage in business was a type of freedom or liberty protected by the Fourteenth Amendment. The majority of the Court refused to find a due process violation, believing that the Fourteenth Amendment applied only to racial discrimination and not to general economic concerns. However, a strong dissent argued that the petitioners in the case were denied both property and liberty interests without due process:

> For the preservation, exercise, and enjoyment of these rights the individual citizen, as a necessity, must be left free to adopt such calling, profession, or trade as may seem to him most conducive to that end. Without this right he cannot be a freeman. This right to choose one's calling is an essential part of that liberty which it is the

---

🏛 **real property**

Land, buildings, and things permanently attached to land and buildings.

🏛 **personal property**

Having to do with movable property, as opposed to land and buildings.

🏛 **monopoly**

Having exclusive control.

object of government to protect; and a calling, when chosen, is a man's property and right. Liberty and property are not protected where these rights are arbitrarily assailed.

In my view, a law which prohibits a large class of citizens from adopting a lawful employment, or from following a lawful employment previously adopted, does deprive them of liberty as well as property, without due process of law. Their right of choice is a portion of their liberty; their occupation is their property. (Justice Bradley dissent)

Eventually, the Supreme Court changed its interpretation of both the Fifth and Fourteenth Amendments, holding that both amendments provided protection to economic interests. As a result, for a while, the Due Process Clause became an important consideration and limitation in the enactment of state and federal economic legislation, especially in the areas of labor laws and general business regulation.

Substantive Due Process and Labor Laws

Thirty-three years after the *Slaughter-House Cases*, in *Lochner v. New York*, the Supreme Court again considered the question of due process and economic liberty. The issue in this case was simple. If an employer wants to allow an employee to work overtime and the employee wants to work overtime, can a law prevent them from doing so? In the *Lochner* case, the petitioner, Lochner, was accused of violating a New York law that limited the number of work hours for someone in the baking industry, even if both employer and employee were in agreement about the overtime work. Petitioner claimed that the law violated substantive due process provisions of the Fourteenth Amendment because (1) the right to enter into contracts is a freedom or liberty protected by the Due Process Clause; (2) the New York law deprived the petitioner of that liberty; and (3) the deprivation was without any legitimate state purpose. The Supreme Court agreed that freedom to contract was a liberty protected by the Fourteenth Amendment. However, the Court stated that it was not an absolute liberty, and states could enact laws under their police powers to protect the safety, health, or morals of society. Such laws must be reasonable and must not arbitrarily interfere with the right to contract. In a 5–4 decision, the Court held that the law in *Lochner* was unreasonable and arbitrary and therefore unconstitutional. The decision and one of the dissents follow.

Lochner v. New York
198 U.S. 45 (1905)

Mr. Justice Peckham, after making the foregoing statement of the facts, delivered the opinion of the court:

The indictment charges that the plaintiff violated the labor law of the state of New York, in that he wrongfully and unlawfully required and permitted an employee working for him to work more than sixty hours in one week. The employee may desire to earn the extra money which would arise from his working more than

the prescribed time, but this statute forbids the employer from permitting the employee to earn it.

The statute necessarily interferes with the right of contract between the employer and employees, concerning the number of hours in which the latter may labor in the bakery of the employer. The general right to make a contract in relation to his business is part of the liberty of the individual protected by the 14th Amendment of the

(continued)

(continued)

Federal Constitution. Under that provision no state can deprive any person of life, liberty, or property without due process of law. The right to purchase or to sell labor is part of the liberty protected by this amendment, unless there are circumstances which exclude the right. There are, however, certain powers, existing in the sovereignty of each state in the Union, somewhat vaguely termed police powers. Those powers, broadly stated, relate to the safety, health, morals, and general welfare of the public. Both property and liberty are held on such reasonable conditions as may be imposed by the governing power of the state in the exercise of those powers, and with such conditions the 14th Amendment was not designed to interfere.

The state, therefore, has power to prevent the individual from making certain kinds of contracts, and in regard to them the Federal Constitution offers no protection. Contracts in violation of a statute, either of the Federal or state government, or a contract to let one's property for immoral purposes, or to do any other unlawful act, could obtain no protection from the Federal Constitution, as coming under the liberty of person or of free contract. Therefore, when the state, in the assumed exercise of its police powers, has passed an act which seriously limits the right to labor or the right of contract in regard to their means of livelihood between persons who are employer and employee it becomes of great importance to determine which shall prevail, the right of the individual to labor for such time as he may choose, or the right of the state to prevent the individual from laboring, or from entering into any contract to labor, beyond a certain time prescribed by the state.

In every case that comes before this court, therefore, where legislation of this character is concerned, and where the protection of the Federal Constitution is sought, the question necessarily arises: Is this a fair, reasonable, and appropriate exercise of the police power of the state, or is it an unreasonable, unnecessary, and arbitrary interference with the right of the individual to his personal liberty, or to enter into those contracts in relation to labor which may seem to him appropriate or necessary for the support of himself and his family? The question whether this act is valid as a labor law, pure and simple, may be dismissed in a few words. There is no reasonable ground for interfering with the liberty of person or the right of free contract, by determining the hours of labor, in the occupation of a baker. Viewed in the light of a purely labor law, with no reference whatever to the question of health, we think that a law like the one before us involves neither the safety, the

morals, nor the welfare, of the public, and that the interest of the public is not in the slightest degree affected by such an act. The law must be upheld, if at all, as a law pertaining to the health of the individual engaged in the occupation of a baker. It does not affect any other portion of the public than those who are engaged in that occupation. Clean and wholesome bread does not depend upon whether the baker works but ten hours per day or only sixty hours a week. The limitation of the hours of labor does not come within the police power on that ground.

We think the limit of the police power has been reached and passed in this case. There is, in our judgment, no reasonable foundation for holding this to be necessary or appropriate as a health law to safeguard the public health, or the health of the individuals who are following the trade of a baker. The judgment of the Court of Appeals of New York, as well as that of the Supreme Court and of the County Court of Oneida County, must be reversed and the case remanded to the County Court for further proceedings not inconsistent with this opinion.

Reversed.

Mr. Justice Harlan (with whom Mr. Justice White and Mr. Justice Day concurred) dissenting:

I take it to be firmly established that what is called the liberty of contract may, within certain limits, be subjected to regulations designed and calculated to promote the general welfare, or to guard the public health, the public morals, or the public safety. Granting, then, that there is a liberty of contract, what are the conditions under which the judiciary may declare such regulations to be in excess of legislative authority and void? Upon this point there is no room for dispute; for the rule is universal that a legislative enactment, Federal or state, is never to be disregarded or held invalid unless it be, beyond question, plainly and palpably in excess of legislative power. If there be doubt as to the validity of the statute, that doubt must therefore be resolved in favor of its validity, and the courts must keep their hands off, leaving the legislature to meet the responsibility for unwise legislation. If the end which the legislature seeks to accomplish be one to which its power extends, and if the means employed to that end, although not the wisest or best, are yet not plainly and palpably unauthorized by law, then the court cannot interfere.

Let these principles be applied to the present case. It is plain that this statute was enacted in order to protect the physical well-being of those who work in bakery and

(continued)

(continued)

confectionery establishments. The statute must be taken as expressing the belief of the people of New York that, as a general rule, and in the case of the average man, labor in excess of sixty hours during a week in such establishments may endanger the health of those who thus labor. Whether or not this be wise legislation it is not the province of the court to inquire. Under our systems of government the courts are not concerned with the wisdom or policy of legislation. So that, in determining the question of power to interfere with liberty of contract, the court may inquire whether the means devised by the state are germane to an end which may be lawfully accomplished and have a real or substantial relation to the protection of health, as involved in the daily work of the persons, male and female, engaged in bakery and confectionery establishments. But

when this inquiry is entered upon I find it impossible, in view of common experience, to say that there is here no real or substantial relation between the means employed by the state and the end sought to be accomplished by its legislation. Nor can I say that the statute has no appropriate or direct connection with that protection to health which each state owes to her citizens; or that it is not promotive of the health of the employees in question or that the regulation prescribed by the state is utterly unreasonable and extravagant or wholly arbitrary. Still less can I say that the statute is, beyond question, a plain, palpable invasion of rights secured by the fundamental law. Therefore I submit that this court will transcend its functions if it assumes to annul the statute of New York.

The judgment, in my opinion, should be affirmed.

The *Lochner* decision ushered in a brief era in which the Court struck down numerous laws dealing with labor relations and business operation. Nevertheless, the Court upheld laws when it found a legitimate state interest, such as maximum work hours for women and for certain occupations, safety laws for the mining industry, prohibitions on child labor for dangerous jobs, as well as laws regulating workers' compensation.

By the 1930s the Great Depression raised new economic and labor concerns in the country. The Court reacted to the changing economy and the need for government intervention by changing its approach to analyzing laws that interfered with economic liberty. The Court continued, and still continues, to recognize that the concept of liberty includes economic freedom. However, it now gives great deference to legislative enactments that interfere with this freedom. It presumes that laws are valid and will not declare a law unconstitutional as long as it has some legitimate government purpose and is not arbitrary or irrational. After 1937, the Court overruled many of its prior precedents but upheld laws that imposed minimum wage requirements and required collective bargaining.

Substantive Due Process and Regulation of Businesses

Using its general police powers, both the state and federal governments have enacted many laws regulating businesses. Whenever the government imposes regulations on businesses, it interferes with the property rights of the business owner. Therefore, such regulations must be consistent with substantive due process, which requires that the laws be related to some legitimate government purpose and not be arbitrary. Among the types of laws the Court considered and upheld are:

- Laws setting maximum rates businesses can charge. Numerous businesses, including public utilities, insurance companies, dairies, and even attorneys have been subject to such laws (see Exhibit 10-1 for an example of such a state law)
- Consumer protection laws restricting business practices, such as price fixing and fraudulent advertising
- Safety requirements for industries, such as the railroad
- Laws requiring licensing for certain trades and professions

Exhibit 10-1 California State Law Limiting Attorney Fees

(California Business and Professions Code)

6146. (a) An attorney shall not contract for or collect a contingency fee for representing any person seeking damages in connection with an action for injury or damage against a health care provider based upon such person's alleged professional negligence in excess of the following limits:

(1) Forty percent of the first fifty thousand dollars ($50,000) recovered.

(2) Thirty-three and one-third percent of the next fifty thousand dollars ($50,000) recovered.

(3) Twenty-five percent of the next five hundred thousand dollars ($500,000) recovered.

(4) Fifteen percent of any amount on which the recovery exceeds six hundred thousand dollars ($600,000).

The limitations shall apply regardless of whether the recovery is by settlement, arbitration, or judgment, or whether the person for whom the recovery is made is a responsible adult, an infant, or a person of unsound mind.

© Cengage Learning 2013

In the case of *Nebbia v. New York*, 291 U.S. 502 (1934), the Court expressed its view of due process and business regulations. This case concerned a New York state law fixing the minimum price that a business could charge for milk. As a result of severe economic problems in the dairy business, the state of New York created a Milk Control Board. This board investigated the industry and recommended price controls. Petitioner, a grocer, refused to follow the Board's price guideline and was criminally prosecuted. He was convicted and appealed. Eventually the case reached the Supreme Court. The majority opinion follows.

Nebbia v. New York
291 U.S. 502 (1934)

Mr. Justice Roberts delivered the opinion of the Court.

The question for decision is whether the Federal Constitution prohibits a state from fixing the selling price of milk. We first inquire as to the occasion for the legislation and its history.

During 1932 the prices received by farmers for milk were much below the cost of production. On March 10, 1932, the senate and assembly resolved, "That a joint Legislative committee is hereby created . . . to investigate the causes of the decline of the price of milk to producers and the resultant effect of the low prices upon the dairy industry and the future supply of milk to the cities of the State." The committee organized May 6, 1932, and its activities lasted nearly a year. Under its direction an extensive research program was prosecuted by experts and official bodies and employees of the state and municipalities, which resulted in the assembling of much pertinent information. As a result of the study a report embracing the conclusions and recommendations of the committee, was presented to the Legislature April 10, 1933. The conscientious effort and thoroughness

exhibited by the report lend weight to the committee's conclusions.

In part those conclusions are:

Milk is an essential item of diet. It cannot long be stored. It is an excellent medium for growth of bacteria. These facts necessitate safeguards in its production and handling for human consumption which greatly increase the cost of the business. Failure of producers to receive a reasonable return for their labor and investment over an extended period threaten a relaxation of vigilance against contamination.

The production and distribution of milk is a paramount industry of the state, and largely affects the health and prosperity of its people. Dairying yields fully one-half of the total income from all farm products. Curtailment or destruction of the dairy industry would cause a serious economic loss to the people of the state.

In addition to the general price decline, other causes for the low price of milk include a periodic increase in the number of cows and in milk production, the prevalence of unfair and destructive trade practices in the distribution of milk, leading to a demoralization of prices in the

(continued)

(continued)

metropolitan area and other markets, and the failure of transportation and distribution charges to be reduced in proportion to the reduction in retail prices for milk and cream.

Various remedies were suggested, amongst them united action by producers, the fixing of minimum prices for milk and cream by state authority, and the imposition of certain graded taxes on milk dealers proportioned so as to equalize the cost of milk and cream to all dealers and so remove the cause of price-cutting.

The Legislature adopted chapter 158 as a method of correcting the evils. Section 312(e) on which the prosecution in the present case is founded, provides: "After the board shall have fixed prices to be charged or paid for milk in any form it shall be unlawful for a milk dealer to sell or buy or offer to sell or buy milk at any price less or more than such price . . . ."

The appellant urges that the enforcement of section 312(e) denied the appellant the due process secured to him by the Fourteenth Amendment.

Under our form of government the use of property and the making of contracts are normally matters of private and not of public concern. The general rule is that both shall be free of governmental interference. But neither property rights nor contract rights are absolute; for government cannot exist if the citizen may at will use his property to the detriment of his fellows, or exercise his freedom of contract to work them harm. Equally fundamental with the private right is that of the public to regulate it in the common interest.

The Fifth Amendment, in the field of federal activity, and the Fourteenth, as respects state action, do not prohibit governmental regulation for the public welfare. They merely condition the exertion of the admitted power, by securing that the end shall be accomplished by methods consistent with due process. And the guaranty of due process, as has often been held, demands only that the law shall not be unreasonable, arbitrary, or capricious, and that the means selected shall have a real and substantial relation to the object sought to be attained. It results that a regulation valid for one sort of business, or in given circumstances, may be invalid for another sort, or for the same business under other circumstances, because the reasonableness of each regulation depends upon the relevant facts.

The state may control the use of property in various ways; may prohibit advertising bill boards except of a prescribed size and location, or their use for certain kinds of advertising; may in certain circumstances authorize encroachments by party walls in cities; may fix the height of buildings, the character of materials, and methods of construction, the adjoining area which must be left open, and may exclude from residential sections offensive trades, industries and structures likely injuriously to affect the public health or safety; or may establish zones within which certain types of buildings or businesses are permitted and others excluded.

Laws passed for the suppression of immorality, in the interest of health, to secure fair trade practices, and to safeguard the interests of depositors in banks, have been found consistent with due process.

The Constitution does not guarantee the unrestricted privilege to engage in a business or to conduct it as one pleases. Certain kinds of business may be prohibited; and the right to conduct a business, or to pursue a calling, may be conditioned. Regulation of a business to prevent waste of the state's resources may be justified. And statutes prescribing the terms upon which those conducting certain businesses may contract, or imposing terms if they do enter into agreements, are within the state's competency. Legislation concerning sales of goods, and incidentally affecting prices, has repeatedly been held valid. In this class fall laws forbidding unfair competition by the charging of lower prices in one locality than those exacted in another, by giving trade inducements to purchasers, and by other forms of price discrimination.

So far as the requirement of due process is concerned, and in the absence of other constitutional restriction, a state is free to adopt whatever economic policy may reasonably be deemed to promote public welfare, and to enforce that policy by legislation adapted to its purpose. The courts are without authority either to declare such policy, or, when it is declared by the legislature, to override it. If the laws passed are seen to have a reasonable relation to a proper legislative purpose, and are neither arbitrary nor discriminatory, the requirements of due process are satisfied, and judicial determination to that effect renders a court *functus officio*. Tested by these considerations we find no basis in the due process clause of the Fourteenth Amendment for condemning the provisions of the Agriculture and Markets Law here drawn into question.

The judgment is affirmed.

Since 1937, the Supreme Court has not struck down any state or federal economic regulation because it violates the liberty of contract guaranteed by the Fifth or Fourteenth Amendments. Because of this, some critics believe that the concept of economic due process has little, if any, relevance. Lower courts, however, continue to apply the doctrine. An example of this is the federal court of appeals decision dealing with the freedom to choose a career, an important economic liberty. No reasonable person questions the right of the government to impose some limits on this right. If the state allowed anyone to practice medicine or give legal advice, serious harm could result. Educational and licensing requirements make sense. However, sometimes these regulations are completely irrational and arbitrary. A contemporary example of this is seen in a federal court of appeals decision regarding a Tennessee law requiring that only licensed funeral directors could sell caskets. To become a licensed funeral director required two years of study either in an accredited mortuary school or as an apprentice. The result of the Tennessee law was the increased cost of caskets. The law was challenged by individuals who operated two independent casket stores, but who were not licensed as funeral directors. The district court ruled in their favor and the state appealed. The appellate court decision follows.

Craigmiles v. Giles
312 F.3d 220 (6th Cir. 2002)

The Supreme Court has established a tripartite rubric for analyzing challenges under the Equal Protection and Due Process clauses. When a statute regulates certain "fundamental rights" (*e.g.*, voting or abortion) or distinguishes between people on the basis of certain "suspect characteristics" (*e.g.*, race or national origin), the statute is subject to "strict scrutiny." *Zablocki v. Redhail*, 434 U.S. 374, 388 (1978). To survive strict scrutiny, the regulation must serve a compelling state purpose and be narrowly tailored to achieving that purpose. The Supreme Court has identified other classifications, such as gender and illegitimacy, which are less "suspect," and are therefore subject only to intermediate scrutiny, under which the regulation need only serve an "important" state interest and the means employed need only be "substantially related" to that interest.

All other regulations are subject to "rational basis" review, requiring only that the regulation bear some rational relation to a legitimate state interest. *Romer v. Evans*, 517 U.S. 620, 632 (1996). Even foolish and misdirected provisions are generally valid if subject only to rational basis review. As we have said, a statute is subject to a "strong presumption of validity" under rational basis review, and we will uphold it "if there is any reasonably conceivable state of facts that could provide a rational basis." *Walker v. Bain*, 257 F.3d 660, 668 (6th Cir. 2001).

All of the parties concede that rational basis review is the proper standard for evaluating the FDEA. While feared by many, morticians and casket retailers have not achieved the protected status that requires a higher level of scrutiny under our Equal Protection jurisprudence. According to the district court, the amendment was designed only for the economic protection of funeral home operators.

At trial, the plaintiffs adduced evidence that funeral home operators sell caskets at prices substantially over total costs. The FDEA has the effect, at least, of preventing individuals who are not licensed funeral directors from selling caskets, potentially at a lower price. In this case, the district court found that funeral home operators generally mark up the price of caskets 250 to 600 percent, whereas casket retailers sell caskets at much smaller margins. *See Craigmiles*, 110 F. Supp. 2d at 664.

The question before this court is whether requiring those who sell funeral merchandise to be licensed funeral directors bears a rational relationship to any legitimate purpose other than protecting the economic interests of licensed funeral directors.

The weakness of Tennessee's proffered explanations indicates that the 1972 amendment adding the retail sale of funeral merchandise to the definition of funeral directing was nothing more than an attempt to prevent economic competition. Indeed, Tennessee's justifications for

(continued)

(continued)

the 1972 amendment come close to striking us with "the force of a five-week-old, unrefrigerated dead fish," *United States v. Searan*, 259 F.3d 434, 447 (6th Cir. 2001); *United States v. Perry*, 908 F.2d 56, 58 (6th Cir. 1990), a level of pungence almost required to invalidate a statute under rational basis review. Only a handful of provisions have been invalidated for failing rational basis review. *See Romer v. Evans*, 517 U.S. 620 (1996); *City of Cleburne v. Cleburne Living Center*, 473 U.S. 432 (1985); *Peoples Rights Org., Inc. v. City of Columbus*, 152 F.3d 522 (6th Cir. 1998). We hold that this case should be among this handful.

The district court was unable to find any way in which the application of the FDEA to the plaintiffs promoted public health or safety. The plaintiffs, of course, would not handle the bodies, much less engage in any embalming services. As the plaintiffs' businesses operated at the time of the Board's order, consumers after a relative's death would simply purchase a casket from the plaintiffs. The plaintiffs would then deliver the purchased casket to the funeral home that would be handling the body. The district court did not enjoin the enforcement of the FDEA to anything other than the retailing of funeral merchandise.

Tennessee also argues that the funeral directors' education and training would increase their ability to advise consumers on which casket would be most protective in particular cases. However, the availability of casket retailers will not prevent funeral directors from continuing to dispense this advice. Only the price of the caskets that the funeral directors may recommend might be affected.

The district court also held that the licensing requirement was not rationally related to the state's interest in consumer protection. The State of Tennessee argues that the FDEA closely regulates the conduct of funeral directors, preventing them from making fraudulent misrepresentations or selling a previously used casket. The state contends that if casket retailers need not be funeral directors, then the retailers would not be subject to these regulations and consumers would be at risk.

There are a few problems with this argument. First, some of the regulations in Section 317(b) of the Act are generally applicable to retailers already, enforced by civil and criminal sanctions. For example, it is not as if casket retailers would be free to "engage in misrepresentation or fraud" if not covered by the FDEA. *See* Tenn. Code Ann. 62-5-317(b)(1).

Finally, the state argues that the course of study required for licensure trains directors in the best ways to treat individuals who have suffered profound loss. Unlicensed casket retailers, without this psychological training, we are told, may aggravate the grief of the decedent's survivors who are shopping for a casket. However, even those who purchase from casket retailers will still need a licensed funeral director for arranging services and handling the body, at which time the survivors may still receive the benefit of the funeral director's psychological training. Moreover, survivors must deal with a panoply of vendors in order to make funeral arrangements, from churches to food vendors for a wake, none of whom is required to have this psychological training. This justification is very weak, indeed.

Finding no rational relationship to any of the articulated purposes of the state, we are left with the more obvious illegitimate purpose to which licensure provision is very well tailored. The licensure requirement imposes a significant barrier to competition in the casket market. By protecting licensed funeral directors from competition on caskets, the FDEA harms consumers in their pocketbooks. If consumer protection were the aim of the 1972 amendment, the General Assembly had several direct means of achieving that end. None of the justifications offered by the state satisfies the slight review required by rational basis review under the Due Process and Equal Protection clauses of the Fourteenth Amendment. As this court has said, "rational basis review, while deferential, is not toothless." *Peoples Rights*, 152 F.3d at 532 (citing *Mathews v. Lucas*, 427 U.S. 495, 510 (1976)).

Judicial invalidation of economic regulation under the Fourteenth Amendment has been rare in the modern era. *See West Coast Hotel v. Parrish*, 300 U.S. 379 (1937). Our decision today is not a return to *Lochner*, by which this court would elevate its economic theory over that of legislative bodies. *See Lochner v. New York*, 198 U.S. 45 (1905). No sophisticated economic analysis is required to see the pretextual nature of the state's proffered explanations for the 1972 amendment. We are not imposing our view of a well-functioning market on the people of Tennessee. Instead, we invalidate only the General Assembly's naked attempt to raise a fortress protecting the monopoly rents that funeral directors extract from consumers. This measure to privilege certain businessmen over others at the expense of consumers is not animated by a legitimate governmental purpose and cannot survive even rational basis review.

For all of the foregoing reasons, we AFFIRM the district court's order enjoining the application of the FDEA to the plaintiffs' businesses as they operated before the Board's cease and desist order.

The Fifth Amendment Takings Clause

IF A STATE DECIDES TO build a new freeway and privately owned homes are situated on the desired freeway path, the government has the right to take these homes. This is because of the power of **eminent domain**, a power shared by all state and federal governments. Specific rules for taking property pursuant to eminent domain are found in state and federal codes. Although the power of eminent domain is not found in the Constitution, it is an inherent power of government that allows privately owned property to be taken for a public use. The power is subject to the Fifth Amendment: "nor shall private property be taken for public use, without just compensation." This provision is referred to as the *Takings Clause*. Although the Fifth Amendment applies only to federal government, the Court has held that this provision is incorporated in the Due Process Clause of the Fourteenth Amendment and therefore also applies to states.

Public Use

The power of eminent domain exists only when the government takes property for a public use, a term given broad meaning by the Court. It includes traditional public uses, such as roadways and waterways, but also includes such uses as public parks, preserving historical landmarks, and beautification of a neighborhood. The power of eminent domain is an important power of redevelopment agencies that are responsible for revitalizing neighborhoods and cities. Redevelopment plans often include improving transportations systems, building new and affordable housing, parks, and cultural institutions. An essential part of many redevelopment plans is encouraging and assisting private developers to invest in shopping centers, hotels, and other necessary community establishments. The question arises, then, whether such use is a public use. The Supreme Court answered this question in the affirmative in *Berman v. Parker*, 348 U.S. 26 (1954). Consider the situation faced by the appellant in the case. He owned a department store in Washington, D.C. He kept his property in good repair and ran a successful business. In spite of this, his property was taken under eminent domain as part of a redevelopment plan whose stated purpose was to eliminate areas that were injurious to the public health, safety, morals, and welfare of the public and to develop a general plan to include housing, business, industry, recreation, education, public buildings, and other general categories of public and private uses of the land. The government planned to lease or sell the property to private developers to further the general intent of the plan. In *Berman*, the store owner challenged the taking, claiming that this was unconstitutional because the property was not in any disrepair and therefore not injurious to the public health or welfare and that furthermore the property was to be redeveloped for private and not public use. The Court rejected both claims stating (1) redevelopment plans must be viewed as a general plan, and the condition of any one property was not relevant, and (2) a public use does not preclude development by private individuals. The Court elaborated on the second point saying:

> Once the object is within the authority of Congress, the means by which it will be attained is also for Congress to determine. Here one of the means chosen is the use of private enterprise for redevelopment of the area. Appellants argue that this makes the project a taking from one businessman for the benefit of another businessman. But the means of executing the project are for Congress and Congress alone to determine, once the public purpose has been established. The public end may be as well or better served through an agency of private enterprise than through a department of government—or so the Congress might conclude. We cannot say that public ownership is the sole method of promoting the public purposes of community redevelopment projects.

In rendering its decision, the Court made another important point. The question of public use is one that is generally within the scope of the legislature not the Court. When any legislative body makes the decision to take property through eminent domain for a particular use, the Court must grant great deference to its decision:

> We do not sit to determine whether a particular housing project is or is not desirable. The concept of the public welfare is broad and inclusive. The values it represents are spiritual as well as physical, aesthetic, as well as monetary. It is within the power of the legislature to determine that the community should be beautiful as well as healthy, spacious as well as clean, well-balanced as well as carefully patrolled. In the present case, the Congress and its authorized agencies have made determinations that take into account a wide variety of values. It is not for us to reappraise them. If those who govern the District of Columbia decide that the Nation's Capital should be beautiful as well as sanitary, there is nothing in the Fifth Amendment that stands in the way.

A Point of Law

Berman v. Parker, 348 U.S. 26 (1954)

Property is properly taken for a public use even though it will be developed by private companies if the property is taken as part of a general plan to improve a neighborhood.

Taking: Physical versus Regulatory

condemnation

A governmental taking of private property with payment, but not necessarily with consent.

Before any government is required to pay just compensation for property it must be "taken." The Supreme Court has identified two types of *taking* that require compensation: a physical taking and a regulatory taking. A physical taking often occurs through a **condemnation** proceeding instituted by the government. In a condemnation proceeding, title is transferred to the government in return for just compensation. However, a physical taking can also occur through a limited occupation or invasion of the property caused by governmental activity. For example, a physical taking was found when low military flights over private property destroyed the property's use as a chicken farm. *United States v. Causby*, 328 U.S. 256 (1946). A physical taking was also found when a government-owned dam repeatedly flooded private property. *United States v. Cress*, 243 U.S. 316 (1917). The justification for requiring compensation when property is taken is that the landowner loses all or some of the economic value of his property.

inverse condemnation

A lawsuit against the government to demand payment for an informal or irregular taking of private property.

A physical taking is not the only way in which a property owner can experience a financial loss. Several types of government regulations, such as zoning, land use, and environmental laws, also lower the value of property. Sometimes the term **inverse condemnation** is used to describe this type of situation. As the Supreme Court said in a 1922 case, *Pennsylvania Coal Co. v. Mahon*, 260 U.S. 393: "The general rule at least is that while property may be regulated to a certain extent, if regulation goes too far it will be recognized as a taking." How far is too far is a difficult question to answer. In several cases the Court lists three factors it considers:

1. the character of the governmental action,
2. the economic impact, and
3. the interference with reasonable investment-backed expectations.

The Court generally holds that if the regulation authorizes actual physical occupation of the property, there is a taking, and compensation will be allowed regardless of the extent of damages. If there is no physical occupation by the government, then the Court focuses on the economic impact of the regulation or to what degree the regulation destroys reasonable investment expectations of the property owners. In 1992, in *Lucas v. S.C. Coastal Council*, 505 U.S. 1003, the Supreme Court offered some clarification of its view regarding regulation and taking. This case involved a coastal regulation that prohibited the construction of any home along the coast. Prior to the enactment of the law, the petitioner, Lucas, purchased beachfront property for almost one million dollars planning to construct a home. He claimed that the law resulted in a taking. The Supreme Court agreed. In discussing whether a regulation becomes a taking the Court said:

> Our decision in *Mahon* offered little insight into when, and under what circumstances, a given regulation would be seen as going "too far" for purposes of the Fifth Amendment. In 70-odd years of succeeding "regulatory takings" jurisprudence, we have generally eschewed any "set formula" for determining how far is too far, preferring to "engage in . . . essentially ad hoc, factual inquiries." We have, however, described at least two discrete categories of regulatory action as compensable without case-specific inquiry into the public interest advanced in support of the restraint. The first encompasses regulations that compel the property owner to suffer a physical "invasion" of his property. In general (at least with regard to permanent invasions), no matter how minute the intrusion, and no matter how weighty the public purpose behind it, we have required compensation. For example, in *Loretto v. Teleprompter Manhattan CATV Corp.*, 458 U.S. 419 (1982), we determined that New York's law requiring landlords to allow television cable companies to emplace cable facilities in their apartment buildings constituted a taking, *id.*, at 435–440, even though the facilities occupied, at most, only 1 1/2 cubic feet of the landlords' property, see *id.*, at 438, n. 16.
>
> The second situation in which we have found categorical treatment appropriate is where regulation denies all economically beneficial or productive use of land. As we have said on numerous occasions, the Fifth Amendment is violated when land use regulation does not substantially advance legitimate state interests or denies an owner economically viable use of his land.
>
> We have never set forth the justification for this rule. Perhaps it is simply, as Justice Brennan suggested, that total deprivation of beneficial use is, from the landowner's point of view, the equivalent of a physical appropriation.

In *Lucas*, there was a *total* loss of economic value. In cases where the loss was less than total, the Court often finds that there is no taking under the Fifth Amendment. The following cases illustrate this:

- A rezoning law that reduced the value of property from $10,000 to $2,500 did not result in a taking because the property was not totally destroyed. *Euclid v. Ambler Realty Co.*, 272 U.S. 365 (1926).
- A city ordinance that placed restrictions on the development of individual historic landmarks and resulted in petitioner's inability to build offices was not a taking even though a several million dollar loss resulted. The Court reasoned that the petitioner retained substantial use of all of its land. *Penn Cent. Transp. Co. v. New York City*, 438 U.S. 104 (1978).

A Point of Law

Pennsylvania Coal Co. v. Mahon, 260 U.S. 393 (1922)

Lucas v. S.C. Coastal Council, 505 U.S. 1003 (1992)

When the government takes physical occupation of all or part of property, whether through eminent domain (condemnation), through its activities, or through regulations, it is a "taking," and the government must pay just compensation. Where government regulations, such as land use, zoning, or environmental laws, negatively affect the value of the property, then the court examines each case to determine if the regulation goes "too far" in destroying the value of the property.

In 2002, the Supreme Court further clarified how it reviews regulatory takings in a case dealing with regulations that imposed a thirty-two-month moratorium on the building of houses along the shores of Lake Tahoe. The landowners here argued that the *Lucas* case applied because they were totally deprived of the use of their property for almost three years. The parties argued that the Court was not required to consider the economic impact of the regulation nor its effect on investors because the thirty-two-month moratorium was the same as a total physical taking. The Court disagreed. In its decision, the Court emphasizes that different tests had to be applied when the taking was regulatory rather than physical. The Court also affirmed that decisions in these cases had to be made on a case-by-case basis. The following is an excerpt from the majority opinion in the case.

Tahoe-Sierra Preservation Council, Inc. v. Tahoe Regional Planning Agency

535 U.S. 302 (2002)

The Tahoe Regional Planning Agency was created by the states of California and Nevada to deal with deterioration of the clarity of the waters of Lake Tahoe. Eventually the agency adopted a 32-month moratorium on building. The Tahoe-Sierra Preservation Council represents the many landowners affected by the moratorium.

JUSTICE STEVENS delivered the opinion of the Court.

The question presented is whether a moratorium on development imposed during the process of devising a comprehensive land-use plan constitutes a taking of property requiring compensation under the Takings Clause of the United States Constitution.

Petitioners contend that the mere enactment of a temporary regulation that, while in effect, denies a property owner all viable economic use of her property gives rise to an unqualified constitutional obligation to compensate her for the value of its use during that period. Under their proposed rule, there is no need to evaluate the landowners' investment-backed expectations, the actual impact of the regulation on any individual, the importance of the public interest served by the regulation, or the reasons for imposing the temporary restriction. For petitioners, it is enough that a regulation imposes a temporary deprivation—no matter how brief—of all economically viable use to trigger a rule that a taking has occurred. Petitioners assert that our opinions in *First English* and *Lucas* have already endorsed their view, and that it is a logical application of the principle that the Takings Clause was "designed to bar Government from forcing some people alone to bear burdens which, in all fairness and justice, should be borne by the public as a whole." *Armstrong v. United States*, 364 U.S. 40, 49 (1960).

(continued)

(continued)

The text of the Fifth Amendment itself provides a basis for drawing a distinction between physical takings and regulatory takings. Its plain language requires the payment of compensation whenever the government acquires private property for a public purpose, whether the acquisition is the result of a condemnation proceeding or a physical appropriation. But the Constitution contains no comparable reference to regulations that prohibit a property owner from making certain uses of her private property. Our jurisprudence involving condemnations and physical takings is as old as the Republic and, for the most part, involves the straightforward application of *per se* rules. Our regulatory takings jurisprudence, in contrast, is of more recent vintage and is characterized by "essentially ad hoc, factual inquiries," *Penn Central*, 438 U.S., at 124, designed to allow "careful examination and weighing of all the relevant circumstances."

When the government physically takes possession of an interest in property for some public purpose, it has a categorical duty to compensate the former owner, *United States v. Pewee Coal Co.*, 341 U.S. 114, 115 (1951), regardless of whether the interest that is taken constitutes an entire parcel or merely a part thereof. Thus, compensation is mandated when a leasehold is taken and the government occupies the property for its own purposes, even though that use is temporary. Similarly, when the government appropriates part of a rooftop in order to provide cable TV access for apartment tenants, *Loretto v. Teleprompter Manhattan CATV Corp.*, 458 U.S. 419 (1982); or when its planes use private airspace to approach a government airport, *United States v. Causby*, 328 U.S. 256 (1946), it is required to pay for that share no matter how small. But a government regulation that merely prohibits landlords from evicting tenants unwilling to pay a higher rent, *Block v. Hirsh*, 256 U.S. 135 (1921); that bans certain private uses of a portion of an owner's property, *Village of Euclid v. Ambler Realty Co.*, 272 U.S. 365 (1926); *Keystone Bituminous Coal Assn. v. DeBenedictis*, 480 U.S. 470 (1987); or that forbids the private use of certain airspace, *Penn Central Transp. Co. v. New York City*, 438 U.S. 104 (1978), does not constitute a categorical taking. "The first category of cases requires courts to apply a clear rule; the second necessarily entails complex factual assessments of the purposes and economic effects of government actions." *Yee v. Escondido*, 503 U.S. 519, 523 (1992). See also *Loretto*, 458 U.S., at 440; *Keystone*, 480 U.S., at 489, n. 18.

This longstanding distinction between acquisitions of property for public use, on the one hand, and regulations prohibiting private uses, on the other, makes it inappropriate to treat cases involving physical takings as controlling precedents for the evaluation of a claim that there has been a "regulatory taking," and vice versa. For the same reason that we do not ask whether a physical appropriation advances a substantial government interest or whether it deprives the owner of all economically valuable use, we do not apply our precedent from the physical takings context to regulatory takings claims. Land-use regulations are ubiquitous and most of them impact property values in some tangential way—often in completely unanticipated ways. Treating them all as *per se* takings would transform government regulation into a luxury few governments could afford. By contrast, physical appropriations are relatively rare, easily identified, and usually represent a greater affront to individual property rights.

As we noted in *Lucas*, it was Justice Holmes' opinion in *Pennsylvania Coal Co. v. Mahon*, 260 U.S. 393 (1922), that gave birth to our regulatory takings jurisprudence. In subsequent opinions we have repeatedly and consistently endorsed Holmes' observation that "if regulation goes too far it will be recognized as a taking." *Id.*, at 415. Justice Holmes did not provide a standard for determining when a regulation goes "too far," but he did reject the view expressed in Justice Brandeis' dissent that there could not be a taking because the property remained in the possession of the owner and had not been appropriated or used by the public. After *Mahon*, neither a physical appropriation nor a public use has ever been a necessary component of a "regulatory taking."

In the decades following that decision, we have "generally eschewed" any set formula for determining how far is too far, choosing instead to engage in "essentially ad hoc, factual inquiries." *Lucas*, 505 U.S., at 1015 (quoting *Penn Central*, 438 U.S., at 124). Indeed, we still resist the temptation to adopt *per se* rules in our cases involving partial regulatory takings, preferring to examine "a number of factors" rather than a simple "mathematically precise" formula. Justice Brennan's opinion for the Court in *Penn Central* did, however, make it clear that even though multiple factors are relevant in the analysis of regulatory takings claims, in such cases we must focus on "the parcel as a whole."

Neither *Lucas* nor any of our other regulatory takings cases compels us to accept petitioners'

(continued)

(continued)

categorical submission. In fact, these cases make clear that the categorical rule in *Lucas* was carved out for the "extraordinary case" in which a regulation permanently deprives property of all value; the default rule remains that, in the regulatory taking context, we require a more fact specific inquiry. Nevertheless, we will consider whether the interest in protecting individual property owners from bearing public burdens "which, in all fairness and justice, should be borne by the public as a whole," *Armstrong v. United States*, 364 U.S., at 49, justifies creating a new rule for these circumstances.

In rejecting petitioners' *per se* rule, we do not hold that the temporary nature of a land-use restriction precludes finding that it effects a taking; we simply recognize that it should not be given exclusive significance one way or the other.

We conclude, therefore, that the interest in "fairness and justice" will be best served by relying on the familiar *Penn Central* approach when deciding cases like this, rather than by attempting to craft a new categorical rule.

Accordingly, the judgment of the Court of Appeals is affirmed.

It is so ordered.

Something to Consider

Review the language of the Fifth Amendment regarding taking of property. (See Appendix A.) The Court emphasizes the difference between a physical taking for a public use and a regulatory taking and further states that this distinction is clear from the plain language of the Amendment. Do you agree?

Taking: Judicial

In 2010, the Supreme Court decided a case involving a restoration of Florida beaches, *Stop the Beach Renourishment, Inc. v. Florida Dept. of Environmental Protection*, 560 U.S. __ (2010). The restoration project involved the deposit of a great deal of sand resulting in changes to the coastline. Private beachfront owners claimed that, as a result, they lost part of their beachfront property to the state. The matter was litigated in the Florida courts and eventually, the Florida Supreme Court decided that the state did not violate the Fifth or the Fourteenth Amendment by taking property without just compensation. The U.S. Supreme Court reviewed Florida statutory and common law, and the justices hearing the case (one justice did not take part in the decision) unanimously agreed that no taking occurred. However, the case raised another issue, one of first impression before the Supreme Court. In this case it was claimed that the ultimate taking resulted from judicial action, rather than a direct physical taking or regulatory action. Four justices believed that a violation of the Takings Clause could result from a "judicial taking," and four justices did not believe this issue needed to be addressed to rule in this case. As a result of the tie, the issue remains open. Read the excerpt from the Court's opinion here to understand the argument for recognizing a judicial taking.

 Stop the Beach Renourishment, Inc. v. Florida Dept. of Environmental Protection

560 U.S. __ (2010)

Before coming to the parties' arguments in the present case, we discuss some general principles of our takings jurisprudence. The Takings Clause—"nor shall private property be taken for public use, without just compensation," U.S. Const., Amdt. 5—applies as fully to the taking of a landowner's riparian rights as it does to the taking of an estate in land. See *Yates* v. *Milwaukee*, 10 Wall. 497, 504 (1871). Moreover, though the classic taking is a transfer of property to the State or to another private party by eminent domain, the Takings Clause

(continued)

(continued)

applies to other state actions that achieve the same thing. Thus, when the government uses its own property in such a way that it destroys private property, it has taken that property. See *United States v. Causby*, 328 U.S. 256, 261–262 (1946). Similarly, our doctrine of regulatory takings "aims to identify regulatory actions that are functionally equivalent to the classic taking." *Lingle v. Chevron U.S.A. Inc.*, 544 U.S. 528, 539 (2005). Thus, it is a taking when a state regulation forces a property owner to submit to a permanent physical occupation, *Loretto v. Teleprompter Manhattan CATV Corp.*, 458 U.S. 419, 425–426 (1982), or deprives him of all economically beneficial use of his property, *Lucas v. South Carolina Coastal Council*, 505 U.S. 1003, 1019 (1992). Finally (and here we approach the situation before us), States effect a taking if they recharacterize as public property what was previously private property. See *Webb's Fabulous Pharmacies, Inc. v. Beckwith*, 449 U.S. 155, 163–165 (1980).

* * * *

The Takings Clause (unlike, for instance, the Ex Post Facto Clauses, see Art. I, §9, cl. 3; §10, cl. 1) is not addressed to the action of a specific branch or branches. It is concerned simply with the act, and not with the governmental actor ("nor shall private property *be taken*" (emphasis added)). There is no textual justification for saying that the existence or the scope of a State's power to expropriate private property without just compensation varies according to the branch of government effecting the expropriation. Nor does common sense recommend such a principle. It would be absurd to allow a State to do by judicial decree what the Takings Clause forbids it to do by legislative fiat. See *Stevens v. Cannon Beach*, 510 U.S. 1207, 1211–1212 (1994).

Property Subject to the Takings Clause

The Fifth Amendment Takings Clause applies to any property taken by the government, not just real property. As with other provisions of the Constitution dealing with property, in the case of the Takings Clause the Supreme Court gives the term property a broad definition. Property includes personal property as well as intangible property interests. The following are examples of types of interests included in the term "property" for the Takings Clause:

- Trade secret information used in the development of pesticides was property. Here the Court also emphasized that investors contributed millions of dollars to develop the product. When disclosing the trade secret destroyed the value of the investment, there was a taking. *Ruckelshaus v. Monsanto Co.*, 467 U.S. 986 (1984).
- One state supreme court (California) ruled that the right to a professional football team, the Oakland Raiders, was property for the purposes of eminent domain. *City of Oakland v. Oakland Raiders*, 32 Cal. 3d 60 (1982). However, a subsequent appellate decision ruled that exercising eminent domain in this case would violate the Commerce Clause. The U.S. Supreme Court denied the petition for writ of certiorari.
- Interest on money in an attorney's trust account is property subject to the Takings Clause. Several states have laws requiring such interest to be given to a bar association fund used for needy parties. In a 2003 case, *Brown v. Washington Legal Found.*, 538 U.S. 216, the Court found that the use of this interest by the bar association was a taking subject to the Fifth Amendment. However, the Court also found that without these special trust accounts, the clients would not earn interest on their money and that therefore they suffered no economic loss and were not entitled to compensation.

Just Compensation

If the government takes property for public use, the Fifth Amendment requires that just compensation be paid to the property owner. Just compensation is generally determined by the fair market value of the property taken. Fair market value is what a willing seller will pay a willing buyer. In condemnation proceedings, often the only issue before the court is the determination of this value. Such trials involve lengthy and often tedious expert testimony regarding the worth of the property.

Taking versus Forfeiture

Many jurisdictions, both federal and state, have enacted a variety of forfeiture laws. These laws allow the government to seize property used in connection with or the proceeds of a crime. No compensation is required when property is forfeited. In some instances, the property in question is not owned by the criminal but by an innocent third party. Many laws allow the government to seize the property even if owned by an innocent party, although some forfeiture laws have an innocent party exception. Innocent parties who suffer the loss of property often challenge the forfeiture on two points: (1) that the taking violates due process and (2) that the taking is in violation of the Fifth Amendment Takings Clause because no compensation is paid. In two recent cases, the Supreme Court rejected these claims and upheld laws that permit the government seizure. In 2002, the Court upheld a law allowing a government housing program to evict a woman whose teenage son was arrested for possession of drugs. *Department of Housing and Urban Development v. Rucker*, 535 U.S. 125 (2002). In 1996, the Court upheld a law that allowed a state to seize an automobile used by the petitioner's husband who was engaged in an act of prostitution. The majority and dissenting opinions in that case follow.

Bennis v. Michigan
516 U.S. 442 (1996)

CHIEF JUSTICE REHNQUIST delivered the opinion of the Court.

Petitioner was a joint owner, with her husband, of an automobile in which her husband engaged in sexual activity with a prostitute. A Michigan court ordered the automobile forfeited as a public nuisance, with no offset for her interest, notwithstanding her lack of knowledge of her husband's activity. We hold that the Michigan court order did not offend the Due Process Clause of the Fourteenth Amendment or the Takings Clause of the 5th Amendment.

We granted certiorari in order to determine whether Michigan's abatement scheme has deprived petitioner of her interest in the forfeited car without due process, in violation of the Fourteenth Amendment, or has taken her interest for public use without compensation, in violation of the Fifth Amendment as incorporated by the Fourteenth Amendment. We affirm.

The gravamen of petitioner's due process claim is not that she was denied notice or an opportunity to contest the abatement of her car; she was accorded both. Rather, she claims she was entitled to contest the abatement by showing she did not know her husband would use it to violate Michigan's indecency law. But a long and unbroken line of cases holds that an owner's interest in property may be forfeited by reason of the use to which the property is put even though the owner did not know that it was to be put to such use.

Our earliest opinion to this effect is Justice Story's opinion for the Court in *The Palmyra*, 12 Wheat. 1 (1827). The Palmyra, which had been commissioned as a privateer by the King of Spain and had attacked a United States vessel, was captured by a United States war ship and brought into Charleston, South Carolina, for adjudication. On the Government's appeal from the Circuit

(continued)

(continued)

Court's acquittal of the vessel, it was contended by the owner that the vessel could not be forfeited until he was convicted for the privateering. The Court rejected this contention, explaining: "The thing is here primarily considered as the offender, or rather the offence is attached primarily to the thing." *Id.*, at 14.

In *Dobbins's Distillery v. United States*, 96 U.S. 395, 401 (1878), this Court upheld the forfeiture of property used by a lessee in fraudulently avoiding federal alcohol taxes, observing: "Cases often arise where the property of the owner is forfeited on account of the fraud, neglect, or misconduct of those intrusted with its possession, care, and custody, even when the owner is otherwise without fault . . . and it has always been held . . . that the acts of the possessors bind the interest of the owner . . . whether he be innocent or guilty."

In *Van Oster v. Kansas*, 272 U.S. 465 (1926), this Court upheld the forfeiture of a purchaser's interest in a car misused by the seller. Van Oster purchased an automobile from a dealer but agreed that the dealer might retain possession for use in its business. The dealer allowed an associate to use the automobile, and the associate used it for the illegal transportation of intoxicating liquor. *Id.*, at 465–466. The State brought a forfeiture action pursuant to a Kansas statute, and Van Oster defended on the ground that the transportation of the liquor in the car was without her knowledge or authority. This Court rejected Van Oster's claim.

In *Calero-Toledo v. Pearson Yacht Leasing Co.*, 416 U.S. 663 (1974), the most recent decision on point, the Court reviewed the same cases discussed above, and concluded that "the innocence of the owner of property subject to forfeiture has almost uniformly been rejected as a defense." *Id.*, at 683. Petitioner is in the same position as the various owners involved in the forfeiture cases beginning with *The Palmyra* in 1827. She did not know that her car would be used in an illegal activity that would subject it to forfeiture. But under these cases the Due Process Clause of the Fourteenth Amendment does not protect her interest against forfeiture by the government.

The dissent also suggests that *The Palmyra* line of cases "would justify the confiscation of an ocean liner just because one of its passengers sinned while on board." Post, at 5. None of our cases have held that an ocean liner may be confiscated because of the activities of one passenger. We said in *Goldsmith-Grant*, and we repeat here, that "when such application shall be made it will be time enough to pronounce upon it." 254 U.S., at 512.

In any event, for the reasons pointed out in *Calero-Toledo* and *Van Oster*, forfeiture also serves a deterrent purpose distinct from any punitive purpose. Forfeiture of property prevents illegal uses "both by preventing further illicit use of the property and by imposing an economic penalty, thereby rendering illegal behavior unprofitable." *Calero-Toledo, supra*, at 687.

Petitioner also claims that the forfeiture in this case was a taking of private property for public use in violation of the Takings Clause of the Fifth Amendment, made applicable to the States by the Fourteenth Amendment. But if the forfeiture proceeding here in question did not violate the Fourteenth Amendment, the property in the automobile was transferred by virtue of that proceeding from petitioner to the State. The government may not be required to compensate an owner for property which it has already lawfully acquired under the exercise of governmental authority other than the power of eminent domain.

We conclude today, as we concluded 75 years ago, that the cases authorizing actions of the kind at issue are "too firmly fixed in the punitive and remedial jurisprudence of the country to be now displaced." *Goldsmith-Grant, supra*, at 511. The State here sought to deter illegal activity that contributes to neighborhood deterioration and unsafe streets. The Bennis automobile, it is conceded, facilitated and was used in criminal activity. Both the trial court and the Michigan Supreme Court followed our longstanding practice, and the judgment of the Supreme Court of Michigan is therefore Affirmed.

JUSTICE STEVENS, with whom JUSTICE SOUTER and JUSTICE BREYER join, dissenting.

For centuries prostitutes have been plying their trade on other people's property. Assignations have occurred in palaces, luxury hotels, cruise ships, college dormitories, truck stops, back alleys and back seats. A profession of this vintage has provided governments with countless opportunities to use novel weapons to curtail its abuses. As far as I am aware, however, it was not until 1988 that any State decided to experiment with the punishment of innocent third parties by confiscating property in which, or on which, a single transaction with a prostitute has been consummated.

The logic of the Court's analysis would permit the States to exercise virtually unbridled power to confiscate vast amounts of property where professional criminals have engaged in illegal acts. Some airline passengers have

(continued)

(continued)

marijuana cigarettes in their luggage; some hotel guests are thieves; some spectators at professional sports events carry concealed weapons; and some hitchhikers are prostitutes. The State surely may impose strict obligations on the owners of airlines, hotels, stadiums, and vehicles to exercise a high degree of care to prevent others from making illegal use of their property, but neither logic nor history supports the Court's apparent assumption that their complete innocence imposes no constitutional impediment to the seizure of their property simply because it provided the locus for a criminal transaction.

Apart from the lack of a sufficient nexus between petitioner's car and the offense her husband committed, I would reverse because petitioner is entirely without responsibility for that act. Fundamental fairness prohibits the punishment of innocent people.

The majority insists that it is a settled rule that the owner of property is strictly liable for wrongful uses to which that property is put. Even assuming that strict liability applies to "innocent" owners, we have consistently recognized an exception for truly blameless individuals. The Court's opinion in *Calero-Toledo v. Pearson Yacht Leasing Co.*, 416 U.S., at 688–690, established the proposition that the Constitution bars the punitive forfeiture of property when its owner alleges and proves that he took all reasonable steps to prevent its illegal use. The majority dismisses this statement as "obiter dictum," but we have assumed that such a principle existed, or expressly reserved the question, in a line of cases dating back nearly 200 years. In one of its earliest decisions, the Court, speaking through Chief Justice Marshall, recognized as "unquestionably a correct legal principle" that "a forfeiture can only be applied to those cases in which

the means that are prescribed for the prevention of a forfeiture may be employed." *Peisch v. Ware*, 4 Cranch 347, 363 (1808). In other contexts, we have regarded as axiomatic that persons cannot be punished when they have done no wrong. I would hold now what we have always assumed: that the principle is required by due process.

The unique facts of this case demonstrate that petitioner is entitled to the protection of that rule. The subject of this forfeiture was certainly not contraband. It was not acquired with the proceeds of criminal activity and its principal use was entirely legitimate. It was an ordinary car that petitioner's husband used to commute to the steel mill where he worked. Petitioner testified that they had been married for nine years; that she had acquired her ownership interest in the vehicle by the expenditure of money that she had earned herself; that she had no knowledge of her husband's plans to do anything with the car except "come directly home from work," as he had always done before; and that she even called "Missing Persons" when he failed to return on the night in question. App. 8–10. Her testimony is not contradicted and certainly is credible. Without knowledge that he would commit such an act in the family car, or that he had ever done so previously, surely petitioner cannot be accused of failing to take "reasonable steps" to prevent the illicit behavior. She is just as blameless as if a thief, rather than her husband, had used the car in a criminal episode.

While I am not prepared to draw a bright line that will separate the permissible and impermissible forfeitures of the property of innocent owners, I am convinced that the blatant unfairness of this seizure places it on the unconstitutional side of that line.

I therefore respectfully dissent.

Something to Consider

Do you think that the reasoning in the majority opinion or in the dissent is more persuasive? Why?

The Contract Clause

ARTICLE I, SECTION 10 PROHIBITS ANY state from passing any law "impairing the Obligation of Contracts . . . ." This section applies only to the states and has no federal counterpart. However, any federal law that does impair the obligation of contracts might be a violation of the Due Process or the Takings Clauses. In the case of *Home Bldg. & Loan Assn. v. Blaisdell*, 290 U.S. 398 (1934), the Supreme Court explains the historical reason for the Contract Clause:

The reasons which led to the adoption of that clause, and of the other prohibitions of section 10 of article 1, are not left in doubt, and have frequently been described with eloquent emphasis. The widespread distress following the revolutionary period and the plight of debtors had called forth in the States an ignoble array of legislative schemes for the defeat of creditors and the invasion of contractual obligations. Legislative interferences had been so numerous and extreme that the confidence essential to prosperous trade had been undermined and the utter destruction of credit was threatened. It was necessary to interpose the restraining power of a central authority in order to secure the foundations even of "private faith." The occasion and general purpose of the contract clause are summed up in the terse statement of Chief Justice Marshall in *Ogden v. Saunders*, 12 Wheat. 213, 354, 355: "The power of changing the relative situation of debtor and creditor, of interfering with contracts, a power which comes home to every man, touches the interest of all, and controls the conduct of every individual in those things which he supposes to be proper for his own exclusive management, had been used to such an excess by the state legislatures, as to break in upon the ordinary intercourse of society, and destroy all confidence between man and man. This mischief had become so great, so alarming, as not only to impair commercial intercourse, and threaten the existence of credit, but to sap the morals of the people, and destroy the sanctity of private faith. To guard against the continuance of the evil, was an object of deep interest with all the truly wise, as well as the virtuous, of this great community, and was one of the important benefits expected from a reform of the government."

In interpreting the section of the Constitution prohibiting states from passing any law impairing the obligation of contracts, the Court has concentrated on addressing the following questions:

1. What does "law" include?
2. What is the "obligation of contracts"?
3. Does the state police power authorize laws that impair contractual obligations?

"Law" and the Contract Clause

Relying on the traditional notion that the legislature makes law and the courts interpret law, in most instances the Court interprets the term *law* in this constitutional provision to include only legislative action. Case law that affects or impairs the obligation of contracts is generally held to not violate the contract clause. The following language in the case of *Central Land Co. v. Laidley*, 159 U.S. 103 (1895), explains:

> In order to come within the provision of the constitution of the United States, which declares that no state shall pass any law impairing the obligation of contracts, not only must the obligation of a contract have been impaired, but it must have been impaired by some act of the legislative power of the state, and not by a decision of its judicial department only.

The *Central Land Co.* case involved a dispute between two parties claiming ownership to the same piece of property. The factual chronology was as follows:

1. S sold land to B_1.
2. Twelve years later, S sold same land to B_2.
3. A state court subsequently declared the first deed invalid.
4. B_1 challenged the state court decision as being in violation of the contract clause.

Acknowledging that the state court may have acted improperly, the Supreme Court nevertheless refused to find any violation of the Constitution, holding that the term *law* as it is used in Article 1, Section 10 applies to legislative acts, not court decisions.

Obligation of Contracts

Article 1, Section 10 does not prohibit laws that impair all aspects of contracts. It is limited to laws that impair the *obligation* of contracts. The obligation of a contract is the duty of the parties to perform. It does not refer to the agreement itself. For example, if A and B agree that A will sell to B and B will purchase from A a piece of property for $1 million, the obligation of the contract is A's duty to transfer the property and B's duty to pay the million dollars. The obligation is the duty of a party to perform, that is, pay money or sell the property. If both parties have already performed, there no longer is any obligation. Thus, this constitutional provision applies only to existing contracts where one or both parties have not yet performed.

The Contract Clause versus State Police Power

In the case of *Home Bldg. & Loan Assn. v. Blaisdell*, 290 U.S. 398 (1934), the Supreme Court stated that the Contract Clause was not an absolute prohibition on state laws that interfered with contract obligations. This case involved a state law that extended the redemption period for those who defaulted on their mortgages. The law was a response to the harsh economic times during the Depression. This law obviously impaired obligations of contracts in that the homeowners were no longer obligated to cure their default within the time limits set by law when the contracts were made. The Court made the point that the obligation of the contract included not only what was actually contained in the contract, but what the laws demanded of the parties at the time the contract was entered into. In spite of this, the Supreme Court held that the general police powers of the state allowed this law because it promoted the general welfare of the people and was only a temporary impairment. The Court emphasized that whether a law is a proper exercise of police power must be decided on a case-by-case basis.

Ethical Decisions—Everyday Choices

The Facts: Jackson is an attorney who represents a local redevelopment agency. He learns that the agency is seriously considering the development of a new shopping center that he believes will greatly enhance the value of neighboring property. Before this information is made public, Jackson tells his father-in-law, who is a real estate developer, knowing that his father-in-law might want to purchase property in the neighboring area before its value escalates. Jackson is aware of confidentiality requirements, but does not see how this disclosure would harm his client, the redevelopment agency.

The Problem: Can Jackson disclose information he acquired in his representation of a client, when the disclosure does not harm his client?

Guiding Principles: Attorneys have an obligation to preserve confidential information of their clients. They also have an ethical obligation not to engage in any activity that creates the impression of impropriety.

Chapter Summary

The Constitution protects property rights and economic interests through the Due Process Clauses (Fifth and Fourteenth Amendments), the Takings Clause (Fifth Amendment), and the Contract Clause (Article 1, Section 10). The Due Process Clauses provide both procedural and substantive protections. The clauses protect traditional forms of property as well as economic freedoms or liberty, such as the freedom to enter into contracts. Laws that affect property or economic interests must have a legitimate state interest and not be arbitrary or irrational. In the past, the Due Process Clauses have been used by the Court to strike down labor laws and laws that regulated businesses. In modern times, the Court rarely, if ever, finds such laws unconstitutional. As long as such laws serve a legitimate state interest and are not arbitrary, they are constitutional.

The Fifth Amendment Takings Clause, is applied to the states through the Due Process Clause of the Fourteenth Amendment. It prohibits government from taking property for public use without just compensation. This clause limits the government's power of eminent domain, which allows government to take property for public use. Public use includes such uses as roadways, public parks, preserving historical landmarks, and beautification of a neighborhood, even when the development is actually done by private parties and ownership of the property is eventually turned over to private parties. In addition to eminent domain, property can be taken by government activities that result in occupation or invasion of land or by regulations resulting in a physical occupation or in an economic loss. Regulations, such as zoning and land-use laws, effect a taking if they result in a serious enough loss to the landowner. Whether there is a taking is determined by the Court on a case-by-case basis. The Court considers the following factors: the nature of the government action, the economic impact, and the interference with reasonable investment-backed expectations. The Court also considers if there is physical occupation of the land. Property subject to the Takings Clause includes not only real and personal property, but also intangible interests, such as trade secrets. Just compensation is the fair market value of the property. Not all government taking of property is subject to the Fifth Amendment requirement of just compensation. Criminal laws, known as forfeiture laws, that allow government to take or seize property used in connection with crimes are examples of this.

The Contract Clause prohibits any state from passing any law that interferes with the obligation of contracts. This section of the Constitution applies only to states, not to the federal government. The term *law* as used in this provision applies to statutory law, not case law. An obligation of a contract is the duty of the parties to perform. This provision of the Constitution is not absolute. In some situations states can use their general police powers to enact laws that do interfere with contractual obligations.

Key Terms

real property	monopoly	condemnation
personal property	eminent domain	inverse condemnation

Questions for Review

1. Which provisions of the Constitution protect property rights and economic interests? Briefly describe the protections granted by each provision.
2. How does substantive due process protect property interests?
3. How has the Supreme Court used the Due Process Clause to strike down labor laws and business regulations?
4. Compare and contrast the taking of property through the power of eminent domain with regulatory taking of property.
5. What factors or criteria does the Supreme Court use to determine if a law or regulation results in a taking for Fifth Amendment purposes?
6. What are some examples of laws or regulations that resulted in a taking for Fifth Amendment purposes?
7. What is the difference between a taking and a forfeiture?

8. What types of law come under the provisions of the Contract Clause?
9. What is meant by the term *obligation of contracts*?
10. How does state police power affect the Contract Clause?

Questions for Analysis

1. Review the situation described in Living **with the Constitution** at the beginning of this chapter. Does the rent control ordinance involve (a) a violation of due process, (b) a taking without just compensation, or (c) a violation of the Contract Clause? Discuss.
2. Answer the following questions about *Lochner v. New York*:
   a. The Court describes certain kinds of contracts that are not protected by the Constitution. What are they?
   b. Why did the Court think the police power was exceeded by New York?
   c. Why did Justice Harlan dissent?
3. According to the Court in *Nebbia v. New York*, what are some ways that the government can curtail the use of private property?
4. Several cases in this chapter mention state "police power." What does this mean?

Assignments and Projects

1. Brief the case *Bennis v. Michigan*.
2. The Environment and Natural Resources Division of the U.S. Department of Justice plays an important role in the exercise of eminent domain power by the federal government. Research this organization and write a short paper on its activities.
3. Locate the oral arguments for *Bennis v. Michigan*. (Hint: Check the Web sites for the Supreme Court and the Oyez Project). Listen to the arguments and summarize the one that you think is most persuasive.

Putting It into Practice

1. Assume that a client has received notice that his home is to be taken for a proposed freeway. He wants to be sure that he receives a fair price for his home. Go on the Internet and locate at least two appraisers who might be hired as expert witnesses in the event the case goes to trial.

Group Activities

1. In small groups, discuss the following questions: In *Tahoe-Sierra Preservation Council, Inc.*, the Court found that depriving a person of his property for almost three years did not necessarily involve a "taking." Do you agree?

2. If you completed Assignment and Project number 3, in small groups compare the summaries of your arguments. Would you have voted the same way as the Court did?

11 Freedom of Expression

Congress shall make no law ... abridging the freedom of speech, or of the press; or the right of people peaceably to assemble, and to petition the Government for a redress of grievances.

First Amendment to the U.S. Constitution

Chapter Outline

Chapter Objectives

When you complete this chapter you should be able to:

1. list the five rights included in freedom of expression.

2. summarize the theories explaining constitutional protection of speech.

3. describe the different types of speech that are constitutionally protected.

4. explain how political campaign finance laws involve freedom of speech issues.

5. describe the types of speech that are not constitutionally protected.

6. discuss the free speech issues of students in public schools.

7. provide examples of situations not protected by the right to assembly.

8. compare and contrast the right to a free press with the rights of criminal defendants.

9. explain the reporter's privilege and its limitations.

10. describe circumstances in which the press can be required to disseminate information.

Looking Back

Before reading this chapter, review the following terms and concepts from the previous chapters:

Strict scrutiny Whenever a law targets a suspect class or burdens a fundamental right, the Court reviews the law with the highest degree of scrutiny. A fundamental right is a constitutional right. (Chapter 8)

Incorporation doctrine Most of the rights found in the Bill of Rights are "incorporated" or included in the concept of due process, and they apply to the states through the Fourteenth Amendment. (Chapter 7)

Magna Carta A statement of rights prepared by the nobles of England and presented to King John in response to abuses of power. Many of the concepts in this document influenced the framers of the Constitution. (Chapter 1)

English Bill of Rights A later statement of rights in response to abuses by the English king that also influenced the framers of the Constitution. (Chapter 1)

Court Syllabus When the Supreme Court issues an opinion, it also issues a short summary of the case, known as the Court Syllabus. (Chapter 1)

Living with the Constitution

Jaime Mendes, a junior at Smalltown High School was upset with a grade he received on an English essay dealing with the immigration policy of the United States. After receiving the low grade, Jaime posted the following article on Facebook: "A Small-Minded Teacher at Smalltown H.S. Avoid Mr. G's junior English class! He can't teach. He can't grade. And he won't tolerate any opinions that are different from his." Two days after this was posted, several students came to school wearing shirts with the slogan: Smalltown NOT Small-minded. The principal learned about Jaime's Facebook posting and ordered him to remove it. He refused and was suspended from school. Jaime believes his First Amendment rights were violated.

THE FIRST AMENDMENT IS THE most important Amendment. The First Amendment and the rights falling under the general heading of *freedom of expression*, form the foundation of American government. Freedom of expression includes speech, press, assembly, petition, and religion. These are the first freedoms, those essential for democracy. American citizens use these rights in the process of self-government. This chapter focuses on the first four of these rights. Freedom of religion is covered in the next chapter.

Background

THE FIRST AMENDMENT WAS DRAFTED as a direct reaction against the restrictions placed on English citizens. In England, until the late 1600s, all publications required a government license. At the same time, the law of **seditious libel** made it a crime to criticize the government of England. First Amendment rights were designed to guarantee that Americans would not live under such restraints.

A great deal of commentary is written on the intent of the Framers of the Constitution. In some instances their intent is clear. However, the intent of the Framers when it comes to the First Amendment is not at all clear. Many scholars agree that there is little in the history of the Constitution to clarify the intent of the drafters. For this reason, the Supreme Court cases often focus on other constitutional provisions when faced with freedom of expression questions.

In the 1920s, the Supreme Court began to seriously focus on the five rights encompassed in freedom of expression, beginning with the right to free speech. The Espionage Act of 1917 prohibited interference with the draft for the war. It also prohibited: "any disloyal, profane, scurrilous, or abusive language about the form of the government of the United States." In 1919, for the first time, the Supreme Court ruled on free speech issues. The Court held that the Espionage Act of 1917 was not a violation of the First Amendment. *Schenck v. United States*, 249 U.S. 47 (1919). In this case, Justice Holmes penned the famous expression: "The most stringent protection of free speech would not protect a man in falsely shouting fire in a theatre and causing a panic." The Court then pointed out that under some circumstances Congress has a right to regulate speech. Whether a regulation is constitutional depends on all the circumstances. The Espionage Act existed during a time of war and thus Congress had a greater interest in regulating the speech mentioned in the Act. At this point, the Supreme Court began a journey toward defining free speech and its limitations. By the late 1940s, the high court incorporated all five rights into the Fourteenth Amendment, thus making them applicable to the states.

Freedom of Speech

What Speech Is

Speech includes spoken words and other forms of expression. The Court divides speech into two categories: pure speech and speech-plus. *Pure speech* includes activities involving spoken words, such as debates. *Speech-plus* is a combination of action and speech, such as a demonstration. Both receive some constitutional protection.

Why Speech Is Protected

There are several theories as to why speech is protected. Each theory has merit but no one theory definitively answers the question: Why is speech protected?

🏛 **seditious libel**

Publishing something to stir up class hatred or contempt for the government. The First Amendment invalidated seditious libel laws in the United States.

Marketplace of Ideas: Justice Oliver Wendell Holmes was the first to use the marketplace of ideas metaphor. In his opinion, *truth* emerges from disagreement. Justice Holmes stated:

> The best test of truth is the power of the thought to get itself accepted in the competition of the market, and that truth is the only ground upon which their wishes safely can be carried out. That at any rate is the theory of our Constitution. It is an experiment, as all life is an experiment. *Abrams v. United States*, 250 U.S. 616, 630 (1919).

Political Speech: Political speech is a key part of American self-governance. American democracy is founded on free speech. This is the most highly protected form of speech.

Tolerance: The protection of speech promotes tolerance. If tolerance is the goal, then protection of distasteful speech is an act of tolerance.

Autonomy: Self-expression or autonomy is another theory as to why speech is protected. In *Procunier v. Martinez*, Justice Thurgood Marshall stated:

> The First Amendment serves not only the needs of the polity but also those of the human spirit—a spirit that demands self-expression. Such expression is an integral part of the development of ideas and a sense of identity. To suppress expression is to reject the basic human desire for recognition and affront the individual's worth and dignity. 416 U.S. 396, 427 (1974).

A flaw in the autonomy rationale is that some speech, for example hate speech, may damage the autonomy of others.

These theories run through the Supreme Court decisions involving freedom of expression. Clearly, the Court has not settled on any one theory to be used in all circumstances. Justice Brandeis, in 1927, said this:

> Those who won our independence believed that the final end of the State was to make men free to develop their faculties; and that in its government the deliberative forces should prevail over the arbitrary. They valued liberty both as an end and as a means. They believed liberty to be the secret of happiness and courage to be the secret of liberty. They believed that freedom to think as you will and to speak as you think are means indispensable to the discovery and spread of political truth; that without free speech and assembly discussion would be futile; that with them, discussion affords ordinarily adequate protection against the dissemination of noxious doctrine; that the greatest menace to freedom is an inert people; that public discussion is a political duty; and that this should be a fundamental principle of the American government. They recognized the risks to which all human institutions are subject. But they knew that order cannot be secured merely through fear of punishment for its infraction; that it is hazardous to discourage thought, hope and imagination; that fear breeds repression; that repression breeds hate; that hate menaces stable government; that the path of safety lies in the opportunity to discuss freely supposed grievances and proposed remedies; and that the fitting remedy for evil counsels is good ones. Believing in the power of reason as applied through public discussion, they eschewed silence coerced by law—the argument of force in its worst form. Recognizing the occasional tyrannies of governing majorities, they amended the Constitution so that free speech and assembly should be guaranteed. *Whitney v. California*, 274 U.S. 357, 375 (1927).

Symbolic Speech

Symbolic speech, also referred to as *expressive conduct*, is action that delivers a message, without using spoken language. Examples of symbolic speech are burning an American flag and burning a draft card.

In *Texas v. Johnson*, the Supreme Court held that the act of burning an American flag is protected by the First Amendment. Texas law prohibited the desecration of the U.S. flag. Specifically, the law prohibited this act of flag burning if it is done in such a way that the "actor knows it will seriously offend" other people. Defendant Johnson burned a flag outside of the 1984 Republican National Convention. His action was part of a large political demonstration. The Court held that "government may not prohibit the expression of an idea simply because society finds the idea itself offensive or disagreeable." An excerpt from the Court Syllabus follows.

Texas v. Johnson
491 U.S. 397 (1989)

Held: Johnson's conviction for flag desecration is inconsistent with the First Amendment.

(a) Under the circumstances, Johnson's burning of the flag constituted expressive conduct, permitting him to invoke the First Amendment. The State conceded that the conduct was expressive. Occurring as it did at the end of a demonstration coinciding with the Republican National Convention, the expressive, overtly political nature of the conduct was both intentional and overwhelmingly apparent.

(b) Texas has not asserted an interest in support of Johnson's conviction that is unrelated to the suppression of expression and would therefore permit application of the test set forth in *United States v. O'Brien*, 391 U.S. 367, whereby an important governmental interest in regulating nonspeech can justify incidental limitations on First Amendment freedoms when speech and nonspeech elements are combined in the same course of conduct. An interest in preventing breaches of the peace is not implicated on this record. Expression may not be prohibited on the basis that an audience that takes serious offense to the expression may disturb the peace, since the government cannot assume that every expression of a provocative idea will incite a riot but must look to the actual circumstances surrounding the expression. Johnson's expression of dissatisfaction with the Federal Government's policies also does not fall within the class of "fighting words" likely to be seen as a direct personal insult or an invitation to exchange fisticuffs. This Court's holding does not forbid a State to prevent "imminent lawless action" and, in fact, Texas has a law specifically prohibiting breaches of the peace. Texas' interest in preserving the flag as a symbol of nationhood and national unity is related to expression in this case and, thus, falls outside the *O'Brien* test.

(c) The latter interest does not justify Johnson's conviction. The restriction on Johnson's political expression is content based, since the Texas statute is not aimed at protecting the physical integrity of the flag in all circumstances, but is designed to protect it from intentional and knowing abuse that causes serious offense to others. It is therefore subject to "the most exacting scrutiny." *Boos v. Barry*, 485 U.S. 312. The government may not prohibit the verbal or nonverbal expression of an idea merely because society finds the idea offensive or disagreeable, even where our flag is involved. Nor may a State foster its own view of the flag by prohibiting expressive conduct relating to it, since the government may not permit designated symbols to be used to communicate a limited set of messages. Moreover, this Court will not create an exception to these principles protected by the First Amendment for the American flag alone.

Congress quickly reacted to the holding in *Texas v. Johnson* by passing the Flag Protection Act of 1989. This Act prohibited flag desecration whether or not bystanders were offended. One year later, the Court held that this Act also violates the First Amendment. The Court specifically found fault with the law because it punished any person "who knowingly mutilates, defaces, physically defiles . . . or tramples upon any flag." The Court held that this language banned disrespect for the flag, rather than physical desecration of it. The Court reasoned that the Act punished a person for the *reason* he or she burned the flag. This, according to the Court, is a violation of free speech. Careful review of Supreme Court cases reveals many instances where Congress reacts to a Supreme Court decision by passing an Act, only to have the Supreme Court find the Act unconstitutional at a future date.

In *United States v. O'Brien* (1968), the Court reached a different result in a case involving the burning of a draft card. Defendant O'Brien burned his draft card as a protest against the Vietnam War. Here the Court held that the law was constitutional because physical destruction of the card interfered with legitimate government purposes, specifically the power to raise an army. Interference with free speech rights was just incidental. Read a summary of the Court's reasoning below.

United States v. O'Brien
391 U.S. 367 (1968)

Held:

1. The 1965 Amendment to 50 U.S.C. App. §462(b)(3) is constitutional as applied in this case.
   (a) The 1965 Amendment plainly does not abridge free speech on its face.
   (b) When "speech" and "nonspeech" elements are combined in the same course of conduct, a sufficiently important governmental interest in regulating the nonspeech element can justify incidental limitations on First Amendment freedoms.
   (c) A governmental regulation is sufficiently justified if it is within the constitutional power of the Government and furthers an important or substantial governmental interest unrelated to the suppression of free expression, and if the incidental restriction on alleged First Amendment freedom is no greater than is essential to that interest. The 1965 Amendment meets all these requirements.
   (d) The 1965 Amendment came within Congress' "broad and sweeping" power to raise and support armies and make all laws necessary to that end.
   (e) The registration certificate serves purposes in addition to initial notification, e.g., it proves that the described individual has registered for the draft; facilitates communication between registrants and local boards; and provides a reminder that the registrant must notify his local board of changes in address or status. The regulatory scheme involving the certificates includes clearly valid prohibitions against alteration, forgery, or similar deceptive misuse.
   (f) The pre-existence of the non-possession regulation does not negate Congress' clear interest in providing alternative statutory avenues of prosecution to assure its interest in preventing destruction of the Selective Service certificates.
   (g) The governmental interests protected by the 1965 Amendment and the non-possession regulation, though overlapping, are not identical.
   (h) The 1965 Amendment is a narrow and precisely drawn provision which specifically protects the Government's substantial interest in an efficient and easily administered system for raising armies.
   (i) O'Brien was convicted only for the willful frustration of that governmental interest. The non-communicative impact of his conduct for which he was convicted makes his case readily distinguishable from *Stromberg v. California*, 283 U.S. 359 (1931).
2. The 1965 Amendment is constitutional as enacted.

Congress' purpose in enacting the law affords no basis for declaring an otherwise constitutional statute invalid. *McCray v. United States*, 195 U.S. 27 (1904).

Something to Consider
The Court reasoned that "a governmental regulation is sufficiently justified if it is within the constitutional power of the Government and furthers an important or substantial governmental interest unrelated to the suppression of free expression and if the incidental restriction on alleged First Amendment freedom is no greater than is essential to that interest." Do you agree?

A Point of Law

Texas v. Johnson, 491 U.S. 397 (1989)

United States v. O'Brien, 391 U.S. 367 (1968)

The First Amendment protects speech and nonspeech activities that are expressive conduct. However, this protection is not absolute and, where there is a sufficient government interest in regulating the nonspeech activity, an incidental restriction on freedom of speech is constitutional.

Courtesy of National Archives and Record Administration

Public Forum

The right to speak in a public forum is fundamental. A public forum may be a public park or a street. In one case, *Pruneyard Shopping Center v. Robins,* 447 U.S. 74 (1980), the Court also treated a privately owned shopping center as a public forum. In designated and traditional public forums, the government may regulate the "time, place, and manner" of speech. But it cannot bar the right of freedom of expression. Regulation of speech in a public forum must be "content neutral." There must be no discrimination based on the content of the speech. On the other hand, in two recent cases, the Supreme Court upheld the right of the government to limit expression on public (government) property. In *Pleasant Grove City, Utah v. Summum,* 555 U.S. 460 (2009), the Court held that a city had the right to refuse to place a privately donated religious monument on public property. In this case, the Court reasoned that by placing the monument on government property, the message of the monument would become a government message or government speech. The case syllabus explains: "Because city parks play an important role in defining the identity that a city projects to its residents and the outside world, cities take care in accepting donated monuments, selecting those that portray what the government decision makers view as appropriate for the place in question, based on esthetics, history, and local culture. The accepted monuments are meant to convey and have the effect of conveying a government message and thus constitute government speech."

In the second case, *Christian Legal Soc. Chapter of Univ. of Cal. Hastings College of Law v. Martinez,* 561 U.S.__(2010), the Court upheld the right of a public college to limit the use of various college facilities to college groups that did not violate the college's anti-discrimination policy. One group, Christian Legal Society, was bound by national bylaws regarding sexual orientation that violated the college policy. The group was therefore denied access to various college facilities and claimed its First and Fourteenth Amendment rights were violated. The Court disagreed, finding the regulation to be reasonable.

Compelling a Person to Speak

People have the right not to speak. In 1943, the Court upheld this right not to speak in *West Virginia State Bd. of Educ. v. Barnette.* The Court held that Jehovah's Witness children were wrongfully expelled from school when they refused to salute the flag, because compelling the children to recite the Pledge of Allegiance was a violation of their First and Fourteenth Amendment rights.

Political Campaign Finance Laws

The controversy over campaign finance laws rages on today. Two key issues are whether limitations can be placed on contributions to a political candidate and whether the political candidate can be limited in the amount he or she spends campaigning for office. There are strong arguments on both sides of these issues. In 1976, in *Buckley v. Valeo,* the Court held that "money is speech" in political campaigns, and, as such, it is protected by the First Amendment. In *Buckley,* the Court considered two aspects of the Federal Election Campaign Act of 1971. The Act limited political contributions to candidates for federal office and limited expenditures by political candidates. It also required that candidates keep extensive records and file regular statements disclosing the identity of contributors. The Court found that the limitation on contributions was constitutional but not the limitation on expenditures. The following is a summary of the Court's holding and reasoning.

⚖ Buckley v. Valeo
424 U.S. 1 (1976)

Held:

1. This litigation presents an Art. III "case or controversy," since the complaint discloses that at least some of the appellants have a sufficient "personal stake" in a determination of the constitutional validity of each of the challenged provisions to present "a real and substantial controversy admitting of specific relief through a decree of a conclusive character, as distinguished from an opinion advising what the law would be upon a hypothetical state of facts." *Aetna Life Ins. Co. v. Haworth,* 300 U.S. 227, 241.

2. The Act's contribution provisions are constitutional, but the expenditure provisions violate the First Amendment.
   (a) The contribution provisions, along with those covering disclosure, are appropriate legislative weapons against the reality or appearance of improper influence stemming from the dependence of candidates on large campaign contributions, and the ceilings imposed accordingly serve the basic governmental interest in safeguarding the integrity of the electoral process without directly impinging upon the rights of individual citizens

(continued)

(continued)

and candidates to engage in political debate and discussion.

(b) The First Amendment requires the invalidation of the Act's independent expenditure ceiling, its limitation on a candidate's expenditures from his own personal funds, and its ceilings on overall campaign expenditures, since those provisions place substantial and direct restrictions on the ability of candidates, citizens, and associations to engage in protected political expression, restrictions that the First Amendment cannot tolerate.

3. The Act's disclosure and recordkeeping provisions are constitutional.

(a) The general disclosure provisions, which serve substantial government interests in informing the electorate and preventing the corruption of the political process, are not overbroad insofar as they apply to contributions to minor parties and independent candidates. No blanket exemption for minor parties is warranted since such parties in order to prove injury as a result of application to them of the disclosure provisions need show only a reasonable probability that the compelled disclosure of a party's contributors' names will subject them to threats, harassment, or reprisals in violation of their First Amendment associational rights.

(b) The provision for disclosure by those who make independent contributions and expenditures, as narrowly construed to apply only (1) when they make contributions earmarked for political purposes or authorized or requested by a candidate or his agent to some person other than a candidate or political committee and (2) when they make an expenditure for a communication that expressly advocates the election or defeat of a clearly identified candidate is not unconstitutionally vague and does not constitute a prior restraint but is a reasonable and minimally restrictive method of furthering First Amendment values by public exposure of the federal election system.

(c) The extension of the recordkeeping provisions to contributions as small as those just above $10 and the disclosure provisions to contributions above $100 is not on this record overbroad since it cannot be said to be unrelated to the informational and enforcement goals of the legislation.

In 2003, Congress enacted the Bipartisan Campaign Reform Act of 2002 (BCRA). This Act prohibits national party committees and their agents from soliciting, receiving, directing, or spending any "soft money." It also prohibits corporations and unions from using general treasury funds for communications that are intended to, or have the effect of, influencing federal election outcomes. *Soft money* refers to contributions that are illegal if contributed in connection with a federal election, but are allowed if made to political parties in connection with state or local elections. Since 2003 the Supreme Court has decided several cases dealing with the constitutionality of various provisions of the Act as well as with other issues related to campaign finance. Some of the important decisions are as follows:

- In *McConnell v. Federal Election Commission*, 537 U.S. 1171 (2003), the Supreme Court, in a 5–4 decision, upheld the major provisions of the BCRA, finding no First Amendment violation. The Court found only a "marginal impact on political speech" because it determined that the law did not limit the total amount any political party could spend, but only the source of that money. In fact, the Court reasoned, the law tended to "increase the dissemination of information by forcing parties, candidates, and officeholders to solicit from a wider array of potential donors."

- In *Davenport v. Washington Educ. Ass'n*, 551 U.S. 177 (2007), the Court upheld a Washington state law that required public sector labor unions to receive authorization from nonunion members before spending their union fees for expenditures or contributions connected to attempts to influence elections.

- In *Ysursa v. Pcoatello Educ. Ass'n*, 555 U.S. 353 (2009), labor unions challenged an Idaho state law that permitted payroll deductions from a nonunion employee for union dues, but not for political activities of the union. The Court held that the law did not restrict political speech, and the First Amendment does not require the state to aid the political activities of unions.

- In *Citizens United v. Federal Election Com'n*, 558 U.S. ___ (2010), the Court reexamined its First Amendment jurisprudence and established that independent political speech of corporations and unions may not be barred. The Court reexamined provisions of the BCRA prohibiting corporations from funding public broadcasts or communications referring to clearly identified candidates within thirty days of a federal election. The Court found this provision violated the First Amendment. The Court overruled prior cases that held political speech of corporations could be restricted. The Court specifically overruled *McConnell* insofar as it was contrary to the decision in *Citizen's United*. The Court stated that "the Government may regulate corporate political speech through disclaimer and disclosure requirements, but it may not suppress that speech altogether."

The issue of campaign finance reform remains a controversial issue.

Obscenity

Obscenity is not protected by the First Amendment. In *Miller v. California*, 413 U.S. 15 (1973), the Court ruled that conduct or speech was obscene if it met all of these guidelines:

1. "whether the average person, applying contemporary community standards, would find that the work, taken as a whole, appeals to the **prurient interest**"
2. "whether the work depicts or describes, in a patently offensive way, sexual conduct specifically defined by the applicable state law" and
3. "whether the work, taken as a whole, lacks serious artistic, political, or scientific value."

prurient interest
A shameful or obsessive interest in immoral or sexual things. "Appealing to prurient interest" is one of many factors involved in deciding whether speech is obscene.

There is no national standard for obscenity. It is not surprising that community standards vary widely on this issue. It is important to remember that speech may be indecent and *not* be legally obscene. This distinction formed the basis of one of the reasons the Supreme Court found the Communications Decency Act of 1996 unconstitutional. The Communications Decency Act of 1996 was intended to protect minors from receiving objectionable material over the Internet. The language of the Act prohibited obscene or indecent material or material that depicted sexual activities in a patently offensive way. The Court found the terms *indecent* and *patently offensive* problematic and overbroad. The following summary is from *Reno v. American Civil Liberties Union*.

Reno v. American Civil Liberties Union
521 U.S. 844 (1997)

Two provisions of the Communications Decency Act of 1996 (CDA or Act) seek to protect minors from harmful material on the Internet, Title 47 U.S.C.A. §223(a)(1)(B)(ii) (Supp. 1997) criminalizes the "knowing" transmission of "obscene or indecent" messages to any recipient under 18 years of age. Section 223(d) prohibits the "knowing" sending or displaying to a person under 18 of any message "that, in context, depicts or describes, in terms patently offensive as measured by contemporary community standards, sexual or excretory activities or organs." A number of plaintiffs filed suit challenging the constitutionality of §§223(a)(1) and 223(d). After making extensive findings of fact, a three-judge District Court convened pursuant to the Act entered a preliminary injunction against enforcement of both challenged provisions. The court's judgment enjoins the Government from enforcing §223(a)(1)(B)'s

(continued)

(continued)

prohibitions insofar as they relate to "indecent" communications, but expressly preserves the Government's right to investigate and prosecute the obscenity or child pornography activities prohibited therein. The injunction against enforcement of §223(d) is unqualified because that section contains no separate reference to obscenity or child pornography. The Government appealed to this Court under the Act's special review provisions, arguing that the District Court erred in holding that the CDA violated both the First Amendment because it is overbroad and the Fifth Amendment because it is vague.

Held:

The CDA's "indecent transmission" and "patently offensive display" provisions abridge "the freedom of speech" protected by the First Amendment.

(a) Although the CDA's vagueness is relevant to the First Amendment overbreadth inquiry, the judgment should be affirmed without reaching the Fifth Amendment issue.

(b) A close look at the precedents relied on by the Government—*Ginsberg v. New York*, 390 U.S. 629, 20 L. Ed. 2d 195, 88 S. Ct. 1274; *FCC v. Pacifica Foundation*, 438 U.S. 726, 57 L. Ed. 2d 1073, 98 S. Ct. 3026; *and Renton v. Playtime Theatres, Inc.*, 475 U.S. 41, 89 L. Ed. 2d 29, 106 S. Ct. 925—raises, rather than relieves, doubts about the CDA's constitutionality. The CDA differs from the various laws and orders upheld in those cases in many ways, including that it does not allow parents to consent to their children's use of restricted materials; is not limited to commercial transactions; fails to provide any definition of "indecent" and omits any requirement that "patently offensive" material lack socially redeeming value; neither limits its broad categorical prohibitions to particular times nor bases them on an evaluation by an agency familiar with the medium's unique characteristics; is punitive; applies to a medium that, unlike radio, receives full First Amendment protection; and cannot be properly analyzed as a form of time, place, and manner regulation because it is a content-based blanket restriction on speech. These precedents, then, do not require the Court to uphold the CDA and are fully consistent with the application of the most stringent review of its provisions.

(c) The special factors recognized in some of the Court's cases as justifying regulation of the broadcast media—the history of extensive government regulation of broadcasting, the scarcity of available frequencies at its inception, and its "invasive" nature, are not present in cyberspace.

(d) Regardless of whether the CDA is so vague that it violates the Fifth Amendment, the many ambiguities concerning the scope of its coverage render it problematic for First Amendment purposes. For instance, its use of the undefined terms "indecent" and "patently offensive" will provoke uncertainty among speakers about how the two standards relate to each other and just what they mean. The vagueness of such a content-based regulation, coupled with its increased deterrent effect as a criminal statute, raise special First Amendment concerns because of its obvious chilling effect on free speech. Contrary to the Government's argument, the CDA is not saved from vagueness by the fact that its "patently offensive" standard repeats the second part of the three-prong obscenity test set forth in *Miller v. California*, 413 U.S. 15, 24, 37 L. Ed. 2d 419, 93 S. Ct. 2607. The second *Miller* prong reduces the inherent vagueness of its own "patently offensive" term by requiring that the proscribed material be "specifically defined by the applicable state law." Each of *Miller*'s other two prongs also critically limits the uncertain sweep of the obscenity definition. Just because a definition including three limitations is not vague, it does not follow that one of those limitations, standing alone, is not vague. The CDA's vagueness undermines the likelihood that it has been carefully tailored to the congressional goal of protecting minors from potentially harmful materials.

(e) The CDA lacks the precision that the First Amendment requires when a statute regulates the content of speech. Although the Government has an interest in protecting children from potentially harmful materials, *see, e.g., Ginsberg*, 390 U.S. at 639, the CDA pursues that interest by suppressing a large amount of speech that adults have a constitutional right to send and receive, *see, e.g., Sable*, at 126. Its breadth is wholly unprecedented. The CDA's burden on adult speech is unacceptable if less restrictive alternatives would be at least as effective in achieving the Act's legitimate purposes. *See, e.g., Sable*, 492 U.S. at 126. The Government has not proved otherwise. On the other hand, the District Court found that currently available user-based software suggests that

(continued)

(continued)

a reasonably effective method by which parents can prevent their children from accessing material which the parents believe is inappropriate will soon be widely available. Moreover, the arguments in this Court referred to possible alternatives such as requiring that indecent material be "tagged" to facilitate parental control, making exceptions for messages with artistic or educational value, providing some tolerance for parental choice, and regulating some portions of the Internet differently than others. Particularly in the light of the absence of any detailed congressional findings, or even hearings addressing the CDA's special problems, the Court is persuaded that the CDA is not narrowly tailored.

(f) The Government's argument that its "significant" interest in fostering the Internet's growth provides an independent basis for upholding the CDA's constitutionality is singularly unpersuasive. The dramatic expansion of this new forum contradicts the factual basis underlying this contention: that the unregulated availability of "indecent" and "patently offensive" material is driving people away from the Internet.

Something to Consider

Explain why the Court held that the "indecent transmission" and "patently offensive display" provisions of the Communications Decency Act of 1996 abridge the freedom of speech protected by the First Amendment. Do you agree with the Court? Why or why not?

In 2002, the Child Pornography Prevention Act of 1996 was also struck down by the high Court. This Act prohibited virtual child pornography as well as pornography involving actual minors. Furthermore, the Act prohibited any depictions that appeared to be minors engaged in sexually explicit conduct. The Court held the law ignored the *Miller* standard of obscenity and was too broad. A summary of *Ashcroft v. Free Speech Coalition* follows here.

Ashcroft v. Free Speech Coalition

535 U.S. 234 (2002)

The Child Pornography Prevention Act of 1996 (CPPA) expands the federal prohibition on child pornography to include not only pornographic images made using actual children, 18 U.S.C. §2256(8)(A), but also "any visual depiction, including any photograph, film, video, picture, or computer or computer-generated image or picture" that "is, or appears to be, of a minor engaging in sexually explicit conduct," §2256(8)(B), and any sexually explicit image that is "advertised, promoted, presented, described, or distributed in such a manner that conveys the impression" it depicts "a minor engaging in sexually explicit conduct," §2256(8)(D). Thus, §2256(8)(B) bans a range of sexually explicit images, sometimes called "virtual child pornography," that appear to depict minors but were produced by means other than using real children, such as through the use of youthful-looking adults or computer-imaging technology. Section 2256(8)(D) is aimed at preventing the production or distribution of pornographic material pandered as child pornography. Fearing that the CPPA threatened their activities, respondents, an adult-entertainment trade association and others, filed this suit alleging that the "appears to be" and "conveys the impression" provisions are overbroad and vague, chilling production of works protected by the First Amendment. The District Court disagreed and granted the Government summary judgment, but the Ninth Circuit reversed. Generally, pornography can be banned only if it is obscene under *Miller v. California*, 413 U.S. 15, 37 L. Ed. 2d 419, 93 S. Ct. 2607, but pornography depicting actual children can be proscribed whether or not the images are obscene because of the State's interest in protecting the children exploited by the production

(continued)

(continued)

process, *New York v. Ferber*, 458 U.S. 747, 758, 73 L. Ed. 2d 1113, 102 S. Ct. 3348, and in prosecuting those who promote such sexual exploitation, *id.* at 761. The Ninth Circuit held the CPPA invalid on its face, finding it to be substantially overbroad because it bans materials that are neither obscene under *Miller* nor produced by the exploitation of real children as in *Ferber*.

Held:

The prohibitions of §§2256(8)(B) and 2256(8)(D) are overbroad and unconstitutional.

(a) Section 2256(8)(B) covers materials beyond the categories recognized in *Ferber* and *Miller*, and the reasons the Government offers in support of limiting the freedom of speech have no justification in this Court's precedents or First Amendment law.

(1) The CPPA is inconsistent with *Miller*. It extends to images that are not obscene under the *Miller* standard, which requires the Government to prove that the work in question, taken as a whole, appeals to the prurient interest, is patently offensive in light of community standards, and lacks serious literary, artistic, political, or scientific value, 413 U.S. at 24. Materials need not appeal to the prurient interest under the CPPA, which proscribes any depiction of sexually explicit activity, no matter how it is presented. It is not necessary, moreover, that the image be patently offensive. Pictures of what appear to be 17-year-olds engaging in sexually explicit activity do not in every case contravene community standards. The CPPA also prohibits speech having serious redeeming value, proscribing the visual depiction of an idea—that of teenagers engaging in sexual activity—that is a fact of modern society and has been a theme in art and literature for centuries. A number of acclaimed movies, filmed without any child actors, explore themes within the wide sweep of the statute's prohibitions. If those movies contain a single graphic depiction of sexual activity within the statutory definition, their possessor would be subject to severe punishment without inquiry into the literary value of the work. This is inconsistent with an essential First Amendment rule: A work's artistic merit does not depend on the presence of a single explicit scene. *See, e.g., Book Named "John Cleland's Memoirs of a Woman of Pleasure" v. Attorney General of Mass.*, 383 U.S. 413, 419, 16 L. Ed. 2d 1, 86 S. Ct. 975. Under *Miller*, redeeming value is judged by considering the work as a whole. Where the scene is part of the narrative, the work itself does not for this reason become obscene, even though the scene in isolation might be offensive. *See Kois v. Wisconsin*, 408 U.S. 229, 231, 33 L. Ed. 2d 312, 92 S. Ct. 2245 (per curiam). The CPPA cannot be read to prohibit obscenity, because it lacks the required link between its prohibitions and the affront to community standards prohibited by the obscenity definition.

(2) While the Government asserts that the images can lead to actual instances of child abuse, the causal link is contingent and indirect. The harm does not necessarily follow from the speech, but depends upon some unquantified potential for subsequent criminal acts.

(3) The Court rejects other arguments offered by the Government to justify the CPPA's prohibitions. The contention that the CPPA is necessary because pedophiles may use virtual child pornography to seduce children runs afoul of the principle that speech within the rights of adults to hear may not be silenced completely in an attempt to shield children from it. That the evil in question depends upon the actor's unlawful conduct, defined as criminal quite apart from any link to the speech in question, establishes that the speech ban is not narrowly drawn. The argument that virtual child pornography whets pedophiles' appetites and encourages them to engage in illegal conduct is unavailing because the mere tendency of speech to encourage unlawful acts is not a sufficient reason for banning it, *Stanley v. Georgia*, 394 U.S. 557, 566, 22 L. Ed. 2d 542, 89 S. Ct. 1243, absent some showing of a direct connection between the speech and imminent illegal conduct, *see, e.g., Brandenburg v. Ohio*, 395 U.S. 444, 447, 23 L. Ed. 2d 430, 89 S. Ct. 1827 (per curiam). The overbreadth doctrine prohibits the Government from banning unprotected speech if a substantial amount of protected speech is prohibited or chilled in the process. *See Broadrick v. Oklahoma*, 413 U.S. 601, 612, 37 L. Ed. 2d 830, 93 S. Ct. 2908.

(b) Section 2256(8)(D) is also substantially overbroad. The Court disagrees with the Government's view that the only difference between that provision and §2256(8)(B)'s "appears to be" provision is that §2256(8)(D) requires the jury to assess the material at issue in light of the manner in which it is promoted, but that the determination would still depend principally upon the prohibited work's content. The "conveys the impression" provision requires little

(continued)

(continued)

judgment about the image's content; the work must be sexually explicit, but otherwise the content is irrelevant. Even if a film contains no sexually explicit scenes involving minors, it could be treated as child pornography if the title and trailers convey the impression that such scenes will be found in the movie. The determination turns on how the speech is presented, not on what is depicted. The CPPA does more than prohibit pandering. It bans possession of material pandered as child pornography by someone earlier in the distribution chain, as well as a sexually explicit film that contains no youthful actors but has been packaged to suggest a prohibited movie. Possession is a crime even when the possessor knows the movie was mislabeled. The First Amendment requires a more precise restriction.

....

Something to Consider

Is the Child Pornography Prevention Act of 1996 inconsistent with *Miller v. California*? Explain.

In 2008, in *United States v. Williams*, 553 U.S. 285, the Court held that the Prosecutorial Remedies and Other Tools to End the Exploitation of Children Today Act did not violate the First Amendment. This Act criminalized the solicitation or pandering of child pornography. *Williams* was distinguished from *Ashcroft v. Free Speech Coalition*. As you read the case summary below, notice *how* the case was distinguished from *Free Speech Coalition*.

United States v. Williams

553 U.S. 285 (2008)

Syllabus:

After this Court found facially overbroad a federal statutory provision criminalizing the possession and distribution of material pandered as child pornography, regardless of whether it actually was that, *Ashcroft v. Free Speech Coalition*, 535 U.S. 234, Congress passed the pandering and solicitation provision at issue, 18 U.S.C. § 2252A(a)(3)(B). Respondent Williams pleaded guilty to this offense and others, but reserved the right to challenge his pandering conviction's constitutionality. The District Court rejected his challenge, but the Eleventh Circuit reversed, finding the statute both overbroad under the First Amendment and impermissibly vague under the Due Process Clause. The Supreme Court disagreed.

Held:

1. Section 2252A(a)(3)(B) is not overbroad under the First Amendment.

    (a) A statute is facially invalid if it prohibits a substantial amount of protected speech. Section 2252A(a)(3)(B) generally prohibits offers to provide and requests to obtain child pornography. It targets not the underlying material, but the collateral speech introducing such material into the child-pornography distribution network. Its definition of material or purported material that may not be pandered or solicited precisely tracks the material held constitutionally proscribable in *New York v. Ferber*, 458 U.S. 747 and *Miller v. California*, 413 U.S. 15: obscene material depicting (actual or virtual) children engaged in sexually explicit conduct, and any other material depicting actual children engaged in sexually explicit conduct. The statute's important features include: (1) a scienter requirement; (2) operative verbs that are reasonably read to penalize speech that accompanies or seeks to induce a child pornography transfer from one person to another; (3) a phrase "in a manner that reflects the belief," *ibid.*—that has both the subjective component that the defendant must actually have held the "belief" that the material or purported material was child pornography, and the objective component that the statement or action must manifest that belief; (4) a phrase—"in a manner . . . that

(continued)

(continued)

is intended to cause another to believe," ibid.—that has only the subjective element that the defendant must "intend" that the listener believe the material to be child pornography; and (5) a "sexually explicit conduct" definition that is very similar to that in the New York statute upheld in *Ferber*.

(b) As thus construed, the statute does not criminalize a substantial amount of protected expressive activity. Offers to engage in illegal transactions are categorically excluded from First Amendment protection. *E.g., Pittsburgh Press Co. v. Pittsburgh Comm'n on Human Relations*, 413 U.S. 376, 388. The Eleventh Circuit mistakenly believed that this exclusion extended only to commercial offers to provide or receive contraband. The exclusion's rationale, however, is based not on the less privileged status of commercial speech, but on the principle that offers to give or receive what it is unlawful to possess have no social value and thus enjoy no First Amendment protection. The constitutional defect in *Free Speech Coalition's* pandering provision was that it went beyond pandering to prohibit possessing material that could not otherwise be proscribed. The Eleventh Circuit's erroneous conclusion led it to apply strict scrutiny to § 2252A(a)(3)(B), lodging three fatal objections that lack merit.

2. Section 2252A(a)(3)(B) is not impermissibly vague under the Due Process Clause. A conviction fails to comport with due process if the statute under which it is obtained fails to provide a person of ordinary intelligence fair notice of what is prohibited, or is so standardless that it authorizes or encourages seriously discriminatory enforcement. *Hill v. Colorado*, 530 U.S. 703, 732. In the First Amendment context plaintiffs may argue that a statute is overbroad because it is unclear whether it regulates a substantial amount of protected speech. *Hoffman Estates v. Flipside, Hoffman Estates, Inc.*, 455 U.S. 489, 494-495. The Eleventh Circuit mistakenly believed that "in a manner that reflects the belief" and "in a manner . . . that is intended to cause another to believe" were vague and standardless phrases that left the public with no objective measure of conformance. What renders a statute vague, however, is not the possibility that it will sometimes be difficult to determine whether the incriminating fact it establishes has been proved; but rather the indeterminacy of what that fact is. *See, e.g., Coates v. Cincinnati*, 402 U.S. 611, 614. There is no such indeterminacy here. The statute's requirements are clear questions of fact. It may be difficult in some cases to determine whether the requirements have been met, but courts and juries every day pass upon the reasonable import of a defendant's statements and upon "knowledge, belief and intent." *American Communications Ass'n v. Douds*, 339 U.S. 382, 411.

444 F.3d 1286, reversed.

A Point of Law

Miller v. California, 413 U.S. 15 (1973)

Reno v. American Civil Liberties Union, 521 U.S. 844 (1997)

Ashcroft v. Free Speech Coalition, 535 U.S. 234 (2002)

United States v. Williams, 553 U.S. 285 (2008)

Laws prohibiting obscenity are constitutional but such laws must be specifically limited to obscene material. Laws that are overbroad and include material not defined as obscene are unconstitutional even if such material is indecent or offensive.

🏛 **defamation**

Transmission to others of false statements that harm the reputation, business, or property rights of a person.

Defamation

Defamation is not protected under the First Amendment, unless the person defamed is a public official or public figure or unless the defamatory statements relate to matters of public concern. In these situations, the First Amendment provides *limited* protection. To defame a person is to

libel

Written defamation. Publicly communicated, false written statements that injure a person's reputation, business, or property rights. To libel certain public figures, the written statement must also be made with at least a "reckless disregard" for whether the statement is true or false.

injure the reputation of another person by spreading falsehoods. Defamation takes two forms. Defamation using written or recorded words is **libel**. Defamation using spoken words is **slander**. If the statements are true, a person cannot prove defamation. The Court has struggled with balancing the rights of a person not to have his or her reputation injured against the right of free speech and free press. Because of this, in defamation cases involving public figures or public officials, the Court crafted special rules that provide limited First Amendment protections.

If a public figure or public official is defamed, it is difficult for that person to recover damages in a defamation lawsuit. A public figure or public official usually has some access to the media to reply or rebut the defamatory statement. This access is generally not available to private persons. The rules applied in cases involving the defamation of a public person, relating to their performance of public duties are set out in *New York Times Co. v. Sullivan*, 376 U.S. 254 (1964).

New York Times Co. v. Sullivan
376 U.S. 254 (1964)

Respondent, an elected official in Montgomery, Alabama, brought suit in a state court alleging that he had been libeled by an advertisement in corporate petitioner's newspaper, the text of which appeared over the names of the four individual petitioners and many others. The advertisement included statements, some of which were false, about police action allegedly directed against students who participated in a civil rights demonstration and against a leader of the Civil Rights Movement; respondent claimed the statements referred to him because his duties included supervision of the police department. The trial judge instructed the jury that such statements were "libelous per se," legal injury being implied without proof of actual damages, and that for the purpose of compensatory damages malice was presumed, so that such damages could be awarded against petitioners if the statements were found to have been published by them and to have related to respondent. As to punitive damages, the judge instructed that mere negligence was not evidence of actual malice and would not justify an award of punitive damages; he refused to instruct that actual intent to harm or recklessness had to be found before punitive damages could be awarded, or that a verdict for respondent should differentiate between compensatory and punitive damages. The jury found for respondent and the State Supreme Court affirmed.

Held: A State cannot under the First and Fourteenth Amendments award damages to a public official for defamatory falsehood relating to his official conduct unless he proves "actual malice"—that the statement was made with knowledge of its falsity or with reckless disregard of whether it was true or false.

(a) Application by state courts of a rule of law, whether statutory or not, to award a judgment in a civil action, is "state action" under the Fourteenth Amendment.

(b) Expression does not lose constitutional protection to which it would otherwise be entitled because it appears in the form of a paid advertisement.

(c) Factual error, content defamatory of official reputation, or both, are insufficient to warrant an award of damages for false statements unless "actual malice"— knowledge that statements are false or in reckless disregard of the truth— is alleged and proved.

(d) State court judgment entered upon a general verdict which does not differentiate between punitive damages, as to which under state law actual malice must be proved, and general damages, as to which it is "presumed," precludes any determination as to the basis of the verdict and requires reversal, where presumption of malice is inconsistent with federal constitutional requirements.

(e) The evidence was constitutionally insufficient to support the judgment for respondent, since it failed to support a finding that the statements were made with actual malice or that they related to respondent.

....

Something to Consider

Using *New York Times Co. v. Sullivan*, what are the rules to be applied in defamation cases involving public officials relating to the performance of their public duties?

slander

Spoken defamation. The speaking of false words that injure another person's reputation, business, or property rights.

Three years after *New York Times*, the Court extended the *New York Times* rules to defamatory statements involving a public figure. *Curtis Pub. Co. v. Butts*, 388 U.S. 130 (1967), and *Associated Press v. Walker*, 389 U.S. 889 (1967). In *Butts*, the Court found that the athletic director of the University of Georgia, a nationally known former coach, was a public figure and the *New York Times* rules applied. In *Walker*, a nationally known military general was found to be a public figure.

A Point of Law

New York Times Co. v. Sullivan, 376 U.S. 254 (1964)

Curtis Pub. Co. v. Butts, 388 U.S. 130 (1967)

Associated Press v. Walker, 389 U.S. 889 (1967)

A state cannot award money damages for defamation of a public figure or public officer unless actual malice is shown. Actual malice is knowledge of the falsehood or a reckless disregard of the truth. Included in public figures or officers are government officials, athletic directors who are nationally known, and military generals.

PRIVATE PERSON AS PLAINTIFF AND MATTERS OF PUBLIC CONCERN

In 1974, in *Gertz v. Robert Welch, Inc.*, the Court refused to extend the *New York Times* rule to a libel action brought by private persons, even though a matter of public concern was involved. In *Gertz*, the Court said that a person who was neither a public official nor a public person need not prove that defamatory statements were published with knowledge of their falsity or in reckless disregard of the truth. However, an award of punitive damages by private parties did require such proof.

Gertz v. Robert Welch, Inc.

418 U.S. 323 (1974)

A Chicago policeman named Nuccio was convicted of murder. The victim's family retained petitioner, a reputable attorney, to represent them in civil litigation against Nuccio. An article appearing in respondent's magazine alleged that Nuccio's murder trial was part of a Communist conspiracy to discredit the local police, and it falsely stated that petitioner had arranged Nuccio's "frame-up," implied that petitioner had a criminal record, and labeled him a "Communist-fronter." Petitioner brought this diversity libel action against respondent. After the jury returned a verdict for petitioner, the District Court decided

that the standard enunciated in *New York Times Co. v. Sullivan*, 376 U.S. 254, which bars media liability for defamation of a public official absent proof that the defamatory statements were published with knowledge of their falsity or in reckless disregard of the truth, should apply to this suit. The court concluded that that standard protects media discussion of a public issue without regard to whether the person defamed is a public official as in *New York Times Co. v. Sullivan*, or a public figure, as in *Curtis Publishing Co. v. Butts*, 388 U.S. 130. The court found that petitioner had failed to prove knowledge of

(continued)

(continued)

falsity or reckless disregard for the truth and therefore entered judgment n.o.v. for respondent. The Court of Appeals affirmed.

Held:

1. A publisher or broadcaster of defamatory falsehoods about an individual who is neither a public official nor a public figure may not claim the *New York Times* protection against liability for defamation on the ground that the defamatory statements concern an issue of public or general interest.

   (a) Because private individuals characteristically have less effective opportunities for rebuttal than do public officials and public figures, they are more vulnerable to injury from defamation. Because they have not voluntarily exposed themselves to increased risk of injury from defamatory falsehoods, they are also more deserving of recovery. The state interest in compensating injury to the reputation of private individuals is therefore greater than for public officials and public figures.

   (b) To extend the *New York Times* standard to media defamation of private persons whenever an issue of general or public interest is involved would abridge to an unacceptable degree the legitimate state interest in compensating private individuals for injury to reputation and would occasion the additional difficulty of forcing courts to decide on an ad hoc basis which publications and broadcasts address issues of general or public interest and which do not.

   (c) So long as they do not impose liability without fault, the States may define for themselves the appropriate standard of liability for a publisher or broadcaster of defamatory falsehood which injures a private individual and whose substance makes substantial danger to reputation apparent.

2. The States, however, may not permit recovery of presumed or punitive damages when liability is not based on knowledge of falsity or reckless disregard for the truth, and the private defamation plaintiff who establishes liability under a less demanding standard than the *New York Times* test may recover compensation only for actual injury.

3. Petitioner was neither a public official nor a public figure.

   (a) Neither petitioner's past service on certain city committees nor his appearance as an attorney at the coroner's inquest into the death of the murder victim made him a public official.

   (b) Petitioner was also not a public figure. Absent clear evidence of general fame or notoriety in the community and pervasive involvement in ordering the affairs of society, an individual should not be deemed a public figure for all aspects of his life. Rather, the public-figure question should be determined by reference to the individual's participation in the particular controversy giving rise to the defamation. Petitioner's role in the Nuccio affair did not make him a public figure.

PRIVATE PERSONS AS PLAINTIFF AND MATTERS NOT INVOLVING PUBLIC CONCERN

In *Dun & Bradstreet v. Greenmoss Builders*, 472 U.S. 749 (1985), the Court again considered the issue of punitive damages in defamation cases involving private persons. *Gertz* was distinguished from this case because the defamatory statement in *Dun & Bradstreet* did not involve public concerns. *Dun & Bradstreet* involved a case where the petitioner credit reporting agency sent out a report to five subscribers stating that respondent, a construction company, had filed for bankruptcy. The report was false and contained gross misrepresentations as to respondent's assets and liabilities. At trial, an issue arose regarding punitive damages and whether *Gertz* applied to the case. The Supreme Court ultimately decided that since the case did not involve public officials or figures and since the matter was entirely private and not of general interest, punitive damages did not require a showing of actual malice. Table 11-1 summarizes defamation issues and protections under the First Amendment.

Table 11-1 Defamation and the First Amendment

Parties Defamed	First Amendment Protections	Cases
Public Official	Any damages for defamation require actual malice, that is, proof that the statement was made with knowledge of its falsity or with reckless disregard of whether it was true or false	*New York Times Co. v. Sullivan*, 376 U.S. 254 (1964)
Public Figure	Same as public official	*Curtis Pub. Co. v. Butts*, 388 U.S. 130 (1967) and *Associated Press v. Walker*, 389 U.S. 889 (1967)
Private Party but defamatory statements involve matters of public concern	No special First Amendment protection for actual damages; punitive damages require actual malice, that is, proof that the statement was made with knowledge of its falsity or with reckless disregard of whether it was true or false	*Gertz v. Robert Welch, Inc.*, 418 U.S. 323 (1974)
Private Party and defamatory statements are private matters	No special First Amendment protection for actual or punitive damages	*Dun & Bradstreet v. Greenmoss Builders*, 472 U.S. 749 (1985)

© Cengage Learning 2013

Something to Consider

Further reading in this area:

Hustler Magazine v. Falwell, 485 U.S. 46 (1988): Public figures cannot recover for intentional infliction of emotional distress unless they can prove the false statement was made with actual malice.

Time, Inc. v. Firestone, 424 U.S. 448 (1976): For First Amendment purposes, not all newsworthy persons are public figures.

Fighting Words

Fighting words are not protected under the First Amendment. Fighting words are insulting and abusive language/words directed face-to-face to a specific person that are likely to result in violence. In the case of *Chaplinsky v. New Hampshire*, the Supreme Court discusses the relationship between the First Amendment and fighting words.

Chaplinsky v. New Hampshire
315 U.S. 568 (1942)

MR. JUSTICE MURPHY delivered the opinion of the Court.

Appellant, a member of the sect known as Jehovah's Witnesses, was convicted in the municipal court of Rochester, New Hampshire, for violation of the Public Laws of New Hampshire:

"No person shall address any offensive, derisive or annoying word to any other person who is lawfully in any street or other public place, nor call him by any offensive or derisive name, nor make any noise or exclamation in his presence and hearing with intent to deride,

(continued)

(continued)

offend or annoy him, or to prevent him from pursuing his lawful business or occupation."

The complaint charged that appellant, "with force and arms, in a certain public place in said city of Rochester, to wit, on the public sidewalk on the easterly side of Wakefield Street, near unto the entrance of the City Hall, did unlawfully repeat, the words following, addressed to the complainant, that is to say, 'You are a God damned racketeer' and 'a damned Fascist and the whole government of Rochester are Fascists or agents of Fascists,' the same being offensive, derisive and annoying words and names."

There is no substantial dispute over the facts. Chaplinsky was distributing the literature of his sect on the streets of Rochester on a busy Saturday afternoon. Members of the local citizenry complained to the City Marshal, Bowering, that Chaplinsky was denouncing all religion as a "racket." Bowering told them that Chaplinsky was lawfully engaged, and then warned Chaplinsky that the crowd was getting restless. Some time later, a disturbance occurred and the traffic officer on duty at the busy intersection started with Chaplinsky for the police station, but did not inform him that he was under arrest or that he was going to be arrested. On the way, they encountered Marshal Bowering, who had been advised that a riot was under way and was therefore hurrying to the scene. Bowering repeated his earlier warning to Chaplinsky, who then addressed to Bowering the words set forth in the complaint.

Chaplinsky's version of the affair was slightly different. He testified that, when he met Bowering, he asked him to arrest the ones responsible for the disturbance. In reply, Bowering cursed him and told him to come along. Appellant admitted that he said the words charged in the complaint, with the exception of the name of the Deity.

Over appellant's objection the trial court excluded, as immaterial, testimony relating to appellant's mission "to preach the true facts of the Bible," his treatment at the hands of the crowd, and the alleged neglect of duty on the part of the police. This action was approved by the court below, which held that neither provocation nor the truth of the utterance would constitute a defense to the charge.

It is now clear that "Freedom of speech and freedom of the press, which are protected by the First Amendment from infringement by Congress, are among the fundamental personal rights and liberties which are protected by the Fourteenth Amendment from invasion by state action." *Lovell v. Griffin*, 303 U.S. 444, 450. Freedom of

worship is similarly sheltered. *Cantwell v. Connecticut*, 310 U.S. 296, 303.

Appellant assails the statute as a violation of all three freedoms, speech, press and worship, but only an attack on the basis of free speech is warranted. The spoken, not the written, word is involved. And we cannot conceive that cursing a public officer is the exercise of religion in any sense of the term. But even if the activities of the appellant which preceded the incident could be viewed as religious in character, and therefore entitled to the protection of the Fourteenth Amendment, they would not cloak him with immunity from the legal consequences for concomitant acts committed in violation of a valid criminal statute.

We turn, therefore, to an examination of the statute itself.

Allowing the broadest scope to the language and purpose of the Fourteenth Amendment, it is well understood that the right of free speech is not absolute at all times and under all circumstances. There are certain well-defined and narrowly limited classes of speech, the prevention and punishment of which have never been thought to raise any Constitutional problem. These include the lewd and obscene, the profane, the libelous, and the insulting or "fighting" words—those which by their very utterance inflict injury or tend to incite an immediate breach of the peace. It has been well observed that such utterances are no essential part of any exposition of ideas, and are of such slight social value as a step to truth that any benefit that may be derived from them is clearly outweighed by the social interest in order and morality. "Resort to epithets or personal abuse is not in any proper sense communication of information or opinion safeguarded by the Constitution, and its punishment as a criminal act would raise no question under that instrument." *Cantwell v. Connecticut*, 310 U.S. 296, 309–310.

The state statute here challenged comes to us authoritatively construed by the highest court of New Hampshire. It has two provisions—the first relates to words or names addressed to another in a public place; the second refers to noises and exclamations. The court said: "The two provisions are distinct. One may stand separately from the other. Assuming, without holding, that the second were unconstitutional, the first could stand if constitutional." We accept that construction of severability and limit our consideration to the first provision of the statute.

(continued)

(continued)

On the authority of its earlier decisions, the state court declared that the statute's purpose was to preserve the public peace, no words being "forbidden except such as have a direct tendency to cause acts of violence by the persons to whom, individually, the remark is addressed." It was further said: "The word 'offensive' is not to be defined in terms of what a particular addressee thinks . . . . The test is what men of common intelligence would understand would be words likely to cause an average addressee to fight . . . . The English language has a number of words and expressions which by general consent are 'fighting words' when said without a disarming smile . . . . Such words, as ordinary men know, are likely to cause a fight. So are threatening, profane or obscene revilings. Derisive and annoying words can be taken as coming within the purview of the statute as heretofore interpreted only when they have this characteristic of plainly tending to excite the addressee to a breach of the peace . . . . The statute, as construed, does no more than prohibit the face-to-face words plainly likely to cause a breach of the peace by the addressee, words whose speaking constitutes a breach of the peace by the speaker—including 'classical fighting words', words in current use less 'classical' but equally likely to cause violence, and other disorderly words, including profanity, obscenity and threats."

We are unable to say that the limited scope of the statute as thus construed contravenes the Constitutional right of free expression. It is a statute narrowly drawn and limited to define and punish specific conduct lying within the domain of state power, the use in a public place of words likely to cause a breach of the peace. *Cf. Cantwell v. Connecticut*, 310 U.S. 296, 311; *Thornhill v. Alabama*, 310 U.S. 88, 105. This conclusion necessarily disposes of appellant's contention that the statute is so vague and indefinite as to render a conviction thereunder a violation of due process. A statute punishing verbal acts, carefully drawn so as not unduly to impair liberty of expression, is not too vague for a criminal law. *Cf. Fox v. Washington*, 236 U.S. 273, 277.

Nor can we say that the application of the statute to the facts disclosed by the record substantially or unreasonably impinges upon the privilege of free speech. Argument is unnecessary to demonstrate that the appellations "damned racketeer" and "damned Fascist" are epithets likely to provoke the average person to retaliation, and thereby cause a breach of the peace.

The refusal of the state court to admit evidence of provocation and evidence bearing on the truth or falsity of the utterances, is open to no Constitutional objection. Whether the facts sought to be proved by such evidence constitute a defense to the charge, or may be shown in mitigation, are questions for the state court to determine. Our function is fulfilled by a determination that the challenged statute, on its face and as applied, does not contravene the Fourteenth Amendment.

Affirmed.

Something to Consider

Does this case have any applicability today in light of current language practices?

Hate Speech

Hate speech is a somewhat new classification of speech. Hate speech is derogatory language about race, gender, religion, or sexual orientation. This often involves ethnic and racial slurs. Some cities and educational institutions have enacted hate speech codes of conduct. These codes prohibit derogatory comments based on race, gender, religion, or sexual orientation. The Court is carefully building a body of case law decisions designed to address the serious issues involving hate speech and the First Amendment.

One of the most abhorrent expressions of hate is the practice of cross burning, a practice often associated with the Ku Klux Klan. Two cases illustrate the Court's changing attitude toward this. The first case, decided in 1992, is *R.A.V. v. City of St. Paul*, 505 U.S. 377. In this case, the Court held unconstitutional a local ordinance that prohibited the display of a symbol that one knows or has reason to know "arouses anger, alarm or resentment in others on the basis of race, color, creed, religion or gender." The petitioner was convicted of violating this ordinance by burning a cross on the lawn of a black family. The Court found the ordinance unconstitutional and therefore set aside the conviction. The Court focused on the language of the statute that banned expressive conduct that was designed to arouse anger or resentment on the basis of race, color, creed, religion, or gender. More recently, however, the Court considered a state law that made it a felony "for any person . . . , with the intent of intimidating any person or group . . . , to burn . . . a cross on the property of another, a highway or other public place," and specifies that "[a]ny such burning . . . shall be prima facie evidence of an intent to intimidate a person or group." In this case, the Court found that the part of the law banning cross burning was constitutional, but the section providing that the act of cross burning was prima facie evidence of an intent to intimidate was unconstitutional. Again, the Court focused on specific language in the code section. The Court also pointed out that cross burning is often used to intimidate and presents a message of intended violence. As such it is not protected by the First Amendment. However, the intimidating nature of the conduct must be proved by evidence other than the cross burning itself. Otherwise, the statute conflicts with the holding in *R.A.V. v. City of St. Paul*. The Court Syllabi for both of these cases follow.

R.A.V. v. City of St. Paul
505 U.S. 377 (1992)

After allegedly burning a cross on a black family's lawn, petitioner R.A.V. was charged under, the St. Paul, Minnesota, Bias-Motivated Crime Ordinance, which prohibits the display of a symbol which one knows or has reason to know "arouses anger, alarm or resentment in others on the basis of race, color, creed, religion or gender." The trial court dismissed this charge on the ground that the ordinance was substantially overbroad and impermissibly content based, but the State Supreme Court reversed. It rejected the overbreadth claim because the phrase "arouses anger, alarm or resentment in others" had been construed in earlier state cases to limit the ordinance's reach to "fighting words" within the meaning of this Court's decision in *Chaplinsky v. New Hampshire*, 315 U.S. 568, 572, 86 L. Ed. 1031, 62 S. Ct. 766, a category of expression unprotected by the First Amendment. The court also concluded that the ordinance was not impermissibly content based because it was narrowly tailored to serve a compelling governmental interest in protecting the community against bias-motivated threats to public safety and order.

Held: The ordinance is facially invalid under the First Amendment.

(a) This Court is bound by the state court's construction of the ordinance as reaching only expressions constituting "fighting words." However, R.A.V.'s request that the scope of the *Chaplinsky* formulation be modified, thereby invalidating the ordinance as substantially overbroad, need not be reached, since the ordinance unconstitutionally prohibits speech on the basis of the subjects the speech addresses.

(b) A few limited categories of speech, such as obscenity, defamation, and fighting words, may be regulated because of their constitutionally proscribable content. However, these categories are not entirely invisible to the Constitution, and government may not regulate them based on hostility, or favoritism, towards a non-proscribable message they contain. Thus the regulation of "fighting words" may not be based on non-proscribable content. It may, however, be underinclusive, addressing some offensive instances and leaving other, equally offensive, ones alone, so long as the selective proscription is not based on content, or there is no realistic possibility that regulation of ideas is afoot.

(c) The ordinance, even as narrowly construed by the State Supreme Court, is facially unconstitutional

(continued)

(continued)

because it imposes special prohibitions on those speakers who express views on the disfavored subjects of "race, color, creed, religion or gender." At the same time, it permits displays containing abusive invective if they are not addressed to those topics. Moreover, in its practical operation the ordinance goes beyond mere content, to actual viewpoint, discrimination. Displays containing "fighting words"

that do not invoke the disfavored subjects would seemingly be useable ad libitum by those arguing in favor of racial, color, etc., tolerance and equality, but not by their opponents. St. Paul's desire to communicate to minority groups that it does not condone the "group hatred" of bias-motivated speech does not justify selectively silencing speech on the basis of its content.

Something to Consider

Explain what the Court in *R.A.V. v. City of St. Paul* means when it states:

[T]he regulation of 'fighting words' may not be based on non-proscribable content. It may, however, be under-inclusive, addressing some offensive instances and leaving other, equally offensive, ones alone, so long as the selective proscription is not based on content, or there is no realistic possibility that regulation of ideas is afoot.

Virginia v. Black
538 U.S. 343 (2003)

Respondents were convicted separately of violating a Virginia statute that makes it a felony "for any person . . . , with the intent of intimidating any person or group . . . , to burn . . . a cross on the property of another, a highway or other public place," and specifies that "[a]ny such burning . . . shall be prima facie evidence of an intent to intimidate a person or group." When respondent Black objected on First Amendment grounds to his trial court's jury instruction that cross burning by itself is sufficient evidence from which the required "intent to intimidate" could be inferred, the prosecutor responded that the instruction was taken straight out of the Virginia Model Instructions.

Held: The judgment is affirmed in part, vacated in part, and remanded.

Justice O'Connor delivered the opinion of the Court with respect to Parts I, II, and III, concluding that a State, consistent with the First Amendment, may ban cross burning carried out with the intent to intimidate.

(a) Burning a cross in the United States is inextricably intertwined with the history of the Ku Klux Klan, which, following its formation in 1866, imposed a reign of terror throughout the South, whipping, threatening, and murdering blacks, southern whites who

disagreed with the Klan, and "carpetbagger" northern whites. The Klan has often used cross burnings as a tool of intimidation and a threat of impending violence, although such burnings have also remained potent symbols of shared group identity and ideology, serving as a central feature of Klan gatherings. To this day, however, regardless of whether the message is a political one or is also meant to intimidate, the burning of a cross is a "symbol of hate." *Capitol Square Review and Advisory Bd. v. Pinette*, 515 U.S. 753, 771. While cross burning does not inevitably convey a message of intimidation, often the cross burner intends that the recipients of the message fear for their lives. And when a cross burning is used to intimidate, few if any messages are more powerful.

(b) The protections the First Amendment affords speech and expressive conduct are not absolute. This Court has long recognized that the government may regulate certain categories of expression consistent with the Constitution. *See, e.g., Chaplinsky v. New Hampshire*, 315 U.S. 568, 571–572. For example, the First Amendment permits a State to ban "true threats," *e.g., Watts v. United States*, 394 U.S. 705, 708 (*per curiam*), which encompass those statements where the

(continued)

(continued)

speaker means to communicate a serious expression of an intent to commit an act of unlawful violence to a particular individual or group of individuals, *see, e.g., id.,* at 708. The speaker need not actually intend to carry out the threat. Rather, a prohibition on true threats protects individuals from the fear of violence and the disruption that fear engenders, as well as from the possibility that the threatened violence will occur. *R.A.V.,* at 388. Intimidation in the constitutionally proscribable sense of the word is a type of true threat, where a speaker directs a threat to a person or group of persons with the intent of placing the victim in fear of bodily harm or death. Respondents do not contest that some cross burnings fit within this meaning of intimidating speech, and rightly so. As the history of cross burning in this country shows, that act is often intimidating, intended to create a pervasive fear in victims that they are a target of violence.

(c) The First Amendment permits Virginia to outlaw cross burnings done with the intent to intimidate because burning a cross is a particularly virulent form of intimidation. Instead of prohibiting all intimidating messages, Virginia may choose to regulate this subset of intimidating messages in light of cross burning's long and pernicious history as a signal of impending violence. A ban on cross burning carried out with the intent to intimidate is fully consistent with this Court's holding in *R.A.V.* Virginia's statute does not run afoul of the First Amendment insofar as it bans cross burning with intent to intimidate. Unlike the statute at issue in *R.A.V.,* the Virginia statute does not single out for opprobrium only that speech directed toward "one of the specified disfavored topics." *Id.,* at 391. It does not matter whether an individual burns a cross with intent to intimidate because

of the victim's race, gender, or religion, or because of the victim's "political affiliation, union membership, or homosexuality." *Ibid.* Thus, just as a State may regulate only that obscenity which is the most obscene due to its prurient content, so too may a State choose to prohibit only those forms of intimidation that are most likely to inspire fear of bodily harm.

JUSTICE O'CONNOR, joined by THE CHIEF JUSTICE, JUSTICE STEVENS, and JUSTICE BREYER, concluded in Parts IV and V that the Virginia statute's prima facie evidence provision, as interpreted through the jury instruction given in respondent Black's case and as applied therein, is unconstitutional on its face. As construed by the instruction, the prima facie provision strips away the very reason why a State may ban cross burning with the intent to intimidate. The provision permits a jury to convict in every cross burning case in which defendants exercise their constitutional right not to put on a defense. And even where a defendant like Black presents a defense, the provision makes it more likely that the jury will find an intent to intimidate regardless of the particular facts of the case. It permits the Commonwealth to arrest, prosecute, and convict a person based solely on the fact of cross burning itself. As so interpreted, it would create an unacceptable risk of the suppression of ideas. *E.g., Secretary of State of Md. v. Joseph H. Munson Co.,* 467 U.S. 947, 965, n.13. The act of burning a cross may mean that a person is engaging in constitutionally proscribable intimidation, or it may mean only that the person is engaged in core political speech. The prima facie evidence provision blurs the line between these meanings, ignoring all of the contextual factors that are necessary to decide whether a particular cross burning is intended to intimidate. The First Amendment does not permit such a shortcut.

Recently, the Court affirmed its position that hate speech alone was not unconstitutional. In *Snyder v. Phelps,* ___U.S.___, 131 S.Ct. 1207 (2011), the Court considered a case where a religious group picketed the funeral of a young soldier killed in the Iraq war. Knowing that the young man was homosexual, the picketers carried extremely offensive and hateful signs, such as "God hates fags" and "Thank God for dead soldiers." The soldier's father sued the church members for intentional infliction of emotional distress and, at the trial level, was awarded large damages. The Supreme Court reversed the trial court stating that the church group was protected by the First Amendment because it was speaking out on an issue of public concern and was picketing on property where it had a right to be. The Court stated that the "speech was at a public place on a matter of public concern, that speech is entitled to 'special protection' under the First Amendment. Such speech cannot be restricted simply because it is upsetting or arouses contempt. 'If there is a bedrock principle underlying the First Amendment, it is that the government may not prohibit the expression of an idea simply because society finds the idea itself offensive or disagreeable.' *Texas v. Johnson.* Indeed, 'the point of all speech protection . . . is to shield just those choices of content that in someone's eyes are misguided, or even hurtful.' *Hurley v. Irish-American Gay, Lesbian and Bisexual Group of Boston, Inc.*"

Another current issue related to hate speech is the trend of state governments to impose stronger penalties on criminal offenders when the crime is motivated by race concerns. This issue is discussed in the case of *Wisconsin v. Mitchell*, which follows.

Notice the Court's use of the reasoning in *R.A.V. v. City of St. Paul* in this 1993 case. This is a good example of one case building upon the next. The *Mitchell* case below is also an instructive example of statutory interpretation.

Wisconsin v. Mitchell
508 U.S. 476 (1993)

Pursuant to a Wisconsin statute, respondent Mitchell's sentence for aggravated battery was enhanced because he intentionally selected his victim on account of the victim's race. The State Court of Appeals rejected his challenge to the law's constitutionality, but the State Supreme Court reversed. Relying on *R.A.V. v. St. Paul*, 505 U.S. 377, it held that the statute violates the First Amendment by punishing what the legislature has deemed to be offensive thought and rejected the State's contention that the law punishes only the conduct of intentional victim selection. It also found that the statute was unconstitutionally overbroad because the evidentiary use of a defendant's prior speech would have a chilling effect on those who fear they may be prosecuted for offenses subject to penalty enhancement. Finally, it distinguished anti-discrimination laws, which have long been held constitutional, on the ground that they prohibit objective acts of discrimination, whereas the state statute punishes the subjective mental process.

Held:

Mitchell's First Amendment rights were not violated by the application of the penalty-enhancement provision in sentencing him.

(a) While Mitchell correctly notes that this Court is bound by a state court's interpretation of a state statute, the State Supreme Court did not construe the instant statute in the sense of defining the meaning of a particular word or phrase. Rather, it characterized the statute's practical effect for First Amendment purposes. Thus, after resolving any ambiguities in the statute's meaning, this Court may form its own judgment about the law's operative effect. The State's argument that the statute punishes only conduct does not dispose of Mitchell's claim, since the fact remains that the same criminal conduct is more heavily punished if the victim is selected because of his protected status than if no such motive obtains.

(b) In determining what sentence to impose, sentencing judges have traditionally considered a wide variety of factors in addition to evidence bearing on guilt, including a defendant's motive for committing the offense. While it is equally true that a sentencing judge may not take into consideration a defendant's abstract beliefs, however obnoxious to most people, the Constitution does not erect a per se barrier to the admission of evidence concerning one's beliefs and associations at sentencing simply because they are protected by the First Amendment. *Dawson v. Delaware*, 503 U.S. 159; *Barclay v. Florida*, 463 U.S. 939 (plurality opinion). That *Dawson* and *Barclay* did not involve the application of a penalty-enhancement provision does not make them inapposite. *Barclay* involved the consideration of racial animus in determining whether to sentence a defendant to death, the most severe "enhancement" of all; and the state legislature has the primary responsibility for fixing criminal penalties. Motive plays the same role under the state statute as it does under federal and state anti-discrimination laws, which have been upheld against constitutional challenge. Nothing in *R.A.V. v. St. Paul*, compels a different result here.

(continued)

(continued)

The ordinance at issue there was explicitly directed at speech, while the one here is aimed at conduct unprotected by the First Amendment. Moreover, the State's desire to redress what it sees as the greater individual and societal harm inflicted by bias-inspired conduct provides an adequate explanation for the provision over and above mere disagreement with offenders' beliefs or biases.

(c) Because the statute has no "chilling effect" on free speech, it is not unconstitutionally overbroad. The prospect of a citizen suppressing his bigoted beliefs for fear that evidence of those beliefs will be introduced against him at trial if he commits a serious offense against person or property is too speculative a hypothesis to support this claim. Moreover, the First Amendment permits the admission of previous declarations or statements to establish the elements of a crime or to prove motive or intent, subject to evidentiary rules dealing with relevancy, reliability, and the like. *Haupt v. United States*, 330 U.S. 631.

Speech Intended to Incite Illegal Action

Speech that incites illegal action is not protected by the First Amendment. In 1919, the Court held that speech that creates a "clear and present danger" of illegal action is not covered by the First Amendment protections. The defendant in *Schenck v. United States* was convicted for distributing materials encouraging men to resist the draft.

In 1951, the Court upheld the Smith Act in *Dennis v. United States,* 341 U.S. 494 (1951). The Smith Act, among other purposes, was intended to discourage membership in the Communist Party. In addition, it prohibited advocating the violent overthrow of the American government. Six years later in *Yates v. United States*, 356 U.S. 363 (1958) the Court clarified that the Smith Act prohibited the advocacy of violent revolution as a concrete specific idea rather than as an abstract idea.

In the 1960s, the Court crafted the current guidelines for the punishment of speech that incites illegal action. Such action must be probable and "imminent." Those guidelines are explained in the following case.

Brandenburg v. Ohio
395 U.S. 444 (1969)

Per Curiam Opinion

The appellant, a leader of a Ku Klux Klan group, was convicted under the Ohio Criminal Syndicalism statute for "advocat[ing] . . . the duty, necessity, or propriety of crime, sabotage, violence, or unlawful methods of terrorism as a means of accomplishing industrial or political reform" and for "voluntarily assembl[ing] with any society, group, or assemblage of persons formed to teach or advocate the doctrines of criminal syndicalism." Ohio Rev. Code Ann. § 2923.13. He was fined $1,000 and sentenced to one to 10 years' imprisonment. The appellant challenged the constitutionality of the criminal syndicalism statute under the First and Fourteenth Amendments to the United States Constitution, but the intermediate appellate court of Ohio affirmed his conviction without opinion. The Supreme Court of Ohio dismissed his appeal.

We reverse.

The record shows that a man, identified at trial as the appellant, telephoned an announcer-reporter on the staff of a Cincinnati television station and invited him to come to a Ku Klux Klan "rally" to be held at a farm in Hamilton County. With the cooperation of the organizers, the reporter and a cameraman attended the meeting and filmed the events. Portions of the films were later broadcast on the local station and on a national network.

(continued)

(continued)

The prosecution's case rested on the films and on testimony identifying the appellant as the person who communicated with the reporter and who spoke at the rally. The State also introduced into evidence several articles appearing in the film, including a pistol, a rifle, a shotgun, ammunition, a Bible, and a red hood worn by the speaker in the films.

One film showed 12 hooded figures, some of whom carried firearms. They were gathered around a large wooden cross, which they burned. No one was present other than the participants and the newsmen who made the film. Most of the words uttered during the scene were incomprehensible when the film was projected, but scattered phrases could be understood that were derogatory of Negroes and, in one instance, of Jews. Another scene on the same film showed the appellant, in Klan regalia, making a speech. The speech, in full, was as follows:

"This is an organizers' meeting. We have had quite a few members here today which are—we have hundreds, hundreds of members throughout the State of Ohio. I can quote from a newspaper clipping from the Columbus, Ohio Dispatch, five weeks ago Sunday morning. The Klan has more members in the State of Ohio than does any other organization. We're not a revengent organization, but if our President, our Congress, our Supreme Court, continues to suppress the white, Caucasian race, it's possible that there might have to be some revengeance taken."

"We are marching on Congress July the Fourth, four hundred thousand strong. From there we are dividing into two groups, one group to march on St. Augustine, Florida, the other group to march into Mississippi. Thank you."

The second film showed six hooded figures one of whom, later identified as the appellant, repeated a speech very similar to that recorded on the first film. The reference to the possibility of "revengeance" was omitted, and one sentence was added: "Personally, I believe the nigger should be returned to Africa, the Jew returned to Israel." Though some of the figures in the films carried weapons, the speaker did not.

The Ohio Criminal Syndicalism Statute was enacted in 1919. From 1917 to 1920, identical or quite similar laws were adopted by 20 States and two territories. E.

Dowell, *A History of Criminal Syndicalism Legislation in the United States* 21 (1939). In 1927, this Court sustained the constitutionality of California's Criminal Syndicalism Act, Cal. Penal Code §§11400–11402, the text of which is quite similar to that of the laws of Ohio. *Whitney v. California*, 274 U.S. 357 (1927). The Court upheld the statute on the ground that, without more, "advocating" violent means to effect political and economic change involves such danger to the security of the State that the State may outlaw it. *Cf. Fiske v. Kansas*, 274 U.S. 380 (1927). But *Whitney* has been thoroughly discredited by later decisions. *See Dennis v. United States*, 341 U.S. 494, at 507 (1951). These later decisions have fashioned the principle that the constitutional guarantees of free speech and free press do not permit a State to forbid or proscribe advocacy of the use of force or of law violation except where such advocacy is directed to inciting or producing imminent lawless action and is likely to incite or produce such action. As we said in *Noto v. United States*, 367 U.S. 290, 297–298 (1961), "the mere abstract teaching . . . of the moral propriety or even moral necessity for a resort to force and violence, is not the same as preparing a group for violent action and steeling it to such action." *See also Herndon v. Lowry*, 301 U.S. 242, 259–261 (1937); *Bond v. Floyd*, 385 U.S. 116, 134 (1966). A statute which fails to draw this distinction impermissibly intrudes upon the freedoms guaranteed by the First and Fourteenth Amendments. It sweeps within its condemnation speech which our Constitution has immunized from governmental control. Measured by this test, Ohio's Criminal Syndicalism Act cannot be sustained. The Act punishes persons who "advocate or teach the duty, necessity, or propriety" of violence "as a means of accomplishing industrial or political reform"; or who publish or circulate or display any book or paper containing such advocacy; or who "justify" the commission of violent acts "with intent to exemplify, spread or advocate the propriety of the doctrines of criminal syndicalism"; or who "voluntarily assemble" with a group formed "to teach or advocate the doctrines of criminal syndicalism." Neither the indictment nor the trial judge's instructions to the jury in any way refined the statute's bald definition of the crime in terms of mere advocacy not distinguished from incitement to imminent lawless action.

Accordingly, we are here confronted with a statute which, by its own words and as applied, purports to punish mere advocacy and to forbid, on pain of criminal

(continued)

(continued)

punishment, assembly with others merely to advocate the described type of action. Such a statute falls within the condemnation of the First and Fourteenth Amendments.

The contrary teaching of *Whitney v. California*, cannot be supported, and that decision is therefore overruled. Reversed.

Something to Consider

The general rule is that a call for specific illegal action is not protected speech. However, a call for violent opposition to civil rights laws is protected speech.

How do you explain why a "cry for specific illegal action" is treated so differently from a "violent opposition to civil rights laws"?

Speech that is Harmful or Violent

In recent years, the Supreme Court considered cases involving laws enacted to prohibit conduct viewed by most as abhorrent. The first case, *United States v. Stevens*, 559 U.S. ___ (2010) involved a federal law criminalizing the "commercial creation, sale, or possession of certain depictions of animal cruelty." In finding the law unconstitutional, the Supreme Court emphasized that the law criminalized the *portrayal* of animal cruelty rather than the act of animal cruelty. As such it involved speech, just as other media such as movies. The Court noted that this case involved a new category of speech and refused to hold that it was included in the types of speech not protected by the First Amendment. The second case, *Brown v. Entertainment Merchant's Assoc.*, 564 U.S. ___ (2011), involved a state law making it a crime to sell or rent violent video games to minors. It also required labeling of the video games. The law applied to video games. The Act covers games "in which the range of options available to a player includes killing, maiming, dismembering, or sexually assaulting an image of a human being." The Court followed its decision in *Stevens*, holding the law was unconstitutional because there was no precedent for protecting this type of speech. The Court noted that speech about violence is not obscene. The Court further stated that "a new category of unprotected speech cannot be created by the legislature." A strong dissent made the following points:

> [T]he majority's different conclusion creates a serious anomaly in First Amendment law. *Ginsberg* makes clear that a State can prohibit the sale to minors of depictions of nudity; today the Court makes clear that a State cannot prohibit the sale to minors of the most violent interactive video games. But what sense does it make to forbid selling to a 13-year-old boy a magazine with an image of a nude woman, while protecting a sale to that 13-year-old of an interactive video game in which he actively, but virtually, binds and gags the woman, then tortures and kills her? What kind of First Amendment would permit the government to protect children by restricting sales of that extremely violent video game *only* when the woman—bound, gagged, tortured, and killed—is also topless?

School Speech /Speech in Educational Institutions

In 1965, a brother and sister wore black armbands to school in protest of the war in Vietnam. The school suspended both students. The Court in *Tinker v. Des Moines Independent School Dist*, 393 U.S. 503 (1969), held that the wearing of the black armband was symbolic speech and, as such, protected under the First Amendment. The Court was careful to exclude student speech that could materially and substantially disrupt the classroom.

Students do *not* enjoy the same freedom of speech rights as adults. In the 1980s, the Court once again directed its attention to the free speech rights of students. In the case of *Bethel School Dist. v. Fraser*, the Court considered whether a school could discipline a student for giving a sexually explicit speech during an assembly. In a second case, *Hazelwood School Dist. v. Kuhlmeier*, the Court considered whether a school could censor articles in a school paper. Following are excerpts from the Court's Syllabi in each case.

Bethel School Dist. v. Fraser
478 U.S. 675 (1986)

Held:
1. The First Amendment did not prevent the School District from disciplining respondent for giving the offensively lewd and indecent speech at the assembly. *Tinker v. Des Moines Independent Community School Dist.*, 393 U.S. 503, distinguished. Under the First Amendment, the use of an offensive form of expression may not be prohibited to adults making what the speaker considers a political point, but it does not follow that the same latitude must be permitted to children in a public school. It is a highly appropriate function of public school education to prohibit the use of vulgar and offensive terms in public discourse. Nothing in the Constitution prohibits the states from insisting that certain modes of expression are inappropriate and subject to sanctions. The inculcation of these values is truly the work of the school, and the determination of what manner of speech is inappropriate properly rests with the school board. First Amendment jurisprudence recognizes an interest in protecting minors from exposure to vulgar and offensive spoken language, *FCC v. Pacifica Foundation*, 438 U.S. 726, as well as limitations on the otherwise absolute interest of the speaker in reaching an unlimited audience where the speech is sexually explicit and the audience may include children, *Ginsberg v. New York*, 390 U.S. 629. Petitioner School District acted entirely within its permissible authority in imposing sanctions upon respondent in response to his offensively lewd and indecent speech, which had no claim to First Amendment protection.

Something to Consider
Why does the Court draw a distinction between adults and children in *Bethel School Dist. v. Fraser?* Do you agree with the Court's reasoning?

Hazelwood School Dist. v. Kuhlmeier
484 U.S. 260 (1988)

Held: Respondents' First Amendment rights were not violated.
(a) First Amendment rights of students in the public schools are not automatically coextensive with the rights of adults in other settings, and must be applied in light of the special characteristics of the school environment. A school need not tolerate student speech that is inconsistent with its basic educational mission, even though the government could not censor similar speech outside the school.
(b) The school newspaper here cannot be characterized as a forum for public expression. School facilities may be deemed to be public forums only if school authorities have by policy or by practice opened the facilities for indiscriminate use by the general public, or by some segment of the public, such as student

(continued)

(continued)

organizations. If the facilities have instead been reserved for other intended purposes, communicative or otherwise, then no public forum has been created, and school officials may impose reasonable restrictions on the speech of students, teachers, and other members of the school community. The school officials in this case did not deviate from their policy that the newspaper's production was to be part of the educational curriculum and a regular classroom activity under the journalism teacher's control as to almost every aspect of publication. The officials did not evince any intent to open the paper's pages to indiscriminate use by its student reporters and editors, or by the student body generally. Accordingly, school officials were entitled to regulate the paper's contents in any reasonable manner.

(c) The standard for determining when a school may punish student expression that happens to occur on school premises is not the standard for determining when a school may refuse to lend its name and resources to the dissemination of student expression. *Tinker v. Des Moines Independent Community School Dist.*, 393 U.S. 503, distinguished. Educators do not offend the First Amendment by exercising editorial control over the style and content of student speech in school-sponsored expressive activities so long as their actions are reasonably related to legitimate pedagogical concerns.

(d) The school principal acted reasonably in this case in requiring the deletion of the pregnancy article, the divorce article, and the other articles that were to appear on the same pages of the newspaper.

In a more recent school speech case the Court held that the First Amendment is not violated when school officials suspend a student who refuses to take down a pro-drug banner at a school-sponsored event. School officials are entitled to safeguard those entrusted to their care from speech that could reasonably be regarded as encouraging illegal drug use. *Morse v. Frederick*, 551 U.S. 383 (2007).

Morse v. Frederick
551 U.S. 383 (2007)

Syllabus:

At a school-sanctioned and school-supervised event, petitioner Morse, the high school principal, saw students unfurl a banner stating "BONG HiTS 4 JESUS," which she regarded as promoting illegal drug use. Consistent with established school policy prohibiting such messages at school events, Morse directed the students to take down the banner. When one of the students who had brought the banner to the event--respondent Frederick--refused, Morse confiscated the banner and later suspended him. The school superintendent upheld the suspension, explaining, *inter alia*, that Frederick was disciplined because his banner appeared to advocate illegal drug use in violation of school policy. Petitioner school board also upheld the suspension. Frederick filed suit under 42 U.S.C. § 1983,

alleging that the school board and Morse had violated his First Amendment rights. The District Court granted petitioner's summary judgment, ruling that they were entitled to qualified immunity and that they had not infringed Frederick's speech rights. The Ninth Circuit reversed. Accepting that Frederick acted during a school-authorized activity and that the banner expressed a positive sentiment about marijuana use, the court nonetheless found a First Amendment violation because the school punished Frederick without demonstrating that his speech threatened substantial disruption. It also concluded that Morse was not entitled to qualified immunity because Frederick's right to display the banner was so clearly established that a reasonable principal in Morse's position would have understood that her actions were unconstitutional.

(continued)

(continued)

Held: Because schools may take steps to safeguard those entrusted to their care from speech that can reasonably be regarded as encouraging illegal drug use, the school officials in this case did not violate the First Amendment by confiscating the pro-drug banner and suspending Frederick.

(a) Frederick's argument that this is not a school speech case is rejected. The event in question occurred during normal school hours and was sanctioned by Morse as an approved social event at which the district's student-conduct rules expressly applied. Teachers and administrators were among the students and were charged with supervising them. Frederick stood among other students across the street from the school and directed his banner toward the school, making it plainly visible to most students. Under these circumstances, Frederick cannot claim he was not at school.

(b) The Court agrees with Morse that those who viewed the banner would interpret it as advocating or promoting illegal drug use, in violation of school policy. At least two interpretations of the banner's words–that they constitute an imperative encouraging viewers to smoke marijuana or, alternatively, that they celebrate drug use–demonstrate that the sign promoted such use. This pro-drug interpretation gains further plausibility from the paucity of alternative meanings the banner might bear.

(c) A principal may, consistent with the First Amendment, restrict student speech at a school event, when that speech is reasonably viewed as promoting illegal drug use. In *Tinker v. Des Moines Independent Community School Dist.,* 393 U.S. 503, the Court declared, in holding that a policy prohibiting high school students from wearing antiwar armbands violated the First Amendment, *id.,* at 504, that student expression may not be suppressed unless school officials reasonably conclude that it will "materially and substantially disrupt the work and discipline of the school," *id.,* at 513. The Court in *Bethel School Dist. No. 403 v. Fraser,* however, upheld the suspension of a student who delivered a high school assembly speech employing "an elaborate, graphic, and explicit sexual metaphor," *id.,* at 678. Analyzing the case

under *Tinker,* the lower courts had found no disruption, and therefore no basis for discipline. 478 U.S., at 679-80. This Court reversed, holding that the school was "within its permissible authority in imposing sanctions . . . in response to [the student's] offensively lewd and indecent speech." Id. Two basic principles may be distilled from *Fraser.* First, it demonstrates that "the constitutional rights of students in public school are not automatically coextensive with the rights of adults in other settings." Id. Had Fraser delivered the same speech in a public forum outside the school context, he would have been protected. *See id.,* at 682-83. In school, however, his First Amendment rights were circumscribed "in light of the special characteristics of the school environment." Tinker, supra, at 506. Second, *Fraser* established that *Tinker'*s mode of analysis is not absolute, since the *Fraser* Court did not conduct the "substantial disruption" analysis. Subsequently, the Court has held in the Fourth Amendment context that "while children assuredly do not 'shed their constitutional rights . . . at the schoolhouse gate,' . . . the nature of those rights is what is appropriate for children in school," *Vernonia Sch. Dist. 47J v. Acton,* 515 U.S. 646, 655-56, and has recognized that deterring drug use by schoolchildren is an "important--indeed, perhaps compelling" interest, *id.,* at 661. Drug abuse by the Nation's youth is a serious problem. For example, Congress has declared that part of a school's job is educating students about the dangers of drug abuse, see, e.g., the Safe and Drug-Free Schools and Communities Act of 1994, and petitioners and many other schools have adopted policies aimed at implementing this message. Student speech celebrating illegal drug use at a school event, in the presence of school administrators and teachers, poses a particular challenge for school officials working to protect those entrusted to their care. The "special characteristics of the school environment," *Tinker,* 393 U.S., and the governmental interest in stopping student drug abuse allow schools to restrict student expression that they reasonably regard as promoting such abuse. *Id.,* at 508, 509, distinguished. 439 F.3d 1114, reversed and remanded.

Something to Consider

Think about this: "A school need not tolerate student speech that is inconsistent with its basic educational mission, even though the government could not censor similar speech outside the school."

Can you imagine situations where the basic educational mission might vary from one school to another or from one community to another? Discuss.

Commercial Speech

In recent years, the Supreme Court extended some First Amendment protection to speech that proposes a commercial transaction, including advertising of products. This protection, however, has limits. Misleading and untruthful statements are not protected. Furthermore, government can regulate commercial speech where there is a legitimate state goal and where the regulation is the least restrictive way of achieving that goal. The Court's philosophy is set out in the case of *Central Hudson Gas & Electric Service Corp. v. Public Service Commn.*, 447 U.S. 557 (1980):

> If the communication is neither misleading nor related to unlawful activity, the government's power is more circumscribed. The State must assert a substantial interest to be achieved by restrictions on commercial speech. Moreover, the regulatory technique must be in proportion to that interest. The limitation on expression must be designed carefully to achieve the State's goal. Compliance with this requirement may be measured by two criteria. First, the restriction must directly advance the state interest involved; the regulation may not be sustained if it provides only ineffective or remote support for the government's purpose. Second, if the governmental interest could be served as well by a more limited restriction on commercial speech, the excessive restrictions cannot survive.

In 2011 the Supreme Court affirmed the holding of *Central Hudson* in *Sorrell v. IMS Health Inc.*, 564 U.S. __ (2011):

> Under a commercial speech inquiry, it is the State's burden to justify its content-based law as consistent with the First Amendment . . . the State must show at least that the statute directly advances a substantial governmental interest and that the measure is drawn to achieve that interest. See *Central Hudson Gas & Elec. Corp. v. Public Serv. Comm'n of N. Y.*, 447 U.S. 557, 566 (1980). There must be a fit between the legislature's ends and the means chosen to accomplish those ends.

In *Sorrell*, the Supreme Court held that a state law that prohibited pharmacies from selling information about doctor's prescribing practices was unconstitutional and a violation of the First Amendment.

Table 11-2 summarizes cases involving protections related to speech.

Table 11-2 Summary of Free Speech Cases

Case	Free Speech Topic	Rule/Holding
Texas v. Johnson, 491 U.S. 397 (1989)	Symbolic Speech	Expressive conduct, such as burning the flag, is protected by the First Amendment.
United States v. O'Brien, 391 U.S. 367 (1968)	Symbolic Speech	Government can prohibit conduct that incidentally affects free speech if there is a legitimate government purpose in prohibiting the conduct. Burning a draft card is not protected by the First Amendment.
West Virginia State Bd. of Educ. v. Barnette, 319 U.S. 624 (1943)	Compelling Speech	The First Amendment prohibits government from compelling speech, such as the recitation of the Pledge of Allegiance by students in a public school.
Buckley v. Valeo, 424 U.S. 1 (1976)	Campaign Finance Laws	Laws restricting the amount a political candidate can spend violate the First Amendment because "money is speech." Laws limiting contributions are constitutional.

Table 11-2 *(continued)*

Case	Free Speech Topic	Rule/Holding
Davenport v. Washington Educ. Ass'n, 551 U.S. 177 (2007)	Campaign Finance Laws	The Court upheld a Washington state law that required public sector labor unions to receive authorization from nonunion members before spending their union fees for expenditures or contributions connected to attempts to influence elections.
Ysursa v. Pcoatello Educ. Ass'n, 555 U.S. 353 (2009)	Campaign Finance Laws	The Court held that an Idaho law banning payroll deductions for local government employees for political union activities does not infringe the unions' First Amendment rights.
Citizens United v. Federal Election Com'n, 558 U.S. ___ (2010)	Campaign Finance Laws	The Court held that portions of a federal law violated the First Amendment where the law suppressed political speech of a corporation by prohibiting independent corporate expenditures for "electioneering communications" (overruling *Austin v. Michigan Chamber of Commerce,* 494 U.S. 652 and *McConnell v. Federal Election Com'n,* 540 U.S. 93.)
		However, disclaimer and disclosure provisions of the same law did not violate the First Amendment.
Miller v. California, 413 U.S. 15 (1973)	Obscenity	Obscenity is determined by the following criteria: whether applying contemporary community standards, the work as a whole applies to the prurient interest; whether the work depicts, in a patently offensive way, sexual conduct specifically defined by law; and whether work lacks serious artistic, political, or scientific value.
Reno v. American Civil Liberties Union, 521 U.S. 844 (1997)	Obscenity	The Communication Decency Act of 1996 violated the First Amendment because its prohibitions were too broad; the Act prohibited transmission of all material that was indecent or that depicted sexual activities in a patently offensive manner.
Ashcroft v. Free Speech Coalition, 535 U.S. 234 (2002)	Obscenity	The Child Pornography Prevention Act of 1996, which prohibited any depictions that appeared to be minors engaged in sexually explicit conduct, violated the First Amendment because the law ignored the Miller standard of obscenity and was too broad.
United States v. Williams, 553 U.S. 285 (2008)	Obscenity	A law criminalizing the *solicitation* or *pandering* of child pornography did not violate the First Amendment.
New York Times Co. v. Sullivan, 376 U.S. 254 (1964)	Defamation	Under the First and Fourteenth Amendments, a state cannot award damages to a public official for defamatory falsehood relating to his official conduct unless plaintiff proves "actual malice."
Gertz v. Robert Welch, Inc., 418 U.S. 323 (1974)	Defamation	A state cannot award punitive damages to a private individual unless plaintiff proves actual malice if the defamatory statements relate to a matter of general concern or interest.
Chaplinsky v. New Hampshire, 315 U.S. 568 (1942)	Fighting Words	"Fighting words," are words calculated to provoke a physical response, they are not protected by the First Amendment. Calling a person a "damned racketeer" and "damned Fascist" were fighting words.

Table 11-2 *(continued)*		
Case	**Free Speech Topic**	**Rule/Holding**
R.A.V. v. City of St. Paul, 505 U.S. 377 (1992)	Hate Speech	An ordinance prohibiting the display of a symbol that one knows or has reason to know "arouses anger, alarm or resentment in others on the basis of race, color, creed, religion or gender" was unconstitutional and a conviction of cross burning under the ordinance was overturned.
Virginia v. Black, 538 U.S. 343 (2003)	Hate Speech	A statute making it a felony to burn a cross was not unconstitutional when applied to a situation where the conduct was meant to intimidate. However, a provision of the statute making the conduct prima facie evidence of intent to intimidate did violate the First Amendment.
Snyder v. Phelps, 562 U.S.__ (2011)	Hate Speech	A church group had a First Amendment right to picket the funeral of a gay soldier killed in Iraq and to hold offensive signs as long as they remained on public property and did not violate any local laws regarding picketing.
Wisconsin v. Mitchell, 508 U.S. 476 (1993)	Hate Speech	A state law imposing additional punishment on a criminal defendant who commits a crime motivated by racial hatred does not violate the First Amendment.
Brandenburg v. Ohio, 395 U.S. 444 (1969)	Inciting Illegal Action	Expression that incites illegal actions is not protected by the First Amendment if it presents an imminent danger of illegal action.
Bethel School Dist. v. Fraser, 478 U.S. 675 (1986)	Speech in Schools	A student's First Amendment rights are not violated when the student is disciplined for making a lewd and offensive speech at an assembly.
Hazelwood School Dist. v. Kuhlmeier, 484 U.S. 260 (1988)	Speech in Schools	A student's First Amendment rights are not violated when the school censors a school newspaper.
Morse v. Frederick, 551 U.S. 383 (2007).	Speech in Schools	A school did not violate a student's First Amendment rights where the student waved a banner promoting the use of marijuana at a school-sponsored event and where this violated school policy.
Pleasant Grove City, Utah v. Summum, 555 U.S. 460 (2009)	Public Forum	Free speech public forum doctrine does not apply to a city's decision to accept or reject a donated monument for placement in a city park; such a monument is government rather than private speech and is not subject to First Amendment.
Legal Soc. Chapter of Univ. of Cal., Hastings College of Law v. Martinez, 561 U. S. ___ (2010)	Public Forum	A public school can impose/require that a student group comply with the school's antidiscrimination policy as a condition to using selected school facilities.
United States v. Stevens, 559 U.S. ___ (2010)	Harmful or Violent Speech	A federal law criminalizing the portrayal of animal cruelty was unconstitutional.
Brown v. Entertainment Merchant's Assoc., 564 U.S. __ (2011)	Harmful or Violent Speech	A law making it a crime to sell or rent violent video games to minors was unconstitutional.
Central Hudson Gas & Electric Corp. v. Public Service Commn., 447 U.S. 557 (1980)	Commercial Speech	Advertising is protected under the First Amendment unless it is misleading or deceptive or there is a legitimate state goal and the regulation is the least restrictive way of achieving that goal.

Peaceable Assembly and the Right to Petition

As the Bill of Rights was under construction, serious attention was given to the right to petition the government. This may be because the English king ignored petitions from the American colonies. In 1689, the English Bill of Rights gave all subjects the right to petition. The process for petition to a government may be rooted in the Magna Carta of 1215. Through this document, English noblemen forced the king of England to respond to their petitions. The right to petition the government has not generated a great deal of Supreme Court case law.

The right to peaceable assembly takes a central role in Supreme Court case law. In 1937, in *De Jonge v. Oregon,* 299 U.S. 353 (1937), the Court applied the freedom of assembly to the states through the Fourteenth Amendment. The key here is the right to *peaceful* assembly. Citizens may not riot. Citizens may not block public roads.

Two cases illustrate and explain the Court's view of the right to assemble, *Cox v. New Hampshire*, 312 U.S. 569 (1941), and *Feiner v. New York*, 340 U.S. 315 (1951). In *Cox,* the Court held that the government can place reasonable "time, place and manner" restrictions on the right to assembly and found that requiring permits to march was a reasonable restriction. In *Feiner,* the Court addressed the issue of a "breach of the peace" caused or threatened by a public gathering. Again, the Court, held that reasonable restrictions could be imposed in this situation. Here the Court upheld a criminal statute based on disorderly conduct. Excerpts from both cases follow.

Cox v. New Hampshire
312 U.S. 569 (1941)

Mr. Chief Justice Hughes delivered the opinion of the Court.

Appellants are five "Jehovah's Witnesses" who, with sixty-three others of the same persuasion, were convicted in the municipal court of Manchester, New Hampshire, for violation of a state statute prohibiting a "parade or procession" upon a public street without a special license.

The statutory prohibition is:

No theatrical or dramatic representation shall be performed or exhibited, and no parade or procession upon any public street or way, and no open-air public meeting upon any ground abutting thereon, shall be permitted, unless a special license therefore shall first be obtained from the selectmen of the town, or from a licensing committee for cities hereinafter provided for.

The sole charge against appellants was that they were "taking part in a parade or procession" on public streets without a permit as the statute required. They were not prosecuted for distributing leaflets, or for conveying information by placards or otherwise, or for issuing invitations to a public meeting, or for holding a public meeting, or for maintaining or expressing religious beliefs. Their right to do any one of these things apart from engaging in a "parade or procession" upon a public street is not here involved and the question of the validity of a statute addressed to any other sort of conduct than that complained of is not before us.

Civil liberties, as guaranteed by the Constitution, imply the existence of an organized society maintaining public order without which liberty itself would be lost in the excesses of unrestrained abuses. The authority of a municipality to impose regulations in order to assure the safety and convenience of the people in the use of public highways has never been regarded as inconsistent with civil liberties but rather as one of the means of safeguarding the good order upon which they ultimately depend. The control of travel on the streets of cities is the most familiar illustration of this recognition of social need.

(continued)

(continued)

Where a restriction of the use of highways in that relation is designed to promote the public convenience in the interest of all, it cannot be disregarded by the attempted exercise of some civil right which in other circumstances would be entitled to protection. As regulation of the use of the streets for parades and processions is a traditional exercise of control by local government, the question in a particular case is whether that control is exerted so as not to deny or unwarrantedly abridge the right of assembly and the opportunities for the communication of thought and the discussion of public questions immemorially associated with resort to public places. *Lovell v. Griffin*, 303 U.S. 444, 451.

In the instant case, we are aided by the opinion of the Supreme Court of the State, which construed the statute and defined the limitations of the authority conferred for the granting of licenses for parades and processions. Recognizing the importance of the civil liberties invoked by appellants, the court thought it significant that the statute prescribed "no measures for controlling or suppressing the publication on the highways of facts and opinions, either by speech or by writing"; that communication "by the distribution of literature or by the display of placards and signs" was in no respect regulated by the statute; that the regulation with respect to parades and processions was applicable only "to organized formations of persons using the highways"; and that "the defendants, separately, or collectively in groups not constituting a parade or procession," were "under no contemplation of the Act." In this light, the court thought that interference with liberty of speech and writing seemed slight; that the distribution of pamphlets and folders by the groups "traveling in unorganized fashion" would have had as large a circulation, and that "signs carried by members of the groups not in marching formation would have been as conspicuous, as published by them while in parade or procession."

It was with this view of the limited objective of the statute that the state court considered and defined the duty of the licensing authority and the rights of the appellants to a license for their parade, with regard only to considerations of time, place and manner so as to conserve the public convenience. The obvious advantage of requiring application for a permit was noted as giving the public authorities notice in advance so as to afford opportunity for proper policing. And the court further observed that, in fixing time and place, the license served "to prevent confusion by overlapping parades or processions, to secure convenient use of the streets by other travelers, and to minimize the risk of disorder." But the court held that the licensing board was not vested with arbitrary power or an unfettered discretion; that its discretion must be exercised with "uniformity of method of treatment upon the facts of each application, free from improper or inappropriate considerations and from unfair discrimination"; that a "systematic, consistent and just order of treatment, with reference to the convenience of public use of the highways, is the statutory mandate." The defendants, said the court, "had a right, under the Act, to a license to march when, where and as they did, if after a required investigation it was found that the convenience of the public in the use of the streets would not thereby be unduly disturbed, upon such conditions or changes in time, place and manner as would avoid disturbance."

If a municipality has authority to control the use of its public streets for parades or processions, as it undoubtedly has, it cannot be denied authority to give consideration, without unfair discrimination, to time, place and manner in relation to the other proper uses of the streets. We find it impossible to say that the limited authority conferred by the licensing provisions of the statute in question as thus construed by the state court contravened any constitutional right. . . .

The judgment of the Supreme Court of New Hampshire is: Affirmed.

....

Something to Consider

Notice the use, in 1941, of the language "time, place and manner" in the *Cox v. New Hampshire* decision. The Court was beginning to fashion the language guiding the courts today when issues arise concerning the proper use of public streets. Reread the statutory prohibition in *Cox*. How is it limited in time, place, and manner?

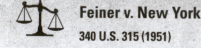

Feiner v. New York
340 U.S. 315 (1951)

MR. CHIEF JUSTICE VINSON delivered the opinion of the Court.

Petitioner was convicted of the offense of disorderly conduct, a misdemeanor under the New York penal laws, and was sentenced to thirty days in the county penitentiary. Petitioner claims that the conviction is in violation of his right of free speech under the Fourteenth Amendment.

On the evening of March 8, 1949, petitioner Irving Feiner was addressing an open-air meeting at the corner of South McBride and Harrison Streets in the City of Syracuse. At approximately 6:30 p. m., the police received a telephone complaint concerning the meeting, and two officers were detailed to investigate. One of these officers went to the scene immediately, the other arriving some twelve minutes later. They found a crowd of about seventy-five or eighty people, both Negro and white, filling the sidewalk and spreading out into the street. Petitioner, standing on a large wooden box on the sidewalk, was addressing the crowd through a loud-speaker system attached to an automobile. Although the purpose of his speech was to urge his listeners to attend a meeting to be held that night in the Syracuse Hotel, in its course he was making derogatory remarks concerning President Truman, the American Legion, the Mayor of Syracuse, and other local political officials.

The police officers made no effort to interfere with petitioner's speech, but were first concerned with the effect of the crowd on both pedestrian and vehicular traffic. They observed the situation from the opposite side of the street, noting that some pedestrians were forced to walk in the street to avoid the crowd. Since traffic was passing at the time, the officers attempted to get the people listening to petitioner back on the sidewalk. The crowd was restless and there was some pushing, shoving and milling around. One of the officers telephoned the police station from a nearby store, and then both policemen crossed the street and mingled with the crowd without any intention of arresting the speaker.

At this time, petitioner was speaking in a "loud, high-pitched voice." He gave the impression that he was endeavoring to arouse the Negro people against the whites, urging that they rise up in arms and fight for equal rights. The statements before such a mixed audience "stirred up a little excitement." Some of the onlookers made remarks to the police about their inability to handle the crowd and at least one threatened violence if the police did not act. There were others who appeared to be favoring petitioner's arguments. Because of the feeling that existed in the crowd both for and against the speaker, the officers finally "stepped in to prevent it from resulting in a fight." One of the officers approached the petitioner, not for the purpose of arresting him, but to get him to break up the crowd. He asked petitioner to get down off the box, but the latter refused to accede to his request and continued talking. The officer waited for a minute and then demanded that he cease talking. Although the officer had thus twice requested petitioner to stop over the course of several minutes, petitioner not only ignored him but continued talking. During all this time, the crowd was pressing closer around petitioner and the officer. Finally, the officer told petitioner he was under arrest and ordered him to get down from the box, reaching up to grab him. Petitioner stepped down, announcing over the microphone that "the law has arrived, and I suppose they will take over now." In all, the officer had asked petitioner to get down off the box three times over a space of four or five minutes. Petitioner had been speaking for over a half hour.

The courts below recognized petitioner's right to hold a street meeting at this locality, to make use of loud-speaking equipment in giving his speech, and to make derogatory remarks concerning public officials and the American Legion. They found that the officers in making the arrest were motivated solely by a proper concern for the preservation of order and protection of the general welfare, and that there was no evidence which could lend color to a claim that the acts of the police were a cover for suppression of petitioner's views and opinions. Petitioner was thus neither arrested nor convicted for the making or the content of his speech. Rather, it was the reaction which it actually engendered.

The language of *Cantwell v. Connecticut*, 310 U.S. 296 (1940), is appropriate here. "The offense known as breach of the peace embraces a great variety of conduct destroying or menacing public order and tranquility. It includes not only violent acts but acts and words likely to produce violence in others. No one would have the hardihood to suggest that the principle of freedom of speech sanctions incitement to riot or that religious liberty connotes the privilege to exhort others to physical attack upon those belonging to another sect. When clear and present danger of riot, disorder, interference with traffic upon the

(continued)

(continued)

public streets, or other immediate threat to public safety, peace, or order, appears, the power of the State to prevent or punish is obvious." 310 U.S. at 308. The findings of the New York courts as to the condition of the crowd and the refusal of petitioner to obey the police requests, supported as they are by the record of this case, are persuasive that the conviction of petitioner for violation of public peace, order and authority does not exceed the bounds of proper state police action. This Court respects, as it must, the interest of the community in maintaining peace and order on its streets. *Schneider v. State*, 308 U.S. 147, 160 (1939); *Kovacs v. Cooper*, 336 U.S. 77, 82 (1949). We cannot say that the preservation of that interest here encroaches on the constitutional rights of this petitioner.

We are well aware that the ordinary murmurings and objections of a hostile audience cannot be allowed to silence a speaker, and are also mindful of the possible danger of giving overzealous police officials complete discretion to break up otherwise lawful public meetings.

"A State may not unduly suppress free communication of views, religious or other, under the guise of conserving desirable conditions." *Cantwell v. Connecticut*, at 308. But we are not faced here with such a situation. It is one thing to say that the police cannot be used as an instrument for the suppression of unpopular views, and another to say that, when as here the speaker passes the bounds of argument or persuasion and undertakes incitement to riot, they are powerless to prevent a breach of the peace. Nor in this case can we condemn the considered judgment of three New York courts approving the means which the police, faced with a crisis, used in the exercise of their power and duty to preserve peace and order. The findings of the state courts as to the existing situation and the imminence of greater disorder coupled with petitioner's deliberate defiance of the police officers convince us that we should not reverse this conviction in the name of free speech.

Affirmed.

Something to Consider

Review the language in *Feiner* from *Cantwell v. Connecticut:* "The offense known as breach of the peace embraces a great variety of conduct destroying or menacing public order and tranquility. It includes not only violent acts but acts and words likely to produce violence in others. . . . . When clear and present danger of riot, disorder, interference with traffic upon the public streets, or other immediate threat to public safety, peace, or order, appears, the power of the State to prevent or punish is obvious."

Using this language as a guide, can you identify situations where "words are [or have been] likely to produce violence in others?"

Freedom of the Press—The Press Clause of the First Amendment

THE FIRST AMENDMENT PROTECTS AGAINST Congress or a state passing a law that abridges freedom of the press. An important issue involving the press is whether it has special immunity from certain laws. For example, the press has argued that it has a right not to testify before a grand jury. The Court held that the press has no such right. The press also argued that it has a special right to attend civil and criminal trials. Again, the Court does not agree.

Freedom of the Press and the Right of a Defendant to a Fair Trial

PRE-TRIAL PUBLICITY

In *Sheppard v. Maxwell*, 384 U.S. 333 (1966), the Court held that the carnival atmosphere in the courtroom violated the defendant's right to a fair trial. This atmosphere was created by the pre-trial and the trial publicity. A murder conviction was reversed as a result of the "carnival atmosphere" in the courtroom throughout the trial. An excerpt from the case follows:

Sheppard v. Maxwell
384 U.S. 333 (1966)

Petitioner's wife was bludgeoned to death July 4, 1954. From the outset officials focused suspicion on petitioner, who was arrested on a murder charge July 30 and indicted August 17. His trial began October 18 and terminated with his conviction December 21, 1954. During the entire pretrial period, virulent and incriminating publicity about petitioner and the murder made the case notorious, and the news media frequently aired charges and countercharges besides those for which petitioner was tried. Three months before trial he was examined for more than five hours without counsel in a televised three-day inquest conducted before an audience of several hundred spectators in a gymnasium. Over three weeks before trial, the newspapers published the names and addresses of prospective jurors causing them to receive letters and telephone calls about the case. The trial began two weeks before a hotly contested election at which the chief prosecutor and the trial judge were candidates for judgeships. Newsmen were allowed to take over almost the entire small courtroom, hounding petitioner, and most of the participants. Twenty reporters were assigned seats by the court within the bar and in close proximity to the jury and counsel, precluding privacy between petitioner and his counsel. The movement of the reporters in the courtroom caused frequent confusion and disrupted the trial; and in the corridors and elsewhere in and around the courthouse, they were allowed free rein by the trial judge. A broadcasting station was assigned space next to the jury room. Before the jurors began deliberations, they were not sequestered and had access to all news media though the court made "suggestions" and "requests" that the jurors not expose themselves to comment about the case. Though they were sequestered during the five days and four nights of their deliberations, the jurors were allowed to make inadequately supervised telephone calls during that period. Pervasive publicity was given to the case throughout the trial, much of it involving incriminating matter not introduced at the trial, and the jurors were thrust into the role of celebrities. At least some of the publicity deluge reached the jurors. At the very inception of the proceedings and later, the trial judge announced that neither he nor anyone else could restrict the prejudicial news accounts. Despite his awareness of the excessive pretrial publicity, the trial judge failed to take effective measures against the massive publicity that continued throughout the trial or to take adequate steps to control the conduct of the trial. The petitioner filed a habeas corpus petition contending that he did not receive a fair trial. The District Court granted the writ.

The Court of Appeals reversed.

Held:

1. The massive, pervasive, and prejudicial publicity attending petitioner's prosecution prevented him from receiving a fair trial consistent with the Due Process Clause of the Fourteenth Amendment.

   (a) Though freedom of discussion should be given the widest range compatible with the fair and orderly administration of justice, it must not be allowed to divert a trial from its purpose of adjudicating controversies according to legal procedures based on evidence received only in open court.

   (b) Identifiable prejudice to the accused need not be shown if, as in *Estes v. Texas*, 381 U.S. 532, and even more so in this case, the totality of the circumstances raises the probability of prejudice.

   (c) The trial court failed to invoke procedures which would have guaranteed petitioner a fair trial, such as adopting stricter rules for use of the courtroom by newsmen as petitioner's counsel requested, limiting their number, and more closely supervising their courtroom conduct. The court should also have insulated the witnesses; controlled the release of leads, information, and gossip to the press by police officers, witnesses, and counsel; proscribed extrajudicial statements by any lawyer, witness, party, or court official divulging prejudicial matters; and requested the appropriate city and county officials to regulate release of information by their employees.

2. The case is remanded to the District Court with instructions to release petitioner from custody unless he is tried again within a reasonable time.

   Reversed and remanded.

Something to Consider

According to the Supreme Court in *Sheppard v. Maxwell*, what could the trial judge have done to avoid the carnival atmosphere?

Fairness of Trials and Prior Restraints

Conflicts sometimes exist between the First and Sixth Amendments in connection with criminal trials and the right of the press to report on the proceedings. The press has a right, under the First Amendment, to report events. On the other hand, the defendant has a right to a fair and impartial trial, a trial where jurors are not biased or prejudiced by what they read or see. A trial judge must do what he or she can so that no one's rights are violated. One remedy frowned upon by the Court is a prior restraint on the press. A prior restraint is an order from the court prohibiting or interfering with the right to publish or speak. This is in contrast to a remedy, such as a criminal conviction or civil judgment, that takes place after the speech or publication. As a general rule, a trial judge must not use prior restraints on the press in an effort to ensure the fairness of a trial when less drastic means are available. In *Nebraska Press Assn. v. Stuart*, 427 U.S. 539 (1976), a pre-trial restraining order prohibited the press from making public any confessions made by the defendant, except confessions made directly to the press. The trial court also prohibited the press from publishing facts strongly implicative of the defendant's guilt. In addition, the trial judge restrained publication of testimony and evidence given at the preliminary hearing. The Supreme Court held that the petitioner's First Amendment rights were violated. Even though this case was "moot" before it came before the Court, the Justices heard the case because it was the type of case that was capable of reoccurring. An excerpt from the Syllabus follows:

Nebraska Press Association v. Stuart
427 U.S. 539 (1976)

Respondent Nebraska state trial judge, in anticipation of a trial for a multiple murder which had attracted widespread news coverage, entered an order which, as modified by the Nebraska Supreme Court, restrained petitioner newspaper, broadcasters, journalists, news media associations, and national newswire services from publishing or broadcasting accounts of confessions or admissions made by the accused to law enforcement officers or third parties, except members of the press, and other facts "strongly implicative" of the accused. The modification of the order had occurred in the course of an action by petitioners, which had sought a stay of the trial court's original order and in which the accused and the State of Nebraska intervened. This Court granted certiorari to determine whether the order violated the constitutional guarantee of freedom of the press. The order expired by its own terms when the jury was impaneled. Respondent was convicted; his appeal is pending in the Nebraska Supreme Court.

Held:

1. The case is not moot simply because the order has expired, since the controversy between the parties is "capable of repetition, yet evading review."

2. While the guarantees of freedom of expression are not an absolute prohibition under all circumstances, the barriers to prior restraint remain high and the presumption against its use continues intact. Although it is unnecessary to establish a priority between First Amendment rights and the Sixth Amendment right to a fair trial under all circumstances, as the authors of the Bill of Rights themselves declined to do, the protection against prior restraint should have particular force as applied to reporting of criminal proceedings.

3. The heavy burden imposed as a condition to securing a prior restraint was not met in this case.

(a) On the pretrial record the trial judge was justified in concluding that there would be intense and pervasive pretrial publicity concerning the case, and he could also reasonably conclude, based on common human experience, that publicity might impair the accused's right to a fair trial. His conclusion as to the impact of such publicity on prospective jurors was of necessity speculative, however, dealing as he was with factors unknown and unknowable.

(continued)

(continued)

(b) There is no finding that measures short of prior restraint on the press and speech would not have protected the accused's rights; the Nebraska Supreme Court no more than implied that alternative measures might not suffice, and the record lacks evidence that would support such a finding.

(c) It is not clear that prior restraint on publication would have effectively protected the accused's rights, in view of such practical problems as the limited territorial jurisdiction of the trial court issuing the restraining order, the difficulties inherent in predicting what information will in fact undermine the jurors' impartiality, the problem of drafting an order that will effectively keep prejudicial information from prospective jurors, and the fact that in this case the events occurred in a small community where rumors would travel swiftly by word of mouth.

(d) To the extent that the order prohibited the reporting of evidence adduced at the open preliminary hearing held to determine whether the accused should be bound over for trial, it violated the settled principle that "there is nothing that proscribes the press from reporting events that transpire in the courtroom," *Sheppard v. Maxwell*, 384 U.S. 333, 362–363, and the portion of the order restraining publication of other facts "strongly implicative" of the accused is too vague and too broad to survive the scrutiny given to restraints on First Amendment rights.

Reversed.

Something to Consider

Reread the following language from the case: "While the guarantees of freedom of expression are not an absolute prohibition under all circumstances, the barriers to prior restraint remain high and the presumption against its use continues intact. Although it is unnecessary to establish a priority between First Amendment rights and the Sixth Amendment right to a fair trial under all circumstances, as the authors of the Bill of Rights themselves declined to do, the protection against prior restraint should have particular force as applied to reporting of criminal proceedings." Does the Court seem to favor one amendment over the other?

Access to Prisoners and Courtrooms

The public has a right to attend trials. This is a presumptive right under the First Amendment. However, when a judge has a compelling reason for closing a courtroom, this right may be overridden. The public has no right to visit with or interview prisoners. However, prison authorities may grant this right. The press has no special right of access to courtrooms or jails or prisons. The rights of the public and the press are the same when it comes to the issues of access to courtrooms and prisoners. In *Richmond Newspapers, Inc. v. Virginia*, 448 U.S. 555 (1980), the Court explained its basic reasoning.

> As we have shown, and as was shown in both the Court's opinion and the dissent in *Gannett,* 443 U.S. at 384, 386, n. 15, 418-425, the historical evidence demonstrate conclusively that, at the time when our organic laws were adopted, criminal trials both here and in England had long been presumptively open. This is no quirk of history; rather, it has long been recognized as an indispensable attribute of an Anglo-American trial. Both Hale in the 17th century and Blackstone in the 18th saw the importance of openness to the proper functioning of a trial; it gave assurance that the proceedings were conducted fairly to all concerned, and it discouraged perjury, the misconduct of participants, and decisions based on secret bias or partiality.

In this case, all counsel agreed the court should be closed. It was the press who objected. The Supreme Court agreed with the press that the courtroom should remain open.

A few years after *Richmond Newspapers, Inc.* the Court in *Globe Newspaper Co. v. Superior Court*, 457 U.S. 596 (1982). reaffirmed its position. Although the Court recognized that some situations might justify closing a courtroom to the public, the right is not absolute, even when the testimony involves a minor witness who was the victim of a sexual assault. A law requiring closure of the courtroom in all such cases was found unconstitutional. Cases had to be evaluated on a case-by-case basis.

Reporters' Privilege

Did You Know?

Oliver Wendell Holmes retired from the U.S. Supreme Court at the age of ninety. Justice Holmes served on the Massachusetts Supreme Court for twenty years before serving twenty-nine years on the U.S. Supreme Court.

Courtesy of Historical/CORBIS

Reporters and journalists often claim that the First Amendment gives them the privilege not to disclose confidential sources used in researching and writing a story. However, the Supreme Court has not officially recognized such a privilege, although many states have laws creating such privileges. Absent a law to the contrary, there is no special privilege exempting reporters from (1) search warrants, and (2) testifying before a grand jury. Reporters have no special privilege permitting them to refuse to testify during a deposition. The media may be liable in a civil suit for breach of a promise not to disclose the identity of a source. In general, reporters and other media are treated like other members of the public when it comes to search warrants, subpoenas, and breaches of promise. For example, in *Zurcher v. Stanford Daily*, 436 U.S. 547 (1978), the Court allowed a search warrant, rather than a subpoena, for a search of the *Stanford Daily* offices (a student newspaper). Police believed the office contained evidence of a crime, namely, photographs showing conflict between police officers and students during a demonstration at the Stanford University Hospital.

When Government May Require the Press to Disseminate Certain Messages

PRINT MEDIA

The government cannot require newspapers to provide free space to political candidates. This usually involves "reply" space in the paper. However, the rule is different for broadcast media. Electronic media differ from printed media because they are granted a monopoly through the licenses given by the Federal Communications Commission (FCC).

BROADCAST MEDIA

🏛 **fairness doctrine**

A former Federal Communications Commission rule that broadcasters must present, or give others a chance to present, all sides of major public issues if they present one side.

Due to spectrum scarcity (a limited number of frequencies) for television and radio, some government regulation is permitted. The reasoning behind this is that this regulation enhances fairness and access. In the past, the FCC adopted rules that fostered fairness and access. These rules are sometimes referred to as the **fairness doctrine or** "equal time doctrine." Under these doctrines, the federal government may require television and radio stations to provide reply time to respond to political editorials and personal attacks. The Supreme Court generally upholds these regulations and the case of *Red Lion Broadcasting Co. v. FCC* explains. However, these doctrines are created in regulations of the FCC rather than case law, and these regulations vary from time to time. The following is an excerpt from *Red Lion Broadcasting Co. v. FCC* illustrating the Supreme Court's rulings regarding government regulation in connection with political issues and candidates:

Red Lion Broadcasting Co. v. FCC

395 U.S. 367 (1969)

Together with No. 717, United States et al. v. Radio Television News Directors Assn., on certiorari to the United States Court of Appeals for the Seventh Circuit, argued April 3, 1969.

The Federal Communications Commission (FCC) has for many years imposed on broadcasters a "fairness doctrine," requiring that public issues be presented by broadcasters and that each side of those issues be given fair coverage. In No. 2, the FCC declared that petitioner Red Lion Broadcasting Co. had failed to meet its obligation under the fairness doctrine when it carried a program which constituted a personal attack on one Cook, and ordered it to send a transcript of the broadcast to Cook and provide reply time, whether or not Cook would pay for it. The Court of Appeals upheld the FCC's position. After the commencement of the Red Lion litigation the FCC began a rule-making proceeding to make the personal attack aspect of the fairness doctrine more precise and more readily enforceable, and to specify its rules relating to political editorials. The rules, as adopted and amended, were held unconstitutional by the Court of Appeals in RTNDA (No. 717), as abridging the freedoms of speech and press.

Held:

1. The history of the fairness doctrine and of related legislation shows that the FCC's action in the *Red Lion* case did not exceed its authority, and that in adopting the new regulations the FCC was implementing congressional policy.

   (a) The fairness doctrine began shortly after the Federal Radio Commission was established to allocate frequencies among competing applicant in the public interest, and insofar as there is an affirmative obligation of the broadcaster to see that both

sides are presented, the personal attack doctrine and regulations do not differ from the fairness doctrine.

   (b) The FCC's statutory mandate to see that broadcasters operate in the public interest and Congress' reaffirmation, in the 1959 amendment to 315 of the Communications Act, of the FCC's view that the fairness doctrine inhered in the public interest standard, support the conclusion that the doctrine and its component personal attack and political editorializing regulations are a legitimate exercise of congressionally delegated authority.

2. The fairness doctrine and its specific manifestations in the personal attack and political editorial rules do not violate the First Amendment.

   (a) The First Amendment is relevant to public broadcasting, but it is the right of the viewing and listening public, and not the right of the broadcasters, which is paramount.

   (b) The First Amendment does not protect private censorship by broadcasters who are licensed by the Government to use a scarce resource which is denied to others.

   (c) The danger that licensees will eliminate coverage of controversial issues as a result of the personal attack and political editorial rules is at best speculative, and, in any event, the FCC has authority to guard against this danger.

   (d) There was nothing vague about the FCC's specific ruling in the *Red Lion* case and the regulations at issue in No. 717 could be employed in precisely the same way as the fairness doctrine in *Red Lion*. It is not necessary to decide every aspect of the fairness doctrine to decide these cases. Problems involving more extreme applications or more

(continued)

(continued)

difficult constitutional questions will be dealt with if and when they arise.

(e) It has not been shown that the scarcity of broadcast frequencies, which impelled governmental regulation, is entirely a thing of the past, as new uses for the frequency spectrum have kept pace with improved technology and more efficient utilization of that spectrum.

Something to Consider

The Court held that since the "marketplace" is limited, enforcing fairness is constitutional. Discuss this concept. Should this concept apply to online social media sites, such as Facebook?

The First Amendment does not require broadcasters to accept paid editorial advertisements. In the early 1970s, the Democratic National Committee, along with a group in opposition to the Vietnam War, were denied access when they attempted to purchase air time to broadcast their views on issues of wide general public interest and importance. The Court found no constitutional violation.

Taxes and the Press

COMPENSATION FOR VICTIMS OF CRIME

In 1991, the Supreme Court struck down the state of New York's "Son of Sam" law. This law required that funds earned by an accused or convicted criminal for the right to her or his story be given to the victim of the crime.

Simon & Schuster, Inc. v. Members of the N.Y. State Crime Victims Bd.

502 U.S. 105 (1991)

Among other things, New York's "Son of Sam" law provides that an "entity" contracting with a person "accused or convicted of a crime" for the production of a book or other work describing the crime must pay to respondent Crime Victims Board any moneys owed to that person under the contract; requires the Board to deposit such funds in an escrow account for payment to any victim who, within five years, obtains a civil judgment against the accused or convicted person and to the criminal's other creditors; and defines "person convicted of a crime" to include "any person who has voluntarily and intelligently admitted the commission of a crime for which such person is not prosecuted." After it discovered that petitioner publisher had signed an agreement with an author who had contracted with admitted organized crime figure Henry Hill for the production of a book about Hill's life, the Board, inter alia, determined that petitioner had violated the Son of Sam law and ordered it to turn over all money payable to Hill. Petitioner then brought suit under 42 U.S.C. §1983, seeking a declaration that the law violates the First Amendment, and an injunction barring the law's enforcement. The District Court found the law to be consistent with the Amendment, and the Court of Appeals affirmed.

Held: The Son of Sam law is inconsistent with the First Amendment.

(continued)

(continued)

(a) Whether the First Amendment "speaker" is considered to be Hill, whose income the New York law places in escrow because of the story he has told, or petitioner, which can publish books about crime with the assistance of only those criminals willing to forgo remuneration for at least five years, the law singles out speech on a particular subject for a financial burden that it places on no other speech and no other income and, thus, is presumptively inconsistent with the Amendment. *Leathers v. Medlock*, 499 U.S. 439, 447; *Arkansas Writers' Project, Inc. v. Ragland*, 481 U.S. 221, 230. The fact that the law escrows speech-derived income, rather than taxing a percentage of it outright as did the law invalidated in Arkansas Writers' Project, cannot serve as the basis for disparate treatment under the Amendment, since both forms of financial burden operate as disincentives to speak. Moreover, the Board's assertion that discriminatory financial treatment is suspect only when the legislature intends to suppress certain ideas is incorrect, since this Court has long recognized that even regulations aimed at proper governmental concerns can restrict unduly the exercise of rights under the Amendment. Furthermore, the Board's claim that the law is permissible under the Amendment because it focuses generally on an "entity," rather than specifically on the media, falters, first, on semantic grounds, since any entity that enters into a contract with a convicted person to transmit that person's speech becomes, by definition, a medium of communication, and, second, on constitutional grounds, since the governmental power to impose content-based financial disincentives on speech does not vary with the identity of the speaker. Accordingly, in order to justify the differential treatment imposed by the law, the State must show that its regulation is necessary to serve a compelling state interest, and is narrowly drawn to achieve that end. *Id.*, at 231.

(b) The State has a compelling interest in compensating victims from the fruits of crime. *Cf. Caplin & Drysdale, Chartered v. United States*, 491 U.S. 617, 629. However, contrary to the Board's assertion, the State has little if any interest in limiting such compensation to the proceeds of the wrongdoer's speech about the crime. The Board cannot explain why the State should have any greater interest in compensating victims from the proceeds of criminals' "storytelling" than from any of their other assets, nor offer any justification for a distinction between this expressive activity and any other activity in connection with its interest in transferring the fruits of crime from criminals to their victims. *Cf., e.g., Arkansas Writers' Project*, at 231. Like the governmental entities in the latter and similar cases, the Board has taken the effect of the statute and posited that effect as the State's interest.

(c) The New York law is not narrowly tailored to achieve the State's objective of compensating victims from the profits of crime. The law is significantly overinclusive, since it applies to works on any subject provided that they express the author's thoughts or recollections about his crime, however tangentially or incidentally, and since its broad definition of "person convicted of a crime" enables the Board to escrow the income of an author who admits in his work to having committed a crime, whether or not he was ever actually accused or convicted. These two provisions combine to encompass a wide range of existing and potential works that do not enable a criminal to profit from his crime while a victim remains uncompensated.

Something to Consider

Explain why the court in *Simon & Schuster, Inc. v. Members of the New York State Crime Victims Bd.* held New York's "Son of Sam" law presumptively unconstitutional.

Sales Tax on the Sale of Cable Television Services

An Arkansas sales tax applied to cable television services. However, receipts from the sale of newspapers and magazines were exempted from the tax applied to cable television services. The cable services sued. The Court found the tax survived a First Amendment challenge because this tax (1) did not discriminate on the basis of the content of the speech, (2) the tax was not intended to create a danger of suppression of ideas, and (3) it did not have the *effect* of creating a danger of suppression of ideas.

Leathers v. Medlock
499 U.S. 439 (1991)

Arkansas' Gross Receipts Act imposes a tax on receipts from the sale of all tangible personal property and specified services, but expressly exempts, inter alia, certain receipts from newspaper and magazine sales. In 1987, Act 188 amended the Gross Receipts Act to impose the tax on cable television. Petitioners in No. 90-38, a cable television subscriber, a cable operator, and a cable trade organization (cable petitioners), brought this class action in the State Chancery Court, contending that their expressive rights under the First Amendment and their rights under the Equal Protection Clause of the Fourteenth Amendment were violated by the extension of the tax to cable services, the exemption from the tax of newspapers and magazines, and the exclusion from the list of services subject to the tax of scrambled satellite broadcast television services to home dish antennae owners. In 1989, shortly after the Chancery Court upheld the constitutionality of Act 188, Arkansas adopted Act 769, which extended the tax to, among other things, all television services to paying customers. On appeal, the State Supreme Court held that the tax was not invalid after the passage of Act 769 because the Constitution does not prohibit the differential taxation of different media. However, believing that the First Amendment does prohibit discriminatory taxation among members of the same medium, and that cable and scrambled satellite television services were "substantially the same," the Supreme Court held that the tax was unconstitutional for the period during which it applied to cable but not satellite broadcast services.

Held:

1. Arkansas' extension of its generally applicable sales tax to cable television services alone, or to cable and satellite services, while exempting the print media, does not violate the First Amendment.
   (a) Although cable television, which provides news, information, and entertainment to its subscribers, is engaged in "speech" and is part of the "press" in much of its operation, the fact that it is taxed differently from other media does not, by itself, raise First Amendment concerns. The Arkansas tax presents none of the First Amendment difficulties that have led this Court to strike down differential taxation of speakers. *See, e.g., Grosjean v. American Press Co.*, 297 U.S. 233; *Minneapolis Star & Tribune Co. v. Minnesota Comm'r of Revenue*, 460 U.S. 575; *Arkansas Writers' Project, Inc. v. Ragland*, 481 U.S. 221. It is a tax of general applicability covering all tangible personal property and a broad range of services and, thus, does not single out the press, and thereby threaten to hinder it as a watchdog of government activity. Furthermore, there is no indication that Arkansas has targeted cable television in a purposeful attempt to interfere with its First Amendment activities, nor is the tax structured so as to raise suspicion that it was intended to do so. Arkansas has not selected a small group of speakers to bear fully the burden of the tax, since, even if the State Supreme Court's finding that cable and satellite television are the same medium is accepted, Act 188 extended the tax uniformly to the approximately 100 cable systems then operating in the State. Finally, the tax is not content-based, since there is nothing in the statute's language that refers to the content of mass media communications, and since the record contains no evidence that the variety of programming cable television offers subscribers differs systematically in its message from that communicated by satellite broadcast programming, newspapers, or magazines.
   (b) Thus, cable petitioners can prevail only if the Arkansas tax scheme presents "an additional basis" for concluding that the State has violated their First Amendment rights. *See Arkansas Writers* at 233. This Court's decisions do not support their argument that such a basis exists here, because the tax discriminates among media and discriminated for a time within a medium.

(continued)

(continued)

Taken together, cases such as *Regan v. Taxation with Representation of Washington*, 461 U.S. 540, *Mabee v. White Plains Publishing Co.*, 327 U.S. 178, and *Oklahoma Press Publishing Co. v. Walling*, 327 U.S. 186, establish that differential taxation of speakers, even members of the press, does not implicate the First Amendment unless the tax is directed at, or presents the danger of suppressing, particular ideas. Nothing about Arkansas' choice to exclude or exempt certain media from its tax has ever suggested an interest in censoring the expressive activities of cable television. Nor does anything in the record indicate that this broad-based, content-neutral tax is likely to stifle the free exchange of ideas.

2. The question whether Arkansas' temporary tax distinction between cable and satellite services violated the Equal Protection Clause must be addressed by the State Supreme Court on remand.

Affirmed in part, reversed in part, and remanded.

❧ Ethical Decisions—Everyday Choices ❧

The Facts: On the evening news, Elizabeth (an attorney) hears about a crackdown on Web sites containing pornographic images of children. She hears the name of one of the sites that was shut down, but the person managing the Web site has not yet been identified. She recognizes the name of the site as being one of the names on a list of Web sites involved in a client's business transaction.

The Problem: Can Elizabeth alert authorities about the identity of her client who is the person managing the Web site containing pornographic images of children?

Guiding Principles: Elizabeth has an ethical duty to protect client confidentiality. However, a lawyer may reveal information to the extent the lawyer believes it is necessary to prevent her client from committing criminal acts that she reasonably believes are likely to result in *substantial* bodily harm.

Chapter Summary

Freedom of expression includes speech, press, assembly, petition, and religion. First Amendment rights were designed to guarantee that Americans would not live under restraints on freedom of expression.

Several theories help to explain why speech is protected by the Constitution. It is the "marketplace of ideas," and thus promotes truth; it includes "political speech," which is the cornerstone of American government; it promotes "tolerance" and "autonomy" that strengthen the worth of the individual. All of these theories influence Supreme Court decisions regarding freedom of speech. Speech includes spoken words and other forms of expression. This includes symbolic speech, which is action that delivers a message. Symbolic speech can be constitutionally protected as is the right to speak in a public forum. Also constitutionally protected is the right not to be forced to speak, for example, being forced to recite the Pledge of Allegiance. Political campaign finance laws also involve free speech rights since "money is speech" in political campaigns.

Not all speech is constitutionally protected. The following is a list of types of speech that receive no constitutional protection: obscenity, fighting words, and speech intended to incite illegal action. Some types of speech, such as defamation, hate speech, speech in public schools, and commercial speech, receive some limited protection. A defamation action requires a showing that the defendant had actual malice when the plaintiff is a public figure or public official. The award of punitive damages also requires actual malice if the defamatory statement concerns a matter of public concern. Hate speech is protected when no intimidating or otherwise illegal conduct is associated with the speech. Students in public schools do have some rights of free speech. However, it is not coextensive with the rights of adults in other settings, and it must be applied in light of the special characteristics of the school environment. A school need not tolerate student speech that is inconsistent with its basic educational mission, even though the government could not censor similar speech outside the school. However, regulation of speech in a public school must be reasonably related to the educational mission. Commercial speech is generally protected unless it is misleading or untruthful.

The First Amendment protects the right to petition and the right to assemble. Although these rights have not generated much case law, the Court has made it clear that the right to assembly means a peaceful assembly and does not give citizens the right to riot or block public streets.

The First Amendment protects against Congress or a state passing a law that abridges freedom of the press. Like freedom of speech, freedom of the press is not an absolute freedom, as the Supreme Court decided in several cases. Restrictions on the press arise in connection with the right of a criminal defendant to a fair trial. In order to avoid a carnival atmosphere and a potentially unfair trial, a judge can place limitations on the press. However, the Court cannot place a prior restraint on what the press can publish when less drastic measures are available. As a result of freedom of the press, reporters have a privilege to keep certain information confidential, but this privilege has limitations. Reporters are not exempt from search warrants and subpoenas. The press has the right to advocate or allow political positions and messages. However, because of the unique influence of television and radio in society, the Court created what might be called a "fairness doctrine." Under this doctrine the federal government may require television and radio stations to provide reply time to respond to political editorials and personal attacks. However, a state cannot force a publisher to compensate crime victims from profits derived from works written by criminals.

Key Terms

seditious libel	defamation	slander
prurient interest	libel	fairness doctrine

Questions for Review

1. What are the five rights included in freedom of expression?
2. Discuss the theories explaining why speech should be constitutionally protected.
3. What are the different types of speech that are constitutionally protected?
4. Why do political campaign finance laws involve freedom of speech issues?
5. What types of speech are not constitutionally protected?
6. What are some of the free speech issues of students in public schools?
7. What types of conduct are not protected by the right to assembly?
8. Compare and contrast the right to a free press with the rights of criminal defendants.
9. What is reporters' privilege, and what are some of its limitations?
10. When can the government require the press to disseminate information?

Questions for Analysis

1. Why did the Supreme Court believe that burning the American flag was protected by the First Amendment but that burning a draft card was not?
2. According to the Supreme Court in *Miller v. California*, what are the guidelines for determining obscenity? Do these standards work for obscene material posted on the Internet?
3. According to *Gertz v. Robert Welch, Inc.*, what makes a person a public figure?
4. Both *R.A.V. v. City of St. Paul* and *Wisconsin v. Mitchell* deal with ordinances based on racial prejudice. Why did the Court find one statute invalid while the other was valid?
5. Several Supreme Court cases dealing with freedom of the press are highly critical of laws that impose a prior restraint on the press. What is meant by "prior restraint," and why is the Court so critical of such rules?
6. In *Citizens United v. Federal Election Com'n*, 558 U.S. ___, (2010), why did the Court uphold part of a statute requiring disclosure of certain independent expenditures for political campaigns while striking down the part prohibiting corporate campaign contributions?
7. How did the Court distinguish *United States v. Williams*, 553 U.S. 285 (2008), from *Ashcroft v. Free Speech Coalition*, 535 U.S. 234 (2002)?
8. Explain why the "public forum doctrine" is not applicable to monuments on public property. *See Pleasant Grove City, Utah v. Summum*, 555 U.S. 460 (2009).

Assignments and Projects

1. Following the format provided in previous chapters, brief *Cox v. New Hampshire*, 312 U.S. 569 (1941).
2. Locate and read *Miller v. California*, 413 U.S. 15 (1973). Do you believe the three "guidelines" articulated in *Miller* adequately "guide" later courts? Why or why not? Should there be another approach? If so, what do you suggest?
3. Locate and read *Columbia Broadcasting System, Inc. v. Democratic Natl. Committee*, 412 U.S. 94 (1973). How did the Court justify holding that the First Amendment does not require broadcasters to accept paid editorial advertisements?
4. Read the excerpt from the Brief on the Merits in the *Morse v. Frederick*, 551 U.S. 383 (2007) school speech case. (Appendix G) Notice how the author uses the school speech cases (*Tinker*, *Fraser*, and *Kuhlmeier*) to make his argument. Write a short summary of the argument made in the Brief on the Merits.

Putting It into Practice

1. Review the Mendes facts in Living with the Constitution at the beginning of this chapter. Assume that your law firm represents Jaime Mendes. Write a letter to the school appealing Jaime's suspension.
2. In the event that a letter does not achieve the desired result, a lawsuit may need to be filed. This type of lawsuit is often based on the U.S. Code, Title 42, section 1983 (42 U.S.C. § 1983). Locate and read a copy of this code section. Write a paragraph explaining if this code section applies to the Mendes case.

Group Activities

....

1. Discuss the following question in small groups: Should a school be able to discipline a student for remarks made by the student on a social media site, such as Facebook or Twitter, if those remarks are unfairly critical of a teacher?

2. Oral arguments from many Supreme Court cases can now be accessed from various sources, including the Internet. Locate the oral arguments for *Morse v. Frederick,* 551 U.S. 383 (2007). Listen to the oral argument made by the first advocate, Mr. Kenneth Starr. Discuss what makes this argument persuasive. What do you notice about how the justices ask questions?

3. An excerpt from the written argument (Brief on the Merits) filed in *Morse v. Frederick*, 551 U.S. 383 (2007), by Mr. Kenneth Starr, is in Appendix G. Compare the content of the brief with the content of the argument. What do you notice?

12 Freedom of Religion

The freedom to hold religious beliefs and opinions is absolute.

Supreme Court Chief Justice Earl Warren

Chapter Objectives

When you complete this chapter you should be able to

1. quote the language of the First Amendment that guarantees freedom of religion.

2. compare and contrast the Establishment Clause with the Free Exercise Clause.

3. describe how the Supreme Court explains the term *religion*.

4. identify the three major theories regarding interpretation of the Establishment Clause.

5. explain the effect of the First Amendment on prayer in public schools.

6. describe how the teaching of evolution created a freedom of religion issue.

7. summarize the arguments for and against grants of tax exemption to religious institutions.

8. analyze circumstances under which the government can give financial aid to religious schools.

9. explain the relevance under the Free Exercise Clause of the difference between religious conduct and religious beliefs.

10. describe how the Supreme Court applies the Free Exercise Clause to claims for unemployment benefits, compulsory education, and Sunday closing laws.

Looking Back

Before reading this chapter, review the following concepts from previous chapters:

Incorporation doctrine The rights established by the Bill of Rights originally applied only to the federal government. However, the Supreme Court decided that most of the rights expressly stated in the Bill of Rights also apply to the states because they are incorporated through the Fourteenth Amendment that prohibits any state from taking away a person's life, liberty, or property without due process of law. (Chapter 7)

Strict scrutiny One standard used by the Supreme Court to review the constitutionality of laws; under this standard, a law is constitutional only if it is *necessary* to achieve a *compelling* state interest. Laws that burden a fundamental right are reviewed under this standard. (Chapter 8)

Rational basis test One standard used by the Supreme Court to review the constitutionality of laws; under this test, a law is constitutional as long as it has a *reasonable* relationship to *legitimate* government interests. (Chapter 8)

Standing A person's right to bring a lawsuit because he or she is directly affected by the issues raised. Taxpayers generally do not have standing to challenge the way their tax money is spent. However, an exception exists when the taxpayer bases a challenge on a violation of the Establishment Clause. (Chapter 3)

Living with the Constitution

Simonds Elementary School, a public school, received a number of complaints about its proposed Christmas program. The children are presenting a short skit based on the Dickens novel, *A Christmas Carol.* When the skit ends, there will be a short intermission after which parents and students will be invited to remain for a group singing of Christmas carols, including the traditional "Silent Night." The principal of the school is sure that the skit does not intrude on anyone's religious beliefs. The skit is clearly not religious, and the singing is entirely voluntary. In spite of the complaints, the school plans to go ahead with the program as planned.

"CONGRESS SHALL MAKE NO LAW respecting an establishment of religion; or prohibiting the free exercise thereof." This is the opening language of the First Amendment. These two seemingly simple clauses are at the center of an ongoing debate over what this language means and what the framers of the Bill of Rights intended. Historians and scholars do not agree about what Congress actually intended when it voted for this First Amendment language. One thing is certain: The United States has seen tremendous change since the First Amendment was ratified. Today, the United States is a much more religiously diverse country than in the eighteenth century. Interestingly, public schools continue to play a vital role in the Court's review and interpretation of the religion clauses. But, it is important to keep in mind that public education, as we now know it, did not exist when the Bill of Rights was ratified. These differences make using history in the interpretation of the religion clauses problematic. This chapter discusses the First Amendment right to freedom of religion and its application in society today.

Religious Protections of the First Amendment

THE FIRST AMENDMENT PROVIDES TWO protections regarding religion. It prohibits Congress from making any law regarding the establishment of religion, as well as any law prohibiting the free exercise of religion. "Congress shall make no law respecting an establishment of religion" is referred to as the **Establishment Clause**. "[P]rohibiting the free exercise thereof" is known as the **Free Exercise Clause**. The Supreme Court has held that these clauses apply to the states as well as to the federal government. Through *Cantwell v. Connecticut*, 310 U.S. 296 (1940), the Free Exercise Clause was applied to the states. In *Everson v. Board of Education*, 330 U.S. 1 (1947), the Court incorporated and applied the Establishment Clause to the states. The Establishment Clause is directed at the actions of governments. The Free Exercise Clause safeguards a person's individual liberty.

There is an inherent tension between the two religion clauses, and, at times, this tension is difficult to reconcile. Justice Stewart, in his dissenting opinion in the *School Dist. v. Schempp* case, focuses on the following example as a tension between the clauses. When the government provides and compensates ministers for soldiers in the armed services, it may establish religion. However, if the government declines to do so, it may deny the free exercise of religion. Mandatory school prayer is another example of the government establishing religion when prayer is allowed, but it denies the free exercise of religious beliefs for persons who do not believe in these prayers.

The Court fashioned a three-part test to be used for the Establishment Clause. The government violates the Establishment Clause if (1) the government's primary purpose is to advance religion, or (2) if the principal effect is to inhibit or aid religion, or (3) if there is government entanglement with religion. This is the *Lemon v. Kurtzman* test. 403 U.S. 602 (1971). The problem with this is that when government takes action to protect the free exercise of religion, its purpose is to advance religion, and the effect is to facilitate free exercise. The result is that government is aiding religion. This issue was also addressed in the *Everson* case. This case concerned the constitutionality of a New Jersey policy of reimbursing the parents of Catholic school students for the cost of busing their children to school. The Court considered both the Establishment and Free Exercise Clause stating:

> New Jersey cannot consistently with the "establishment of religion" clause of the First Amendment contribute tax-raised funds to the support of an institution which teaches the tenets and faith of any church. On the other hand, other language of the amendment commands that New Jersey cannot hamper its citizens in the free exercise of their own religion. Consequently, it cannot exclude individual

---

🏛 **Establishment Clause**

That part of the First Amendment to the U.S. Constitution that states "Congress shall make no law respecting an *establishment* of religion."

🏛 **Free Exercise Clause**

That part of the First Amendment to the U.S. Constitution that states "Congress shall make no law ... prohibiting the *free exercise [of religion].*"

> Catholics, Lutherans, Mohammedans, Baptists, Jews, Methodists, Non-believers, Presbyterians, or the members of any other faith, because of their faith, or lack of it, from receiving the benefits of public welfare legislation. While we do not mean to intimate that a state could not provide transportation only to children attending public schools, we must be careful, in protecting the citizens of New Jersey against state-established churches, to be sure that we do not inadvertently prohibit New Jersey from extending its general State law benefits to all its citizens without regard to their religious belief.

The Court concluded that the state policy did not violate the First Amendment.

The Court recognizes this inherent tension in other cases. In *Walz v. Tax Com. of New York*, 397 U.S. 664, 668–69 (1970), the Court said: "[A] neutral course between the two Religion Clauses, both of which are cast in absolute terms, and either of which if expanded to a logical extreme, would tend to clash with the other."

Although a conflict sometimes exists, both Establishment and Free Exercise Clauses protect religious actions and religious beliefs. In this way the clauses are compatible. In a concurring opinion, Justice Brennan stated that the "Establishment Clause [is] a co-guarantor, with the Free Exercise Clause, of religious liberty. The Framers did not trust the liberty of religious beliefs to either clause alone." *School Dist. v. Schempp*, 374 U.S. 203, 256 (1963). His point is that the Establishment Clause also protects individual liberty. Almost thirty years later, the Court held that "a state-created orthodoxy puts at grave risk that freedom of belief and conscience which are the sole assurance that religious faith is real, not imposed." *Lee v. Weisman*, 505 U.S. 577, 592 (1992). In *Weisman*, the Court held that a clergy-led prayer at a high school graduation ceremony was unconstitutional.

What Is Religion?

THE COURT, TO DATE, HAS avoided defining "religion." It may not be possible to create a definition that includes the diverse spiritual practices and beliefs now present in the United States. There is concern that a definition of religion, that is, choosing one definition, is the "establishment" of religion. Again, the tension between the clauses is apparent. Under the Free Exercise Clause a very broad definition is necessary to protect religious conduct. On the other hand, under the Establishment Clause a very narrow definition is needed to limit the constraints on government.

In *Everson v. Board of Education*, 330 U.S. 1 (1947), in a dissenting opinion, one justice rejected the notion of two definitions of religion. "Religion appears only once in the Amendment. But the word governs two prohibitions and governs them alike. It does not have two meanings, one narrow to forbid 'an establishment' and another much broader, for 'securing' the free exercise thereof." 330 U.S. at 32 (Rutledge, J., dissenting).

The Court has considered the issue of the definition of religion. In 1890, in *Davis v. Beason*, 133 U.S. 333, the Court stated: "[T]he term 'religion' has reference to one's view of his relations to his Creator, and to the obligations they impose of reverence for His being and character, and obedience to His will." The Court's view of religion over one hundred years ago probably fit the beliefs of many citizens at that time. Today, American society is very different.

Attempts at Defining Religion: Selective Service Act

In 1965, the Court heard a case in which four men, claiming conscientious objector status, refused to serve in the armed forces in the Vietnam War. *United States v. Seeger*, 380 U.S. 163 (1965). In *Seeger*, the Court worked with the Universal Training and Selective Service

Act that authorized the military draft. This Act exempted from combat duty persons "who by reason of their religious training and belief are conscientiously opposed to participation in war in any form." 380 U.S. 163, 164–165 (1965). The Act defined "religious training and belief" as "an individual's belief in relation to a Supreme Being involving duties superior to those arising from any human relation," but this did not include "essentially political, sociological, or philosophical views or a merely personal moral code." One of the men in *Seeger* denied any belief in a Supreme Being, yet he sought a religious exemption from the Vietnam War draft. The Court held:

> Congress in using the expression "Supreme Being" rather than the designation "God" was merely clarifying the meaning of religious tradition and belief so as to embrace all religions and to exclude essentially political, sociological, or philosophical views [and] the test of belief "in a relation to a Supreme Being" is whether a given belief that is sincere and meaningful occupies a place in the life of its possessor or parallel to the orthodox belief in God.

Interestingly, the Court recognized all four men as conscientious objectors on religious grounds. However, the Court stopped short of providing a test for assessing whether or not a specific viewpoint is religious under this definition. It is critical to remember that the Supreme Court defined religion only while interpreting a statutory provision. This was not a constitutional interpretation.

United States v. Seeger is set forth below in an edited format. The focus of this edited version of the case is on Mr. Seegers's situation.

United States v. Seeger
380 U.S. 163 (1965)

MR. JUSTICE CLARK delivered the opinion of the Court.

These cases involve claims of conscientious objectors under 6(j) of the Universal Military Training and Service Act, 50 U.S.C. App. 456(j) (1958 ed.), which exempts from combatant training and service in the armed forces of the United States those persons who by reason of their religious training and belief are conscientiously opposed to participation in war in any form. The parties raise the basic question of the constitutionality of the section which defines the term "religious training and belief," as used in the Act, as "an individual's belief in a relation to a Supreme Being involving duties superior to those arising from any human relation, but [not including] essentially political, sociological, or philosophical views or a merely personal moral code." The constitutional attack is launched under the First Amendment's Establishment and Free Exercise Clauses and is twofold: (1) The section does not exempt nonreligious conscientious objectors; and (2) it discriminates between different forms of religious expression in violation of the Due Process Clause of the Fifth Amendment.

We have concluded that Congress, in using the expression "Supreme Being" rather than the designation "God," was merely clarifying the meaning of religious training and belief so as to embrace all religions and to exclude essentially political, sociological, or philosophical views. We believe that under this construction, the test of belief "in a relation to a Supreme Being" is whether a given belief that is sincere and meaningful occupies a place in the life of its possessor parallel to that filled by the orthodox belief in God of one who clearly qualifies for the exemption. Where such beliefs have parallel positions in the lives of their respective holders we cannot say that one is "in a relation to a Supreme Being" and the other is not.

The Facts

Seeger was convicted in the District Court for the Southern District of New York of having refused to submit to induction in the armed forces. Although he did not adopt verbatim the printed Selective Service System form, he declared that he was conscientiously opposed to participation in war in any form by reason of his

(continued)

(continued)

"religious" belief; that he preferred to leave the question as to his belief in a Supreme Being open, "rather than answer 'yes' or 'no'"; that his "skepticism or disbelief in the existence of God" did "not necessarily mean lack of faith in anything whatsoever"; that his was a "belief in and devotion to goodness and virtue for their own sakes, and a religious faith in a purely ethical creed." R. 69–70, 73. He cited such personages as Plato, Aristotle and Spinoza for support of his ethical belief in intellectual and moral integrity "without belief in God, except in the remotest sense." R. 73. His belief was found to be sincere, honest, and made in good faith; and his conscientious objection to be based upon individual training and belief, both of which included research in religious and cultural fields. Seeger's claim, however, was denied solely because it was not based upon a "belief in a relation to a Supreme Being" as required by 6(j) of the Act. At trial Seeger's counsel admitted that Seeger's belief was not in relation to a Supreme Being as commonly understood, but contended that he was entitled to the exemption because "under the present law Mr. Seeger's position would also include definitions of religion which have been stated more recently," R. 49, and could be "accommodated" under the definition of religious training and belief in the Act, R. 53. He was convicted and the Court of Appeals reversed, holding that the Supreme Being requirement of the section distinguished "between internally derived and externally compelled beliefs" and was, therefore, an "impermissible classification" under the Due Process Clause of the Fifth Amendment. 326 F.2d 846.

Interpretation of 6(j)

1. The crux of the problem lies in the phrase "religious training and belief" which Congress has defined as "belief in a relation to a Supreme Being involving duties superior to those arising from any human relation." The section excludes those persons who, disavowing religious belief, decide on the basis of essentially political, sociological or economic considerations that war is wrong and that they will have no part of it. The statute further excludes those whose opposition to war stems from a "merely personal moral code," a phrase to which we shall have occasion to turn later in discussing the application of 6(j) to these cases. We also pause to take note of what is not involved in this litigation. No party claims to be an atheist or attacks the statute on this ground. Our question, therefore, is the narrow one: Does the term "Supreme Being" as used in 6(j) mean the orthodox God or the broader concept of a power or being, or a faith, "to which all else is subordinate or upon which all else is ultimately dependent"? *Webster's New International Dictionary* (Second Edition). In considering this question we resolve it solely in relation to the language of 6(j) and not otherwise.

2. Few would quarrel, we think, with the proposition that in no field of human endeavor has the tool of language proved so inadequate in the communication of ideas as it has in dealing with the fundamental questions of man's predicament in life, in death or in final judgment and retribution. Over 250 sects inhabit our land. Some believe in a purely personal God, some in a supernatural deity; others think of religion as a way of life envisioning as its ultimate goal the day when all men can live together in perfect understanding and peace. There are those who think of God as the depth of our being; others, such as the Buddhists, strive for a state of lasting rest through self-denial and inner purification; in Hindu philosophy, the Supreme Being is the transcendental reality which is truth, knowledge and bliss.

In spite of the elusive nature of the inquiry, we are not without certain guidelines. In amending the 1940 Act, Congress adopted almost intact the language of Chief Justice Hughes in *United States v. Macintosh*:

> The essence of religion is belief in a relation to God involving duties superior to those arising from any human relation.

By comparing the statutory definition with those words, however, it becomes readily apparent that the Congress deliberately broadened them by substituting the phrase "Supreme Being" for the appellation "God." And in so doing it is also significant that Congress did not elaborate on the form or nature of this higher authority which it chose to designate as "Supreme Being." By so refraining it must have had in mind the admonitions of the Chief Justice when he said in the same opinion that even the word "God" had myriad meanings for men of faith:

(continued)

(continued)

[P]utting aside dogmas with their particular conceptions of deity, freedom of conscience itself implies respect for an innate conviction of paramount duty. The battle for religious liberty has been fought and won with respect to religious beliefs and practices, which are not in conflict with good order, upon the very ground of the supremacy of conscience within its proper field.

Moreover, the Senate Report on the bill specifically states that 6(j) was intended to re-enact "substantially the same provisions as were found" in the 1940 Act. That statute, of course, refers to "religious training and belief" without more. Admittedly, all of the parties here purport to base their objection on religious belief. It appears, therefore, that we need only look to this clear statement of congressional intent as set out in the report. Under the 1940 Act it was necessary only to have a conviction based upon religious training and belief; we believe that is all that is required here. Within that phrase would come all sincere religious beliefs which are based upon a power or being, or upon a faith, to which all else is subordinate or upon which all else is ultimately dependent. The test might be stated in these words: A sincere and meaningful belief which occupies in the life of its possessor a place parallel to that filled by the God of those admittedly qualifying for the exemption comes within the statutory definition. This construction avoids imputing to Congress an intent to classify different religious beliefs, exempting some and excluding others, and is in accord with the well-established congressional policy of equal treatment for those whose opposition to service is grounded in their religious tenets.

We recognize the difficulties that have always faced the trier of fact in these cases. We hope that the test that we lay down proves less onerous. The examiner is furnished a standard that permits consideration of criteria with which he has had considerable experience. While the applicant's words may differ, the test is simple of application. It is essentially an objective one, namely, does the claimed belief occupy the same place in the life of the objector as an orthodox belief in God holds in the life of one clearly qualified for exemption?

Moreover, it must be remembered that in resolving these exemption problems one deals with the beliefs of different individuals who will articulate them in a multitude of ways. In such an intensely personal area, of course, the claim of the registrant that his belief is an essential part of a religious faith must be given great weight.

The validity of what he believes cannot be questioned. Some theologians, and indeed some examiners, might be tempted to question the existence of the registrant's "Supreme Being" or the truth of his concepts. But these are inquiries foreclosed to Government. As Mr. Justice Douglas stated in *United States v. Ballard*, 322 U.S. 78, 86 (1944): "Men may believe what they cannot prove. They may not be put to the proof of their religious doctrines or beliefs. Religious experiences which are as real as life to some may be incomprehensible to others." Local boards and courts in this sense are not free to reject beliefs because they consider them "incomprehensible." Their task is to decide whether the beliefs professed by a registrant are sincerely held and whether they are, in his own scheme of things, religious.

But we hasten to emphasize that while the "truth" of a belief is not open to question, there remains the significant question whether it is "truly held." This is the threshold question of sincerity which must be resolved in every case. It is, of course, a question of fact—a prime consideration to the validity of every claim for exemption as a conscientious objector. The Act provides a comprehensive scheme for assisting the Appeal Boards in making this determination, placing at their service the facilities of the Department of Justice, including the Federal Bureau of Investigation and hearing officers.

Application of 6(j) to the Instant Cases

In summary, Seeger professed "religious belief" and "religious faith." He did not disavow any belief "in a relation to a Supreme Being"; indeed he stated that "the cosmic order does, perhaps, suggest a creative intelligence." He decried the tremendous "spiritual" price man must pay for his willingness to destroy human life. In light of his beliefs and the unquestioned sincerity with which he held them, we think the Board, had it applied the test we propose today, would have granted him the exemption. We think it clear that the beliefs which prompted his objection occupy the same place in his life as the belief in a traditional deity holds in the lives of his friends, the Quakers.

It may be that Seeger did not clearly demonstrate what his beliefs were with regard to the usual understanding of the term "Supreme Being." But as we have said Congress did not intend that to be the test. We therefore affirm the judgment the *Seeger* case.

In 1970, the Court revisited this issue in *Welsh v. United States,* 398 U.S. 333 (1970). Welsh also sought an exemption from the draft on religious grounds. On his application form he crossed out the phrase "religious training." Justice Black held that "Seeger and Welsh affirmed on their applications that they held deep convictions and scruples against taking part in wars where people were killed. Both strongly believed that killing in war was wrong, unethical, and immoral, and their consciences forbade them to take part in such an evil practice." *Id.* at 337. The Court appears to reiterate that the key is to determine "whether or not the registrant's beliefs are religious [and] whether these beliefs play the role of a religion and function as a religion in the registrant's life." *Id.* at 340.

Further guidance is found in the following language from the case:

> Most of the great religions of today and of the past have embodied the idea of a Supreme Being or a Supreme Reality—a God—who communicates to man in some way a consciousness of what is right and should be done, of what is wrong and therefore should be shunned. If an individual deeply and sincerely holds beliefs that are purely ethical or moral in source and content but that nevertheless impose upon him a duty of conscience to refrain from participating in any war at any time, those beliefs certainly occupy in the life of that individual "a place parallel to that [of] . . . God" in traditionally religious persons. *Welsh,* 398 U.S. at 340.

Again, this is a case involving statutory construction, not constitutional interpretation.

Welsh and *Seeger* broaden the definition of religion to include nontheistic beliefs. These definitions protect moral judgments whether they are based on philosophy or religion. An Establishment-Clause problem does not arise because the definitions do not provide special status to religion-based moral judgments over secular judgments. What these cases do not provide is guidance on what is a religious belief to judges who will hear future cases.

The courts continue to expand the *Seeger* definition. In order for a belief or creed to be considered a religion, the following criteria must be met: (1) there must be a belief in God or the person must hold a parallel belief that is central in the person's life, (2) the religion must incorporate a moral code that goes beyond individual belief, (3) there must be some associational ties, some group of people brought together by common beliefs, and (4) the belief must be sincere.

A Point of Law

United States v. Seeger, 380 U.S. 163 (1965)

Welsh v. United States, 398 U.S. 333 (1970)

As used in the Selective Service Act, the term *religious belief* does not mean belief in any one God. Rather it means a moral, ethical, or religious belief about what is right or wrong and that this belief is held with the strength of traditional religious convictions.

The Establishment Clause

Separation of Church and State

The Establishment Clause was intended to prohibit state-sponsored religion and led to the doctrine of *separation of church and state*. Thomas Jefferson may have been the first person to refer to a "wall of separation between Church and State." This was a new and uniquely American vision. But the Establishment Clause did not immediately put an end to state-sponsored churches. Some states continued their tax-supported churches into the nineteenth century. The Supreme Court in *Everson*, taking guidance from Jefferson, stated: "The First Amendment has erected a wall between church and state. That wall must be kept high and impregnable." 330 U.S. 1, 18 (1947).

Major Theories on Establishment Clause Interpretation

There are three major theories as to what the Establishment Clause means and how it should be interpreted.

STRICT SEPARATION THEORY

🏛 **strict separation theory**
A theory related to the interpretation of the Establishment Clause holding that religion and government should be separated to the greatest extent possible.

The **strict separation theory** states that religion and government should be separated to the greatest extent possible. Under this theory, government is to be secular and religion is left to society. There are sound arguments to support the strict separation theory. This separation helps to protect religious liberty. Government involvement in religion is bound to be divisive in a country as religiously diverse as the United States.

As with most theories there are problems. An absolute prohibition of government assistance to religion may threaten the free exercise of religion. A complete wall between Church and State may not be possible. Maybe the question becomes one of how high and how impregnable the wall should be.

NEUTRALITY THEORY

🏛 **neutrality theory**
A theory related to the interpretation of the Establishment Clause holding that government should not prefer religion over secularism or favor one religion over others.

Under the **neutrality theory**, the government must remain neutral toward religion. The government cannot prefer religion over secularism or favor one religion over others. Essentially, government must minimize the extent to which it discourages or encourages religious disbelief or belief. The Supreme Court fashioned a **symbolic endorsement test** to be used in the evaluation of the neutrality of a government's actions. Under this test, a government violates the Establishment Clause when it "symbolically endorses" one religion or if it generally endorses secularism or religion. This test is criticized for its potential ambiguity. People perceive symbols differently. Justice Kennedy wrote this about the endorsement test: "Either the endorsement test must invalidate scores of traditional practices recognizing the place religion holds in our culture or it must be twisted and stretched to avoid inconsistency with practices we know to have been permitted in the past, while condemning similar practices with no greater endorsement effect simply by reason of their lack of historical antecedent. Neither result is acceptable." *County of Allegheny v. American Civil Liberties Union, Greater Pittsburgh*, 492 U.S. 573, 674 (1989).

🏛 **symbolic endorsement test**
A theory related to the interpretation of the Establishment Clause holding that government violates the Establishment Clause when it "symbolically endorses" one religion or if it generally endorses secularism or religion.

ACCOMMODATION THEORY

🏛 **accommodation theory**
An interpretation of the Establishment Clause wherein the Court affirms the importance of religion in American society and accommodates its presence in our government.

The **accommodation theory** supports an interpretation of the Establishment Clause to mean that the Court should affirm the importance of religion in American society, and it should accommodate its presence in our government. The Court centers its discussion of this theory around the concept of "government coercion." In *Lee v. Weisman*, 505 U.S. 577 (1992), the Court discussed what constitutes government coercion. The issue in *Weisman* was whether clergy-led prayers at public school graduations were unconstitutional. The majority opinion found such prayers to be inherently coercive. The Court supported this discussion by explaining that students are pressured to attend graduation ceremonies and to not leave during the prayers. The Court was deeply divided on this issue. Those who argue against the accommodation approach feel that little or nothing will violate the Establishment Clause.

Public Display of Religious Symbols

The Establishment Clause and the various theories regarding its interpretation have played a major role in several cases dealing with the display of religious items on public property. The Court has considered the constitutionality of government-sponsored displays of items such as the Christian crèche, the Jewish menorah, replicas of the Ten Commandments, and a Christian cross. Not only do the case decisions seem to differ, but the justices have a difficult time agreeing with one another in the same case. In deciding these cases, the Court has focused on whether the display has a primary secular purpose. In 1989, the Court decided a case involving two separate public displays, one involving a Christian crèche and the other a display of the Jewish Menorah. The result of the case was not unanimous and the justices differed widely in their reasoning. Read the following Court Syllabus for *County of Allegheny v. American Civil Liberties Union, Greater Pittsburg* and the breakdown of the decision.

County of Allegheny v. American Civil Liberties Union, Greater Pittsburgh
492 U.S. 573 (1989)

This litigation concerns the constitutionality of two recurring holiday displays located on public property in downtown Pittsburgh. The first, a crèche depicting the Christian Nativity scene, was placed on the Grand Staircase of the Allegheny County Courthouse, which is the "main," "most beautiful," and "most public" part of the courthouse. The crèche was donated by the Holy Name Society, a Roman Catholic group, and bore a sign to that effect. Its manger had at its crest an angel bearing a banner proclaiming "Gloria in Excelsis Deo," meaning "Glory to God in the Highest." The second of the holiday displays in question was an eighteen-foot Chanukah menorah or candelabrum, which was placed just outside the City-County Building next to the city's forty-five-foot decorated Christmas tree. At the foot of the tree was a sign bearing the mayor's name and containing text declaring the city's "salute to liberty." The menorah is owned by Chabad, a Jewish group, but is stored, erected, and removed each year by the city. Respondents, the Greater Pittsburgh Chapter of the American Civil Liberties Union and seven local residents, filed suit seeking permanently to enjoin the county from displaying the crèche and the city from displaying the menorah on the ground that the displays violated the Establishment Clause of the First Amendment, made applicable to state governments by the Fourteenth Amendment. The District Court denied relief, relying on *Lynch v. Donnelly*, 465 U.S. 668, which held that a city's inclusion of a crèche in its annual Christmas display in a private park did not violate the Establishment Clause. The Court of Appeals reversed, distinguishing *Lynch v. Donnelly*, and holding that the crèche and the menorah in the present case must be understood as an impermissible governmental endorsement of Christianity and Judaism under *Lemon v. Kurtzman*, 403 U.S. 602.

Held:

The judgment is affirmed in part and reversed in part, and the cases are remanded. 842 F.2d 655.

JUSTICE BLACKMUN delivered the opinion of the Court with respect to Parts III-A, IV, and V, concluding that:

(continued)

(continued)

1. Under *Lemon v. Kurtzman*, 403 U.S., at 612, a "practice which touches upon religion, if it is to be permissible under the Establishment Clause," must not, inter alia, "advance [or] inhibit religion in its principal or primary effect." Although, in refining the definition of governmental action that unconstitutionally "advances" religion, the Court's subsequent decisions have variously spoken in terms of "endorsement," "favoritism," "preference," or "promotion," the essential principle remains the same: The Clause, at the very least, prohibits government from appearing to take a position on questions of religious belief or from "making adherence to a religion relevant in any way to a person's standing in the political community." *Lynch v. Donnelly*, 465 U.S., at 687 (O'CONNOR, J., concurring).

2. When viewed in its overall context, the crèche display violates the Establishment Clause. The crèche angel's words endorse a patently Christian message: Glory to God for the birth of Jesus Christ. Moreover, in contrast to *Lynch*, nothing in the crèche's setting detracts from that message. Although the government may acknowledge Christmas as a cultural phenomenon, it may not observe it as a Christian holy day by suggesting that people praise God for the birth of Jesus.

JUSTICE BLACKMUN concluded in Part VI that the menorah display does not have the prohibited effect of endorsing religion, given its "particular physical setting." Its combined display with a Christmas tree and a sign saluting liberty does not impermissibly endorse both the Christian and Jewish faiths, but simply recognizes that both Christmas and Chanukah are part of the same winter-holiday season, which has attained a secular status in our society. The widely accepted view of the Christmas tree as the preeminent secular symbol of the Christmas season emphasizes this point. The tree, moreover, by virtue of its size and central position in the display, is clearly the predominant element, and the placement of the menorah beside it is readily understood as simply a recognition that Christmas is not the only traditional way of celebrating the season. The absence of a more secular alternative to the menorah negates the inference of endorsement. Similarly, the presence of the mayor's sign confirms that in the particular context the government's association with a religious symbol does not represent sponsorship of religious beliefs but simply a recognition

of cultural diversity. Given all these considerations, it is not sufficiently likely that a reasonable observer would view the combined display as an endorsement or disapproval of his individual religious choices.

JUSTICE O'CONNOR also concluded that the city's display of a menorah, together with a Christmas tree and a sign saluting liberty, does not violate the Establishment Clause. The Christmas tree, whatever its origins, is widely viewed today as a secular symbol of the Christmas holiday. Although there may be certain secular aspects to Chanukah, it is primarily a religious holiday and the menorah its central religious symbol and ritual object. By including the menorah with the tree, however, and with the sign saluting liberty, the city conveyed a message of pluralism and freedom of belief during the holiday season, which, in this particular physical setting, could not be interpreted by a reasonable observer as an endorsement of Judaism or Christianity or disapproval of alternative beliefs.

JUSTICE KENNEDY, joined by THE CHIEF JUSTICE, JUSTICE WHITE, and JUSTICE SCALIA, concluded that both the menorah display and the crèche display are permissible under the Establishment Clause.

(a) The test set forth in *Lemon v. Kurtzman*, 403 U.S. 602, 612—which prohibits the "principal or primary effect" of a challenged governmental practice from either advancing or inhibiting religion—when applied with the proper sensitivity to our traditions and case law, supports the conclusion that both the crèche and the menorah are permissible displays in the context of the holiday season. The requirement of neutrality inherent in the *Lemon* formulation does not require a relentless extirpation of all contact between government and religion. Government policies of accommodation, acknowledgement, and support for religion are an accepted part of our political and cultural heritage, and the Establishment Clause permits government some latitude in recognizing the central role of religion in society.

(b) In permitting the displays of the menorah and the crèche, the city and county sought merely to "celebrate the season," and to acknowledge the historical background and the religious as well as secular nature of the Chanukah and Christmas holidays. This interest falls well within the tradition of governmental accommodation and acknowledgment of religion that has marked our history from the beginning. If government

(continued)

(continued)

is to participate in its citizens' celebration of a holiday that contains both a secular and a religious component, enforced recognition of only the secular aspect would signify the callous indifference toward religious faith that our cases and traditions do not require; for by commemorating the holiday only as it is celebrated by non-adherents, the government would be refusing to acknowledge the plain fact, and the historical reality, that many of its citizens celebrate the religious aspects of the holiday as well. There is no suggestion here that the government's power to coerce has been used to further Christianity or Judaism or that the city or the county contributed money to further any one faith or intended to use the crèche or the menorah to proselytize. Thus, the crèche and menorah are purely passive symbols of religious holidays and their use is permissible under *Lynch*. If *Marsh*, allows Congress and the state legislatures to begin each day with a state-sponsored prayer offered by a government-employed chaplain, a menorah or crèche, displayed in the limited context of the holiday season, cannot be invalid. The facts that, unlike the crèche in *Lynch*, the menorah and crèche at issue were both located on government property and were not surrounded by secular holiday paraphernalia are irrelevant, since the displays present no realistic danger of moving the government down the forbidden road toward an establishment of religion.

The outcome in the *Allegheny* case was a five-to-four vote that the nativity scene was unconstitutional. The vote was six-to-three that the menorah was allowable. This case clearly shows that no one theory of the interpretation of the Establishment Clause has the support of a clear majority of the Supreme Court justices.

In 2000, the issue of public displays of religious items again came to the Supreme Court in two cases involving displays of replicas of the Ten Commandments. In *McCreary v. ACLU*, 545 U.S. 844 (2005), in a 5–4 decision, the Supreme Court held that a display of the Ten Commandments in a Kentucky courthouse violated the Establishment Clause. The Court held that the display was not part of a secular display and had a religious goal. In *Van Orden v. Perry*, 545 U.S. 677 (2005) the same Supreme Court decided 5–4 that a display of the Ten Commandments on the grounds of the Texas state capitol did not violate the Establishment Clause. Justice Breyer was the one justice who voted differently in each case. His concurring opinion in *Van Orden v. Perry* helps to explain.

Van Orden v. Perry
545 U.S. 677 (2005)

JUSTICE BREYER, concurring in the judgment.

The Court has made clear that government must "neither engage in nor compel religious practices," that it must "effect no favoritism among sects or between religion and nonreligion," and that it must "work deterrence of no religious belief." *Schempp, supra*, at 305 (concurring opinion). The government must avoid excessive interference with, or promotion of, religion. See generally *County of Allegheny v. American Civil Liberties Union, Greater Pittsburgh Chapter*, 492 U.S. 573, 593—594 (1989). But the Establishment Clause does not compel the government to purge from the public sphere all that in any way partakes of the religious. See, *e.g., Marsh v. Chambers*, 463 U.S. 783 (1983). Such absolutism is not only inconsistent with our national traditions, see, *e.g., Lemon v. Kurtzman*, 403 U.S. 602, 614 (1971); *Lynch v. Donnelly*, 465 U.S. 668, 672—678 (1984), but would also tend to promote the kind of social conflict the Establishment Clause seeks to avoid.

Thus the Court has found no single mechanical formula that can accurately draw the constitutional line in every case. Where the Establishment Clause is at issue, tests designed to measure "neutrality" alone are

(continued)

(continued)

insufficient, both because it is sometimes difficult to determine when a legal rule is "neutral." Ibid.

Neither can this Court's other tests readily explain the Establishment Clause's tolerance, for example, of the prayers that open legislative meetings, see *Marsh, supra*; certain references to, and invocations of, the Deity in the public words of public officials; the public references to God on coins, decrees, and buildings; or the attention paid to the religious objectives of certain holidays, including Thanksgiving.

If the relation between government and religion is one of separation, but not of mutual hostility and suspicion, one will inevitably find difficult borderline cases. And in such cases, I see no test-related substitute for the exercise of legal judgment. That judgment is not a personal judgment. Rather, as in all constitutional cases, it must reflect and remain faithful to the underlying purposes of the Clauses, and it must take account of context and consequences measured in light of those purposes. While the Court's prior tests provide useful guideposts—and might well lead to the same result the Court reaches today, no exact formula can dictate a resolution to such fact-intensive cases.

The case before us is a borderline case. It concerns a large granite monument bearing the text of the Ten Commandments located on the grounds of the Texas State Capitol. On the one hand, the Commandments' text undeniably has a religious message, invoking, indeed emphasizing, the Diety. On the other hand, focusing on the text of the Commandments alone cannot conclusively resolve this case. Rather, to determine the message that the text here conveys, we must examine how the text is *used*. And that inquiry requires us to consider the context of the display. In certain contexts, a display of the tablets of the Ten Commandments can convey not simply a religious message but also a secular moral message (about proper standards of social conduct). And in certain contexts, a display of the tablets can also convey a historical message (about a historic relation between those standards and the law)—a fact that helps to explain the display of those tablets in dozens of courthouses throughout the Nation, including the Supreme Court of the United States. Here the tablets have been used as part of a display that communicates not simply a religious message, but a secular message as well. The circumstances surrounding the display's placement on the capitol grounds and its physical setting suggest that the State itself intended the latter, nonreligious aspects of the tablets' message to

predominate. And the monument's 40-year history on the Texas state grounds indicates that that has been its effect. The group that donated the monument, the Fraternal Order of Eagles, a private civic (and primarily secular) organization, while interested in the religious aspect of the Ten Commandments, sought to highlight the Commandments' role in shaping civic morality as part of that organization's efforts to combat juvenile delinquency. The Eagles' consultation with a committee composed of members of several faiths in order to find a nonsectarian text underscores the group's ethics-based motives. The tablets, as displayed on the monument, prominently acknowledge that the Eagles donated the display, a factor which, though not sufficient, thereby further distances the State itself from the religious aspect of the Commandments' message. The physical setting of the monument, moreover, suggests little or nothing of the sacred. The monument sits in a large park containing 17 monuments and 21 historical markers, all designed to illustrate the "ideals" of those who settled in Texas and of those who have lived there since that time. The setting does not readily lend itself to meditation or any other religious activity. But it does provide a context of history and moral ideals. It (together with the display's inscription about its origin) communicates to visitors that the State sought to reflect moral principles, illustrating a relation between ethics and law that the State's citizens, historically speaking, have endorsed. That is to say, the context suggests that the State intended the display's moral message—an illustrative message reflecting the historical "ideals" of Texans—to predominate.

If these factors provide a strong, but not conclusive, indication that the Commandments' text on this monument conveys a predominantly secular message, a further factor is determinative here. As far as I can tell, 40 years passed in which the presence of this monument, legally speaking, went unchallenged (until the single legal objection raised by petitioner). And I am not aware of any evidence suggesting that this was due to a climate of intimidation. Hence, those 40 years suggest more strongly than can any set of formulaic tests that few individuals, whatever their system of beliefs, are likely to have understood the monument as amounting, in any significantly detrimental way, to a government effort to favor a particular religious sect, primarily to promote religion over nonreligion, to "engage in" any "religious practic[e]," to "compel" any "religious practic[e]," or to "work deterrence" of any "religious belief." *Schempp*, 374 U.S., at

(continued)

(continued)

305 (Goldberg, J., concurring). Those 40 years suggest that the public visiting the capitol grounds has considered the religious aspect of the tablets' message as part of what is a broader moral and historical message reflective of a cultural heritage.

This case, moreover, is distinguishable from instances where the Court has found Ten Commandments displays impermissible. The display is not on the grounds of a public school, where, given the impressionability of the young, government must exercise particular care in separating church and state. See, e.g., *Weisman*, 505 U.S., at 592; *Stone v. Graham*, 449 U.S. 39 (1980) *(per curiam)*. This case also differs from *McCreary County*, where the short (and stormy) history of the courthouse Commandments' displays demonstrates the substantially religious objectives of those who mounted them, and the effect of this readily apparent objective upon those who view them. That history there indicates a governmental effort substantially to promote religion, not simply an effort primarily to reflect, historically, the secular impact of a religiously inspired document. And, in today's world, in a Nation of so many different religious and comparable nonreligious fundamental beliefs, a more contemporary state effort to focus attention upon a religious text is certainly likely to prove divisive in a way that this longstanding, pre-existing monument has not.

For these reasons, I believe that the Texas display—serving a mixed but primarily nonreligious purpose, not primarily "advanc[ing]" or "inhibit[ing]" religion," and not creating an "excessive government entanglement with religion,"–might satisfy this Court's more formal Establishment Clause tests. But, as I have said, in reaching the conclusion that the Texas display falls on the permissible side of the constitutional line, I rely less upon a literal application of any particular test than upon consideration of the basic purposes of the First Amendment's Religion Clauses themselves. This display has stood apparently uncontested for nearly two generations. That experience helps us understand that as a practical matter of *degree* this display is unlikely to prove divisive. And this matter of degree is, I believe, critical in a borderline case such as this one.

At the same time, to reach a contrary conclusion here, based primarily upon on the religious nature of the tablets' text would, I fear, lead the law to exhibit a hostility toward religion that has no place in our Establishment Clause traditions. Such a holding might well encourage disputes concerning the removal of longstanding depictions of the Ten Commandments from public buildings across the Nation. And it could thereby create the very kind of religiously based divisiveness that the Establishment Clause seeks to avoid.

In light of these considerations, I cannot agree with today's plurality's analysis. Nor can I agree with Justice Scalia's dissent in *McCreary County*. I do agree with Justice O'Connor's statement of principles in *McCreary County* though I disagree with her evaluation of the evidence as it bears on the application of those principles to this case.

I concur in the judgment of the Court.

Education and Religion

School Prayer

In the early 1960s, the Supreme Court handed down a series of what turned out to be very unpopular decisions. Beginning with *Engel v. Vitale* in 1962 (370 U.S. 421), the Court struck down a policy that called for the voluntary recitation of a prayer by children in public schools at the beginning of each day. Only Justice Stewart dissented. He compared the recitation of the prayer to other recognitions of religion and God. Specifically, he cited the president's oath of office, the pledge of allegiance to the flag, and the invocation spoken prior to all oral arguments before the Supreme Court. In 1963, in *School Dist. v. Schempp*, and a companion case, *Murray v. Curlett*, 374 U.S. 203 (1963), the Court invalidated the practice of reading the Bible and the recitation of the Lord's Prayer in public schools. This is now commonly referred to as the Supreme Court's ban on school prayer.

A Point of Law

Engel v. Vitale, 370 U.S. 421 (1962)

School Dist. v. Schempp, 374 U.S. 203 (1963)

A public school that endorses or requires the recitation of prayer or reading the Bible in school violates the First Amendment protections regarding freedom of religion.

Even though a majority of Americans do not support the ban on school prayer, the Court continues to maintain its position first asserted in the early 1960s. It is important to understand that the Court never said that it is unconstitutional for students to pray at school. The Court stands behind its rulings that state schools may not endorse, require, or sanction prayer.

The Issue of Evolution

In 1925, a controversy over the teaching of evolution in the public schools earned international notoriety. A high school biology teacher, John Scopes, was brought to trial for teaching the evolution theory. This was a violation of a new Tennessee law. See Exhibit 12-1 for the statute at issue in the *Scopes* case. This famous trial is often referred to as the "Monkey Trial." The dispute brought two very talented men face-to-face in this famous trial. Clarence Darrow, a talented trial lawyer, represented Mr. Scopes and William Jennings Bryant, a famous orator and politician, spoke on behalf of the State of Tennessee. In a trial that achieved world-wide attention, Scopes was convicted of violating the Tennessee statute. However, the Tennessee Supreme Court reversed the conviction on technical grounds. This reversal of the *Scopes* conviction prevented the U.S. Supreme Court from considering the evolution issue.

Exhibit 12-1   Tennessee Evolution Law

PUBLIC ACTS OF THE STATE OF TENNESSEE

PASSED BY THE SIXTY - FOURTH GENERAL ASSEMBLY

1925

CHAPTER NO. 27

House Bill No. 185

AN ACT prohibiting the teaching of the Evolution Theory in all the Universities, Normals and all other public schools of Tennessee, which are supported in whole or in part by the public school funds of the State, and to provide penalties for the violations thereof.

Section 1. Be it enacted by the General Assembly of the State of Tennessee, That it shall be unlawful for any teacher in any of the Universities, Normals and all other public schools of the State which are supported in whole or in part by the public school funds of the State, to teach any theory that denies the story of the Divine Creation of man as taught in the Bible, and to teach instead that man has descended from a lower order of animals.

Section 2. Be it further enacted, That any teacher found guilty of the violation of this Act, Shall be guilty of a misdemeanor and upon conviction, shall be fined not less than One Hundred $ (100.00) Dollars nor more than Five Hundred ($ 500.00) Dollars for each offense.

Section 3. Be it further enacted, That this Act take effect from and after its passage, the public welfare requiring it.

Passed March 13, 1925

Exhibit 12-2 is an excerpt taken from the trial transcript in the *Scopes* case. In an unusual move, Mr. Darrow called Mr. Bryan to the stand and questioned him. This dialog is a famous exchange of ideas and beliefs. It helps set the scene around this 1925 evolution trial. A more complete version of this famous dialogue is found in Appendix F.

In 1968, the Supreme Court took its opportunity to resolve the evolution–creationism conflict. In *Epperson v. Arkansas*, 393 U.S. 97 (1968), the Court held that states cannot "prevent its teachers from discussing the theory of evolution because it is contrary to the belief of some that the Book of Genesis must be the exclusive source of doctrine as to the origins of man."

Exhibit 12-2 Darrow's Examination of Bryan

Examination of W.J. Bryan by Clarence Darrow, of counsel for the defense:

Q—You have given considerable study to the Bible, haven't you, Mr. Bryan?
A—Yes, sir, I have tried to.

Q—Then you have made a general study of it?
A—Yes, I have; I have studied the Bible for about fifty years, or sometime more than that, but, of course, I have studied it more as I have become older than when I was but a boy.

Q—You claim that everything in the Bible should be literally interpreted?
A—I believe everything in the Bible should be accepted as it is given there: some of the Bible is given illustratively, for instance: "Ye are the salt of the earth." I would not insist that man was actually salt, or that he had flesh of salt, but it is used in the sense of salt as saving God's people.

Q—But when you read that Jonah swallowed the whale—or that the whale swallowed Jonah—excuse me please—how do you literally interpret that?
A—When I read that a big fish swallowed Jonah—it does not say whale. . . .That is my recollection of it. A big fish, and I believe it, and I believe in a God who can make a whale and can make a man and make both what He pleases.

Q—Now, you say, the big fish swallowed Jonah, and he there remained how long—three days— and then he spewed him upon the land. You believe that the big fish was made to swallow Jonah?
A—I am not prepared to say that; the Bible merely says it was done.

Q—You don't know whether it was the ordinary run of fish, or made for that purpose?
A—You may guess; you evolutionists guess. . . .

Q—You are not prepared to say whether that fish was made especially to swallow a man or not?
A—The Bible doesn't say, so I am not prepared to say.

Q—But do you believe He made them—that He made such a fish and that it was big enough to swallow Jonah?
A—Yes, sir. Let me add: One miracle is just as easy to believe as another.

Q—Just as hard?
A—It is hard to believe for you, but easy for me. A miracle is a thing performed beyond what man can perform. When you get within the realm of miracles; and it is just as easy to believe the miracle of Jonah as any other miracle in the Bible.

Q—Perfectly easy to believe that Jonah swallowed the whale?
A—If the Bible said so; the Bible doesn't make as extreme statements as evolutionists do. . . .

Q—The Bible says Joshua commanded the sun to stand still for the purpose of lengthening the day, doesn't it, and you believe it?
A—I do.

(continued)

(continued)

Q—Do you believe at that time the entire sun went around the earth?
A—No, I believe that the earth goes around the sun.

Q—Do you believe that the men who wrote it thought that the day could be lengthened or that the sun could be stopped?
A—I don't know what they thought.

© Cengage Learning 2013

In 1987, Louisiana's Creationism Act was challenged. The issue in *Edwards v. Aguillard*, 482 U.S. 578 (1987), was whether Louisiana could mandate that creation science be provided with equal time in the classroom along with the evolution theory. The Supreme Court said "no." The Court explained that the Louisiana Creationism Act was drafted to endorse a specific religious doctrine. The Act was not intended to provide different points of view in Louisiana classrooms.

One response to the *Epperson* and *Aguillard* cases comes from fundamentalist Christians. They believe that the Supreme Court fosters a religion of secular humanism. Secular humanism is a philosophy embodying the position that morality is a human invention and that moral choice is a matter of personal value.

In 1988, the Supreme Court declined to hear a case brought by fundamentalist parents. These Tennessee parents sued a school board over the local public school's reading curriculum. The parents strongly objected to the humanist perspective provided in the curriculum. The plaintiffs won in the trial court, but the appellate court overruled the trial court's decision. The Supreme Court declined review of the case. The decision of the appellate court stands. *Mozert v. Hawkins County Public Schools*, 827 F.2d 1058 (6th Cir. 1988).

A Point of Law

Epperson v. Arkansas, 393 U.S. 97 (1968)

Edwards v. Aguillard, 482 U.S. 578 (1987)

School curriculum cannot endorse a specific religious belief, such as creationism, although it can present different points of view.

Financial Aid to Religion

Threshold Standing Issues

Cases questioning the constitutionality of financial aid to religion often present a threshold issue related to the standing of the individual or group bring the lawsuit. Such cases are sometimes initiated by taxpayers, claiming that they have the right to sue because it is their money that is spent to further some religion. Recall from Chapter 3 that taxpayers rarely have standing to challenge a law based on taxpayer status. One exception, however, is in cases where the Establishment or Free Exercise Clause is involved. This issue was discussed in Chapter 3.

Tax Exemptions for Churches

Churches enjoy an exemption from local property taxes, and church incomes are exempt from state and federal income tax. In addition to churches, some private nonprofit organizations qualify as charitable institutions. It is argued that tax exemptions are indirect subsidies. If this is true, this tax exempt status violates the separation of church and state requirement. However, to tax churches may be characterized as an infringement of the Free Exercise Clause.

Two cases are key in this area: *Walz v. Tax Com.*, 397 U.S. 664 (1970) and *Texas Monthly, Inc. v. Bullock*, 489 U.S. 1 (1989). In *Walz*, the Supreme Court held a state law, giving property tax exemptions for real and personal property that was used exclusively for religious, charitable, or educational purposes, constitutional. The Court stated that "[t]he legislative purpose of a property tax exemption is neither advancement nor the inhibition of religion, it is neither sponsorship nor hostility." *Walz*, 397 U.S. at 672. The Court held that the real purpose of tax exempt status is to assist nonprofit institutions that the government sees as important to communities.

In *Texas Monthly*, the Court held a tax exemption that was solely available to religious organizations was unconstitutional. This case involved a state sales and use tax exemption for periodicals that were distributed or published by a religious faith and that embodied only writings promoting that faith. Books consisting of nothing but writings sacred to a religious faith were also under scrutiny.

The Court distinguished *Walz* from *Texas Monthly*, 489 U.S. by finding that "the benefits derived by religious organizations flowed to a large number of non-religious groups as well . . . . Insofar as that subsidy is conferred upon a wide array of nonsectarian groups as well as religious organizations . . . , the fact that religious groups benefit incidentally does not deprive the subsidy of the secular purpose and primary effect mandated by the Establishment Clause. However, when government directs a subsidy exclusively to religious organizations that is not required by the Free Exercise Clause . . . , it provides unjustifiable awards of assistance to religious organizations and cannot but convey a message of endorsement to slighted members of the community." *Texas Monthly*, 489 U.S. at 11, 14–15.

As a result of *Walz* and *Texas Monthly*, states may provide tax exemptions to religious organizations only if nonreligious charitable groups are also beneficiaries.

A Point of Law

Walz v. Tax Com., 397 U.S. 664 (1970)

Texas Monthly, Inc. v. Bullock, 489 U.S. 1 (1989)

Government can provide tax exemptions for religious organizations if the organization benefits the community. However, a tax exemption designed solely for religious groups violates the Establishment Clause.

Aid to Parochial Schools and Students

Aid to parochial elementary and secondary schools is the source of a great deal of litigation. The constitutionality of many types of assistance has been considered. Textbooks, tuition tax credits, medical diagnostic tests, audiovisual equipment, transportation, and more have been considered by the Court. An important New Jersey case came before the Supreme Court in 1947. The issue was whether a local school district could reimburse parents for their expenses incurred transporting their children to and from parochial schools. The Court held that the transportation reimbursements were furthering New Jersey's legitimate interest of moving school children "regardless of their religion, safely and expeditiously to and from accredited schools." *Everson v. Board of Education*, 330 U.S. 1 (1947). This was a deeply divided Court. Justice Rutledge stated: "Like St. Paul's freedom, religious liberty with a great price must be bought. And for those who exercise it most fully, by insisting upon religious education for their children mixed with secular, by the terms of our Constitution the price is greater than for others." The child benefit theory from *Everson* is still in effect today.

When the case law in this area is considered as a whole, there is a pattern to the principles applied by the Court. First, the aid is not allowed if it is to be received only by nonpublic schools. Assistance is permissible only if it is equally available to public school students. Second, the Court fashioned a presumption against aid received directly by the schools. Aid provided directly to the students is more likely to be upheld. Third, aid that can easily be used in religious instruction is not allowed.

In *Committee for Public Education & Religious Liberty v. Nyquist*, 413 U.S. 756 (1973), the Court addressed the issues of reimbursements and tax credits to students attending nonpublic schools. The Court held that the reimbursements were unconstitutional. Even though the payments went directly to students, the aid was available only to nonpublic school students. As you read the following case, pay close attention to the Court's reasoning concerning the Establishment Clause.

Committee for Public Education & Religious Liberty v. Nyquist
413 U.S. 756 (1973)

Amendments to New York's Education and Tax Laws established three financial aid programs for nonpublic elementary and secondary schools. The first section provides for direct money grants to "qualifying" nonpublic schools to be used for "maintenance and repair" of facilities and equipment to ensure the students' "health, welfare and safety." A "qualifying" school is a nonpublic, nonprofit elementary or secondary school serving a high concentration of pupils from low-income families. The annual grant is $30 per pupil, or $40 if the facilities are more than 25 years old, which may not exceed 50% of the average per-pupil cost for equivalent services in the public schools. Legislative findings concluded that the State "has a primary responsibility to ensure the health, welfare and safety of children attending . . . nonpublic schools"; that the "fiscal crisis in nonpublic education . . . has caused a diminution of proper maintenance and repair programs, threatening the health, welfare and safety

of nonpublic school children" in low-income urban areas; and that "a healthy and safe school environment" contributes "to the stability of urban neighborhoods." Section 2 establishes a tuition reimbursement plan for parents of children attending nonpublic elementary or secondary schools. To qualify, a parent's annual taxable income must be less than $5,000. The amount of reimbursement is $50 per grade school child and $100 per high school student so long as those amounts do not exceed 50% of actual tuition paid. The legislature found that the right to select among alternative educational systems should be available in a pluralistic society, and that any sharp decline in nonpublic school pupils would massively increase public school enrollment and costs, seriously jeopardizing quality education for all children. Reiterating a declaration contained in the first section, the findings concluded that "such assistance is clearly secular, neutral and non-ideological." The third program,

(continued)

(continued)

contained in §§ 3, 4, and 5 of the challenged law, is designed to give tax relief to parents failing to qualify for tuition reimbursement. Each eligible taxpayer-parent is entitled to deduct a stipulated sum from his adjusted gross income for each child attending a nonpublic school. The amount of the deduction is unrelated to the amount of tuition actually paid and decreases as the amount of taxable income increases. These sections are also prefaced by a series of legislative findings similar to those accompanying the previous sections. Almost 20% of the State's students, some 700,000 to 800,000, attend nonpublic schools, approximately 85% of which are church affiliated. While practically all the schools entitled to receive maintenance and repair grants "are related to the Roman Catholic Church and teach Catholic religious doctrine to some degree," institutions qualifying under the remainder of the statute include a substantial number of other church-affiliated schools. The District Court held that § 1, the maintenance and repair grants, and § 2, the tuition reimbursement grants, were invalid, but that the income tax provisions of §§ 3, 4, and 5 did not violate the Establishment Clause.

Held:

1. The propriety of a legislature's purpose may not immunize from further scrutiny a law that either has a primary effect that advances religion or fosters excessive church-state entanglements.
2. The maintenance and repair provisions of the New York statute violate the Establishment Clause because their inevitable effect is to subsidize and advance the religious mission of sectarian schools. Those provisions do not properly guarantee the secularity of state aid by limiting the percentage of assistance to 50% of comparable aid to public schools. Such statistical assurances fail to provide an adequate guarantee that aid will not be utilized to advance the religious activities of sectarian schools.
3. The tuition reimbursement grants, if given directly to sectarian schools, would similarly violate the Establishment Clause, and the fact that they are delivered to the parents rather than the schools does not compel a contrary result, as the effect of the aid is unmistakably to provide financial support for nonpublic, sectarian institutions.
   (a) The fact that the grant is given as reimbursement for tuition already paid, and that the recipient is not required to spend the amount received on education, does not alter the effect of the law.
   (b) The argument that the statute provides "a statistical guarantee of neutrality" since the tuition reimbursement is only 15% of the educational costs in nonpublic schools and the compulsory education laws require more than 15% of school time to be devoted to secular courses, is merely another variant of the argument rejected as to maintenance and repair costs.
   (c) The State must maintain an attitude of "neutrality," neither "advancing" nor "inhibiting" religion, and it cannot, by designing a program to promote the free exercise of religion, erode the limitations of the Establishment Clause.
4. The system of providing income tax benefits to parents of children attending New York's nonpublic schools also violates the Establishment Clause because, like the tuition reimbursement program, it is not sufficiently restricted to assure that it will not have the impermissible effect of advancing the sectarian activities of religious schools. *Walz v. Tax Com.*, 397 U.S. 664, distinguished.
5. Because the challenged sections have the impermissible effect of advancing religion, it is not necessary to consider whether such aid would yield an entanglement with religion. But it should be noted that, apart from any administrative entanglement of the State in particular religious programs, assistance of the sort involved here carries grave potential for entanglement in the broader sense of continuing and expanding political strife over aid to religion.

Issues similar to the concerns raised in *Nyquist* are addressed in a 2002 case. The Court's Syllabus follows.

Zelman v. Simmons-Harris
536 U.S. 639 (2002)

Ohio's Pilot Project Scholarship Program gives educational choices to families in any Ohio school district that is under state control pursuant to a federal-court order. The program provides tuition aid for certain students in the Cleveland City School District, the only covered district, to attend participating public or private schools of their parent's choosing and tutorial aid for students who choose to remain enrolled in public school. Both religious and non-religious schools in the district may participate, as may public schools in adjacent school districts. Tuition aid is distributed to parents according to financial need, and where the aid is spent depends solely upon where parents choose to enroll their children. The number of tutorial assistance grants provided to students remaining in public school must equal the number of tuition aid scholarships. In the 1999-2000 school year, 82% of the participating private schools had a religious affiliation, none of the adjacent public schools participated, and 96% of the students participating in the scholarship program were enrolled in religiously affiliated schools. Sixty percent of the students were from families at or below the poverty line. Cleveland schoolchildren also have the option of enrolling in community schools, which are funded under state law but run by their own school boards and receive twice the per-student funding as participating private schools, or magnet schools, which are public schools emphasizing a particular subject area, teaching method, or service, and for which the school district receives the same amount per student as it does for a student enrolled at a traditional public school. Respondents, Ohio taxpayers, sought to enjoin the program on the ground that it violated the Establishment Clause. The Federal District Court granted them summary judgment, and the Sixth Circuit affirmed.

Held: The program does not offend the Establishment Clause.

(a) Because the program was enacted for the valid secular purpose of providing educational assistance to poor children in a demonstrably failing public school system, the question is whether the program nonetheless has the forbidden effect of advancing or inhibiting religion. *See Agostini v. Felton*, 521 U.S. 203, 222, 138 L. Ed. 2d 391, 117 S. Ct. 1997-223. This Court's jurisprudence makes clear that a government aid program is not readily subject to challenge under the Establishment Clause if it is neutral with respect to religion and provides assistance directly to a broad class of citizens who, in turn, direct government aid to religious schools wholly as a result of their own genuine and independent private choice. *See*, 463 U.S. 388, 77 L. Ed. 2d 721, 103, S. Ct. 3062. Under such a program, government aid reaches religious institutions only by way of the deliberate choices of numerous individual recipients. The incidental advancement of a religious mission, or the perceived endorsement of a religious message, is reasonably attributable to the individual aid recipients not the government, whose role ends with the disbursement of benefit.

(b) The instant program is one of true private choice, consistent with the *Mueller* line of cases, and thus constitutional. It is neutral in all respects towards religion, and is part of Ohio's general and multifaceted undertaking to provide educational opportunities to children in a failed school district. It confers educational assistance directly to a broad class of individuals defined without reference to religion and permits participation of all district schools—religious or non-religious—and adjacent public schools. The Establishment Clause question whether Ohio is coercing parents into sending their children to religious schools must be answered by evaluating all options Ohio provides Cleveland schoolchildren, only one of which is to obtain a scholarship and then choose a religious school. Cleveland's preponderance of religiously affiliated schools did not result from the program, but is a phenomenon common to many American cities. Eighty-two percent of Cleveland's private schools are religious, as are 81% of Ohio's private schools. To attribute constitutional significance to the 82% figure would lead to the absurd result that a neutral school-choice program might be permissible in parts of Ohio where the percentage is lower, but not in Cleveland, where Ohio has deemed such programs most sorely needed. The constitutionality of a neutral educational aid program simply does not turn on whether and why, in a particular area, at a particular time, most private schools are religious, or most recipients choose

(continued)

(continued)

to use the aid at a religious school. Finally, contrary to respondents' argument, *Committee for Public Ed. & Religious Liberty v. Nyquist*, 413 U.S. 756, 37 L. Ed. 2d 948, 93 S. Ct. 2955—a case that expressly reserved judgment on the sort of program challenged here—does not govern neutral educational assistance programs that offer aid directly to a broad class of individuals defined without regard to religion.

Reversed.

Something to Consider

How might one reconcile the *Nyquist* (1973) and *Zelman* (2002) decisions? Compare the reasoning used by the Court in these two cases.

Aid to Religious Colleges and Universities

The Court draws important distinctions between universities and colleges and elementary and secondary schools. The Court allows more government assistance to the religious institutions of higher education. It notes the difference in age of students and their ability to understand that government aid is not an endorsement of a religion. In addition, the Court states that institutions of higher education are not as saturated with religious doctrine as are their elementary and secondary counterparts.

Following is the summary of one case that is instructive on the issue of government aid to universities and colleges. In *Tilton v. Richardson*, 403 U.S. 672 (1971), the Court upheld a law that allowed federal funds to be used for construction of campus facilities that were not designed to be used for religious instruction. However, the Court held unconstitutional a part of the law allowing institutions to use these facilities for religious purposes after 20 years.

Tilton v. Richardson
403 U.S. 672 (1971)

The Higher Education Facilities Act of 1963 provides federal construction grants for college and university facilities, excluding "any facility used or to be used for sectarian instruction or as a place for religious worship, or . . . primarily in connection with any part of the program of a school or department of divinity." The United States retains a 20-year interest in any facility constructed with funds under the Act, and if, during this period, the recipient violates the statutory conditions, the Government is entitled to recovery of funds. Four church-related colleges and universities in Connecticut received federal construction grants for five facilities. Appellants attempted to show, in a three-judge court, that the recipient institutions were "sectarian" by introducing evidence of their relations with religious authorities, the curricula content, and other indicia of religious character. Appellee colleges introduced testimony that they had fully complied with the statutory conditions and that their religious affiliations did not interfere with their secular educational functions. The court held that the Act authorized grants to church-related schools, and sustained its constitutionality, finding that the Act had neither the purpose nor the effect of promoting religion.

Held: The Act is constitutional except for that portion providing for a 20-year limitation on the religious use of the facilities constructed with federal funds.

(continued)

(continued)

THE CHIEF JUSTICE, joined by MR. JUSTICE HARLAN, MR. JUSTICE STEWART, and MR. JUSTICE BLACKMUN, concluded that:

1. The Act includes colleges and universities with religious affiliations.
2. Congress' objective of providing more opportunity for college education is a legitimate secular goal entirely appropriate for governmental action.
3. The record fully supports the District Court's findings that the colleges involved have not violated the statutory restrictions; it provides no basis for assuming that religiosity necessarily permeates the secular education of the colleges; and it yields no evidence that religion seeps into the use of any of the five facilities.
4. The limitation of federal interest in the facilities to a period of 20 years violates the Religion Clauses of the First Amendment, as the unrestricted use of valuable property after 20 years is in effect a contribution to a religious body.
5. This case is distinguished from *Lemon v. Kurtzman*; (a) there is less danger here than in church-related primary and secondary schools dealing with impressionable children that religion will permeate the area of secular education, since religious indoctrination is not a substantial purpose or activity of these church-related colleges, (b) the facilities provided here are themselves religiously neutral, with correspondingly less need for government surveillance, and (c) the government aid here is a one-time, single-purpose construction grant, with only minimal need for inspection. Cumulatively, these factors lessen substantially the potential for divisive religious fragmentation in the political arena.
6. The implementation of the Act does not inhibit the free exercise of religion in violation of the First Amendment.

MR. JUSTICE WHITE concurred in the judgment in this case.

MR. JUSTICE DOUGLAS, joined by MR. JUSTICE BLACK and MR. JUSTICE MARSHALL, agreed only with that part of the plurality opinion relating to the limitation of federal interest in the facilities to 20 years, concluding that a reversion of a facility at the end of that period to a parochial school would be unconstitutional as a gift of taxpayers' funds.

The Free Exercise Clause

THE SUPREME COURT CONSISTENTLY HOLDS that governmental regulation of religious beliefs is unconstitutional. The purpose of the Free Exercise Clause is to secure religious liberty for individuals through the prohibition of governmental restraints on the free exercise of religion. At the core of the Free Exercise Clause is the freedom of conscience. The government cannot discriminate against or penalize individuals or groups because of their religious beliefs. The government cannot compel individuals to affirm any specific belief.

The first case to construe the Free Exercise Clause was *Reynolds v. United States*, 98 U.S. 145 (1878). In *Reynolds,* the Court stated: "Congress was deprived of all legislative power over mere opinion, but was left free to reach actions." The freedom to act is clearly separated from the freedom to believe.

Religious Conduct

Statutes regulate conduct or actions. In the landmark case *Reynolds v. United States*, the Court upheld a federal anti-polygamy statute. A Mormon man argued that he had a religious duty to have more than one wife. This decision produced the belief–conduct distinction. The Court held that laws "cannot interfere with mere religious beliefs or opinions, they may with practices." Even though the motivation to have more than one wife is a religious motivation, only the belief is protected; the conduct, polygamy in this case, is not protected under the Free Exercise Clause. The Supreme Court consistently affirms protection for religiously motivated conduct, but it is willing to draw lines of distinction when the conduct is dangerous or illegal.

In the 1960s, a time of social change, the Court's approach to the Free Exercise Clause changed. In 1963, the Court declared that strict scrutiny should be employed when a court evaluated a law burdening the free exercise of religion. In *Sherbert v. Verner*, 374 U.S. 398 (1963), a woman was denied unemployment benefits. Her employer discharged her because she refused to work on her Saturday Sabbath. The Court held the denial of unemployment benefits unconstitutional. Over time, the Court developed the compelling state interest test. Under this approach, freedom of religion is a fundamental right that is abridged only if it is necessary to protect a compelling state interest.

For almost three decades, the Court followed the strict scrutiny test or the compelling state interest approach. Then, in 1990, the Court heard *Employment Division v. Smith*, 494 U.S. 872 (1990). This case produced a significant change in the Court's approach to determining when religious freedom is entitled to the protection provided by the Constitution. In *Smith*, the Court held that the Free Exercise Clause may not be employed to challenge a law of general applicability. A law may burden a religious practice and be constitutional as long as it does not target religious behavior for punishment. In addition, the law cannot be motivated by an intent to interfere with religion.

Following is the syllabus from the *Smith* case. In 1993, the Court struck down a city ordinance that prohibited ritual sacrifice of animals. The ordinance was unconstitutional because it was directed at one specific religious sect. *Church of Lukumi Babalu Aye v. City of Hialeah*, 508 U.S. 520 (1993). The result of these cases was that neutral laws of general applicability had to meet a rational basis scrutiny. Laws directed at religious practices must meet strict scrutiny.

Employment Division v. Smith
494 U.S. 872 (1990)

Respondents Smith and Black were fired by a private drug rehabilitation organization because they ingested peyote, a hallucinogenic drug, for sacramental purposes at a ceremony of their Native American Church. Their applications for unemployment compensation were denied by the State of Oregon under a state law disqualifying employees discharged for work-related "misconduct." Holding that the denials violated respondents' First Amendment free exercise rights, the State Court of Appeals reversed. The State Supreme Court affirmed, but this Court vacated the judgment and remanded for a determination whether sacramental peyote use is proscribed by the State's controlled substance law, which makes it a felony to knowingly or intentionally possess the drug. Pending that determination, the Court refused to decide whether such use is protected by the Constitution. On remand, the State Supreme Court held that sacramental peyote use violated, and was not excepted from, the state-law prohibition, but concluded that that prohibition was invalid under the Free Exercise Clause.

Held: The Free Exercise Clause permits the State to prohibit sacramental peyote use and thus to deny unemployment benefits to persons discharged for such use.

(continued)

(continued)

(a) Although a State would be "prohibiting the free exercise [of religion]" in violation of the Clause if it sought to ban the performance of (or abstention from) physical acts solely because of their religious motivation, the Clause does not relieve an individual of the obligation to comply with a law that incidentally forbids (or requires) the performance of an act that his religious belief requires (or forbids) if the law is not specifically directed to religious practice and is otherwise constitutional as applied to those who engage in the specified act for non-religious reasons. *See, e. g., Reynolds v. United States*, 98 U.S. 145, 166–167. The only decisions in which this Court has held that the First Amendment bars application of a neutral, generally applicable law to religiously motivated action are distinguished on the ground that they involved not the Free Exercise Clause alone, but that Clause in conjunction with other constitutional protections. *See, e. g., Cantwell v. Connecticut*, 310 U.S. 296, 304–307; *Wisconsin v. Yoder*, 406. U.S. 205.

(b) Respondents' claim for a religious exemption from the Oregon law cannot be evaluated under the balancing test set forth in the line of cases following *Sherbert v. Verner*, 374 U.S. 398, 402–403, whereby governmental actions that substantially burden a religious practice must be justified by a "compelling governmental interest." That test was developed in a context—unemployment compensation eligibility rules—that lent itself to individualized governmental assessment of the reasons for the relevant conduct. The test is inapplicable to an across-the-board criminal prohibition on a particular form of conduct. A holding to the contrary would create an extraordinary right to ignore generally applicable laws that are not supported by "compelling governmental interest" on the basis of religious belief. Nor could such a right be limited to situations in which the conduct prohibited is "central" to the individual's religion, since that would enmesh judges in an impermissible inquiry into the centrality of particular beliefs or practices to a faith. Cf. *Hernandez v. Commissioner*, 490 U.S. 680, 699. Thus, although it is constitutionally permissible to exempt sacramental peyote use from the operation of drug laws, it is not constitutionally required.

Jehovah's Witnesses Cases

Prior to *Cantwell v. Connecticut*, the Court primarily used the Due Process Clause of the Fourteenth Amendment to provide religious freedom. A good number of cases in the 1940s involved members of the Jehovah's Witnesses. In *Murdock v. Pennsylvania*, 319 U.S. 105 (1943), the Court held that a state law requiring payment of a license tax for the privilege of religious solicitation was unconstitutional.

The Court in *Cantwell* held that the state law prohibiting door-to-door solicitation for religious or charitable causes, without prior approval of a state agency, was unconstitutional. The Court invalidated the state statute and reversed several breach of the peace convictions. In doing so the Court stated:

> In the realm of religious faith, and in that of political belief, sharp differences arise. In both fields the tenets of one man may seem the rankest error to his neighbor. To persuade others to his point of view, the pleader, as we know, resorts to exaggeration, to vilification of men who have been, or are, permanent in church or state, and even to false statement. But the people of this nation have ordained in the light of history, that, in spite of the probability of excesses and abuses, these liberties are, in the long view, essential to enlightened opinion and right conduct on the part of citizens of a democracy.

Even though the Court settled on the strict scrutiny test when evaluating law that infringed on the free exercise of religion, there were only two types of cases where the Supreme Court found laws unconstitutional for violating the free exercise of religion. Statues that denied benefits to persons who quit their jobs for religious purposes were held unconstitutional. In addition, the compulsory school attendance laws, as they apply to the Amish, were invalidated. Between 1960 and 1990, in all other free exercise cases, the laws at issue were upheld.

Unemployment Benefits

The *Sherbert* decision held that government cannot deny unemployment benefits to persons who leave their jobs for religious reasons. In *Thomas v. Review Bd. of Indiana Employment Serv. Div.*, 450 U.S. 707 (1981), a man was transferred to work in an armaments section of the factory where he was employed. He objected to working in this part of the factory, and he based his objection on religious grounds. He quit his job, rather than work in the armaments section. He applied for, and was denied, unemployment benefits. The Court found this denial unconstitutional.

The Court used *Sherbert* and *Thomas* in deciding *Hobbie v. Unemployment Appeals Comm'n*, 480 U.S. 136 (1987). In *Hobbie*, the state was required to pay unemployment benefits to a woman who was discharged because she refused to work on her Sabbath.

Compulsory Education: Amish Children

In *Wisconsin v. Yoder*, 406 U.S. 205 (1972), Amish parents were granted an exemption from compulsory school attendance for their fourteen- to fifteen-year-old children. The parents objected to high school education because of the exposure of their children to influences that conflict with their beliefs. The Court stated: "The record in this case abundantly supports the claim that the traditional way of life of the Amish is not merely a matter of personal preference, but one of deep religious conviction, shared by an organized group, and intimately related to daily living." The Court added this on the issue of compulsory education as it applied to the Amish students and families:

> The impact of the compulsory-attendance law on respondents' practice of the Amish religion is not only severe, but inescapable, for the Wisconsin law affirmatively compels them, under threat of criminal sanction, to perform acts undeniably at odds with fundamental tenets of their religious beliefs. *See Braunfeld v. Braun*, 366 U.S. 599, 605 (1961). Nor is the impact of the compulsory-attendance law confined to grave interference with important Amish religious tenets from a subjective point of view. It carries with it precisely the kind of objective danger to the free exercise of religion that the First Amendment was designed to prevent. As the record shows, compulsory school attendance to age 16 for Amish children carries with it a very real threat of undermining the Amish community and religious practice as they exist today; they must either abandon belief and be assimilated into society at large, or be forced to migrate to some other and more tolerant region.

Sunday Closing Laws

In *Braunfeld v. Braun*, 366 U.S. 599 (1961), a free exercise challenge to Sunday closing laws was rejected. The Sunday closing laws were challenged by Orthodox Jews who argued that their religion required that their businesses be closed on their Saturday Sabbath, and it was hard for them to follow their religion if they were also required to be closed on Sundays. The Court disagreed.

Religious Freedom Restoration Act

In 1993, the Religious Freedom Restoration Act, 42 U.S.C. §2000bb, was enacted. This Act negated the effect of *Employment Division v. Smith*. It restored the standard of strict scrutiny for the analysis of the Free Exercise Clause even in situations involving neutral laws of general applicability. The purpose of this Act, as stated in the Act, was: "to restore the compelling interest test as set forth in *Sherbert v. Verner*, and *Wisconsin v. Yoder*, and to guarantee its application in all cases where free exercise of religion is substantially burdened; and to provide a claim or defense to persons whose religious exercise is substantially burdened by government."

The life of the Act was short. In 1997, in *City of Boerne v. Flores*, the Court held the Act to be unconstitutional. The Act was found to be an unconstitutional exercise of power under the Fourteenth Amendment because it was inconsistent with *Employment Division v. Smith* (1990).

The Act as it exists today was clarified in a later case, *Gonzales v. O Centro Espirita Beneficiente Uniao Do Vegetal*, 546 U.S. 418 (2006). Here, the Court affirmed that the Act was unconstitutional as to states because it was beyond the power of Congress. However, it was not unconstitutional as to the federal government. The Act required the federal government to apply strict scrutiny and to find a compelling government interest before it could apply any law that interfered with the free exercise of religion. In this case, respondents were a religious group that used a controlled substance in its religious services.

Religious Land Use and Institutionalized Persons Act

In another attempt to protect the free exercise of religion, in 2000, Congress enacted the Religious Land Use and Institutionalized Persons Act of 2000. First, the Act provides protection in two areas. It provides that no government shall impose a land use regulation that imposes a substantial burden on a person's religious exercise without showing that there is a compelling government interest and that the regulation is the least restrictive manner of furthering that interest. Second, the Act provides that no government shall impose a substantial burden on the religious exercise of a person residing in or confined to an institution without showing a compelling government reason and without showing that the imposition of the burden is the least restrictive means of furthering the compelling interest.

The Supreme Court decided two important cases related to the Act, *Cutter v. Wilkinson*, 544 U.S. 709 (2005) and *Sossamon v. Texas*, 563 U.S. __ (2011). In the earlier case, *Cutter v. Wilkinson*, the Court affirmed the constitutionality of the Act. The following excerpt from the case explains.

Cutter v. Wilkinson
544 U.S. 709 (2005)

JUSTICE GINSBURG delivered the opinion of the Court.

Petitioners here, are current and former inmates of institutions operated by the Ohio Department of Rehabilitation and Correction and assert that they are adherents of "nonmainstram" religions: the Satanist, Wicca, and Asatru religions, and the Church of Jesus Christ Christian. They complain that Ohio prison officials (respondents here), in violation of RLUIPA, have failed to accommodate their religious exercise "in a variety of different ways, including retaliating and discriminating against them for exercising their nontraditional faiths, denying them access to religious literature, withholding religious ceremonial items and failing to provide a chaplain trained in their faith."[R]espondents have stipulated that petitioners are members of bona fide religions and that they are sincere in their beliefs. In response to petitioners' complaints, respondent prison officials have mounted a facial challenge to the institutionalized-persons provision of RLUIPA; respondents contend, inter alia, that the Act improperly advances religion in violation of the First Amendment's Establishment Clause. The appeals court held, as the prison officials urged, that the portion of RLUIPA applicable to institutionalized persons, violates the Establishment Clause. We reverse the Court of Appeals.

I

A

RLUIPA is the latest of long-running congressional efforts to accord religious exercise heightened protection from government-imposed burdens, consistent with this Court's precedents. Ten years before RLUIPA's enactment, the Court held, in *Employment Div., Dept. of Human Resources of Ore. v. Smith,* 494 U.S. 872, 878—882 (1990), that the First Amendment's Free Exercise Clause does not inhibit enforcement of otherwise valid laws of general application that incidentally burden religious conduct. In particular, we ruled that the Free Exercise Clause did not bar Oregon from enforcing its blanket ban on peyote possession with no allowance for sacramental use of the drug. Accordingly, the State could deny unemployment benefits to persons dismissed from their jobs because of their religiously inspired peyote use. *Id.,* at 874, 890.

Responding to *Smith,* Congress enacted the Religious Freedom Restoration Act of 1993 (RFRA), 107 Stat. 1488, 42 U.S.C. § 2000bb et seq. In *City of Boerne,* this Court invalidated RFRA as applied to States and their subdivisions, holding that the Act exceeded Congress' remedial powers under the Fourteenth Amendment. Id., at 532—536.

Congress again responded, this time by enacting RLUIPA. Less sweeping than RFRA, and invoking federal authority under the Spending and Commerce Clauses, RLUIPA targets two areas: Section 2 of the Act concerns land-use regulation, 42 U.S.C. § 2000cc; §3 relates to religious exercise by institutionalized persons, §2000cc—1. Section 3, at issue here, provides that "[n]o [state or local] government shall impose a substantial burden on the religious exercise of a person residing in or confined to an institution," unless the government shows that the burden furthers "a compelling governmental interest" and does so by "the least restrictive means." §2000cc—1(a)(1)—(2). "A person may assert a violation of [RLUIPA] as a claim or defense in a judicial proceeding and obtain appropriate relief against a government." §2000cc—2(a).

II

A

The Religion Clauses of the First Amendment provide: "Congress shall make no law respecting an establishment of religion, or prohibiting the free exercise thereof." The first of the two Clauses, commonly called the Establishment Clause, commands a separation of church and state. The second, the Free Exercise Clause, requires government respect for, and noninterference with, the religious beliefs and practices of our Nation's people. While the two Clauses express complementary values, they often exert conflicting pressures. See *Locke,* 540 U.S., at 718 ("These two Clauses . . . are frequently in tension."); *Walz,* 397 U.S., at 668—669

(continued)

(continued)

[W]e hold that §3 of RLUIPA fits within the corridor between the Religion Clauses: On its face, the Act qualifies as a permissible legislative accommodation of religion that is not barred by the Establishment Clause.

Foremost, we find RLUIPA's institutionalized-persons provision compatible with the Establishment Clause because it alleviates exceptional government-created burdens on private religious exercise. Properly applying RLUIPA, courts must take adequate account of the burdens a requested accommodation may impose on nonbeneficiaries; and they must be satisfied that the Act's prescriptions are and will be administered neutrally among different faiths, see *Kiryas Joel*, 512 U.S. 687-788

"[T]he 'exercise of religion' often involves not only belief and profession but the performance of . . . physical acts [such as] assembling with others for a worship service [or] participating in sacramental use of bread and wine . . . ." Smith, 494 U.S., at 877. Section 3 covers state-run institutions–mental hospitals, prisons, and the like–in which the government exerts a degree of control unparalleled in civilian society and severely disabling to private religious exercise. 42 U.S.C. § 2000cc—1(a);

§1997; RLUIPA thus protects institutionalized persons who are unable freely to attend to their religious needs and are therefore dependent on the government's permission and accommodation for exercise of their religion.10

We do not read RLUIPA to elevate accommodation of religious observances over an institution's need to maintain order and safety. Our decisions indicate that an accommodation must be measured so that it does not override other significant interests.

Should inmate requests for religious accommodations become excessive, impose unjustified burdens on other institutionalized persons, or jeopardize the effective functioning of an institution, the facility would be free to resist the imposition. In that event, adjudication in as-applied challenges would be in order.

* * *

For the reasons stated, the judgment of the United States Court of Appeals for the Sixth Circuit is reversed, and the case is remanded for further proceedings consistent with this opinion.

It is so ordered.

By its terms, RLIUPA allows an instituted person to claim money damages from an entity that violates his or her First Amendment rights. Alternatively, a person could sue for an injunction to prevent behavior that violates the Act. A few years after *Cutter,* in *Sossamon v. Texas*, the Supreme Court ruled that individuals could not sue a state for money damages because of the doctrine of sovereign immunity of the states under the Eleventh Amendment. The Act allows individuals to sue both for money damages, if their right to free exercise of religion was violated, and also for an injunction, stopping a government from continued violation of the Act. *Sossamon* initially involved a case where a state government prevented inmates from attending religious services. By the time the case reached the Supreme Court, the state had changed its policy. An injunction was no longer required because the state was no longer doing anything wrong. The doctrine of sovereign immunity prevented the inmate from recovering money damages from the state.

Something to Consider

American history contains many examples of one group of people trying to convert another group to the Christian religion. In 1805, Red Jacket, a Seneca Indian Chief, made the following comments during a speech:

"Brother: you say there is but one way to worship and serve the Great Spirit. If there is but one religion, why do you white people differ so much about it? Why not all agreed, as you can all read the book?

(continued)

(continued)

"Brother: we do not understand these things. We are told that your religion was given to your forefathers, and has been handed down from father to son. We also have a religion, which was given to our forefathers, and has been handed down to us, their children. We worship in that way. It teaches us to be thankful for all the favors we receive; to love each other, and to be united. We never quarrel about religion.

"Brother: the Great Spirit has made us all, but He has made a great difference between his white and red children. He has given us different complexions and different customs. To you He has given the arts. To these He has not opened our eyes. We know these things to be true. Since He has made so great a difference between us in other things, why may we not conclude that He has given us a different religion according to our understanding? The Great Spirit does right. He knows what is best for his children; we are satisfied.

"Brother: we do not wish to destroy your religion, or take it from you. We only want to enjoy our own."

Source: Religious Liberty Archive: Rothgerber Johnson & Lyons LLP, Colorado Springs, Colorado.
Original Source: *IV A Library of American Literature* 36–38, Edmund C. Stedman and Ellen M. Hutchinson, eds., 1892.

See Table 12-1 for a review of important First Amendment cases.

Table 12-1 First Amendment Religion Cases

Case	Topic	Rule
Lemon v. Kurtzman, 403 U.S. 602 (1971)	Establishment Clause	Government action violates the Establishment Clause if (1) its primary purpose is to advance religion, or (2) its principal effect is to inhibit or aid religion, or (3) if government is entangled with religion.
United States v. Seeger, 380 U.S. 163 (1965)	Test for belief in a Supreme Being	Whether a given belief is sincere and meaningful and occupies a place in the life of its possessor parallel to that filled by an orthodox belief in God.
County of Allegheny v. American Civil Liberties Union, Greater Pittsburgh, 492 U.S. 573, 674 (1989); *Van Orden v. Perry*, 545 U.S. 677 (2005); *McCreary v. ACLU*, 545 U.S. 844 (2005)	Religious displays on public property	Displays such as a Christian crèche, Jewish menorah, or a replica of the Ten Commandments violate the Establishment Clause if the principal effect is to endorse religion, but not if they are part of a primarily secular display.
Engel v. Vitale, 370 U.S. 421 (1962); *School Dist. v. Schempp*, 374 U.S. 203 (1963)	School prayer	A public school that endorses or requires the recitation of prayer or reading the Bible in school violates the First Amendment protections regarding freedom of religion.
Epperson v. Arkansas, 393 U.S. 97 (1968)	Evolution	Public school cannot prevent teaching of evolution.
Walz v. Tax Com. of New York, 397 U.S. 664 (1970)	Tax exemptions for religious organizations	Government can provide tax exemptions for religious organizations if the organization benefits the community.

Table 12-1 *(continued)*

Case	Topic	Rule
Everson v. Board of Education, 330 U.S. 1 (1947)	Financial aid to religious schools	Transportation costs for parochial schoolchildren did not violate the First Amendment because the state had a legitimate interest in safely and expeditiously moving schoolchildren.
Committee for Public Education & Religious Liberty v. Nyquist, 413 U.S. 756 (1973)	Financial aid to religious schools	Reimbursements/tax credits given only to students of religious schools violates the First Amendment.
Zelman v. Simmons-Harris, 536 U.S. 639 (2002)	Financial aid to religious schools	Tuition aid offered to both public and private students does not violate the First Amendment.
Tilton v. Richardson, 403 U.S. 672 (1971)	Financial aid to religious colleges	Aid to colleges does not violate First Amendment if used for secular purposes, but not if used for religious purposes.
Sherbert v. Verner, 374 U.S. 398 (1963),	Free Exercise—Strict scrutiny	Violation of the Free Exercise Clause to deny unemployment benefits to a woman discharged because of her refusal to work on her Sabbath.
Employment Division v. Smith, 494 U.S. 872 (1990)	Free Exercise—Laws of general application	Free Exercise Clause may not be employed to challenge a law of general applicability.
Gonzales v. O Centro Espirita Beneficiente Uniao Do Vegetal, 546 U.S. 418 (2006)	Religious Freedom Restoration Act	Act was held to be unconstitutional as applied to States.
Cutter v. Wilkinson, 544 U.S. 709 (2005)	RLUIPA	Act was held to be constitutional as to federal government
Sossamon v. Texas, 563 U. S. ___ (2011)	RLUIPA	Act does not authorize lawsuits for money damages against states because of sovereign immunity under the Eleventh Amendment.

© Cengage Learning 2013

❧ **Ethical Decisions—Everyday Choices** ❧

The Facts: Ramon passed the bar exam last year. His sole-practitioner practice has been slow. In fact he handled only three small traffic-related cases. The parents of fourteen-year-old David asked Ramon to represent them in a case against the local Rough and Ready School District. Their religion prohibits participation in contact sports. The school requires all male students to play football as part of the compulsory physical education program. Ramon knows nothing about this area of the law but he is eager to learn what he needs to know in order to represent David and his parents.

The Problem: Is Ramon competent to represent his clients?

Guiding Principles: A lawyer must provide competent representation to all clients. Competent representation requires: requisite skill, legal knowledge, thoroughness, and preparation reasonably necessary for the specific representation.

Chapter Summary

The First Amendment prohibits Congress from making any law regarding the establishment of religion or the free exercise of religion. This applies to the states under the Due Process Clause of the Fourteenth Amendment. The Establishment Clause is directed at the actions of governments. The Free Exercise Clause safeguards a person's individual liberty. According to the Supreme Court, the government violates the Establishment Clause if (1) the government's primary purpose is to advance religion, or (2) if the principal effect is to inhibit or aid religion, or (3) if there is government entanglement with religion. Unfortunately, when the government takes action to assure the free exercise of religion, it often results in advancing one religion. In such a situation, the Court must decide which law prevails.

An initial question faced by the Court in interpreting this part of the First Amendment is the definition of religion. The Supreme Court has developed the following criteria: (1) there must be a belief in God or the person must hold a parallel belief that is central in the person's life, (2) the religion must incorporate a moral code that goes beyond individual belief, (3) there must be some associational ties, some group of people brought together by common beliefs, and (4) the belief must be sincere.

The Establishment Clause was intended to prohibit state-sponsored religion and led to the doctrine of "separation of church and state." In interpreting cases under this clause, the Supreme Court has referred to and applied three major theories: the strict separation theory, the neutrality theory, and the accommodation theory. The strict separation theory states that religion and government should be separated to the greatest extent possible. Under the neutrality theory, the government must remain neutral toward religion. The accommodation theory holds that the Court should affirm the importance of religion in American society, and it should accommodate its presence in our government.

The First Amendment religious freedoms resulted in several Supreme Court cases related to education. The Supreme Court has ruled that prayer in public schools violates the First Amendment. It has also ruled that states cannot ban the teaching of evolution, nor can they mandate that the creation theory be given the same emphasis as evolution. Financial aid to religious institutions has also raised First Amendment issues.

Government can provide tax exemptions for religious organizations if the organization benefits the community. However, a tax exemption designed solely for religious groups violates the Establishment Clause. Financial aid to religious schools has been allowed where the aid is available to public schools as well as to private religious schools. Aid is more likely to be found constitutional if it involves colleges and universities rather than elementary or high schools.

The Free Exercise Clause of the First Amendment prohibits any regulation of one's beliefs. However, sometimes the Court upholds laws that regulate religious conduct. The Free Exercise Clause cannot be employed to challenge a law of general applicability. A law may burden a religious practice and be constitutional as long as it does not target religious behavior for punishment. In addition, the law cannot be motivated by an intent to interfere with religion.

Key Terms

Establishment Clause	strict separation theory	symbolic endorsement test
Free Exercise Clause	neutrality theory	accommodation theory

Questions for Review

1. What language in the First Amendment guarantees freedom of religion?
2. Compare and contrast the Establishment Clause with the Free Exercise Clause.
3. How does the Supreme Court explain the term *religion*?
4. What are the three major theories regarding interpretation of the Establishment Clause?
5. What is the effect of the First Amendment on prayer in public schools?

6. How does the teaching of evolution create a freedom of religion issue?
7. What are the arguments for and against grants of tax exemption to religious institutions?
8. Analyze circumstances under which the government can give financial aid to religious schools.
9. What is the relevance under the Free Exercise Clause between religious conduct and religious beliefs?
10. How has the Supreme Court applied the Free Exercise Clause to claims for unemployment benefits, compulsory education, and Sunday closing laws?

Questions for Analysis

1. Answer the following questions regarding the *Seeger* case:
   a. What was the judicial history of the *Seeger* case?
   b. According to the Supreme Court, what should be the test for determining belief in a Supreme Being?
   c. How did Seeger describe his belief in a Supreme Being?
   d. Why was Seeger's claim denied by the Selective Service Board?
   e. How did Congress define "religious training and belief" as the phrase is used in the Selective Service Act?
2. Answer the following questions regarding the *Allegheny* case:
   a. Why did the crèche display violate the Establishment Clause?
   b. Is it all right for government to celebrate Christmas? Explain.
   c. Why did Justice Blackmun think that the menorah did not violate the First Amendment?
   d. Which Establishment Clause theory did Justices Kennedy, White, and Scalia apply? What was their conclusion?
3. Answer the following questions regarding *Committee for Public Education & Religious Liberty v. Nyquist*:
   a. What type of aid did the state give to religious schools in this case?
   b. What did the Supreme Court say about the aid?
   c. Compare the result in this case with the result in *Zelman v. Simmons-Harris*.
4. Answer the following questions regarding *Van Orden v. Perry*.
   a. What facts led Justice Bryer to conclude that the Ten Commandment display had a secular purpose?
   b. What test did Justice Bryer use to analyze whether the display violated the Establishment Clause?

Assignments and Projects

1. Following the format provided in previous chapters, brief the case of *United States v. Seeger*.
2. Locate and describe at least three organizations whose purpose is to promote religious freedom.
3. In *Hosanna-Tabor Evangelical Lutheran Church and School v. EEOC*, 565 U.S. ____ (2012) the Court held that the Free Exercise and Establishment Clauses bars law suits brought by ministers against churches, where the claim against the church is violation of employment discrimination laws. Write a case brief for this decision. The case can be located on the Internet.

Putting It into Practice

1. Review the facts found in Living with the Constitution at the beginning of this chapter. Assume that you represent Peter and Julie Jacobs, parents of two children attending Simonds Elementary School. They object strongly to the inclusion of religious songs in the program and have retained a law firm to seek an injunction to stop or at least limit the performance. Draft a letter to be sent from the law firm to the school principal, Terry Bannon, demanding that there be no religious content in the program.

2. Create a design for a Christmas holiday display to be placed in the local city headquarters. The mayor of the city made it clear that she wants the display to represent the true spirit of Christmas, including some appropriate religious symbols.

Group Activity

Consider the following situation: For over a century, the Capitol City town square was used for public speeches, gatherings, and festivals advocating and celebrating a variety of causes, both secular and religious. State law makes the square available "for use by the public . . . for free discussion of public questions, or for activities of a broad public purpose." To use the square, a group must simply fill out an official application form and meet several criteria that primarily concern safety, sanitation, and noninterference with other uses of the square. The Ku Klux Klan applied to use the square to display a cross and the city denied the permit, claiming it would violate the Establishment Clause. Discuss the pros and cons of the city's argument and then vote on how you would decide the issue. (Check the case of *Capitol Square Review and Advisory Bd. v. Pinette*, 515 U.S. 753 (1995) to see how the Supreme Court resolved this.)

13 The Right to Privacy Under Due Process and the Equal Protection Clause

Live and Let Live

Proverb

Live and Let Die

James Bond movie / Ian Fleming novel

Chapter Outline

Chapter Objectives

When you complete this chapter you should be able to

1. describe the constitutional sources for the right to privacy.

2. identify and explain the standard used by the Supreme Court to review laws or government practices that interfere with the right to privacy.

3. list specific examples of conduct protected by the constitutional right to privacy.

4. explain the relationship of the Ninth Amendment to the right to privacy.

5. explain why the Court struck down a law limiting the right to marry of individuals who owed child support.

6. explain why the Supreme Court invalidated a law authorizing the sterilization of repeat felons for crimes involving moral turpitude.

7. describe specific rights affirmed by the Supreme Court related to contraceptives.

8. describe situations in which the Court has limited the decision of *Roe v. Wade*.

9. summarize the Court's reason for overturning a Texas state law criminalizing sexual conduct between members of the same sex.

10. explain the Supreme Court's view regarding an individual's right to reject medical care.

Looking Back

Before reading this chapter, review the following terms and concepts from the previous chapters:

Strict scrutiny The standard of review used by the Supreme Court when it reviews laws or government practices targeting a suspect class or infringing upon a fundamental right. Under this standard, a law or practice is unconstitutional unless it is necessary to achieve a compelling government interest. (Chapter 8)

Fundamental right A right that is expressed or implied in the Constitution. (Chapter 8)

Liberty A right protected by the Due Process Clauses; it includes not only freedom from physical restraint but also the freedom to make personal choices about one's life. (Chapter 9)

Living with the Constitution

Thomas Reily, a CFO for a large corporation, was recently convicted of securities fraud and sentenced to four years in prison. At the time of his arrest, Reily was engaged to be married. After three months of imprisonment, Reily and his fiancé decided that they wanted to proceed with the marriage. Prison officials refused to allow him to marry.

🏛 **fundamental right**

The basic rights, such as the right to vote and the right to travel, most strongly protected by the Constitution.

THE CONSTITUTION DOES NOT PROVIDE a specific right to privacy. Privacy is an aspect of liberty. The Due Process Clauses and the Equal Protection Clause protect the right to privacy. Privacy is considered a **fundamental right**. The government cannot infringe upon a fundamental right unless the standard of strict scrutiny is met. The Supreme Court has identified rights such as marriage, procreation, sexual orientation, sexual activity, medical care decisions, voting, access to the courts, and travel to be fundamental rights. Whenever government action infringes upon such liberties, strict scrutiny is applied by the Court. Remember, this means that the government must show that governmental action is necessary to achieve a compelling governmental purpose.

When the Supreme Court is presented with a privacy issue, there are usually four basic questions the Court seeks to answer: (1) Do the facts present a fundamental right? (2) Is this fundamental right infringed? (3) Does the government present a compelling purpose for the infringement of the fundamental right? (strict scrutiny) (4) Is the means necessary to achieve the governmental purpose? Not every case presents all four questions, and there is no specific formula for answering the questions. A difficulty here is that these questions require the Court to make value judgments. As you read the cases in this chapter, focus on these four issues and pay close attention to how the Court answers these value judgment questions.

The Right to Privacy

THE LIBERTIES GENERALLY FALLING UNDER the broad category of "privacy" evolved over the years. Privacy issues involving fundamental rights include: freedom of speech, freedom of religion, economic rights, protection from unreasonable searches and seizures, protection from self-incrimination, protection from double jeopardy, the right to a speedy trial, the right to bail, and the protections against cruel and unusual punishment. These topics are covered elsewhere in this text. This chapter introduces the following liberties: marriage, contraception, abortion, sexual orientation, sexual activity, and the right to die. This is by no means an all-inclusive list.

The Ninth Amendment

THERE ARE NO SPECIFIC NINTH Amendment rights. The Ninth Amendment states: "The enumeration in the Constitution of certain rights, shall not be construed to disparage others retained by the people." This Amendment provides the Court the justification necessary to protect **unenumerated rights**, such as the right to privacy.

🏛 **unenumerated rights**

Those rights not mentioned specifically in the Constitution.

The Ninth Amendment is rarely invoked by the Supreme Court. However, in *Griswold v. Connecticut,* 381 U.S. 479 (1965), in a concurring opinion, one justice outlined the history of this Amendment and its application to fundamental rights such as privacy. In *Griswold,* the Court affirmed a constitutional right to privacy for a married couple's choice to use contraception. The case involved a state law intruding on this right. This concurrence follows. A summary of the majority view in the *Griswold* case is found later in this chapter.

Griswold v. Connecticut
381 U.S. 479 (1965)

MR. JUSTICE GOLDBERG, whom THE CHIEF JUSTICE and MR. JUSTICE BRENNAN JOIN, concurring.

I agree with the Court that Connecticut's birth-control law unconstitutionally intrudes upon the right of marital privacy, and I join in its opinion and judgment. Although I have not accepted the view that "due process" as used in the Fourteenth Amendment incorporates all of the first eight Amendments, I do agree that the concept of liberty protects those personal rights that are fundamental, and is not confined to the specific terms of the Bill of Rights. My conclusion that the concept of liberty is not so restricted and that it embraces the right of marital privacy though that right is not mentioned explicitly in the Constitution is supported both by numerous decisions of this Court, referred to in the Court's opinion, and by the language and history of the Ninth Amendment. In reaching the conclusion that the right of marital privacy is protected, as being within the protected penumbra of specific guarantees of the Bill of Rights, the Court refers to the Ninth Amendment. I add these words to emphasize the relevance of that Amendment to the Court's holding.

> The Court stated many years ago that the Due Process Clause protects those liberties that are "so rooted in the traditions and conscience of our people as to be ranked as fundamental."

[I]n *Meyer v. Nebraska*, 262 U.S. 390, 399 (1923), the Court, referring to the Fourteenth Amendment, stated:

> While this Court has not attempted to define with exactness the liberty thus guaranteed, the term has received much consideration and some of the included things have been definitely stated. Without doubt, it denotes not merely freedom from bodily restraint but also [for example,] the right . . . to marry, establish a home and bring up children . . . .

This Court, in a series of decisions, has held that the Fourteenth Amendment absorbs and applies to the States those specifics of the first eight amendments which express fundamental personal rights. The language and history of the Ninth Amendment reveal that the Framers of the Constitution believed that there are additional fundamental rights, protected from governmental infringement, which exist alongside those fundamental rights specifically mentioned in the first eight constitutional amendments.

The Ninth Amendment reads, "The enumeration in the Constitution, of certain rights, shall not be construed to deny or disparage others retained by the people." The Amendment is almost entirely the work of James Madison. It was introduced in Congress by him and passed the House and Senate with little or no debate and virtually no change in language. It was proffered to quiet expressed fears that a bill of specifically enumerated rights could not be sufficiently broad to cover all essential rights and that the specific mention of certain rights would be interpreted as a denial that others were protected.

Mr. Justice Story wrote of this argument against a bill of rights and the meaning of the Ninth Amendment:

> In regard to . . . [a] suggestion, that the affirmance of certain rights might disparage others, or might lead to argumentative implications in favor of other powers, it might be sufficient to say that such a course of reasoning could never be sustained upon any solid basis . . . But a conclusive answer is, that such an attempt may be interdicted (as it has been) by a positive declaration in such a bill of rights that the enumeration of certain rights shall not be construed to deny or disparage others retained by the people. *Story, Commentaries on the Constitution of the United States* 626–627 (5th ed. 1891).

These statements of Madison and Story make clear that the Framers did not intend that the first eight amendments be construed to exhaust the basic and fundamental rights which the Constitution guaranteed to the people.

The Ninth Amendment to the Constitution may be regarded by some as a recent discovery and may be forgotten by others, but since 1791 it has been a basic part

(continued)

(continued)

of the Constitution which we are sworn to uphold. To hold that a right so basic and fundamental and so deep-rooted in our society as the right of privacy in marriage may be infringed because that right is not guaranteed in so many words by the first eight amendments to the Constitution is to ignore the Ninth Amendment and to give it no effect whatsoever. Moreover, a judicial construction that this fundamental right is not protected by the Constitution because it is not mentioned in explicit terms by one of the first eight amendments or elsewhere in the Constitution would violate the Ninth Amendment, which specifically states that "[t]he enumeration in the Constitution, of certain rights, shall not be construed to deny or disparage others retained by the people." (Emphasis added.)

A dissenting opinion suggests that my interpretation of the Ninth Amendment somehow "broaden[s] the powers of this Court." Rather, the Ninth Amendment shows a belief of the Constitution's authors that fundamental rights exist that are not expressly enumerated in the first eight amendments and an intent that the list of rights included there not be deemed exhaustive. As any student of this Court's opinions knows, this Court has held, often unanimously, that the Fifth and Fourteenth Amendments protect certain fundamental personal liberties from abridgment by the Federal Government or the States. The Ninth Amendment simply shows the intent of the Constitution's authors that other fundamental personal rights should not be denied such protection or disparaged in any other way simply because they are not specifically listed in the first eight constitutional amendments. I do not see how this broadens the authority of the Court; rather it serves to support what this Court has been doing in protecting fundamental rights.

In sum, the Ninth Amendment simply lends strong support to the view that the "liberty" protected by the Fifth and Fourteenth Amendments from infringement by the Federal Government or the States is not restricted to rights specifically mentioned in the first eight amendments. *Cf. United Public Workers v. Mitchell*, 330 U.S. 75, 94–95.

In determining which rights are fundamental, judges are not left at large to decide cases in light of their personal and private notions. Rather, they must look to the "traditions and [collective] conscience of our people" to determine whether a principle is "so rooted [there] . . . as to be ranked as fundamental." *Snyder v. Massachusetts*, 291 U.S. 97, 105. The inquiry is whether a right involved

"is of such a character that it cannot be denied without violating those 'fundamental principles of liberty and justice which lie at the base of all our civil and political institutions'. . . ." *Powell v. Alabama*, 287 U.S. 45, 67. "Liberty" also "gains content from the emanations of . . . specific [constitutional] guarantees" and "from experience with the requirements of a free society." *Poe v. Ullman*, 367 U.S. 497, 517 (dissenting opinion of MR. JUSTICE DOUGLAS).

I agree fully with the Court that, applying these tests, the right of privacy is a fundamental personal right, emanating "from the totality of the constitutional scheme under which we live." *Id.*, at 521.

The Connecticut statutes here involved deal with a particularly important and sensitive area of privacy—that of the marital relation and the marital home. This Court recognized in *Meyer v. Nebraska*, that the right "to marry, establish a home and bring up children" was an essential part of the liberty guaranteed by the Fourteenth Amendment. 262 U.S., at 399. In *Pierce v. Society of Sisters*, 268 U.S. 510, the Court held unconstitutional an Oregon Act which forbade parents from sending their children to private schools because such an act "unreasonably interferes with the liberty of parents and guardians to direct the upbringing and education of children under their control." 268 U.S., at 534–535. As this Court said in *Prince v. Massachusetts*, 321 U.S. 158, at 166, the *Meyer* and *Pierce* decisions "have respected the private realm of family life which the state cannot enter."

I agree with MR. JUSTICE HARLAN's statement in his dissenting opinion in *Poe v. Ullman*, 367 U.S. 497, 551–552: "Certainly the safeguarding of the home does not follow merely from the sanctity of property rights. The home derives its pre-eminence as the seat of family life. And the integrity of that life is something so fundamental that it has been found to draw to its protection the principles of more than one explicitly granted Constitutional right. . . . Of this whole 'private realm of family life' it is difficult to imagine what is more private or more intimate than a husband and wife's marital relations."

The entire fabric of the Constitution and the purposes that clearly underlie its specific guarantees demonstrate that the rights to marital privacy and to marry and raise a family are of similar order and magnitude as the fundamental rights specifically protected.

(continued)

(continued)

Although the Constitution does not speak in so many words of the right of privacy in marriage, I cannot believe that it offers these fundamental rights no protection. The fact that no particular provision of the Constitution explicitly forbids the State from disrupting the traditional relation of the family—a relation as old and as fundamental as our entire civilization—surely does not show that the Government was meant to have the power to do so. Rather, as the Ninth Amendment expressly recognizes, there are fundamental personal rights such as this one, which are protected from abridgment by the Government though not specifically mentioned in the Constitution.

My Brother STEWART, while characterizing the Connecticut birth control law as "an uncommonly silly law," *post*, at 527, would nevertheless let it stand on the ground that it is not for the courts to "substitute their social and economic beliefs for the judgment of legislative bodies, who are elected to pass laws." *Post*, at 528. Elsewhere, I have stated that "[w]hile I quite agree with Mr. Justice Brandeis that . . . 'a . . . State may . . . serve as a laboratory; and try novel social and economic experiments,' *New State Ice Co. v. Liebmann*, 285 U.S. 262, 280, 311 (dissenting opinion), I do not believe that this includes the power to experiment with the fundamental liberties of citizens. . . ." The vice of the dissenters' views is that it would permit such experimentation by the States in the area of the fundamental personal rights of its citizens. I cannot agree that the Constitution grants such power either to the States or to the Federal Government.

The logic of the dissents would sanction federal or state legislation that seems to me even more plainly unconstitutional than the statute before us. Surely the Government, absent a showing of a compelling subordinating state interest, could not decree that all husbands and wives must be sterilized after two children have been born to them. Yet by their reasoning such an invasion of marital privacy would not be subject to constitutional challenge because, while it might be "silly," no provision of the Constitution specifically prevents the Government from curtailing the marital right to bear children and raise a family. While it may shock some of my Brethren that the Court today holds that the Constitution protects the right of marital privacy, in my view it is far more shocking to believe that the personal liberty guaranteed by the Constitution does not include protection against such totalitarian limitation of family size, which is at complete variance with our constitutional concepts. Yet, if upon a showing of a slender basis of rationality, a law outlawing voluntary birth control by married persons is valid, then, by the same reasoning, a law requiring compulsory birth control also would seem to be valid. In my view, however, both types of law would unjustifiably intrude upon rights of marital privacy which are constitutionally protected.

In a long series of cases this Court has held that where fundamental personal liberties are involved, they may not be abridged by the States simply on a showing that a regulatory statute has some rational relationship to the effectuation of a proper state purpose. "Where there is a significant encroachment upon personal liberty, the State may prevail only upon showing a subordinating interest which is compelling," *Bates v. Little Rock*, 361 U.S. 516, 524. The law must be shown "necessary, and not merely rationally related, to the accomplishment of a permissible state policy." *McLaughlin v. Florida*, 379 U.S. 184, 196. See *Schneider v. Irvington*, 308 U.S. 147, 161.

Although the Connecticut birth-control law obviously encroaches upon a fundamental personal liberty, the State does not show that the law serves any "subordinating [state] interest which is compelling" or that it is "necessary . . . to the accomplishment of a permissible state policy." The State, at most, argues that there is some rational relation between this statute and what is admittedly a legitimate subject of state concern—the discouraging of extra-marital relations. It says that preventing the use of birth-control devices by married persons helps prevent the indulgence by some in such extramarital relations. The rationality of this justification is dubious, particularly in light of the admitted widespread availability to all persons in the State of Connecticut, unmarried as well as married, of birth-control devices for the prevention of disease, as distinguished from the prevention of conception, see *Tileston v. Ullman*, 129 Conn. 84, 26 A.2d 582. But, in any event, it is clear that the state interest in safeguarding marital fidelity can be served by a more discriminately tailored statute, which does not, like the present one, sweep unnecessarily broadly, reaching far beyond the evil sought to be dealt with and intruding upon the privacy of all married couples. See *Aptheker v. Secretary of State*, 378 U.S. 500, 514; *NAACP v. Alabama*, 377 U.S. 288, 307–308; *McLaughlin v. Florida*, at 196. Here, as elsewhere, where, "[p]recision of regulation must be the touchstone in an area so closely touching our most precious freedoms." *NAACP v. Button*, 371 U.S. 415, 438. The State of Connecticut

(continued)

(continued)

does have statutes, the constitutionality of which is beyond doubt, which prohibit adultery and fornication. *See* Conn. Gen. Stat. 53-218, 53-219 *et seq.* These statutes demonstrate that means for achieving the same basic purpose of protecting marital fidelity are available to Connecticut without the need to "invade the area of protected freedoms." *NAACP v. Alabama*, at 307. *See McLaughlin v. Florida*, at 196.

Finally, it should be said of the Court's holding today that it in no way interferes with a State's proper regulation of sexual promiscuity or misconduct. As my Brother HARLAN so well stated in his dissenting opinion in *Poe v. Ullman*, at 553.

Adultery, homosexuality and the like are sexual intimacies which the State forbids . . . but the intimacy of husband and wife is necessarily an essential and accepted feature of the institution of marriage, an institution which the State not only must allow, but which always and in every age it has fostered and protected. It is one thing when the State exerts its power either to forbid extramarital sexuality . . . or to say who may marry, but it is quite another when, having acknowledged a marriage and the intimacies inherent in it, it undertakes to regulate by means of the criminal law the details of that intimacy.

In sum, I believe that the right of privacy in the marital relation is fundamental and basic—a personal right "retained by the people" within the meaning of the Ninth Amendment. Connecticut cannot constitutionally abridge this fundamental right, which is protected by the Fourteenth Amendment from infringement by the States. I agree with the Court that petitioners' convictions must therefore be reversed.

The Right to Marry

IN 1923, THE SUPREME COURT specifically held that the right to marry is a liberty protected by the Due Process Clause of the Constitution. The Court in *Meyer v. Nebraska*, 262 U.S. 390 (1923), provides a very broad definition of the word *liberty* as it pertains to aspects of family autonomy. Liberty "denotes not merely freedom from bodily restraint, but also the right of the individual to contract, to engage in any of the common occupations of life, to acquire useful knowledge, to marry, to establish home and bring up children, to worship God according to the dictates of his own conscience, and generally to enjoy those privileges long recognized at common law as essential to the orderly pursuit of happiness by free men."

In *Zablocki v. Redhail*, 434 U.S. 374 (1978), the Court was presented with a situation where a state refused to grant a marriage license to anyone who had minor children whom she or he was obligated to support unless the person applying for the license could prove payment of the child support. Using the Equal Protection Clause of the Constitution, the Court invalidated the law because it seriously interfered with a person's fundamental right to marry. The short syllabus for the *Zablocki* case follows.

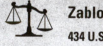

Zablocki v. Redhail
434 U.S. 374 (1978)

Wisconsin statute providing that any resident of that State "having minor issue not in his custody and which he is under obligation to support by any court order or judgment" may not marry without a court approval order, which cannot be granted absent a showing that the support obligation has been met and that children covered by the support order "are not then and are not likely thereafter to become public charges," held to violate the Equal Protection Clause of the Fourteenth Amendment.

(a) Since the right to marry is of fundamental importance, *e.g., Loving v. Virginia*, 388 U.S. 1, and the statutory classification involved here significantly

(continued)

(continued)

interferes with the exercise of that right, "critical examination" of the state interests advanced in support of the classification is required. *Massachusetts Board of Retirement v. Murgia*, 427 U.S. 307, 312, 314.

(b) The state interests assertedly served by the challenged statute unnecessarily impinge on the right to marry. If the statute is designed to furnish an opportunity to counsel persons with prior child-support obligations before further such obligations are incurred, it neither expressly requires counselling nor provides for automatic approval after counseling is completed. The statute cannot be justified as encouraging an applicant to support his children. By the proceeding the State, which already possesses numerous other means for exacting compliance with support obligations, merely prevents the applicant from getting married, without ensuring support of the applicant's prior children. Though it is suggested that the statute protects the ability of marriage applicants to meet prior support obligations before new ones are incurred, the statute is both under inclusive (as it does not limit new financial commitments other than those arising out of the contemplated marriage) and over-inclusive (since the new spouse may better the applicant's financial situation).

Two justices wrote separate concurring opinions in *Zablocki*. Both concurring opinions agreed with the majority opinion outcome, but would have used an equal protection analysis rather than the due process analysis.

Something to Consider

Read the entire *Zablocki* case and the concurring opinions. Do you find the due process or the equal protection analysis more compelling? Explain.

A Point of Law

Meyer v. Nebraska, 262 U.S. 390 (1923)

Zablocki v. Redhail, 434 U.S. 374 (1978)

The term *liberty* as used in the Constitution includes the freedom to marry. A state denies persons of liberty without due process and thus violates the Fourteenth Amendment by refusing to issue a marriage license to those who have children unless they prove payment of child support.

The Right to Reproductive Freedom

CONSTITUTIONAL PROTECTION EXTENDS to protect the right to procreate. However, the Supreme Court allowed sterilization in one case, *Buck v. Bell*, 274 U.S. 200 (1927). *Buck v. Bell* involved a sterilization of a young mentally disabled woman whose mother and daughter shared a similar disability. After *Buck*, the Court again addressed the question of sterilization in 1942, in *Skinner v. Oklahoma*. Here, the Supreme Court invalidated a law authorizing the sterilization of repeat felons for crimes involving moral turpitude. The Oklahoma Habitual Criminal Sterilization Act was designed to cleanse the public gene pool of the children of repeat felons. This law exempted white-collar criminals from the sterilization requirement. Using a strict scrutiny analysis, the Court held that the Act deprived certain persons of the right to procreate. The Court used an equal protection approach in this case because the case involved one group of repeat felons versus another. This would have been a due process case if the Act had stated that all repeat felons were to be treated the same. In his opinion, Justice Douglas makes it clear that the right to procreate is a fundamental right of privacy.

Skinner v. Oklahoma
316 U.S. 535 (1942)

MR. JUSTICE DOUGLAS delivered the opinion of the Court.

This case touches a sensitive and important area of human rights. Oklahoma deprives certain individuals of a right which is basic to the perpetuation of a race—the right to have offspring. Oklahoma has decreed the enforcement of its law against petitioner, overruling his claim that it violated the Fourteenth Amendment. Because that decision raised grave and substantial constitutional questions, we granted the petition for certiorari.

The statute involved is Oklahoma's Habitual Criminal Sterilization Act. Okl.St.Ann. Tit. 57, §171. That Act defines an "habitual criminal" as a person who, having been convicted two or more times for crimes "amounting to felonies involving moral turpitude" either in an Oklahoma court or in a court of any other State, is thereafter convicted of such a felony in Oklahoma and is sentenced to a term of imprisonment in an Oklahoma penal institution. §173. Machinery is provided for the institution by the Attorney General of a proceeding against such a person in the Oklahoma courts for a judgment that such person shall be rendered sexually sterile. §§176, 177. Notice, an opportunity to be heard, and the right to a jury trial are provided. §§177–181. The issues triable in such a proceeding are narrow and confined. If the court or jury finds that the defendant is an "habitual criminal" and that he "may be rendered sexually sterile without detriment to his or her general health," then the court "shall render judgment to the effect that said defendant be rendered sexually sterile" §182, by the operation of vasectomy in case of a male and of salpingectomy in case of a female. §174. Only one other provision of the Act is material here and that is §195 which provides that "offenses arising out of the violation of the prohibitory laws, revenue acts, embezzlement, or political offenses, shall not come or be considered within the terms of this Act."

Petitioner was convicted in 1926 of the crime of stealing chickens and was sentenced to the Oklahoma State Reformatory. In 1929 he was convicted of the crime of robbery with fire arms and was sentenced to the reformatory. In 1934 he was convicted again of robbery with firearms and was sentenced to the penitentiary. He was confined there in 1935 when the Act was passed. In 1936 the Attorney General instituted proceedings against him. Petitioner in his answer challenged the Act as unconstitutional by reason of the Fourteenth Amendment. A jury trial was had. The court instructed the jury that the crimes of which petitioner had been convicted were felonies involving moral turpitude and that the only question for the jury was whether the operation of vasectomy could be performed on petitioner without detriment to his general health. The jury found that it could be. A judgment directing that the operation of vasectomy be performed on petitioner was affirmed by the Supreme Court of Oklahoma by a five to four decision. 189 Okl. 235, 115 P.2d 123.

Several objections to the constitutionality of the Act have been pressed upon us. It is urged that the Act cannot be sustained as an exercise of the police power in view of the state of scientific authorities respecting inheritability of criminal traits. It is argued that due process is lacking because under this Act, unlike the act upheld *in Buck v. Bell*, 274 U.S. 200, 47 S. Ct. 584, the defendant is given no opportunity to be heard on the issue as to whether he is the probable potential parent of socially undesirable offspring. *See Davis v. Berry*, D.C., 216 F. 413; *Williams v. Smith*, 190 Ind. 526, 131 N.E. 2. It is also suggested that the Act is penal in character and that the sterilization provided for is cruel and unusual punishment and violative of the Fourteenth Amendment. *See Davis v. Berry. Cf. State v. Feilen*, 70 Wash. 65, 126 P. 75, 41 L.R.A., N.S., 418, Ann.Cas.1914B, 512; *Mickle v. Henrichs*, D.C.,

(continued)

(continued)

262 F. 687. We pass those points without intimating an opinion on them, for there is a feature of the Act which clearly condemns it. That is its failure to meet the requirements of the equal protection clause of the Fourteenth Amendment.

We do not stop to point out all of the inequalities in this Act. A few examples will suffice. In Oklahoma grand larceny is a felony. Okl. St. Ann. Tit. 21, §1705(5). Larceny is grand larceny when the property taken exceeds $20 in value. *Id.* §1704. Embezzlement is punishable "in the manner prescribed for feloniously stealing property of the value of that embezzled." *Id.* §1462. Hence he who embezzles property worth more than $20 is guilty of a felony. A clerk who appropriates over $20 from his employer's till (*Id.* §1456) and a stranger who steals the same amount are thus both guilty of felonies. If the latter repeats his act and is convicted three times, he may be sterilized. But the clerk is not subject to the pains and penalties of the Act no matter how large his embezzlements nor how frequent his convictions. A person who enters a chicken coop and steals chickens commits a felony (*Id.* §1719); and he may be sterilized if he is thrice convicted. If, however, he is a bailee of the property and fraudulently appropriates it, he is an embezzler. *Id.* §1455. Hence no matter how habitual his proclivities for embezzlement are and no matter how often his conviction, he may not be sterilized. Thus the nature of the two crimes is intrinsically the same and they are punishable in the same manner. Furthermore, the line between them follows close distinctions—distinctions comparable to those highly technical ones which shaped the common law as to "trespass" or "taking". Bishop, Criminal Law, 9th Ed., Vol. 2, 760, 799, *et seq.* There may be larceny by fraud rather than embezzlement even where the owner of the personal property delivers it to the defendant, if the latter has at that time "a fraudulent intention to make use of the possession as a means of converting such property to his own use, and does so convert it". *Bivens v. State*, 6 Okl. Cr. 521, 529, 120 P. 1033, 1036. If the fraudulent intent occurs later and the defendant converts the property, he is guilty of embezzlement. *Bivens v. State; Flohr v. Territory*, 14 Okl. 477, 78 P. 565. Whether a particular act is larceny by fraud or embezzlement thus turns not on the intrinsic quality of the act but on when the felonious intent arose—a question for the jury under appropriate instructions. *Bivens v. State; Riley v. State*, 64 Okl. Cr. 183, 78 P.2d 712.

We are dealing here with legislation which involves one of the basic civil rights of man. Marriage and procreation are fundamental to the very existence and survival of the race. The power to sterilize, if exercised, may have subtle, far reaching and devastating effects. In evil or reckless hands it can cause races or types which are inimical to the dominant group to wither and disappear. There is no redemption for the individual whom the law touches. Any experiment which the State conducts is to his irreparable injury. He is forever deprived of a basic liberty. We mention these matters not to reexamine the scope of the police power of the States. We advert to them merely in emphasis of our view that strict scrutiny of the classification which a State makes in a sterilization law is essential, lest unwittingly or otherwise invidious discriminations are made against groups or types of individuals in violation of the constitutional guaranty of just and equal laws. The guaranty of 'equal protection of the laws is a pledge of the protection of equal laws.' *Yick Wo v. Hopkins*, 118 U.S. 356, 369, 6 S. Ct. 1064, 1070. When the law lays an unequal hand on those who have committed intrinsically the same quality of offense and sterilizes one and not the other, it has made as an invidious a discrimination as if it had selected a particular race or nationality for oppressive treatment. *Yick Wo v. Hopkins; Gaines v. Canada*, 305 U.S. 337, 59 S. Ct. 232. Sterilization of those who have thrice committed grand larceny with immunity for those who are embezzlers is a clear, pointed, unmistakable discrimination. Oklahoma makes no attempt to say that he who commits larceny by trespass or trick or fraud has biologically inheritable traits which he who commits embezzlement lacks. Oklahoma's line between larceny by fraud and embezzlement is determined, as we have noted, "with reference to the time when the fraudulent intent to convert the property to the taker's own use" arises. *Riley v. State*, 64 Okl.Cr. page 189, 78 P.2d page 715. We have not the slightest basis for inferring that that line has any significance in eugenics nor that the inheritability of criminal traits follows the neat legal distinctions which the law has marked between those two offenses. In terms of fines and imprisonment the crimes of larceny and embezzlement rate the same under the Oklahoma code. Only when it comes to sterilization are the pains and penalties of the law different. The equal protection clause would indeed be a formula of empty words if such conspicuously artificial lines could be drawn. *See Smith v. Wayne Probate Judge*, 231 Mich. 409, 420, 421, 204 N.W. 140, 40 A.L.R. 515. In *Buck v. Bell*, the Virginia statute was upheld though it applied only to feebleminded persons in

(continued)

(continued)

institutions of the State. But it was pointed out that "so far as the operations enable those who otherwise must be kept confined to be returned to the world, and thus open the asylum to others, the equality aimed at will be more nearly reached." 274 U.S. page 208, 47 S. Ct. page 585. Here there is no such saving feature. Embezzlers are forever free. Those who steal or take in other ways are not. If such a classification were permitted, the technical common law concept of a "trespass" (Bishop, Criminal Law, 9th Ed., vol. 1, 566, 567) based on distinctions which are "very largely dependent upon history for explanation" (Holmes, The Common Law, p. 73) could readily become a rule of human genetics.

It is true that the Act has a broad severability clause. But we will not endeavor to determine whether its application would solve the equal protection difficulty. The Supreme Court of Oklahoma sustained the Act without reference to the severability clause. We have therefore a situation where the Act as construed and applied to petitioner is allowed to perpetuate the discrimination which we have found to be fatal. Whether the severability clause would be so applied as to remove this particular constitutional objection is a question which may be more appropriately left for adjudication by the Oklahoma court. *Dorchy v. Kansas,* 264 U.S. 286, 44 S. Ct. 323. That is reemphasized here by our uncertainty as to what excision, if any, would be made as a matter of Oklahoma law. *Cf. Smith v. Cahoon,* 283 U.S. 553, 51 S. Ct. 582. It is by no means clear whether if an excision were made, this particular constitutional difficulty might be solved by enlarging on the one hand or contracting on the other (cf. MR. JUSTICE BRANDEIS dissenting, *National Life Insurance Co. v. United States,* 277 U.S. 508, 534, 535, 48 S. Ct. 591, 598) the class of criminals who might be sterilized.

Reversed.

Something to Consider

One thing is clear: The right to procreate is a fundamental right. *Buck v. Bell* was not expressly overruled in *Skinner.* Why do you think the Court avoided overruling *Buck*? Do you think that World War II and the Nazi concept of a master race had an impact on this decision? Explain.

Contraception

RECENT DECADES PRODUCED A great deal of Supreme Court activity surrounding the issue of contraception. One of the initial issues involved the right of a married couple to receive information about contraceptives. Later, the Court held that married and unmarried persons have a constitutional right to access contraceptives.

In *Griswold v. Connecticut,* 381 U.S. 479 (1965), the Court invalidated a law that made it a crime to give information or advice about contraceptives to married persons.

Griswold v. Connecticut
381 U.S. 479 (1965)

MR. JUSTICE DOUGLAS delivered the opinion of the Court.

Appellant Griswold is Executive Director of the Planned Parenthood League of Connecticut. Appellant Buxton is a licensed physician and a professor at the Yale Medical School who served as Medical Director for the League at its Center in New Haven—a center open and operating from November 1 to November 10, 1961, when appellants were arrested.

They gave information, instruction, and medical advice to married persons as to the means of preventing conception. They examined the wife and prescribed the best contraceptive device or material for her use. Fees

(continued)

(continued)

were usually charged, although some couples were serviced free.

The statutes whose constitutionality is involved in this appeal are §§53-32 and 54-196 of the General Statutes of Connecticut (1958 rev.). The former provides:

Any person who uses any drug, medicinal article or instrument for the purpose of preventing conception shall be fined not less than fifty dollars or imprisoned not less than sixty days nor more than one year or be both fined and imprisoned.

Section 54-196 provides:

Any person who assists, abets, counsels, causes, hires or commands another to commit any offense may be prosecuted and punished as if he were the principal offender.

The appellants were found guilty as accessories and fined $100 each, against the claim that the accessory statute as so applied violated the Fourteenth Amendment. The Appellate Division of the Circuit Court affirmed. The Supreme Court of Errors affirmed that judgment. 151 Conn. 544, 200 A. 2d 479. We noted probable jurisdiction. 379 U.S. 926.

We think that appellants have standing to raise the constitutional rights of the married people with whom they had a professional relationship. *Tileston v. Ullman*, 318 U.S. 44, is different, for there the plaintiff seeking to represent others asked for a declaratory judgment. In that situation we thought that the requirements of standing should be strict, lest the standards of "case or controversy" in Article III of the Constitution become blurred. Here those doubts are removed by reason of a criminal conviction for serving married couples in violation of an aiding-and-abetting statute. Certainly the accessory should have standing to assert that the offense which he is charged with assisting is not, or cannot constitutionally be, a crime.

Coming to the merits, we are met with a wide range of questions that implicate the Due Process Clause of the Fourteenth Amendment. We do not sit as a super-legislature to determine the wisdom, need, and propriety of laws that touch economic problems, business affairs, or social conditions. This law, however, operates directly on an intimate relation of husband and wife and their physician's role in one aspect of that relation.

The association of people is not mentioned in the Constitution nor in the Bill of Rights. The right to educate a child in a school of the parents' choice—whether public or private or parochial—is also not mentioned. Nor is the right to study any particular subject or any foreign language. Yet the First Amendment has been construed to include certain of those rights.

By *Pierce v. Society of Sisters*, the right to educate one's children as one chooses is made applicable to the States by the force of the First and Fourteenth Amendments. By *Meyer v. Nebraska*, the same dignity is given the right to study the German language in a private school. In other words, the State may not, consistently with the spirit of the First Amendment, contract the spectrum of available knowledge. The right of freedom of speech and press includes not only the right to utter or to print, but the right to distribute, the right to receive, the right to read (*Martin v. Struthers*, 319 U.S. 141, 143) and freedom of inquiry, freedom of thought, and freedom to teach (*See Wieman v. Updegraff*, 344 U.S. 183, 195)—indeed the freedom of the entire university community. *Sweezy v. New Hampshire*, 354 U.S. 234, 249–250, 261–263; *Barenblatt v. United States*, 360 U.S. 109, 112; *Baggett v. Bullitt*, 377 U.S. 360, 369. Without those peripheral rights the specific rights would be less secure. And so we reaffirm the principle of the *Pierce* and the *Meyer* cases.

In *NAACP v. Alabama*, 357 U.S. 449, 462, we protected the "freedom to associate and privacy in one's associations," noting that freedom of association was a peripheral First Amendment right. Disclosure of membership lists of a constitutionally valid association, we held, was invalid "as entailing the likelihood of a substantial restraint upon the exercise by petitioner's members of their right to freedom of association." *Ibid.* In other words, the First Amendment has a penumbra where privacy is protected from governmental intrusion. In like context, we have protected forms of "association" that are not political in the customary sense but pertain to the social, legal, and economic benefit of the members. *NAACP v. Button*, 371 U.S. 415, 430–431. In *Schware v. Board of Bar Examiners*, 353 U.S. 232, we held it not permissible to bar a lawyer from practice, because he had once been a member of the Communist Party. The man's "association with that Party" was not shown to be "anything more than a political faith in a political party" (*Id.*, at 244) and was not action of a kind proving bad moral character. *Id.*, at 245–246.

Those cases involved more than the "right of assembly"—a right that extends to all irrespective of

(continued)

(continued)

their race or ideology. *De Jonge v. Oregon*, 299 U.S. 353. The right of "association," like the right of belief (*Board of Education v. Barnette*, 319 U.S. 624), is more than the right to attend a meeting; it includes the right to express one's attitudes or philosophies by membership in a group or by affiliation with it or by other lawful means. Association in that context is a form of expression of opinion; and while it is not expressly included in the First Amendment its existence is necessary in making the express guarantees fully meaningful.

The foregoing cases suggest that specific guarantees in the Bill of Rights have penumbras, formed by emanations from those guarantees that help give them life and substance. *See Poe v. Ullman*, 367 U.S. 497, 516–522 (dissenting opinion). Various guarantees create zones of privacy. The right of association contained in the penumbra of the First Amendment is one, as we have seen. The Third Amendment in its prohibition against the quartering of soldiers "in any house" in time of peace without the consent of the owner is another facet of that privacy. The Fourth Amendment explicitly affirms the "right of the people to be secure in their persons, houses, papers, and effects, against unreasonable searches and seizures." The Fifth Amendment in its Self-Incrimination Clause enables the citizen to create a zone of privacy which government may not force him to surrender to his detriment. The Ninth Amendment provides: "The enumeration in the Constitution, of certain rights, shall not be construed to deny or disparage others retained by the people."

The Fourth and Fifth Amendments were described in *Boyd v. United States*, 116 U.S. 616, 630, as protection against all governmental invasions "of the sanctity of a man's home and the privacies of life." We recently referred in *Mapp v. Ohio*, 367 U.S. 643, 656, to the Fourth Amendment as creating a "right to privacy, no less important than any other right carefully and particularly reserved to the people." *See* Beaney, The Constitutional

Right to Privacy, 1962 Sup. Ct. Rev. 212; *Griswold*, The Right to be Let Alone, 55 Nw. U. L. Rev. 216 (1960).

We have had many controversies over these penumbral rights of "privacy and repose." *See, e. g., Breard v. Alexandria*, 341 U.S. 622, 626, 644; *Public Utilities Comm'n v. Pollak*, 343 U.S. 451; *MonRoe v. Pape*, 365 U.S. 167; *Lanza v. New York*, 370 U.S. 139; *Frank v. Maryland*, 359 U.S. 360; *Skinner v. Oklahoma*, 316 U.S. 535, 541. These cases bear witness that the right of privacy which presses for recognition here is a legitimate one.

The present case, then, concerns a relationship lying within the zone of privacy created by several fundamental constitutional guarantees. And it concerns a law which, in forbidding the use of contraceptives rather than regulating their manufacture or sale, seeks to achieve its goals by means having a maximum destructive impact upon that relationship. Such a law cannot stand in light of the familiar principle, so often applied by this Court, that a "governmental purpose to control or prevent activities constitutionally subject to state regulation may not be achieved by means which sweep unnecessarily broadly and thereby invade the area of protected freedoms." *NAACP v. Alabama*, 377 U.S. 288, 307. Would we allow the police to search the sacred precincts of marital bedrooms for telltale signs of the use of contraceptives? The very idea is repulsive to the notions of privacy surrounding the marriage relationship.

We deal with a right of privacy older than the Bill of Rights—older than our political parties, older than our school system. Marriage is a coming together for better or for worse, hopefully enduring, and intimate to the degree of being sacred. It is an association that promotes a way of life, not causes; a harmony in living, not political faiths; a bilateral loyalty, not commercial or social projects. Yet it is an association for as noble a purpose as any involved in our prior decisions.

Reversed.

Something to Consider

Review the concurring opinion written by Justice Goldberg found earlier in this chapter. Summarize what the justice wrote about the Ninth Amendment being the authority for the Court to protect non-enumerated rights.

Seven years after the *Griswold* case, the Supreme Court took the opportunity to address the question of the right of unmarried persons to receive contraceptives. A Massachusetts law criminalizing the distribution of contraceptives to unmarried persons was challenged. The Court held that the law violated the rights of unmarried persons to be treated as married couples in situations involving access to contraceptives. Not surprisingly, the Court used the Equal Protection Clause to recognize the fundamental right of unmarried adults to have equal access to contraceptives. The decision is based on an individual's right to make decisions concerning procreation. An excerpt from the Court Syllabus explains the Court's reasoning.

Eisenstadt v. Baird
405 U.S. 438 (1972)

By providing dissimilar treatment for married and unmarried persons who are similarly situated, the statute violates the Equal Protection Clause of the Fourteenth Amendment.

(a) The deterrence of fornication, a 90-day misdemeanor under Massachusetts law, cannot reasonably be regarded as the purpose of the statute, since the statute is riddled with exceptions making contraceptives freely available for use in premarital sexual relations and its scope and penalty structure are inconsistent with that purpose.

(b) Similarly, the protection of public health through the regulation of the distribution of potentially harmful articles cannot reasonably be regarded as the purpose of the law, since, if health were the rationale, the statute would be both discriminatory and overbroad, and federal and state laws already regulate the distribution of drugs unsafe for use except under the supervision of a licensed physician.

(c) Nor can the statute be sustained simply as a prohibition on contraception per se, for whatever the rights of the individual to access to contraceptives may be, the rights must be the same for the unmarried and the married alike. If under *Griswold*, the distribution of contraceptives to married persons cannot be prohibited, a ban on distribution to unmarried persons would be equally impermissible, since the constitutionally protected right of privacy inheres in the individual, not the marital couple. If, on the other hand, *Griswold* is no bar to a prohibition on the distribution of contraceptives, a prohibition limited to unmarried persons would be underinclusive and invidiously discriminatory.

Something to Consider
Justice Douglas, in his concurring opinion in *Eisenstadt*, believed that the law should have been invalidated because (in his opinion) it violated the First Amendment. Why do you think he would hold this opinion?

Five years after *Eisenstadt*, the Supreme Court held that minors have a right to obtain contraceptives (non-prescription). A New York law prohibited the sale of non-prescription contraceptives to anyone less than sixteen years of age. The State of New York argued that the ban on contraceptives to minors would deter underage sex; the Court did not agree. The Court held that a law inhibiting the privacy rights of minors is valid only if the law advances a significant state interest. An excerpt from the Court Syllabus explains.

Carey v. Population Services International
431 U.S. 678 (1977)

MR. JUSTICE BRENNAN delivered the opinion of the Court with respect to Parts I, II, III, and V, finding that:

1. Appellee Population Planning Associates (PPA), a corporation that makes mail-order sales of non-medical contraceptive devices from its North Carolina offices and regularly advertises its products in New York periodicals and fills mail orders from New York residents without limiting availability of the products to persons of any particular age, has the requisite standing to maintain the action not only in its own right

(continued)

(continued)

but also on behalf of its potential customers, *Craig v. Boren*, 429 U.S. 190, and therefore there is no occasion to decide the standing of the other appellees.

2. Regulations imposing a burden on a decision as fundamental as whether to bear or beget a child may be justified only by compelling state interests, and must be narrowly drawn to express only those interests.

3. The provision prohibiting distribution of non-medical contraceptives to persons 16 or over except through licensed pharmacists clearly burdens the right of such individuals to use contraceptives if they so desire, and the provision serves no compelling state interests. It cannot be justified by an interest in protecting health insofar as it applies to non-hazardous contraceptives or in protecting potential life, nor can it be justified by a concern that young people not sell contraceptives, or as being designed to serve as a quality control device or as facilitating enforcement of the other provisions of the statute.

4. The prohibition of any advertisement or display of contraceptives that seeks to suppress completely any information about the availability and price of contraceptives cannot be justified on the ground that advertisements of contraceptive products would offend and embarrass those exposed to them and that permitting them would legitimize sexual activity of young people. These are classically not justifications validating suppression of expression protected by the First Amendment, and here the advertisements in question merely state the availability of products that are not only entirely legal but constitutionally protected.

MR. JUSTICE BRENNAN, joined by MR. JUSTICE STEWART, MR. JUSTICE MARSHALL, and MR. JUSTICE BLACKMUN, concluded in Part IV that the provision prohibiting distribution of contraceptives to persons under 16, as applied to nonprescription contraceptives, cannot be justified as a permissible regulation of minors' morality in furtherance of the State's policy against promiscuous sexual intercourse among the young.

(a) The right to privacy in connection with decisions affecting procreation extends to minors as well as to adults, and since a State may not impose a blanket prohibition, or even a blanket requirement of parental consent, on the choice of a minor to terminate her pregnancy, *Planned Parenthood of Missouri v. Danforth*, 428 U.S. 52, the constitutionality of a blanket prohibition of the distribution of contraceptives to minors is a fortiori foreclosed.

(b) The argument that sexual activity may be deterred by increasing the hazards attendant on it has been rejected by the Court as a justification for restrictions on the freedom to choose whether to bear or beget a child. *Eisenstadt v. Baird*, 405 U.S. 438, 448; *Roe v. Wade*, 410 U.S. 113, 148. Moreover, there is substantial doubt whether limiting access to contraceptives will in fact substantially discourage early sexual behavior. When a State, as here, burdens the exercise of a fundamental right, its attempt to justify that burden as a rational means for the accomplishment of some state policy requires more than the unsupported assertion (appellants here having conceded that there is no evidence that teenage extramarital sexual activity increases in proportion to the availability of contraceptives) that the burden is connected to such a policy.

(c) That under another provision of the statute a minor under 16 may be supplied with a contraceptive by a physician does not save the challenged provision, especially where appellants asserted no medical necessity for imposing a limitation on the distribution of nonprescription contraceptives to minors.

Abortion Rights

THE RIGHT TO AN ABORTION is one of the unenumerated rights involving reproductive autonomy. Controversy surrounds the abortion decisions. Strong opinions and emotions are found on both sides of the issues involved in the abortion rulings. This is a complicated area of the law. The issues travel beyond the simple "right to an abortion." Some state regulation of abortion is constitutional; other regulations are not constitutional. There is the question of using government facilities or funds for abortions. There are also consent issues, including consent of the spouse and consent of the parent of a pregnant minor.

Approximately forty years ago, in *Roe v. Wade*, the Supreme Court held that a woman has a fundamental right to decide to terminate her pregnancy prior to viability. The Court held that (1) the government cannot prohibit an abortion prior to the time at which the fetus can survive outside the womb on its own (viability); and (2) that government regulation of abortions must meet strict scrutiny. *Roe v. Wade* involved a factual situation where Texas law criminalized all abortions except those where the life of the mother was in danger. As you read the *Roe* decision, notice that Justice Blackmun focuses on the right to privacy after presenting an exhaustive history of abortion. The Court found the right to abortion to be protected under the Due Process Clause. Compare this with the *Griswold* decision where Justice Douglass found privacy in the Bill of Rights. Also note the dissenting opinion by Justice Rehnquist. Many of the abortion cases have strong dissents.

Roe v. Wade
410 U.S. 113 (1973)

MR. JUSTICE BLACKMUN delivered the opinion of the Court.

The principal thrust of appellant's attack on the Texas statutes is that they improperly invade a right, said to be possessed by the pregnant woman, to choose to terminate her pregnancy. Appellant would discover this right in the concept of personal "liberty" embodied in the Fourteenth Amendment's Due Process Clause; or in personal, marital, familial, and sexual privacy said to be protected by the Bill of Rights or its penumbras, or among those rights reserved to the people by the Ninth Amendment.

Three reasons have been advanced to explain historically the enactment of criminal abortion laws in the 19th century and to justify their continued existence. It has been argued occasionally that these laws were the product of a Victorian social concern to discourage illicit sexual conduct. Texas, however, does not advance this justification in the present case, and it appears that no court or commentator has taken the argument seriously.

A second reason is concerned with abortion as a medical procedure. When most criminal abortion laws were first enacted, the procedure was a hazardous one for the woman. This was particularly true prior to the development of antisepsis. Thus, it has been argued that a State's real concern in enacting a criminal abortion law was to protect the pregnant woman, that is, to restrain her from submitting to a procedure that placed her life in serious jeopardy.

Modern medical techniques have altered this situation. Appellants and various amici refer to medical data indicating that abortion in early pregnancy, that is, prior to the end of the first trimester, although not without its risk, is now relatively safe. Consequently, any interest of the State in protecting the woman from an inherently hazardous procedure, except when it would be equally dangerous for her to forgo it, has largely disappeared. Of course, important state interests in the areas of health and medical standards do remain. The State has a legitimate interest in seeing to it that abortion, like any other medical procedure, is performed under circumstances that insure maximum safety for the patient. Moreover, the risk to the woman increases as her pregnancy continues. Thus, the State retains a definite interest in protecting the woman's own health and safety when an abortion is proposed at a late stage of pregnancy.

The third reason is the State's interest—some phrase it in terms of duty—in protecting prenatal life. Some of the argument for this justification rests on the theory that a new human life is present from the moment of conception. The State's interest and general obligation to protect life then extends, it is argued, to prenatal life. In assessing the State's interest, recognition may be given to the less rigid claim that as long as at least potential life is involved, the State may assert interests beyond the protection of the pregnant woman alone.

It is with these interests, and the weight to be attached to them, that this case is concerned.

The Constitution does not explicitly mention any right of privacy. In a line of decisions, however, going back perhaps as far as *Union Pacific R. Co. v. Botsford*, 141 U.S. 250, 251 (1891), the Court has recognized that a right of personal privacy, or a guarantee of certain areas or zones of privacy, does exist under the Constitution.

(continued)

(continued)

[D]ecisions make it clear that only personal rights that can be deemed "fundamental" or "implicit in the concept of ordered liberty," *Palko v. Connecticut*, 302 U.S. 319, 325 (1937), are included in this guarantee of personal privacy. They also make it clear that the right has some extension to activities relating to marriage, *Loving v. Virginia*, 388 U.S. 1, 12 (1967); procreation, *Skinner v. Oklahoma*, 316 U.S. 535, 541–542 (1942); contraception, *Eisenstadt v. Baird*, 405 U.S., at 453–454; *Id.*, at 460, 463; family relationships, *Prince v. Massachusetts*, 321 U.S. 158, 166 (1944); and child rearing and education, *Pierce v. Society of Sisters*, 268 U.S. 510, 535 (1925), *Meyer v. Nebraska*.

This right of privacy is broad enough to encompass a woman's decision whether or not to terminate her pregnancy. The detriment that the State would impose upon the pregnant woman by denying this choice altogether is apparent. Specific and direct harm medically diagnosable even in early pregnancy may be involved. Maternity, or additional offspring, may force upon the woman a distressful life and future. Psychological harm may be imminent. Mental and physical health may be taxed by child care. There is also the distress, for all concerned, associated with the unwanted child, and there is the problem of bringing a child into a family already unable, psychologically and otherwise, to care for it. In other cases, as in this one, the additional difficulties and continuing stigma of unwed motherhood may be involved. All these are factors the woman and her responsible physician necessarily will consider in consultation.

On the basis of elements such as these, appellant and some amici argue that the woman's right is absolute and that she is entitled to terminate her pregnancy at whatever time, in whatever way, and for whatever reason she alone chooses. With this we do not agree. The Court's decisions recognizing a right of privacy also acknowledge that some state regulation in areas protected by that right is appropriate. As noted above, a State may properly assert important interests in safeguarding health, in maintaining medical standards, and in protecting potential life. At some point in pregnancy, these respective interests become sufficiently compelling to sustain regulation of the factors that govern the abortion decision. The privacy right involved, therefore, cannot be said to be absolute.

We, therefore, conclude that the right of personal privacy includes the abortion decision, but that this right is not unqualified and must be considered against important state interests in regulation.

Where certain "fundamental rights" are involved, the Court has held that regulation limiting these rights may be justified only by a "compelling state interest," and that legislative enactments must be narrowly drawn to express only the legitimate state interests at stake.

The District Court held that the appellee failed to meet his burden of demonstrating that the Texas statute's infringement upon *Roe*'s rights was necessary to support a compelling state interest, and that, although the appellee presented "several compelling justifications for state presence in the area of abortions," the statutes outstripped these justifications and swept "far beyond any areas of compelling state interest." 314 F. Supp., at 1222–1223. Appellant and appellee both contest that holding. Appellant, as has been indicated, claims an absolute right that bars any state imposition of criminal penalties in the area. Appellee argues that the State's determination to recognize and protect prenatal life from and after conception constitutes a compelling state interest. As noted above, we do not agree fully with either formulation.

A. The appellee and certain amici argue that the fetus is a "person" within the language and meaning of the Fourteenth Amendment. In support of this, they outline at length and in detail the well-known facts of fetal development.

The Constitution does not define "person" in so many words. Section 1 of the Fourteenth Amendment contains three references to "person." The first, in defining "citizens," speaks of "persons born or naturalized in the United States." The word also appears both in the Due Process Clause and in the Equal Protection Clause. "Person" is used in other places in the Constitution. But in nearly all these instances, the use of the word is such that it has application only postnatally. None indicates, with any assurance, that it has any possible pre-natal application.

All this, together with our observation that throughout the major portion of the 19th century prevailing legal abortion practices were far freer than they are today, persuades us that the word "person," as used in the Fourteenth Amendment, does not include the unborn. This conclusion, however, does not of itself fully answer the contentions raised by Texas, and we pass on to other considerations.

B. The pregnant woman cannot be isolated in her privacy. She carries an embryo and, later, a fetus, if one accepts the medical definitions of the developing young

(continued)

(continued)

in the human uterus. The situation therefore is inherently different from marital intimacy, or bedroom possession of obscene material, or marriage, or procreation, or education, with which *Eisenstadt* and *Griswold*, *Stanley*, *Loving*, *Skinner*, and *Pierce* and *Meyer* were respectively concerned. As we have intimated above, it is reasonable and appropriate for a State to decide that at some point in time another interest, that of health of the mother or that of potential human life, becomes significantly involved. The woman's privacy is no longer sole and any right of privacy she possesses must be measured accordingly.

Texas urges that, apart from the Fourteenth Amendment, life begins at conception and is present throughout pregnancy, and that, therefore, the State has a compelling interest in protecting that life from and after conception. We need not resolve the difficult question of when life begins. When those trained in the respective disciplines of medicine, philosophy, and theology are unable to arrive at any consensus, the judiciary, at this point in the development of man's knowledge, is not in a position to speculate as to the answer.

It should be sufficient to note briefly the wide divergence of thinking on this most sensitive and difficult question. There has always been strong support for the view that life does not begin until live birth.

In areas other than criminal abortion, the law has been reluctant to endorse any theory that life, as we recognize it, begins before live birth or to accord legal rights to the unborn except in narrowly defined situations and except when the rights are contingent upon live birth. For example, the traditional rule of tort law denied recovery for prenatal injuries even though the child was born alive. That rule has been changed in almost every jurisdiction. In most States, recovery is said to be permitted only if the fetus was viable, or at least quick, when the injuries were sustained, though few courts have squarely so held. In short, the unborn have never been recognized in the law as persons in the whole sense.

In view of all this, we do not agree that, by adopting one theory of life, Texas may override the rights of the pregnant woman that are at stake. We repeat, however, that the State does have an important and legitimate interest in preserving and protecting the health of the pregnant woman, whether she be a resident of the State or a nonresident who Seeks medical consultation and treatment there, and that it has still another important and legitimate interest in protecting the potentiality of human life. These interests are separate and distinct. Each grows in substantiality as the woman approaches term and, at a point during pregnancy, each becomes "compelling."

With respect to the State's important and legitimate interest in the health of the mother, the "compelling" point, in the light of present medical knowledge, is at approximately the end of the first trimester. It follows that, from and after this point, a State may regulate the abortion procedure to the extent that the regulation reasonably relates to the preservation and protection of maternal health.

This means, on the other hand, that, for the period of pregnancy prior to this "compelling" point, the attending physician, in consultation with his patient, is free to determine, without regulation by the State, that, in his medical judgment, the patient's pregnancy should be terminated. If that decision is reached, the judgment may be effectuated by an abortion free of interference by the State.

With respect to the State's important and legitimate interest in potential life, the "compelling" point is at viability. This is so because the fetus then presumably has the capability of meaningful life outside the mother's womb. State regulation protective of fetal life after viability thus has both logical and biological justifications. If the State is interested in protecting fetal life after viability, it may go so far as to proscribe abortion during that period, except when it is necessary to preserve the life or health of the mother.

To summarize and to repeat:

1. A state criminal abortion statute of the current Texas type, that excepts from criminality only a life-saving procedure on behalf of the mother, without regard to pregnancy stage and without recognition of the other interests involved, is violative of the Due Process Clause of the Fourteenth Amendment.

   (a) For the stage prior to approximately the end of the first trimester, the abortion decision and its effectuation must be left to the medical judgment of the pregnant woman's attending physician.

   (b) For the stage subsequent to approximately the end of the first trimester, the State, in promoting its interest in the health of the mother, may, if it chooses, regulate the abortion procedure in ways that are reasonably related to maternal health.

   (c) For the stage subsequent to viability, the State in promoting its interest in the potentiality of human

(continued)

(continued)

life (410 U.S. 113, 165) may, if it chooses, regulate, and even proscribe, abortion except where it is necessary, in appropriate medical judgment, for the preservation of the life or health of the mother.

2. The State may define the term "physician," as it has been employed in the preceding paragraphs of this Part XI of this opinion, to mean only a physician currently licensed by the State, and may proscribe any abortion by a person who is not a physician as so defined.

The judgment of the District Court as to intervenor Hallford is reversed, and Dr. Hallford's complaint in intervention is dismissed. In all other respects, the judgment of the District Court is affirmed. Costs are allowed to the appellee.

It is so ordered.

MR. JUSTICE REHNQUIST, dissenting.

The Court's opinion brings to the decision of this troubling question both extensive historical fact and a wealth of legal scholarship. While the opinion thus commands my respect, I find myself nonetheless in fundamental disagreement with those parts of it that invalidate the Texas statute in question, and therefore dissent.

I have difficulty in concluding, as the Court does, that the right of "privacy" is involved in this case. Texas, by the statute here challenged, bars the performance of a medical abortion by a licensed physician on a plaintiff such as *Roe*.

If the Court means by the term "privacy" no more than that the claim of a person to be free from unwanted state regulation of consensual transactions may be a form of "liberty" protected by the Fourteenth Amendment, there is no doubt that similar claims have been upheld in our earlier decisions on the basis of that liberty.

I agree with the statement of MR. JUSTICE STEWART in his concurring opinion that the "liberty," against deprivation of which without due process the Fourteenth Amendment protects, embraces more than the rights found in the Bill of Rights. But that liberty is not guaranteed absolutely against deprivation, only against deprivation without due process of law. The test traditionally applied in the area of social and economic legislation is whether or not a law such as that challenged has a rational relation to a valid

state objective. The Due Process Clause of the Fourteenth Amendment undoubtedly does place a limit, albeit a broad one, on legislative power to enact laws such as this. If the Texas statute were to prohibit an abortion even where the mother's life is in jeopardy, I have little doubt that such a statute would lack a rational relation to a valid state objective. But the Court's sweeping invalidation of any restrictions on abortion during the first trimester is impossible to justify under that standard, and the conscious weighing of competing factors that the Court's opinion apparently substitutes for the established test is far more appropriate to a legislative judgment than to a judicial one.

The decision here to break pregnancy into three distinct terms and to outline the permissible restrictions the State may impose in each one, for example, partakes more of judicial legislation than it does of a determination of the intent of the drafters of the Fourteenth Amendment.

The fact that a majority of the States reflecting, after all, the majority sentiment in those States, have had restrictions on abortions for at least a century is a strong indication, it seems to me, that the asserted right to an abortion is not "so rooted in the traditions and conscience of our people as to be ranked as fundamental," *Snyder v. Massachusetts*, 401 U.S. 97, 105 (1934). Even today, when society's views on abortion are changing, the very existence of the debate is evidence that the "right" to an abortion is not so universally accepted as the appellant would have us believe.

Even if one were to agree that the case that the Court decides were here, and that the enunciation of the substantive constitutional law in the Court's opinion were proper, the actual disposition of the case by the Court is still difficult to justify. The Texas statute is struck down in toto, even though the Court apparently concedes that at later periods of pregnancy Texas might impose these selfsame statutory limitations on abortion. My understanding of past practice is that a statute found to be invalid as applied to a particular plaintiff, but not unconstitutional as a whole, is not simply "struck down" but is, instead, declared unconstitutional as applied to the fact situation before the Court. *Yick Wo v. Hopkins*, 118 U.S. 356 (1886); *Street v. New York*, 394 U.S. 576 (1969).

For all of the foregoing reasons, I respectfully dissent.

Something to Consider

In *Roe*, Justice Blackmun stated: "This right of privacy, whether it be founded in the Fourteenth Amendment's conception of personal liberty and restrictions upon state action, or . . . in the Ninth Amendment's reservation of right to the people is broad enough to encompass a woman's decision whether or not to terminate her pregnancy." Why do you believe the Court chose to base this right to abortion under the Due Process Clause of the Fourteenth Amendment, rather than the Ninth Amendment?

The debate over *Roe v. Wade* continues today. A major criticism of the *Roe* decision is that it protects an unenumerated right that cannot be inferred from the Constitution. Another criticism of *Roe* is that the Court should have used equal protection as the basis for the decision. Finally, many argue that the Court did not give appropriate weight to the state's interest in protecting the life of the fetus. There are strong and compelling arguments on both sides of these issues.

In 1989, *Webster v. Reproductive Health Services* came before the Supreme Court. In this case, the Court held that a state may prohibit the use of public facilities and public employees to perform abortions. The *Webster* decision came from a deeply divided Court. In his dissent in *Webster*, Justice Blackmun stated: "Today, *Roe v. Wade* and the fundamental constitutional right of women to decide whether to terminate a pregnancy survive, but are not secure. . . . [T]he plurality discards a landmark case of the last generation and casts into darkness the hopes and visions of every woman in this country who had come to believe that the Constitution guaranteed her right to exercise some control over her unique ability to bear children. . . . For today, at least, the law of abortion stands undisturbed. For today, the women of this Nation still retain the liberty to control their destinies. But the signs are evident and very ominous, and a chill wind blows." The following is an excerpt from the Court Syllabus.

Webster v. Reproductive Health Services
492 U.S. 490 (1989)

Appellees, state-employed health professionals and private nonprofit corporations providing abortion services, brought suit in the District Court for declaratory and injunctive relief challenging the constitutionality of a Missouri statute regulating the performance of abortions.

The statute, inter alia:

(1) sets forth "findings" in its preamble that "[t]he life of each human being begins at conception," and that "unborn children have protectable interests in life, health, and well-being," §1.205.1(1), (2), and requires that all state laws be interpreted to provide unborn children with the same rights enjoyed by other persons, subject to the Federal Constitution and this Court's precedents, §1.205.2;

(2) specifies that a physician, prior to performing an abortion on any woman whom he has reason to believe is 20 or more weeks pregnant, must ascertain whether the fetus is "viable" by performing "such medical examinations and tests as are necessary to make a finding of [the fetus'] gestational age, weight, and lung maturity," §188.029;

(3) prohibits the use of public employees and facilities to perform or assist abortions not necessary to save the mother's life, §§188.210, 188.215; and

(4) makes it unlawful to use public funds, employees, or facilities for the purpose of "encouraging or counseling" a woman to have an abortion not necessary to save her life, §§188.205, 188.210, 188.215.

The District Court struck down each of the above provisions, among others, and enjoined their enforcement. The Court of Appeals affirmed, ruling that the provisions in question violated this Court's decisions in *Roe v. Wade*, 410 U.S. 113, and subsequent cases.

Held:

The judgment is reversed.

THE CHIEF JUSTICE delivered the opinion of the Court with respect to Parts I, II-A, II-B, and II-C, concluding that:

1. This Court need not pass on the constitutionality of the Missouri statute's preamble. In invalidating the preamble, the Court of Appeals misconceived the meaning of the dictum in *Akron v. Akron Center for Reproductive Health, Inc.*, 462 U.S. 416, 444, that "a State may not adopt one theory of when life begins to justify its regulation of abortions." That statement means only that a State could not "justify" any abortion regulation otherwise invalid under *Roe v. Wade* on the ground that it embodied the State's view about when life begins. The preamble does not by its terms regulate abortions or any other aspect of appellees' medical practice, and §1.205.2 can be interpreted to

(continued)

(continued)

do no more than offer protections to unborn children in tort and probate law, which is permissible under *Roe v. Wade* at 161–162. This Court has emphasized that *Roe* implies no limitation on a State's authority to make a value judgment favoring childbirth over abortion, *Maher v. Roe*, and the preamble can be read simply to express that sort of value judgment. The extent to which the preamble's language might be used to interpret other state statutes or regulations is something that only the state courts can definitively decide, and, until those courts have applied the preamble to restrict appellees' activities in some concrete way, it is inappropriate for federal courts to address its meaning. *Alabama State Federation of Labor v. McAdory.*

2. The restrictions in §§188.210 and 188.215 of the Missouri statute on the use of public employees and facilities for the performance or assistance of nontherapeutic abortions do not contravene this Court's abortion decisions. The Due Process Clauses generally confer no affirmative right to governmental aid, even where such aid may be necessary to secure life, liberty, or property interests of which the government may not deprive the individual. *DeShaney v. Winnebago County Dept. of Social Services.* Thus, in *Maher v. Roe; Poelker v. Doe;* and *Harris v. McRae*, this Court upheld governmental regulations withholding public funds for nontherapeutic abortions but allowing payments for medical services related to childbirth, recognizing that a government's decision to favor childbirth over abortion through the allocation of public funds does not violate *Roe v. Wade.* A State may implement that same value judgment through the allocation of other public resources, such as hospitals and medical staff. There is no merit to the claim that *Maher, Poelker,* and *McRae* must be distinguished on the grounds that preventing access to a public facility narrows or forecloses the availability of abortion. Just as in those cases, Missouri's decision to use public facilities and employees to encourage childbirth over abortion places no governmental obstacle in the path of a woman who chooses to terminate her pregnancy, but leaves her with the same choices as if the State had decided not to operate any hospitals at all. The challenged provisions restrict her ability to obtain an abortion only to the extent that she chooses to use a physician affiliated with a public hospital. Also without merit is the assertion that *Maher, Poelker,* and *McRae* must be distinguished on the ground that, since the evidence shows that all of a public facility's costs in providing abortion services are recouped when the patient pays such that no public funds are expended, the Missouri statute goes beyond expressing a preference for childbirth over abortion by creating an obstacle to the right to choose abortion that cannot stand absent a compelling state interest. Nothing in the Constitution requires States to enter or remain in the abortion business or entitles private physicians and their patients access to public facilities for the performance of abortions. Indeed, if the State does recoup all of its costs in performing abortions and no state subsidy, direct or indirect, is available, it is difficult to see how any procreational choice is burdened by the State's ban on the use of its facilities or employees for performing abortions. The cases in question all support the view that the State need not commit any resources to performing abortions, even if it can turn a profit by doing so.

THE CHIEF JUSTICE, joined by JUSTICE WHITE and JUSTICE KENNEDY, concluded in Parts II-D and III that:

1. Section 188.029 of the Missouri statute—which specifies, in its first sentence, that a physician, before performing an abortion on a woman he has reason to believe is carrying an unborn child of 20 or more weeks gestational age, shall first determine if the unborn child is viable by using that degree of care, skill, and proficiency that is commonly exercised by practitioners in the field; but which then provides, in its second sentence, that, in making the viability determination, the physician shall perform such medical examinations and tests as are necessary to make a finding of the unborn child's gestational age, weight, and lung maturity—is constitutional, since it permissibly furthers the State's interest in protecting potential human life.

2. This case affords no occasion to disturb *Roe*'s holding that a Texas statute which criminalized all nontherapeutic abortions unconstitutionally infringed the right to an abortion derived from the Due Process Clause. *Roe* is distinguishable on its facts, since

(continued)

(continued)

Missouri has determined that viability is the point at which its interest in potential human life must be safeguarded.

JUSTICE O'CONNOR, agreeing that it was plain error for the Court of Appeals to interpret the second sentence of §188.029 as meaning that doctors must perform tests to find gestational age, fetal weight, and lung maturity, concluded that the section was constitutional as properly interpreted by the plurality, and that the plurality should therefore not have proceeded to reconsider *Roe v. Wade*.

JUSTICE SCALIA would reconsider and explicitly overrule *Roe v. Wade*. Avoiding the *Roe* question by deciding this case in as narrow a manner as possible is not required by precedent and not justified by policy. To do so is

needlessly to prolong this Court's involvement in a field where the answers to the central questions are political rather than juridical, and thus to make the Court the object of the sort of organized pressure that political institutions in a democracy ought to receive. It is particularly perverse to decide this case as narrowly as possible in order to avoid reading the inexpressibly "broader-than-was-required-by-the-precise-facts" structure established by *Roe v. Wade*. The question of *Roe*'s validity is presented here, inasmuch as §188.029 constitutes a legislative imposition on the judgment of the physician concerning the point of viability and increases the cost of an abortion. It does palpable harm, if the States can and would eliminate largely unrestricted abortion, skillfully to refrain from telling them so.

Something to Consider

Justice O'Connor cast the fifth vote for the outcome in *Webster*. She stated: "When the constitutional invalidity of a State's abortion statute actually turns on the constitutional validity of *Roe v. Wade*, there will be time enough to reexamine *Roe*. And to do so carefully." Why do you believe Justice O'Connor was unwilling to overrule Roe? Consider Justice Scalia's comment: "Avoiding the Roe question by deciding with this case in as narrow a manner as possible is not required by precedent and not justified by policy. To do so needlessly is to prolong this Court's involvement in a field where the answers to the central questions are political rather than juridical, and thus to make the Court the object of the sort of organized pressure that political institutions in a democracy ought to receive. It is particularly perverse to decide this case as narrowly as possible in order to avoid reading the inexpressibly 'broader-than-was-required-by-the-precise-facts' structure established by *Roe v. Wade*." Discuss these diverse viewpoints.

Three years later, in 1992, *Planned Parenthood v. Casey* came before the Court. Here the Court tested the constitutionality of a state law that imposed several different "notice" requirements that were a condition of having an abortion, even in the first trimester. The law required that the woman be provided with certain information at least 24 hours prior to the procedure, that a minor have parental consent, and that a married woman be required to sign a statement that she notified her husband. The Court was presented with the opportunity to address *Roe*. There was surprise and dismay when the Court did not overrule *Roe*. However, the Court rejected the trimester approach of *Roe* that afforded women an absolute right to an abortion in the first trimester. The Court also rejected the "strict scrutiny" approach to reviewing laws that burdened the right and applied a lesser standard referred to by the Court as "undue burden." The Court made it clear that it retained the core of the *Roe* decision and that women have the fundamental right to decide whether to terminate a pregnancy. The Court upheld the parts of the law requiring notice to the woman undergoing the procedure and parental consent, noting that exceptions existed. It found the section requiring that a married woman notify her husband to be unduly burdensome and held it to be unconstitutional. As with many of the abortion cases, the justices were divided as to reasoning and conclusions.

Planned Parenthood v. Casey

505 U.S. 833 (1992)

At issue are five provisions of the Pennsylvania Abortion Control Act of 1982: §3205, which requires that a woman seeking an abortion give her informed consent prior to the procedure, and specifies that she be provided with certain information at least twenty-four hours before the abortion is performed; §3206, which mandates the informed consent of one parent for a minor to obtain an abortion, but provides a judicial bypass procedure; §3209, which commands that, unless certain exceptions apply, a married woman seeking an abortion must sign a statement indicating that she has notified her husband; §3203, which defines a "medical emergency" that will excuse compliance with the foregoing requirements; and §§3207(b), 3214(a), and 3214(f), which impose certain reporting requirements on facilities providing abortion services. Before any of the provisions took effect, the petitioners, five abortion clinics and a physician representing himself and a class of doctors who provide abortion services, brought this suit seeking a declaratory judgment that each of the provisions was unconstitutional on its face, as well as injunctive relief. The District Court held all the provisions unconstitutional, and permanently enjoined their enforcement. The Court of Appeals affirmed in part and reversed in part, striking down the husband notification provision but upholding the others.

Held:

JUSTICE O'CONNOR, JUSTICE KENNEDY, and JUSTICE SOUTER delivered the opinion of the Court with respect to Parts I, II, and III, concluding that:

Consideration of the fundamental constitutional question resolved by *Roe v. Wade*, principles of institutional integrity, and the rule of stare decisis require that *Roe*'s essential holding be retained and reaffirmed as to each of its three parts:

(1) a recognition of a woman's right to choose to have an abortion before fetal viability and to obtain it without undue interference from the State, whose pre-viability interests are not strong enough to support an abortion prohibition or the imposition of substantial obstacles to the woman's effective right to elect the procedure;

(2) a confirmation of the State's power to restrict abortions after viability, if the law contains exceptions for pregnancies endangering a woman's life or health; and

(3) the principle that the State has legitimate interests from the outset of the pregnancy in protecting the health of the woman and the life of the fetus that may become a child.

(a) A reexamination of the principles that define the woman's rights and the State's authority regarding abortions is required by the doubt this Court's subsequent decisions have cast upon the meaning and reach of *Roe*'s central holding, by the fact that The Chief Justice would overrule *Roe*, and by the necessity that state and federal courts and legislatures have adequate guidance on the subject.

(b) *Roe* determined that a woman's decision to terminate her pregnancy is a "liberty" protected against state interference by the substantive component of the Due Process Clause of the Fourteenth Amendment. Neither the Bill of Rights nor the specific practices of States at the time of the Fourteenth Amendment's adoption marks the outer limits of the substantive sphere of such "liberty." Rather, the adjudication of substantive due process claims may require this Court to exercise its reasoned judgment in determining the boundaries between the individual's liberty and the demands of organized society. The Court's decisions have afforded constitutional protection to personal decisions relating to marriage, *See, e.g., Loving v. Virginia*, procreation, *Skinner v. Oklahoma ex rel Williamson*, family relationships, *Prince v. Massachusetts*, child rearing and education, *Pierce v. Society of Sisters*, and contraception, *Griswold v. Connecticut*, and have recognized the right of the individual to be free from unwarranted governmental intrusion into matters so fundamentally affecting a person as the decision whether to bear or beget a child, *Eisenstadt v. Baird*. *Roe*'s central holding properly invoked the reasoning and tradition of these precedents.

(c) Application of the doctrine of stare decisis confirms that *Roe*'s essential holding should be reaffirmed. In reexamining that holding, the Court's judgment is informed by a series of prudential and pragmatic considerations designed to test the consistency of overruling the holding with the ideal of the rule of law, and to gauge the respective costs of reaffirming and overruling.

(continued)

(continued)

(d) Although *Roe* has engendered opposition, it has in no sense proven unworkable, representing as it does a simple limitation beyond which a state law is unenforceable.

(e) The *Roe* rule's limitation on state power could not be repudiated without serious inequity to people who, for two decades of economic and social developments, have organized intimate relationships and made choices that define their views of themselves and their places in society, in reliance on the availability of abortion in the event that contraception should fail. The ability of women to participate equally in the economic and social life of the Nation has been facilitated by their ability to control their reproductive lives. The Constitution serves human values, and while the effect of reliance on *Roe* cannot be exactly measured, neither can the certain costs of overruling *Roe* for people who have ordered their thinking and living around that case be dismissed.

(f) No evolution of legal principle has left *Roe*'s central rule a doctrinal anachronism discounted by society. If *Roe* is placed among the cases exemplified by *Griswold*, it is clearly in no jeopardy, since subsequent constitutional developments have neither disturbed, nor do they threaten to diminish, the liberty recognized in such cases.

(g) No change in *Roe*'s factual underpinning has left its central holding obsolete, and none supports an argument for its overruling. Although subsequent maternal health care advances allow for later abortions safe to the pregnant woman, and post-*Roe* neonatal care developments have advanced viability to a point somewhat earlier, these facts go only to the scheme of time limits on the realization of competing interests. Thus, any later divergences from the factual premises of *Roe* have no bearing on the validity of its central holding, that viability marks the earliest point at which the State's interest in fetal life is constitutionally adequate to justify a legislative ban on nontherapeutic abortions. The soundness or unsoundness of that constitutional judgment in no sense turns on when viability occurs. Whenever it may occur, its attainment will continue to serve as the critical fact.

(h) [B]ecause neither the factual underpinnings of *Roe*'s central holding nor this Court's understanding of it has changed (and because no other indication of weakened precedent has been shown), the Court could not pretend to be reexamining *Roe* with any justification beyond a present doctrinal disposition to come out differently from the *Roe* Court. That is an inadequate basis for overruling a prior case.

(i) Overruling *Roe*'s central holding would not only reach an unjustifiable result under stare decisis principles, but would seriously weaken the Court's capacity to exercise the judicial power and to function as the Supreme Court of a Nation dedicated to the rule of law. Where the Court acts to resolve the sort of unique, intensely divisive controversy reflected in *Roe*, its decision has a dimension not present in normal cases, and is entitled to rare precedential force to counter the inevitable efforts to overturn it and to thwart its implementation. Only the most convincing justification under accepted standards of precedent could suffice to demonstrate that a later decision overruling the first was anything but a surrender to political pressure and an unjustified repudiation of the principle on which the Court staked its authority in the first instance. Moreover, the country's loss of confidence in the Judiciary would be underscored by condemnation for the Court's failure to keep faith with those who support the decision at a cost to themselves. A decision to overrule *Roe*'s essential holding under the existing circumstances would address error, if error there was, at the cost of both profound and unnecessary damage to the Court's legitimacy and to the Nation's commitment to the rule of law.

An examination of *Roe v. Wade*, and subsequent cases, reveals a number of guiding principles that should control the assessment of the Pennsylvania statute:

(a) To protect the central right recognized by *Roe* while at the same time accommodating the State's profound interest in potential life, *See Id.*, at 162, the undue burden standard should be employed. An undue burden exists, and therefore a provision of law is invalid, if its purpose or effect is to place substantial obstacles in the path of a woman seeking an abortion before the fetus attains viability.

(b) *Roe*'s rigid trimester framework is rejected. To promote the State's interest in potential life throughout pregnancy, the State may take measures to ensure that the woman's choice is informed. Measures

(continued)

designed to advance this interest should not be invalidated if their purpose is to persuade the woman to choose childbirth over abortion. These measures must not be an undue burden on the right.

(c) As with any medical procedure, the State may enact regulations to further the health or safety of a woman seeking an abortion, but may not impose unnecessary health regulations that present a substantial obstacle to a woman seeking an abortion.

(d) Adoption of the undue burden standard does not disturb *Roe*'s holding that, regardless of whether exceptions are made for particular circumstances, a State may not prohibit any woman from making the ultimate decision to terminate her pregnancy before viability.

(e) *Roe*'s holding that "subsequent to viability, the State, in promoting its interest in the potentiality of human life, may, if it chooses, regulate, and even proscribe, abortion except where it is necessary, in appropriate medical judgment, for the preservation of the life or health of the mother" is also reaffirmed. *Id.*, at 164–165.

JUSTICE O'CONNOR, JUSTICE KENNEDY, and JUSTICE SOUTER delivered the opinion of the Court with respect to Parts V-A and V-C, concluding that:

1. As construed by the Court of Appeals, §3203's medical emergency definition is intended to assure that compliance with the State's abortion regulations would not in any way pose a significant threat to a woman's life or health, and thus does not violate the essential holding of *Roe*, at 164. Although the definition could be interpreted in an unconstitutional manner, this Court defers to lower federal court interpretations of state law unless they amount to "plain" error.

2. Section 3209's husband notification provision constitutes an undue burden, and is therefore invalid. A significant number of women will likely be prevented from obtaining an abortion just as surely as if Pennsylvania had outlawed the procedure entirely. The fact that §3209 may affect fewer than one percent of women seeking abortions does not save it from facial invalidity, since the proper focus of constitutional inquiry is the group for whom the law is a restriction, not the group for whom it is irrelevant. Furthermore, it cannot be claimed that the father's interest in the fetus' welfare is equal to the mother's protected liberty, since it is an inescapable biological fact that state

regulation with respect to the fetus will have a far greater impact on the pregnant woman's bodily integrity than it will on the husband. Section 3209 embodies a view of marriage consonant with the common law status of married women, but repugnant to this Court's present understanding of marriage and of the nature of the rights secured by the Constitution. *See Planned Parenthood of Central Mo. v. Danforth.*

JUSTICE O'CONNOR, JUSTICE KENNEDY, and JUSTICE SOUTER, joined by JUSTICE STEVENS, concluded in Part V-E that all of the statute's record keeping and reporting requirements, except that relating to spousal notice, are constitutional. The reporting provision relating to the reasons a married woman has not notified her husband that she intends to have an abortion must be invalidated, because it places an undue burden on a woman's choice.

JUSTICE O'CONNOR, JUSTICE KENNEDY, and JUSTICE SOUTER concluded in Parts V-B and V-D that:

1. Section 3205's informed consent provision is not an undue burden on a woman's constitutional right to decide to terminate a pregnancy. To the extent *Akron I*, and *Thornburgh*, find a constitutional violation when the government requires, as it does here, the giving of truthful, non-misleading information about the nature of the abortion procedure, the attendant health risks and those of childbirth, and the "probable gestational age" of the fetus, those cases are inconsistent with *Roe*'s acknowledgment of an important interest in potential life, and are overruled. Requiring that the woman be informed of the availability of information relating to the consequences to the fetus does not interfere with a constitutional right of privacy between a pregnant woman and her physician, since the doctor-patient relation is derivative of the woman's position, and does not underlie or override the abortion right.

2. Section 3206's one-parent consent requirement and judicial bypass procedure are constitutional. *See, e.g., Ohio v. Akron Center for Reproductive Health*, at 519.

JUSTICE BLACKMUN concluded that application of the strict scrutiny standard of review required by this Court's abortion precedents results in the invalidation of all the challenged provisions in the Pennsylvania statute, including the reporting requirements, and therefore concurred in the judgment that the requirement that a pregnant woman report her reasons for failing to provide spousal notice is unconstitutional.

(continued)

(continued)

THE CHIEF JUSTICE, joined by JUSTICE WHITE, JUSTICE SCALIA, and JUSTICE THOMAS, concluded that:

1. Although *Roe v. Wade*, is not directly implicated by the Pennsylvania statute, which simply regulates, and does not prohibit, abortion, a reexamination of the "fundamental right" *Roe* accorded to a woman's decision to abort a fetus, with the concomitant requirement that any state regulation of abortion survive "strict scrutiny," *Id.*, at 154–156, is warranted by the confusing and uncertain state of this Court's post-*Roe* decisional law.

2. The *Roe* Court reached too far when it analogized the right to abort a fetus to the rights involved in *Pierce v. Society of Sisters*; *Meyer v. Nebraska*; *Loving v. Virginia*; and *Griswold v. Connecticut*, and thereby deemed the right to abortion to be "fundamental." None of these decisions endorsed an all-encompassing "right of privacy," as *Roe*, at 152–153, claimed. Because abortion involves the purposeful termination of potential life, the abortion decision must be recognized as sui generis, different in kind from the rights protected in the earlier cases under the rubric of personal or family privacy and autonomy. And the historical traditions of the American people—as evidenced by the English common law and by the American abortion statutes in existence both at the time of the Fourteenth Amendment's adoption and *Roe*'s issuance—do not support the view that the right to terminate one's pregnancy is "fundamental." Thus, enactments abridging that right need not be subjected to strict scrutiny.

3. The undue burden standard adopted by the joint opinion of JUSTICES O'CONNOR, KENNEDY, and SOUTER has no basis in constitutional law, and will not result in the sort of simple limitation, easily applied, which the opinion anticipates.

4. The correct analysis is that set forth by the plurality opinion in *Webster*: a woman's interest in having an abortion is a form of liberty protected by the Due Process Clause, but States may regulate abortion procedures in ways rationally related to a legitimate state interest.

5. Section 3205's requirements are rationally related to the State's legitimate interest in assuring that a woman's consent to an abortion be fully informed. That such information might create some uncertainty and persuade some women to forgo abortions only demonstrates that it might make a difference, and is therefore relevant to a woman's informed choice. The waiting period helps ensure that a woman's decision to abort is a well-considered one, and rationally furthers the State's legitimate interest in maternal health and in unborn life. It may delay, but does not prohibit, abortions; and both it and the informed consent provisions do not apply in medical emergencies.

6. The statute's parental consent provision is entirely consistent with this Court's previous decisions involving such requirements. *See, e.g., Planned Parenthood Ass. of Kansas City, M., Inc. v. Ashcroft*. It is reasonably designed to further the State's important and legitimate interest "in the welfare of its young citizens, whose immaturity, inexperience, and lack of judgment may sometimes impair their ability to exercise their rights wisely." *Hodgson*, at 444.

JUSTICE SCALIA, joined by THE CHIEF JUSTICE, JUSTICE WHITE, and JUSTICE THOMAS, concluded that a woman's decision to abort her unborn child is not a constitutionally protected "liberty," because (1) the Constitution says absolutely nothing about it, and (2) the longstanding traditions of American society have permitted it to be legally proscribed. *See, e.g., Ohio v. Akron Center for Reproductive Health*, (SCALIA, J., concurring). The Pennsylvania statute should be upheld in its entirety under the rational basis test.

In summary, Justice O'Connor employed an undue burden test in *Webster*. After viability, a state may prohibit or restrict abortion. Prior to viability, a state may not impose an undue burden on a woman's decision to end her pregnancy.

A recent development in the area of constitutional protection for reproductive autonomy involves the issue of "partial birth abortions." In 2000, the Court struck down a Nebraska law prohibiting the abortion procedure known as dilation and extraction. In *Stenberg v. Carhart*, 530 U.S. 914 (2000), the Court narrowly reaffirmed the *Casey* decision.

In a 5–4 vote, the Court held that (1) the statute at issue had no exception for the life or health of the mother (required by *Roe* and *Casey*) and (2) the statute was worded too broadly.

Following *Stenberg v. Carhart*, the U.S. Congress enacted a federal law, the Partial-Birth Abortion Ban Act of 2003. The Act was much more specific than the Nebraska law in describing the procedure that was banned. In two cases that were consolidated by the Supreme Court, (*Gonzales v. Carhart* and *Gonzales v. Planned Parenthood*) the Court was asked to rule on the constitutionality of the statute. Three challenges to the statute were made: (1) it was void because it was too vague, (2) it placed an undue burden on the woman, and (3) it contained no exception for medical necessity. The Court upheld the law, finding the detailed description of the medical procedure along with the necessary intent were sufficient for a doctor of ordinary intelligence to understand. The following excerpt explains why the Court also held that the law did not place an undue burden on the woman and why a medical necessity was not needed.

Gonzales v. Carhart
550 U.S. 124 (2007)

Following this Court's *Stenberg v. Carhart*, 530 U. S. 914, decision that Nebraska's "partial birth abortion" statute violated the Federal Constitution, as interpreted in *Planned Parenthood of Southeastern Pa. v. Casey*, 505 U. S. 833, and *Roe v. Wade*, 410 U. S. 113, Congress passed the Partial-Birth Abortion Ban Act of 2003 (Act) to proscribe a particular method of ending fetal life in the later stages of pregnancy. The Act does not regulate the most common abortion procedures used in the first trimester of pregnancy, when the vast majority of abortions take place. The procedure that prompted the federal Act and various state statutes, including Nebraska's, is a variation of the standard D&E, and is herein referred to as "intact D&E."

[R]espondent abortion doctors challenged the Act's constitutionality on its face, and the Federal District Court granted a permanent injunction prohibiting petitioner Attorney General from enforcing the Act in all cases but those in which there was no dispute the fetus was viable. The Court found the Act unconstitutional because it (1) lacked an exception allowing the prohibited procedure where necessary for the mother's health and (2) covered not merely intact D&E but also other D&Es. Affirming, the Eighth Circuit found that a lack of consensus existed in the medical community as to the banned procedure's necessity, and thus *Stenberg* required legislatures to err on the side of protecting women's health by including a health exception. [R]espondent abortion advocacy

groups brought suit challenging the Act. The District Court enjoined the Attorney General from enforcing the Act, concluding it was unconstitutional on its face because it (1) unduly burdened a woman's ability to choose a second-trimester abortion, (2) was too vague, and (3) lacked a health exception as required by *Stenberg*. The Ninth Circuit agreed and affirmed.

Held: Respondents have not demonstrated that the Act, as a facial matter, is void for vagueness, or that it imposes an undue burden on a woman's right to abortion based on its overbreadth or lack of a health exception.

1. The *Casey* Court reaffirmed what it termed *Roe*'s three-part "essential holding": First, a woman has the right to choose to have an abortion before fetal viability and to obtain it without undue interference from the State. Second, the State has the power to restrict abortions after viability, if the law contains exceptions for pregnancies endangering the woman's life or health. And third, the State has legitimate interests from the pregnancy's outset in protecting the health of the woman and the life of the fetus that may become a child. 505 U. S., at 846. Though all three are implicated here, it is the third that requires the most extended discussion. In deciding whether the Act furthers the Government's legitimate interest in protecting fetal life, the Court assumes, *inter alia,* that an undue burden on the previability abortion right exists if a regulation's "purpose or effect is to place

(continued)

(continued)

a substantial obstacle in the [woman's] path," *id.,* at 878, but that "[r]egulations which do no more than create a structural mechanism by which the State . . . may express profound respect for the life of the unborn are permitted, if they are not a substantial obstacle to the woman's exercise of the right to choose," *id.,* at 877. *Casey* struck a balance that was central to its holding, and the Court applies *Casey*'s standard here. A central premise of *Casey*'s joint opinion—that the government has a legitimate, substantial interest in preserving and promoting fetal life—would be repudiated were the Court now to affirm the judgments below.

2. The Act, on its face, is not void for vagueness and does not impose an undue burden from any overbreadth..

3. The Act, measured by its text in this facial attack, does not impose a "substantial obstacle" to late-term, but previability, abortions, as prohibited by the *Casey* plurality, 505 U. S., at 878. Pp. 26–37.

(a) The contention that the Act's congressional purpose was to create such an obstacle is rejected. The Act's stated purposes are protecting innocent human life from a brutal and inhumane procedure and protecting the medical community's ethics and reputation. The government undoubtedly "has an interest in protecting the integrity and ethics of the medical profession." *Washington* v. *Glucksberg,* 521 U. S. 702. Moreover, *Casey* reaffirmed that the government may use its voice and its regulatory authority to show its profound respect for the life within the woman. See, *e.g.,* 505 U. S., at 873. The Act's ban on abortions involving partial delivery of a living fetus furthers the Government's objectives. Congress determined that such abortions are similar to the killing of a newborn infant. This Court has confirmed the validity of drawing boundaries to prevent practices that extinguish life and are close to actions that are condemned. *Glucksberg, supra,* at 732–735, and n. 23. The Act also recognizes that respect for human life finds an ultimate expression in a mother's love for her child. Whether to have an abortion requires a difficult and painful moral decision, *Casey,* 505 U. S., at 852–853, which some women come to regret. In a decision so fraught with emotional consequence, some doctors may prefer not to disclose precise details of the abortion procedure to be

used. It is, however, precisely this lack of information that is of legitimate concern to the State. *Id.,* at 873. The State's interest in respect for life is advanced by the dialogue that better informs the political and legal systems, the medical profession, expectant mothers, and society as a whole of the consequences that follow from a decision to elect a late-term abortion. The objection that the Act accomplishes little because the standard D&E is in some respects as brutal, if not more, than intact D&E, is unpersuasive. It was reasonable for Congress to think that partial-birth abortion, more than standard D&E, undermines the public's perception of the doctor's appropriate role during delivery, and perverts the birth process. Pp. 26–30.

(b) The Act's failure to allow the banned procedure's use where " 'necessary, in appropriate medical judgment, for preservation of the [mother's] health,' " *Ayotte* v. *Planned Parenthood of Northern New Eng.,* 546 U. S. 320, does not have the effect of imposing an unconstitutional burden on the abortion right. The Court assumes the Act's prohibition would be unconstitutional, under controlling precedents, if it "subject[ed] [women] to significant health risks." *Id.,* at 328. Whether the Act creates such risks was, however, a contested factual question below: The evidence presented in the trial courts and before Congress demonstrates both sides have medical support for their positions. The Court's precedents instruct that the Act can survive facial attack when this medical uncertainty persists. See, *e.g., Kansas* v. *Hendricks,* 521 U. S. 346, n. 3. This traditional rule is consistent with *Casey,* which confirms both that the State has an interest in promoting respect for human life at all stages in the pregnancy, and that abortion doctors should be treated the same as other doctors. Medical uncertainty does not foreclose the exercise of legislative power in the abortion context any more than it does in other contexts. Other considerations also support the Court's conclusion, including the fact that safe alternatives to the prohibited procedure, such as D&E, are available. In addition, if intact D&E is truly necessary in some circumstances, a prior injection to kill the fetus allows a doctor to perform the procedure, given that the Act's prohibition only applies

(continued)

(continued)

to the delivery of "a living fetus," 18 U. S. C. §1531(b)(1)(A). *Planned Parenthood of Central Mo. v. Danforth*, 428 U. S. 52, distinguished. The Court rejects certain of the parties' arguments. On the one hand, the Attorney General's contention that the Act should be upheld based on the congressional findings alone fails because some of the Act's recitations are factually incorrect and some of the important findings have been superseded. Also unavailing, however, is respondents' contention that an abortion regulation must contain a health exception if "substantial medical authority supports the proposition that banning a particular procedure could endanger women's health, " *Stenberg*, 530 U. S., at 938. Interpreting *Stenberg* as leaving no margin for legislative error in the face of medical uncertainty is too exacting a standard. Marginal safety considerations, including the balance of risks, are within the legislative competence where, as here, the regulation is rational and pursues legitimate ends, and standard, safe medical options are available.

4. These facial attacks should not have been entertained in the first instance. In these circumstances the proper means to consider exceptions is by as-applied challenge. Cf. *Wisconsin Right to Life, Inc. v. Federal Election Comm'n*, 546 U. S. ___, ___. This is the proper manner to protect the woman's health if it can be shown that in discrete and well-defined instances a condition has or is likely to occur in which the procedure prohibited by the Act must be used. No as-applied challenge need be brought if the Act's prohibition threatens a woman's life, because the Act already contains a life exception. 18 U. S. C. § 1531(a).

KENNEDY, J., delivered the opinion of the Court, in which ROBERTS, C. J., and SCALIA, THOMAS, and ALITO, J. J., joined. THOMAS, J., filed a concurring opinion, in which SCALIA, J., joined. GINSBURG, J., filed a dissenting opinion, in which STEVENS, SOUTER, and BREYER, J. J., joined.

The following language is from the dissent by Justice Ginsburg:

Seven years ago, in *Stenberg v. Carhart*, 530 U. S. 914 (2000), the Court invalidated a Nebraska statute criminalizing the performance of a medical procedure that, in the political arena, has been dubbed "partial-birth abortion." With fidelity to the *Roe-Casey* line of precedent, the Court held the Nebraska statute unconstitutional in part because it lacked the requisite protection for the preservation of a woman's health. *Stenberg*, 530 U. S., at 930; cf. *Ayotte v. Planned Parenthood of Northern New Eng.*, 546 U. S. 320, 327 (2006).

Today's decision is alarming. It refuses to take *Casey* and *Stenberg* seriously. It tolerates, indeed applauds, federal intervention to ban nationwide a procedure found necessary and proper in certain cases by the American College of Obstetricians and Gynecologists (ACOG). It blurs the line, firmly drawn in *Casey*, between previability and postviability abortions. And, for the first time since *Roe*, the Court blesses a prohibition with no exception safeguarding a woman's health.

I dissent from the Court's disposition. Retreating from prior rulings that abortion restrictions cannot be imposed absent an exception safeguarding a woman's health, the Court upholds an Act that surely would not survive under the close scrutiny that previously attended state-decreed limitations on a woman's reproductive choices.

Constitutional Protection for Sexual Acts and Sexual Orientation

UNTIL VERY RECENTLY, THE SUPREME Court was unwilling to provide constitutional protection for sexual activity or sexual orientation. In the now outdated *Bowers v. Hardwick*, the Court held that the constitutional right to privacy did not include a right for consenting adults to engage in homosexual activity, even if that activity took place in a private home.

Bowers v. Hardwick
478 U.S. 186 (1986)

After being charged with violating the Georgia statute criminalizing sodomy by committing that act with another adult male in the bedroom of his home, respondent Hardwick (respondent) brought suit in Federal District Court, challenging the constitutionality of the statute insofar as it criminalized consensual sodomy. The court granted the defendants' motion to dismiss for failure to state a claim. The Court of Appeals reversed and remanded, holding that the Georgia statute violated respondent's fundamental rights.

Held:
The Georgia statute is constitutional.

(a) The Constitution does not confer a fundamental right upon homosexuals to engage in sodomy. None of the fundamental rights announced in this Court's prior cases involving family relationships, marriage, or procreation bear any resemblance to the right asserted in this case. And any claim that those cases stand for the proposition that any kind of private sexual conduct between consenting adults is constitutionally insulated from state proscription is unsupportable.

(b) Against a background in which many States have criminalized sodomy and still do, to claim that a right to engage in such conduct is "deeply rooted in this Nation's history and tradition" or "implicit in the concept of ordered liberty" is, at best, facetious.

(c) There should be great resistance to expand the reach of the Due Process Clauses to cover new fundamental rights. Otherwise, the Judiciary necessarily would take upon itself further authority to govern the country without constitutional authority. The claimed right in this case falls far short of overcoming this resistance.

(d) The fact that homosexual conduct occurs in the privacy of the home does not affect the result. *Stanley v. Georgia*, distinguished.

(e) Sodomy laws should not be invalidated on the asserted basis that majority belief that sodomy is immoral is an inadequate rationale to support the laws.

Seventeen years later, the *Bowers* case was overruled by *Lawrence v. Texas*. Notice the shift in language and approach in *Lawrence*.

Lawrence v. Texas
539 U.S. 558 (2003)

The Court in Lawrence *affirms that human dignity is protected by the Fourteenth Amendment and that the United States Constitution precludes government intrusion into the realm of consensual adult intimacy and one's choice of an intimate partner. The Court reaffirms the critical role that decisions whether to marry or raise children bear in shaping one's identity.*

Responding to a reported weapons disturbance in a private residence, Houston police entered petitioner Lawrence's apartment and saw him and another adult man, petitioner Garner, engaging in a private, consensual sexual act. Petitioners were arrested and convicted of deviate sexual intercourse in violation of a Texas statute forbidding two persons of the same sex to engage in certain intimate sexual conduct. In affirming, the State Court of Appeals held, inter alia, that the statute was not unconstitutional under the Due Process Clause of the Fourteenth Amendment. The court considered *Bowers v. Hardwick*, controlling on that point.

(continued)

(continued)

Held: The Texas statute making it a crime for two persons of the same sex to engage in certain intimate sexual conduct violates the Due Process Clause.

(a) Resolution of this case depends on whether petitioners were free as adults to engage in private conduct in the exercise of their liberty under the Due Process Clause. For this inquiry the Court deems it necessary to reconsider its *Bowers* holding. The *Bowers* Court's initial substantive statement—"The issue presented is whether the Federal Constitution confers a fundamental right upon homosexuals to engage in sodomy . . . ," discloses the Court's failure to appreciate the extent of the liberty at stake. To say that the issue in *Bowers* was simply the right to engage in certain sexual conduct demeans the claim the individual put forward, just as it would demean a married couple were it said that marriage is just about the right to have sexual intercourse. Although the laws involved in *Bowers* and here purport to do not more than prohibit a particular sexual act, their penalties and purposes have more far-reaching consequences, touching upon the most private human conduct, sexual behavior, and in the most private of places, the home. They seek to control a personal relationship that, whether or not entitled to formal recognition in the law, is within the liberty of persons to choose without being punished as criminals. The liberty protected by the Constitution allows homosexual persons the right to choose to enter upon relationships in the confines of their homes and their own private lives and still retain their dignity as free persons.

(b) Having misapprehended the liberty claim presented to it, the *Bowers* Court stated that proscriptions against sodomy have ancient roots. It should be noted, however, that there is no longstanding history in this country of laws directed at homosexual conduct as a distinct matter. Early American sodomy laws were not directed at homosexuals as such but instead sought to prohibit non-procreative sexual activity more generally, whether between men and women or men and men. Moreover, early sodomy laws seem not to have been enforced against consenting adults acting in private. Instead, sodomy prosecutions often involved predatory acts against those who could not or did not consent: relations between men and minor girls or boys, between adults involving force, between adults implicating disparity in status, or between men and animals. The longstanding criminal prohibition of homosexual sodomy upon which *Bowers* placed such reliance is as consistent with a general condemnation of non-procreative sex as it is with an established tradition of prosecuting acts because of their homosexual character. Far from possessing "ancient roots," *ibid.*, American laws targeting same-sex couples did not develop until the last third of the 20th century. Even now, only nine States have singled out same-sex relations for criminal prosecution. Thus, the historical grounds relied upon in *Bowers* are more complex than the majority opinion and the concurring opinion by Chief Justice Burger there indicated. They are not without doubt and, at the very least, are overstated. The *Bowers* Court was, of course, making the broader point that for centuries there have been powerful voices to condemn homosexual conduct as immoral, but this Court's obligation is to define the liberty of all, not to mandate its own moral code, *Planned Parenthood of Southeastern Pa. v. Casey*. The Nation's laws and traditions in the past half century are most relevant here. They show an emerging awareness that liberty gives substantial protection to adult persons in deciding how to conduct their private lives in matters pertaining to sex. *See County of Sacramento v. Lewis*.

(c) *Bowers'* deficiencies became even more apparent in the years following its announcement. The 25 States with laws prohibiting the conduct referenced in *Bowers* are reduced now to 13, of which 4 enforce their laws only against homosexual conduct. In those States, including Texas, that still proscribe sodomy (whether for same-sex or heterosexual conduct), there is a pattern of non-enforcement with respect to consenting adults acting in private. *Casey*, at 851—which confirmed that the Due Process Clause protects personal decisions relating to marriage, procreation, contraception, family relationships, child rearing, and education—and *Romer v. Evans*, 624—which struck down class-based legislation directed at homosexuals—cast *Bowers'* holding into even more doubt. The stigma the Texas criminal statute imposes, moreover, is not trivial. Although the offense is but a minor misdemeanor, it remains a criminal offense with all that imports for the dignity of the persons charged, including notation of convictions on their records and on job application forms, and registration as sex offenders under state law. Where a case's foundations have sustained serious erosion, criticism from other sources is of greater significance. In the United States, criticism of *Bowers* has been substantial and continuing, disapproving of its reasoning in

(continued)

(continued)

all respects, not just as to its historical assumptions. And, to the extent *Bowers* relied on values shared with a wider civilization, the case's reasoning and holding have been rejected by the European Court of Human Rights, and that other nations have taken action consistent with an affirmation of the protected right of homosexual adults to engage in intimate, consensual conduct. There has been no showing that in this country the governmental interest in circumscribing personal choice is somehow more legitimate or urgent. Stare decisis is not an inexorable command. *Payne v. Tennessee*. *Bowers*' holding has not induced detrimental reliance of the sort that could counsel against overturning it once there are compelling reasons to do so. *Casey*, at 855–856. *Bowers* causes uncertainty, for the precedents before and after it contradict its central holding.

(d) *Bowers*' rationale does not withstand careful analysis. In his dissenting opinion in *Bowers* Justice Stevens concluded that (1) the fact a State's governing majority has traditionally viewed a particular practice as immoral is not a sufficient reason for upholding a law prohibiting the practice, and (2) individual decisions concerning the intimacies of physical relationships, even when not intended to produce offspring, are a form of "liberty" protected by due process. That analysis should have controlled *Bowers*, and it controls here. *Bowers* was not correct when it was decided, is not correct today, and is hereby overruled. This case does not involve minors, persons who might be injured or coerced, those who might not easily refuse consent, or public conduct or prostitution. It does involve two adults who, with full and mutual consent, engaged in sexual practices common to a homosexual lifestyle. Petitioners' right to liberty under the Due Process Clause gives them the full right to engage in private conduct without government intervention. *Casey*, at 847. The Texas statute furthers no legitimate state interest which can justify its intrusion into the individual's personal and private life.

Same Sex Marriage

At some point, the U.S. Supreme Court will undoubtedly address the issue of same sex marriage. Until then, state and lower federal courts struggle with the issue. "The history of constitutional law 'is the story of the extension of constitutional rights and protections to people once ignored or excluded.'" *Goodridge* (see following case) quoting *United States v. Virginia*, 518 U.S. 515, 557 (1996). In November of 2003, the Massachusetts Supreme Court answered a question not reached in *Lawrence*: "Whether the Commonwealth may use its formidable regulatory authority to bar same-sex couples from civil marriage is a question not previously addressed by a Massachusetts appellate court."

Goodridge v. Department of Public Health

440 Mass. 309 (2003)

Marriage is a vital social institution. The exclusive commitment of two individuals to each other nurtures love and mutual support; it brings stability to our society. For those who choose to marry, and for their children, marriage provides an abundance of legal, financial, and social benefits. In return it imposes weighty legal, financial, and social obligations. The question before us is whether, consistent with the Massachusetts Constitution, the Commonwealth may deny the protections, benefits, and obligations conferred by civil marriage to two individuals of the same sex who wish to marry. We conclude that it may not. The Massachusetts Constitution affirms the dignity and equality of all individuals. It forbids the creation of second-class citizens. In reaching our conclusion we have given full deference to the arguments made by the Commonwealth. But it has failed to identify any constitutionally adequate reason for denying civil marriage to same-sex couples.

(continued)

(continued)

We are mindful that our decision marks a change in the history of our marriage law. Many people hold deep-seated religious, moral, and ethical convictions that marriage should be limited to the union of one man and one woman, and that homosexual conduct is immoral. Many hold equally strong religious, moral, and ethical convictions that same-sex couples are entitled to be married, and that homosexual persons should be treated no differently than their heterosexual neighbors. Neither view answers the question before us. Our concern is with the Massachusetts Constitution as a charter of governance for every person properly within its reach. "Our obligation is to define the liberty of all, not to mandate our own moral code." *Lawrence v. Texas*, 123 S. Ct. 2472, 2480 (2003), quoting *Planned Parenthood of Southeastern Pa. v. Casey*, 505 U.S. 833, 850 (1992).

Whether the Commonwealth may use its formidable regulatory authority to bar same-sex couples from civil marriage is a question not previously addressed by a Massachusetts appellate court. It is a question the United States Supreme Court left open as a matter of Federal law in *Lawrence*, at 2484, where it was not an issue. There, the Court affirmed that the core concept of common human dignity protected by the Fourteenth Amendment to the United States Constitution precludes government intrusion into the deeply personal realms of consensual adult expressions of intimacy and one's choice of an intimate partner. The Court also reaffirmed the central role that decisions whether to marry or have children bear in shaping one's identity. *Id.*, at 2481. The Massachusetts Constitution is, if anything, more protective of individual liberty and equality than the Federal Constitution; it may demand broader protection for fundamental rights; and it is less tolerant of government intrusion into the protected spheres of private life.

Barred access to the protections, benefits, and obligations of civil marriage, a person who enters into an intimate, exclusive union with another of the same sex is arbitrarily deprived of membership in one of our community's most rewarding and cherished institutions. That exclusion is incompatible with the constitutional principles of respect for individual autonomy and equality under law.

I

The plaintiffs are fourteen individuals from five Massachusetts counties. The plaintiffs include business executives, lawyers, an investment banker, educators, therapists, and a computer engineer. Many are active in church, community, and school groups. They have employed such legal means as are available to them—for example, joint adoption, powers of attorney, and joint ownership of real property—to secure aspects of their relationships. Each plaintiff attests a desire to marry his or her partner in order to affirm publicly their commitment to each other and to secure the legal protections and benefits afforded to married couples and their children.

The Department of Public Health (department) is charged by statute with safeguarding public health. Among its responsibilities, the department oversees the registry of vital records and statistics (registry), which "enforce[s] all laws" relative to the issuance of marriage licenses and the keeping of marriage records, and which promulgates policies and procedures for the issuance of marriage licenses by city and town clerks and registers.

In March and April, 2001, each of the plaintiff couples attempted to obtain a marriage license from a city or town clerk's office. In each case, the clerk either refused to accept the notice of intention to marry or denied a marriage license to the couple on the ground that Massachusetts does not recognize same-sex marriage. Because obtaining a marriage license is a necessary prerequisite to civil marriage in Massachusetts, denying marriage licenses to the plaintiffs was tantamount to denying them access to civil marriage itself, with its appurtenant social and legal protections, benefits, and obligations.

II

Although the plaintiffs refer in passing to "the marriage statutes," they focus, quite properly, on G. L. c. 207, the marriage licensing statute, which controls entry into civil marriage. As a preliminary matter, we summarize the provisions of that law.

In short, for all the joy and solemnity that normally attend a marriage, G. L. c. 207, governing entrance to marriage, is a licensing law. The plaintiffs argue that because nothing in that licensing law specifically prohibits marriages between persons of the same sex, we may interpret the statute to permit "qualified same sex couples" to obtain marriage licenses, thereby avoiding the question whether the law is constitutional. This claim lacks merit. We interpret statutes to carry out the Legislature's intent, determined by the words of a statute interpreted according to "the ordinary and approved usage of the

(continued)

(continued)

language." *Hanlon v. Rollins*, 286 Mass. 444, 447 (1934). The everyday meaning of "marriage" is "[t]he legal union of a man and woman as husband and wife," *Black's Law Dictionary* 986 (7th ed. 1999), and the plaintiffs do not argue that the term "marriage" has ever had a different meaning under Massachusetts law.

The only reasonable explanation is that the Legislature did not intend that same-sex couples be licensed to marry. We conclude, as did the trial court judge, that G. L. c. 207 may not be construed to permit same-sex couples to marry.

III

A

The larger question is whether, as the department claims, government action that bars same-sex couples from civil marriage constitutes a legitimate exercise of the State's authority to regulate conduct, or whether, as the plaintiffs claim, this categorical marriage exclusion violates the Massachusetts Constitution. We have recognized the long-standing statutory understanding, derived from the common law, that "marriage" means the lawful union of a woman and a man. But that history cannot and does not foreclose the constitutional question.

The plaintiffs' claim that the marriage restriction violates the Massachusetts Constitution can be analyzed in two ways. Does it offend the Constitution's guarantees of equality before the law? Or do the liberty and due process provisions of the Massachusetts Constitution secure the plaintiffs' right to marry their chosen partner?

We begin by considering the nature of civil marriage itself. Simply put, the government creates civil marriage. In Massachusetts, civil marriage is, and since pre-Colonial days has been, precisely what its name implies: a wholly secular institution. Civil marriage is created and regulated through exercise of the police power. "Police power" (now more commonly termed the State's regulatory authority) is an old-fashioned term for the Commonwealth's lawmaking authority, as bounded by the liberty and equality guarantees of the Massachusetts Constitution and its express delegation of power from the people to their government. In broad terms, it is the Legislature's power to enact rules to regulate conduct, to the extent that such laws are "necessary to secure the health, safety, good order, comfort, or general welfare of the community" (citations omitted). Opinion of the Justices, 341 Mass. 760, 785 (1960).

Without question, civil marriage enhances the "welfare of the community." It is a "social institution of the highest importance." *French v. McAnarney*. Civil marriage anchors an ordered society by encouraging stable relationships over transient ones. It is central to the way the Commonwealth identifies individuals, provides for the orderly distribution of property, ensures that children and adults are cared for and supported whenever possible from private rather than public funds, and tracks important epidemiological and demographic data.

Marriage also bestows enormous private and social advantages on those who choose to marry. Civil marriage is at once a deeply personal commitment to another human being and a highly public celebration of the ideals of mutuality, companionship, intimacy, fidelity, and family. Because it fulfils yearnings for security, safe haven, and connection that express our common humanity, civil marriage is an esteemed institution, and the decision whether and whom to marry is among life's momentous acts of self-definition.

Tangible as well as intangible benefits flow from marriage. The marriage license grants valuable property rights to those who meet the entry requirements, and who agree to what might otherwise be a burdensome degree of government regulation of their activities. The benefits accessible only by way of a marriage license are enormous, touching nearly every aspect of life and death. The department states that "hundreds of statutes" are related to marriage and to marital benefits.

It is undoubtedly for these concrete reasons, as well as for its intimately personal significance, that civil marriage has long been termed a "civil right." *See, e.g., Loving v. Virginia*, 388 U.S. 1, 12 (1967) ("Marriage is one of the 'basic civil rights of man,' fundamental to our very existence and survival"), quoting *Skinner v. Oklahoma*, 316 U.S. 535, 541 (1942); *Milford v. Worcester*, 7 Mass. 48, 56 (1810) (referring to "civil rights incident to marriages"). The United States Supreme Court has described the right to marry as "of fundamental importance for all individuals" and as "part of the fundamental 'right of privacy' implicit in the Fourteenth Amendment's Due Process Clause." *Zablocki v. Redhail*, 434 U.S. 374, 384 (1978). *See Loving v. Virginia*, ("The freedom to marry has long been recognized as one of the vital personal rights essential to the orderly pursuit of happiness by free men").

(continued)

(continued)

Without the right to marry—or more properly, the right to choose to marry—one is excluded from the full range of human experience and denied full protection of the laws for one's "avowed commitment to an intimate and lasting human relationship." *Baker v. State*, at 229. Because civil marriage is central to the lives of individuals and the welfare of the community, our laws assiduously protect the individual's right to marry against undue government incursion. Laws may not "interfere directly and substantially with the right to marry." *Zablocki v. Redhail*, at 387.

B

The Massachusetts Constitution protects matters of personal liberty against government incursion as zealously, and often more so, than does the Federal Constitution, even where both Constitutions employ essentially the same language. *See Planned Parenthood League of Mass., Inc. v. Attorney Gen.*, 424 Mass. 586, 590 (1997). That the Massachusetts Constitution is in some instances more protective of individual liberty interests than is the Federal Constitution is not surprising. Fundamental to the vigor of our Federal system of government is that "state courts are absolutely free to interpret state constitutional provisions to accord greater protection to individual rights than do similar provisions of the United States Constitution." *Arizona v. Evans*, 514 U.S. 1, 8 (1995).

The individual liberty and equality safeguards of the Massachusetts Constitution protect both "freedom from" unwarranted government intrusion into protected spheres of life and "freedom to" partake in benefits created by the State for the common good. Both freedoms are involved here. Whether and whom to marry, how to express sexual intimacy, and whether and how to establish a family—these are among the most basic of every individual's liberty and due process rights. And central to personal freedom and security is the assurance that the laws will apply equally to persons in similar situations. "Absolute equality before the law is a fundamental principle of our own Constitution." Opinion of the Justices, 211 Mass. 618, 619 (1912). The liberty interest in choosing whether and whom to marry would be hollow if the Commonwealth could, without sufficient justification, foreclose an individual from freely choosing the person with whom to share an exclusive commitment in the unique institution of civil marriage.

The Massachusetts Constitution requires, at a minimum, that the exercise of the State's regulatory authority not be "arbitrary or capricious." *Commonwealth v. Henry's Drywall Co.*, 366 Mass. 539, 542 (1974). Under both the equality and liberty guarantees, regulatory authority must, at very least, serve "a legitimate purpose in a rational way"; a statute must "bear a reasonable relation to a permissible legislative objective." *Rushworth v. Registrar of Motor Vehicles*, 413 Mass. 265, 270 (1992). Any law failing to satisfy the basic standards of rationality is void. The plaintiffs challenge the marriage statute on both equal protection and due process grounds. Because the statute does not survive rational basis review, we do not consider the plaintiffs' arguments that this case merits strict judicial scrutiny.

The department posits three legislative rationales for prohibiting same-sex couples from marrying: (1) providing a "favorable setting for procreation"; (2) ensuring the optimal setting for child rearing, which the department defines as "a two-parent family with one parent of each sex"; and (3) preserving scarce State and private financial resources. We consider each in turn.

The judge in the Superior Court endorsed the first rationale, holding that "the state's interest in regulating marriage is based on the traditional concept that marriage's primary purpose is procreation." This is incorrect. Our laws of civil marriage do not privilege procreative heterosexual intercourse between married people above every other form of adult intimacy and every other means of creating a family. General Laws c. 207 contains no requirement that the applicants for a marriage license attest to their ability or intention to conceive children by coitus. Fertility is not a condition of marriage, nor is it grounds for divorce. People who have never consummated their marriage, and never plan to, may be and stay married. *See Franklin v. Franklin*, 154 Mass. 515, 516 (1891) ("The consummation of a marriage by coition is not necessary to its validity"). People who cannot stir from their deathbed may marry. While it is certainly true that many, perhaps most, married couples have children together (assisted or unassisted), it is the exclusive and permanent commitment of the marriage partners to one another, not the begetting of children, that is the sine qua non of civil marriage.

The department's first stated rationale, equating marriage with unassisted heterosexual procreation, shades imperceptibly into its second: that confining

(continued)

(continued)

marriage to opposite-sex couples ensures that children are raised in the "optimal" setting. Protecting the welfare of children is a paramount State policy. Restricting marriage to opposite-sex couples, however, cannot plausibly further this policy. "The demographic changes of the past century make it difficult to speak of an average American family. The composition of families varies greatly from household to household." *Troxel v. Granville*, 530 U.S. 57, 63 (2000). Massachusetts has responded supportively to "the changing realities of the American family," *id.*, at 64, and has moved vigorously to strengthen the modern family in its many variations. Moreover, we have repudiated the common-law power of the State to provide varying levels of protection to children based on the circumstances of birth. *Powers v. Wilkinson*, 399 Mass. 650, 661 (1987) ("Ours is an era in which logic and compassion have impelled the law toward unburdening children from the stigma and the disadvantages heretofore attendant upon the status of illegitimacy"). The "best interests of the child" standard does not turn on a parent's sexual orientation or marital status. See *e.g., Doe v. Doe*, 16 Mass. App. Ct. 499, 503 (1983) (parent's sexual orientation insufficient ground to deny custody of child in divorce action). *See also E.N.O. v. L.M.M.* at 829–830 (best interests of child determined by considering child's relationship with biological and de facto same-sex parents); *Silvia v. Silvia*, 9 Mass. App. Ct. 339, 341 & n.3 (1980) (collecting support and custody statutes containing no gender distinction).

The department has offered no evidence that forbidding marriage to people of the same sex will increase the number of couples choosing to enter into opposite-sex marriages in order to have and raise children. There is thus no rational relationship between the marriage statute and the Commonwealth's proffered goal of protecting the "optimal" child rearing unit. Moreover, the department readily concedes that people in same-sex couples may be "excellent" parents. These couples (including four of the plaintiff couples) have children for the reasons others do—to love them, to care for them, to nurture them. But the task of child rearing for same-sex couples is made infinitely harder by their status as outliers to the marriage laws.

In this case, we are confronted with an entire, sizable class of parents raising children who have absolutely no access to civil marriage and its protections because they are forbidden from procuring a marriage license. It

cannot be rational under our laws, and indeed it is not permitted, to penalize children by depriving them of State benefits because the State disapproves of their parents' sexual orientation.

The third rationale advanced by the department is that limiting marriage to opposite-sex couples furthers the Legislature's interest in conserving scarce State and private financial resources. The marriage restriction is rational, it argues, because the General Court logically could assume that same-sex couples are more financially independent than married couples and thus less needy of public marital benefits, such as tax advantages, or private marital benefits, such as employer-financed health plans that include spouses in their coverage.

An absolute statutory ban on same-sex marriage bears no rational relationship to the goal of economy. First, the department's conclusory generalization—that same-sex couples are less financially dependent on each other than opposite-sex couples—ignores that many same-sex couples, such as many of the plaintiffs in this case, have children and other dependents (here, aged parents) in their care. The department does not contend, nor could it, that these dependents are less needy or deserving than the dependents of married couples. Second, Massachusetts marriage laws do not condition receipt of public and private financial benefits to married individuals on a demonstration of financial dependence on each other; the benefits are available to married couples regardless of whether they mingle their finances or actually depend on each other for support.

The department suggests additional rationales for prohibiting same-sex couples from marrying, which are developed by some amici. It argues that broadening civil marriage to include same-sex couples will trivialize or destroy the institution of marriage as it has historically been fashioned. Certainly our decision today marks a significant change in the definition of marriage as it has been inherited from the common law, and understood by many societies for centuries. But it does not disturb the fundamental value of marriage in our society.

Here, the plaintiffs seek only to be married, not to undermine the institution of civil marriage. They do not want marriage abolished. They do not attack the binary nature of marriage, the consanguinity provisions, or any of the other gate-keeping provisions of the marriage licensing law. Recognizing the right of an individual to marry a person of the same sex will not diminish the

(continued)

(continued)

validity or dignity of opposite-sex marriage, any more than recognizing the right of an individual to marry a person of a different race devalues the marriage of a person who marries someone of her own race. If anything, extending civil marriage to same-sex couples reinforces the importance of marriage to individuals and communities. That same-sex couples are willing to embrace marriage's solemn obligations of exclusivity, mutual support, and commitment to one another is a testament to the enduring place of marriage in our laws and in the human spirit.

It has been argued that, due to the State's strong interest in the institution of marriage as a stabilizing social structure, only the Legislature can control and define its boundaries. Accordingly, our elected representatives legitimately may choose to exclude same-sex couples from civil marriage in order to assure all citizens of the Commonwealth that (1) the benefits of our marriage laws are available explicitly to create and support a family setting that is, in the Legislature's view, optimal for child rearing, and (2) the State does not endorse gay and lesbian parenthood as the equivalent of being raised by one's married biological parents. These arguments miss the point. The Massachusetts Constitution requires that legislation meet certain criteria and not extend beyond certain limits. It is the function of courts to determine whether these criteria are met and whether these limits are exceeded. In most instances, these limits are defined by whether a rational basis exists to conclude that legislation will bring about a rational result. The Legislature in the first instance, and the courts in the last instance, must ascertain whether such a rational basis exists. To label the court's role as usurping that of the Legislature, *see, e.g.*, post at (Cordy, J., dissenting), is to misunderstand the nature and purpose of judicial review. We owe great deference to the Legislature to decide social and policy issues, but it is the traditional and settled role of courts to decide constitutional issues.

The history of constitutional law "is the story of the extension of constitutional rights and protections to people once ignored or excluded." *United States v. Virginia*, 518 U.S. 515, 557 (1996) (construing equal protection clause of the Fourteenth Amendment to prohibit categorical exclusion of women from public military institute). This statement is as true in the area of civil marriage as in any other area of civil rights. *See, e.g.*, *Turner v. Safley*, 482 U.S. 78 (1987); *Loving v. Virginia*, 388 U.S. 1 (1967). As a public institution and a right of fundamental importance, civil marriage is an evolving paradigm. The common law was exceptionally harsh toward women who became wives: a woman's legal identity all but evaporated into that of her husband. *See generally* C.P. Kindregan, Jr., & M.L. Inker, *Family Law and Practice* §§ 1.9 and 1.10 (3d ed. 2002). Thus, one early Nineteenth Century jurist could observe matter of factly that, prior to the abolition of slavery in Massachusetts, "the condition of a slave resembled the connection of a wife with her husband, and of infant children with their father. He is obliged to maintain them, and they cannot be separated from him." *Winchendon v. Hatfield*, 4 Mass. 123, 129 (1808). But since at least the middle of the Nineteenth Century, both the courts and the Legislature have acted to ameliorate the harshness of the common-law regime. In *Bradford v. Worcester*, 184 Mass. 557, 562 (1904), we refused to apply the common-law rule that the wife's legal residence was that of her husband to defeat her claim to a municipal "settlement of paupers." In *Lewis v. Lewis*, 370 Mass. 619, 629 (1976), we abrogated the common-law doctrine immunizing a husband against certain suits because the common-law rule was predicated on "antediluvian assumptions concerning the role and status of women in marriage and in society." *Id.*, at 621. Alarms about the imminent erosion of the "natural" order of marriage were sounded over the demise of anti-miscegenation laws, the expansion of the rights of married women, and the introduction of "no-fault" divorce. Marriage has survived all of these transformations, and we have no doubt that marriage will continue to be a vibrant and revered institution.

The department has had more than ample opportunity to articulate a constitutionally adequate justification for limiting civil marriage to opposite-sex unions. It has failed to do so. The department has offered purported justifications for the civil marriage restriction that are starkly at odds with the comprehensive network of vigorous, gender-neutral laws promoting stable families and the best interests of children. It has failed to identify any relevant characteristic that would justify shutting the door to civil marriage to a person who wishes to marry someone of the same sex.

The marriage ban works a deep and scarring hardship on a very real segment of the community for no rational reason. The absence of any reasonable relationship between, on the one hand, an absolute disqualification of same-sex couples who wish to enter into civil marriage and, on the other, protection of public health, safety, or

(continued)

(continued)

general welfare, suggests that the marriage restriction is rooted in persistent prejudices against persons who are (or who are believed to be) homosexual. "The Constitution cannot control such prejudices but neither can it tolerate them. Private biases may be outside the reach of the law, but the law cannot, directly or indirectly, give them effect." *Palmore v. Sidoti*, 466 U.S. 429, 433 (1984) (construing Fourteenth Amendment). Limiting the protections, benefits, and obligations of civil marriage to opposite-sex couples violates the basic premises of individual liberty and equality under law protected by the Massachusetts Constitution.

IV

We consider next the plaintiffs' request for relief. We preserve as much of the statute as may be preserved in the face of the successful constitutional challenge.

We construe civil marriage to mean the voluntary union of two persons as spouses, to the exclusion of all others. This reformulation redresses the plaintiffs' constitutional injury and furthers the aim of marriage to promote stable, exclusive relationships. It advances the two legitimate State interests the department has identified: providing a stable setting for child rearing and conserving State resources. It leaves intact the Legislature's broad discretion to regulate marriage. *See Commonwealth v. Stowell*, 389 Mass. 171, 175 (1983).

In their complaint the plaintiffs request only a declaration that their exclusion and the exclusion of other qualified same-sex couples from access to civil marriage violates Massachusetts law. We declare that barring an individual from the protections, benefits, and obligations of civil marriage solely because that person would marry a person of the same sex violates the Massachusetts Constitution. We vacate the summary judgment for the department. We remand this case to the Superior Court for entry of judgment consistent with this opinion. Entry of judgment shall be stayed for 180 days to permit the Legislature to take such action as it may deem appropriate in light of this opinion. *See, e.g., Michaud v. Sheriff of Essex County*, 390 Mass. 523, 535–536 (1983).

So ordered.

Something to Consider

Less than two decades passed between the *Bowers* (1986) and *Lawrence* (2003) decisions. *Goodridge* was also decided in 2003. How do you account for what appears to be a rapid shift in judicial reasoning in these cases?

Although the Supreme Court has yet to rule on this issue, some lower federal courts have addressed the question. The arguments supporting this issue are based on the U.S. constitutional rights of privacy, equal protection, and due process. In one lower court case, *Perry v. Brown* (formerly *Perry v. Schwarzenegger*), a California District Court affirmed the right of a same-sex couple to marry. The court's conclusions were based primarily on due process and equal protection arguments, but in its order the court concluded that the right of the same-sex couple to marry was a fundamental right of privacy related to marriage. The following language from the court order illustrates:

> The Supreme Court recognizes that, wholly apart from procreation, choice and privacy play a pivotal role in the marital relationship. *See Griswold*, 381 U.S. at 485-486. Race restrictions on marital partners were once common in most states but are now seen as archaic, shameful or even bizarre. When the Supreme Court invalidated race restrictions in *Loving*, the definition of the right to marry did not change. 388 U.S. at 12. Instead, the Court recognized that race restrictions, despite their historical prevalence, stood in stark contrast to the concepts of liberty and choice inherent in the right to marry. *Id.* . . . The right to marry has been historically and remains the right to choose a spouse and, with mutual consent, join together and form a household. Race and gender restrictions shaped marriage during eras of race and gender inequality, but such restrictions were never part of the historical core of the institution of marriage.

The Court of Appeals recently upheld the decision in this case. For additional discussion on this issue, see Chapter 7.

The Right to Die

THE RIGHT TO PRIVACY is not limited to matters of a sexual nature. The right to privacy also includes the right to accept or reject medical care.

In 1990, the Court decided *Cruzan v. Director, Missouri Department of Health*, a case dealing with the right to withdraw medical treatment. The Court also discussed a related procedural due process question that commonly arises in these cases—what standards should be used by a court to determine the wishes of patients who are unable to make their wishes known. In *Cruzan*, the Court held that individuals have a due process right to reject medical care. However, the majority also held that a state law requiring clear and convincing evidence of the patient's wishes was valid. The opinion and a dissent from that case follows.

Cruzan v. Director, Missouri Department of Health
497 U.S. 261 (1990)

CHIEF JUSTICE REHNQUIST delivered the opinion of the Court.

Petitioner Nancy Beth Cruzan was rendered incompetent as a result of severe injuries sustained during an automobile accident. Co-petitioners Lester and Joyce Cruzan, Nancy's parents and co-guardians, sought a court order directing the withdrawal of their daughter's artificial feeding and hydration equipment after it became apparent that she had virtually no chance of recovering her cognitive faculties. The Supreme Court of Missouri held that, because there was no clear and convincing evidence of Nancy's desire to have life-sustaining treatment withdrawn under such circumstances, her parents lacked authority to effectuate such a request. We granted certiorari, and now affirm.

Before the turn of the century, this Court observed that "no right is held more sacred, or is more carefully guarded by the common law, than the right of every individual to the possession and control of his own person, free from all restraint or interference of others, unless by clear and unquestionable authority of law." *Union Pacific R. Co. v. Botsford*, (1891). This notion of bodily integrity has been embodied in the requirement that informed consent is generally required for medical treatment.

The logical corollary of the doctrine of informed consent is that the patient generally possesses the right not to consent, that is, to refuse treatment. Until about 15 years ago and the seminal decision in *In re Quinlan*, 70 N.J. 10, 355 A.2d 647, *cert. denied sub nom. Garger v. New Jersey*, (1976), the number of right-to-refuse-treatment decisions were relatively few. In the *Quinlan* case, young Karen Quinlan suffered severe brain damage as the result of anoxia, and entered a persistent vegetative state. Karen's father sought judicial approval to disconnect his daughter's respirator. The New Jersey Supreme Court granted the relief, holding that Karen had a right of privacy grounded in the Federal Constitution to terminate treatment. Recognizing that this right was not absolute, however, the court balanced it against asserted state interests. Noting that the State's interest "weakens and the individual's right to privacy grows as the degree of bodily invasion increases and the prognosis dims," the court concluded that the state interests had to give way in that case. The court also concluded that the "only practical way" to prevent the loss of Karen's privacy right due to her incompetence was to allow her guardian and family to decide "whether she would exercise it in these circumstances." *Ibid.*

After *Quinlan*, however, most courts have based a right to refuse treatment either solely on the common law right to informed consent or on both the common law right and a constitutional privacy right. In this Court, the

(continued)

(continued)

question is simply and starkly whether the United States Constitution prohibits Missouri from choosing the rule of decision which it did. This is the first case in which we have been squarely presented with the issue of whether the United States Constitution grants what is in common parlance referred to as a "right to die." The Fourteenth Amendment provides that no State shall "deprive any person of life, liberty, or property, without due process of law." The principle that a competent person has a constitutionally protected liberty interest in refusing unwanted medical treatment may be inferred from our prior decisions.

Just this Term, in the course of holding that a State's procedures for administering antipsychotic medication to prisoners were sufficient to satisfy due process concerns, we recognized that prisoners possess "a significant liberty interest in avoiding the unwanted administration of antipsychotic drugs under the Due Process Clause of the Fourteenth Amendment." *Washington v. Harper*, at 222 (1990).

But determining that a person has a "liberty interest" under the Due Process Clause does not end the inquiry; "whether respondent's constitutional rights have been violated must be determined by balancing his liberty interests against the relevant state interests." *Youngberg v. Romeo* (1982). For purposes of this case, we assume that the United States Constitution would grant a competent person a constitutionally protected right to refuse lifesaving hydration and nutrition.

Petitioners go on to assert that an incompetent person should possess the same right in this respect as is possessed by a competent person. The difficulty with petitioners' claim is that, in a sense, it begs the question: an incompetent person is not able to make an informed and voluntary choice to exercise a hypothetical right to refuse treatment or any other right. Such a "right" must be exercised for her, if at all, by some sort of surrogate. Here, Missouri has in effect recognized that, under certain circumstances, a surrogate may act for the patient in electing to have hydration and nutrition withdrawn in such a way as to cause death, but it has established a procedural safeguard to assure that the action of the surrogate conforms as best it may to the wishes expressed by the patient while competent. Missouri requires that evidence of the incompetent's wishes as to the withdrawal of treatment be proved by clear and convincing evidence. The question, then, is whether the United States Constitution forbids the establishment of this procedural requirement by the State. We hold that it does not.

Whether or not Missouri's clear and convincing evidence requirement comports with the United States Constitution depends in part on what interests the State may properly seek to protect in this situation. Missouri relies on its interest in the protection and preservation of human life, and there can be no gainsaying this interest.

But in the context presented here, a State has more particular interests at stake. The choice between life and death is a deeply personal decision of obvious and overwhelming finality. We believe Missouri may legitimately seek to safeguard the personal element of this choice through the imposition of heightened evidentiary requirements. It cannot be disputed that the Due Process Clause protects an interest in life as well as an interest in refusing life-sustaining medical treatment. Not all incompetent patients will have loved ones available to serve as surrogate decision makers. And even where family members are present, "[t]here will, of course, be some unfortunate situations in which family members will not act to protect a patient." *In re Jobes*, 108 N.J. 394, 419, 529 A.2d 434, 477 (1987). A State is entitled to guard against potential abuses in such situations. Similarly, a State is entitled to consider that a judicial proceeding to make a determination regarding an incompetent's wishes may very well not be an adversarial one, with the added guarantee of accurate fact finding that the adversary process brings with it. Finally, we think a State may properly decline to make judgments about the "quality" of life that a particular individual may enjoy, and simply assert an unqualified interest in the preservation of human life to be weighed against the constitutionally protected interests of the individual.

In our view, Missouri has permissibly sought to advance these interests through the adoption of a "clear and convincing" standard of proof to govern such proceedings.

In sum, we conclude that a State may apply a clear and convincing evidence standard in proceedings where a guardian seeks to discontinue nutrition and hydration of a person diagnosed to be in a persistent vegetative state.

The judgment of the Supreme Court of Missouri is Affirmed.

JUSTICE BRENNAN, with whom JUSTICE MARSHALL and JUSTICE BLACKMUN join, dissenting.

Today the Court, while tentatively accepting that there is some degree of constitutionally protected liberty interest in avoiding unwanted medical treatment,

(continued)

(continued)

including life-sustaining medical treatment such as artificial nutrition and hydration, affirms the decision of the Missouri Supreme Court. The majority opinion, as I read it, would affirm that decision on the ground that a State may require "clear and convincing" evidence of Nancy Cruzan's prior decision to forgo life-sustaining treatment under circumstances such as hers in order to ensure that her actual wishes are honored. Because I believe that Nancy Cruzan has a fundamental right to be free of unwanted artificial nutrition and hydration, which right is not outweighed by any interests of the State, and because I find that the improperly biased procedural obstacles imposed by the Missouri Supreme Court impermissibly burden that right, I respectfully dissent. Nancy Cruzan is entitled to choose to die with dignity.

The right to be free of unwanted medical intervention, like other constitutionally protected interests, may not be absolute. As the majority recognizes, Missouri has a parens patriae interest in providing Nancy Cruzan,

now incompetent, with as accurate as possible a determination of how she would exercise her rights under these circumstances.

Accuracy must be our touchstone. Missouri may constitutionally impose only those procedural requirements that serve to enhance the accuracy of a determination of Nancy Cruzan's wishes or are at least consistent with an accurate determination. The Missouri "safeguard" that the Court upholds today does not meet that standard. The rules by which an incompetent person's wishes are determined must represent every effort to determine those wishes. The rule that the Missouri court adopted and that this Court upholds, however, skews the result away from a determination that as accurately as possible reflects the individual's own preferences and beliefs. It is a rule that transforms human beings into passive subjects of medical technology.

I respectfully dissent.

Something to Consider

"Whether or not Missouri's clear and convincing evidence requirement comports with the United States Constitution depends in part on what interests the State may properly seek to protect in this situation." What State interests was Missouri seeking to protect in *Cruzan*?

Although the Constitution affords the right to reject medical care, the Supreme Court has not ruled that an individual has a fundamental right to commit suicide. In 2006, in *Gonzales v. Oregon*, 546 U.S. 243 (2006), the Supreme Court acknowledged that the federal government could not prevent a doctor from assisting in a suicide provided that the doctor did not violate any federal or state laws (here the doctor prescribed a regulated, but legal, drug). The doctor in this case was also in compliance with state law that permitted physician assisted suicide.

The Supreme Court also ruled that a patient does not have a right to use a federally prohibited drug, such as marijuana, even though state law allowed for it when medically necessary. *Gonzales v. Raich*, 545 U.S. 1 (2005).

Table 13-1 provides an overview of the privacy cases discussed in this chapter.

Table 13-1 Overview of Privacy Cases		
Case	**Privacy Interest**	**Decision**
Meyer v. Nebraska, 262 U.S. 390 (1923)	Marriage	Recognized freedom to marry as a type of liberty protected by the Fourteenth Amendment.
Zablocki v. Redhail, 434 U.S. 374 (1978)	Marriage	A state law denying a marriage license to those who have children unless they prove payment of child support violated the constitutional right of privacy.
Griswold v. Connecticut, 381 U.S. 479 (1965)	Procreation	A law prohibiting a married couple's use of contraceptives violated the constitutional right of privacy.

Table 13-1 Overview of Privacy Cases *(continued)*

Eisenstadt v. Baird, 405 U.S. 438 (1972)	Procreation	A law prohibiting an unmarried person's use of contraceptives violated the constitutional right of privacy.
Carey v. Population Servs. Intl., 431 U.S. 678 (1977)	Procreation	A law prohibiting dissemination of contraceptives to minors violates the Constitution unless narrowly written to preserve a compelling state interest.
Skinner v. Oklahoma, 316 U.S. 535 (1942)	Procreation	A law requiring sterilization of repeat felons, excluding white-collar criminals, violated the constitutional right of equal protection.
Roe v. Wade, 410 U.S. 113 (1973)	Abortion	A law denying the right of a woman to terminate a pregnancy in the early stages violates the constitutional right of privacy.
Webster v. Reproductive Health Services, 492 U.S. 490 (1989)	Abortion	A law prohibiting the use of public employees and facilities for the performance or assistance of nontherapeutic abortions did not violate the constitutional right of privacy.
Planned Parenthood. v. Casey, 505 U.S. 833 (1992)	Abortion	Affirmed the essential holding of *Roe v. Wade* regarding a woman's right to terminate a pregnancy.
Stenberg v. Carhart, 530 U.S. 914 (2000)	Abortion	Again affirmed the essential holding of *Roe v. Wade* and held a law prohibiting "partial birth abortions" was unconstitutional because it was overbroad since it contained no provisions for threats to the mother's health.
Gonzales v. Carhart 550 U.S. 124 (2007)	Abortion	A federal law, the Partial-Birth Abortion Ban Act of 2003 was held to be not facially unconstitutional; the test for evaluating abortion laws is whether the law imposes an undue burden on the woman, not strict scrutiny.
Bowers v. Hardwick, 478 U.S. 186 (1986)	Same-Sex Issues	A law criminalizing homosexual activity did not violate the Constitution.
Lawrence v. Texas, 539 U.S. 558 (2003)	Same-Sex Issues	Overruled *Bowers* and affirmed that sexual activity between consenting adults of the same sex was protected by the constitutional right of privacy.
Goodridge v. Department of Pub. Health, 440 Mass. 309 (2003)	Same-Sex Issues (Marriage)	A state case affirming the right of a same-sex couple to marry under a state constitutional right of privacy.
Cruzan v. Director Missouri Department of Health, 497 U.S. 261 (1990)	Right to Die	The right to reject medical care is protected by the constitutional right of privacy, but a state can require a clear and convincing standard of a person's wishes to reject such care.

© Cengage Learning 2013

❧ **Ethical Decisions—Everyday Choices** ❧

The Facts: A small group of citizens asked Attorney Mila to represent them in a civil action against their Internet service provider. Apparently, the service provider allowed several U.S. government agencies to monitor the Internet and email use of these citizens. It looks like the action could turn into a huge class action suit. The citizens asked Mila to take this case on a contingency fee basis. She is willing to do this, but the clients are shocked to find out Mila will charge them 50 percent of whatever damages may eventually be awarded.

The Problem: Is the 50 percent contingency fee reasonable?

Guiding Principles: Attorney fees must be "reasonable." Some of the factors used to arrive at what is reasonable are: time, labor, difficulty, skill required, preclusion of acceptance of other employment, local fees, the amount involved, and the result obtained. Mila may need to focus on this one case. It could turn into a situation where it is her only case for a year, or more. The litigation will be complicated and there may be many plaintiffs.

Chapter Summary

The right to privacy is not expressly stated in the Constitution, although it is protected by the Due Process and Equal Protection Clauses of the Fifth and Fourteenth Amendments because it is considered to be part of "liberty." The Court considers the right to privacy to be a fundamental right and therefore any government action that infringes upon this right is reviewed under the standard of strict scrutiny.

In most cases, the Supreme Court bases its analysis of privacy issues on the Due Process or Equal Protection Clauses of the Constitution. Some justices, however, prefer to rely on the Ninth Amendment that protects "unenumerated" rights.

The right to privacy includes many specific rights, including rights relating to marriage, procreation, contraception, abortion, sex, and the right to die. The Supreme Court acknowledged that the right to marry is included in the right to privacy and that states could not limit this right without a compelling government purpose. It also acknowledged that privacy extends to reproduction issues. Government cannot order sterilization of selected criminals nor can it deny access to contraceptives to either married or unmarried parties. One of the most controversial privacy issues is the right of a woman to choose an abortion. This right was affirmed in the landmark decision, *Roe v. Wade*. Since the *Roe* decision, the Court has recognized the right of government to enact laws affecting this right, such as the right of government not to pay for an abortion and the right of parents of a pregnant minor to be informed of the procedure. However, the Court still acknowledges the basic right of a woman to choose.

In recent years, the Supreme Court addressed the issue of whether the constitutional right of privacy protects sexual acts between consenting adults of the same sex. At first, the Supreme Court refused to extend constitutional protection to this area. However, most recently the Court did recognize that the Due Process Clause and the right to privacy protect such conduct. The Supreme Court has not ruled on the issue of same-sex marriage, although state courts and lower federal courts have done so.

Another emerging issue relates to the right of the individual regarding medical choices. To date, the Court has allowed patients to reject medical care but has not directly ruled on the issue of the right of a patient to commit suicide.

Key Terms

fundamental right

unenumerated rights

Questions for Review

1. What are the constitutional sources for the right to privacy?
2. What standard is used by the Supreme Court to review laws or government practices that interfere with the right to privacy?
3. What are some specific examples of conduct protected by the constitutional right to privacy?
4. What is the relationship of the Ninth Amendment to the right to privacy?
5. Why did the Court strike down a law limiting the right to marry of individuals who owed child support?
6. Why did the Supreme Court invalidate a law authorizing the sterilization of repeat felons for crimes involving moral turpitude?
7. What specific rights related to contraceptives are affirmed by the Supreme Court?
8. How has the Court limited the decision of *Roe v. Wade*?
9. What was the Court's reason for overturning a Texas state law criminalizing sexual conduct between members of the same sex?
10. What is the Supreme Court's view regarding an individual's right to reject medical care?

Questions for Analysis

1. In both *Griswold* and *Roe v. Wade*, the Supreme Court talks about a "penumbra of rights." What does this mean and why is it important?
2. Answer the following regarding *Skinner v. Oklahoma*.
   a. Were the defendant's procedural due process rights violated? Explain.
   b. Did the Court outlaw forced sterilization in all circumstances? Explain.
3. The Court in *Lawrence v. Texas* held that the Texas law criminalizing homosexual conduct violated the Due Process Clause. Was the Court referring to substantive due process or procedural due process? Explain.
4. Review the hypothetical case in Living with the Constitution. Do you think Reily has a constitutional right to marry while in prison? Why or why not?

Assignments and Projects

1. Brief the case of *Roe v. Wade*, using the format from previous chapters.
2. Justice Brennan wrote the *Carey* decision. He stated: "'Compelling' is of course the key word; where a decision as fundamental as that whether to bear or beget a child is involved, regulations imposing a burden on it may be justified only by compelling state interests, and must be narrowly drawn to express only those interests." Justice Brennan drew the distinction between a "significant state interest" and a "compelling state interest." Read the full case and explain the difference between these two types of state interests.
3. Read the selection from the brief of one of the petitions in *Gonzales v. Carhart* found in Appendix G. Summarize the argument.

Putting It into Practice

Review the facts in the hypothetical case in Living with the Constitution at the beginning of the chapter. Assume that you work for a firm that represents Reily and his fiancé. You have researched their situation and found a federal code section, 42 U.S.C. §1983, that permits an individual to sue a government official if his or her constitutional rights are violated. Since Reily claims that he has a constitutional right to marry, he wants to file a lawsuit under this section. Appendix C contains a form provided by the federal courts for lawsuits under this section. Based on the facts you know, complete this form as much as possible. Also, write a letter to your client Reily asking for necessary information to complete the form.

Group Activity

Compare the short extract from *Gonzales v. Carhart* found in Appendix G with the extract from the case dealing with "undue burden." What do you notice? Did the Court agree with everything that the government argued? Is there any difference in the tone of the language?

14 Criminal Justice and the Constitution

Our reason is our law.

John Milton, *Paradise Lost*

Chapter Outline

Chapter Objectives

When you complete this chapter you should be able to

1. list the amendments in the Bill of Rights that provide constitutional protection in criminal cases.

2. explain the importance of the Fourteenth Amendment and the Incorporation Doctrine to the constitutional rights of those accused of crimes.

3. define the exclusionary rule.

4. discuss the arguments for and against the exclusionary rule.

5. summarize the types of protections found in the Fourth Amendment.

6. summarize the types of protections found in the Fifth Amendment.

7. discuss the importance of the *Miranda* decision.

8. summarize the protections found in the Sixth Amendment.

9. summarize the protections found in the Eighth Amendment.

10. list the constitutional rights that apply to juvenile proceedings and those rights that do not apply.

Looking Back

Before reading this chapter, review the following concepts and cases from previous chapters.

Incorporation Doctrine The Bill of Rights originally applied only to the federal government. The Due Process Clause of the Fourteenth Amendment incorporated most of the rights expressed in the Bill of Rights, making them applicable to the states. (Chapter 7)

Bill of Rights The first ten amendments to the Constitution. These were added to the Constitution to assure that certain rights and freedoms would not be abridged by the federal government. (Chapters 1 and 7)

Due process The right to due process is found in both the Fifth and Fourteenth Amendments. It guarantees that government not deprive a person of life, liberty, or property without due process and applies in both civil and criminal cases. (Chapter 9)

Juvenile court system Special courts and procedures established by states to handle cases where juveniles commit crimes. Although these courts are designed to promote rehabilitation, they often impose punishments as severe as those imposed on adults. (Chapter 9)

Living with the Constitution

Teresa Branigan is a homicide detective with the Metro Police Department. She was on the force for fourteen years; six were as a homicide detective, and she investigated hundreds of homicide cases. She is currently investigating a possible homicide of Stacey Stevenson. Stacey's husband, Jerry, reported her missing approximately three weeks ago. Since then, no one has seen or heard from Stacey Stevenson. Branigan's investigation discovered the following facts: The Stevensons were married four years; they separated two times. The police were called to the Stevenson residence on two occasions because of domestic disturbances, although no charges were ever filed. A woman living in a nearby town reported to the police that she had an affair with Stevenson, but broke up with him when she learned he was married. From the beginning of her investigation, Branigan suspected that Jerry Stevenson killed his wife. Earlier today, Branigan received a phone call from an anonymous caller telling her that he had just left a downtown club where the caller heard a man confess to murdering his wife. The man, who had been drinking heavily, was boasting that he killed his wife, buried her body in his backyard, and that the cops would never catch him. He also claimed that he had an airline ticket for South America and was leaving the country that evening. The caller never identified himself, but said he recognized Stevenson from photos in the newspaper. Branigan wants to search the Stevenson's backyard and detain or arrest Jerry Stevenson.

THE MAGNA CARTA AND THE ENGLISH Bill of Rights heavily influenced the framers of the Constitution. Both of these documents guarantee rights to those accused of crimes, and many of these rights are also found in the U.S. Constitution, specifically in the Fourth, Fifth, Sixth, and Eighth Amendments. Police procedures, such as searches, arrests, and interrogations, as well as criminal trials and sentencing, are regulated by the Constitution. Recall from earlier chapters that the first ten amendments, the Bill of Rights, originally imposed limitations only on the power of the *federal* government. These amendments did not limit the power of *state* governments. However, after the Fourteenth Amendment was adopted, through a series of cases, the Supreme Court extended most of the provisions in the Bill of Rights to the states. This is the Incorporation Doctrine. Today, with very limited exceptions, the provisions of the Bill of Rights dealing with the criminal justice system apply to federal and state governments. Keep in mind, however, that states have the power, through their constitutions and laws, to grant greater protections to parties accused of state crimes. The subject of criminal procedure is a broad, complex subject and a detailed explanation of the rules and procedures in criminal cases is beyond the scope of this text. This chapter presents an overview of the major constitutional protections dealing with the criminal justice system and the consequences for violations of these protections.

The Constitution does not establish specific or detailed rules about the actual court procedures in criminal cases. For federal cases, detailed rules are found in the Federal Rules of Criminal Procedure. For state cases, rules are found in state codes and rules of court. The Constitution establishes general principles or rights that apply in all cases. For example, the Constitution mandates a "speedy trial," but does not specify any exact time limits. Words like *reasonable*, *probable cause*, *speedy*, and *due process* are used. As with other rights embodied in the Constitution, the members of the Supreme Court often disagree about the interpretation of these terms. Today, especially, most of the Supreme Court decisions in this area are not unanimous and many are decided by one-or two-vote margins.

The Exclusionary Rule

🏛 **exclusionary rule**

A reason why even relevant evidence will be kept out of a trial. 2. Often refers to the rule that illegally gathered evidence may not be used in a criminal trial.

🏛 **fruit of the poisonous tree**

The rule that evidence gathered as a result of evidence gained in an illegal search or questioning cannot be used against the person searched or questioned even if the later evidence was gathered lawfully.

ONE OF THE MOST CONTROVERSIAL rules of criminal procedure is the **exclusionary rule.** The exclusionary rule provides that evidence obtained in violation of a person's constitutional rights is inadmissible in a criminal case. The rule applies to evidence that is a direct result of an illegal police action, as well as to evidence that is an indirect result (the **fruit of the poisonous tree**). The controversy surrounding this rule stems from two factors. First, the rule is not expressly stated in the Constitution. It is a result of Supreme Court interpretation. Second, the rule sometimes results in guilty people going free, an inevitable result of excluding incriminating evidence.

The Supreme Court first applied the exclusionary rule in 1914 in *Weeks v. United States*, 232 U.S. 383, a case involving an illegal search and seizure conducted by a deputy U.S. Marshal. The Court held that the Fourth Amendment required that illegally obtained evidence not be used in court. After this decision, the exclusionary rule applied in federal cases, but not state cases. In the years following the *Weeks* decision, many states created state exclusionary rules. However, by the 1960s, there were still a large number of states that allowed illegally obtained evidence to be used. The issue was presented to the Supreme Court in *Mapp v. Ohio*. In this case, local police searched a woman's home without a warrant and without any other justification. In the course of the search they found obscene material, and she was charged with its possession. The validity of her conviction was eventually heard by the Supreme Court. The Court decided that the exclusionary rule applied to states as well as to the federal government because it was a requirement of due process under the Fourteenth Amendment. An excerpt from the case follows.

Mapp v. Ohio
367 U.S. 643 (1961)

MR. JUSTICE CLARK delivered the opinion of the Court.

The State says that even if the search were made without authority, or otherwise unreasonably, it is not prevented from using the unconstitutionally seized evidence at trial, citing *Wolf v. Colorado*, 338 U.S. 25 (1949), in which this Court did indeed hold "that in a prosecution in a State court for a State crime the Fourteenth Amendment does not forbid the admission of evidence obtained by an unreasonable search and seizure." On this appeal, of which we have noted probable jurisdiction, it is urged once again that we review that holding.

While in 1949, prior to the *Wolf* case, almost two-thirds of the States were opposed to the use of the exclusionary rule, now, despite the *Wolf* case, more than half of those since passing upon it, by their own legislative or judicial decision, have wholly or partly adopted or adhered to the *Weeks* rule.

Significantly, among those now following the rule is California, which, according to its highest court, was "compelled to reach that conclusion because other remedies have completely failed to secure compliance with the constitutional provisions. . . ." *People v. Cahan*, 44 Cal. 2d 434, 445, 282 P.2d 905, 911 (1955).

We are aware of no restraint conditioning the enforcement of any other basic constitutional right. This Court has not hesitated to enforce as strictly against the States as it does against the Federal Government the rights of free speech and of a free press, the rights to notice and to a fair, public trial, including, as it does, the right not to be convicted by use of a coerced confession, however logically relevant it be, and without regard to its reliability. *Rogers v. Richmond*, 365 U.S. 534 (1961). And nothing could be more certain than that when a coerced confession is involved, "the relevant rules of evidence" are overridden without regard to "the incidence of such conduct by the police," slight or frequent. Why should not the same rule apply to what is tantamount to coerced testimony by way of unconstitutional seizure of goods, papers, effects, documents, etc.? We find that, as to the Federal Government, the Fourth and Fifth Amendments and, as to the States, the freedom from unconscionable invasions of privacy and the freedom from convictions based upon coerced confessions do enjoy an "intimate relation" in their perpetuation of "principles of humanity and civil liberty secured . . . only after years of struggle," *Bram v. United States*, 168 U.S. 532, 543–544 (1897). They express "supplementing phases of the same constitutional purpose—to maintain inviolate large areas of personal privacy." *Feldman v. United States*, 322 U.S. 487, 489–490 (1944). The philosophy of each Amendment and of each freedom is complementary to, although not dependent upon, that of the other in its sphere of influence—the very least that together they assure in either sphere is that no man is to be convicted on unconstitutional evidence. *Cf. Rochin v. California*, 342 U.S. 165, 173 (1952).

Moreover, our holding that the exclusionary rule is an essential part of both the Fourth and Fourteenth Amendments is not only the logical dictate of prior cases, but it also makes very good sense. There is no war between the Constitution and common sense. Presently, a federal prosecutor may make no use of evidence illegally seized, but a State's attorney across the street may, although he supposedly is operating under the enforceable prohibitions of the same Amendment. Thus the State, by admitting evidence unlawfully seized, serves to encourage disobedience to the Federal Constitution which it is bound to uphold.

There are those who say, as did Justice (then Judge) Cardozo, that under our constitutional exclusionary doctrine "the criminal is to go free because the constable has blundered." *People v. Defore*, 242 N.Y., at 21, 150 N.E., at 587. In some cases this will undoubtedly be the result. But, as was said in *Elkins*, "there is another consideration—the imperative of judicial integrity." 364 U.S., at 222. The criminal goes free, if he must, but it is the law that sets him free. Nothing can destroy a government more quickly than its failure to observe its own laws, or worse, its disregard of the charter of its own existence. As Mr. Justice Brandeis, dissenting, said in *Olmstead v. United States*, 277 U.S. 438, 485 (1928): "Our Government is the potent, the omnipresent teacher. For good or for ill, it teaches the whole people by its example. . . . If the Government becomes a lawbreaker, it breeds contempt for law; it invites every man to become a law unto himself; it invites anarchy." Nor can it lightly be assumed that, as a practical matter, adoption of the exclusionary rule fetters law enforcement.

(continued)

(continued)

The ignoble shortcut to conviction left open to the State tends to destroy the entire system of constitutional restraints on which the liberties of the people rest. Having once recognized that the right to privacy embodied in the Fourth Amendment is enforceable against the States, and that the right to be secure against rude invasions of privacy by state officers is, therefore, constitutional in origin, we can no longer permit that right to remain an empty promise. Because it is enforceable in the same manner and to like effect as other basic rights secured by the Due Process Clause, we can no longer permit it to be revocable at the whim of any police officer who, in the name of law enforcement itself, chooses to suspend its enjoyment. Our decision, founded on reason and truth, gives to the individual no more than that which the Constitution guarantees him, to the police officer no less than that to which honest law enforcement is entitled, and, to the courts, that judicial integrity so necessary in the true administration of justice.

The judgment of the Supreme Court of Ohio is reversed and the cause remanded for further proceedings not inconsistent with this opinion.

Reversed and remanded.

Something to Consider

The Court states that the decision to require the exclusionary rule in state criminal proceedings is based on "reason and truth." Do you agree with this? Is it reasonable to allow guilty persons to go free?

The exclusionary rule applies to cases in which police conduct an illegal search or arrest or illegally obtain a confession. It also applies when there has been an unconstitutional denial of the right to counsel. In the years following the *Mapp* decision, the Supreme Court interpreted numerous cases dealing with the exclusionary rule and created several exceptions to the rule. The result today is that in many situations illegally obtained evidence can be used. The exceptions to the exclusionary rule include:

execute

Complete, make, perform, do, or carry out; for example, an official carrying out (executing) a court's order.

1. Good Faith Exception—If police have a search warrant that appears to be valid, but for some reason is not, evidence found while **executing** the warrant can be used if the officers acted in good faith. *United States v. Leon*, 468 U.S. 897 (1984). This rule was applied in a recent case, *Herring v. U.S.* 555 U.S. 135 (2009), when a warrant was withdrawn but not removed from a database. A search pursuant to the warrant uncovered contraband. In holding that the exclusionary rule did not apply, the Court said:

   > To trigger the exclusionary rule, police conduct must be sufficiently deliberate that exclusion can meaningfully deter it, and sufficiently culpable that such deterrence is worth the price paid by the justice system. As laid out in our cases, the exclusionary rule serves to deter deliberate, reckless, or grossly negligent conduct, or in some circumstances recurring or systemic negligence.

2. Impeachment Exception—If a defendant testifies in his or her own behalf, illegally obtained evidence can usually be used to attack the credibility of his or her statements. The illegally obtained evidence cannot be used by the prosecution to prove guilt, but the defendant will not be allowed to lie about the evidence. *Harris v. New York*, 401 U.S. 222 (1971) and *United States v. Havens*, 446 U.S. 620 (1980).

standing

A person's right to bring (start) or join a lawsuit because he or she is directly affected by the issues raised. This is called "standing to sue."

3. Standing—The person seeking to invoke the exclusionary rule must have personal interest in the property searched in violation of the Fourth Amendment. For example, passengers in a car have no basis to invoke the exclusionary rule when the car is illegally searched since they have no personal interest in the car and therefore, they lack **standing** to challenge the search. *Rakas v. Illinois*, 439 U.S. 128, 139 (1978).

4. Independent Source and Inevitable Discovery—If the prosecution can show that there was a separate legal source for the illegally obtained evidence or that it would have inevitably been discovered through some legal means, the evidence is admissible even though it was actually obtained through an illegal means. *United States v. Karo*, 468 U.S. 705 (1984).

5. Attenuation—When the link between the illegal activity and the evidence eventually discovered is remote, the evidence is admissible. For example, in one case, the Court refused to exclude a station-house confession made by a suspect whose arrest at his home had violated the Fourth Amendment because the questioning in the police station was too far removed from the illegal arrest at the defendant's home. *New York v. Harris*, 495 U.S. 14 (1990).

The Fourth Amendment: Search and Seizure

Amendment IV

The right of the people to be secure in their persons, houses, papers, and effects, against unreasonable searches and seizures, shall not be violated, and no Warrants shall issue, but upon probable cause, supported by Oath or affirmation, and particularly describing the place to be searched, and the persons or things to be seized.

THE FOURTH AMENDMENT PROVIDES PROTECTIONS in the area known as *search and seizure*. This includes all types of searches including searches of homes, cars, and individuals, and all types of seizures including seizures of property and persons. It includes limited searches and seizures such as "pat-downs" and detentions, as well as full searches and arrests. The basic protections offered by the Fourth Amendment are:

1. All searches must be reasonable.
2. All seizures must be reasonable.
3. If there is a warrant, it must be based on probable cause, signed by a neutral magistrate, and specifically describe the place or person to be searched or the person or items to be seized. (Note that the Fourth Amendment does not state when or if warrants are required; it only sets out standards for the warrant.)

Definitions of Search and Seizure

It is important to determine whether police activity is a search or a seizure, because only then does the Fourth Amendment apply. At one point in time, the Supreme Court equated search with a physical intrusion or trespass on property. If police did not physically intrude upon the property interest of a person, there was no search. Such a definition, however, does not fit in a technological age and the Court now makes it clear that searches protect people, not property. One test is whether the police intrude into an area in which a person has a reasonable expectation of privacy. Thus, the Fourth Amendment applies to all manners of searching, including the use of technological devices to listen, see, or otherwise detect information. However, the Fourth Amendment does not protect individuals who leave property in "plain view" because police see this without searching. A leading case dealing with the definition of a search is *Katz v. United States*, a case involving a wiretap of a public telephone. The Court held that this was a search because an individual has a reasonable expectation of privacy during his conversation, even though he was using a public telephone. The case follows.

The term *seizure* as used in the Fourth Amendment refers to either taking of property or persons and includes temporary takings. In particular, in addition to arrest, which is an obvious seizure of a person, it also includes a detention, which is a temporary stop for investigative purposes.

Katz v. United States
389 U.S. 347 (1967)

MR. JUSTICE STEWART delivered the opinion of the Court.

The petitioner was convicted in the District Court for the Southern District of California under an indictment charging him with transmitting wagering information by telephone. At trial the Government was permitted, over the petitioner's objection, to introduce evidence of the petitioner's end of telephone conversations, overheard by FBI agents who had attached an electronic listening and recording device to the outside of the public telephone booth from which he had placed his calls. In affirming his conviction, the Court of Appeals rejected the contention that the recordings had been obtained in violation of the Fourth Amendment, because "there was no physical entrance into the area occupied by the petitioner." We granted certiorari in order to consider the constitutional questions thus presented.

The Fourth Amendment protects people, not places. What a person knowingly exposes to the public, even in his own home or office, is not a subject of Fourth Amendment protection. But what he seeks to preserve as private, even in an area accessible to the public, may be constitutionally protected.

The Government stresses the fact that the telephone booth from which the petitioner made his calls was constructed partly of glass, so that he was as visible after he entered it as he would have been if he had remained outside. But what he sought to exclude when he entered the booth was not the intruding eye—it was the uninvited ear. He did not shed his right to do so simply because he made his calls from a place where he might be seen. No less than an individual in a business office, in a friend's apartment, or in a taxicab, a person in a telephone booth may rely upon the protection of the Fourth Amendment. One who occupies it, shuts the door behind him, and pays the toll that permits him to place a call is surely entitled to assume that the words he utters into the mouthpiece will not be broadcast to the world. To read the Constitution more narrowly is to ignore the vital role that the public telephone has come to play in private communication.

Indeed, we have expressly held that the Fourth Amendment governs not only the seizure of tangible items, but extends as well to the recording of oral statements, over-heard without any "technical trespass under . . . local property law." *Silverman v. United States*, 365 U.S. 505, 511. Once this much is acknowledged, and once it is recognized that the Fourth Amendment protects people—and not simply "areas"—against unreasonable searches and seizures, it becomes clear that the reach of that Amendment cannot turn upon the presence or absence of a physical intrusion into any given enclosure.

The question remaining for decision, then, is whether the search and seizure conducted in this case complied with constitutional standards. In that regard, the Government's position is that its agents acted in an entirely defensible manner: They did not begin their electronic surveillance until investigation of the petitioner's activities had established a strong probability that he was using the telephone in question to transmit gambling information to persons in other States, in violation of federal law. Moreover, the surveillance was limited, both in scope and in duration, to the specific purpose of establishing the contents of the petitioner's unlawful telephonic communications. The agents confined their surveillance to the brief periods during which he used the telephone booth, and they took great care to overhear only the conversations of the petitioner himself.

Accepting this account of the Government's actions as accurate, it is clear that this surveillance was so narrowly circumscribed that a duly authorized magistrate could constitutionally have authorized the very limited search and seizure that the Government asserts in fact took place. It is apparent that the agents in this case acted with restraint. Yet the inescapable fact is that this

(continued)

(continued)

restraint was imposed by the agents themselves, not by a judicial officer. This Court has never sustained a search upon the sole ground that officers reasonably expected to find evidence of a particular crime and voluntarily confined their activities to the least intrusive means consistent with that end. Searches conducted without warrants have been held unlawful "notwithstanding facts unquestionably showing probable cause," *Agnello v. United States*, 269 U.S. 20, 33, for the Constitution requires "that the deliberate, impartial judgment of a judicial officer . . . be interposed between the citizen and the police. . . ." *Wong Sun v. United States*, 371 U.S. 471, 481–482. The government agents here ignored "the procedure of antecedent justification . . . that is central to the Fourth Amendment," a procedure that we hold to be a constitutional precondition of the kind of electronic surveillance involved in this case. Because the surveillance here failed to meet that condition, and because it led to the petitioner's conviction, the judgment must be reversed.

It is so ordered.

Something to Consider

Reread the Fourth Amendment. What provisions of that amendment were violated by the police officers in the *Katz* case?

Telephone booths have changed drastically since the *Katz* era. The basic rule of *Katz*, though, is still applicable in our more technological world. The case of *Kyllo v. U.S.*, 533 U.S. 27 (2001) illustrates. In *Kyllo*, police used a thermal imaging device to scan a home to determine if the amount of heat emanating from it was consistent with the high-intensity lamps typically used for indoor marijuana growth. The agents did not have a warrant. The Supreme Court found that this was an intrusion into the home—a place where individuals have the greatest expectation of privacy.

Reasonableness and Probable Cause

🏛 **rational suspicion**

Reasonable belief that a person is involved in criminal activity; it is more than a hunch but less than probable cause.

🏛 **probable cause**

The U.S. constitutional requirement that law enforcement officers present sufficient facts to convince a judge to issue a search warrant or an arrest warrant and the requirement that no warrant should be issued unless it is more likely than not that the objects sought will be found in the place to be searched or that a crime has been committed by the person to be arrested.

🏛 **affidavit**

A written statement sworn to before a person officially permitted by law to administer an oath.

Whether a search or seizure is reasonable obviously depends on the circumstances of the search or seizure. This requirement relates to (1) the justification for the search or seizure, (2) the manner in which the search or seizure is carried out, and (3) whether or not a warrant is needed. Police cannot conduct a search or seizure based on a hunch or suspicion. There must be proper justification. The Court allows limited searches and seizures (detentions and pat-downs) when an officer has **rational suspicion** to believe that the individual might be involved in criminal activity. Rational suspicion is more than just a hunch, but less than **probable cause.** With some exceptions, probable cause is required before a police officer can search or arrest. Probable cause is determined by evaluating the facts and circumstances known to the police officer before he or she searches or arrests. If a reasonable person under the same or similar circumstances would believe that there is contraband to be found or that an individual committed a crime, then probable cause exists. However, the term *reasonable* as used in the Fourth Amendment means more than just having probable cause. It means that the search or arrest must be conducted in a reasonable way. Thus, the use of excessive force violates the requirement of reasonableness. Under many circumstances the requirement of reasonableness also requires that police have a warrant.

Warrants

A warrant is an order from a court allowing police to search or arrest. Under the Constitution, police cannot obtain a warrant without showing the court they have probable cause to search or arrest. This is generally done in the form of an **affidavit** submitted to the court.

Furthermore, an arrest warrant must describe with particularity who is to be arrested and the crimes for which the person is to be arrested, and a search warrant must describe with particularity what person or place is to be searched and what items are to be seized. Warrants must also be signed by neutral magistrates or judges. These constitutional requirements were a response to a practice during Revolutionary times allowing soldiers to obtain general warrants not particularly describing items or individuals.

The Fourth Amendment describes the requirements of the warrant, but it does not set out any situations in which a warrant is required. It simply provides that searches or seizures be reasonable. However, the Court decided that in general a search or seizure is unreasonable if no warrant was obtained unless the search or seizure comes within one of the court-created exceptions. Those exceptions include such circumstances as:

 exigent (exigency)

A sudden event that requires immediate attention; an urgent state of affairs. Exigent circumstances may permit law officers to conduct the search or arrest of a person without a warrant.

- the consent of the individual to be searched
- **exigent** circumstances
- automobile searches (as long as there is probable cause to believe the automobile contains contraband)
- airport and border searches
- search of open fields
- search of abandoned property

In the recent case of *Whren v. United States*, the Supreme Court discusses issues related to the reasonableness of searches and the warrant requirements. *Whren* was a unanimous decision.

Whren v. United States
517 U.S. 806 (1996)

Factual Background: Police suspected that individuals in a vehicle might be involved in drug activity. However, they lacked probable cause to do anything. The vehicle made a turn without signaling and police stopped them for this violation. After approaching the vehicle, officers observed drugs in plain view. The occupants were eventually convicted of drug charges and appealed, claiming that the stop was unreasonable and therefore invalid.

JUSTICE SCALIA delivered the opinion of the Court.

The Fourth Amendment guarantees "the right of the people to be secure in their persons, houses, papers, and effects, against unreasonable searches and seizures." Temporary detention of individuals during the stop of an automobile by the police, even if only for a brief period and for a limited purpose, constitutes a "seizure" of "persons" within the meaning of this provision. An automobile stop is thus subject to the constitutional imperative that it not be "unreasonable" under the circumstances. As a general matter, the decision to stop an automobile is reasonable

where the police have probable cause to believe that a traffic violation has occurred.

Petitioners accept that Officer Soto had probable cause to believe that various provisions of the District of Columbia traffic code had been violated. They argue, however, that "in the unique context of civil traffic regulations" probable cause is not enough. Since, they contend, the use of automobiles is so heavily and minutely regulated that total compliance with traffic and safety rules is nearly impossible, a police officer will almost invariably be able to catch any given motorist in a technical violation. This creates the temptation to use traffic stops as a means of investigating other law violations, as to which no probable cause or even articulable suspicion exists. Petitioners, who are both black, further contend that police officers might decide which motorists to stop based on decidedly impermissible factors, such as the race of the car's occupants. To avoid this danger, they say, the Fourth Amendment test for traffic stops should be, not the normal one (applied by

(continued)

(continued)

the Court of Appeals) of whether probable cause existed to justify the stop; but rather, whether a police officer, acting reasonably, would have made the stop for the reason given.

Petitioners contend that the standard they propose is consistent with our past cases' disapproval of police attempts to use valid bases of action against citizens as pretexts for pursuing other investigatory agendas. We are reminded that in *Florida v. Wells*, 495 U.S. 1, 4 (1990), we stated that "an inventory search must not be used as a ruse for a general rummaging in order to discover incriminating evidence"; that in *Colorado v. Bertine*, 479 U.S. 367, 372 (1987), in approving an inventory search, we apparently thought it significant that there had been "no showing that the police, who were following standard procedures, acted in bad faith or for the sole purpose of investigation"; and that in *New York v. Burger*, 482 U.S. 691, 716–717, n. 27 (1987), we observed, in upholding the constitutionality of a warrantless administrative inspection, that the search did not appear to be "a 'pretext' for obtaining evidence of . . . violation of . . . penal laws." But only an undiscerning reader would regard these cases as endorsing the principle that ulterior motives can invalidate police conduct that is justifiable on the basis of probable cause to believe that a violation of law has occurred. In each case we were addressing the validity of a search conducted in the absence of probable cause. Our quoted statements simply explain that the exemption from the need for probable cause (and warrant), which is accorded to searches made for the purpose of inventory or administrative regulation, is not accorded to searches that are not made for those purposes. *See Bertine*, at 371–372; *Burger*, at 702–703.

Petitioners' difficulty is not simply a lack of affirmative support for their position. Not only have we never held, outside the context of inventory search or administrative inspection (discussed above), that an officer's motive invalidates objectively justifiable behavior under the Fourth Amendment; but we have repeatedly held and asserted the contrary. In *United States v. Villamonte-Marquez*, 462 U.S. 579, 584, n. 3 (1983), we held that an otherwise valid warrantless boarding of a vessel by customs officials was not rendered invalid "because the customs officers were accompanied by a Louisiana state policeman, and were following an informant's tip that a vessel in the ship channel was thought to be carrying marihuana." We flatly dismissed the idea that an ulterior motive might serve to strip the agents of their legal justification. In *United States v. Robinson*, 414 U.S. 218 (1973), we held that a traffic-violation arrest (of the sort here) would not be rendered invalid by the fact that it was "a mere pretext for a narcotics search," *id.*, at 221, n. 1; and that a lawful postarrest search of the person would not be rendered invalid by the fact that it was not motivated by the officer-safety concern that justifies such searches, *see id.*, at 236. *See also Gustafson v. Florida*, 414 U.S. 260, 266 (1973). We think these cases foreclose any argument that the constitutional reasonableness of traffic stops depends on the actual motivations of the individual officers involved. We of course agree with petitioners that the Constitution prohibits selective enforcement of the law based on considerations such as race. But the constitutional basis for objecting to intentionally discriminatory application of laws is the Equal Protection Clause, not the Fourth Amendment. Subjective intentions play no role in ordinary, probable-cause Fourth Amendment analysis.

Petitioners urge as an extraordinary factor in this case that the "multitude of applicable traffic and equipment regulations" is so large and so difficult to obey perfectly that virtually everyone is guilty of violation, permitting the police to single out almost whomever they wish for a stop. But we are aware of no principle that would allow us to decide at what point a code of law becomes so expansive and so commonly violated that infraction itself can no longer be the ordinary measure of the lawfulness of enforcement. And even if we could identify such exorbitant codes, we do not know by what standard (or what right) we would decide, as petitioners would have us do, which particular provisions are sufficiently important to merit enforcement.

For the run-of-the-mine case, which this surely is, we think there is no realistic alternative to the traditional common-law rule that probable cause justifies a search and seizure.

Here the District Court found that the officers had probable cause to believe that petitioners had violated the traffic code. That rendered the stop reasonable under the Fourth Amendment, the evidence thereby discovered admissible, and the upholding of the convictions by the Court of Appeals for the District of Columbia Circuit correct.

Judgment affirmed.

Contemporary Issues

The constitutional prohibition on unreasonable searches and seizures continues to raise legal questions and problems. Technology enables law enforcement to look into areas of people's lives in ways that were unheard of when the Fourth Amendment was adopted. Drugs and weapons in schools and the terrorist events of September 11, 2001, have prompted calls for greater security. Although the national climate has changed drastically in the last two hundred years, the general provisions of the Fourth Amendment still apply. Searches and arrests must be reasonable. It is the Court's responsibility to determine precisely what that means. Some recent cases illustrate how the Court approaches this task (see Table 14-1).

Table 14-1 Recent Search and Seizure Cases

Kyllo v. United States, 533 U.S. 27 (2001)	Use of thermal detecting devices to investigate excessive heat produced in a home is a search and requires a warrant.
Ferguson v. City of Charleston, 532 U.S. 67 (2001)	Drug testing of new mothers by a state hospital, to detect criminal activity that was reported to law enforcement, was unreasonable.
Board. of Educ. v. Earls, 536 U.S. 822 (2002)	Drug testing required by schools for students wishing to participate in extracurricular activities is reasonable.
Brendlin v. California, 551 U.S. 249 (2007)	When a vehicle is stopped by police, a passenger in the car is considered to be "seized" for Fourth Amendment purposes.
Arizona v. Gant, 556 U.S. 332 (2009)	A search of an automobile incident to a lawful arrest is often justified without a warrant but it is not justified after the driver is arrested, handcuffed, and placed in the back of a police car.
Safford Unified School District v. Redding 557 U.S. 364 (2009)	A strip search of a young girl violated the Fourth Amendment when it was based on a tip from another student that the young girl had ibuprofen in violation of school policy.

© Cengage Learning 2013

The Fifth Amendment: Self-Incrimination, Grand Jury, and Double Jeopardy

Amendment V

No person shall be held to answer for a capital, or otherwise infamous crime, unless on a presentment or indictment of a Grand Jury, except in cases arising in the land or naval forces, or in the Militia, when in actual service in time of War or public danger; nor shall any person be subject for the same offence to be twice put in jeopardy of life or limb; nor shall be compelled in any criminal case to be a witness against himself, nor be deprived of life, liberty, or property, without due process of law; nor shall private property be taken for public use, without just compensation.

THE FIFTH AMENDMENT CONTAINS a variety of safeguards for those accused of crimes. An individual cannot be compelled to be a witness against him or herself. A person accused of a serious crime has the right to a grand jury hearing before indictment. An individual cannot be subject to multiple prosecutions for the same crime. An accused has a general right to due process in a criminal proceeding.

Miranda warning

The warning that must be given to a person arrested or taken into custody by a police officer or other official prior to any interrogation. The warning includes the fact that what you say may be held against you and that you have the rights to remain silent, to contact a lawyer, and to have a free court-appointed lawyer if you are poor. If this warning is not given properly, statements made by the defendant during custody may be inadmissible in court. The warning is required by the 1966 case *Miranda v. Arizona*, 384 U.S. 436.

Self-Incrimination

The self-incrimination provision of the Fifth Amendment prohibits government from using physical or psychological force to obtain a confession (or any statements) from an individual. It applies to testimonial evidence, not to evidence such as fingerprints or physical specimens containing DNA. The purpose of this safeguard is to make sure that any statements are voluntary and credible.

The Fifth Amendment prohibition against self-incrimination resulted in one of the most famous and controversial Supreme Court cases, *Miranda v. Arizona*, 384 U.S. 436 (1966). At the time of the *Miranda* decision, the Court was concerned with questionable interrogation techniques that were sometimes used by police. Influenced by this, the Court imposed the duty on police to inform suspects of certain rights prior to custodial interrogations. These rights are known as the *Miranda rights* or **Miranda warnings**. *Miranda* warnings are not required when a person is arrested and questioned. They are required when police conduct "custodial interrogations." In the years following *Miranda*, the Court interpreted what it meant by *custodial interrogation*. Generally, this means questioning following an arrest or significant deprivation of liberty. The Court's syllabus in the *Miranda* decision follows.

Miranda v. Arizona
384 U.S. 436 (1966)

In each of these cases the defendant while in police custody was questioned by police officers, detectives, or a prosecuting attorney in a room in which he was cut off from the outside world. None of the defendants was given a full and effective warning of his rights at the outset of the interrogation process. In all four cases the questioning elicited oral admissions, and in three of them signed statements as well, which were admitted at their trials. All defendants were convicted and all convictions, except in No. 584, were affirmed on appeal. Held:

1. The prosecution may not use statements, whether exculpatory or inculpatory, stemming from questioning initiated by law enforcement officers after a person has been taken into custody or otherwise deprived of his freedom of action in any significant way, unless it demonstrates the use of procedural safeguards effective to secure the Fifth Amendment's privilege against self-incrimination.

(a) The atmosphere and environment of incommunicado interrogation as it exists today is inherently intimidating and works to undermine the privilege against self-incrimination. Unless adequate preventive measures are taken to dispel the compulsion inherent in custodial surroundings, no statement obtained from the defendant can truly be the product of his free choice.

(b) The privilege against self-incrimination, which has had a long and expansive historical development, is the essential mainstay of our adversary system and guarantees to the individual the "right to remain silent unless he chooses to speak in the unfettered exercise of his own will," during a period of custodial interrogation as well as in the courts or during the course of other official investigations.

(c) The decision in *Escobedo v. Illinois*, 378 U.S. 478, stressed the need for protective devices to make the process of police interrogation conform to the dictates of the privilege.

(d) In the absence of other effective measures the following procedures to safeguard the Fifth Amendment privilege must be observed: The person in custody must, prior to interrogation, be clearly informed that he has the right to remain silent, and that anything he says will be used against him in court; he must be clearly informed that he has the right to consult with a lawyer and to have the lawyer with him during interrogation, and that, if he is indigent, a lawyer will be appointed to represent him.

(continued)

(continued)

(e) If the individual indicates, prior to or during questioning, that he wishes to remain silent, the interrogation must cease; if he states that he wants an attorney, the questioning must cease until an attorney is present.

(f) Where an interrogation is conducted without the presence of an attorney and a statement is taken, a heavy burden rests on the Government to demonstrate that the defendant knowingly and intelligently waived his right to counsel.

(g) Where the individual answers some questions during in-custody interrogation he has not waived his privilege and may invoke his right to remain silent thereafter.

(h) The warnings required and the waiver needed are, in the absence of a fully effective equivalent, prerequisites to the admissibility of any statement, inculpatory or exculpatory, made by a defendant.

2. The limitations on the interrogation process required for the protection of the individual's constitutional rights should not cause an undue interference with a proper system of law enforcement, as demonstrated by the procedures of the FBI and the safeguards afforded in other jurisdictions.

3. In each of these cases the statements were obtained under circumstances that did not meet constitutional standards for protection of the privilege against self-incrimination.

After the *Miranda* decision, the Court decided several cases creating exceptions to the rule. One major exception is that non-*Mirandized* confessions can be used to contradict or impeach a defendant's testimony if the defendant voluntarily testifies at trial. *Harris v. New York*, 401 U.S. 222 (1971). In a recent case, *Chavez v. Martinez* 538 U.S. 760 (2003), the Court again limited the application of the *Miranda* decision. This case arose not from a criminal case but a civil action for money damages based on a provision of the United States Code (42 U.S.C. §1983) that allows a person to sue when his constitutional rights are denied by government officials. Martinez was involved in a police altercation and was shot. While being treated at the hospital, he was interrogated for a lengthy time by petitioner Chavez, a police officer. At no time was Martinez read his *Miranda* rights. During the interrogation, Martinez made several incriminating statements, but he was never prosecuted criminally. He later filed this civil lawsuit claiming his constitutional rights were violated because he was not read his *Miranda* rights. The Supreme Court disagreed and held that the *Miranda* rights protect a constitutional right—the right against self-incrimination—but are not constitutional rights themselves.

> Rules designed to safeguard a constitutional right, however, do not extend the scope of the constitutional right itself, just as violations of judicially crafted prophylactic rules do not violate the constitutional rights of any person. As we explained, we have allowed the Fifth Amendment privilege to be asserted by witnesses in noncriminal cases in order to safeguard the core constitutional right defined by the Self-Incrimination Clause—the right not to be compelled in any criminal case to be a witness against oneself. We have likewise established the *Miranda* exclusionary rule as a prophylactic measure to prevent violations of the right protected by the text of the Self-Incrimination Clause—the admission into evidence in criminal case of confessions obtained through coercive custodial questioning.

The Supreme Court also allowed the prosecution to use a confession obtained in violation of the right to counsel in *Kansas v. Ventris*, 556 U.S. 586 (2009). In this case, police engaged the services of a cell mate of the defendant to act as an undercover informant. The Court held that statements made to this individual by the defendant violated the defendant's Sixth Amendment right to counsel because the defendant was not advised of his right to counsel.

Nevertheless, the statements could be used in court to contradict or impeach the defendant's testimony.

The *Miranda* decision is often criticized, and many legal scholars think that one day it may be overruled. However, as recently as 2000, the Supreme Court affirmed the continued validity of the decision. In 2000, the Court was asked to interpret a provision of the U.S. Code enacted after the *Miranda* decision in which Congress made statements admissible unless they were not voluntary. The Court found that such a law was not permissible. The Court further expressly refused to overrule the *Miranda* decision. The Court syllabus follows.

Dickerson v. United States
530 U.S. 428 (2000)

In the wake of *Miranda v. Arizona*, 384 U.S. 436, in which the Court held that certain warnings must be given before a suspect's statement made during custodial interrogation could be admitted in evidence, *id.*, at 479, Congress enacted 18 U.S.C. §3501, which in essence makes the admissibility of such statements turn solely on whether they were made voluntarily. Petitioner, under indictment for bank robbery and related federal crimes, moved to suppress a statement he had made to the Federal Bureau of Investigation, on the ground he had not received "*Miranda* warnings" before being interrogated. The District Court granted his motion, and the Government took an interlocutory appeal. In reversing, the Fourth Circuit acknowledged that petitioner had not received *Miranda* warnings, but held that §3501 was satisfied because his statement was voluntary. It concluded that *Miranda* was not a constitutional holding, and that, therefore, Congress could by statute have the final say on the admissibility question.

Held: Miranda and its progeny in this Court govern the admissibility of statements made during custodial interrogation in both state and federal courts.

(a) *Miranda*, being a constitutional decision of this Court, may not be in effect overruled by an Act of Congress. Given §3501's express designation of voluntariness as the touchstone of admissibility, its omission of any warning requirement, and its instruction for trial courts to consider the totality of the circumstances surrounding the giving of the confession, this Court agrees with the Fourth Circuit that Congress intended §3501 to overrule *Miranda*. The law is clear as to whether Congress has constitutional authority to do so. This Court has supervisory authority over the federal courts to prescribe binding rules of evidence and procedure. While Congress has ultimate authority to modify or set aside any such rules that are not constitutionally required, it may not supersede this Court's decisions interpreting and applying the Constitution. That *Miranda* announced a constitutional rule is demonstrated, first and foremost, by the fact that both *Miranda* and two of its companion cases applied its rule to proceedings in state courts, and that the Court has consistently done so ever since. The Court does not hold supervisory power over the state courts, as to which its authority is limited to enforcing the commands of the Constitution. The conclusion that *Miranda* is constitutionally based is also supported by the fact that that case is replete with statements indicating that the majority thought it was announcing a constitutional rule. Although *Miranda* invited legislative action to protect the constitutional right against coerced self-incrimination, it stated that any legislative alternative must be at least as effective in appraising accused persons of their right of silence and in assuring a continuous opportunity to exercise it.

A contrary conclusion is not required by the fact that the Court has subsequently made exceptions from the *Miranda* rule. No constitutional rule is immutable, and the sort of refinements made by such cases are merely a normal part of constitutional law. Finally, although the Court agrees with the court-appointed *amicus curiae* that there are more remedies available for abusive police conduct than there were when *Miranda* was decided—*e.g.*, a suit under *Bivens v. Six Unknown Named Agents*, 403 U.S. 388, 29 L. Ed. 2d 619, 91 S.

(continued)

(continued)

Ct. 1999—it does not agree that such additional measures supplement §3501's protections sufficiently to create an adequate substitute for the *Miranda* warnings. *Miranda* requires procedures that will warn a suspect in custody of his right to remain silent and assure him that the exercise of that right will be honored, while §3501 explicitly eschews a requirement of preinterrogation warnings in favor of an approach that looks to the administration of such warnings as only one factor in determining the voluntariness of a suspect's confession. Section 3501, therefore, cannot be sustained if *Miranda* is to remain the law.

(b) This Court declines to overrule *Miranda*. Whether or not this Court would agree with *Miranda*'s reasoning and its rule in the first instance, *stare decisis* weighs heavily against overruling it now. Even in constitutional cases, *stare decisis* carries such persuasive force that the Court has always required a departure from precedent to be supported by some special justification. There is no such justification here. *Miranda* has become embedded in routine police practice to the point where the warnings have become part of our national culture. While the Court has overruled its precedents when subsequent cases have undermined their doctrinal underpinnings, that has not happened to *Miranda*. If anything, subsequent cases have reduced *Miranda*'s impact on legitimate law enforcement while reaffirming the decision's core ruling. The rule's disadvantage is that it may result in a guilty defendant going free. But experience suggests that §3501's totality-of-the-circumstances test is more difficult than *Miranda* for officers to conform to, and for courts to apply consistently. The requirement that *Miranda* warnings be given does not dispense with the voluntariness inquiry, but cases in which a defendant can make a colorable argument that a self-incriminating statement was compelled despite officers' adherence to *Miranda* are rare.

Something to Consider

Read the case of *Chavez v. Martinez*, 538 U.S. 760 (2003). Do you think this decision reflects a change of the Court's view that *Miranda* is a constitutional rule that cannot be changed by the legislature?

Grand Jury

infamous (infamy)

The loss of a good reputation because of a conviction of a major crime and the loss of certain legal rights that accompanies this loss of reputation. An infamous crime used to be defined by type (such as treason), but is now defined by punishment possible (such as over a year in prison).

indicted (indictment)

A sworn written accusation of a crime made against a person by a prosecutor to a grand jury. If the grand jury approves it as a true bill, the indictment becomes the document used against the person as a defendant in pretrial and trial proceedings. [pronounce: in-ditement]

The Fifth Amendment requires a grand jury hearing for all capital or **infamous** crimes. This means that before a person can be charged or **indicted** for the crime, the members of the grand jury must find sufficient evidence to establish probable cause that the defendant committed a crime. The grand jury operates as a check on prosecutors by providing a safeguard against frivolous charges being filed against someone. The creation of the grand jury was not something new to the founders of the Constitution, as the Supreme Court described:

> The grand jury is an integral part of our constitutional heritage which was brought to this country with the common law. The Framers, most of them trained in the English law and traditions, accepted the grand jury as a basic guarantee of individual liberty; notwithstanding periodic criticism, much of which is superficial, overlooking relevant history, the grand jury continues to function as a barrier to reckless or unfounded charges. "Its adoption in our Constitution as the sole method for preferring charges in serious criminal cases shows the high place it held as an instrument of justice." *Costello v. United States*, 350 U.S. 359, 362 (1956). Its historic office has been to provide a shield against arbitrary or oppressive action, by insuring that serious criminal accusations will be brought only upon the considered judgment of a representative body of citizens acting under oath and under judicial instruction and guidance. *United States v. Mandujano*, 425 U.S. 564 (1976).

subpoena

A court's order to a person that he or she appear in court to testify (give evidence) in a case. Some administrative agencies may also issue subpoenas. [pronounce: suh-pee-na]

The Fifth Amendment is not specific about the grand jury or its proceedings. In the federal system, this is governed by Rule 6 of the Federal Rules of Criminal Procedure. The grand jury consists of between sixteen to twenty-three individuals selected from the community who review evidence presented to them by a prosecutor. It also has investigative powers and can **subpoena** individuals to testify. Grand juries meet in private and even an accused is not present. If the grand jurors find there is probable cause to believe a person committed a crime, they issue an indictment. The indictment is a type of complaint charging a person with a crime. It is filed in court after it is issued. See Exhibit 14-1 for an excerpt from an indictment.

Exhibit 14-1   Excerpt from Indictment (Zacarias Moussaoui)

IN THE UNITED STATES DISTRICT COURT
FOR THE EASTERN DISTRICT OF VIRGINIA
ALEXANDRIA DIVISION

UNITED STATES OF AMERICA
-v-
ZACARIAS MOUSSAOUI,
a/k/a "Shaqil,"
a/k/a "Abu Khalid al Sahrawi,"

Defendant.

CRIMINAL NO:

Conspiracy to Commit Acts of Terrorism
Transcending National Boundaries
(18 U.S.C. §§ 2332b(a)(2) & (c))
(Count One)

Conspiracy to Commit Aircraft Piracy
(49 U.S.C. §§ 46502(a)(1)(A) and (a)(2)(B))
(Count Two)

Conspiracy to Destroy Aircraft
(18 U.S.C. §§ 32(a)(7) & 34)
(Count Three)

Conspiracy to Use Weapons of Mass Destruction
(18 U.S.C. § 2332a(a))
(Count Four)

Conspiracy to Murder United States Employees
(18 U.S.C. §§ 1114 & 1117)
(Count Five)

Conspiracy to Destroy Property
(18 U.S.C. §§ 844(f), (i), (n))
(Count Six)

DECEMBER 2001 TERM—AT ALEXANDRIA
INDICTMENT

THE GRAND JURY CHARGES THAT:

COUNT ONE

(Conspiracy to Commit Acts of Terrorism Transcending National Boundaries). . .

The Defendant

13. ZACARIAS MOUSSAOUI, a/k/a "Shaqil," a/k/a "Abu Khalid al Sahrawi," was born in France of Moroccan descent on May 30, 1968. Before 2001 he was a resident of the United Kingdom. MOUSSAOUI held a masters degree from Southbank University in the United Kingdom and traveled widely.

(continued)

(continued)

MOUSSAOUI's Supporting Conspirators

14. Ramzi Bin al-Shibh, a/k/a "Ahad Sabet," a/k/a "Ramzi Mohamed Abdellah Omar," was born in Yemen on May 1, 1972. He entered Germany in or about 1995 and afterwards lived in Hamburg, where he shared an apartment with hijacker Mohammed Atta (#11) in 1998 and 1999. Bin al-Shibh also was employed with Atta as a warehouse worker at a computer company in Hamburg.

15. Mustafa Ahmed al-Hawsawi, a/k/a "Mustafa Ahmed," was born in Jeddah, Saudi Arabia on August 5, 1968.

The Charge

16. From in or about 1989 until the date of the filing of this Indictment, in the Eastern District of Virginia, the Southern District of New York, and elsewhere, the defendant, ZACARIAS MOUSSAOUI, a/k/a "Shaqil," a/k/a "Abu Khalid al Sahrawi," with other members and associates of al Qaeda and others known and unknown to the Grand Jury, unlawfully, wilfully and knowingly combined, conspired, confederated and agreed to kill and maim persons within the United States, and to create a substantial risk of serious bodily injury to other persons by destroying and damaging structures, conveyances, and other real and personal property within the United States, in violation of the laws of States and the United States, in circumstances involving conduct transcending national boundaries, and in which facilities of interstate and foreign commerce were used in furtherance of the offense, the offense obstructed, delayed, and affected interstate and foreign commerce, the victim was the United States Government, members of the uniformed services, and officials, officers, employees, and agents of the governmental branches, departments, and agencies of the United States, and the structures, conveyances, and other real and personal property were, in whole or in part, owned, possessed, and leased to the United States and its departments and agencies, resulting in the deaths of thousands of persons on September 11, 2001.

The Fifth Amendment grand jury requirement is not incorporated into the concept of due process under the Fourteenth Amendment. Thus, states are not required to provide grand jury hearings to those accused of serious crimes.

Double Jeopardy

The purpose of the double jeopardy clause is fairly obvious. It is intended to prevent the state from harassing individuals by charging them repeatedly for the same crimes. Double jeopardy applies only to criminal cases, not civil actions. Where the same act can result in both a criminal and civil case, in most instances no double jeopardy problem arises. However, in one case, *United States v. Halper*, 490 U.S. 435 (1989), the Court found that double jeopardy did apply where a person who was convicted of a criminal case was then sued civilly. In this case, the manager of a company that provided medical services for patients eligible for federal Medicare benefits, was convicted of submitting sixty-five false claims for government reimbursement in violation of the federal criminal false-claims statute. He was sentenced to prison and fined $5000. The government then sued him and won under the federal False Claims Act. Under the terms of that act, the manager was liable for a civil penalty of $2000 on each of the sixty-five false claims, as well as for twice the amount of the government's actual damages of $585 and the costs of the action. The Supreme Court found this to be double jeopardy because of the punitive nature of the civil case:

> In the rare case such as the present, where a prolific but small-gauge offender previously has sustained a criminal penalty, and the civil penalty sought in a subsequent proceeding bears no rational relation to the goal of compensating the Government for its loss, but rather appears to qualify as "punishment" in the plain

meaning of the word, the defendant is entitled to an accounting of the Government's damages and costs in order to allow the trial court, in its discretion, to determine whether the penalty sought in fact constitutes a second punishment violative of the Clause and to set the size of the civil sanction the Government may receive without crossing the line between permissible remedy and prohibited punishment.

🏛 **civil commitment**

Confinement by a noncriminal process in a mental hospital or other treatment facility for insanity or for alcohol or drug addiction. The usual justification for confining a person who has not committed a crime is that he or she "is a danger to self or others."

🏛 **mistrial**

A trial that the judge ends and declares will have no legal effect because of a major defect in procedure or because of the death of a juror, a deadlocked jury, or other major problem.

On the other hand, the Court found that **civil commitment** of convicted sex offenders is not double jeopardy.

In spite of the double jeopardy clause, at times a defendant can be tried more than once for the same offense. If a **mistrial** occurs, the case can be retried. A common basis for a mistrial is a hung jury, which is a jury that deadlocks and cannot reach a verdict. Likewise, if a defendant appeals a conviction and wins on appeal, the government can retry the person without violating the double jeopardy provision. Also where a defendant's actions violate the laws of two separate governments (that is, federal and state or two separate states), the defendant can be tried in all of the jurisdictions. The Supreme Court affirmed this right in the case of *United States v. Lanza*, 260 U.S. 377 (1922). The following language expresses the Court's reasoning:

> We have here two sovereignties, deriving power from different sources, capable of dealing with the same subject matter within the same territory. Each may, without interference by the other, enact laws to secure prohibition, with the limitation that no legislation can give validity to acts prohibited by the amendment. Each government in determining what shall be an offense against its peace and dignity is exercising its own sovereignty, not that of the other.
>
> It follows that an act denounced as a crime by both national and state sovereignties is an offense against the peace and dignity of both and may be punished by each. The Fifth Amendment, like all the other guaranties in the first eight amendments, applies only to proceedings by the federal government (*Barron v. City of Baltimore*, 7 Pet. 243), and the double jeopardy therein forbidden is a second prosecution under authority of the federal government after a first trial for the same offense under the same authority. Here the same act was an offense against the state of Washington, because a violation of its law, and also an offense against the United States under the National Prohibition Act. The defendants thus committed two different offenses by the same act, and a conviction by a court of Washington of the offense against that state is not a conviction of the different offense against the United States, and so is not double jeopardy.

The Sixth Amendment: Right to Counsel and a Fair Trial

Amendment VI

In all criminal prosecutions, the accused shall enjoy the right to a speedy and public trial, by an impartial jury of the State and district wherein the crime shall have been committed, which district shall have been previously ascertained by law, and to be informed of the nature and cause of the accusation; to be confronted with the witnesses against him; to have compulsory process for obtaining witnesses in his favor, and to have the Assistance of Counsel for his defence.

THE SIXTH AMENDMENT PROVIDES THE accused with the right to counsel as well as setting forth specific requirements to assure a fair trial.

Right to Counsel

The right to counsel expressed in the Sixth Amendment presents several issues for the courts. Important questions include:

1. Does the Fourteenth Amendment incorporate this right into the Due Process Clause so that it applies to state cases as well as federal cases, and does the right require that the government provide lawyers without cost to defendants who cannot afford their own lawyers?
2. How competent or expert must a lawyer be?
3. At what stages is a defendant entitled to have an attorney?

RIGHT TO COURT APPOINTED COUNSEL IN STATE CASES

 indigent

A poor person. An indigent criminal defendant is entitled to a free court-appointed lawyer.

The original intent of the Sixth Amendment right to counsel was to prevent the government from denying an individual access to a lawyer. The question of court-appointed lawyers for **indigent** defendants was not a consideration. Nevertheless, one of the most important early questions faced by the Court dealt with this issue. The Court considered this issue, along with whether the right to counsel was incorporated in the Due Process Clause in the famous case of *Powell v. Alabama*, 287 U.S. 45 (1932), a case also known as the *Scottsboro* case. In this 1932 case, the Supreme Court ruled that the Sixth and Fourteenth Amendments required states to provide lawyers to indigent defendants accused of *capital* crimes. A little over ten years later, the Court was asked to decide if this right applied to all felony cases. In *Betts v. Brady*, 316 U.S. 455 (1942), the Court decided that it did not. The right to court-appointed counsel in non-capital felony cases depended on whether a defendant had "special circumstances" making it difficult or impossible to defend him or herself. Special circumstances included such factors as illiteracy and mental incompetence. This rule proved to be unworkable at the trial level, and, in 1963, in the famous case of *Gideon v. Wainwright*, the Court overruled *Betts v. Brady* and decided that an indigent defendant accused of a felony did have the right to counsel in felony cases.

Gideon v. Wainwright

372 U.S. 335 (1963)

MR. JUSTICE BLACK delivered the opinion of the Court.

Petitioner was charged in a Florida state court with having broken and entered a poolroom with intent to commit a misdemeanor. This offense is a felony under Florida law. Appearing in court without funds and without a lawyer, petitioner asked the court to appoint counsel for him, whereupon the following colloquy took place:

The COURT: Mr. Gideon, I am sorry, but I cannot appoint Counsel to represent you in this case.

Under the laws of the State of Florida, the only time the Court can appoint Counsel to represent a Defendant is when that person is charged with a capital offense.

Put to trial before a jury, Gideon conducted his defense about as well as could be expected from a layman. He made an opening statement to the jury, cross-examined the State's witnesses, presented witnesses in his own defense, declined to testify himself, and made a short argument "emphasizing his innocence to the charge

(continued)

(continued)

contained in the Information filed in this case." The jury returned a verdict of guilty, and petitioner was sentenced to serve five years in the state prison. Later, petitioner filed in the Florida Supreme Court this habeas corpus petition attacking his conviction and sentence on the ground that the trial court's refusal to appoint counsel for him denied him rights "guaranteed by the Constitution and the Bill of Rights by the United States Government." The State Supreme Court, "upon consideration thereof" but without an opinion, denied all relief. Since 1942, when *Betts v. Brady*, 316 U.S. 455, was decided by a divided Court, the problem of a defendant's federal constitutional right to counsel in a state court has been a continuing source of controversy and litigation in both state and federal courts. To give this problem another review here, we granted certiorari. Since Gideon was proceeding in forma pauperis, we appointed counsel to represent him and requested both sides to discuss in their briefs and oral arguments the following: "Should this Court's holding in *Betts v. Brady*, 316 U.S. 455, be reconsidered?"

Upon full reconsideration we conclude that *Betts v. Brady* should be overruled.

The Sixth Amendment provides, "In all criminal prosecutions, the accused shall enjoy the right . . . to have the Assistance of Counsel for his defense." We have construed this to mean that in federal courts counsel must be provided for defendants unable to employ counsel unless the right is competently and intelligently waived. Betts argued that this right is extended to indigent defendants in state courts by the Fourteenth Amendment. In response the Court stated that, while the Sixth Amendment laid down "no rule for the conduct of the States, the question recurs whether the constraint laid by the Amendment upon the national courts expresses a rule so fundamental and essential to a fair trial, and so, to due process of law, that it is made obligatory upon the States by the Fourteenth Amendment." 316 U.S., at 465. In order to decide whether the Sixth Amendment's guarantee of counsel is of this fundamental nature, the Court in *Betts* set out and considered "relevant data on the subject . . . afforded by constitutional and statutory provisions subsisting in the colonies and the States prior to the inclusion of the Bill of Rights in the national Constitution, and in the constitutional, legislative, and judicial history of the States to the present date." 316 U.S., at 465. On the basis of this historical data the Court concluded that "appointment of counsel is not a fundamental right, essential to a fair trial." 316 U.S., at 471.

We think the Court in *Betts* had ample precedent for acknowledging that those guarantees of the Bill of Rights which are fundamental safeguards of liberty immune from federal abridgment are equally protected against state invasion by the Due Process Clause of the Fourteenth Amendment. This same principle was recognized, explained, and applied in *Powell v. Alabama*, 287 U.S. 45 (1932), a case upholding the right of counsel, where the Court held that the Fourteenth Amendment "embraced" those "'fundamental principles of liberty and justice which lie at the base of all our civil and political institutions,'" even though they had been "specifically dealt with in another part of the federal Constitution." 287 U.S., at 67. In many cases other than *Powell* and *Betts*, this Court has looked to the fundamental nature of original Bill of Rights guarantees to decide whether the Fourteenth Amendment makes them obligatory on the States. Explicitly recognized to be of this "fundamental nature" and therefore made immune from state invasion by the Fourteenth, or some part of it, are the First Amendment's freedoms of speech, press, religion, assembly, association, and petition for redress of grievances. For the same reason, though not always in precisely the same terminology, the Court has made obligatory on the States the Fifth Amendment's command that private property shall not be taken for public use without just compensation, the Fourth Amendment's prohibition of unreasonable searches and seizures, and the Eighth's ban on cruel and unusual punishment.

We accept *Betts v. Brady's* assumption, based as it was on our prior cases, that a provision of the Bill of Rights which is "fundamental and essential to a fair trial" is made obligatory upon the States by the Fourteenth Amendment. We think the Court in *Betts* was wrong, however, in concluding that the Sixth Amendment's guarantee of counsel is not one of these fundamental rights. Ten years before *Betts v. Brady*, this Court, after full consideration of all the historical data examined in *Betts*, had unequivocally declared that "the right to the aid of counsel is of this fundamental character." *Powell v. Alabama*, 287 U.S. 45, 68 (1932). While the Court at the close of its *Powell* opinion did by its language, as this Court frequently does, limit its holding to the particular facts and circumstances of that case, its conclusions about the fundamental nature of the right to counsel are unmistakable.

Reason and reflection require us to recognize that in our adversary system of criminal justice, any person

(continued)

(continued)

haled into court, who is too poor to hire a lawyer, cannot be assured a fair trial unless counsel is provided for him. This seems to us to be an obvious truth. Governments, both state and federal, quite properly spend vast sums of money to establish machinery to try defendants accused of crime. Lawyers to prosecute are everywhere deemed essential to protect the public's interest in an orderly society. Similarly, there are few defendants charged with crime, few indeed, who fail to hire the best lawyers they can get to prepare and present their defenses. That government hires lawyers to prosecute and defendants who have the money hire lawyers to defend are the strongest indications of the widespread belief that lawyers in criminal courts are necessities, not luxuries. The right of one charged with crime to counsel may not be deemed fundamental and essential to fair trials in some countries, but it is in ours. From the very beginning, our state and national constitutions and laws have laid great emphasis on procedural and substantive safeguards designed to assure fair trials before impartial tribunals in which every defendant stands equal before the law. This noble ideal cannot be realized if the poor man charged with crime has to face his accusers without a lawyer to assist him.

The Court in *Betts v. Brady* departed from the sound wisdom upon which the Court's holding in *Powell v. Alabama* rested. Florida, supported by two other States, has asked that *Betts v. Brady* be left intact. Twenty-two States, as friends of the Court, argue that *Betts* was "an anachronism when handed down" and that it should now be overruled. We agree.

The judgment is reversed and the cause is remanded to the Supreme Court of Florida for further action not inconsistent with this opinion.

Reversed.

The right to court-appointed counsel was later extended to misdemeanor cases. In *Argersinger v. Hamlin*, 407 U.S. 25 (1972), the Court stated:

> We must conclude, therefore, that the problems associated with misdemeanor and petty offenses often require the presence of counsel to insure the accused a fair trial. Mr. Justice Powell suggests that these problems are raised even in situations where there is no prospect of imprisonment. We need not consider the requirements of the Sixth Amendment as regards the right to counsel where loss of liberty is not involved, however, for here petitioner was in fact sentenced to jail. And, as we said in *Baldwin v. New York*, 399 U.S. at 73, "the prospect of imprisonment for however short a time will seldom be viewed by the accused as a trivial or 'petty' matter and may well result in quite serious repercussions affecting his career and his reputation."
>
> We hold, therefore, that absent a knowing and intelligent waiver, no person may be imprisoned for any offense, whether classified as petty, misdemeanor, or felony, unless he was represented by counsel at his trial.

THE RIGHT TO COMPETENT COUNSEL

In *Strickland v. Washington*, 466 U.S. 668 (1984), the Supreme Court stated: "The Sixth Amendment recognizes the right to the assistance of counsel because it envisions counsel's playing a role that is critical to the ability of the adversarial system to produce just results. An accused is entitled to be assisted by an attorney, whether retained or appointed, who plays the role necessary to ensure that the trial is fair." Certainly, if counsel is incompetent, he or she does not play a critical role in the trial.

Determining if an attorney is effective or competent is difficult because during a criminal trial an attorney is often required to exercise his or her judgment. Sometimes that judgment proves to be wrong, but it does not necessarily mean that the attorney was incompetent. Such was the case in *Strickland*. In this case, the defendant pleaded guilty to three brutal murders.

At the time of the plea, the judge told the defendant he had a great deal of respect for individuals who assumed responsibility for their actions. At a later hearing to determine if the defendant would receive the death penalty, his attorney decided not to call any character witnesses and not to demand a presentence probation report. Witnesses would have testified that the defendant was generally a good person, and the report would have shown that he did not have a serious prior criminal history. However, the defense attorney feared that cross-examination of the witnesses and contradicting evidence would have done more harm than the benefit derived from producing the evidence. The attorney hoped that the judge's previous comments indicated the possibility that some leniency would be shown. It was not, and the defendant was sentenced to die. The defendant then appealed, claiming that he did not receive adequate counsel. The Supreme Court disagreed saying:

> A convicted defendant's claim that counsel's assistance was so defective as to require reversal of a conviction or death sentence has two components. First, the defendant must show that counsel's performance was deficient. This requires showing that counsel made errors so serious that counsel was not functioning as the "counsel" guaranteed the defendant by the Sixth Amendment. Second, the defendant must show that the deficient performance prejudiced the defense. This requires showing that counsel's errors were so serious as to deprive the defendant of a fair trial, a trial whose result is reliable. Unless a defendant makes both showings, it cannot be said that the conviction or death sentence resulted from a breakdown in the adversary process that renders the result unreliable.
>
> The Court has not elaborated on the meaning of the constitutional requirement of effective assistance in the latter class of cases—that is, those presenting claims of "actual ineffectiveness." In giving meaning to the requirement, however, we must take its purpose—to ensure a fair trial—as the guide. The benchmark for judging any claim of ineffectiveness must be whether counsel's conduct so undermined the proper functioning of the adversarial process that the trial cannot be relied on as having produced a just result.

The Court found that in *Strickland* the attorney had a reasonable basis for his decisions and that, in any event, nothing would have changed the outcome of the hearing. Compare the *Strickland* case to *Wiggins v. Smith*, a 2003 case also dealing with the failure to introduce evidence in a capital case. The following syllabus explains the facts and the holding of the case.

Wiggins v. Smith
539 U.S. 510 (2003)

In 1989, petitioner Wiggins was convicted of capital murder by a Maryland judge and subsequently elected to be sentenced by a jury. His public defenders, Schlaich and Nethercott, moved to bifurcate the sentencing, representing that they planned to prove that Wiggins did not kill the victim by his own hand and then, if necessary, to present a mitigation case. The court denied the motion. At sentencing, Nethercott told the jury in her opening statement that they would hear, among other things, about Wiggins' difficult life, but such evidence was never introduced. Before closing arguments and outside the presence of the jury Schlaich made a proffer to the court to preserve the bifurcation issue for appeal, detailing the mitigation case counsel would have presented. Schlaich never mentioned Wiggins' life history or family background. The jury sentenced Wiggins to death, and the Maryland Court of Appeals affirmed. Represented by new counsel, Wiggins sought postconviction relief, arguing that his

(continued)

(continued)

trial counsel had rendered ineffective assistance by failing to investigate and present mitigating evidence of his dysfunctional background. He presented expert testimony by a forensic social worker about the severe physical and sexual abuse he had suffered at the hands of his mother and while under the care of a series of foster parents. Schlaich testified that he did not remember retaining a forensic social worker to prepare a social history before sentencing, even though state funds were available for that purpose, and explained that he and Nethercott had decided to focus on retrying the factual case and disputing Wiggins' direct responsibility for the murder. The trial court denied the petition, and the State Court of Appeals affirmed, concluding that trial counsel had made a reasoned choice to proceed with what they considered their best defense. Subsequently, the Federal District Court granted Wiggins relief on his federal habeas petition, holding that the Maryland courts' rejection of his ineffective assistance claim involved an unreasonable application of clearly established federal law. In reversing, the Fourth Circuit found trial counsel's strategic decision to focus on Wiggins' direct responsibility to be reasonable.

Held: The performance of Wiggins' attorneys at sentencing violated his Sixth Amendment right to effective assistance of counsel.

(a) An ineffective assistance claim has two components: A petitioner must show that counsel's performance was deficient, and that the deficiency prejudiced the defense. *Strickland* v. *Washington*, 466 U.S. 668, 687. Performance is deficient if it falls below an objective standard of reasonableness, which is defined in terms of prevailing professional norms. *Id.*, at 688. Here, as in *Strickland*, counsel claim that their limited investigation into petitioner's background reflected a tactical judgment not to present mitigating evidence and to pursue an alternative strategy instead. In evaluating petitioner's claim, this Court's principal concern is not whether counsel should have presented a mitigation case, but whether the investigation supporting their decision not to introduce mitigating evidence of Wiggins' background was *itself reasonable.* The Court thus conducts an objective review of their performance, measured for reasonableness under prevailing professional norms, including a context-dependent consideration of the challenged conduct as seen from counsel's perspective at the time of that conduct. *Id.*, at 688, 689.

(b) Counsel did not conduct a reasonable investigation. Their decision not to expand their investigation beyond a presentence investigation (PSI) report and Baltimore City Department of Social Services (DSS) records fell short of the professional standards prevailing in Maryland in 1989. Standard practice in Maryland capital cases at that time included the preparation of a social history report. Although there were funds to retain a forensic social worker, counsel chose not to commission a report. Their conduct similarly fell short of the American Bar Association's capital defense work standards. Moreover, in light of the facts counsel discovered in the DSS records concerning Wiggins' alcoholic mother and his problems in foster care, counsel's decision to cease investigating when they did was unreasonable. Any reasonably competent attorney would have realized that pursuing such leads was necessary to making an informed choice among possible defenses, particularly given the apparent absence of aggravating factors from Wiggins' background.

(c) Counsel's failures prejudiced Wiggins' defense. To establish prejudice, a defendant must show that there is a reasonable probability that, but for counsel's unprofessional errors, the proceeding's result would have been different. *Strickland*, at 694. This Court assesses prejudice by reweighing the aggravating evidence against the totality of the mitigating evidence adduced both at trial and in the habeas proceedings. *Williams* v. *Taylor*, 397–398. The mitigating evidence counsel failed to discover and present here is powerful. Wiggins experienced severe privation and abuse while in the custody of his alcoholic, absentee mother and physical torment, sexual molestation, and repeated rape while in foster care. His time spent homeless and his diminished mental capacities further augment his mitigation case. He thus has the kind of troubled history relevant to assessing a defendant's moral culpability. *Penry* v. *Lynaugh*, 492 U.S. 302, 319. Given the nature and extent of the abuse, there is a reasonable probability that a competent attorney, aware of this history, would have introduced it at sentencing, and that a jury confronted with such mitigating evidence would have returned with a different sentence. The only significant mitigating factor the jury heard was that Wiggins had no prior convictions. Had it been able to place his excruciating

(continued)

(continued)

life history on the mitigating side of the scale, there is a reasonable probability that at least one juror would have struck a different balance. Wiggins had no record of violent conduct that the State could have introduced to offset this powerful mitigating narrative. Thus, the available mitigating evidence, taken as a whole, might well have influenced the jury's appraisal of his moral culpability.

The Court reaffirmed the *Strickland* and *Wiggins* approach to evaluating the competency of counsel in *Bobby v. Van Hook*, 558 U.S.__ (2009), and *Wong v. Belmontes*, 558 U.S.___ (2009), although neither case was reversed on the grounds of incompetency of counsel. In *Bobby v. Van Hook*, the Court found that the lower court erroneously relied on ABA standards, treating the standards as "inexorable commands" rather than just guides. The Court further concluded that even if counsel was ineffective, the defendant suffered no prejudice. In *Wong*, the Court also found no prejudice from the acts of the attorney. Both of these cases were death penalty situations where ineffective counsel claims stemmed from allegations that the defense attorneys did not adequately investigate or present mitigating evidence in the penalty phase of the cases. In both cases the Court recognized that an attorney's judgment is involved in investigative and evidentiary decisions and that as long as this meets a minimal objective standard of reasonableness, counsel is not "ineffective."

STAGES AT WHICH RIGHT TO COUNSEL APPLIES

The Sixth Amendment specifically applies to "criminal prosecutions." Criminal prosecutions consist of a number of stages or proceedings, not just the trial. In any case, there might be several court and out-of-court proceedings such as pretrial hearings and motions, line-ups, and interrogations. After a trial, there are often sentencing hearings and appeals. The Supreme Court affirmed the right to counsel in the following important proceedings:

- Custodial interrogation
- Line-ups
- Pretrial proceedings
- Sentencing hearings
- Appeals

The Court's philosophy on the right to counsel at early stages in the criminal proceeding is expressed in *Brewer v. Williams* (a case also known as the "Christian Burial Case"). The Court's syllabus follows.

Brewer v. Williams
430 U.S. 387 (1977)

Respondent was arrested, arraigned, and committed to jail in Davenport, Iowa, for abducting a 10-year-old girl in Des Moines, Iowa. Both his Des Moines lawyer and his lawyer at the Davenport arraignment advised respondent not to make any statements until after consulting with the Des Moines lawyer upon being returned to Des Moines, and the police officers who were to accompany respondent on the automobile drive back to Des Moines agreed not to question him during the trip. During the trip, respondent expressed no willingness to be

(continued)

(continued)

interrogated in the absence of an attorney, but instead stated several times that he would tell the whole story after seeing his Des Moines lawyer. However, one of the police officers, who knew that respondent was a former mental patient and was deeply religious, sought to obtain incriminating remarks from respondent by stating to him during the drive that he felt they should stop and locate the girl's body because her parents were entitled to a Christian burial for the girl, who was taken away from them on Christmas Eve. Respondent eventually made several incriminating statements in the course of the trip, and finally directed the police to the girl's body. Respondent was tried and convicted of murder, over his objections to the admission of evidence relating to or resulting from any statements he made during the automobile ride, and the Iowa Supreme Court affirmed, holding, as did the trial court, that respondent had waived his constitutional right to the assistance of counsel. Respondent then petitioned for habeas corpus in Federal District Court, which held that the evidence in question had been wrongly admitted at respondent's trial on the ground, *inter alia*, that he had been denied his constitutional right to the assistance of counsel, and further ruled that he had not waived that right. The Court of Appeals affirmed. Petitioner warden claims that the District Court, in making its findings of fact, disregarded 28 U.S.C. §2254(d), which provides that, subject to certain exceptions, federal habeas corpus courts shall accept as correct the factual determinations made by state courts.
Held:

1. The District Court correctly applied 28 U.S.C. § 2254(d) in its resolution of the disputed evidentiary facts where it appears that it made no findings of fact in conflict with those of the Iowa courts, and that its additional findings of fact based upon its examination of the state court record were conscientiously and carefully explained, and were approved by the Court of Appeals as being supported by the record.

2. Respondent was deprived of his constitutional right to assistance of counsel. . . .

   (a) The right to counsel granted by the Sixth and Fourteenth Amendments means at least that a person is entitled to a lawyer's help at or after the time that judicial proceedings have been initiated against him, and here there is no doubt that judicial proceedings had been initiated against respondent before the automobile trip started, since a warrant had been issued for his arrest, he had been arraigned, and had been committed to jail.

   (b) An individual against whom adversary proceedings have commenced has a right to legal representation when the government interrogates him, *Massiah v. United States,* 377 U.S. 201, and since here the police officer's "Christian burial speech" was tantamount to interrogation, respondent was entitled to the assistance of counsel at the time he made the incriminating statements.

3. The circumstances of record provide, when viewed in light of respondent's assertions of his right to counsel, no reasonable basis for finding that respondent waived his right to the assistance of counsel, the record falling far short of sustaining the State's burden to prove "an intentional relinquishment or abandonment of a known right or privilege." *Johnson v. Zerbst,* 304 U.S. 458, 464.

Right to a Fair Trial

Several provisions of the Sixth Amendment are intended to guarantee that a defendant in a criminal case receives a fair trial. These rights include the following:

1. The right to a speedy and public trial

The Supreme Court explains the right to a speedy trial as follows: "This guarantee is an important safeguard to prevent undue and oppressive incarceration prior to trial, to minimize anxiety and concern accompanying public accusation and to limit the possibilities that long delay will impair the ability of an accused to defend himself." *United States v. Ewell,* 383 U.S. 116 (1966). The right to a speedy trial is guaranteed by two types of laws:

To bring a defendant before a judge to hear the charges and to enter a plea (guilty, not guilty, etc.). [pronounce: ah-rayn]

🏛 **statute of limitation**

1. A restriction. 2. A time limit. For example, a statute of limitations is a law that sets a maximum amount of time after something happens for it to be taken to court, such as a "three-year statute" for lawsuits based on a contract or a "six-year statute" for a criminal prosecution.

statutes of limitations for prosecution of crimes and laws setting time limits for prosecutors to **arraign** and try defendants. Statutes of limitations impose time limits for prosecution of most crimes, although some crimes have no statute of limitations. When a **statute of limitation** expires, a case can no longer be prosecuted. Recently, this rule created controversy in relationship to accused child molesters whose crimes did not come to light until well after the statute of limitations expired. In an effort to circumvent this, one state enacted a law lengthening the statute of limitations and applying to all past crimes. In reviewing this law, the Supreme Court held that a law enacted after expiration of a previously applicable limitations period violates the *Ex Post Facto* Clause when it is applied to revive a previously time-barred prosecution. *Stogner v. California*, 539 U.S. 607 (2003). In addition to statutes of limitations, the federal rules, as well as state laws and rules, impose strict time limits on court proceedings following an individual's arrest.

The right to a public trial is described by the Court as follows:

> The historical evidence demonstrates conclusively that at the time when our organic laws were adopted, criminal trials both here and in England had long been presumptively open. This is no quirk of history; rather, it has long been recognized as an indispensable attribute of an Anglo-American trial. Both Hale in the 17th century and Blackstone in the 18th saw the importance of openness to the proper functioning of a trial; it gave assurance that the proceedings were conducted fairly to all concerned, and it discouraged perjury, the misconduct of participants, and decisions based on secret bias or partiality.

Trials and pretrial proceedings (except a grand jury hearing) are generally open to the public, although the Court allows certain pretrial proceedings to be closed when there is a compelling reason. Although the press has some rights under this provision in conjunction with their rights under the First Amendment, a public trial does not guarantee the right to have cameras in the courtroom, as some members of the media would argue.

2. The right to trial by an impartial jury

The right to a jury trial was not a new concept to the framers of the Constitution. It is well-rooted in English common law. Under the English system, criminal juries consisted of twelve persons who unanimously decided the case. The American system, however, does not have the same requirements. The Supreme Court upholds juries with as few as six persons (in noncapital cases). With twelve-person juries, it also upholds laws that permit less than unanimous decisions.

Selecting an impartial jury has two requirements. First, the jurors must be selected from a pool that represents a cross section of the community. The selection process cannot eliminate or discriminate against any group. In most cases, such discrimination is also a violation of the Equal Protection Clause. (See Chapter 8.) Second, each individual chosen for the jury must be free from bias or prejudice. The process of **voir dire** helps to determine if any bias exists.

🏛 **voir dire**

(French) "To see, to say"; "to state the truth." The preliminary in-court questioning of a prospective witness (or juror) to determine competency to testify (or suitability to decide a case). [pronounce: vwahr deer]

The importance of the jury to criminal cases has been emphasized by the Court in two recent cases, *Apprendi v. New Jersey*, 530 U.S. 466 (2000) and *Ring v. Arizona*, 536 U.S. 584 (2002). In the first case, Apprendi was convicted of possession of firearms after shooting at the house of an African-American family. At sentencing, the prosecutor asked for an enhanced sentence under the state's hate crime, which allowed the judge, rather than the jury, to determine if the crime was motivated by racial hatred. The judge in the case found that it was a hate crime and added several years to the sentence normally imposed for possession of firearms. The Supreme Court reversed, stating that the Constitution requires that any fact increasing the penalty for a crime beyond the statutory maximum, other than the fact of a prior conviction, must be submitted to a jury and proved beyond a reasonable doubt. In *Ring v. Arizona*, the Court reviewed the role of the jury in a death penalty case. Under Arizona law, Ring, who was convicted of murder by a jury, could have received the death penalty only if there were aggravating circumstances. (In this case, the prosecutor had to prove that Ring, who was convicted of a murder, was the actual killer of the victim, not just a participant in the crime.) The law permitted this finding to be made by the judge rather than the jury. The judge found that he was the actual killer and sentenced him to death. The Supreme Court reversed, citing *Apprendi* and held that the factual determinations needed to find aggravating circumstances must be made by a jury.

The question of what constitutes an impartial jury arose recently in *Skilling v. U.S.*, 561 U.S. ___(2010), a case involving the criminal trial of one of the executives of Enron. Skilling was charged with a variety of crimes related to securities fraud that contributed to the bankruptcy of the once prominent company. He was convicted and appealed raising several issues, including the argument that he was denied a fair trial, primarily because of pretrial publicity. The following excerpt from the Court's opinion discusses the issue of a fair trial.

Skilling v. U.S.
561 U.S. __ (2010)

Skilling's fair-trial claim thus raises two distinct questions. First, did the District Court err by failing to move the trial to a different venue based on a presumption of prejudice? Second, did actual prejudice contaminate Skilling's jury?

When does the publicity dim prospects that the trier can judge a case, as due process requires, impartially, unswayed by outside influence? Because most cases of consequence garner at least some pretrial publicity, courts have considered this question in diverse settings. We begin our discussion by addressing the presumption of prejudice from which the Fifth Circuit's analysis in Skilling's case proceeded. The foundation precedent is *Rideau v. Louisiana*, 373 U. S. 723 (1963).

Wilbert Rideau robbed a bank in a small Louisiana town, kidnaped three bank employees, and killed one of them. Police interrogated Rideau in jail without counsel present and obtained his confession. Without informing Rideau, no less seeking his consent, the police filmed the interrogation. On three separate occasions shortly before the trial, a local television station broadcast the film to audiences ranging from 24,000 to 53,000 individuals. Rideau moved for a change of venue, arguing that he could not receive a fair trial in the parish where the crime occurred, which had a population of approximately 150,000 people. The trial court denied the motion, and a jury eventually convicted Rideau. The Supreme Court of Louisiana upheld the conviction.

We reversed. "What the people [in the community] saw on their television sets," we observed, "was Rideau, in jail, flanked by the sheriff and two state troopers, admitting in detail the commission of the robbery, kidnapping, and murder." *Id.*, at 725. "[T]o the tens of thousands of people who saw and heard it," we explained, the interrogation "in a very real sense *was* Rideau's trial—at which he pleaded guilty." *Id.*, at 726. We therefore "d[id] not hesitate to hold, without pausing to examine a particularized transcript of the *voir dire*," that "[t]he kangaroo court proceedings" trailing the televised confession violated due process. *Id.*, at 726–727.

Similarly, in *Sheppard* v. *Maxwell*, 384 U. S. 333 (1966), news reporters extensively covered the story of Sam Sheppard, who was accused of bludgeoning his pregnant wife to death. "[B]edlam reigned at the courthouse during the trial and newsmen took over practically the entire courtroom," thrusting jurors "into the role of celebrities." *Id.*, at 353, 355. Pretrial media coverage, which we characterized as "months [of] virulent publicity about Sheppard and the murder," did not alone deny due process, we noted. *Id.*, at 354. But Sheppard's case involved

(continued)

(continued)

more than heated reporting pretrial: We upset the murder conviction because a "carnival atmosphere" pervaded the trial, *id.,* at 358.

In each of these cases, we overturned a "conviction obtained in a trial atmosphere that [was] utterly corrupted by press coverage"; our decisions, however, "cannot be made to stand for the proposition that juror exposure to . . . news accounts of the crime . . . alone presumptively deprives the defendant of due process." *Murphy* v. *Florida,* 421 U. S. 794, 798–799 (1975). Prominence does not necessarily produce prejudice, and juror *impartiality,* we have reiterated, does not require *ignorance. Irvin* v. *Dowd,* 366 U. S. 717, 722 (1961)

Important differences separate Skilling's prosecution from those in which we have presumed juror prejudice. First, we have emphasized in prior decisions the size and characteristics of the community in which the crime occurred. In *Rideau,* for example, we noted that the murder was committed in a parish of only 150,000 residents. Houston, in contrast, is the fourth most populous city in the Nation: At the time of Skilling's trial, more than 4.5 million individuals eligible for jury duty resided in the Houston area. Given this large, diverse pool of potential jurors, the suggestion that 12 impartial individuals could not be empaneled is hard to sustain.

Second, although news stories about Skilling were not kind, they contained no confession or other blatantly prejudicial information of the type readers or viewers could not reasonably be expected to shut from sight. Rideau's dramatically staged admission of guilt, for instance, was likely imprinted indelibly in the mind of anyone who watched it.

Third, unlike cases in which trial swiftly followed a widely reported crime, *e.g., Rideau,* 373 U. S., at 724, over four years elapsed between Enron's bankruptcy and Skilling's trial. Although reporters covered Enron-related news throughout this period, the decibel level of media attention diminished somewhat in the years following Enron's collapse.

Finally, and of prime significance, Skilling's jury acquitted him of nine insider-trading counts. Similarly, earlier instituted Enron-related prosecutions yielded no overwhelming victory for the Government.

We next consider whether actual prejudice infected Skilling's jury. *Voir dire,* Skilling asserts, did not adequately detect and defuse juror bias. "[T]he record . . . affirmatively confirm[s]" prejudice, he maintains, because

several seated jurors "prejudged his guilt.". We disagree with Skilling's characterization of the *voir dire* and the jurors selected through it.

No hard-and-fast formula dictates the necessary depth or breadth of *voir dire.* See *United States* v. *Wood,* 299 U. S. 123, 145–146 (1936) ("Impartiality is not a technical conception. It is a state of mind. For the ascertainment of this mental attitude of appropriate indifference, the Constitution lays down no particular tests and procedure is not chained to any ancient and artificial formula."). Jury selection, we have repeatedly emphasized, is "particularly within the province of the trial judge." *Ristaino* v. *Ross,* 424 U. S. 589, 594–595 (1976)

When pretrial publicity is at issue, "primary reliance on the judgment of the trial court makes [especially] good sense" because the judge "sits in the locale where the publicity is said to have had its effect" and may base her evaluation on her "own perception of the depth and extent of news stories that might influence a juror." *Mu'Min,* 500 U. S., at 427.

Reviewing courts are properly resistant to second-guessing the trial judge's estimation of a juror's impartiality, for that judge's appraisal is ordinarily influenced by a host of factors impossible to capture fully in the record—among them, the prospective juror's inflection, sincerity, demeanor, candor, body language, and apprehension of duty. See *Reynolds,* 98 U. S., at 156–157. In contrast to the cold transcript received by the appellate court, the in-the-moment *voir dire* affords the trial court a more intimate and immediate basis for assessing a venire member's fitness for jury service. We consider the adequacy of jury selection in Skilling's case, therefore, attentive to the respect due to district-court determinations of juror impartiality and of the measures necessary to ensure that impartiality.

The District Court, moreover, did not simply take venire members who proclaimed their impartiality at their word. As noted, all of Skilling's jurors had already affirmed on their questionnaires that they would have no trouble basing a verdict only on the evidence at trial. Nevertheless, the court followed up with each individually to uncover concealed bias. This face-to-face opportunity to gauge demeanor and credibility, coupled with information from the questionnaires regarding jurors' backgrounds, opinions, and sources of news, gave the court a sturdy foundation to assess fitness for jury service. The jury's not-guilty verdict on nine insider-trading

(continued)

(continued)

counts after nearly five days of deliberation, meanwhile, suggests the court's assessments were accurate. Skilling, we conclude, failed to show that his *voir dire* fell short of constitutional requirements.

In sum, Skilling failed to establish that a presumption of prejudice arose or that actual bias infected the jury that tried him. Jurors, the trial court correctly comprehended, need not enter the box with empty heads in order to determine the facts impartially. "It is sufficient if the juror[s] can lay aside [their] impression[s] or opinion[s] and render a verdict based on the evidence presented in court." *Irvin*, 366 U. S., at 723. Taking account of the full record, rather than incomplete exchanges selectively culled from it, we find no cause to upset the lower courts' judgment that Skilling's jury met that measure. We therefore affirm the Fifth Circuit's ruling that Skilling received a fair trial.

3. Other rights assuring a fair trial

In addition to the right to a speedy and public trial by an impartial jury, the Sixth Amendment also requires:

1. that the defendant be informed of the nature of the charges against him or her,
2. that juries be selected from the district in which the crime was committed, and
3. that the defense has the right to compel the attendance of witnesses as well as the right to confront witnesses.

The Federal Rules of Criminal Procedure and state rules and codes contain provisions that give effect to these provisions. Defendants are normally informed of their offenses at an arraignment, a court hearing at which the defendant is told of the charges and given the opportunity to enter a plea. The requirement that juries be selected from the district in which the crime occurred generally requires that the trial take place in that locality. However, if the defense can show that it cannot get a fair trial, it can ask the court to change venue to another area. The right to call witnesses gives the defense the right to have subpoenas issued. When properly served with a subpoena, a witness must attend the court hearing or risk serious sanctions including arrest. The right to confront witnesses is the right to cross-examine a witness whose testimony is used against a person. This generally means that the prosecutor cannot use written or oral statements from witnesses to events. The witness must testify so that the defense can cross-examine.

The Eighth Amendment: Bail and Cruel and Unusual Punishment

Amendment VIII

Excessive bail shall not be required, nor excessive fines imposed, nor cruel and unusual punishments inflicted.

Bail

The Eighth Amendment states that bail cannot be *excessive*. It does not create a *right* to bail. Courts are allowed to deny bail in a variety of circumstances. If the defendant poses a flight risk or a threat to society, bail can be denied. It can also be denied for capital offenses. However, if bail is granted, the amount must not be more than necessary to assure the defendant's presence at trial.

Cruel and Unusual Punishment: Proportionality

Defining the phrase *cruel and unusual punishment* presents challenges for the Court. As the Court stated in *Wilkerson v. Utah*, 99 U.S. 130 (1878): "Difficulty would attend the effort to define with exactness the extent of the constitutional provision which provides that cruel and unusual punishments shall not be inflicted; but it is safe to affirm that punishments of torture . . . and all others in the same line of unnecessary cruelty, are forbidden by that amendment to the Constitution." In a later case, the Court decided that cruel and unusual punishment could apply to nonphysical as well as physical punishment. In *Trop v. Dulles*, 356 U.S. 86 (1958), the Court held that loss of citizenship for wartime desertion from the military was cruel and unusual. The Court stated:

> We believe, as did Chief Judge Clark in the court below, that use of denationalization as a punishment is barred by the Eighth Amendment. There may be involved no physical mistreatment, no primitive torture. There is instead the total destruction of the individual's status in organized society. It is a form of punishment more primitive than torture, for it destroys for the individual the political existence that was centuries in the development. The punishment strips the citizen of his status in the national and international political community. His very existence is at the sufferance of the country in which he happens to find himself. . . . In short, the expatriate has lost the right to have rights. This punishment is offensive to cardinal principles for which the Constitution stands.

🏛 **proportionality**

The term given to the concept that the punishment for a crime must bear some relationship to the nature or seriousness of the crime. The Eighth Amendment prohibition on cruel and unusual punishment requires that punishment for a crime cannot be grossly disproportionate to the crime but it need not be strictly in proportion to the offense charged.

One of the more difficult questions facing the Court in interpreting this Amendment is whether the punishment must fit the crime. The Court refers to this concept as **proportionality**. The Court recognized this principle in *Weems v. United States*, 217 U.S. 349 (1910), where the Court held that fifteen years of incarceration at hard labor with chains on the ankles, loss of all civil rights, and perpetual surveillance for the offense of falsifying public documents, constituted cruel and unusual punishment because it was too excessive for the crime.

In more modern times, the issue of proportionality arises in the context of laws that impose severe punishment, including life sentences, for repeat offenders (three strikes laws). The rule that emerged is that the punishment for a crime cannot be grossly disproportionate to the crime but it need not be strictly in proportion to the offense charged. In the case of laws that harshly punish repeat offenders, the Court looks at the nature of the prior convictions. In two cases, the Supreme Court upheld life sentences for individuals convicted of minor offenses when the prior convictions were serious felonies. *Rummel v. Estelle*, 445 U.S. 263 (1980), and *Ewing v. California*, 538 U.S. 11 (2003). In another case, however, the Court found the imposition of a life sentence to be cruel and unusual when a defendant had several prior convictions, but none of them involved serious injury to other persons. *Solem v. Helm*, 463 U.S. 277 (1983). (The cases were decided by 6–3 or 5–4 votes.)

CRUEL AND UNUSUAL PUNISHMENT: THE DEATH PENALTY

One of the most controversial issues before the nation and the Court is the death penalty. On several occasions, the Court was asked to rule on the relationship of the death penalty to the Eighth Amendment provision on cruel and unusual punishment. In doing this the Court declared the death penalty unconstitutional in 1972, reinstated it in 1976, and in several subsequent cases explained some of its parameters and limitations.

🏛 **per curiam**

(Latin) "By the court." Describes an opinion backed by all the judges in a particular court and usually with no one judge's name on it. [pronounce: per cure-ee-am]

In 1972, in a **per curiam** opinion, the Supreme Court issued a landmark decision, *Furman v. Georgia*, declaring all death penalty laws in the United States unconstitutional. A majority agreed that the death penalty was unconstitutional but they did not agree on the reason. Three justices felt that it should be declared unconstitutional because it was applied in a discriminatory way. Two justices felt that the death penalty should be abolished entirely because by its nature it was cruel and unusual. Four justices thought it should be upheld. Several of the justices wrote concurring or dissenting opinions. Following is the per curiam opinion and selections from the concurring and dissenting opinions reflecting the various philosophies of the Court.

Furman v. Georgia
408 U.S. 238 (1972)

Per Curiam. Petitioner in No. 69-5003 was convicted of murder in Georgia and was sentenced to death pursuant to Ga. Code Ann. 26-1005 (Supp. 1971) (effective prior to July 1, 1969). 225 Ga. 253, 167 S.E.2d 628 (1969). Petitioner in No. 69-5030 was convicted of rape in Georgia and was sentenced to death pursuant to Ga. Code Ann. 26-1302 (Supp. 1971) (effective prior to July 1, 1969). 225 Ga. 790, 171 S.E.2d 501 (1969). Petitioner in No. 69-5031 was convicted of rape in Texas and was sentenced to death pursuant to Tex. Penal Code, Art. 1189 (1961). 447 S.W.2d 932 (Ct. Crim. App. 1969). Certiorari was granted limited to the following question: "Does the imposition and carrying out of the death penalty in these cases constitute cruel and unusual punishment in violation of the Eighth and Fourteenth Amendments?" 403 U.S. 952 (1971). The Court holds that the imposition and carrying out of the death penalty in these cases constitute cruel and unusual punishment in violation of the Eighth and Fourteenth Amendments. The judgment in each case is therefore reversed insofar as it leaves undisturbed the death sentence imposed, and the cases are remanded for further proceedings.

So ordered.

Mr. Justice Douglas, concurring.

It has been assumed in our decisions that punishment by death is not cruel, unless the manner of execution can be said to be inhuman and barbarous. *In re Kemmler*, 136 U.S. 436, 447. The generality of a law inflicting capital punishment is one thing. What may be said of the validity of a law on the books and what may be done with the law in its application do, or may, lead to quite different conclusions.

It would seem to be incontestable that the death penalty inflicted on one defendant is "unusual" if it discriminates against him by reason of his race, religion, wealth, social position, or class, or if it is imposed under a procedure that gives room for the play of such prejudices.

There is evidence that the provision of the English Bill of Rights of 1689, from which the language of the Eighth Amendment was taken, was concerned primarily with selective or irregular application of harsh penalties and that its aim was to forbid arbitrary and discriminatory penalties of a severe nature. The words "cruel and unusual" certainly include penalties that are barbaric. But the words, at least when read in light of the English proscription against selective and irregular use of penalties, suggest that it is "cruel and unusual" to apply the death penalty—or any other penalty—selectively to minorities whose numbers are few, who are outcasts of society, and who are unpopular, but whom society is willing to see suffer though it would not countenance general application of the same penalty across the board.

A study of capital cases in Texas from 1924 to 1968 reached the following conclusions:

> Application of the death penalty is unequal: most of those executed were poor, young, and ignorant.
>
> Seventy-five of the 460 cases involved co-defendants, who, under Texas law, were given separate trials. In several instances where a white and a Negro were co-defendants, the white was sentenced to life imprisonment or a term of years, and the Negro was given the death penalty.
>
> Another ethnic disparity is found in the type of sentence imposed for rape. The Negro convicted of rape is far more likely to get the death penalty than a term sentence, whereas whites and Latins are far more likely to get a term sentence than the death penalty.

(continued)

(continued)

One searches our chronicles in vain for the execution of any member of the affluent strata of this society. The Leopolds and Loebs are given prison terms, not sentenced to death.

We cannot say from facts disclosed in these records that these defendants were sentenced to death because they were black. Yet our task is not restricted to an effort to divine what motives impelled these death penalties. Rather, we deal with a system of law and of justice that leaves to the uncontrolled discretion of judges or juries the determination whether defendants committing these crimes should die or be imprisoned. Under these laws no standards govern the selection of the penalty. People live or die, dependent on the whim of one man or of 12.

Thus, these discretionary statutes are unconstitutional in their operation. They are pregnant with discrimination and discrimination is an ingredient not compatible with the idea of equal protection of the laws that is implicit in the ban on "cruel and unusual" punishments.

I concur in the judgments of the Court.

MR. JUSTICE BRENNAN, concurring.

The Cruel and Unusual Punishments Clause, like the other great clauses of the Constitution, is not susceptible of precise definition. Yet we know that the values and ideals it embodies are basic to our scheme of government. And we know also that the Clause imposes upon this Court the duty, when the issue is properly presented, to determine the constitutional validity of a challenged punishment, whatever that punishment may be.

Ours would indeed be a simple task were we required merely to measure a challenged punishment against those that history has long condemned. That narrow and unwarranted view of the Clause, however, was left behind with the 19th century. Our task today is more complex. We know "that the words of the [Clause] are not precise, and that their scope is not static." We know, therefore, that the Clause must draw its meaning from the evolving standards of decency that mark the progress of a maturing society. That knowledge, of course, is but the beginning of the inquiry.

There are, then, four principles by which we may determine whether a particular punishment is "cruel and unusual." In sum, the punishment of death is inconsistent with all four principles: Death is an unusually severe and degrading punishment; there is a strong probability that it is inflicted arbitrarily; its rejection by contemporary society is virtually total; and there is no reason to believe that it serves any penal purpose more effectively than the less severe punishment of imprisonment. The function of these principles is to enable a court to determine whether a punishment comports with human dignity. Death, quite simply, does not.

When this country was founded, memories of the Stuart horrors were fresh and severe corporal punishments were common. Death was not then a unique punishment. The practice of punishing criminals by death, moreover, was widespread and by and large acceptable to society. Indeed, without developed prison systems, there was frequently no workable alternative. Since that time, successive restrictions, imposed against the background of a continuing moral controversy, have drastically curtailed the use of this punishment. Today death is a uniquely and unusually severe punishment. When examined by the principles applicable under the Cruel and Unusual Punishments Clause, death stands condemned as fatally offensive to human dignity. The punishment of death is therefore "cruel and unusual," and the States may no longer inflict it as a punishment for crimes. Rather than kill an arbitrary handful of criminals each year, the States will confine them in prison. "The State thereby suffers nothing and loses no power. The purpose of punishment is fulfilled, crime is repressed by penalties of just, not tormenting, severity, its repetition is prevented, and hope is given for the reformation of the criminal." *Weems v. United States*, 217 U.S., at 381.

I concur in the judgments of the Court.

MR. JUSTICE REHNQUIST, with whom THE CHIEF JUSTICE, MR. JUSTICE BLACKMUN, and MR. JUSTICE POWELL join, dissenting.

The Court's judgments today strike down a penalty that our Nation's legislators have thought necessary since our country was founded. My Brothers Douglas, Brennan, and Marshall would at one fell swoop invalidate laws enacted by Congress and 40 of the 50 state legislatures. My Brothers Stewart and White, asserting reliance on a more limited rationale—the reluctance of judges and juries actually to impose the death penalty in the majority of capital cases—join in the judgments in these cases. Whatever its precise rationale, today's holding necessarily brings into sharp relief the fundamental question of the role of judicial review in a democratic society. How can government by the elected representatives of the people

(continued)

(continued)

co-exist with the power of the federal judiciary, whose members are constitutionally insulated from responsiveness to the popular will, to declare invalid laws duly enacted by the popular branches of government?

The answer, of course, is found in Hamilton's Federalist Paper No. 78 and in Chief Justice Marshall's classic opinion in *Marbury v. Madison*, 1 Cranch 137 (1803). An oft-told story since then, it bears summarization once more. Sovereignty resides ultimately in the people as a whole and, by adopting through their States a written Constitution for the Nation and subsequently adding amendments to that instrument, they have both granted certain powers to the National Government, and denied other powers to the National and the State Governments. Courts are exercising no more than the judicial function conferred upon them by Art. III of the Constitution when they assess, in a case before them, whether or not a particular legislative enactment is within the authority granted by the Constitution to the enacting body, and whether it runs afoul of some limitation placed by the Constitution on the authority of that body. For the theory is that the people themselves have spoken in the Constitution, and

therefore its commands are superior to the commands of the legislature, which is merely an agent of the people.

If there can be said to be one dominant theme in the Constitution, perhaps more fully articulated in the Federalist Papers than in the instrument itself, it is the notion of checks and balances. The Framers were well aware of the natural desire of office holders as well as others to seek to expand the scope and authority of their particular office at the expense of others. They sought to provide against success in such efforts by erecting adequate checks and balances in the form of grants of authority to each branch of the government in order to counteract and prevent usurpation on the part of the others.

The very nature of judicial review makes the courts the least subject to Madisonian check in the event that they shall, for the best of motives, expand judicial authority beyond the limits contemplated by the Framers. It is for this reason that judicial self-restraint is surely an implied, if not an expressed, condition of the grant of authority of judicial review. The Court's holding in these cases has been reached, I believe, in complete disregard of that implied condition.

Since a majority of the members of the Court did not express the opinion that the death penalty per se was cruel and unusual, the legislatures of thirty-five states rewrote the death penalty statutes in their states in an effort to create a death penalty law that would be found constitutional. In the case of *Gregg v. Georgia*, 428 U.S. 153 (1976), the Supreme Court again reviewed a death penalty statute. In this case, the Supreme Court (in a 7–2 decision) found that the death penalty did not always violate the Eighth and Fourteenth Amendments. It gave several reasons. First, capital punishment was recognized by the framers of the Constitution and had been in existence for approximately 200 years. Second, society obviously felt the necessity for such a law as was indicated by the number of states that rewrote their death penalty statutes after *Furman*. Third, the Court mentioned that the death penalty serves two principal social purposes: retribution and deterrence of capital crimes by prospective offenders.

The Court stated:

> In sum, we cannot say that the judgment of the Georgia Legislature that capital punishment may be necessary in some cases is clearly wrong. Considerations of federalism, as well as respect for the ability of a legislature to evaluate, in terms of its particular State, the moral consensus concerning the death penalty and its social utility as a sanction, require us to conclude, in the absence of more convincing. . . .

🏛 **bifurcated trial**

Separate hearings for different issues in the same case; for example, for guilt and sanity or guilt and punishment in a criminal trial or for liability and damages in a complicated auto injury trial.

In finding the revised Georgia statute constitutional, the Court noted two features of the law. First, it provided for a **bifurcated trial**, which is a trial that takes place in two stages. In the first stage, the jury determined basic guilt or innocence. In the second stage, which occurred only with a finding of guilt, the jury decided the sentence based on direction from the Court. Second, a sentence of death was automatically appealed to the state supreme court who reviewed the case to make sure it was supported by the evidence and that it was not arbitrary or capricious. The Supreme Court did not mandate either of these procedures, but did recommend them.

Since the defendant in *Gregg v. Georgia* was convicted of murder, the Court did not have to consider if the death penalty could be imposed for lesser crimes. This issue came before the Court shortly after *Gregg*, in *Coker v. Georgia*, 433 U.S. 584 (1977), when the defendant was charged with rape of an adult woman. In this case, a majority found that the death penalty was disproportionate to the crime and therefore unconstitutional. A strong dissent argued that in this case the death penalty should have been upheld because of the past record of the defendant who committed this crime after escaping from prison. He was in prison for past rapes and murder.

In 2008, in *Kennedy v. Louisiana*, 554 U.S. 407, the Court faced another difficult and emotional case involving the rape of a child. In a 5–4 decision, the Court held that the imposition of the death penalty was disproportionate for even this type of crime, because no death resulted.

In two relatively recent cases, the Supreme Court considered whether mentally retarded individuals could be executed. In 1989 in *Penry v. Lynaugh*, 492 U.S. 302 (1989), the Court held that executing a mentally retarded individual did not violate the cruel and unusual punishment provision of the Eighth Amendment. However, in 2002, the Court revisited this issue in *Atkins v. Virginia* and decided that executing a mentally retarded individual did violate the Eighth Amendment. *Atkins* involved a defendant with an I.Q. of approximately fifty-nine who was sentenced to death for murder. In deciding the case, the Court made the following points:

1. Excessive punishment should be measured by current standards of decency (not by what was common when the Bill of Rights was adopted).
2. The best measure of decency is state legislatures.
3. When there is some consensus among the state legislatures, the Court should follow their lead, unless there is some constitutional objection.
4. Regarding the question of executing the mentally retarded, in the past few years fourteen states eliminated the death penalty for those of lower mental ability and, in practice, many other states did not impose the penalty.

In light of this, the Supreme Court found that the death penalty for mentally retarded individuals violates the Constitution. The following language from the Court's syllabus explains:

> Mentally retarded persons frequently know the difference between right and wrong and are competent to stand trial, but, by definition, they have diminished capacities to understand and process information, to communicate, to abstract from mistakes and learn from experience, to engage in logical reasoning, to control impulses, and to understand others' reactions. Their deficiencies do not warrant an exemption from criminal sanctions, but diminish their personal culpability.

As the Court abolished the death penalty for the mentally retarded, it also abolished it for juveniles. In 2005 in *Roper v. Simmons,* 543 U.S. 551 the Supreme Court ruled that a person who was under 18 at the time a crime was committed could not be executed.

The Juvenile Justice System

JUVENILES WHO COMMIT CRIMES present special concerns and difficulties for government. Some youthful offenders may not have the same degree of maturity and judgment as adult offenders, and sometimes the nature of the crimes committed reflect immature choices rather than serious criminal intent. However, some juvenile offenders commit crimes as serious as those of the most hardened adult criminals. In an effort to handle the unique problems of juvenile offenders, by the middle of the twentieth century, all states established special court procedures. Generally, the philosophy behind the juvenile court system was that the state acted in place of the parents (*parens patriae*). Philosophically, the juvenile system emphasized rehabilitation more than the adult criminal justice system. Also, court proceedings were generally not referred to as *criminal* proceedings. Based on these factors, states justified the establishment of informal court procedures that often ignored the constitutional rights enjoyed by adults accused of crimes. Realistically, however, many juveniles faced lengthy commitment and harsh penalties for the offenses they committed. Eventually, the Supreme Court ruled that juvenile procedures that deprived a person of liberty are governed by the Due Process Clause of the Fourteenth Amendment and that most rights guaranteed to an adult offender were also guaranteed to a juvenile. The exceptions are the right to bail and the right to a jury trial. The leading Supreme Court case is *In re Gault*, found in Chapter 9, Due Process.

The distinction between juveniles and adults is also seen in two recent cases. First was *Graham v. Florida*, 560 U.S. __(2010), in which the Court found that juveniles could not be sentenced to life imprisonment without the possibility of parole for non-homicide cases. Second was *J.D.B. v. North Carolina*, 564 U.S. __(2011) where the Court decided that a juvenile's age was a circumstance to be considered in determining if the juvenile was "in custody" for *Miranda* purposes.

Did You Know?

William O. Douglas served on the U.S. Supreme Court for thirty-six years. He was appointed to the Court by President Franklin D. Roosevelt in 1939.

Courtesy of Oscar White/Historical/CORBIS

❧ Ethical Decisions—Everyday Choices ❧

The Facts: Brooke is a public defender representing an accused murderer, Jones. Alice is Brooke's paralegal. Jones told Brooke and Alice that at the time of the murder he was with his friend Smith. When Brooke and Alice question Smith, Smith denies that he was with Jones at the time of the murder and adds that Jones told him he had in fact committed the crime. The prosecutor is unaware of Smith. Without Smith's testimony, there is a good chance that Jones will be found not guilty at trial and released.

The Problem: Should either Brooke or Alice keep Smith's identity a secret, knowing that a murderer might escape punishment?

Guiding Principles: Attorneys have an ethical duty to protect confidential information received from their clients as well as a duty to act diligently in representing their clients. On the other hand, they have a duty to be honest in their dealings with the court. Paralegals are bound by these same ethical duties.

Chapter Summary

Police procedures such as searches, arrests, and interrogations, as well as criminal trials and sentencing, are regulated by the Constitution in the Fourth, Fifth, Sixth, and Eighth Amendments. Most of the provisions of these amendments apply to the states through the Fourteenth Amendment. The Constitution provides general guidelines or rules that apply in criminal cases. Specific rules are found in the Federal Rules of Criminal Procedure and in state codes and rules. Members of the Supreme Court often disagree when interpreting the language of the amendments dealing with criminal procedure. For this reason, most cases are not unanimous decisions.

In order to enforce various provisions of the Constitution related to the criminal justice system, the Supreme Court created the exclusionary rule. This rule provides that evidence obtained in violation of the Constitution is not admissible at trial. The rule is controversial and the Court created several exceptions to its application.

The Fourth Amendment provides protections in the area known as *search and seizure*. The basic protections offered by the Fourth Amendment are: (1) All searches must be reasonable; (2) All seizures must be reasonable; (3) If there is a warrant, it must be based on probable cause, signed by a neutral magistrate, and must specifically describe the place or person to be searched or the person to be arrested or the items to be seized. Although the Constitution does not expressly require warrants before searches or seizures, the Court ruled that any search or seizure conducted without a warrant is presumed to be unconstitutional, and the state must justify its action.

The Fifth Amendment contains a variety of safeguards for those accused of crimes. An individual cannot be compelled to be a witness against himself. The government cannot use physical or psychological force to obtain a confession. Furthermore, in the landmark case of *Miranda v. Arizona*, the Court held that before any custodial interrogation occurs, a suspect must be advised of certain rights, including the right to remain silent and the right to an attorney. A person accused of a serious crime has the right to a grand jury hearing before indictment. The grand jury determines if there is sufficient evidence against the accused to warrant a trial. This right is not incorporated into the concept of due process found in the Fourteenth Amendment and thus, states are not required to afford a grand jury hearing. An individual cannot be subject to multiple prosecutions for the same crime (double jeopardy). Finally, the Fifth Amendment contains a general right to due process in a criminal proceeding.

The Sixth Amendment provides the accused with the right to counsel as well as setting forth specific requirements to assure a fair trial. The right to counsel includes the right to court-appointed (and paid) counsel for indigent defendants. To assure a fair trial, the Sixth Amendment also gives the defendant the following rights: a speedy and public trial, trial by an impartial jury, the right to be informed of the charges, the right to confront witnesses against him or her, and the right to subpoena witnesses.

The Eighth Amendment prohibits government from imposing excessive bail or cruel and unusual punishment. Bail is not guaranteed to a defendant and can be denied. If set, however, it must be reasonable. Regarding the prohibition on cruel and unusual punishment, one question that plagues the Court is whether the punishment for a crime is in proportion to the seriousness of the offense (proportionality). Although the Court recognizes such a principle, recent Court decisions hold that only sentences that are grossly disproportionate are unconstitutional. The question of cruel and unusual punishment was addressed in several cases dealing with the death penalty. According to the Court, the death penalty itself is not cruel and unusual punishment. However, the Court did rule the death penalty unconstitutional when applied to the mentally retarded or to juveniles.

Although juvenile proceedings are often characterized as noncriminal cases, the Supreme Court recognized that the penalties imposed on juveniles are often as severe as those imposed upon adult offenders. Consequently, the Court held that most of the rights afforded to adult offenders under the Constitution also apply to juveniles accused of crimes. Two major exceptions are the provisions regarding bail and the right to a jury trial.

Key Terms

exclusionary rule	exigent	indigent
fruit of the poisonous tree	*Miranda* warnings	arraign
execute	infamous	statute of limitation
standing	indicted	*voir dire*
rational suspicion	subpoena	proportionality
probable cause	civil commitment	per curiam
affidavit	mistrial	bifurcated trial

Questions for Review

1. Which amendments in the Bill of Rights provide constitutional protection in criminal cases?
2. What is the importance of the Fourteenth Amendment and the Incorporation Doctrine to constitutional rights of those accused of crimes?
3. What is the exclusionary rule?
4. What are some of the arguments for and against the exclusionary rule?
5. What types of police activities are governed by the Fourth Amendment?
6. What rights are found in the Fifth Amendment?
7. What is the importance of the *Miranda* decision?
8. What rights are found in the Sixth Amendment?
9. What rights are found in the Eighth Amendment?
10. Which constitutional rights apply to juvenile proceedings, and which do not?

Questions for Analysis

1. Review the hypothetical case in Living in America. Do you think that it is reasonable for Detective Branigan to detain Stevenson? Does she have probable cause to arrest Stevenson? Does she have probable cause to search the Stevenson backyard? Assuming that she does have probable cause to arrest and search, do you think she needs a warrant to do either or both? Explain.
2. Review the cases in the chapter dealing with the right to counsel. Do you think a person can get a fair trial without a lawyer? If not, how can the Court allow defendants to represent themselves at trial?
3. Consider the following facts: In a trial for murder, the court allowed a police officer to testify as to statements that a mortally wounded victim made. The defendant claimed that this violated his constitutional right to confront witnesses. Is the defendant correct? Discuss. (*See Michigan v. Bryant*, 562 U.S. __(2011))

Assignments and Projects

1. Visit a local court that hears criminal cases. Sit in on some pretrial hearings. Describe the proceeding, and explain how the constitutional rights discussed in this chapter affected or influenced the hearing.
2. Read the selection from the government's brief in *Skilling v. U.S.* in Appendix G. Summarize the argument.

Putting It into Practice

Review the hypothetical case in Living with the Constitution. Assume that Detective Branigan decided to apply for a search warrant to search the Stevenson backyard. Complete the Application for a Search Warrant found in Appendix C.

Group Activity

Reread the brief in *Skilling v. U.S.* found in Appendix G. The government maintains that Skilling had a fair trial. Discuss arguments that Skilling might make that he did not receive a fair trial.

The Constitution of the United States

We the people of the United States, in order to form a more perfect union, establish justice, insure domestic tranquility, provide for the common defense, promote the general welfare, and secure the blessings of liberty to ourselves and our posterity, do ordain and establish this Constitution for the United States of America.

Article I

Section 1

All legislative powers herein granted shall be vested in a Congress of the United States, which shall consist of a Senate and House of Representatives.

Section 2

The House of Representatives shall be composed of members chosen every second year by the people of the several states, and the electors in each state shall have the qualifications requisite for electors of the most numerous branch of the state legislature.

No person shall be a Representative who shall not have attained to the age of twenty five years, and been seven years a citizen of the United States, and who shall not, when elected, be an inhabitant of that state in which he shall be chosen.

Representatives and direct taxes shall be apportioned among the several states which may be included within this union, according to their respective numbers, which shall be determined by adding to the whole number of free persons, including those bound to service for a term of years, and excluding Indians not taxed, three fifths of all other Persons. The actual Enumeration shall be made within three years after the first meeting of the Congress of the United States, and within every subsequent term of ten years, in such manner as they shall by law direct. The number of Representatives shall not exceed one for every thirty thousand, but each state shall have at least one Representative; and until such enumeration shall be made, the state of New Hampshire shall be entitled to choose three, Massachusetts eight, Rhode Island and Providence Plantations one, Connecticut five, New York six, New Jersey four, Pennsylvania eight, Delaware one, Maryland six, Virginia ten, North Carolina five, South Carolina five, and Georgia three.

When vacancies happen in the Representation from any state, the executive authority thereof shall issue writs of election to fill such vacancies.

The House of Representatives shall choose their speaker and other officers; and shall have the sole power of impeachment.

Section 3

The Senate of the United States shall be composed of two Senators from each state, chosen by the legislature thereof, for six years; and each Senator shall have one vote.

Immediately after they shall be assembled in consequence of the first election, they shall be divided as equally as may be into three classes. The seats of the Senators of the first class shall be vacated at the expiration of the second year, of the second class at the expiration of the fourth year, and the third class at the expiration of the sixth year, so that one third may be chosen every second year; and if vacancies happen by resignation, or otherwise, during the recess of the legislature of any state, the executive thereof may make temporary appointments until the next meeting of the legislature, which shall then fill such vacancies.

No person shall be a Senator who shall not have attained to the age of thirty years, and been nine years a citizen of the United States and who shall not, when elected, be an inhabitant of that state for which he shall be chosen.

The Vice President of the United States shall be President of the Senate, but shall have no vote, unless they be equally divided.

The Senate shall choose their other officers, and also a President pro tempore, in the absence of the Vice President, or when he shall exercise the office of President of the United States.

The Senate shall have the sole power to try all impeachments. When sitting for that purpose, they shall be on oath or affirmation. When the President of the United States is tried, the Chief Justice shall preside: And no person shall be convicted without the concurrence of two thirds of the members present.

Judgment in cases of impeachment shall not extend further than to removal from office, and disqualification to hold and enjoy any office of honor, trust or profit under the United States: but the party convicted shall nevertheless be liable and subject to indictment, trial, judgment and punishment, according to law.

Section 4

The times, places and manner of holding elections for Senators and Representatives, shall be prescribed in each state by the legislature thereof; but the Congress may at any time by law make or alter such regulations, except as to the places of choosing Senators.

The Congress shall assemble at least once in every year, and such meeting shall be on the first Monday in December, unless they shall by law appoint a different day.

Section 5

Each House shall be the judge of the elections, returns and qualifications of its own members, and a majority of each shall constitute a quorum to do business; but a smaller number may adjourn from day to day, and may be authorized to compel the attendance of absent members, in such manner, and under such penalties as each House may provide.

Each House may determine the rules of its proceedings, punish its members for disorderly behavior, and, with the concurrence of two thirds, expel a member.

Each House shall keep a journal of its proceedings, and from time to time publish the same, excepting such parts as may in their judgment require secrecy; and the yeas and nays of the members of either House on any question shall, at the desire of one fifth of those present, be entered on the journal.

Neither House, during the session of Congress, shall, without the consent of the other, adjourn for more than three days, nor to any other place than that in which the two Houses shall be sitting.

Section 6

The Senators and Representatives shall receive a compensation for their services, to be ascertained by law, and paid out of the treasury of the United States. They shall in all cases, except treason, felony and breach of the peace, be privileged from arrest during their attendance at the session of their respective Houses, and in going to and returning from the same; and for any speech or debate in either House, they shall not be questioned in any other place.

No Senator or Representative shall, during the time for which he was elected, be appointed to any civil office under the authority of the United States, which shall have been created, or the emoluments whereof shall have been increased during such time: and no person holding any office under the United States, shall be a member of either House during his continuance in office.

Section 7

All bills for raising revenue shall originate in the House of Representatives; but the Senate may propose or concur with amendments as on other Bills.

Every bill which shall have passed the House of Representatives and the Senate, shall, before it become a law, be presented to the President of the United States; if he approve he shall sign it, but if not he shall return it, with his objections to that House in which it shall have originated, who shall enter the objections at large on their journal, and proceed to reconsider it. If after such reconsideration two thirds of that House shall agree to pass the bill, it shall be sent, together with the objections, to the other House, by which it shall likewise be reconsidered, and if approved by two thirds of that House, it shall become a law. But in all such cases the votes of both Houses shall be determined by yeas and nays, and the names of the persons voting for and against the bill shall be entered on the journal of each House respectively. If any bill shall not be returned by the President within ten days (Sundays excepted) after it shall have been presented to him, the same shall be a law, in like manner as if he had signed it, unless the Congress by their adjournment prevent its return, in which case it shall not be a law.

Every order, resolution, or vote to which the concurrence of the Senate and House of Representatives may be necessary (except on a question of adjournment) shall be presented to the President of the United States; and before the same shall take effect, shall be approved by him, or being disapproved by him, shall be repassed by two thirds of the Senate and House of Representatives, according to the rules and limitations prescribed in the case of a bill.

Section 8

The Congress shall have power to lay and collect taxes, duties, imposts and excises, to pay the debts and provide for the common defense and general welfare of the United States; but all duties, imposts and excises shall be uniform throughout the United States;

To borrow money on the credit of the United States;

To regulate commerce with foreign nations, and among the several states, and with the Indian tribes;

To establish a uniform rule of naturalization, and uniform laws on the subject of bankruptcies throughout the United States;

To coin money, regulate the value thereof, and of foreign coin, and fix the standard of weights and measures;

To provide for the punishment of counterfeiting the securities and current coin of the United States;

To establish post offices and post roads;

To promote the progress of science and useful arts, by securing for limited times to authors and inventors the exclusive right to their respective writings and discoveries;

To constitute tribunals inferior to the Supreme Court;

To define and punish piracies and felonies committed on the high seas, and offenses against the law of nations;

To declare war, grant letters of marque and reprisal, and make rules concerning captures on land and water;

To raise and support armies, but no appropriation of money to that use shall be for a longer term than two years;

To provide and maintain a navy;

To make rules for the government and regulation of the land and naval forces;

To provide for calling forth the militia to execute the laws of the union, suppress insurrections and repel invasions;

To provide for organizing, arming, and disciplining, the militia, and for governing such part of them as may be employed in the service of the United States, reserving to the states respectively, the appointment of the officers, and the authority of training the militia according to the discipline prescribed by Congress;

To exercise exclusive legislation in all cases whatsoever, over such District (not exceeding ten miles square) as may, by cession of particular states, and the acceptance of Congress, become the seat of the government of the United States, and to exercise like authority over all places purchased by the consent of the legislature of the state in which the same shall be, for the erection of forts, magazines, arsenals, dockyards, and other needful buildings;—And

To make all laws which shall be necessary and proper for carrying into execution the foregoing powers, and all other powers vested by this Constitution in the government of the United States, or in any department or officer thereof.

Section 9

The migration or importation of such persons as any of the states now existing shall think proper to admit, shall not be prohibited by the Congress prior to the year one thousand eight hundred and eight, but a tax or duty may be imposed on such importation, not exceeding ten dollars for each person.

The privilege of the writ of habeas corpus shall not be suspended, unless when in cases of rebellion or invasion the public safety may require it.

No bill of attainder or ex post facto Law shall be passed.

No capitation, or other direct, tax shall be laid, unless in proportion to the census or enumeration herein before directed to be taken.

No tax or duty shall be laid on articles exported from any state.

No preference shall be given by any regulation of commerce or revenue to the ports of one state over those of another: nor shall vessels bound to, or from, one state, be obliged to enter, clear or pay duties in another.

No money shall be drawn from the treasury, but in consequence of appropriations made by law; and a regular statement and account of receipts and expenditures of all public money shall be published from time to time.

No title of nobility shall be granted by the United States: and no person holding any office of profit or trust under them, shall, without the consent of the Congress, accept of any present, emolument, office, or title, of any kind whatever, from any king, prince, or foreign state.

Section 10

No state shall enter into any treaty, alliance, or confederation; grant letters of marque and reprisal; coin money; emit bills of credit; make anything but gold and silver coin a tender in payment of debts; pass any bill of attainder, ex post facto law, or law impairing the obligation of contracts, or grant any title of nobility.

No state shall, without the consent of the Congress, lay any imposts or duties on imports or exports, except what may be absolutely necessary for executing its inspection laws: and the net produce of all duties and imposts, laid by any state on imports or exports, shall be for the use of the treasury of the United States; and all such laws shall be subject to the revision and control of the Congress.

No state shall, without the consent of Congress, lay any duty of tonnage, keep troops, or ships of war in time of peace, enter into any agreement or compact with another state, or with a foreign power, or engage in war, unless actually invaded, or in such imminent danger as will not admit of delay.

Article II

Section 1

The executive power shall be vested in a President of the United States of America. He shall hold his office during the term of four years, and, together with the Vice President, chosen for the same term, be elected, as follows:

Each state shall appoint, in such manner as the Legislature thereof may direct, a number of electors, equal to the whole number of Senators and Representatives to which the State may be entitled in the Congress: but no Senator or Representative, or person holding an office of trust or profit under the United States, shall be appointed an elector.

The electors shall meet in their respective states, and vote by ballot for two persons, of whom one at least shall not be an inhabitant of the same state with themselves. And they shall make a list of all the persons voted for, and of the number of votes for each; which list they shall sign and certify, and transmit sealed to the seat of the government of the United States, directed to the President of the Senate. The President of the Senate shall, in the presence of the Senate and House of Representatives, open all the certificates, and the votes shall then be counted. The person having the greatest number of votes shall be the President, if such number be a majority of the whole number of electors appointed; and if there be more than one who have such majority, and have an equal number of votes, then the House of Representatives shall immediately choose by ballot one of them for President; and if no person have a majority, then from the five highest on the list the said House shall in like manner choose the President. But in choosing the President, the votes shall be taken by States, the representation from each state having one vote; A quorum for this purpose shall consist of a member or members from two thirds of the states, and a majority of all the states shall be necessary to a choice. In every case, after the choice of the President, the person having the greatest number of votes of the electors shall be the Vice President. But if there should remain two or more who have equal votes, the Senate shall choose from them by ballot the Vice President.

The Congress may determine the time of choosing the electors, and the day on which they shall give their votes; which day shall be the same throughout the United States.

No person except a natural born citizen, or a citizen of the United States, at the time of the adoption of this Constitution, shall be eligible to the office of President; neither shall any person be eligible to that office who shall not have attained to the age of thirty five years, and been fourteen Years a resident within the United States.

In case of the removal of the President from office, or of his death, resignation, or inability to discharge the powers and duties of the said office, the same shall devolve on the Vice President, and the Congress may by law provide for the case of removal, death, resignation or inability, both of the President and Vice President, declaring what officer shall then act as President, and such officer shall act accordingly, until the disability be removed, or a President shall be elected.

The President shall, at stated times, receive for his services, a compensation, which shall neither be increased nor diminished during the period for which he shall have been elected, and he shall not receive within that period any other emolument from the United States, or any of them.

Before he enter on the execution of his office, he shall take the following oath or affirmation:—"I do solemnly swear (or affirm) that I will faithfully execute the office of President of the United States, and will to the best of my ability, preserve, protect and defend the Constitution of the United States."

Section 2

The President shall be commander in chief of the Army and Navy of the United States, and of the militia of the several states, when called into the actual service of the United States; he may require the opinion, in writing, of the principal officer in each of the executive departments, upon any subject relating to the duties of their respective offices, and he shall have power to grant reprieves and pardons for offenses against the United States, except in cases of impeachment.

He shall have power, by and with the advice and consent of the Senate, to make treaties, provided two thirds of the Senators present concur; and he shall nominate, and by and with the advice and consent of the Senate, shall appoint ambassadors, other public ministers and consuls, judges of the Supreme Court, and all other officers of the United States, whose appointments are not herein otherwise provided for, and which shall be established by law: but the Congress may by law vest the appointment of such inferior officers, as they think proper, in the President alone, in the courts of law, or in the heads of departments.

The President shall have power to fill up all vacancies that may happen during the recess of the Senate, by granting commissions which shall expire at the end of their next session.

Section 3

He shall from time to time give to the Congress information of the state of the union, and recommend to their consideration such measures as he shall judge necessary and expedient; he may, on extraordinary occasions, convene both Houses, or either of them, and in case of disagreement between them, with respect to the time of adjournment, he may adjourn them to such time as he shall think proper; he shall receive ambassadors and other public ministers; he shall take care that the laws be faithfully executed, and shall commission all the officers of the United States.

Section 4

The President, Vice President and all civil officers of the United States, shall be removed from office on impeachment for, and conviction of, treason, bribery, or other high crimes and misdemeanors.

Article III

Section 1

The judicial power of the United States, shall be vested in one Supreme Court, and in such inferior courts as the Congress may from time to time ordain and establish. The judges, both of the supreme and inferior courts, shall hold their offices during good behaviour, and shall, at stated times, receive for their services, a compensation, which shall not be diminished during their continuance in office.

Section 2

The judicial power shall extend to all cases, in law and equity, arising under this Constitution, the laws of the United States, and treaties made, or which shall be made, under their authority;—to all cases affecting ambassadors, other public ministers and consuls;—to all cases of admiralty and maritime jurisdiction;—to controversies to which the United States shall be a party;—to controversies between two or more states;—between a state and citizens of another state;—between citizens of different states;—between citizens of the same state claiming lands under grants of different states, and between a state, or the citizens thereof, and foreign states, citizens or subjects.

In all cases affecting ambassadors, other public ministers and consuls, and those in which a state shall be party, the Supreme Court shall have original jurisdiction. In all the other cases before mentioned, the Supreme Court shall have appellate jurisdiction, both as to law and fact, with such exceptions, and under such regulations as the Congress shall make.

The trial of all crimes, except in cases of impeachment, shall be by jury; and such trial shall be held in the state where the said crimes shall have been committed; but when not committed within any state, the trial shall be at such place or places as the Congress may by law have directed.

Section 3

Treason against the United States, shall consist only in levying war against them, or in adhering to their enemies, giving them aid and comfort. No person shall be convicted of treason unless on the testimony of two witnesses to the same overt act, or on confession in open court.

The Congress shall have power to declare the punishment of treason, but no attainder of treason shall work corruption of blood, or forfeiture except during the life of the person attainted.

Article IV

Section 1

Full faith and credit shall be given in each state to the public acts, records, and judicial proceedings of every other state. And the Congress may by general laws prescribe the manner in which such acts, records, and proceedings shall be proved, and the effect thereof.

Section 2

The citizens of each state shall be entitled to all privileges and immunities of citizens in the several states.

A person charged in any state with treason, felony, or other crime, who shall flee from justice, and be found in another state, shall on demand of the executive authority of the state from which he fled, be delivered up, to be removed to the state having jurisdiction of the crime.

No person held to service or labor in one state, under the laws thereof, escaping into another, shall, in consequence of any law or regulation therein, be discharged from such service or labor, but shall be delivered up on claim of the party to whom such service or labor may be due.

Section 3

New states may be admitted by the Congress into this union; but no new states shall be formed or erected within the jurisdiction of any other state; nor any state be formed by the junction of two or more states, or parts of states, without the consent of the legislatures of the states concerned as well as of the Congress.

The Congress shall have power to dispose of and make all needful rules and regulations respecting the territory or other property belonging to the United States; and nothing in this Constitution shall be so construed as to prejudice any claims of the United States, or of any particular state.

Section 4

The United States shall guarantee to every state in this union a republican form of government, and shall protect each of them against invasion; and on application of the legislature, or of the executive (when the legislature cannot be convened) against domestic violence.

Article V

The Congress, whenever two thirds of both houses shall deem it necessary, shall propose amendments to this Constitution, or, on the application of the legislatures of two thirds of the several states, shall call a convention for proposing amendments, which, in either case, shall be valid to all intents and purposes, as part of this Constitution, when ratified by the legislatures of three fourths of the several states, or by conventions in three fourths thereof, as the one or the other mode of ratification may be proposed by the Congress; provided that no amendment which may be made prior to the year one thousand eight hundred and eight shall in any manner affect the first and fourth clauses in the ninth section of the first article; and that no state, without its consent, shall be deprived of its equal suffrage in the Senate.

Article VI

All debts contracted and engagements entered into, before the adoption of this Constitution, shall be as valid against the United States under this Constitution, as under the Confederation.

This Constitution, and the laws of the United States which shall be made in pursuance thereof; and all treaties made, or which shall be made, under the authority of the United States, shall be the supreme law of the land; and the judges in every state shall be bound thereby, anything in the Constitution or laws of any State to the contrary notwithstanding.

The Senators and Representatives before mentioned, and the members of the several state legislatures, and all executive and judicial officers, both of the United States and of the several states, shall be bound by oath or affirmation, to support this Constitution; but no religious test shall ever be required as a qualification to any office or public trust under the United States.

Article VII

The ratification of the conventions of nine states, shall be sufficient for the establishment of this Constitution between the states so ratifying the same.

Done in convention by the unanimous consent of the states present the seventeenth day of September in the year of our Lord one thousand seven hundred and eighty seven and of the independence of the United States of America the twelfth. In witness whereof We have hereunto subscribed our Names,

G. Washington-Presidt. and deputy from Virginia
New Hampshire: John Langdon, Nicholas Gilman
Massachusetts: Nathaniel Gorham, Rufus King
Connecticut: Wm: Saml. Johnson, Roger Sherman
New York: Alexander Hamilton
New Jersey: Wil: Livingston, David Brearly, Wm. Paterson, Jona: Dayton
Pennsylvania: B. Franklin, Thomas Mifflin, Robt. Morris, Geo. Clymer, Thos. Fitz-Simons, Jared Ingersoll, James Wilson, Gouv Morris
Delaware: Geo: Read, Gunning Bedford jun, John Dickinson, Richard Bassett, Jaco: Broom
Maryland: James McHenry, Dan of St Thos. Jenifer, Danl Carroll
Virginia: John Blair—, James Madison Jr.
North Carolina: Wm. Blount, Richd. Dobbs Spaight, Hu Williamson
South Carolina: J. Rutledge, Charles Cotesworth Pinckney, Charles Pinckney, Pierce Butler
Georgia: William Few, Abr Baldwin

The Bill of Rights

Amendments 1-10 of the Constitution

(1791)

Amendment I

Congress shall make no law respecting an establishment of religion, or prohibiting the free exercise thereof; or abridging the freedom of speech, or of the press; or the right of the people peaceably to assemble, and to petition the government for a redress of grievances.

Amendment II

A well regulated militia, being necessary to the security of a free state, the right of the people to keep and bear arms, shall not be infringed.

Amendment III

No soldier shall, in time of peace be quartered in any house, without the consent of the owner, nor in time of war, but in a manner to be prescribed by law.

Amendment IV

The right of the people to be secure in their persons, houses, papers, and effects, against unreasonable searches and seizures, shall not be violated, and no warrants shall issue, but upon probable cause, supported by oath or affirmation, and particularly describing the place to be searched, and the persons or things to be seized.

Amendment V

No person shall be held to answer for a capital, or otherwise infamous crime, unless on a presentment or indictment of a grand jury, except in cases arising in the land or naval forces, or in the militia, when in actual service in time of war or public danger; nor shall any person be subject for the same offense to be twice put in jeopardy of life or limb; nor shall be compelled in any criminal case to be a witness against himself, nor be deprived of life, liberty, or property, without due process of law; nor shall private property be taken for public use, without just compensation.

Amendment VI

In all criminal prosecutions, the accused shall enjoy the right to a speedy and public trial, by an impartial jury of the state and district wherein the crime shall have been committed, which district shall have been previously ascertained by law, and to be informed of the nature and cause of the accusation; to be confronted with the witnesses against him; to have compulsory process for obtaining witnesses in his favor, and to have the assistance of counsel for his defense.

Amendment VII

In suits at common law, where the value in controversy shall exceed twenty dollars, the right of trial by jury shall be preserved, and no fact tried by a jury, shall be otherwise reexamined in any court of the United States, than according to the rules of the common law.

Amendment VIII

Excessive bail shall not be required, nor excessive fines imposed, nor cruel and unusual punishments inflicted.

Amendment IX

The enumeration in the Constitution, of certain rights, shall not be construed to deny or disparage others retained by the people.

Amendment X

The powers not delegated to the United States by the Constitution, nor prohibited by it to the states, are reserved to the states respectively, or to the people.

Amendment XI

(1798)

The judicial power of the United States shall not be construed to extend to any suit in law or equity, commenced or prosecuted against one of the United States by citizens of another state, or by citizens or subjects of any foreign state.

Amendment XII

(1804)

The electors shall meet in their respective states and vote by ballot for President and Vice-President, one of whom, at least, shall not be an inhabitant of the same state with themselves; they shall name in their ballots the person voted for as President, and in distinct ballots the person voted for as Vice-President, and they shall make distinct lists of all persons voted for as President, and of all persons voted for as Vice-President, and of the number of votes for each, which lists they shall sign and certify, and transmit sealed to the seat of the government of the United States, directed to the President of the Senate;—The President of the Senate shall, in the presence of the Senate and House of Representatives, open all the certificates and the votes shall then be counted;—the person having the greatest number of votes for President, shall be the President, if such number be a majority of the whole number of electors appointed; and if no person have such majority, then from the persons having the highest numbers not exceeding three on the list of those voted for as President, the House of Representatives shall choose immediately, by ballot, the President. But in choosing the President, the votes shall be taken by states, the representation from each state having one vote; a quorum for this purpose shall consist of a member or members from two-thirds of the states, and a majority of all the states shall be necessary to a choice. And if the House of Representatives shall not choose a President whenever the right of choice shall devolve upon them, before the fourth day of March next following, then the Vice-President shall act as President, as in the case of the death or other constitutional disability of the President. The person having the greatest number of votes as Vice-President, shall be the Vice-President, if such number be a majority of the whole number of electors appointed, and if no person have a majority, then from the two highest numbers on the list, the Senate shall choose the Vice-President; a quorum for the purpose shall consist of two-thirds of the whole number of Senators, and a majority of the whole number shall be necessary to a choice. But no person constitutionally ineligible to the office of President shall be eligible to that of Vice-President of the United States.

Amendment XIII

(1865)

Section 1

Neither slavery nor involuntary servitude, except as a punishment for crime whereof the party shall have been duly convicted, shall exist within the United States, or any place subject to their jurisdiction.

Section 2

Congress shall have power to enforce this article by appropriate legislation.

Amendment XIV

(1868)

Section 1

All persons born or naturalized in the United States, and subject to the jurisdiction thereof, are citizens of the United States and of the state wherein they reside. No state shall make or enforce any law which shall abridge the privileges or immunities of citizens of the United States; nor shall any state deprive any person of life, liberty, or property, without due process of law; nor deny to any person within its jurisdiction the equal protection of the laws.

Section 2

Representatives shall be apportioned among the several states according to their respective numbers, counting the whole number of persons in each state, excluding Indians not taxed. But when the right to vote at any election for the choice of electors for President and Vice President of the United States, Representatives in Congress, the executive and judicial officers of a state, or the members of the legislature thereof, is denied to any of the male inhabitants of such state, being twenty-one years of age, and citizens of the United States, or in any way abridged, except for participation in rebellion, or other crime, the basis of representation therein shall be reduced in the proportion which the number of such male citizens shall bear to the whole number of male citizens twenty-one years of age in such state.

Section 3

No person shall be a Senator or Representative in Congress, or elector of President and Vice President, or hold any office, civil or military, under the United States, or under any state, who, having previously taken an oath, as a member of Congress, or as an officer of the United States, or as a member of any state legislature, or as an executive or judicial officer of any state, to support the Constitution of the United States, shall have engaged in insurrection or rebellion against the same, or given aid or comfort to the enemies thereof. But Congress may by a vote of two-thirds of each House, remove such disability.

Section 4

The validity of the public debt of the United States, authorized by law, including debts incurred for payment of pensions and bounties for services in suppressing insurrection or rebellion, shall not be questioned. But neither the United States nor any state shall assume or pay any debt or obligation incurred in aid of insurrection or rebellion against the United States, or any claim for the loss or emancipation of any slave; but all such debts, obligations and claims shall be held illegal and void.

Section 5

The Congress shall have power to enforce, by appropriate legislation, the provisions of this article.

Amendment XV

(1870)

Section 1

The right of citizens of the United States to vote shall not be denied or abridged by the United States or by any state on account of race, color, or previous condition of servitude.

Section 2

The Congress shall have power to enforce this article by appropriate legislation.

Amendment XVI

(1913)

The Congress shall have power to lay and collect taxes on incomes, from whatever source derived, without apportionment among the several states, and without regard to any census of enumeration.

Amendment XVII

(1913)

The Senate of the United States shall be composed of two Senators from each state, elected by the people thereof, for six years; and each Senator shall have one vote. The electors in each state shall have the qualifications requisite for electors of the most numerous branch of the state legislatures.

When vacancies happen in the representation of any state in the Senate, the executive authority of such state shall issue writs of election to fill such vacancies: Provided, that the legislature of any state may empower the executive thereof to make temporary appointments until the people fill the vacancies by election as the legislature may direct.

This amendment shall not be so construed as to affect the election or term of any Senator chosen before it becomes valid as part of the Constitution.

Amendment XVIII

(1919)

Section 1

After one year from the ratification of this article the manufacture, sale, or transportation of intoxicating liquors within, the importation thereof into, or the exportation thereof from the United States and all territory subject to the jurisdiction thereof for beverage purposes is hereby prohibited.

Section 2

The Congress and the several states shall have concurrent power to enforce this article by appropriate legislation.

Section 3

This article shall be inoperative unless it shall have been ratified as an amendment to the Constitution by the legislatures of the several states, as provided in the Constitution, within seven years from the date of the submission hereof to the states by the Congress.

Amendment XIX

(1920)

The right of citizens of the United States to vote shall not be denied or abridged by the United States or by any state on account of sex.

Congress shall have power to enforce this article by appropriate legislation.

Amendment XX

(1933)

Section 1

The terms of the President and Vice President shall end at noon on the 20th day of January, and the terms of Senators and Representatives at noon on the 3d day of January, of the years in which such terms would have ended if this article had not been ratified; and the terms of their successors shall then begin.

Section 2

The Congress shall assemble at least once in every year, and such meeting shall begin at noon on the 3d day of January, unless they shall by law appoint a different day.

Section 3

If, at the time fixed for the beginning of the term of the President, the President elect shall have died, the Vice President elect shall become President. If a President shall not have been chosen before the time fixed for the beginning of his term, or if the President elect shall have failed to qualify, then the Vice President elect shall act as President until a President shall have qualified; and the Congress may by law provide for the case wherein neither a President elect nor a Vice President elect shall have qualified, declaring who shall then act as President, or the manner in which one who is to act shall be selected, and such person shall act accordingly until a President or Vice President shall have qualified.

Section 4

The Congress may by law provide for the case of the death of any of the persons from whom the House of Representatives may choose a President whenever the right of choice shall have devolved upon them, and for the case of the death of any of the persons from whom the Senate may choose a Vice President whenever the right of choice shall have devolved upon them.

Section 5

Sections 1 and 2 shall take effect on the 15th day of October following the ratification of this article.

Section 6

This article shall be inoperative unless it shall have been ratified as an amendment to the Constitution by the legislatures of three-fourths of the several states within seven years from the date of its submission.

Amendment XXI

(1933)

Section 1

The eighteenth article of amendment to the Constitution of the United States is hereby repealed.

Section 2

The transportation or importation into any state, territory, or possession of the United States for delivery or use therein of intoxicating liquors, in violation of the laws thereof, is hereby prohibited.

Section 3

This article shall be inoperative unless it shall have been ratified as an amendment to the Constitution by conventions in the several states, as provided in the Constitution, within seven years from the date of the submission hereof to the states by the Congress.

Amendment XXII

(1951)

Section 1

No person shall be elected to the office of the President more than twice, and no person who has held the office of President, or acted as President, for more than two years of a term to which some other person was elected President shall be elected to the office of the President more than once. But this article shall not apply to any person holding the office of President when this article was proposed by the Congress, and shall not prevent any person who may be holding the office of President, or acting as President, during the term within which this article becomes operative from holding the office of President or acting as President during the remainder of such term.

Section 2

This article shall be inoperative unless it shall have been ratified as an amendment to the Constitution by the legislatures of three-fourths of the several states within seven years from the date of its submission to the states by the Congress.

Amendment XXIII

(1961)

Section 1

The District constituting the seat of government of the United States shall appoint in such manner as the Congress may direct:

A number of electors of President and Vice President equal to the whole number of Senators and Representatives in Congress to which the District would be entitled if it were a state, but in no event more than the least populous state; they shall be in addition to those appointed by the states, but they shall be considered, for the purposes of the election of President and Vice President, to be electors appointed by a state; and they shall meet in the District and perform such duties as provided by the twelfth article of amendment.

Section 2

The Congress shall have power to enforce this article by appropriate legislation.

Amendment XXIV

(1964)

Section 1

The right of citizens of the United States to vote in any primary or other election for President or Vice President, for electors for President or Vice President, or for Senator or

Representative in Congress, shall not be denied or abridged by the United States or any state by reason of failure to pay any poll tax or other tax.

Section 2

The Congress shall have power to enforce this article by appropriate legislation.

Amendment XXV

(1967)

Section 1

In case of the removal of the President from office or of his death or resignation, the Vice President shall become President.

Section 2

Whenever there is a vacancy in the office of the Vice President, the President shall nominate a Vice President who shall take office upon confirmation by a majority vote of both Houses of Congress.

Section 3

Whenever the President transmits to the President pro tempore of the Senate and the Speaker of the House of Representatives his written declaration that he is unable to discharge the powers and duties of his office, and until he transmits to them a written declaration to the contrary, such powers and duties shall be discharged by the Vice President as Acting President.

Section 4

Whenever the Vice President and a majority of either the principal officers of the executive departments or of such other body as Congress may by law provide, transmit to the President pro tempore of the Senate and the Speaker of the House of Representatives their written declaration that the President is unable to discharge the powers and duties of his office, the Vice President shall immediately assume the powers and duties of the office as Acting President.

Thereafter, when the President transmits to the President pro tempore of the Senate and the Speaker of the House of Representatives his written declaration that no inability exists, he shall resume the powers and duties of his office unless the Vice President and a majority of either the principal officers of the executive department or of such other body as Congress may by law provide, transmit within four days to the President pro tempore of the Senate and the Speaker of the House of Representatives their written declaration that the President is unable to discharge the powers and duties of his office. Thereupon Congress shall decide the issue, assembling within forty-eight hours for that purpose if not in session. If the Congress, within twenty-one days after receipt of the latter written declaration, or, if Congress is not in session, within twenty-one days after Congress is required to assemble, determines by two-thirds vote of both Houses that the President is unable to discharge the powers and duties of his office, the Vice President shall continue to discharge the same as Acting President; otherwise, the President shall resume the powers and duties of his office.

Amendment XXVI

(1971)

Section 1

The right of citizens of the United States, who are 18 years of age or older, to vote, shall not be denied or abridged by the United States or any state on account of age.

Section 2

The Congress shall have the power to enforce this article by appropriate legislation.

Amendment XXVII

(1992)

No law varying the compensation for the services of the Senators and Representatives shall take effect until an election of Representatives shall have intervened.

Historical Documents

THE MAGNA CARTA
(The Great Charter)

Preamble:

John, by the grace of God, king of England, lord of Ireland, duke of Normandy and Aquitaine, and count of Anjou, to the archbishop, bishops, abbots, earls, barons, justiciaries, foresters, sheriffs, stewards, servants, and to all his bailiffs and liege subjects, greetings. Know that, having regard to God and for the salvation of our soul, and those of all our ancestors and heirs, and unto the honor of God and the advancement of his holy Church and for the rectifying of our realm, we have granted as underwritten by advice of our venerable fathers, Stephen, archbishop of Canterbury, primate of all England and cardinal of the holy Roman Church, Henry, archbishop of Dublin, William of London, Peter of Winchester, Jocelyn of Bath and Glastonbury, Hugh of Lincoln, Walter of Worcester, William of Coventry, Benedict of Rochester, bishops; of Master Pandulf, subdeacon and member of the household of our lord the Pope, of brother Aymeric (master of the Knights of the Temple in England), and of the illustrious men William Marshal, earl of Pembroke, William, earl of Salisbury, William, earl of Warenne, William, earl of Arundel, Alan of Galloway (constable of Scotland), Waren Fitz Gerold, Peter Fitz Herbert, Hubert De Burgh (seneschal of Poitou), Hugh de Neville, Matthew Fitz Herbert, Thomas Basset, Alan Basset, Philip d'Aubigny, Robert of Roppesley, John Marshal, John Fitz Hugh, and others, our liegemen.

1. In the first place we have granted to God, and by this our present charter confirmed for us and our heirs forever that the English Church shall be free, and shall have her rights entire, and her liberties inviolate; and we will that it be thus observed; which is apparent from this that the freedom of elections, which is reckoned most important and very essential to the English Church, we, of our pure and unconstrained will, did grant, and did by our charter confirm and did obtain the ratification of the same from our lord, Pope Innocent III, before the quarrel arose between us and our barons: and this we will observe, and our will is that it be observed in good faith by our heirs forever. We have also granted to all freemen of our kingdom, for us and our heirs forever, all the underwritten liberties, to be had and held by them and their heirs, of us and our heirs forever.

2. If any of our earls or barons, or others holding of us in chief by military service shall have died, and at the time of his death his heir shall be full of age and owe "relief", he shall have his inheritance by the old relief, to wit, the heir or heirs of an earl, for the whole barony of an earl by L100; the heir or heirs of a baron, L100 for a whole barony; the heir or heirs of a knight, 100s, at most, and whoever owes less let him give less, according to the ancient custom of fees.

3. If, however, the heir of any one of the aforesaid has been under age and in wardship, let him have his inheritance without relief and without fine when he comes of age.

4. The guardian of the land of an heir who is thus under age, shall take from the land of the heir nothing but reasonable produce, reasonable customs, and reasonable services, and that without destruction or waste of men or goods; and if we have committed the wardship of the lands of any such minor to the sheriff, or to any other who is responsible to us for its issues, and he has made destruction or waster of what he holds in wardship, we will take of him amends, and the land shall be committed to two lawful and discreet men of that fee, who shall be responsible for the issues to us or to him to whom we shall assign them; and if we have given or sold the wardship of any such land to anyone and he has therein made destruction or waste, he shall lose that wardship, and it shall be transferred to two lawful and discreet men of that fief, who shall be responsible to us in like manner as aforesaid.

5. The guardian, moreover, so long as he has the wardship of the land, shall keep up the houses, parks, fishponds, stanks, mills, and other things pertaining to the land, out of the issues of the same land; and he shall restore to the heir, when he has come to full age, all his land, stocked with ploughs and wainage, according as the season of husbandry shall require, and the issues of the land can reasonable bear.

6. Heirs shall be married without disparagement, yet so that before the marriage takes place the nearest in blood to that heir shall have notice.

7. A widow, after the death of her husband, shall forthwith and without difficulty have her marriage portion and inheritance; nor shall she give anything for her dower, or for her marriage portion, or for the inheritance which her husband and she held on the day of the death of that husband; and she may remain in the house of her husband for forty days after his death, within which time her dower shall be assigned to her.

8. No widow shall be compelled to marry, so long as she prefers to live without a husband; provided always that she gives security not to marry without our consent, if she holds of us, or without the consent of the lord of whom she holds, if she holds of another.

9. Neither we nor our bailiffs will seize any land or rent for any debt, as long as the chattels of the debtor are sufficient to repay the debt; nor shall the sureties of the debtor be distrained so long as the principal debtor is able to satisfy the debt; and if the principal debtor shall fail to pay the debt, having nothing wherewith to pay it, then the sureties shall answer for the debt; and let them have the lands and rents of the debtor, if they desire them, until they are indemnified for the debt which they have paid for him, unless the principal debtor can show proof that he is discharged thereof as against the said sureties.

10. If one who has borrowed from the Jews any sum, great or small, die before that loan be repaid, the debt shall not bear interest while the heir is under age, of whomsoever he may hold; and if the debt fall into our hands, we will not take anything except the principal sum contained in the bond.

11. And if anyone die indebted to the Jews, his wife shall have her dower and pay nothing of that debt; and if any children of the deceased are left under age, necessaries shall be provided for them in keeping with the holding of the deceased; and out of the residue the debt shall be paid, reserving, however, service due to feudal lords; in like manner let it be done touching debts due to others than Jews.

12. No scutage not aid shall be imposed on our kingdom, unless by common counsel of our kingdom, except for ransoming our person, for making our eldest son a knight,

and for once marrying our eldest daughter; and for these there shall not be levied more than a reasonable aid. In like manner it shall be done concerning aids from the city of London.

13. And the city of London shall have all it ancient liberties and free customs, as well by land as by water; furthermore, we decree and grant that all other cities, boroughs, towns, and ports shall have all their liberties and free customs.

14. And for obtaining the common counsel of the kingdom anent the assessing of an aid (except in the three cases aforesaid) or of a scutage, we will cause to be summoned the archbishops, bishops, abbots, earls, and greater barons, severally by our letters; and we will moveover cause to be summoned generally, through our sheriffs and bailiffs, and others who hold of us in chief, for a fixed date, namely, after the expiry of at least forty days, and at a fixed place; and in all letters of such summons we will specify the reason of the summons. And when the summons has thus been made, the business shall proceed on the day appointed, according to the counsel of such as are present, although not all who were summoned have come.

15. We will not for the future grant to anyone license to take an aid from his own free tenants, except to ransom his person, to make his eldest son a knight, and once to marry his eldest daughter; and on each of these occasions there shall be levied only a reasonable aid.

16. No one shall be distrained for performance of greater service for a knight's fee, or for any other free tenement, than is due therefrom.

17. Common pleas shall not follow our court, but shall be held in some fixed place.

18. Inquests of novel disseisin, of mort d'ancestor, and of darrein presentment shall not be held elsewhere than in their own county courts, and that in manner following; We, or, if we should be out of the realm, our chief justiciar, will send two justiciaries through every county four times a year, who shall alone with four knights of the county chosen by the county, hold the said assizes in the county court, on the day and in the place of meeting of that court.

19. And if any of the said assizes cannot be taken on the day of the county court, let there remain of the knights and freeholders, who were present at the county court on that day, as many as may be required for the efficient making of judgments, according as the business be more or less.

20. A freeman shall not be amerced for a slight offense, except in accordance with the degree of the offense; and for a grave offense he shall be amerced in accordance with the gravity of the offense, yet saving always his "contentment"; and a merchant in the same way, saving his "merchandise"; and a villein shall be amerced in the same way, saving his "wainage" if they have fallen into our mercy: and none of the aforesaid amercements shall be imposed except by the oath of honest men of the neighborhood.

21. Earls and barons shall not be amerced except through their peers, and only in accordance with the degree of the offense.

22. A clerk shall not be amerced in respect of his lay holding except after the manner of the others aforesaid; further, he shall not be amerced in accordance with the extent of his ecclesiastical benefice.

23. No village or individual shall be compelled to make bridges at river banks, except those who from of old were legally bound to do so.

24. No sheriff, constable, coroners, or others of our bailiffs, shall hold pleas of our Crown.

25. All counties, hundred, wapentakes, and trithings (except our demesne manors) shall remain at the old rents, and without any additional payment.

26. If anyone holding of us a lay fief shall die, and our sheriff or bailiff shall exhibit our letters patent of summons for a debt which the deceased owed us, it shall be lawful for our sheriff or bailiff to attach and enroll the chattels of the deceased, found upon the lay fief, to the value of that debt, at the sight of law worthy men, provided always that nothing whatever be thence removed until the debt which is evident shall be fully paid to us; and the residue shall be left to the executors to fulfill the will of the deceased; and if there be nothing due from him to us, all the chattels shall go to the deceased, saving to his wife and children their reasonable shares.

27. If any freeman shall die intestate, his chattels shall be distributed by the hands of his nearest kinsfolk and friends, under supervision of the Church, saving to every one the debts which the deceased owed to him.

28. No constable or other bailiff of ours shall take corn or other provisions from anyone without immediately tendering money therefor, unless he can have postponement thereof by permission of the seller.

29. No constable shall compel any knight to give money in lieu of castle-guard, when he is willing to perform it in his own person, or (if he himself cannot do it from any reasonable cause) then by another responsible man. Further, if we have led or sent him upon military service, he shall be relieved from guard in proportion to the time during which he has been on service because of us.

30. No sheriff or bailiff of ours, or other person, shall take the horses or carts of any freeman for transport duty, against the will of the said freeman.

31. Neither we nor our bailiffs shall take, for our castles or for any other work of ours, wood which is not ours, against the will of the owner of that wood.

32. We will not retain beyond one year and one day, the lands those who have been convicted of felony, and the lands shall thereafter be handed over to the lords of the fiefs.

33. All kydells for the future shall be removed altogether from Thames and Medway, and throughout all England, except upon the seashore.

34. The writ which is called praecipe shall not for the future be issued to anyone, regarding any tenement whereby a freeman may lose his court.

35. Let there be one measure of wine throughout our whole realm; and one measure of ale; and one measure of corn, to wit, "the London quarter"; and one width of cloth (whether dyed, or russet, or "halberget"), to wit, two ells within the selvedges; of weights also let it be as of measures.

36. Nothing in future shall be given or taken for a writ of inquisition of life or limbs, but freely it shall be granted, and never denied.

37. If anyone holds of us by fee-farm, either by socage or by burage, or of any other land by knight's service, we will not (by reason of that fee-farm, socage, or burgage), have the wardship of the heir, or of such land of his as if of the fief of that other; nor shall we have wardship of that fee-farm, socage, or burgage, unless such fee-farm owes knight's service. We will not by reason of any small serjeancy which anyone may hold of us by the service of rendering to us knives, arrows, or the like, have wardship of his heir or of the land which he holds of another lord by knight's service.

38. No bailiff for the future shall, upon his own unsupported complaint, put anyone to his "law", without credible witnesses brought for this purposes.

39. No freemen shall be taken or imprisoned or disseised or exiled or in any way destroyed, nor will we go upon him nor send upon him, except by the lawful judgment of his peers or by the law of the land.

40. To no one will we sell, to no one will we refuse or delay, right or justice.
41. All merchants shall have safe and secure exit from England, and entry to England, with the right to tarry there and to move about as well by land as by water, for buying and selling by the ancient and right customs, quit from all evil tolls, except (in time of war) such merchants as are of the land at war with us. And if such are found in our land at the beginning of the war, they shall be detained, without injury to their bodies or goods, until information be received by us, or by our chief justiciar, how the merchants of our land found in the land at war with us are treated; and if our men are safe there, the others shall be safe in our land.
42. It shall be lawful in future for anyone (excepting always those imprisoned or outlawed in accordance with the law of the kingdom, and natives of any country at war with us, and merchants, who shall be treated as if above provided) to leave our kingdom and to return, safe and secure by land and water, except for a short period in time of war, on grounds of public policy- reserving always the allegiance due to us.
43. If anyone holding of some escheat (such as the honor of Wallingford, Nottingham, Boulogne, Lancaster, or of other escheats which are in our hands and are baronies) shall die, his heir shall give no other relief, and perform no other service to us than he would have done to the baron if that barony had been in the baron's hand; and we shall hold it in the same manner in which the baron held it.
44. Men who dwell without the forest need not henceforth come before our justiciaries of the forest upon a general summons, unless they are in plea, or sureties of one or more, who are attached for the forest.
45. We will appoint as justices, constables, sheriffs, or bailiffs only such as know the law of the realm and mean to observe it well.
46. All barons who have founded abbeys, concerning which they hold charters from the kings of England, or of which they have long continued possession, shall have the wardship of them, when vacant, as they ought to have.
47. All forests that have been made such in our time shall forthwith be disafforsted; and a similar course shall be followed with regard to river banks that have been placed "in defense" by us in our time.
48. All evil customs connected with forests and warrens, foresters and warreners, sheriffs and their officers, river banks and their wardens, shall immediately by inquired into in each county by twelve sworn knights of the same county chosen by the honest men of the same county, and shall, within forty days of the said inquest, be utterly abolished, so as never to be restored, provided always that we previously have intimation thereof, or our justiciar, if we should not be in England.
49. We will immediately restore all hostages and charters delivered to us by Englishmen, as sureties of the peace of faithful service.
50. We will entirely remove from their bailiwicks, the relations of Gerard of Athee (so that in future they shall have no bailiwick in England); namely, Engelard of Cigogne, Peter, Guy, and Andrew of Chanceaux, Guy of Cigogne, Geoffrey of Martigny with his brothers, Philip Mark with his brothers and his nephew Geoffrey, and the whole brood of the same.
51. As soon as peace is restored, we will banish from the kingdom all foreign born knights, crossbowmen, serjeants, and mercenary soldiers who have come with horses and arms to the kingdom's hurt.
52. If anyone has been dispossessed or removed by us, without the legal judgment of his peers, from his lands, castles, franchises, or from his right, we will immediately restore them to him; and if a dispute arise over this, then let it be decided by the

five and twenty barons of whom mention is made below in the clause for securing the peace. Moreover, for all those possessions, from which anyone has, without the lawful judgment of his peers, been disseised or removed, by our father, King Henry, or by our brother, King Richard, and which we retain in our hand (or which as possessed by others, to whom we are bound to warrant them) we shall have respite until the usual term of crusaders; excepting those things about which a plea has been raised, or an inquest made by our order, before our taking of the cross; but as soon as we return from the expedition, we will immediately grant full justice therein.

53. We shall have, moreover, the same respite and in the same manner in rendering justice concerning the disafforestation or retention of those forests which Henry our father and Richard our brother afforested, and concerning the wardship of lands which are of the fief of another (namely, such wardships as we have hitherto had by reason of a fief which anyone held of us by knight's service), and concerning abbeys founded on other fiefs than our own, in which the lord of the fee claims to have right; and when we have returned, or if we desist from our expedition, we will immediately grant full justice to all who complain of such things.

54. No one shall be arrested or imprisoned upon the appeal of a woman, for the death of any other than her husband.

55. All fines made with us unjustly and against the law of the land, and all amercements, imposed unjustly and against the law of the land, shall be entirely remitted, or else it shall be done concerning them according to the decision of the five and twenty barons whom mention is made below in the clause for securing the pease, or according to the judgment of the majority of the same, along with the aforesaid Stephen, archbishop of Canterbury, if he can be present, and such others as he may wish to bring with him for this purpose, and if he cannot be present the business shall nevertheless proceed without him, provided always that if any one or more of the aforesaid five and twenty barons are in a similar suit, they shall be removed as far as concerns this particular judgment, others being substituted in their places after having been selected by the rest of the same five and twenty for this purpose only, and after having been sworn.

56. If we have disseised or removed Welshmen from lands or liberties, or other things, without the legal judgment of their peers in England or in Wales, they shall be immediately restored to them; and if a dispute arise over this, then let it be decided in the marches by the judgment of their peers; for the tenements in England according to the law of England, for tenements in Wales according to the law of Wales, and for tenements in the marches according to the law of the marches. Welshmen shall do the same to us and ours.

57. Further, for all those possessions from which any Welshman has, without the lawful judgment of his peers, been disseised or removed by King Henry our father, or King Richard our brother, and which we retain in our hand (or which are possessed by others, and which we ought to warrant), we will have respite until the usual term of crusaders; excepting those things about which a plea has been raised or an inquest made by our order before we took the cross; but as soon as we return (or if perchance we desist from our expedition), we will immediately grant full justice in accordance with the laws of the Welsh and in relation to the foresaid regions.

58. We will immediately give up the son of Llywelyn and all the hostages of Wales, and the charters delivered to us as security for the peace.

59. We will do towards Alexander, king of Scots, concerning the return of his sisters and his hostages, and concerning his franchises, and his right, in the same manner as we shall do towards our owher barons of England, unless it ought to be otherwise according to the charters which we hold from William his father, formerly king of Scots; and this shall be according to the judgment of his peers in our court.

60. Moreover, all these aforesaid customs and liberties, the observances of which we have granted in our kingdom as far as pertains to us towards our men, shall be observed b all of our kingdom, as well clergy as laymen, as far as pertains to them towards their men.

61. Since, moveover, for God and the amendment of our kingdom and for the better allaying of the quarrel that has arisen between us and our barons, we have granted all these concessions, desirous that they should enjoy them in complete and firm endurance forever, we give and grant to them the underwritten security, namely, that the barons choose five and twenty barons of the kingdom, whomsoever they will, who shall be bound with all their might, to observe and hold, and cause to be observed, the peace and liberties we have granted and confirmed to them by this our present Charter, so that if we, or our justiciar, or our bailiffs or any one of our officers, shall in anything be at fault towards anyone, or shall have broken any one of the articles of this peace or of this security, and the offense be notified to four barons of the foresaid five and twenty, the said four barons shall repair to us (or our justiciar, if we are out of the realm) and, laying the transgression before us, petition to have that transgression redressed without delay. And if we shall not have corrected the transgression (or, in the event of our being out of the realm, if our justiciar shall not have corrected it) within forty days, reckoning from the time it has been intimated to us (or to our justiciar, if we should be out of the realm), the four barons aforesaid shall refer that matter to the rest of the five and twenty barons, and those five and twenty barons shall, together with the community of the whole realm, distrain and distress us in all possible ways, namely, by seizing our castles, lands, possessions, and in any other way they can, until redress has been obtained as they deem fit, saving harmless our own person, and the persons of our queen and children; and when redress has been obtained, they shall resume their old relations towards us. And let whoever in the country desires it, swear to obey the orders of the said five and twenty barons for the execution of all the aforesaid matters, and along with them, to molest us to the utmost of his power; and we publicly and freely grant leave to everyone who wishes to swear, and we shall never forbid anyone to swear. All those, moreover, in the land who of themselves and of their own accord are unwilling to swear to the twenty five to help them in constraining and molesting us, we shall by our command compel the same to swear to the effect foresaid. And if any one of the five and twenty barons shall have died or departed from the land, or be incapacitated in any other manner which would prevent the foresaid provisions being carried out, those of the said twenty five barons who are left shall choose another in his place according to their own judgment, and he shall be sworn in the same way as the others. Further, in all matters, the execution of which is entrusted, to these twenty five barons, if perchance these twenty five are present and disagree about anything, or if some of them, after being summoned, are unwilling or unable to be present, that which the majority of those present ordain or command shall be held as fixed and established, exactly as if the whole twenty five had concurred in this; and the said twenty five shall swear that they will faithfully observe all that is aforesaid, and cause it to be observed with all their might. And we shall procure nothing from anyone, directly or indirectly, whereby any part of these concessions and liberties might be revoked or diminished;

and if any such things has been procured, let it be void and null, and we shall never use it personally or by another.

62. And all the will, hatreds, and bitterness that have arisen between us and our men, clergy and lay, from the date of the quarrel, we have completely remitted and pardoned to everyone. Moreover, all trespasses occasioned by the said quarrel, from Easter in the sixteenth year of our reign till the restoration of peace, we have fully remitted to all, both clergy and laymen, and completely forgiven, as far as pertains to us. And on this head, we have caused to be made for them letters testimonial patent of the lord Stephen, archbishop of Canterbury, of the lord Henry, archbishop of Dublin, of the bishops aforesaid, and of Master Pandulf as touching this security and the concessions aforesaid.

63. Wherefore we will and firmly order that the English Church be free, and that the men in our kingdom have and hold all the aforesaid liberties, rights, and concessions, well and peaceably, freely and quietly, fully and wholly, for themselves and their heirs, of us and our heirs, in all respects and in all places forever, as is aforesaid. An oath, moreover, has been taken, as well on our part as on the art of the barons, that all these conditions aforesaid shall be kept in good faith and without evil intent. Given under our hand - the above named and many others being witnesses - in the meadow which is called Runnymede, between Windsor and Staines, on the fifteenth day of June, in the seventeenth year of our reign.

This is but one of three different translations I found of the Magna Carta; it was originally done in Latin, probably by the Archbishop, Stephen Langton. It was in force for only a few months, when it was violated by the king. Just over a year later, with no resolution to the war, the king died, being succeeded by his 9-year old son, Henry III. The Charter (Carta) was reissued again, with some revisions, in 1216, 1217 and 1225. As near as I can tell, the version presented here is the one that preceded all of the others; nearly all of its provisions were soon superseded by other laws, and none of it is effective today. The two other versions I found each professed to be the original, as well. The basic intent of each is the same. —Gerald Murphy (The Cleveland Free-Net - aa300)

Acknowledgments: Prepared by Nancy Troutman (The Cleveland Free-Net - aa345) Distributed by the Cybercasting Services Division of the National Public Telecomputing Network (NPTN). Permission is hereby given to download, reprint, and/or otherwise redistribute this file, provided appropriate point of origin credit is given to the preparer(s) and the National Public Telecomputing Network.

THE ARTICLES OF CONFEDERATION

November 15, 1777

To all to whom these Presents shall come, we the undersigned Delegates of the States affixed to our Names send greeting. Articles of Confederation and perpetual Union between the states of New Hampshire, Massachusetts-bay Rhode Island and Providence Plantations,

Connecticut, New York, New Jersey, Pennsylvania, Delaware, Maryland, Virginia, North Carolina, South Carolina and Georgia.

I. The Style of this Confederacy shall be "The United States of America".

II. Each state retains its sovereignty, freedom, and independence, and every power, jurisdiction, and right, which is not by this Confederation expressly delegated to the United States, in Congress assembled.

III. The said States hereby severally enter into a firm league of friendship with each other, for their common defense, the security of their liberties, and their mutual and general welfare, binding themselves to assist each other, against all force offered to, or attacks made upon them, or any of them, on account of religion, sovereignty, trade, or any other pretense whatever.

IV. The better to secure and perpetuate mutual friendship and intercourse among the people of the different States in this Union, the free inhabitants of each of these States, paupers, vagabonds, and fugitives from justice excepted, shall be entitled to all privileges and immunities of free citizens in the several States; and the people of each State shall free ingress and regress to and from any other State, and shall enjoy therein all the privileges of trade and commerce, subject to the same duties, impositions, and restrictions as the inhabitants thereof respectively, provided that such restrictions shall not extend so far as to prevent the removal of property imported into any State, to any other State, of which the owner is an inhabitant; provided also that no imposition, duties or restriction shall be laid by any State, on the property of the United States, or either of them.

   If any person guilty of, or charged with, treason, felony, or other high misdemeanor in any State, shall flee from justice, and be found in any of the United States, he shall, upon demand of the Governor or executive power of the State from which he fled, be delivered up and removed to the State having jurisdiction of his offense. Full faith and credit shall be given in each of these States to the records, acts, and judicial proceedings of the courts and magistrates of every other State.

V. For the most convenient management of the general interests of the United States, delegates shall be annually appointed in such manner as the legislatures of each State shall direct, to meet in Congress on the first Monday in November, in every year, with a power reserved to each State to recall its delegates, or any of them, at any time within the year, and to send others in their stead for the remainder of the year.

   No State shall be represented in Congress by less than two, nor more than seven members; and no person shall be capable of being a delegate for more than three years in any term of six years; nor shall any person, being a delegate, be capable of holding any office under the United States, for which he, or another for his benefit, receives any salary, fees or emolument of any kind.

   Each State shall maintain its own delegates in a meeting of the States, and while they act as members of the committee of the States.

   In determining questions in the United States in Congress assembled, each State shall have one vote.

   Freedom of speech and debate in Congress shall not be impeached or questioned in any court or place out of Congress, and the members of Congress shall be protected in their persons from arrests or imprisonments, during the time of their going to and from, and attendance on Congress, except for treason, felony, or breach of the peace.

VI. No State, without the consent of the United States in Congress assembled, shall send any embassy to, or receive any embassy from, or enter into any conference, agreement, alliance or treaty with any King, Prince or State; nor shall any person holding any office of profit or trust under the United States, or any of them, accept any present, emolument, office or title of any kind whatever from any King, Prince or foreign State; nor shall the United States in Congress assembled, or any of them, grant any title of nobility.

No two or more States shall enter into any treaty, confederation or alliance whatever between them, without the consent of the United States in Congress assembled, specifying accurately the purposes for which the same is to be entered into, and how long it shall continue.

No State shall lay any imposts or duties, which may interfere with any stipulations in treaties, entered into by the United States in Congress assembled, with any King, Prince or State, in pursuance of any treaties already proposed by Congress, to the courts of France and Spain.

No vessel of war shall be kept up in time of peace by any State, except such number only, as shall be deemed necessary by the United States in Congress assembled, for the defense of such State, or its trade; nor shall any body of forces be kept up by any State in time of peace, except such number only, as in the judgement of the United States in Congress assembled, shall be deemed requisite to garrison the forts necessary for the defense of such State; but every State shall always keep up a well-regulated and disciplined militia, sufficiently armed and accoutered, and shall provide and constantly have ready for use, in public stores, a due number of filed pieces and tents, and a proper quantity of arms, ammunition and camp equipage.

No State shall engage in any war without the consent of the United States in Congress assembled, unless such State be actually invaded by enemies, or shall have received certain advice of a resolution being formed by some nation of Indians to invade such State, and the danger is so imminent as not to admit of a delay till the United States in Congress assembled can be consulted; nor shall any State grant commissions to any ships or vessels of war, nor letters of marque or reprisal, except it be after a declaration of war by the United States in Congress assembled, and then only against the Kingdom or State and the subjects thereof, against which war has been so declared, and under such regulations as shall be established by the United States in Congress assembled, unless such State be infested by pirates, in which case vessels of war may be fitted out for that occasion, and kept so long as the danger shall continue, or until the United States in Congress assembled shall determine otherwise.

VII. When land forces are raised by any State for the common defense, all officers of or under the rank of colonel, shall be appointed by the legislature of each State respectively, by whom such forces shall be raised, or in such manner as such State shall direct, and all vacancies shall be filled up by the State which first made the appointment.

VIII. All charges of war, and all other expenses that shall be incurred for the common defense or general welfare, and allowed by the United States in Congress assembled, shall be defrayed out of a common treasury, which shall be supplied by the several States in proportion to the value of all land within each State, granted or surveyed for any person, as such land and the buildings and improvements thereon shall be estimated according to such mode as the United States in Congress assembled, shall from time to time direct and appoint.

The taxes for paying that proportion shall be laid and levied by the authority and direction of the legislatures of the several States within the time agreed upon by the United States in Congress assembled.

IX.   The United States in Congress assembled, shall have the sole and exclusive right and power of determining on peace and war, except in the cases mentioned in the sixth article

— of sending and receiving ambassadors

— entering into treaties and alliances, provided that no treaty of commerce shall be made whereby the legislative power of the respective States shall be restrained from imposing such imposts and duties on foreigners, as their own people are subjected to, or from prohibiting the exportation or importation of any species of goods or commodities whatsoever

— of establishing rules for deciding in all cases, what captures on land or water shall be legal, and in what manner prizes taken by land or naval forces in the service of the United States shall be divided or appropriated

— of granting letters of marque and reprisal in times of peace

— appointing courts for the trial of piracies and felonies committed on the high seas and establishing courts for receiving and determining finally appeals in all cases of captures, provided that no member of Congress shall be appointed a judge of any of the said courts.

The United States in Congress assembled shall also be the last resort on appeal in all disputes and differences now subsisting or that hereafter may arise between two or more States concerning boundary, jurisdiction or any other causes whatever; which authority shall always be exercised in the manner following. Whenever the legislative or executive authority or lawful agent of any State in controversy with another shall present a petition to Congress stating the matter in question and praying for a hearing, notice thereof shall be given by order of Congress to the legislative or executive authority of the other State in controversy, and a day assigned for the appearance of the parties by their lawful agents, who shall then be directed to appoint by joint consent, commissioners or judges to constitute a court for hearing and determining the matter in question: but if they cannot agree, Congress shall name three persons out of each of the United States, and from the list of such persons each party shall alternately strike out one, the petitioners beginning, until the number shall be reduced to thirteen; and from that number not less than seven, nor more than nine names as Congress shall direct, shall in the presence of Congress be drawn out by lot, and the persons whose names shall be so drawn or any five of them, shall be commissioners or judges, to hear and finally determine the controversy, so always as a major part of the judges who shall hear the cause shall agree in the determination: and if either party shall neglect to attend at the day appointed, without showing reasons, which Congress shall judge sufficient, or being present shall refuse to strike, the Congress shall proceed to nominate three persons out of each State, and the secretary of Congress shall strike in behalf of such party absent or refusing; and the judgement and sentence of the court to be appointed, in the manner before prescribed, shall be final and conclusive; and if any of the parties shall refuse to submit to the authority of such court, or to appear or defend their claim or cause, the court shall nevertheless proceed to pronounce sentence, or judgement, which shall in like manner be final and decisive, the judgement or sentence and other proceedings being in either case transmitted to Congress, and lodged among the acts of Congress for the security of the parties concerned: provided that every commissioner, before he sits in judgement, shall take an oath to be administered by one of the judges of the supreme or superior court of the State, where the cause shall be tried, 'well and truly to hear and determine the matter in question, according to the best of his judgement, without favor, affection or hope of reward': provided also, that no State shall be deprived of territory for the benefit of the United States.

All controversies concerning the private right of soil claimed under different grants of two or more States, whose jurisdictions as they may respect such lands, and the States which passed such grants are adjusted, the said grants or either of them being at the same time claimed to have originated antecedent to such settlement of jurisdiction, shall on the petition of either party to the Congress of the United States, be finally determined as near as may be in the same manner as is before prescribed for deciding disputes respecting territorial jurisdiction between different States.

The United States in Congress assembled shall also have the sole and exclusive right and power of regulating the alloy and value of coin struck by their own authority, or by that of the respective States

— fixing the standards of weights and measures throughout the United States

— regulating the trade and managing all affairs with the Indians, not members of any of the States, provided that the legislative right of any State within its own limits be not infringed or violated

— establishing or regulating post offices from one State to another, throughout all the United States, and exacting such postage on the papers passing through the same as may be requisite to defray the expenses of the said office

— appointing all officers of the land forces, in the service of the United States, excepting regimental officers

— appointing all the officers of the naval forces, and commissioning all officers whatever in the service of the United States

— making rules for the government and regulation of the said land and naval forces, and directing their operations.

The United States in Congress assembled shall have authority to appoint a committee, to sit in the recess of Congress, to be denominated 'A Committee of the States', and to consist of one delegate from each State; and to appoint such other committees and civil officers as may be necessary for managing the general affairs of the United States under their direction

— to appoint one of their members to preside, provided that no person be allowed to serve in the office of president more than one year in any term of three years; to ascertain the necessary sums of money to be raised for the service of the United States, and to appropriate and apply the same for defraying the public expenses

— to borrow money, or emit bills on the credit of the United States, transmitting every half-year to the respective States an account of the sums of money so borrowed or emitted

— to build and equip a navy

— to agree upon the number of land forces, and to make requisitions from each State for its quota, in proportion to the number of white inhabitants in such State; which requisition shall be binding, and thereupon the legislature of each State shall appoint the regimental officers, raise the men and cloath, arm and equip them in a solid-like manner, at the expense of the United States; and the officers and men so cloathed, armed and equipped shall march to the place appointed, and within the time agreed on by the United States in Congress assembled. But if the United States in Congress assembled shall, on consideration of circumstances judge proper that any State should not raise men, or should raise a smaller number of men than the quota thereof, such extra number shall be raised, officered, cloathed, armed and equipped in the same manner as the quota of each State, unless the legislature of such State shall judge that such extra number cannot be safely spread out in the same, in which case they shall raise, officer, cloath, arm and equip as many of such extra number as they judge can be safely spared. And the officers and men so cloathed, armed, and equipped, shall march to the place appointed, and within the time agreed on by the United States in Congress assembled.

The United States in Congress assembled shall never engage in a war, nor grant letters of marque or reprisal in time of peace, nor enter into any treaties or alliances, nor coin money, nor regulate the value thereof, nor ascertain the sums and expenses necessary for the defense and welfare of the United States, or any of them, nor emit bills, nor borrow money on the credit of the United States, nor appropriate money, nor agree upon the number of vessels of war, to be built or purchased, or the number of land or sea forces to be raised, nor appoint a commander in chief of the army or navy, unless nine States assent to the same: nor shall a question on any other point, except for adjourning from day to day be determined, unless by the votes of the majority of the United States in Congress assembled.

The Congress of the United States shall have power to adjourn to any time within the year, and to any place within the United States, so that no period of adjournment be for a longer duration than the space of six months, and shall publish the journal of their proceedings monthly, except such parts thereof relating to treaties, alliances or military operations, as in their judgement require secrecy; and the yeas and nays of the delegates of each State on any question shall be entered on the journal, when it is desired by any delegates of a State, or any of them, at his or their request shall be furnished with a transcript of the said journal, except such parts as are above excepted, to lay before the legislatures of the several States.

X.   The Committee of the States, or any nine of them, shall be authorized to execute, in the recess of Congress, such of the powers of Congress as the United States in Congress assembled, by the consent of the nine States, shall from time to time think expedient to vest them with; provided that no power be delegated to the said Committee, for the exercise of which, by the Articles of Confederation, the voice of nine States in the Congress of the United States assembled be requisite.

XI.   Canada acceding to this confederation, and adjoining in the measures of the United States, shall be admitted into, and entitled to all the advantages of this Union; but no other colony shall be admitted into the same, unless such admission be agreed to by nine States.

XII.   All bills of credit emitted, monies borrowed, and debts contracted by, or under the authority of Congress, before the assembling of the United States, in pursuance of the present confederation, shall be deemed and considered as a charge against the United States, for payment and satisfaction whereof the said United States, and the public faith are hereby solemnly pleged.

XIII. Every State shall abide by the determination of the United States in Congress assembled, on all questions which by this confederation are submitted to them. And the Articles of this Confederation shall be inviolably observed by every State, and the Union shall be perpetual; nor shall any alteration at any time hereafter be made in any of them; unless such alteration be agreed to in a Congress of the United States, and be afterwards confirmed by the legislatures of every State.

   And Whereas it hath pleased the Great Governor of the World to incline the hearts of the legislatures we respectively represent in Congress, to approve of, and to authorize us to ratify the said Articles of Confederation and perpetual Union. Know Ye that we the undersigned delegates, by virtue of the power and authority to us given for that purpose, do by these presents, in the name and in behalf of our respective constituents, fully and entirely ratify and confirm each and every of the said Articles of Confederation and perpetual Union, and all and singular the matters and things therein contained: And we do further solemnly plight and engage the faith of our respective constituents, that they shall abide by the determinations of the United States in Congress assembled, on all questions, which by the said Confederation are submitted to them. And that the Articles thereof shall be inviolably observed by the States we respectively represent, and that the Union shall be perpetual.

   In Witness whereof we have hereunto set our hands in Congress. Done at Philadelphia in the State of Pennsylvania the ninth day of July in the Year of our Lord One Thousand Seven Hundred and Seventy-Eight, and in the Third Year of the independence of America.

   Agreed to by Congress 15 November 1777

   In force after ratification by Maryland, 1 March 1781

Declaration of Independence

In Congress, July 4, 1776

The unanimous Declaration of the thirteen united States of America,

When in the Course of human events,it becomes necessary for one people to dissolve the political bands which have connected them with another, and to assume among the powers of the earth,the separate and equal station to which the Laws of Nature and of Nature's God entitle them,a decent respect to the opinions of mankind requires that they should declare the causes which impel them to the separation.

We hold these truths to be self-evident, that all men are created equal, that they are endowed by their Creator with certain unalienable Rights, that among these are Life, Liberty and the pursuit of Happiness. That to secure these rights, Governments are instituted among Men, deriving their just powers from the consent of the governed, that whenever any Form of Government becomes destructive of these ends, it is the Right of the People to alter or to abolish it, and to institute new Government, laying its foundation on such principles and organizing its powers in such form, as to them shall seem most likely to effect their Safety and Happiness. Prudence, indeed, will dictate that Governments long established should not be changed for light and transient causes; and accordingly all experience hath shewn, that mankind are more disposed to suffer, while evils are sufferable, than to right themselves by abolishing the forms to which they are accustomed. But when a long train of abuses and usurpations, pursuing invariably the same Object evinces a design to reduce them under absolute Despotism, it is their right, it is their duty, to throw off such Government, and to provide new Guards for their future security. Such has been the patient sufferance of these Colonies; and such is now the necessity which constrains them to alter their former Systems of Government.The history of the present King of Great Britain is a history of repeated injuries and usurpations, all having in direct object the establishment of an absolute Tyranny over these States.To prove this, let Facts be submitted to a candid world.

> He has refused his Assent to Laws, the most wholesome and necessary for the public good.
>
> He has forbidden his Governors to pass Laws of immediate and pressing importance, unless suspended in their operation till his Assent should be obtained; and when so suspended, he has utterly neglected to attend to them.
>
> He has refused to pass other Laws for the accommodation of large districts of people, unless those people would relinquish the right of Representation in the Legislature, a right inestimable to them and formidable to tyrants only.
>
> He has called together legislative bodies at places unusual, uncomfortable, and distant from the depository of their public Records, for the sole purpose of fatiguing them into compliance with his measures.
>
> He has dissolved Representative Houses repeatedly, for opposing with manly firmness his invasions on the rights of the people.
>
> He has refused for a long time, after such dissolutions, to cause others to be elected; whereby the Legislative powers, incapable of Annihilation, have returned to the People at large for their exercise; the State remaining in the mean time exposed to all the dangers of invasion from without, and convulsions within.
>
> He has endeavoured to prevent the population of these States; for that purpose obstructing the Laws for Naturalization of Foreigners; refusing to pass

others to encourage their migrations hither, and raising the conditions of new Appropriations of Lands.

He has obstructed the Administration of Justice, by refusing his Assent to Laws for establishing Judiciary powers.

He has made Judges dependent on his Will alone, for the tenure of their offices, and the amount and payment of their salaries.

He has erected a multitude of New Offices, and sent hither swarms of Officers to harass our people, and eat out their substance.

He has kept among us, in times of peace, Standing Armies without the Consent of our legislatures.

He has affected to render the Military independent of and superior to the Civil power.

He has combined with others to subject us to a jurisdiction foreign to our constitution, and unacknowledged by our laws; giving his Assent to their Acts of pretended Legislation:

For Quartering large bodies of armed troops among us:

For protecting them, by a mock Trial, from punishment for any Murders which they should commit on the Inhabitants of these States:

For cutting off our Trade with all parts of the world:

For imposing Taxes on us without our Consent:

For depriving us in many cases, of the benefits of Trial by Jury:

For transporting us beyond Seas to be tried for pretended offences:

For abolishing the free System of English Laws in a neighbouring Province, establishing therein an Arbitrary government, and enlarging its Boundaries so as to render it at once an example and fit instrument for introducing the same absolute rule into these Colonies:

For taking away our Charters, abolishing our most valuable Laws, and altering fundamentally the Forms of our Governments:

For suspending our own Legislatures, and declaring themselves invested with power to legislate for us in all cases whatsoever.

He has abdicated Government here, by declaring us out of his Protection and waging War against us.

He has plundered our seas, ravaged our Coasts, burnt our towns, and destroyed the lives of our people.

He is at this time transporting large Armies of foreign Mercenaries to compleat the works of death, desolation and tyranny, already begun with circumstances of Cruelty & perfidy scarcely paralleled in the most barbarous ages, and totally unworthy the Head of a civilized nation.

He has constrained our fellow Citizens taken Captive on the high Seas to bear Arms against their Country, to become the executioners of their friends and Brethren, or to fall themselves by their Hands.

He has excited domestic insurrections amongst us, and has endeavoured to bring on the inhabitants of our frontiers, the merciless Indian Savages, whose known rule of warfare, is an undistinguished destruction of all ages, sexes and conditions.

In every stage of these Oppressions We have Petitioned for Redress in the most humble terms: Our repeated Petitions have been answered only by repeated injury. A Prince whose character is thus marked by every act which may define a Tyrant, is unfit to be the ruler of a free people.

Nor have We been wanting in attentions to our British brethren. We have warned them from time to time of attempts by their legislature to extend an unwarrantable jurisdiction over us. We have reminded them of the circumstances of our emigration and settlement here. We have appealed to their native justice and magnanimity, and we have conjured them by the ties of our common kindred to disavow these usurpations, which, would inevitably interrupt our connections and correspondence. They too have been deaf to the voice of justice and of consanguinity. We must, therefore, acquiesce in the necessity, which denounces our Separation, and hold them, as we hold the rest of mankind, Enemies in War, in Peace Friends.

We, therefore, the Representatives of the united States of America, in General Congress, Assembled, appealing to the Supreme Judge of the world for the rectitude of our intentions, do, in the Name, and by Authority of the good People of these Colonies, solemnly publish and declare, That these United Colonies are, and of Right ought to be Free and Independent States; that they are Absolved from all Allegiance to the British Crown, and that all political connection between them and the State of Great Britain, is and ought to be totally dissolved; and that as Free and Independent States, they have full Power to levy War, conclude Peace, contract Alliances, establish Commerce, and to do all other Acts and Things which Independent States may of right do. And for the support of this Declaration, with a firm reliance on the protection of divine Providence, we mutually pledge to each other our Lives, our Fortunes and our sacred Honor.

APPENDIX

C

Legal Documents— Constitutional Law and the Courts

Contents

PETITION FOR COMMUTATION

Petition for Commutation of Sentence

Please read the accompanying instructions carefully before completing the application. Type or print the answers in ink. Each question must be answered fully, truthfully and accurately. If the space for any answer is insufficient, you may complete the answer on a separate sheet of paper and attach it to the petition. You may attach any additional documentation that you believe is relevant to your petition. The submission of any material, false information is punishable by up to five years' imprisonment and a fine of not more than $250,000. 18 U.S.C. §§ 1001 and 3571.

Relief sought: *(check one)*

☐ **Reduction of Prison Sentence Only**   ☐ **Reduction of Prison Sentence and Remission**
☐ **Remission of Fine and/or Restitution Only**   ☑ **Other** _____

To The President of the United States:

The undersigned petitioner, a Federal prisoner, prays for commutation of sentence and in support thereof states as follows:

1.   **Full name:** _____
                    First   *Middle*   *Last*

    Reg. No. _____   **Social Security No.** _____

    Confined in the Federal Institution at _____

    Date and place of birth: _____

    Are you a United States citizen?   ☐ yes ☐ no
    If you are not a U.S. citizen, indicate your country of citizenship

    _____

    Have you ever applied for commutation of sentence before?   ☐ yes ☐ no
    If yes, state the date(s) on which you applied, and the date(s) when you were notified of the final decision on your petition(s).

    _____

    _____

Offense(s) For Which Commutation Is Sought

2.   **I was convicted on a plea of** _____ **in the United States District Court**
                                    (guilty, not guilty, nolo contendere)

    for the _____ **District of** _____ **of the crime of:**
                    (Northern, Western, etc.)   *(identify state)*

Offense(s) For Which Commutation Is Sought

_____
(State specific offense(s); provide citation of statute(s) violated, if known)

_____

_____

_____

I was sentenced on _____, _____ to imprisonment for _____, to pay
                (month/day)   _(year)_   _(length of sentence)_

☐ a fine of $ _____, ☐ restitution of $ _____, and to
          (do not include special assessment)

☐ supervised release or ☐ special parole for _____, and/or to probation for

_____. I was _____ years of age when the offense was committed.
(length of sentence)

3.   I began service of the sentence of imprisonment on _____, _____, and I am projected to
                                                        (month/day) _(year)_

be released from confinement on _____, _____.
                                  (month/day)   _(year)_

Are you eligible for parole? ☐ yes ☐ no
If yes, indicate the date when you became eligible for release, and state whether your application for parole was granted or denied

_____

Have you paid in full any fine or restitution imposed on you? ☐ yes ☐ no
If the fine or restitution has not been paid in full, state the remaining balance.

4.   **Did you appeal your conviction or sentence to the United States Court of Appeals?** ☐ yes ☐ no

Is your appeal concluded? ☐ yes ☐ no
If yes, indicate whether your conviction or sentence was affirmed or reversed, the date of the decision, and the citation(s) to any published court opinions. Provide copies of any unpublished court decisions concerning such appeals, if they are available to you.

_____

_____

Did you seek review by the Supreme Court? ☐ yes ☐ no

Is your appeal concluded? ☐ yes ☐ no
If yes, indicate whether your petition was granted or denied and the date of the decision.

_____

_____

Offense(s) For Which Commutation Is Sought

Have you filed a challenge to your conviction or sentence under 28 U.S.C. § 2255 (habeas corpus)?   ☐ yes ☐ no

Is your challenge concluded?   ☐ yes ☐ no

If yes, indicate whether your motion was granted or denied, the date of the decision, and the citation(s) to any published court opinions, if known. Provide copies of any unpublished court decisions concerning such motions, if they are available to you. If you have filed more than one post-conviction motion, provide the requested information for each such motion.

_____

_____

_____

5.   **Provide a complete and detailed account of the offense for which you seek commutation, including the full extent of your involvement. If you need more space, you may complete your answer on a separate sheet of paper and attach it to the petition.**

_____

_____

_____

_____

_____

_____

_____

_____

_____

_____

_____

_____

_____

_____

_____

_____

_____

_____

_____

Other Criminal Record

6. **Aside from the offense for which commutation is sought, have you ever been arrested or taken into custody by any law enforcement authority, or convicted in any court, either as a juvenile or an adult, for any other incident?** ☐ yes ☐ no

   For each such incident, provide: the date, the nature of charge, the law enforcement authority involved, and the final disposition of the incident. You must list every violation, including traffic violations that resulted arrest or in an criminal charge, such as driving under the influence.

Arrests:

_____

_____

_____

_____

_____

_____

_____

_____

_____

_____

_____

Convictions:

_____

_____

_____

_____

_____

_____

_____

_____

_____

_____

_____

_____

_____

_____

Reasons for Seeking Clemency

7.   State your reasons for seeking commutation of sentence. If you need more space, you may complete your answer on a separate sheet of paper and attach it to the petition.

_____

_____

_____

_____

_____

_____

_____

_____

_____

_____

_____

_____

_____

_____

_____

_____

_____

_____

_____

_____

_____

_____

_____

Certification and Personal Oath

I hereby certify that all answers to the above questions and all statement contained herein are true and correct to the best of my knowledge, information, and belief. I understand that any intentional misstatements of material facts contained in this application form may cause adverse action on my petition for executive clemency and may subject me to criminal prosecution.

Respectfully submitted this _____ day of _____, _____.

(month)   (year)

_____
Signature of Petitioner

Excerpt from Petition for Writ of Habeas Corpus (form)

✎AO 241
(Rev. 10/07)

Petition for Relief From a Conviction or Sentence
By a Person in State Custody

(Petition Under 28 U.S.C. § 2254 for a Writ of Habeas Corpus)

Instructions

1. To use this form, you must be a person who is currently serving a sentence under a judgment against you in a state court. You are asking for relief from the conviction or the sentence. This form is your petition for relief.

2. You may also use this form to challenge a state judgment that imposed a sentence to be served in the future, but you must fill in the name of the state where the judgment was entered. If you want to challenge a federal judgment that imposed a sentence to be served in the future, you should file a motion under 28 U.S.C. § 2255 in the federal court that entered the judgment.

3. Make sure the form is typed or neatly written.

4. You must tell the truth and sign the form. If you make a false statement of a material fact, you may be prosecuted for perjury.

5. Answer all the questions. You do not need to cite law. You may submit additional pages if necessary. If you do not fill out the form properly, you will be asked to submit additional or correct information. If you want to submit a brief or arguments, you must submit them in a separate memorandum.

6. You must pay a fee of $5. If the fee is paid, your petition will be filed. If you cannot pay the fee, you may ask to proceed in forma pauperis (as a poor person). To do that, you must fill out the last page of this form. Also, you must submit a certificate signed by an officer at the institution where you are confined showing the amount of

    money that the institution is holding for you. If your account exceeds $_____, you must pay the filing fee.

7. In this petition, you may challenge the judgment entered by only one court. If you want to challenge a judgment entered by a different court (either in the same state or in different states), you must file a separate petition.

8. When you have completed the form, send the original and two copies to the Clerk of the United States District Court at this address:

    > Clerk, United States District Court for
    > Address
    > City, State Zip Code

9. **CAUTION: You must include in this petition all the grounds for relief from the conviction or sentence that you challenge. And you must state the facts that support each ground. If you fail to set forth all the grounds in this petition, you may be barred from presenting additional grounds at a later date.**

10. **CAPITAL CASES: If you are under a sentence of death, you are entitled to the assistance of counsel and should request the appointment of counsel.**

✎AO 241
(Rev. 10/07)

**PETITION UNDER 28 U.S.C. § 2254 FOR WRIT OF
HABEAS CORPUS BY A PERSON IN STATE CUSTODY**

United States District Court	District:	
Name (under which you were convicted):		Docket or Case No.:
Place of Confinement :	Prisoner No.:	
Petitioner (include the name under which you were convicted) v.	Respondent (authorized person having custody of petitioner)	
The Attorney General of the State of		

PETITION

1. (a) Name and location of court that entered the judgment of conviction you are challenging:

    (b) Criminal docket or case number (if you know):

2. (a) Date of the judgment of conviction (if you know):

    (b) Date of sentencing:

3. Length of sentence:

4. In this case, were you convicted on more than one count or of more than one crime?   ❏ Yes   ❏ No

5. Identify all crimes of which you were convicted and sentenced in this case:

6. (a) What was your plea? (Check one)

    ❏ (1)   Not guilty   ❏ (3)   Nolo contendere (no contest)

    ❏ (2)   Guilty   ❏ (4)   Insanity plea

(b) If you entered a guilty plea to one count or charge and a not guilty plea to another count or charge, what did you plead guilty to and what did you plead not guilty to?

(c) If you went to trial, what kind of trial did you have? (Check one)

❏   Jury   ❏   Judge only

7.   Did you testify at a pretrial hearing, trial, or a post-trial hearing?

❏   Yes   ❏   No

8.   Did you appeal from the judgment of conviction?

❏   Yes   ❏   No

9.   If you did appeal, answer the following:

(a) Name of court:

(b) Docket or case number (if you know):

(c) Result:

(d) Date of result (if you know):

(e) Citation to the case (if you know):

(f) Grounds raised:

(g) Did you seek further review by a higher state court?   ❏ Yes   ❏ No

If yes, answer the following:

(1) Name of court:

(2) Docket or case number (if you know):

(3) Result:

(4) Date of result (if you know):

✎AO 241
(Rev. 10/07)

(5) Citation to the case (if you know):

(6) Grounds raised:

(h) Did you file a petition for certiorari in the United States Supreme Court?   ❐ Yes   ❐ No

If yes, answer the following:

(1) Docket or case number (if you know):

(2) Result:

(3) Date of result (if you know):

(4) Citation to the case (if you know):

10.   Other than the direct appeals listed above, have you previously filed any other petitions, applications, or motions concerning this judgment of conviction in any state court?   ❐ Yes   ❐ No

11.   If your answer to Question 10 was "Yes," give the following information:

(a)   (1) Name of court:

(2) Docket or case number (if you know):

(3) Date of filing (if you know):

(4) Nature of the proceeding:

(5) Grounds raised:

(6) Did you receive a hearing where evidence was given on your petition, application, or motion?

❐ Yes   ❐ No

(7) Result:

(8) Date of result (if you know):

(b) If you filed any second petition, application, or motion, give the same information:

    (1) Name of court:

    (2) Docket or case number (if you know):

    (3) Date of filing (if you know):

    (4) Nature of the proceeding:

    (5) Grounds raised:

    (6) Did you receive a hearing where evidence was given on your petition, application, or motion?

❒   Yes   ❒ No

    (7) Result:

    (8) Date of result (if you know):

(c) If you filed any third petition, application, or motion, give the same information:

    (1) Name of court:

    (2) Docket or case number (if you know):

    (3) Date of filing (if you know):

    (4) Nature of the proceeding:

    (5) Grounds raised:

AO 241
(Rev. 10/07)

(6) Did you receive a hearing where evidence was given on your petition, application, or motion?

❐   Yes   ❐   No

(7) Result:

(8) Date of result (if you know):

(d) Did you appeal to the highest state court having jurisdiction over the action taken on your petition, application, or motion?

(1) First petition: ❐   Yes   ❐   No

(2) Second petition: ❐   Yes   ❐   No

(3) Third petition: ❐   Yes   ❐   No

(e) If you did not appeal to the highest state court having jurisdiction, explain why you did not:

12.   For this petition, state every ground on which you claim that you are being held in violation of the Constitution, laws, or treaties of the United States. Attach additional pages if you have more than four grounds. State the facts supporting each ground.

CAUTION: To proceed in the federal court, you must ordinarily first exhaust (use up) your available state-court remedies on each ground on which you request action by the federal court. Also, if you fail to set forth all the grounds in this petition, you may be barred from presenting additional grounds at a later date.

GROUND ONE:

(a) Supporting facts (Do not argue or cite law. Just state the specific facts that support your claim.):

(b) If you did not exhaust your state remedies on Ground One, explain why:

✎AO 241
(Rev. 10/07)

(c)   **Direct Appeal of Ground One:**

(1) If you appealed from the judgment of conviction, did you raise this issue?   ❐ Yes   ❐ No

(2) If you did not raise this issue in your direct appeal, explain why:

(d) **Post-Conviction Proceedings:**

(1) Did you raise this issue through a post-conviction motion or petition for habeas corpus in a state trial court?

❐ Yes   ❐ No

(2) If your answer to Question (d)(1) is "Yes," state:

Type of motion or petition:

Name and location of the court where the motion or petition was filed:

Docket or case number (if you know):

Date of the court's decision:

Result (attach a copy of the court's opinion or order, if available):

(3) Did you receive a hearing on your motion or petition?   ❐ Yes   ❐ No

(4) Did you appeal from the denial of your motion or petition?   ❐ Yes   ❐ No

(5) If your answer to Question (d)(4) is "Yes," did you raise this issue in the appeal? ❐ Yes   ❐ No

(6) If your answer to Question (d)(4) is "Yes," state:

Name and location of the court where the appeal was filed:

Docket or case number (if you know):

Date of the court's decision:

Result (attach a copy of the court's opinion or order, if available):

(7) If your answer to Question (d)(4) or Question (d)(5) is "No," explain why you did not raise this issue:

Civil Rights Complaint (form)

UNITED STATES DISTRICT COURT
FOR THE NORTHERN DISTRICT OF CALIFORNIA

**INSTRUCTIONS FOR FILING A COMPLAINT BY A PRISONER
UNDER THE CIVIL RIGHTS ACT, 42 U.S.C. §§ 1983**

I.   42 U.S.C. §§ 1983

You may file an action under 42 U.S.C. §§ 1983 to challenge federal constitutional or statutory violations by state actors which affect the conditions of your confinement.

A §§ 1983 action may not be used to challenge the length of your sentence or the validity of your conviction. Such claims must be addressed in a petition for a writ of habeas corpus, on the correct forms provided by the clerk of the court.

II.   Filing a §§ 1983 Action

To file a §§ 1983 action, you must submit: (1) an original complaint and (2) a check or money order for $350.00 or an original Prisoner's In Forma Pauperis Application.

This packet includes a complaint form and a Prisoner's In Forma Pauperis Application. When these forms are fully completed, mail the originals to: Clerk of the United States District Court for the Northern District of California, 450 Golden Gate Avenue, Box 36060, San Francisco, CA 94102.

III.   Filing Fees

Under the Deficit Reduction Act of 2005, the filing fee for a § 1983 action filed on or after April 9, 2006 has been increased to $350.00 from $250.00, to be paid at the time of filing. If you are unable to pay the full filing fee at this time, you may petition the court to proceed in forma pauperis, using the Prisoner's In Forma Pauperis Application in this packet. You must fully complete the application and sign and declare under penalty of perjury that the facts stated therein are true and correct.

Each plaintiff must submit his or her own Prisoner's In Forma Pauperis Application. You must use the Prisoner's In Forma Pauperis Application provided with this packet and not any other version.

IV.   Complaint Form

You must complete the entire complaint form. Your responses must be typewritten or legibly handwritten and you must sign and declare under penalty of perjury that the facts stated in the complaint are true and correct. Each plaintiff must sign the complaint.

Under 42 U.S.C. §§ 1997e, you are required to exhaust your administrative remedies before filing a §§ 1983 action; you must indicate clearly on the complaint form whether you have done so.

PrisonerCiv4-06.wpd

1

V.   <u>After Complaint Is Filed</u>

2
You will be notified as soon as the court issues any order in your case. It is your
responsibility to keep the court informed of any changes of address to ensure you receive court
3   orders. Failure to so do may result in dismissal of your action.

4

VI.   <u>Repeat Filers</u>

5
If you are seeking leave to proceed <u>in forma pauperis</u> and, while incarcerated or detained,
you have filed §§ 1983 actions on three or more prior occasions which were dismissed as
6   frivolous, malicious, or for failure to state a claim upon which relief may be granted, you may not
file a new §§ 1983 action unless you are under imminent danger of serious physical injury. 28
7   U.S.C.
§§ 1915(g).

8

VII.   <u>Inquiries and Copying Requests</u>

9
Because of the large volume of cases filed by inmates in this court and very limited court
resources, the court can no longer answer questions concerning the status of your case or provide
10   copies of documents, except at a charge of fifty cents ($0.50) per page. You must therefore keep
copies of all documents submitted to the court for your own records.

11

12

13

14

15

16

17

18

19

20

21

22

23

24

25

26

27

28

1   <u>**COMPLAINT BY A PRISONER UNDER THE CIVIL RIGHTS ACT, 42 U.S.C §§ 1983**</u>

2   Name _____

3   (Last)   (First)   (Initial)

4   Prisoner Number _____

5   Institutional Address _____

6   ==

7   **UNITED STATES DISTRICT COURT**
        NORTHERN DISTRICT OF CALIFORNIA

8

9   _____   )
     (Enter the full name of plaintiff in this action.)   )

10   vs.   )   Case No. _____
)   (To be provided by the Clerk of Court)

11   _____   )

12   _____   )   **COMPLAINT UNDER THE**
)   **CIVIL RIGHTS ACT,**

13   _____   )   **Title 42 U.S.C § 1983**

14   _____   )
     (Enter the full name of the defendant(s) in this action)   )

15   _____   )

16   *[All questions on this complaint form must be answered in order for your action to proceed..]*

17   I.   Exhaustion of Administrative Remedies.

18   [**Note:** You must exhaust your administrative remedies before your claim can go

19   forward. The court will dismiss any unexhausted claims.]

20   A.   Place of present confinement _____

21   B.   Is there a grievance procedure in this institution?

22   YES ( )   NO ( )

23   C.   Did you present the facts in your complaint for review through the grievance

24   procedure?

25   YES ( )   NO ( )

26   D.   If your answer is YES, list the appeal number and the date and result of the

27   appeal at each level of review. If you did not pursue a certain level of appeal,

28   explain why.

COMPLAINT   - 1 -

1   1. Informal appeal _____

2   _____

3   _____

4   2. First formal level_____

5   _____

6   _____

7   3. Second formal level_____

8   _____

9   _____

10   4. Third formal level _____

11   _____

12   _____

13   E.   Is the last level to which you appealed the highest level of appeal available to

14   you?

15   YES ( )   NO ( )

16   F.   If you did not present your claim for review through the grievance procedure,

17 explain why._____

18   _____

19   _____

20 II.   Parties.

21   A.   Write your name and your present address. Do the same for additional plaintiffs,

22   if any.

23   _____

24   _____

25   _____

26   B.   Write the full name of each defendant, his or her official position, and his or her

27   place of employment.

28   _____

COMPLAINT   - 2 -

1 _____
2 _____
3 _____
4 _____
5 III.   Statement of Claim.
6   State here as briefly as possible the facts of your case. Be sure to describe how each
7 defendant is involved and to include dates, when possible. Do not give any legal arguments or
8 cite any cases or statutes. If you have more than one claim, each claim should be set forth in a
9 separate numbered paragraph.
10 _____
11 _____
12 _____
13 _____
14 _____
15 _____
16 _____
17 _____
18 _____
19 _____
20 _____
21 _____
22 _____
23 IV.   Relief.
24   Your complaint cannot go forward unless you request specific relief. State briefly exactly
25 what you want the court to do for you. Make no legal arguments; cite no cases or statutes.
26 _____
27 _____
28 _____

COMPLAINT   - 3 -

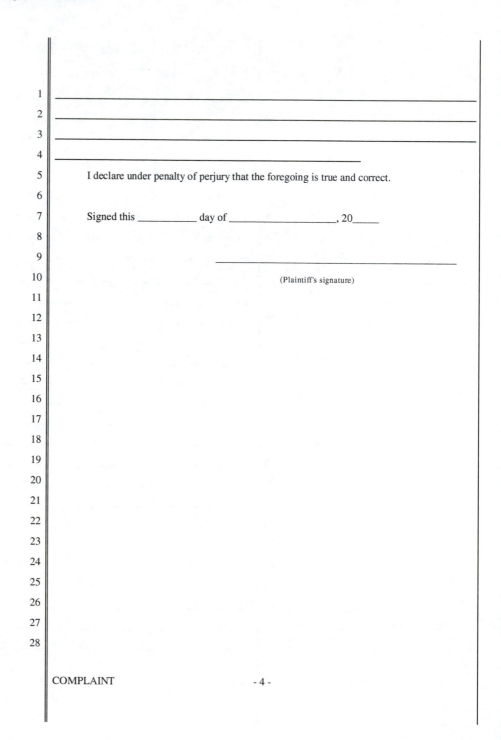

1

2

3

4

5   I declare under penalty of perjury that the foregoing is true and correct.

6

7   Signed this _____ day of _____, 20_____

8

9

10   (Plaintiff's signature)

11

12

13

14

15

16

17

18

19

20

21

22

23

24

25

26

27

28

COMPLAINT   - 4 -

Application and Affidavit for Search Warrant

AO 106 (Rev. 04/10) Application for a Search Warrant

UNITED STATES DISTRICT COURT
for the

In the Matter of the Search of
*(Briefly describe the property to be searched
or identify the person by name and address)*

)
)
)
)
)
)

Case No. _____

APPLICATION FOR A SEARCH WARRANT

I, a federal law enforcement officer or an attorney for the government, request a search warrant and state under penalty of perjury that I have reason to believe that on the following person or property *(identify the person or describe the property to be searched and give its location)*:

located in the _____ District of _____ , there is now concealed *(identify the person or describe the property to be seized)*:

The basis for the search under Fed. R. Crim. P. 41(c) is *(check one or more)*:

❑ evidence of a crime;

❑ contraband, fruits of crime, or other items illegally possessed;

❑ property designed for use, intended for use, or used in committing a crime;

❑ a person to be arrested or a person who is unlawfully restrained.

The search is related to a violation of:

Code Section   *Offense Description*

The application is based on these facts:

❑ Continued on the attached sheet.

❑ Delayed notice of _____ days (give exact ending date if more than 30 days: _____) is requested under 18 U.S.C. § 3103a, the basis of which is set forth on the attached sheet.

_____
Applicant's signature

_____
Printed name and title

Sworn to before me and signed in my presence.

Date: _____

_____
Judge's signature

City and state: _____

_____
Printed name and title

Excerpt from Petition for Writ of Certiorari

No.

IN THE

Supreme Court of the United States

GEORGE W. BUSH,

Petitioner,

v.

PALM BEACH COUNTY CANVASSING BOARD, *ET AL.,*

Respondents.

On Petition For A Writ Of Certiorari
To The Supreme Court Of Florida

PETITION FOR A WRIT OF CERTIORARI

MICHAEL A. CARVIN
COOPER, CARVIN &
  ROSENTHAL, P.L.L.C.
1500 K Street, N.W.
Suite 200
Washington, D.C. 20005
(202) 220-9600

BARRY RICHARD
GREENBERG TRAURIG, P.A.
101 East College Avenue
Post Office Drawer 1838
Tallahassee, FL 32302
(850) 222-6891

THEODORE B. OLSON
  Counsel of Record
DOUGLAS R. COX
THOMAS G. HUNGAR
MARK A. PERRY
GIBSON, DUNN & CRUTCHER LLP
1050 Connecticut Avenue, N.W.
Washington, D.C. 20036
(202) 955-8500

BENJAMIN L. GINSBERG
PATTON BOGGS LLP
2550 M Street, N.W.
Washington, D.C. 20037
(202) 457-6000

[Additional counsel listed on inside front cover]

Counsel for Petitioner

GEORGE J. TERWILLIGER III
TIMOTHY E. FLANIGAN
MARCOS D. JIMÉNEZ
WHITE & CASE LLP
First Union Financial Center
200 South Biscayne Blvd.
Miami, Florida 33131
(305) 371-2700

i

QUESTIONS PRESENTED

The Supreme Court of Florida has held that the Secretary of State cannot certify election results in accordance with preexisting Florida law and must instead wait for the statutorily untimely results of manual recounts conducted in three Florida counties before certifying the results of the November 7, 2000 presidential election. This holding raises three substantial federal questions that warrant immediate review by this Court:

1. Whether post-election judicial limitations on the discretion granted by the legislature to state executive officials to certify election results, and/or post-election judicially created standards for the determination of controversies concerning the appointment of presidential electors, violate the Due Process Clause or 3 U.S.C. § 5, which requires that a State resolve controversies relating to the appointment of electors under "laws enacted prior to" election day.

2. Whether the state court's decision, which cannot be reconciled with state statutes enacted before the election was held, is inconsistent with Article II, Section 1, clause 2 of the Constitution, which provides that electors shall be appointed by each State "in such Manner as the Legislature thereof may direct."

3. Whether the use of arbitrary, standardless, and selective manual recounts that threaten to overturn the results of the election for President of the United States violates the Equal Protection or Due Process Clauses, or the First Amendment.

PARTIES TO THE PROCEEDING

The following individuals and entities are parties to the proceeding in the court below:

Governor George W. Bush, as candidate for President; Katherine Harris, as Secretary of State, State of Florida; Katherine Harris, Bob Crawford, and Laurence C. Roberts, as members of the Elections Canvassing Commission; Matt Butler; Palm Beach County Canvassing Board; Broward County Canvassing Board; Broward County Supervisor of Elections; Robert A. Butterworth, as Attorney General, State of Florida; Florida Democratic Party; and Vice President Albert Gore, Jr., as candidate for President.

iii

TABLE OF CONTENTS

iv

TABLE OF AUTHORITIES-continued

PETITION FOR A WRIT OF CERTIORARI

Petitioner George W. Bush, the candidate of the Republican Party for the office of President of the United States, respectfully prays that a writ of certiorari be issued to review the judgment of the Supreme Court of quirements of the Constitution of the United States and federal law, the state supreme court has embarked on an *ad hoc*, standardless, and lawless exercise of judicial power, which appears designed to thwart the will of the electorate as well as the considered judgments of Florida's executive and legislative branches. Because the selection of presidential electors is governed directly by the Constitution and congressional enactments, as well the utmost *federal* importance.

OPINIONS BELOW

The opinion of the Supreme Court of Florida (App., *infra*, 1a-39a) is not yet reported. The orders of the Circuit Court of the Second Judicial District for the County of Leon, Florida (App., *infra*, 43a-44a & 45a-51a) are not reported. Florida in this case. In plain contravention of the reas by state law, the court's decision involves issues of

JURISDICTION

The judgment of the Supreme Court of Florida was entered on November 21, 2000. The jurisdiction of this Court rests upon 28 U.S.C. § 1257.

The decision below compels the Florida Secretary of State and Elections Canvassing Commission to accept, and include in the State's certification of election returns, untimely election results derived from selective manual recounts being conducted in certain Florida counties. App., *infra*, 42a. The judgment below is therefore "final" for purposes of this Court's jurisdiction under § 1257; indeed, it amounts to the entry of a permanent injunction against the

2

responsible state officials. 548, 551 (1945) (entry of injunction is "an effective determination of the litigation and not of merely interlocutory or intermediate steps therein"). *Market Street Ry. Co. v. Railroad Comm'n*, 324 U.S.

As demonstrated *infra*, petitioner expressly raised below the federal questions presented in this petition. Accordingly, the Florida Supreme Court's failure to address petitioner's federal claims, and its assertion that "[n]either party has raised as an issue on appeal the constitutionality of Florida's election laws" (App., *infra*, 11a, n.10), is no barrier to review by this Court. "The issue of whether a federal question was sufficiently and federal question, as to which this Court is not bound by the decision of the state courts." *Street v. New York*, 394 U.S. 576, 583 (1969). *See also Black v. Cutter Labs.*, 351 U.S. 292, 298 (1956) (this Court has a "duty to ... determine for ourselves precisely the ground on which the judgment rests"). Accordingly, a state court cannot evade this Court's review by failing to discuss federal *Admr.*, 123 U.S. 540, 548 (1887) ("If a federal question is fairly presented by the record, and its decision is actually necessary to the determination of the case, a judgment which rejects a claim, but avoids all reference to it, is as much against the right ... as if it has been specifically referred to and the right directly refused."). properly raised in the state courts is itself ultimately a questions in its opinion. *Chapman v. Goodnow's*

Petition for Writ of Habeas Corpus

IN THE UNITED STATES DISTRICT COURT FOR THE DISTRICT OF COLUMBIA

SHAFIQ RASUL,   )
Detainee, Camp X-Ray   )
Guantanamo Bay Naval Base   )
Guantanamo Bay, Cuba   )
)
SKINA BIBI, as Next Friend of Shafiq Rasul   )
14 Inverness Street   )
London NW1 7HJ   )
United Kingdom   )
)
ASIF IQBAL, Detainee, Camp X-Ray   )
Guantanamo Bay Naval Base   )
Guantanamo Bay, Cuba   )
)
MOHAMMED IQBAL, as Next Friend of Asif Iqbal   )
14 Inverness Street   )
London NW1 7HJ   )
United Kingdom   )
)
DAVID HICKS,   )
Detainee, Camp X-Ray   )
Guantanamo Bay Naval Base   )
Guantanamo Bay, Cuba   )
)
TERRY HICKS,   )
as Next Friend of David Hicks   )
345 King William Street   )
Adelaide, SA 5000   )
Petitioners,   )
)
v.   )
)
GEORGE WALKER BUSH,   )
President of the United States   )
The White House   )
1600 Pennsylvania Ave., N.W.   )
Washington, D.C. 20500   )
)

DONALD RUMSFELD,   )
Secretary, United States   )
Department of Defense   )
1000 Defense Pentagon   )
Washington, D.C. 20301-1000   )
)
BRIGADIER GEN. MICHAEL LEHNERT   )
Commander, Joint Task Force-160   )
Guantanamo Bay Naval Base   )
Guantanamo Bay, Cuba   )
)
COLONEL TERRY CARRICO,   )
Commander, Camp X-Ray,   )
Guantanamo Bay Naval Base   )
Guantanamo Bay, Cuba   )
)
Respondents   )
All sued in their official   )
and individual capacities.   )

Petition for Writ of Habeas Corpus

1. Petitioners David Hicks, Asif Iqbal, and Shafiq Rasul seek the Great Writ. They act on their own behalf and through their Next Friends: Terry Hicks acts for his son David, Mohammed Iqbal acts for his son Asif, and Skina Bibi acts for her son Shafiq Rasul. David Hicks is a citizen of Australia. Mr. Iqbal and Mr. Rasul are citizens of the United Kingdom. They are being held virtually *incommunicado* in respondents' unlawful custody.

I. Jurisdiction

2. Petitioners bring this action under 28 U.S.C. §§2241 and 2242, and invoke this Court's jurisdiction under 28 U.S.C. §§1331, 1350, 1651, 2201, and 2202; 5 U.S.C. §702; as well as the Fifth and Fourteenth Amendments to the United States Constitution, the International Covenant on Civil and Political Rights ("ICCPR"), the American Declaration on the Rights and Duties of Man ("ADRDM"), and Customary International Law. Because they seek declaratory relief, Petitioners also rely on F. R. Civ. P. 57.

3. This Court is empowered under 28 U.S.C. §2241 to grant the Writ of Habeas Corpus, and to entertain the Petition filed by Terry Hicks, Mohammed Iqbal, and Skina Bibi as Next Friend under 28 U.S.C. §2242. This Court is further empowered to declare the rights and other legal relations of the parties herein by 28 U.S.C. §2201, and to effectuate and enforce declaratory relief by all necessary and proper means by 28 U.S.C. §2202, as this case involves an actual controversy within the Court's jurisdiction.

II. Venue

4. Venue is proper in the United States District Court for the District of Columbia, since at least one respondent resides in the district, a substantial part of the events or omissions giving rise to the claim occurred in the district, at least one respondent may be found in

the district, and all respondents are either officers or employees of the United States or any agency thereof acting in their official capacities. 28 U.S.C. §§1391(b); 1391(e).

III. Parties

5. Petitioner David Hicks is an Australian citizen presently incarcerated and held in respondents' unlawful custody at Camp X-Ray, United States Naval Base, Guantanamo Bay, Cuba. See Exhibit A, Birth Certificate of David Hicks.

6. Petitioner Terry Hicks is David Hicks' father. He too is an Australian citizen. Terry Hicks has received a letter from his son, delivered through the Australian Red Cross, asking for legal assistance. Because his son cannot secure access either to legal counsel or the courts of the United States, the elder Mr. Hicks acts as Next Friend. See Exhibit B, Affidavit of Terry Hicks, incorporated by reference herein.

7. Through counsel, Terry Hicks has tried repeatedly to contact his son, and to learn more about his condition and status. The United States has either rebuffed or ignored counsel's requests. In a letter dated January 17, 2002, for instance, Steven Kenny, Australian counsel for Terry and David Hicks, asked the Australian Government to confirm, inter alia, whether David Hicks was being held at Guantanamo, whether the United States intended to charge him with any offense, and whether the Australian Government could work with counsel to secure representation for Mr. Hicks. In the same letter, Mr. Kenny asked the Australian Government to "arrange contact between David and his family." See Exhibit C, Affidavit of Stephen Kenny, Australian Counsel for Petitioners; Letter from Stephen Kenny to Hon. Daryl Williams, Attorney-General (Jan. 17, 2002), all correspondence incorporated herein by reference. The following day, the Australian Government advised counsel that Mr. Hicks was being held in Guantanamo, that he "does not currently have legal representation due to the nature and circumstances of his detention," and that "the matter of access to Mr. Hicks by his family" was "ultimately a matter for the United States." Id. at Letter from Robert Cornall, Attorney-General's Department (Jan. 18, 2002).

8. Mr. Kenny responded the same day, repeating his request for information about Mr. Hicks, and seeking the assistance of the Australian Government "with a view to arranging" legal advice for Mr. Hicks. On February 1, 2002, Mr. Kenny renewed his request for "access by [Terry Hicks] to his son. He wishes to see his son face to face but would appreciate being able to make even a telephone call to him. Will you please make a direct request to the United States authorities for such a meeting." Id. at Letter from Stephen Kenny (Feb. 1, 2002). On February 8, 2002, the Australian Government left no doubt that David Hicks, and all detainees, were cut off: Your request for Mr. Hicks' family to have access to him was referred to the United States authorities. The United States has advised that, at this stage, no family access will be allowed any of the detainees held at Guantanamo Bay. Id. at Letter from Robert Cornall (Feb. 8, 2002)(emphasis added).

9. In addition to his correspondence with the Australian Government, on January 25, Mr. Kenny wrote to President Bush, asking, inter alia, if he would "permit David to be seen by legal counsel," and if he would allow Terry Hicks "to have contact with his son." To date, the United States Government has not responded to this request.

10. Petitioner Asif Iqbal is a citizen of the United Kingdom presently incarcerated and held in respondents' unlawful custody at Camp X-Ray, Guantanamo Bay Naval Station, Guantanamo Bay, Cuba. See Exhibit D, Birth Certificate of Asif Iqbal.

11. Petitioner Mohammed Iqbal is Asif Iqbal's father. He too is a British citizen. Mohammed Iqbal received a telephone call from the Foreign and Commonwealth Office on January 21, 2002, during which he was informed that his son was being detained in Guantanamo Bay. Because his son cannot secure access either to legal counsel or the courts of the United States, Mohammed Iqbal acts as his Next Friend. See Exhibit E, Affidavit of Mohammed Iqbal, incorporated by reference herein.

12. Through counsel, Mohammed Iqbal has attempted to gain access to his son. The United States has declined to accede to counsel's requests. See Exhibit F, First Affidavit of Gareth Peirce, United Kingdom Counsel for Petitioners Asif and Mohammed Iqbal and Shafiq Rasul and Skina Bibi.

13. The British Foreign and Commonwealth Office advised Ms. Peirce that any request for access to Mr. Iqbal must be made to the United States Ambassador in London. Immediately upon receiving instructions from Mr. Iqbal's family, on January 25, 2002, Ms. Peirce telephoned and also sent a faxed request to the Ambassador, seeking immediate access to Mr. Iqbal in Guantanamo Bay in order to provide legal advice. In addition, she asked the Foreign and Commonwealth Office in London to pursue this request directly with the United States government. Ms. Peirce has been advised by the Foreign and Commonwealth Office that this request has been passed to the United States government on behalf of Mr. Iqbal, together with requests by Mr. Iqbal's Member of Parliament that he and Mr. Iqbal's family be permitted access to him. Counsel is advised by the Foreign and Commonwealth Office that as of February 13, 2002, these requests have not received a response, and nor has a request for further consular access to Mr. Iqbal, i.e. a second consular visit, been granted.

14. Petitioner Shafiq Rasul is a citizen of the United Kingdom presently incarcerated and held in respondents' unlawful custody at Camp X-Ray, Guantanamo Bay Naval Station, Guantanamo Bay, Cuba. See Exhibit G, Birth Certificate of Shafiq Rasul.

15. Petitioner Skina Bibi is Shafiq Rasul's mother. She too is a British citizen. Ms. Bibi received a telephone call from the Foreign and Commonwealth Office on January 21, 2002, during which she was informed that her son was being detained in Guantanamo Bay. Skina Bibi has also received news of a message from her son, delivered through the Red Cross, asking for legal representation. Because her son cannot secure access either to legal counsel or the courts of the United States, she acts as his Next Friend. See Exhibit H, Affidavit of Skina Bibi, incorporated by reference herein.

16. Through counsel, Skina Bibi has attempted to gain access to her son. The United States has declined to accede to counsel's requests. See Exhibit I, Second Affidavit of Gareth Peirce, United Kingdom Counsel for the Petitioners Asif and Mohammed Iqbal and Shafiq Rasul and Skina Bibi.

17. The British Foreign and Commonwealth Office advised Ms. Peirce that any request for access to Mr. Rasul must be made to the United States Ambassador in London. Immediately upon receiving instructions from Mr. Rasul's family, on January 25, 2002, Ms. Peirce telephoned and also sent a faxed request to the Ambassador, seeking immediate access to Mr. Rasul in Guantanamo Bay in order to provide legal advice. In addition, she asked the Foreign and Commonwealth Office in London to pursue this request directly with the United States government. Ms. Peirce has been advised by the Foreign and Commonwealth Office that this request has been passed to the United States government on behalf of Mr. Rasul, together with requests by Mr. Rasul's Member of Parliament that he and Mr. Rasul's family be permitted access to him. Counsel is advised by the Foreign and Commonwealth Office that as of February 13, 2002, these requests have not received

a response, and nor has a request for further consular access to Mr. Rasul, i.e. a second consular visit, been granted.

18. Respondent Bush is the President of the United States and Commander in Chief of the United States Military. He is the author of the Order directing that David Hicks, Asif Iqbal, and Shafiq Rasul be detained, and is ultimately responsible for their unlawful detention. He is sued in his official and personal capacities.

19. Respondent Rumsfeld is the Secretary of the United States Department of Defense. Pursuant to the Order described in Para. 18, respondent Rumsfeld has been charged with maintaining the custody and control of the detained petitioners. Respondent Rumsfeld is sued in his official and personal capacities.

20. Respondent Lehnert is the Commander of Joint Task Force-160, the task force running the detention operation at the Guantanamo Naval Station, Guantanamo Bay, Cuba. He has supervisory responsibility for the detained petitioners and is sued in his official and personal capacities.

21. Respondent Carrico is the Commandant of Camp X-Ray, where the detained petitioners are presently held. He is the immediate custodian responsible for their detention, and is sued in his official and personal capacities.

IV. Statement of Facts

22. The detained petitioners are not enemy aliens. David Hicks is an Australian citizen in respondents' unlawful custody. At the time of his seizure by the United States Government, Mr. Hicks was living in Afghanistan. On information and belief, he had no involvement, direct or indirect, in either the terrorist attacks on the United States September 11, 2001, or any act of international terrorism attributed by the United States to al Qaida or any terrorist group. He is not properly subject to the detention Order issued by respondent Bush, and discussed infra in Paras. 28–33.

23. Petitioners Asif Iqbal and Shafiq Rasul are UK citizens in respondents' unlawful custody. No proper or adequate information has been provided by the United States government as to the circumstances of their seizure by U.S. forces. They were in the United Kingdom at all material times before and on September 11, 2001. On information and belief, they had no involvement, direct or indirect, in either the terrorist attacks on the United States on September 11, 2001, or any act of international terrorism attributed by the United States to al Qaida or any terrorist group. They are not properly subject to the detention Order issued by respondent Bush, and discussed infra in Paras. 28–33.

PETITIONERS' SEIZURE BY THE UNITED STATES

24. In the wake of September 11, 2001, the United States, at the direction of respondent Bush, began a massive military campaign against the Taliban, then in power in Afghanistan. On September 18, 2001, a Joint Resolution of Congress authorized the President to use force against the "nations, organizations, or persons" that "planned, authorized, committed, or aided the terrorist attacks on September 11, 2001, or [that] harbored such organizations or persons." Joint Resolution 23, Authorization for Use of Military Force, Public Law 107-40, 115 Stat. 224 (Jan. 18, 2001). The Resolution did not authorize the indefinite detention of persons seized on the field of battle.

25. In the course of the military campaign, and as part of their effort to overthrow the Taliban, the United States provided military assistance to the Northern Alliance, a loosely knit coalition of Afghani and other military groups opposed to the Taliban Government. On information and belief, no American casualties were caused by the Taliban prior to when Mr. Hicks, Mr. Iqbal, and Mr. Rasul were apprehended, and the detained petitioners neither caused nor attempted to cause any harm to American personnel prior to their capture.

26. On or about December 9, 2001, the precise date unknown to counsel but known to respondents, the Northern Alliance captured David Hicks in Afghanistan. On December 17, 2001, the Northern Alliance transferred him to the custody of the United States military. See Exhibit J, Joint News Release of the Australian Attorney General and the Minister for Defense (December 17, 2001). David Hicks has been held in United States custody since that time.

27. No proper or adequate information has been provided by the United States government as to the date or circumstances of Mr. Iqbal's and Mr. Rasul's seizure by U.S. forces. The precise date of their capture by U.S. forces is unknown to counsel but known to respondents. They have been held in United States custody since that time.

THE DETENTION ORDER

28. On November 13, 2001, respondent Bush issued a Military Order authorizing indefinite detention without due process of law. The Order authorizes respondent Rumsfeld to detain anyone respondent Bush has "reason to believe":

    i. is or was a member of the organization known as al Qaida;

    ii. has engaged in, aided or abetted, or conspired to commit, acts of international terrorism, or acts in preparation therefor, that have caused, threaten to cause, or have as their aim to cause, injury to or adverse effects on the United States, its citizens, national security, foreign policy, or economy; or iii. has knowingly harbored one or more individuals described in subparagraphs (i) and (ii) See Exhibit K, Military Order of November 13, 2001. President Bush must make this determination in writing. The Order was neither authorized nor directed by Congress, and is beyond the scope of the Joint Resolution of September 18, 2001.

29. The Military Order vests the President with complete discretion to identify the individuals that fall within its scope. It establishes no standards governing the use of his discretion. Once a person has been detained, the Order contains no provision for him to be notified of the charges he may face. On the contrary, the Order authorizes detainees to be held without charges. It contains no provision for detainees to be notified of their rights under domestic and international law, and provides neither the right to counsel, nor the right to consular access. It provides no right to appear before a neutral tribunal to review the legality of a detainee's continued detention, and no provision for appeal to an Article III court. In fact, the Order expressly bars review by any court. Though the Order directs respondent Rumsfeld to create military tribunals, it sets no deadline for his task. And for those detainees who will not be tried before a tribunal, the Order authorizes indefinite and unreviewable detention, based on nothing more than the President's written determination that an individual is subject to its terms.

30. The United States Government has advised the Australian Government that Mr. Hicks is being held at Camp X-Ray, Guantanamo Bay Naval Station, Guantanamo Bay, Cuba, pursuant to this Order. See Exhibit L, Letter from Robert Cornall, Australian Attorney General's Department, to Stephen Kenny, Australian counsel for Petitioners (Jan. 18, 2002).

31. British Foreign Office Minister Ben Bradshaw advised Parliament on January 21, 2002, that British officials had visited three British citizens being detained at Camp X-Ray, Guantanamo Bay Naval Station, Guantanamo Bay, Cuba, who were held pursuant to this Order. Only one of the detainees was named; the name given was neither Mr. Iqbal nor Mr. Rasul. However, Petitioners Mohammed Iqbal and Skina Bibi received telephone calls from the Foreign and Commonwealth Office January 21, 2002, during which they were informed that their sons were being detained at Camp X-Ray, in Guantanamo Bay.

32. On information and belief, respondent Bush has never certified or determined in any manner, in writing or otherwise, that the detained petitioners are subject to this detention order.

33. The detained petitioners are not properly subject to this detention order.

GUANTANAMO BAY NAVAL STATION

34. On or about January 11, 2002, the United States military began transporting prisoners captured in Afghanistan to Camp X-Ray, at the United States Naval Base, in Guantanamo Bay, Cuba. Guantanamo Bay is a self-sufficient and essentially permanent city with approximately 7,000 military and civilian residents under the complete jurisdiction and control of the United States. Guantanamo Bay occupies nearly thirty-one square miles of land, an area larger than Manhattan, and nearly half the size of the District of Columbia. It has its own schools, generates its own power, provides its own internal transportation, and supplies its own water. Offenses committed by both civilians and foreign nationals living on Guantanamo are brought before federal courts on the mainland, where respondents enjoy the full panoply of Constitutional rights. The United States has occupied Guantanamo Bay since 1903, and has repeatedly declared its intention to remain there indefinitely. For several decades, the United States has resisted claims of national sovereignty made by Cuba over Guantanamo Bay.

35. On or about January 11, 2002, the precise date unknown to counsel but known to respondents, the United States military transferred the detained petitioners to Camp X-Ray, Guantanamo Bay, where they have been held ever since, in the custody of respondents Bush, Rumsfeld, Lehnert, and Carrico.

36. Since gaining control of the detained petitioners, the United States military has held them virtually incommunicado. They have been or will be interrogated repeatedly by agents of the United States Departments of Defense and Justice, though they have not been charged with an offense, nor have they been notified of any pending or contemplated charges. They have made no appearance before either a military or civilian tribunal of any sort, nor have they been provided counsel or the means to contact counsel. They have not been informed of their rights under the United States Constitution, the regulations of the United States Military, the Geneva Convention, the International Covenant on Civil and Political Rights, or the American Declaration on the Rights and Duties of Man. Indeed, the respondents have taken the position that the detainees should not be told of these rights. As a result, the detained petitioners are completely unable either to protect, or to vindicate their rights under domestic and international law.

37. David Hicks has been allowed to write a single, brief letter to his father, which was delivered by the Australian Red Cross. In that letter, he asked his father for legal assistance. See Exhibit B, Affidavit of Terry Hicks.

38. Shafiq Rasul has attempted to pass messages to his family, through the Red Cross. The U.S. authorities did not permit the details of these messages to be delivered. A summary was provided, however, indicating that Mr. Rasul was well and that he had asked for legal representation. See Exhibit H, Affidavit of Skina Bibi. Asif Iqbal communicated with his family, through the Red Cross, when he was detained in Afghanistan. It is unknown whether he has attempted to communicate with his family since his detention in Guantanamo.

39. In published statements, respondents Bush, Rumsfeld, Lehnert and Carrico have indicated the United States may hold the detained petitioners under these conditions indefinitely. See, e.g., Roland Watson, The Times (London), Jan. 18, 2002 ("Donald Rumsfeld, the U.S. Defence Secretary, suggested last night that al-Qaeda prisoners could be held indefinitely at the base. He said that the detention of some would be open-ended as the United States tried to build a case against them."); Lynne Sladky, Associated Press, Jan. 22, 2002 ("Marine Brig. Gen. Mike Lehnert, who is in charge of the detention mission, defended the temporary cells where detainees are being held ... 'We have to look at Camp X-ray as a work in progress...,' Lehnert told CNN. ... Lehnert said plans are to build a more permanent prison 'exactly in accordance with federal prison standards'"); John Mintz, THE WASHINGTON POST, "Extended Detention In Cuba Mulled," Feb. 13, 2002 ("As the Bush administration nears completion of new rules for conducting military trials of foreign detainees, U.S. officials say they envision the naval base at Gantanamo Bay, Cuba, as a site for the tribunals and as a terrorist penal colony for many years to come.")[1]

V. Causes of Action

FIRST CLAIM FOR RELIEF (DUE PROCESS — FIFTH AND FOURTEENTH AMENDMENTS TO THE UNITED STATES CONSTITUTION)

40. Petitioners incorporate paragraphs 1–39 by reference.

41. By the actions described above, respondents, acting under color of law, have violated and continue to violate the Fifth and Fourteenth Amendments to the United States Constitution. Respondent Bush has ordered the prolonged, indefinite, and arbitrary detention of individuals, without Due Process of Law. Respondents Rumsfeld, Lehnert, and Carrico are likewise acting in violation of the Fifth Amendment, since they act at the President's direction. On its face, the Executive Order violates the Fifth and Fourteenth Amendments.

SECOND CLAIM FOR RELIEF (DUE PROCESS — FIFTH AND FOURTEENTH AMENDMENTS TO THE UNITED STATES CONSTITUTION)

42. Petitioners incorporate paragraphs 1–41 by reference.

43. By the actions described above, respondents, acting under color of law, have violated and continue to violate the right of the detained petitioners to be free from arbitrary, prolonged, and indefinite detention, in violation of the Due Process Clause of the Fifth and Fourteenth Amendments to the United States Constitution. The Executive Order, as applied to Mr. Hicks, Mr. Iqbal, and Mr. Rasul, violates the Fifth and Fourteenth Amendments.

THIRD CLAIM FOR RELIEF (DUE PROCESS — INTERNATIONAL LAW)

44. Petitioners incorporate paragraphs 1–43 by reference.

45. By the actions described above, respondents, acting under color of law, have violated and continue to violate Customary International Law, Arts. 9 & 14 of the International Covenant on Civil and Political Rights, and Arts. 18, 25, & 26 of the American Declaration on the Rights and Duties of Man. Respondent Bush has ordered the prolonged, indefinite, and arbitrary detention of individuals, without legal process, in violation of binding obligations of the United States under International Law. Respondents Rumsfeld, Lehnert, and Carrico are likewise acting in violation of International Law, since they act at the President's direction. On its face, the Executive Order violates International Law.

FOURTH CLAIM FOR RELIEF (DUE PROCESS — INTERNATIONAL LAW)

46. Petitioners incorporate paragraphs 1–45 by reference.

47. By the actions described above, respondents, acting under color of law, have violated and continue to violate the right of the detained petitioners to be free from arbitrary, prolonged, and indefinite detention, in violation of Customary International Law, Arts. 9 & 14 of the International Covenant on Civil and Political Rights, and Arts. 18, 25, & 26 of the American Declaration on the Rights and Duties of Man. The Executive Order, as applied to the detained petitioners, violates these and other binding obligations of the United States under International Law.

FIFTH CLAIM FOR RELIEF (DUE PROCESS — FAILURE TO COMPLY WITH U.S. MILITARY REGULATIONS AND INTERNATIONAL HUMANITARIAN LAW)

48. Petitioners incorporate paragraphs 1–47 by reference.

49. By the actions described above, respondents, acting under color of law, have violated and continue to violate the rights accorded to persons seized by the United States Military in times of armed conflict, as established by, inter alia, the regulations of the United States Military, Articles 4 and 5 of Geneva Convention III, Geneva Convention IV, and Customary International Law.

SIXTH CLAIM FOR RELIEF (WAR POWERS CLAUSE)

50. Petitioners incorporate paragraphs 1–49 by reference.

51. By the actions described above, respondents, acting under color of law, have exceeded the constitutional authority of the Executive and have violated and continue to violate the War Powers Clause by ordering the prolonged and indefinite detention of the detained petitioners without Congressional authorization.

SEVENTH CLAIM FOR RELIEF (SUSPENSION OF THE WRIT)

52. Petitioners incorporate paragraphs 1–51 by reference.

53. To the extent the order of November 13, 2001, disallows any challenge to the legality of the detained petitioners' detention by way of habeas corpus, the Order and its enforcement constitute an unlawful Suspension of the Writ, in violation of Article I of the United States Constitution.

VI. Prayer for Relief

WHEREFORE, Petitioners pray for relief as follows:

1. Grant Petitioner Terry Hicks Next Friend status, as Next Friend of David Hicks;

2. Grant Petitioner Mohammed Iqbal Next Friend status, as Next Friend of Asif Iqbal;

3. Grant Petitioner Skina Bibi Next Friend status, as Next Friend of Shafiq Rasul;

4. Order the detained petitioners released from respondents' unlawful custody;

5. Order respondents to allow counsel to meet and confer with the detained petitioners, in private and unmonitored attorney-client conversations;

6. Order respondents to cease all interrogations of the detained petitioners, direct or indirect, while this litigation is pending;

7. Order and declare the Executive Order of November 13, 2001, unlawful as a violation of the Fifth and Fourteenth Amendments to the United States Constitution;

8. Order and declare that the detained petitioners are being held in violation of the Fifth and Fourteenth Amendments to the United States Constitution;

9. Order and declare the Executive Order of November 13, 2001, unlawful as a violation of Customary International Law, the International Covenant on Civil and Political Rights, and the American Declaration on the Rights and Duties of Man;

10. Order and declare that the detained petitioners are being held in violation of Customary International Law, the International Covenant on Civil and Political Rights, and the American Declaration on the Rights and Duties of Man;

11. Order and declare that the detained petitioners are being held in violation of the regulations of the United States Military, the Geneva Convention, and International Humanitarian Law;

12. Order and declare that the Executive Order of November 13, 2001, violates the War Powers Clause;

13. Order and declare that the provision of the Executive Order that bars the detained petitioners from seeking relief in this Court is an unlawful Suspension of the Writ, in violation of Article I of the United States Constitution;

14. To the extent respondents contest any material factual allegations in this Petition, schedule an evidentiary hearing, at which Petitioners may adduce proof in support of their allegations;

15. Such other relief as the Court may deem necessary and appropriate to protect Petitioners' rights under the United States Constitution and International Law.

F

Darrow's Examination of Bryan in the *Scopes* Trial

Examination of W.J. Bryan by Clarence Darrow, of counsel for the defense:

Q   You have given considerable study to the Bible, haven't you, Mr. Bryan?

A   Yes, sir, I have tried to.

Q   Then you have made a general study of it?

A   Yes, I have; I have studied the Bible for about fifty years, or sometime more than that, but, of course, I have studied it more as I have become older than when I was but a boy.

Q   You claim that everything in the Bible should be literally interpreted?

A   I believe everything in the Bible should be accepted as it is given there: some of the Bible is given illustratively, for instance: "Ye are the salt of the earth." I would not insist that man was actually salt, or that he had flesh of salt, but it is used in the sense of salt as saving God's people.

Q   But when you read that Jonah swallowed the whale—or that the whale swallowed Jonah—excuse me please—how do you literally interpret that?

A   When I read that a big fish swallowed Jonah—it does not say whale. . . . That is my recollection of it. A big fish, and I believe it, and I believe in a God who can make a whale and can make a man and make both what He pleases.

Q   Now, you say, the big fish swallowed Jonah, and he there remained how long—three days—and then he spewed him upon the land. You believe that the big fish was made to swallow Jonah?

A   I am not prepared to say that; the Bible merely says it was done.

Q   You don't know whether it was the ordinary run of fish, or made for that purpose?

A   You may guess; you evolutionists guess. . . .

Q   You are not prepared to say whether that fish was made especially to swallow a man or not?

A   The Bible doesn't say, so I am not prepared to say.

Q   But do you believe He made them—that He made such a fish and that it was big enough to swallow Jonah?

A   Yes, sir. Let me add: One miracle is just as easy to believe as another.

Q   Just as hard?

A   It is hard to believe for you, but easy for me. A miracle is a thing performed beyond what man can perform. When you get within the realm of miracles; and it is just as easy to believe the miracle of Jonah as any other miracle in the Bible.

Q   Perfectly easy to believe that Jonah swallowed the whale?

A   If the Bible said so; the Bible doesn't make as extreme statements as evolutionists do. . . .

Q   The Bible says Joshua commanded the sun to stand still for the purpose of lengthening the day, doesn't it, and you believe it?

A   I do.

Q   Do you believe at that time the entire sun went around the earth?

A   No, I believe that the earth goes around the sun.

Q   Do you believe that the men who wrote it thought that the day could be lengthened or that the sun could be stopped?

A   I don't know what they thought.

Q   You don't know?

A   I think they wrote the fact without expressing their own thoughts.

Q   Have you an opinion as to whether or not the men who wrote that thought

Gen. Stewart   I want to object, your honor; it has gone beyond the pale of any issue that could possibly be injected into this lawsuit, except by imagination. I do not think the defendant has a right to conduct the examination any further and I ask your honor to exclude it.

The Witness   It seems to me it would be too exacting to confine the defense to the facts; if they are not allowed to get away from the facts, what have they to deal with?

The Court   Mr. Bryan is willing to be examined. Go ahead.

Mr. Darrow   I read that years ago. Can you answer my question directly? If the day was lengthened by stopping either the earth or the sun, it must have been the earth?

A   Well, I should say so.

Q   Now, Mr. Bryan, have you ever pondered what would have happened to the earth if it had stood still?

A   No.

Q   You have not?

A   No; the God I believe in could have taken care of that, Mr. Darrow.

Q   I see. Have you ever pondered what would naturally happen to the earth if it stood still suddenly?

A   No.

Q	Don't you know it would have been converted into molten mass of matter?
A	You testify to that when you get on the stand, I will give you a chance.
Q	Don't you believe it?
A	I would want to hear expert testimony on that.
Q	You have never investigated that subject?
A	I don't think I have ever had the question asked.
Q	Or ever thought of it?
A	I have been too busy on things that I thought were of more importance than that.
Q	You believe the story of the flood to be a literal interpretation?
A	Yes, sir.
Q	When was that Flood?
A	I would not attempt to fix the date. The date is fixed, as suggested this morning.
Q	About 4004 B.C.?
A	That has been the estimate of a man that is accepted today. I would not say it is accurate.
Q	That estimate is printed in the Bible?
A	Everybody knows, at least, I think most of the people know, that was the estimate given.
Q	But what do you think that the Bible, itself says? Don't you know how it was arrived at?
A	I never made a calculation.
Q	A calculation from what?
A	I could not say.
Q	From the generations of man?
A	I would not want to say that.
Q	What do you think?
A	I do not think about things I don't think about.
Q	Do you think about things you do think about?
A	Well, sometimes.

(Laughter in the courtyard.)

Policeman   Let us have order. . . .

Stewart	Your honor, he is perfectly able to take care of this, but we are attaining no evidence. This is not competent evidence.
Witness	These gentlemen have not had much chance—they did not come here to try this case. They came here to try revealed religion. I am here to defend it and they can ask me any question they please.
The Court	All right.

(Applause from the court yard.)

Darrow	Great applause from the bleachers.
Witness	From those whom you call "Yokels."
Darrow	I have never called them yokels.
Witness	That is the ignorance of Tennessee, the bigotry.
Darrow	You mean who are applauding you? (Applause.)
Witness	Those are the people whom you insult.
Darrow	You insult every man of science and learning in the world because he does believe in your fool religion.
The Court	I will not stand for that.
Darrow	For what he is doing?
The Court	I am talking to both of you. . . .
Q	Wait until you get to me. Do you know anything about how many people there were in Egypt 3,500 years ago, or how many people there were in China 5,000 years ago?
A	No.
Q	Have you ever tried to find out?
A	No, sir. You are the first man I ever heard of who has been in interested in it. *(Laughter.)*
Q	Mr. Bryan, am I the first man you ever heard of who has been interested in the age of human societies and primitive man?
A	You are the first man I ever heard speak of the number of people at those different periods.
Q	Where have you lived all your life?
A	Not near you. *(Laughter and applause.)*
Q	Nor near anybody of learning?
A	Oh, don't assume you know it all.
Q	Do you know there are thousands of books in our libraries on all those subjects I have been asking you about?
A	I couldn't say, but I will take your word for it. . . .

Q	Have you any idea how old the earth is?
A	No.
Q	The Book you have introduced in evidence tells you, doesn't it?
A	I don't think it does, Mr. Darrow.
Q	Let's see whether it does; is this the one?
A	That is the one, I think.
Q	It says B.C. 4004?
A	That is Bishop Usher's calculation.
Q	That is printed in the Bible you introduced?
A	Yes, sir. . . .
Q	Would you say that the earth was only 4,000 years old?
A	Oh, no; I think it is much older than that.
Q	How much?
A	I couldn't say.
Q	Do you say whether the Bible itself says it is older than that?
A	I don't think it is older or not.
Q	Do you think the earth was made in six days?
A	Not six days of twenty-four hours.
Q	Doesn't it say so?
A	No, sir. . . .
The Court	Are you about through, Mr. Darrow?
Darrow	I want to ask a few more questions about the creation.
The Court	I know. We are going to adjourn when Mr. Bryan comes off the stand for the day. Be very brief, Mr. Darrow. Of course, I believe I will make myself clearer. Of course, it is incompetent testimony before the jury. The only reason I am allowing this to go in at all is that they may have it in the appellate court as showing what the affidavit would be.
Bryan	The reason I am answering is not for the benefit of the superior court. It is to keep these gentlemen from saying I was afraid to meet them and let them question me, and I want the Christian world to know that any atheist, agnostic, unbeliever, can question me anytime as to my belief in God, and I will answer him.
Darrow	I want to take an exception to this conduct of this witness. He may be very popular down here in the hills. . . .
Bryan	Your honor, they have not asked a question legally and the only reason they have asked any question is for the purpose, as the question about Jonah was

asked, for a chance to give this agnostic an opportunity to criticize a believer in the world of God; and I answered the question in order to shut his mouth so that he cannot go out and tell his atheistic friends that I would not answer his questions. That is the only reason, no more reason in the world.

Malone   Your honor on this very subject, I would like to say that I would have asked Mr. Bryan—and I consider myself as good a Christian as he is—every question that Mr. Darrow has asked him for the purpose of bring out whether or not there is to be taken in this court a literal interpretation of the Bible, or whether, obviously, as these questions indicate, if a general and literal construction cannot be put upon the parts of the Bible which have been covered by Mr. Darrow's questions. I hope for the last time no further attempt will be made by counsel on the other side of the case, or Mr. Bryan, to say the defense is concerned at all with Mr. Darrow's particular religious views or lack of religious views. We are here as lawyers with the same right to our views. I have the same right to mine as a Christian as Mr. Bryan has to his, and we do not intend to have this case charged by Mr. Darrow's agnosticism or Mr. Bryan's brand of Christianity. *(A great applause.)*

Mr. Darrow:

Q   Mr. Bryan, do you believe that the first woman was Eve?

A   Yes.

Q   Do you believe she was literally made out of Adams's rib?

A   I do.

Q   Did you ever discover where Cain got his wife?

A   No, sir; I leave the agnostics to hunt for her.

Q   You have never found out?

A   I have never tried to find

Q   You have never tried to find?

A   No.

Q   The Bible says he got one, doesn't it? Were there other people on the earth at that time?

A   I cannot say.

Q   You cannot say. Did that ever enter your consideration?

A   Never bothered me.

Q   There were no others recorded, but Cain got a wife.

A   That is what the Bible says.

Q   Where she came from you do not know. All right. Does the statement, "The morning and the evening were the first day," and "The morning and the evening were the second day," mean anything to you?

A   I do not think it necessarily means a twenty-four-hour day.

Q   You do not?

A   No.

Q   What do you consider it to be?

A   I have not attempted to explain it. If you will take the second chapter—let me have the book. *(Examining Bible.)* The fourth verse of the second chapter says: "These are the generations of the heavens and of the earth, when they were created in the day that the Lord God made the earth and the heavens," the word "day" there in the very next chapter is used to describe a period. I do not see that there is any necessity for construing the words, "the evening and the morning," as meaning necessarily a twenty-four-hour day, "in the day when the Lord made the heaven and the earth."

Q   Then, when the Bible said, for instance, "and God called the firmament heaven. And the evening and the morning were the second day," that does not necessarily mean twenty-four hours?

A   I do not think it necessarily does.

Q   Do you think it does or does not?

A   I know a great many think so.

Q   What do you think?

A   I do not think it does.

Q   You think those were not literal days?

A   I do not think they were twenty-four-hour days.

Q   What do you think about it?

A   That is my opinion—I do not know that my opinion is better on that subject than those who think it does.

Q   You do not think that?

A   No. But I think it would be just as easy for the kind of God we believe in to make the earth in six days as in six years or in 6,000,000 years or in 600,000,000 years. I do not think it important whether we believe one or the other.

Q   Do you think those were literal days?

A   My impression is they were periods, but I would not attempt to argue as against anybody who wanted to believe in literal days.

Q   I will read it to you from the Bible: "And the Lord God said unto the serpent, because thou hast done this, thou art cursed above all cattle, and above every beast of the field; upon thy belly shalt thou go and dust shalt thou eat all the days of thy life." Do you think that is why the serpent is compelled to crawl upon its belly?

A   I believe that.

Q   Have you any idea how the snake went before that time?

A	No, sir.
Q	Do you know whether he walked on his tail or not?
A	No, sir. I have no way to know. *(Laughter in audience.)*
Q	Now, you refer to the cloud that was put in heaven after the flood, the rainbow. Do you believe in that?
A	Read it.
Q	All right, Mr. Bryan, I will read it for you.
Bryan	Your Honor, I think I can shorten this testimony. The only purpose Mr. Darrow has is to slur at the Bible, but I will answer his question. I will answer it all at once, and I have no objection in the world, I want the world to know that this man, who does not believe in a God, is trying to use a court in Tennesseee—
Darrow	I object to that.
Bryan	*(Continuing)* to slur at it, and while it will require time, I am willing to take it.
Darrow	I object to your statement. I am exempting you on your fool ideas that no intelligent Christian on earth believes.
The Court	Court is adjourned until 9 o'clock tomorrow morning.

Selections from Attorney Briefs to the Supreme Court in:

1. *United States v. Morrison*
2. *Morse v. Frederick*
3. *Gonzales v. Carhart*
4. *Skilling v. United States*

In the Supreme Court of the United States

UNITED STATES OF AMERICA, PETITIONER
v.
ANTONIO J. MORRISON, ET AL.

CHRISTY BRZONKALA, PETITIONER
v.
ANTONIO J. MORRISON, ET AL.

ON WRIT OF CERTIORARI
TO THE UNITED STATES COURT OF APPEALS
FOR THE FOURTH CIRCUIT

BRIEF FOR THE UNITED STATES

Questions Presented

1. Whether 42 U.S.C. § 13981, the provision of the Violence Against Women Act that creates a private right of action for victims of gender-motivated violence, is a valid exercise of Congress's power under the Commerce Clause of the Constitution.

2. Whether 42 U.S.C. § 13981 is a valid exercise of Congress's power under the Enforcement Clause of the Fourteenth Amendment to the Constitution.

SUMMARY OF ARGUMENT

After four years of investigation, Congress determined that violence against women is pervasive in modern American society to a degree that had previously been unrecognized. Congress found that the problem has been exacerbated by the States' failure to treat violent crimes that primarily victimize women, such as rape and domestic abuse, as seriously as other violent crimes. In addition, Congress found that the problem not only devastates the lives of its victims, but also harms the national economy and interstate commerce in many ways. Based on those findings, Congress exercised its powers under the Commerce Clause and the Enforcement Clause of the Fourteenth Amendment to enact Section 13981, a private right of action that enables victims of gender-motivated violence to seek redress against their assailants. Congress acted well within its constitutional authority in doing so.

1. Section 13981 is an appropriate exercise of Congress's power under the Commerce Clause. Congress had far more than the rational basis that this Court has required to conclude that gender-motivated violence substantially affects interstate commerce. Congress found that gender-motivated violence burdens the national economy and interstate commerce in several distinct ways: by deterring women from seeking jobs, including jobs in interstate businesses, that would require them to work at certain hours or in certain places; by inhibiting women from traveling, interstate as well as intrastate, and from engaging in other economic activity; by impeding victims' ability to work at all, or to work productively, thereby forcing many into dependence, poverty, and even homelessness; and by imposing increased medical and other costs on victims, their employers and insurers, and state and local governments. All of those burdens were documented in the extensive legislative record. Congress reviewed that

record with the understanding that the Commerce Clause had long been regarded as an appropriate source of constitutional authority to regulate activity that creates a barrier to the participation of particular groups in the Nation's commerce. *See, e.g., Katzenbach v. McClung*, 379 U.S. 294 (1964); *Heart of Atlanta Motel v. United States*, 379 U.S. 241 (1964).

Contrary to the court of appeals' reasoning, Congress's commerce power is not confined to the regulation of those intrastate activities that are "commercial" or "economic" in nature. It is not the character of the activity, but the substantiality of its impact on interstate commerce, that determines whether the activity may be regulated under the Commerce Clause. As Justices Kennedy and O'Connor suggested in their concurring opinion in *United States v. Lopez*, 514 U.S. 549, 580 (1995), when Congress exercises its commerce power where "neither the [regulated] actors nor their conduct has a commercial character," the regulation might be sustained if it does not "intrude upon an area of traditional state concern." Nor is Section 13981 unconnected to economic activity. The gender-motivated violence remedied by Section 13981 occurs at, or en route to, workplaces, retail establishments, and interstate transportation terminals as well as in other settings; in addition, Section 13981 is directed not only at gender-motivated violence itself, but also at the inadequate state mechanisms for compensating victims for its economic consequences.

Section 13981 does not, as the court of appeals suggested, present the federalism concerns that were presented by the statute at issue in *Lopez*. First, Section 13981 is an exclusively civil remedy that enables victims of gender-motivated violence to seek redress against their assailants-a remedy that supplements, but does not supplant, any remedy that the victims may have under state law. It does not intrude into the operations of state government, operate against the States, or conscript the States or state officials in its enforcement. Second, Section 13981 was intended as, and patterned after, federal civil rights legislation. The vindication of civil rights has long been recognized to be a paradigmatic national responsibility, not one that has been primarily left to the States. Third, Congress enacted Section 13981 to address a problem that, as the States acknowledged, their own justice systems had failed adequately to address. A statute premised on such systemic state failures does not presage an open-ended expansion of federal power into domains properly reserved to the States. Finally, the Violence Against Women Act, of which Section 13981 is a part, is a prototypical example of cooperative federalism. It contains a number of provisions designed to encourage and enhance the States' own efforts to address gender-motivated violence. Section 13981, especially when viewed in the context of the entire Act, poses no threat to federalism principles.

2. Section 13981 is also an appropriate exercise of Congress's power under Section 5 of the Fourteenth Amendment to remedy and deter violations of the Equal Protection Clause. Congress, employing its unique institutional ability to investigate and assess whether legislation is needed to enforce constitutional guarantees, found that pervasive bias in the state justice systems denies victims of gender-motivated violence the equal protection of the laws. Congress based that determination on an extensive record documenting that inaccurate stereotypes about gender-motivated violence and its victims-reflected in state laws, state evidentiary rules, and, especially, the attitudes of police, prosecutors, judges and other state actors-have caused violent crimes motivated by gender animus to be treated less seriously than other violent crimes. It is well-settled that state action based

on inaccurate stereotypes, including stereotypes relating to gender, may violate the Equal Protection Clause. Congress was entitled to invoke its authority under Section 5 to remedy such violations.

Section 13981 is a suitable remedy for the constitutional violations that Congress identified. As Congress explained, Section 13981 gives victims of gender-motivated violence "an opportunity for legal vindication," in either federal or state court, "that the [victim], not the State, controls." 1990 S. Rep. 42. Section 13981 thus remedies and prevents the discrimination that victims of gender-motivated crimes often face in the state justice systems by giving them an alternative means of obtaining legal redress. Congress's broad enforcement authority under Section 5 is not limited, as the court of appeals believed, to the creation of remedies against the States themselves. A remedy that permits victims of gender-motivated violence to seek the vindication withheld by the States is a wholly permissible means of effectuating the purposes of the Fourteenth Amendment.

Section 13981 is fully consistent with this Court's decisions addressing the scope of Congress's power to enforce the Fourteenth Amendment. Section 13981 is unlike the statutes in this Court's Reconstruction-era decisions, which were predicated on the assumption that private conduct may violate the Equal Protection Clause. Those decisions do not bar Congress from reaching the conduct of private persons, when Congress does so to remedy discrimination by the State or its agents. Nor does Section 13981 suffer from the defects that the Court perceived in *City of Boerne v. Flores*, 521 U.S. 507 (1997). Section 13981, unlike the statute in that case, provides a remedy that is congruent and proportional to the constitutional violations that Congress identified. Section 13981 does not redefine the substantive prohibitions of the Fourteenth Amendment. To the contrary, Section 13981 provides an additional remedy for state action that Congress reasonably found would violate equal protection under the standards announced by this Court. And, in contrast to the situation in *Flores*, Section 13981 is an appropriately limited remedy that does not intrude into the operations of state government.

Morse v. Frederick

2006 U.S. Briefs 278 (2007)

Questions Presented

1. Whether the First Amendment allows public schools, at school-sponsored, faculty-supervised events, to prohibit students from displaying messages promoting the use of illegal substances.

[Issue two is omitted.]

ARGUMENT

Under challenge to address declining academic performance in the age of globalization, American public education finds itself—even at a time of war—as a vitally important subject in the unfolding democratic conversation about the Nation's future. The Ninth Circuit's destabilizing decision in this sensitive arena renders all the more daunting the vital task of teachers, administrators, and volunteer school board members in attending holistically to the needs of millions of students entrusted every school day to their charge. In reversing the district court's grant of summary judgment in favor of the Juneau School Board and Deborah Morse, the Ninth Circuit has dramatically altered the legal landscape of public education law in the United States. As to both the First Amendment and the law of qualified immunity, the court of appeals' uncompromisingly libertarian vision is deeply unsettling to public school educators across the country. The decision below is doubly—and dangerously—wrong. The judgment should be reversed.

I. THE JUNEAU SCHOOL OFFICIALS DID NOT VIOLATE FREDERICK'S FIRST AMENDMENT RIGHTS WHEN THEY DISCIPLINED HIM FOR VIOLATING SCHOOL POLICIES AGAINST PROMOTING ILLEGAL SUBSTANCES AT A SCHOOL ACTIVITY.

A. The "special characteristics" of the school setting require deference for school officials' actions.

Throughout the fifty States (and the District of Columbia), public education serves what this Court long ago described as "a principal instrument in awakening the child to cultural values." *Brown v. Bd. of Educ.,* 347 U.S. 483, 493 (1954). Through government-operated educational institutions, large and small, the vast majority of young Americans are prepared "for later professional training" and for "adjust[ing] normally to [their] environment." *Kuhlmeier,* 484 U.S. at 272 (quoting *Brown,* 347 U.S. at 493). Those who serve as teachers and administrators in this challenging environment are tasked with a weighty and delicate responsibility. In prescribing and controlling student conduct, public educators are inexorably required to balance students' constitutionally-guaranteed liberties with the bedrock duty to educate young minds, including fashioning "the boundaries of socially appropriate behavior." *Fraser,* 478 U.S. at 681. Pursuit of these goals inevitably requires authorities to regulate speech, symbolic and otherwise, in a manner impermissible outside the school setting. *Id.* at 682; *accord Bd. of Educ. v. Earls,* 536 U.S. 822 (2002) (upholding high school's random suspicionless drug testing policy); *Vernonia Sch. Dist. 47J v. Acton,* 515 U.S. 646 (1995) (permitting random drug testing of high school student athletes).

In the First Amendment context, this Court has long emphasized that the rights of students in the public schools "are not automatically coextensive with the rights of adults in other settings." *Fraser,* 478 U.S. at 682 (citing *New Jersey v. T.L.O., 469* U.S. 325, 340-342 (1985)). Thus, while students do not "shed their constitutional rights to freedom of speech or expression at the schoolhouse gate," students' rights must be "applied in light of the *special characteristics* of the school environment." *Tinker,* 393 U.S. at 506 (emphasis added). The "uninhibited, robust, and wide-open" free speech in adult discourse, as ordained in *New York Times Co. v. Sullivan,* 376 U.S. 254, 270 (1964), is manifestly different from the latitude accorded to schoolchildren in a "custodial and tutelary" environment. *Vernonia,* 515 U.S. at 655.

As this Court has acknowledged on numerous occasions, the resolution of conflicts arising in the daily operation of school systems "is primarily the responsibility of parents, teachers, and state and local school officials, and not of federal judges." *Kuhlmeier,* 484 U.S. at 273 (citations omitted). Only when a decision to censor student expression has no valid educational purpose is the First Amendment so *"directly and sharply implicate[d]"* as to require judicial intervention to protect students' constitutional rights. *Id.* (quoting *Epperson v. Arkansas,* 393 U.S. 97, 104 (1968)). Thus, in discerning the proper doctrinal limitations upon the baseline liberty guaranteed by the Free Speech Clause, a guiding principle unifying this Court's teachings is that "[a] school need not tolerate student speech that is inconsistent with its 'basic educational mission.'" *Id.* at 266 (citing *Fraser,* 478 U.S. at 685). Firmly embedded in this Court's student speech jurisprudence, that overarching principle is the beginning and end of this case.

1. *Tinker* protects speech that does not intrude upon the work of the [**38] schools.

The framework for student speech doctrine begins with *Tinker.* In that landmark case, the Court upheld the free speech rights of three students to wear anti-war armbands during the school day as a silent, passive political protest. 393 U.S. at 514. The Court reasoned that wearing black armbands, a traditional sign of mourning, was expressive conduct akin to pure speech, which is entitled to comprehensive protection. *Id.* at 505-06. At the same time, the *Tinker* majority recognized the unique characteristics of a public school and the unavoidable reality that administrators and teachers may suppress student speech, whether in class or out of it, that "intrudes upon the work of the schools or the rights of other students." *Id.* at 508. In the record before it, however, the Court could discern no evidence that the passive wearing of two-inch armbands disrupted school operations. *Id.*

The *Tinker* Court had no occasion to spell out in detail the extent or nature of "disruption" necessary to trigger a school's authority to curtail student speech. The Court described the requisite disruption as "interference, actual or nascent, with the schools' work," which is something more than "undifferentiated fear or apprehension of disturbance." *Id.* Under this standard, if a school administrator reasonably perceives (or forecasts) that a student's expressive conduct is presently interfering (or would eventually interfere) with the school's work, then the administrator is warranted in suppressing the particular expression (or expressive conduct). *Id.* Student speech rising to this level of disruption may occur "in class or out of it" and may "stem[] from time, place, or type of behavior." *Id.* at 513. The Court provided further guidance by distinguishing John Tinker's silent, passive conduct from the disciplinary problems posed by "aggressive, disruptive action or even group demonstrations." *Id.* at 507-08. The *Tinker* Court thus foreshadowed its willingness to approve school intervention when speech is accompanied by antisocial conduct.

Justice Black dissented. He lamented that the broad sweep of the majority decision invited students to "use the schools at their whim as a platform" and that courts, rather than schools, "will allocate to themselves the function of deciding how the pupils' school day will be spent." *Id.* at 517 (Black, J., dissenting). Although his opinion failed to carry the day, Justice Black's plain-spoken words continue to echo through the body of student speech law.

2. *Fraser* permits schools to prohibit student speech that undermines the basic educational mission.

Fraser—the second stage of the student speech decisional trilogy—assured school officials that they retain authority to proscribe student speech that is vulgar, lewd, indecent, obscene, or plainly offensive, even absent a showing of material and substantial disruption to school discipline. 478 U.S. at 683-84. Drawing from *Tinker,* the *Fraser* Court emphasized that inculcating habits and manners of civility—through discouraging offensive language— is "truly the 'work of the schools.'" *Id.* at 683 (quoting *Tinker,* 393 U.S. at 508). To force a school to tolerate indecorous student speech, wrote Chief Justice Burger, "would undermine the school's basic educational mission." *Id.* at 685

Applying this principle, the *Fraser* Court reversed the Ninth Circuit's contrary judgment and upheld a public high school's disciplining a student for delivering a sexually suggestive nominating speech for a student government candidate at a voluntary school assembly. *Id.* That speech referred to the candidate in terms of "an elaborate, graphic, and explicit sexual metaphor," though the speaker's saucy presentation employed neither profanity nor obscenity. *Id.* at 677-78. Under the circumstances, the Court determined that "it was perfectly appropriate for the school to disassociate itself to make the point to the pupils that vulgar speech and lewd conduct is wholly inconsistent with the 'fundamental values' of public school education." *Id.* at 685-86. On that note, the Court embraced Justice Black's broad teaching in *Tinker* that "the Federal Constitution [does not] compel[] . . . teachers, parents, and elected school officials to surrender control of the American public school system to public school students." *Id.* at 686 (quoting *Tinker,* 393 U.S. at 526 (Black, J., dissenting)).

Emphasizing that not all types of speech are accorded identical protection, particularly in view of the "special characteristics" of the educational setting, the *Fraser* Court recognized "the marked distinction between the political 'message' of the armbands in *Tinker* and the sexual content of [Matthew Fraser's] speech." *Id.* at 680. The Court acknowledged that some speech is properly subject to age-appropriate restrictions: "[Fraser's sexually explicit] speech could well be seriously damaging to its less mature audience, many of whom were only 14 years old and on the threshold of awareness of human sexuality." *Id.* at 683. n6 In that regard, the *Fraser* Court echoed Justice Stewart's concurrence in *Tinker,* where the Justice from Cincinnati articulated the view that "[a] State may permissibly determine that, at least in some precisely delineated areas, a child—like someone in a captive audience—is not possessed of that full capacity for individual choice which is the presupposition of First Amendment guarantees." *Tinker,* 393 U.S. at 515 (Stewart, J., concurring) (quoting *Ginsburg v. New York,* 390 U.S. 629, 649-50 (1968) (Stewart, J., concurring in result). Significantly for First Amendment analysis, Fraser's ribald electioneering pronouncements fell well below the standards for "obscenity" established in adult contexts. *See, e.g., Miller v. California,* 413 U.S. 15 (1973). The bedrock point from *Tinker* remained: The public education setting has "special characteristics" profoundly informing First Amendment analysis.

Justice Brennan concurred in the judgment. He agreed that, "under certain circumstances, high school students may properly be reprimanded for giving a speech at a high school assembly which school officials conclude disrupted the school's educational mission." *Fraser,* 478 U.S. at 688-89 (Brennan, J., concurring). In dissent, Justice Stevens similarly recognized the appropriateness of disciplining students for expressive conduct that conflicts with a school's educational mission. *Id.* at 691 (Stevens, J., dissenting). He opined that "a school faculty must regulate the content as well as the style of student speech in carrying out its educational mission." *Id.* (Stevens, J., dissenting).

3. *Kuhlmeier* allows student speech restrictions in school-sponsored activities when pursuant to legitimate pedagogical concerns.

Fraser's deferential approach to school officials' First Amendment calibrations was likewise embraced in *Kuhlmeier.* In this final stage of the Court's school speech trilogy, the Court acknowledged that school officials are entitled to exercise pervasive control over the style and content of student speech that reasonably might be perceived to bear the school's imprimatur. 484 U.S. at 273. Regulation of speech viewed as "school-sponsored"—on account of the school lending its name and resources to the activity—is permitted if the curtailment is reasonably related to "legitimate pedagogical concerns." *Id.* Thus, in *Kuhlmeier,* a school properly exercised its discretion in refusing to publish certain student articles on pregnancy and divorce in a school-funded student newspaper. *Id.* at 276. The Court concluded that suppression of the articles was reasonably related to the tripartite school objectives of (i) protecting the privacy of the individuals referenced in the articles; (ii) shielding younger students from inappropriate subject matter; and (iii) teaching journalistic fairness. *Id.*

The *Kuhlmeier* Court added that "[a] school must also retain the authority to refuse to sponsor student speech that might reasonably be perceived to advocate drug or alcohol use." 484 U.S. at 272. Alluding to Fraser's emphasis on upholding schools' "educational mission," the majority recognized that promoting illegal substances was "inconsistent with 'the shared values of a civilized social order.'" *Id.* (quoting *Fraser,* 478 U.S. at 683). Thus, the Court left no doubt that discouraging illegal substance use reflected a legitimate pedagogical concern.

B. The *Tinker-Fraser-Kuhlmeier* trilogy permitted Juneau school officials to discipline Frederick for promoting illegal substances.

The case at hand fits comfortably within the framework of the school speech trilogy. In sharp contrast to Tinker's anti-war armband, Frederick's "bong hits" banner did not involve the passive expression of a political viewpoint. Rather, his slang marijuana reference was part of an antisocial publicity stunt designed to draw attention away from an important (and historic) school activity. The message that Principal Morse, Superintendent Bader, the unanimous School Board, and Chief Judge Sedwick all reasonably gleaned from this banner—and on which the Ninth Circuit proceeded—was that it expressed a positive sentiment about marijuana use. Frederick cannot reasonably contend otherwise. The message was therefore directly contrary to the school's basic educational mission of promoting a healthy, drug-free lifestyle (as expressed in written School Board policies). In the context of a school-sponsored activity, Principal Morse's restriction of this expression was indisputably consistent with an important pedagogical concern. The trilogy—when distilled to its essential principles—stands for the proposition that students have limited free speech rights balanced against the School District's right to carry out its educational mission and to maintain discipline. Under this body of law, Frederick's claim to First Amendment protection falls woefully short.

1. Discouraging use of illegal substances is an undeniably important educational mission.

Preventing teenage drug use is a critical educational mission of our public schools. "That the nature of the concern is important—indeed perhaps compelling—can hardly be doubted." *Vernonia*, 515 U.S. at 661; *see also Lorillard Tobacco Co. v. Reilly*, 533 U.S. 525, 599 (2001) (Souter, J., concurring in part and dissenting in part) ("[F]ew interests are more 'compelling,' than ensuring that minors do not become addicted to a dangerous drug before they are able to make a mature and informed decision as to the health risks associated with that substance. . . ."). While drug abuse remains a serious problem with adults, the severity is even more pronounced with elementary and secondary schoolchildren:

School years are the time when the physical, psychological, and addictive effects of drugs are most severe. Maturing nervous systems are more critically impaired by intoxicants than mature ones are; childhood losses in learning are lifelong and profound; children grow chemically dependent more quickly than adults, and their record of recovery is depressingly poor. And of course the effects of a drug-infested school are visited not just upon the users, but upon the entire student body and faculty, as the educational process is disrupted.

Vernonia, 515 U.S. at 661-62 (internal citations and quotation marks omitted). Troublingly, "[t]he drug abuse problem among our Nation's youth . . . has only grown worse" in recent years, thus "mak[ing] the war against drugs a pressing concern in every school." *Earls*, 536 U.S. at 834.

In view of this flinty reality, this Court has determined that "'special needs' . . . exist in the public school context" to justify overriding Fourth Amendment privacy interests that would otherwise apply outside the school setting. *Id.* at 843; *Vernonia*, 515 U.S. at 653. Accordingly, the majorities in *Earls* and *Vernonia* upheld random drug testing of students participating in extracurricular activities. 536 U.S. at 837-38; 515 U.S. at 664-65. These precedents once again confirmed that constitutional protections for schoolchildren are inexorably informed (and frequently diluted) by "the *special characteristics* of the school environment." *Tinker*, 393 U.S. at 506 (emphasis added).

Student free speech rights likewise appropriately yield when it comes to promoting illegal substances. "[T]he single most important factor leading schoolchildren to take drugs . . . [is] peer pressure." *Earls*, 536 U.S. at 840 (Breyer, J., concurring). Impressionable adolescents face strong inducements to use drugs as they are bombarded with pro-drug messages from classmates, adults, and the media. Remaining steadfastly consistent with the drug-free-lifestyle message is therefore particularly important while school is in session. Congress recognized this fact in passing the comprehensive Safe and Drug Free Schools and Communities Act, which supports local schools' drug prevention efforts and requires consistency of message that illegal drugs are "wrong and harmful." 20 U.S.C. § 7114(d)(6).

Consistent with Congress' mandate, thousands of local school boards across the country, much like Juneau's, have addressed the drug problem by crafting policies related to drug-abuse prevention, intervention, treatment, and discipline. Pet. at 17-21. These policies are adopted by duly-elected school board members through a public, deliberative process. The Juneau School Board, for example, is required by statute to develop and periodically review its policies governing student rights and responsibilities. Alaska Admin. Code tit. 4, § 07.010. These student conduct rules must substantively and procedurally comply with applicable laws and regulations. *Id.* Through this exercise in constitutional self-government, a common prohibatory theme has emerged: Messages promoting illegal substances are not to be tolerated during school or any school activities. *See* Pet. App. 52a-58a (various anti-drug-message policies adopted in 1985, as revised).

Not surprisingly, lower courts addressing First Amendment challenges to anti-drug school policies had reached a bottom-line consensus—at least prior to *Frederick.* Several courts had recognized that prohibitions on pro-drug messages are constitutional because such expression is "plainly offensive" under *Fraser* and inconsistent with the mission of schools to promote healthy lifestyles (including by seeking at every turn to combat substance abuse). *See, e.g., Boroff,* 220 F.3d at 471 (upholding ban on Marilyn Manson t-shirts because singer promoted drug use); *Nixon v. N. Local Sch. Dist.,* 383 F. Supp. 2d 965, 971 (S.D. Ohio 2005) ("Examples [of offensive speech under *Fraser*] are speech containing vulgar language, graphic sexual innuendos, or speech that promotes suicide, drugs, alcohol, or murder."); *Barber v. Dearborn Pub. Sch.,* 286 F. Supp. 2d 847, 859 (E.D. Mich. 2003) ("[W]hen student speech is . . . lewd, obscene, or vulgar (including related to alcohol or drugs), school officials may curtail that speech."); *Gano v. Sch. Dist. No. 411,* 674 F. Supp. 796, 798-99 (D. Idaho 1987) (upholding prohibition of t-shirt depicting drunken administrators under *Fraser,* noting that schools have a duty to teach about harmful effects of alcohol).

Other courts have observed that there can be little dispute that messages promoting illegal substances cause disruption within schools. *See Williams v. Spencer,* 622 F.2d 1200, 1205-06 (4th Cir. 1980) (taking judicial notice that messages promoting drug use endanger students' health and safety; prohibiting distribution of underground newspaper containing drug paraphernalia advertisements); *cf. McIntire v. Bethel Sch.,* 804 F. Supp. 1415, 1420-21 (W.D. Okla. 1992) ("Reasonable school officials could forecast that the wearing of clothing bearing a message advertising an alcoholic beverage would substantially disrupt or materially interfere with the teaching of the adverse effects of alcohol and that its consumption by minors is illegal and/or would substantially disrupt or materially interfere with school discipline.").

Still other courts have upheld bans on pro-drug messages in the context of school-sponsored activities. *See Bannon v. Sch. Dist. of Palm Beach County,* 387 F.3d 1208, 1219 (11th Cir. 2004) (approving viewpoint discrimination in school-sponsored speech to forbid pro-drug messages); *Planned Parenthood of S. Nev., Inc. v. Clark County Sch. Dist.,* 941 F.2d 817 (9th Cir. 1991) (permitting school policy banning ads in school publications for tobacco and liquor products); *McCann v. Fort Zumwalt Sch. Dist.,* 50 F. Supp. 2d 918, 920 (E.D. Mo. 1999) (upholding prohibition against school band playing song "White Rabbit" because it might "reasonably be perceived" to advocate the use of illegal drugs).

More broadly, discouraging drug use has been universally recognized and sanctioned by school boards, legislatures, courts (including this Court) as a permissible educational goal. n9 The *Frederick* decision appears to be the first case in American jurisprudence in which any court—federal or state—has stripped public school officials of authority to proscribe pro-drug messages. n10 This Court should remove any lingering doubt whether school authorities, pursuant to their basic educational mission, retain discretion to restrict student speech that is reasonably viewed as promoting or advocating the use of substances that are illegal to minors.

. . . . .

In the Supreme Court of the United States

ALBERTO R. GONZALES, ATTORNEY GENERAL, PETITIONER

v.

LEROY CARHART, ET AL.

ON WRIT OF CERTIORARI
TO THE UNITED STATES COURT OF APPEALS
FOR THE EIGHTH CIRCUIT

BRIEF FOR THE PETITIONER

Question Presented

The Partial-Birth Abortion Ban Act of 2003 (the Act), Pub. L. No. 108-105, 117 Stat. 1201 (18 U.S.C. 1531 (Supp. III 2003)), prohibits a physician from knowingly performing a "partial-birth abortion" (as defined in the statute) in or affecting interstate commerce. Act § 3, 117 Stat. 1206-1207. The Act contains an exception for cases in which the abortion is necessary to preserve the life of the mother, but no corresponding exception for the health of the mother. Congress, however, made extensive factual findings, including a finding that "partial-birth abortion is never medically indicated to preserve the health of the mother." § 2(14)(O), 117 Stat. 1206. The question presented is as follows:

Whether, notwithstanding Congress's determination that a health exception was unnecessary to preserve the health of the mother, the Partial-Birth Abortion Ban Act of 2003 is invalid because it lacks a health exception or is otherwise unconstitutional on its face.

ARGUMENT

I. THE ABSENCE OF A HEALTH EXCEPTION DOES NOT RENDER THE ACT FACIALLY INVALID

A. A Statute That Regulates Abortion, But Lacks A Health Exception, Is Not Facially Invalid Unless It Would Cre ate Significant Health Risks, And Thereby Impose An Undue Burden, In A Large Fraction Of Its Applications

B. When Analyzed Under The Proper Standard, The Record Overwhelmingly Supports Congress's Judgment That No Health Exception Was Required

[The arguments for Point IA and IB are omitted.]

C. Even Assuming That Partial-Birth Abortion Has Marginal Health Advantages In Some Cases, A Statute That Prohibits Partial-Birth Abortion Does Not Impose An Undue Burden On A Woman's Access To An Abortion

Even if the Court refused to defer to Congress's considered findings, respondents' trial evidence at most suggested that partial-birth abortion is marginally safer than other abortion procedures in some circumstances. Absent a showing that it would "create significant health risks," however, a statute prohibiting partial-birth abortion does not impose an undue burden on a woman's access to an abortion. *Stenberg,* 530 U.S. at 932 (emphasis added).

Casey's undue-burden standard effectively replaced the strict-scrutiny standard from *Roe. See* 505 U.S. at 876. In adopting the undue-burden standard, the joint opinion in *Casey* emphasized that the government has a "profound interest in potential life," id. at

878, and reasoned that "[t]he very notion that the [government] has a substantial interest in potential life leads to the conclusion that not all [abortion] regulations must be deemed unwarranted," *id.* at 876. Where the regulation at issue limits a specific method of abortion, the difference in safety must be significant enough that elimination of that method places a "substantial obstacle in the path of a woman seeking an abortion," in light of the continuing availability of other methods. *Id.* at 878. A different rule would force courts to make difficult medical judgment calls and would devalue the vital government interests that *Casey* sought to bring back into the equation in reviewing abortion regulations.

The protection of innocent human life-in or out of the womb-is the most compelling interest the government can advance. The Act implicates not only the government's compelling interest in protecting human life, but also the govern ment's specific (and no less compelling) interest in prohibiting a particular type of abortion procedure that closely resembles infanticide. *See, e.g., Stenberg,* 530 U.S. at 960, 962 (Kennedy, J., dissenting) (noting that, "[i]n light of the description of the D&X procedure, it should go without saying that Nebraska's ban on partial birth abortion furthers purposes States are entitled to pursue" and adding that "Nebraska was entitled to find the existence of a consequential moral difference between the [D&X and D&E] procedures"); *id.* at 1006 (Thomas, J., dissenting) (stating that "[t]here is no question that the State of Nebraska has a valid interest-one not designed to strike at the right itself-in prohibiting partial birth abortion" and adding that "States may, without a doubt, express [their] pro found respect [for the life of the unborn] by prohibiting a procedure that approaches infanticide").

In passing the Act, Congress specifically found that partial-birth abortion "blurs the line between abortion and infanticide in the killing of a partially-born child just inches from birth," Act § 2(14)(O), 117 Stat. 1206; that partial-birth abortion "also confuses the medical, legal, and ethical duties of physicians to preserve and promote life," § 2(14)(J), 117 Stat. 1205; and that failing to prohibit the procedure would "promote[] a complete disregard for infant human life," § 2(14)(L), 117 Stat. 1206, and "further coarsen society to the humanity of not only newborns, but all vulnerable and innocent human life, making it increasingly difficult to protect such life," § 2(14)(N), 117 Stat. 1206. In light of the relative strength of the government's interest in prohibiting partial- birth abortion, and the relative weakness of a woman's interest in having access to a particular type of abortion procedure that has no health advantages (according to Congress), or at most marginal health advantages, when compared with other, unregulated types of procedures, the Act is constitutional under *Casey* because it does not impose an undue burden on a woman's access to an abortion.

Holding that the Act is valid only if it contains a health exception would substantially undermine the government's compelling interests in preventing partial-birth abortion. As proponents of the Act appreciated,13 a health exception, no matter how narrowly crafted, would potentially give a physician unfettered discretion in determining when a partial-birth abortion may be performed. *Cf. Stenberg,* 530 U.S. at 972 (Kennedy, J., dissenting). Congress could thus have reason ably determined that a ban on partial-birth abortion that in cludes a health exception would amount to no ban at all.

D. To The Extent That The Court Believes That Stenberg Compels A Different Result, It Should Be Overruled

For the reasons explained above, the Act is constitutional under the principles adopted by the joint opinion in *Casey* and applied by this Court in *Stenberg*, notwithstanding the absence of a health exception. Although this Court reached a contrary result in *Stenberg* with respect to the state statute at issue there, *Stenberg* is distinguishable in a number of important respects from this case. Most notably, the statute at issue here is an Act of Congress accompanied by congressional findings-including the ultimate finding that partial-birth abortion is never medically indicated-that are amply supported by substantial evidence and therefore entitled to deference. In addition, the statute at issue carefully defines partial-birth abortion so that it does not reach the more common D&E procedure. *See* pp. 45-48, *infra*. Moreover, the trial record supporting the constitutionality of the Act is much more extensive than in *Stenberg*, where the trial lasted only one day (whereas the trial in this case lasted two weeks).

If this Court nevertheless concludes for any reason that its decision in *Stenberg* compels the conclusion that the Act is unconstitutional, however, *Stenberg* should be overruled. To be sure, values of stare decisis help ensure continuity in the law as developed by this Court. However, to the extent that the Court construes *Stenberg* to require invalidation of the statute at issue, continuing adherence to *Stenberg* could not further those values, because such a reading of *Stenberg* would be unfaithful to the Court's prior precedents, including *Casey*, *see Stenberg*, 530 U.S. at 957, 960-963, 979 (Kennedy, J., joined by Rehnquist, C.J., dissenting); *id.* at 1005-1020 (Thomas, J., joined by Rehnquist, C.J., and Scalia, J., dissening); *National Abortion Federation v. Gonzales*, 437 F.3d at 292 (Walker, C.J., concurring); it would risk "caus[ing] * * * society as a whole to become insensitive, even disdainful, to life, including life in the human fetus," *Stenberg*, 530 U.S. at 961 (Kennedy, J., dissenting); and it would therefore only further unsettle this Court's abortion jurisprudence. More over, to the extent that *Stenberg* is read to require courts to disregard legislative findings and make fine-tuned judgments about the relative merits of particular medical techniques, it would place judges in an untenable position and would prove unworkable in practice. Indeed, the different analytical approaches reflected in the various lower-court opinions on the constitutionality of the Act demonstrate that *Stenberg* has created confusion and proven unworkable already.

In the Supreme Court of the United States

JEFFREY K. SKILLING, PETITIONER

v.

UNITED STATES OF AMERICA

ON WRIT OF CERTIORARI
TO THE UNITED STATES COURT OF APPEALS
FOR THE FIFTH CIRCUIT

BRIEF FOR THE UNITED STATES

Questions Presented

1. Whether, to convict petitioner of conspiring to commit wire fraud by depriving his employer and its shareholders of the right to petitioner's honest services (18 U.S.C. 1343, 1346), the government was required to prove that petitioner intended to obtain some private gain.

2. Whether 18 U.S.C. 1346 is unconstitutionally vague.

3. Whether the district court erred in denying petitioner's motions for a change of venue.

In the Supreme Court of the United States

ARGUMENT

I. THE DENIAL OF PETITIONER'S VENUE TRANSFER MOTIONS DID NOT VIOLATE HIS FAIR TRIAL RIGHTS

Petitioner contends (Br. 23-38) that the district court violated his due process right to a fair trial and his Sixth Amendment right to an impartial jury by denying his motions for a change of venue. He argues that pretrial publicity surrounding Enron's collapse created an irrebuttable "presumption of prejudice," requiring automatic reversal of his convictions without regard to whether the jury that decided his case was actually biased. Alternatively, petitioner contends that the "presumption of prejudice" obligated the government to prove the impartiality of each juror beyond a reasonable doubt, that the courts below erroneously failed to hold the government to that burden, and that the government could not make such a showing in any event.

The Court should reject those claims. Petitioner received what the Constitution guaranteed him: a trial before a panel of unbiased jurors capable of deciding the case based on the evidence presented in court. Although language in some of this Court's cases speaks of a presumption of juror prejudice from pretrial publicity, no holding of this Court requires the general irrebuttable presumption of jury prejudice that petitioner seeks. And many of this Court's cases attest to the efficacy of the usual trial tools employed to ferret out bias. To the extent a presumption of prejudice exists, it would not apply in this case, and even if it did apply, it would not require "automatic reversal" of petitioner's convictions. Instead, any such presumption would shift to the government the burden to show by a preponderance the actual impartiality of the seated jury. For the reasons the court of appeals identified, the government amply satisfied that showing.

A. Because The Jury That Decided His Case Was Impartial, Petitioner Has Failed To Establish A Constitutional Violation

Petitioner emphasizes the publicity generated by Enron's collapse, contending that such media coverage, combined with the financial impact of the company's bankruptcy, rendered Houston a constitutionally impermissible venue for his trial. That contention is incorrect. The Constitution guarantees a trial before a jury that is actually impartial, not a trial in a venue whose populace has no exposure to the effects of the defendant's crime or adverse pretrial publicity about it. Because no biased juror sat on petitioner's jury, no violation of rights occurred.

1. The Constitution requires trial before an impartial jury

"The constitutional standard of fairness requires that a defendant have a panel of impartial, indifferent jurors." *Murphy v. Florida*, 421 U.S. 794, 799 (1975) (internal quotation marks and citation omitted); *see Smith v. Phillips,* 455 U.S. 209, 217 (1982) ("Due process means a jury capable and willing to decide the case solely on the evidence before it"). That principle is satisfied when no biased juror is actually seated at trial. See *Rivera v. Illinois*, 129 S. Ct. 1446, 1454 (2009) ("[H]aving been tried by a jury on which no biased juror sat, [the defendant] could not tenably assert any violation of his right to due process.") (internal quotation marks, citations, and ellipsis omitted); *see id*. at 1450 ("[i]f all seated jurors are qualified and unbiased," erroneous denial of defendant's peremptory challenge does not warrant reversal); *see also United States v. Martinez-Salazar*, 528 U.S. 304, 316 (2000); *Ross v. Oklahoma*, 487 U.S. 81, 85 (1988); *Patton v. Yount*, 467 U.S. 1025, 1035 (1984) ("The relevant question" is whether the jurors who decided the case "had such fixed opinions that they could not judge impartially the guilt of the defendant.").

A defendant who argues that he was deprived of an impartial jury must establish that claim "not as a matter of speculation but as a demonstrable reality." United States ex rel. *Darcy v. Handy*, 351 U.S. 454, 462 (1956) (citation omitted). Thus, "[t]his Court has long held that the remedy for allegations of juror partiality" is the defendant's "opportunity to prove actual bias" on the part of a seated juror. *Smith*, 455 U.S. at 215; *see Dennis v. United States*, 339 U.S. 162, 171-172 (1950) ("Preservation of the opportunity to prove actual bias is a guarantee of a defendant's right to an impartial jury."). When the defendant's claim of bias arises from allegedly prejudicial publicity, "the appropriate safeguard against such prejudice is the defendant's right to demonstrate that the media's coverage of his case-be it printed or broadcast-compromised the ability of the particular jury that heard the case to adjudicate fairly." *Smith*, 455 U.S. at 217 (quoting *Chandler v. Florida*, 449 U.S. 560, 575 (1981)).

2. Petitioner's jury was impartial

a. Petitioner has failed to establish that any juror who decided his case was actually biased. Voir dire demonstrated that, whatever the beliefs of Houston residents generally, the particular individuals selected for petitioner's jury neither knew nor cared much about Enron's collapse or the resulting media coverage. See p. 12, *supra* (noting that nine jurors did not read the Houston Chronicle, four rarely or never watched television, and ten said that they did not follow the news about Enron). The overwhelming sentiment among the seated jurors was indifference to events that did not concern them and that were by then "old news." J.A. 856a. The juror's statements thus indicated that they were eminently "capable and willing to decide the case solely on the evidence before [them]." *Smith*, 455 U.S. at 217.

Petitioner's own actions during voir dire underscore the absence of actual bias among the seated jurors. Although petitioner moved to strike eight potential jurors for cause, he did not assert such a challenge specifically to 11 of the 12 individuals who sat on the jury. Indeed, counsel for both petitioner and his co-defendant declined to ask a single question of four of the seated jurors, apparently satisfied, after reading those jurors' questionnaires and hearing their responses to the court's initial inquiry, that they did not harbor any bias or partiality.

The jury's verdict confirmed its impartiality. Although the jurors found petitioner guilty on some counts, they also found him not guilty on nine counts. The counts of acquittal, moreover, concerned allegations that petitioner had enriched himself at the expense of Enron shareholders by selling company stock based on inside information. If petitioner were correct that the jury was infected with a venomous anti-Enron sentiment, conviction on those charges, regardless of the sufficiency of the evidence, would have served as an apt means to express the jury's purported desire for "revenge" on behalf of Houston's residents. That the jurors instead unanimously voted to find petitioner not guilty of nine insider trading charges speaks volumes about their ability, irrespective of any pretrial publicity about the case, "conscientiously [to] apply the law and find the facts" based on the evidence at trial. *Lockhart v. McCree*, 476 U.S. 162, 178 (1986).

b. In an effort to establish actual bias, petitioner emphasizes certain comments made by jurors whom he declined to challenge for cause. That effort, however, relies on a selective and incomplete characterization of the record. Petitioner notes, for example, that one juror expressed sympathy on his questionnaire for the "small average worker [who] saves money for retirement all his life." Pet. Br. 14. But petitioner chose not to challenge that juror (or even to ask him any questions) after the juror made clear that he "underst[oo]d that it's the government's job to prove guilt beyond a reasonable doubt" and did not have "any problem" with that requirement; that he "[v]ery seldom" read the Houston Chronicle and never watched the news; and that he had "no opinion" about the defendant's guilt. J.A. 981a-983a. Similarly, petitioner attacks another juror as biased because she stated on her questionnaire that "someone had to be doing something illegal" in connection with Enron's collapse. Br. 14. Petitioner omits to mention, however, that at voir dire the same juror explained that "[b]ecause it never really affected [her]," she "never really paid that much attention" to news about Enron; that she "ha[d] really honestly not formed an opinion" about petitioner's guilt; and that she "[a]bsolutely" could "base [her] decision only on the evidence in the case." J.A. 1010a-1011a. Petitioner did not seek to ask that juror any questions, much less to remove her on grounds that she was biased.

. . . . .

accommodation theory An interpretation of the Establishment Clause wherein the Court affirms the importance of religion in American society and accommodates its presence in our government.

administrative agency A sub-branch of the government set up to carry out the laws. For example, the police department is a local administrative agency and the IRS is a national one.

admiralty A court that handles most maritime (seagoing) matters, such as collisions between ships and shipping claims.

affidavit A written statement sworn to before a person officially permitted by law to administer an oath.

amnesty A wiping out, by the government, of guilt for persons guilty of a crime; a general governmental forgiving; a general pardon.

antifederalists Those persons opposing the ratification of the U.S. Constitution.

arraign To bring a defendant before a judge to hear the charges and to enter a plea (guilty, not guilty, etc.). [pronounce: ah-rayn]

Articles of Confederation The document that held together the thirteen original American colonies before the adoption of the Constitution.

attach Formally seizing property (or a person) in order to bring it under the control of the court. This is usually done by getting a court order to have a law enforcement officer take control of the property.

bicameral Having two chambers. A two-part legislature, such as the U.S. Congress, is bicameral; it is composed of the Senate (the "upper house" or "upper chamber") and the House of Representatives (the "lower house" or "lower chamber").

bifurcated trial Separate hearings for different issues in the same case; for example, for guilt and sanity or guilt and punishment in a criminal trial or for liability and damages in a complicated auto injury trial.

bill of attainder The wiping out of civil rights that may occur when a person is found guilty of a felony or receives a death sentence. It usually includes the government's taking of all the person's property. This practice is no longer done in the United States. A bill of attainder was a legislative act pronouncing a person guilty (usually of treason) without a trial and sentencing the person to death and attainder. This practice is now prohibited by the U.S. Constitution (Article I, Section 9).

case brief A summary of a published opinion in a case. Preparing the summary helps in understanding the opinion and simplifies later review.

case law All reported judicial decisions; the law derived from judges' opinions in lawsuits (as opposed to, for example, the laws passed by a legislature).

checks and balances A restraint.

civil commitment Confinement by a noncriminal process in a mental hospital or other treatment facility for insanity or for alcohol or drug addiction. The usual justification for confining a person who has not committed a crime is that he or she "is a danger to self or others."

clear and convincing evidence Stronger evidence than a preponderance of the evidence (evidence that something is more likely to be true than false) but not as strong as beyond a reasonable doubt. Clear and convincing evidence is required for a few civil lawsuits, such as those involving the reformation of a contract.

commission A written grant of authority to do a particular thing, given by the government to one of its branches or to an individual or organization.

common law Legal principles and obligations developed through court cases rather than legislative action.

commute Changing a criminal punishment to one less severe.

concurrent Running together; having the same authority at the same time. As examples, courts have concurrent jurisdiction when each one has the power to deal with the same case; concurrent sentences are prison terms that run at the same time; and federal and state governments have concurrent power to govern in many areas.

concurring opinion (concur) A concurring opinion, or concurrence, is one in which a judge agrees with the result reached in an opinion by another judge in the same case but not necessarily with the reasoning the other judge used to reach the conclusion.

condemnation A governmental taking of private property with payment, but not necessarily with consent.

conflict preemption The principle that a state law is unconstitutional because it conflicts with a federal law.

constitutional courts Courts created pursuant to the U.S. Constitution.

contempt A willful disobeying of a judge's command or official court order. It is also possible to be in contempt of a legislature or an administrative agency.

Declaration of Independence The July 4, 1776, announcement by the Continental Congress (representatives of the thirteen colonies) that because of specified grievances the colonies were no longer subject to British rule but were free states. The Declaration of Independence is not a part of U.S. law, but its principles are reflected in the U.S. Constitution.

defamation Transmission to others of false statements that harm the reputation, business, or property rights of a person.

discrete and insular minority A phrase used by the Supreme Court to refer to suspect classes of people.

dissenting opinion (dissent) A judge's formal disagreement with the decision of the majority of the judges in a lawsuit. If a judge puts it in writing, then it is called a dissenting opinion.

diversity of citizenship The situation that occurs when persons on one side of a case in federal court come from a different state than persons on the other side.

Dormant Commerce Clause The principle that the Commerce Clause prevents state regulation of interstate commerce even if the specific regulated activity is not covered by federal laws.

duty of tonnage Governmental port charges or port taxes on a boat.

duty A tax on imports or exports.

electoral college A name for the persons chosen by voters to elect the president and vice president of the United States. The electoral college is now almost a formality, since the electoral college generally votes in accordance with the popular vote of a state. Theoretically, however, some electors might decide to vote differently, a choice that could change the result of a close election.

eminent domain The government's right and power to take private land for public use by paying for it.

enabling clause The section or clause in a constitutional article or amendment that grants Congress the power to make laws to enforce the article or amendment.

enjoin Require or command. A court's issuing of an injunction directing someone to do or, more likely, to refrain from doing certain acts.

enumerated powers Mentioned specifically; listed one by one.

Establishment Clause That part of the First Amendment to the U.S. Constitution that states "Congress shall make no law respecting an *establishment* of religion."

et seq. (Latin) Abbreviation for *et sequentes* ("and the following"). For example, "page 27 et seq." means "page twenty-seven and the following pages." Used with a code citation, it means "and the following code sections."

ex post facto laws (Latin) After the fact. An *ex post facto law* is one that retroactively attempts to make an action a crime that was not a crime at the time it was done or a law that attempts to reduce a person's rights based on a past act that was not subject to the law when it was done. Ex post facto laws are prohibited by the U.S. Constitution (Article I, Section 9).

exclusionary rule 1. A reason why even relevant evidence will be kept out of a trial. 2. Often refers to the rule that illegally gathered evidence may not be used in a criminal trial.

exclusive Shutting out all others; sole; one only. For example, if a court has exclusive jurisdiction over a subject, no other court in the area can decide a lawsuit on that subject.

execute Complete, make, perform, do, or carry out; for example, an official carrying out (executing) a court's order.

executive agreement A document, similar to a treaty, that is signed by the president but does not require the approval of the Senate (as a treaty does).

executive immunity The freedom of the president from arrest, criminal prosecution, or civil lawsuits for official acts.

executive order A rule or procedure created by the president or a governor that does not need to be passed by the legislature.

executive privilege The right of the president and subordinates to keep some information (primarily documents) from public disclosure. The privilege is used most often for military and diplomatic secrets.

exigent (exigency) A sudden event that requires immediate attention; an urgent state of affairs. Exigent circumstances may permit law officers to conduct the search or arrest of a person without a warrant.

express preemption The principle that a state law is unconstitutional because a federal law expressly supersedes it.

extradite Extradition; one country (or state) giving up a person to a second country (or state) when the second requests the person for a trial or for punishment after trial.

facially neutral A type of law that does not discriminate by its terms, but may result in discriminatory practices anyway.

fairness doctrine A former Federal Communications Commission rule that broadcasters must present, or give others a chance to present, all sides of major public issues if they present one side.

federal question A legal issue directly involving the U.S. Constitution, statutes, or treaties. Federal courts have jurisdiction in cases involving a federal question.

federalism A system of political organization with several different levels of government (e.g., city, state, and national) coexisting in the same area, with the lower levels having some independent powers.

federalists Those persons supporting the ratification of the U.S. Constitution.

field preemption The principle that a state law is unconstitutional because Congress impliedly usurped total control over the subject matter by enacting federal legislation.

Free Exercise Clause That part of the First Amendment to the U.S. Constitution that states "Congress shall make no law . . . prohibiting the *free exercise* [*of religion*]."

fruit of the poisonous tree The rule that evidence gathered as a result of evidence gained in an illegal search or questioning cannot be used against the person searched or questioned even if the later evidence was gathered lawfully.

full faith and credit The constitutional requirement that each state must treat as valid, and enforce where appropriate, the laws and court decisions of other states. There are exceptions to this rule, especially those cases in which the other state lacked proper jurisdiction.

fundamental right The basic rights, such as the right to vote and the right to travel, most strongly protected by the Constitution.

gerrymandering Creating geographical voting districts in such a way that one group is favored over another.

headnotes A summary of a case, or of an important legal point made in the case, placed at the beginning of the case when it is published. A case may have several headnotes.

immunity The freedom of national, state, and local government officials from prosecution for, or arrest during, most official acts, and their freedom from most tort lawsuits resulting from their official duties.

impeach (impeachment) The first step in the removal from public office of a high public official, such as a governor, judge, or the president. In the case of the president of the United States, the House of Representatives makes an accusation by drawing up articles of impeachment, voting on them, and presenting them to the Senate. This process makes up impeachment. Impeachment, however, is popularly thought to include the process that may take place after impeachment: the trial of the president in the Senate and conviction by two-thirds of the senators.

imposts Taxes; import taxes.

in personam jurisdiction (Latin) Describes a lawsuit brought to enforce rights against another person.

in rem jurisdiction (Latin) Describes a lawsuit brought to enforce rights in a "thing" or property located as opposed to one brought to enforce rights against another person.

Incorporation Doctrine The legal theory used by the Supreme Court to apply the rights found in the Bill of Rights to the states by using the Fourteenth Amendment requirement that states provide due process to all their citizens.

indicted (indictment) A sworn written accusation of a crime made against a person by a prosecutor to a grand jury. If the grand jury approves it as a true bill, the indictment becomes the document used against the person as a defendant in pretrial and trial proceedings. [pronounce: in-ditement]

indigent A poor person. An indigent criminal defendant is entitled to a free court-appointed lawyer.

infamous (infamy) The loss of a good reputation because of a conviction of a major crime and the loss of certain legal rights that accompanies this loss of reputation. An infamous crime used to be defined by type (such as treason), but is now defined by punishment possible (such as over a year in prison).

inferior court Any court but the highest one in a court system; a court with special, limited responsibilities, such as a probate court.

inherent power The powers a government must have to govern, even if not explicitly stated in its governing documents; for example, the constitutional power of the federal government to conduct foreign affairs or the power of the federal courts to protect constitutional rights.

injunction A court order to do or to stop doing a particular thing.

intrastate "Within." For example, intrastate commerce is business carried out entirely within one state, as opposed to interstate commerce. Intra is usually contrasted with inter (meaning either between or among).

inverse condemnation A lawsuit against the government to demand payment for an informal or irregular taking of private property.

invidious discrimination Illegally unequal treatment based on race, color, religion, sex, age, handicap, or national origin.

judgment debtor A person owing money as a result of a judgment in court.

judicial review A court's power to declare a statute unconstitutional and to interpret laws.

justiciable [pronounce: justish-able] Proper to be decided by a particular court. For example, a "justiciable controversy" is a real, rather than hypothetical, dispute. Federal courts may handle only cases that present a justiciable controversy.

legislative courts Courts that have been set up by legislatures (Congress, state legislatures, etc.) rather than those set up originally by the U.S. Constitution or by state constitutions.

libel Written defamation. Publicly communicated, false written statements that injure a person's reputation, business, or property rights. To libel certain public figures, the written statement must also be made with at least a "reckless disregard" for whether the statement is true or false.

liberty to contract The constitutionally-protected right to make and enforce contracts, as limited only by reasonable laws about health, safety, and consumer protection.

magistrate judges [pronounce: maj-eh-strate] A judge, usually with limited functions and powers (e.g., a police court judge). U.S. magistrates conduct pretrial proceedings, try minor criminal matters, and so forth.

majority opinion (opinion) A judge's statement about the conclusions of that judge and other judges who agree with the judge in a case. A majority opinion is written when over half the judges in a case agree about both the result and the reasoning used to reach that result.

martial law Government completely by the military; control of the domestic civilian population by the military in wartime or during a breakdown of civilian control.

Miranda warning The warning that must be given to a person arrested or taken into custody by a police officer or other official prior to any interrogation. The warning includes the fact that what you say may be held against you and that you have the rights to remain silent, to contact a lawyer, and to have a free court-appointed lawyer if you are poor. If this warning is not given properly, no statements made by the defendant during custody may be used by the police or by the prosecutor in court. The warning is required by the 1966 case *Miranda v. Arizona*, 384 U.S. 436.

mistrial A trial that the judge ends and declares will have no legal effect because of a major defect in procedure or because of the death of a juror, a deadlocked jury, or other major problem.

monopoly Having exclusive control.

mootness No longer important or no longer needing a decision because it has already been decided.

Necessary and Proper Clause The clause (Article I, Section 8, Clause 18) of the U.S. Constitution that gives Congress the power to pass all laws appropriate to carry out its functions.

neutrality theory A theory related to the interpretation of the Establishment Clause holding that government should not prefer religion over secularism or favor one religion over others.

opinion A judge's statement of the decision he or she has reached in a case.

original jurisdiction The power of a court to take a case, try it, and decide it (as opposed to appellate jurisdiction, which is the power of a court to hear and decide an appeal).

parallel citation An alternate reference to a case (or other legal document) that is published in more than one place. There is usually one official publication of a court case or a statute. If so, that is the *official* or primary citation, and all others are *parallel citations*.

pardon A president's or governor's release of a person from punishment for a crime.

party A person who is either a plaintiff or a defendant in a lawsuit.

per curiam (Latin) "By the court." Describes an opinion backed by all the judges in a particular court and usually with no one judge's name on it. [pronounce: per cure-ee-am]

peremptory challenges A peremptory challenge to a potential juror is the automatic elimination of that person from the jury by one side before trial without needing to state the reason for the elimination. Each side has the right to a certain number of peremptory challenges, and all other attempts to eliminate a potential juror must be for a reason (which may or may not be accepted by the judge).

personal property Having to do with movable property, as opposed to land and buildings.

plurality opinion (plurality) The greatest number. For example, if Jane gets ten votes and Don and Mary each get seven, Jane has a *plurality* (the most votes), but not a majority (more than half of the votes).

police powers The government's right and power to set up and enforce laws to provide for the safety, health, and general welfare of the people; for example, police power includes the power to license occupations, such as haircutting.

political question An issue that a court may refuse to decide because it concerns a decision properly made by the executive or legislative branch of government and because the court has no adequate standards of review or no adequate way to enforce the court's judgment. Most political questions are international diplomatic issues (e.g., whether or not a foreign country is an independent nation) that are considered by the federal courts to be best left to the president of the United States.

poll tax A tax, now illegal, paid to vote or for the right to vote.

preempts Supersedes.

Presentment clause Clause in the Constitution requiring that bills passed by both the Senate and the House of Representatives be presented to the president for signature; basis of presidential veto power.

presidential proclamation A type of a formal government statement meant for immediate widespread announcement.

probable cause The U.S. constitutional requirement that law enforcement officers present sufficient facts to convince a judge to issue a search warrant or an arrest warrant and the requirement that no warrant should be issued unless it is more likely than not that the objects sought will be found in the place to be searched or that a crime has been committed by the person to be arrested.

procedural due process What constitutes due process of law varies from situation to situation, but the core of the idea is that a person should always have notice and a real chance to present his or her side in a legal dispute.

proportionality The term given to the concept that the punishment for a crime must bear some relationship to the nature or seriousness of the crime. The Eighth Amendment prohibition on cruel and unusual punishment requires that punishment for a crime cannot be grossly disproportionate to the crime but it need not be strictly in proportion to the offense charged.

prurient interest A shameful or obsessive interest in immoral or sexual things. "Appealing to prurient interest" is one of many factors involved in deciding whether speech is obscene.

published When an appellate court decides that a decision in a case should become case law, it orders the case "published." The case then appears in case reporters.

quasi in rem jurisdiction A type of lawsuit "in between" in rem and in personam called "quasi in rem" or "sort of concerning a thing." Quasi in rem actions are really directed against a person, but are formally directed only against property (or vice versa); for example, a mortgage foreclosure.

quasi-suspect class A classification in the law based on factors such as gender or legitimacy that must be strongly justified if the law is challenged.

ratified (ratification) Confirmation and acceptance of a previous act.

rational suspicion Reasonable belief that a person is involved in criminal activity; it is more than a hunch but less than probable cause.

real property Land, buildings, and things permanently attached to land and buildings.

reapportionment Changing the boundaries of legislative districts to reflect changes in population and ensure that each person's vote for representatives carries roughly equal weight.

Reconstruction Amendments The Thirteenth, Fourteenth, and Fifteenth Amendments that were enacted after the Civil War and meant to provide constitutional protection to the newly freed slaves.

remand Send back. For example, a higher court may remand (send back) a case to a lower court, directing the lower court to take some action.

ripeness A case is ripe for selection and decision by the U.S. Supreme Court if the legal issues involved are clear enough, well enough evolved and presented so that a clear decision can come out of the case.

Rule of Four The principle that if at least four of the nine U.S. Supreme Court justices vote to take a case, the Court will hear the case. The Court uses the Rule of Four for cases that reach the Court by certiorari.

saving clause A clause in a statute (or a contract) that states that if part of the statute (or contract) is declared void, the remainder stays in effect; a clause in a statute that preserves certain rights, responsibilities, or liabilities that are in existence as of the adoption of the statute but would otherwise be lost upon its adoption.

seditious libel Publishing something to stir up class hatred or contempt for the government. The First Amendment invalidated seditious libel laws in the United States.

segregation 1. The separation of property into groups. Segregation of assets involves identifying and setting aside the property belonging to one person from a common fund or pot. 2. The unconstitutional practice of separating persons in housing, schooling, and public accommodation, based on race, color, nationality, etc.

separate but equal doctrine The rule, established in the 1896 Supreme Court case *Plessy v. Ferguson* and then rejected as unconstitutional in the 1954 *Brown* decision, that when races are given substantially equal facilities, they may lawfully be segregated.

separation of powers The division of the federal government (and state governments) into legislative (lawmaking), judicial (law-interpreting), and executive (law-carrying-on) branches. Each acts to prevent the others from becoming too powerful.

service of process The delivery (or its legal equivalent, such as publication in a newspaper in some cases) of a legal paper, such as a writ, by an authorized person in a way that meets certain formal requirements. It is the way to notify a person of a lawsuit.

slander Spoken defamation. The speaking of false words that injure another person's reputation, business, or property rights.

special master An individual appointed by the court to preside over a case in place of a judge.

special prosecutor A prosecutor appointed specially to investigate and, if appropriate, prosecute a particular case.

standing A person's right to bring (start) or join a lawsuit because he or she is directly affected by the issues raised. This is called "standing to sue."

stare decisis [pronounce: <u>star</u>-e de-<u>si</u>-sis] (Latin) "Let the decision stand." The rule that when a court has decided a case by applying a legal principle to a set of facts, the court should stick by the principle and apply it to all later cases with clearly similar facts unless there is a strong reason not to, and that courts below must apply the principle in similar cases. These rules help promote fairness and reliability in judicial decision making.

statute of limitation 1. A restriction. 2. A time limit. For example, a statute of limitations is a law that sets a maximum amount of time after something happens for it to be taken to court, such as a "three-year statute" for lawsuits based on a contract or a "six-year statute" for a criminal prosecution.

strict separation theory A theory related to the interpretation of the Establishment Clause holding that religion and government should be separated to the greatest extent possible.

subpoena A court's order to a person that he or she appear in court to testify (give evidence) in a case. Some administrative agencies may also issue subpoenas. [pronounce: suh-pee-na]

substantive due process No law or government procedure should be arbitrary or unfair.

suspect class (suspect classification) Making choices based on factors such as race or nationality. These choices, only rarely legitimate, must be strongly justified if challenged. (Gender is a quasi-suspect classification that must be justified, but not as strongly if challenged.)

Suspension Clause Article I, Section 9 of the U.S. Constitution authorizing the president to suspend the writ of habeas corpus only in times of rebellion or invasion and when required for public safety.

syllabus A headnote, summary, or abstract of a case.

symbolic endorsement test A theory related to the interpretation of the Establishment Clause holding that government violates the Establishment Clause when it "symbolically endorses" one religion or if it generally endorses secularism or religion.

Takings Clause That part of the Fifth Amendment to the U.S. Constitution that prohibits the taking of private property for public use without just compensation.

treaty A formal agreement between countries on a major political subject. The treaty clause of the U.S. Constitution requires the approval of two-thirds of the Senate for any treaty made by the president.

unenumerated rights Those rights not mentioned specifically in the Constitution.

United States Code The official law books containing federal laws organized by subject. They are recompiled every six years, and supplements are published when needed.

voir dire (French) "To see, to say"; "to state the truth." The preliminary in-court questioning of a prospective witness (or juror) to determine competency to testify (or suitability to decide a case). [pronounce: vwahr deer]

writ of certiorari [pronounce: sir-sho-rare-ee] A request for certiorari (or "cert." for short) is similar to an appeal, but it is one that the higher court is not required to decide. It is literally a writ from the higher court asking the lower court for the record of the case.

writ of habeas corpus (habeas corpus) (Latin) "You have the body." A judicial order to someone holding a person to bring that person to court. It is most often used to get a person out of unlawful imprisonment by forcing the captor and the person being held to come to court for a decision on the legality of the imprisonment or other holding (such as keeping a child when someone else claims custody). (pronounce: hay-bee-as core-pus)

writ of mandamus [pronounce: man-day-mus] A writ of mandamus is a court order that directs a public official or government department to do something. It may be sent to the executive branch, the legislative branch, or a lower court.

writ A judge's order requiring that something be done outside the courtroom or authorizing it to be done.

CPSIA information can be obtained
at www.ICGtesting.com
Printed in the USA
FFHW010312190219
50600979-55950FF